BOOKS BY EDMUND WILSON

AXEL'S CASTLE

THE TRIPLE THINKERS

TO THE FINLAND STATION

THE WOUND AND THE BOW

THE SHOCK OF RECOGNITION

MEMOIRS OF HECATE COUNTY

CLASSICS AND COMMERCIALS

THE SHORES OF LIGHT

FIVE PLAYS

RED, BLACK, BLOND AND OLIVE

A PIECE OF MY MIND

THE AMERICAN EARTHQUAKE

APOLOGIES TO THE IROQUOIS

WILSON'S NIGHT THOUGHTS

PATRIOTIC GORE

THE COLD WAR AND THE INCOME TAX

O CANADA

THE BIT BETWEEN MY TEETH

EUROPE WITHOUT BAEDEKER

GALAHAD and I THOUGHT OF DAISY

A PRELUDE

THE DUKE OF PALERMO AND OTHER PLAYS

THE DEAD SEA SCROLLS: 1947–1969

UPSTATE

A WINDOW ON RUSSIA

THE DEVILS AND CANON BARHAM

THE TWENTIES

LETTERS
ON LITERATURE
AND POLITICS

1912–1972

Henri Cartier-Bresson/Magnum Photos

EDMUND WILSON

Edmund Wilson

LETTERS
ON LITERATURE
AND POLITICS
1912–1972

Edited by Elena Wilson

INTRODUCTION BY DANIEL AARON

FOREWORD BY LEON EDEL

ROUTLEDGE & KEGAN PAUL · LONDON AND HENLEY

First published in Great Britain in 1977
by Routledge & Kegan Paul Ltd
39 Store Street,
London WC1E 7DD and
Broadway House,
Newtown Road,
Henley-on-Thames,
Oxon RG9 1EN
Printed in the United States of America

Some of these letters first appeared in *The New York Review
of Books*, *The New Republic*, and *The Papers of Christian
Gauss* (Random House, 1957)

Acknowledgment is made to Condé Nast Publications for
permission to reproduce the photographs of Louise Bogan,
F. Scott Fitzgerald, Christian Gauss, James Joyce, Edna St.
Vincent Millay, John Dos Passos, and Paul Rosenfeld, which
originally appeared in *Vanity Fair*

The illustrations on the part-title pages were chosen from
among many drawings included in Edmund Wilson's letters
to friends or doodled on his telephone note pads

British Library Cataloguing in Publication Data

Wilson, Edmund
    Letters on literature and politics, 1912-1972.
    1.   Literature—Addresses, essays, lectures
  I.   Title   II.   Wilson, Elena
  809   PN501
  ISBN 0-7100-8761-6

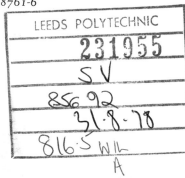

My original idea was merely to print passages which bore on his literary work; the whole subject of his personal relations might better be left for the eventual biographer.

To John Biggs
(On editing F. Scott Fitzgerald)

CONTENTS

FOREWORD

This anthology, edited by Mrs. Edmund Wilson, is designed to make available a volume of Edmund Wilson's literary and political letters in the margin of his posthumous papers, which I am editing in accordance with his wishes. It was felt both by Elena Wilson, who is her husband's literary executor, and by myself that readers and students of Wilson's work should be provided as soon as possible with certain relevant portions of his correspondence. A comprehensive collection is planned for a later date. More than a sampling, the present volume provides sufficient material to show the energy and vitality of Wilson's professional relations with friends and acquaintances; it shows even more the continuity of his imaginative life from his youth to the end.

Mrs. Wilson's anthology follows the design of Wilson's own editing of the literary remains of his friend F. Scott Fitzgerald, *The Crack-Up* of 1945. This was a general "homage" by Wilson and others to the essential achievements of Fitzgerald's career. The present volume is the homage of a widow to her husband's work, in which she herself was involved for many years. She wanted her husband's voice to be the predominant voice —with as little editorial intervention as possible. Professor Daniel Aaron of Harvard, who helped Mrs. Wilson in the earlier stages of this book, has generously supplied the introduction, and we have both given Mrs. Wilson such assistance as might expedite the appearance of so "usable" a volume. For my part, I wish to thank once again the National Endowment for the Humanities, which has taken such a generous view of the need to bring out—sooner rather than later—the splendid heritage of American writing Wilson left behind him.

LEON EDEL
General Editor
The Edmund Wilson Papers

INTRODUCTION

by DANIEL AARON

Writing to his old friend John Dos Passos in 1965, Edmund Wilson explained why he had denied requests to make Dos Passos's letters "available to people who are writing about you . . . I have refused, on the principle that it is only when people are dead that it is time to publish their correspondence."

Wilson's concern for the defenseless dead was in keeping with his notions of privacy. There was a time to "tell all" and a time to be silent. He distrusted the squads of academic detectives dredging up items about his own life and the lives of his friends, and he could not get used to finding his "own day before yesterday turning up as literary history." Most biographies of writers he knew personally seemed to him badly written, misleading, wanting in selective detail, and full of mistakes as well, either because of sloppy research or because the people close to the subjects of the biographers withheld revealing facts.

Wilson's biographers should make fewer mistakes if only because he was one of those writing animals John Jay Chapman referred to who leave "a cocoon as large as a haystack." His letters contain information about himself and others that is hard to come by: changes of address, literary enthusiasms, friendships and antipathies, professional activities and political involvements. They chart the cyclical pattern of his emotional ups and downs; they trace the genesis and development of his books. Wilson, the busy journalist, dashed off a number of notes to request or supply information or to acknowledge letters received, but his correspondence also includes carefully composed, essaylike statements on a profusion of topics. Witty, serious, didactic, critical (the holographs sometimes marked with interlinear corrections and appended afterthoughts), and written in a precise and felicitous prose, they comprise a lively if unsystematic personal history of a gifted man and his literary generation.

He was not a self-conscious letter writer or one who tried to sustain the studied mannerisms of a Henry Adams. Nor did he resort to artifice or entangle himself in circumlocutions. The young, middle-aged, and old Wilson speaks directly through his letters, which are spontaneous and informal for the most part and which undisguisedly reflect his changing moods. On occasion—in response, perhaps, to the misery of a friend or a public outrage or a personal challenge—he can become eloquent, even passionate, but that is not his prevailing tone.

The letters are far-ranging and diverse, but they are essentially about literature and literary culture, subjects that for Wilson embraced the conventional genres; about history and philosophy, the lives of writers, living and dead; and, to use his words, about "all the constructions of intellect and imagination, from poetry, drama, and fiction through Whitehead (metaphysics is the poetry and fiction of people who do not produce concrete images) to Einstein." Writing he considered a discipline as well as a profession. It had its code, its own responsibilities and obligations, which often brought the writer into conflict with the values of the commercial world. To stick to that code took strength and character, something akin to heroism. It required, besides a certain kind of self-effacement, a subordination if not suppression of the personal note to facts and evidence. "I have always made 'validity' rather than 'authenticity' the criterion," he wrote in one of his letters. Edmund Wilson's career in all its phases illustrates very well what the valid literary life with its penalties and satisfactions is all about.

A dedication to literature is apparent even during his preparatory schooldays when young Wilson, luxuriating in books and enjoying the "dignity" of seeing himself in print, adjudicated the claims of Kipling, Stevenson, and George Borrow. Nothing in his early letters points in any other but a literary direction. Family tradition alone would probably have ruled out the likelihood of his choosing a business career, and he was grateful to Princeton for giving him "a sort of eighteenth-century humanism" and for tolerating "whatever it is that inspires people not to take too seriously the ideal of the successful man."

Even before he graduated from college, he was making sententious judgments tinged with self-irony on art and life, announcing intellectual allegiances, turning out precocious parodies, and choosing as his models writers whose character and style met his exacting standards. Boswell, fascinated by the glamour and charm of life and telling "the strict truth about it," had "the true creative genius, which always feels more than it knows." Macaulay—honest, dogmatic, and stubborn like Samuel Johnson— was to be emulated for his "scrupulous thoroughness, his sound literary conscience, and his knowledge and acceptance of his own limitations."

The world war postponed rather than deflected Wilson's literary plans. He enlisted in the medical corps as a matter of course and without illusions, having no hankering to kill Germans or save democracy. The letters depict the war he observed as an amalgam of cruelty, ineptitude, and waste, yet it remained peripheral to his never-to-be-realized hope of owning and editing a "powerful publication" and less real to him than the ideas he was storing up for "my forthcoming books." The painful scenes he witnessed as a hospital orderly and which he was soon to incorporate into his first stories did not interrupt his routine of reading ("my single aim has been literature"). While still in uniform he plotted his future: he would "work on some liberal magazine or newspaper" and do something for the literary credit of America.

The mood of Wilson and his friends at the end of the war in which most of them had served was at bottom less despairing than readers of their fiction and poetry might imagine. However disenchanted and cynical they sounded, neither they nor their country had suffered irreparable damage, and they conveyed their disgust with America's business civilization in a high-spirited way. They had their breakdowns and crack-ups, to be sure, and Wilson commiserated with his literary generation's public and private despair. With untypical grandiloquence in 1922, he could fault his Princeton mentor and friend, Christian Gauss, for holding stereotyped notions about "happy youth," and he resorted to the most violent imagery to describe its disasters: "painful parturition," "drowning men," "extreme disgust with life," a battleground for wild beasts. All the same, his letters of the twenties are generally breezy and expectant. He was too stimulated by the American scene, too deep in the Great Cause of literature to sink into the pessimism he sympathized with yet deprecated in some of his friends who were overwhelmed by personal problems and at odds with or in flight from Philistia.

Most American writers, he acknowledged—Whitman was a notable exception—had written books "to tell what a terrible place America is," but all of this "devastating criticism" cleared the way for its becoming culturally inhabitable. Far from suffering neglect, the American "highbrow and artist" was now endangered by unwarranted attention and the ease, as he put it in a letter to Fitzgerald, with which "a traditionless and half-educated public (I mean the growing public for really good stuff) can be impressed, delighted, and satisfied." It was an encouraging sign that Americans were at last beginning to speak their own idiom, but it would take time for artists to affect a commercial and industrial society whose only cultural foundation was "one layer of eighteenth-century civilization." He was prepared to argue at the end of the twenties, nonetheless, "that our civilization is in some respects far superior to anything previously known and that it is our high destiny to step in and speak the true prophetic words to declining Europe." Such was the role he envisaged for himself and his literary fraternity, men and women writers whom he had known during and since his college days and whom he recruited as contributors to *Vanity Fair* and *The New Republic*.

A chronic skepticism, quickened by his reading of Charles Beard's historical writing, worked against this optimism, and Wilson himself had no aptitude for the prophetic role adopted by some of his evangelical friends. But he belonged to the American family of Matthew Arnold, the patriot-castigators and spreaders of light, whose view of culture is best expressed in Lionel Trilling's definition: "the locus of the meeting of literature with social actions and attitudes and manners." Intellectuals, Wilson believed then and later, "ought to identify themselves a little more with the general life of the country." He hoped to prove himself " 'a soldier in the Liberation War of humanity' and to speak for the 'younger generation' who were 'knocking at the door.' "

When he assumed his place as the armed critic in the twenties, he had read the cultural pundits and missionaries who preceded him and singled out what he considered admirable and usable in their writing. He had also noted their deficiencies, the critical appraiser invariably checking the enthusiast. Brilliant John Jay Chapman, so robust and unaffected and elegant, the quirky moralist and the finest exemplar of "a trained and public-spirited caste," was intellectually wayward and insensitive to new forms of literary expression. Honest and learned Paul Elmer More knew what he thought and said what he meant; his philosophical system embraced all culture. But he was a prig. He could not respond disinterestedly to art that clashed with his prim and arrogant aesthetic. Van Wyck Brooks, more to Wilson's liking, was at his best a beautiful and incisive writer and conversant with European literature. He showed how one could criticize American culture without ceasing to love it. He believed in standards. But he had nothing of interest to say about philosophy, politics, or economics, and he was not really a sensitive discriminator. His literary judgments never deepened, and he recoiled from the modernists. James Gibbons Huneker, on the other hand, welcomed the new and the different. He was a kind of showman for the arts, a man to be admired for his versatility and professional competence—but he was more enthusiastic than penetrating. H. L. Mencken seemed to Wilson a writer of authentic genius as Huneker was not, but Wilson esteemed the prose writer of originality, the professional journalist (the best since Poe), the good-natured hurler of dead cats, not the excoriator of boobs and the bogus Nietzschean.

The young critic who held these opinions was better equipped than most of his generation to instruct educated Americans who wanted to be instructed without being bored. He had acquired a solid background in classical and foreign literatures and had learned to elucidate complex ideas precisely in rhythmic, "well-drilled" sentences. Although he disdained the posturings of literary Bohemia, he was an avid student of European modernism and demonstrated in his own writing and attitudes

xviii

his links not only with traditional culture and history but also with the new and experimental.

If Wilson sharply disavowed the anti-modernist opinions of Paul Elmer More and Van Wyck Brooks, he wanted like them to call attention to the variety and freshness of the national literary landscape. His almost proprietary feeling toward the country he alternately defended and chastised derived in part from what might be called ancestral conditioning. Family ties reached north to New England (he frequently referred to his connection with the Mather line while disclaiming any admiration for the Yankees) and to the South. The Talcottville house in New York State, however, represented quintessential America, for it gave him some sense of how Americans used to live and provided spiritual sustenance. As the frequent backward glances in the letters might suggest, he had not cut himself off from the past so drastically as he thought, and the pull of the past symbolized by that old stone house grew stronger as he aged. He and his college mates may have gleefully violated the taboos of their fathers, but the tensions between themselves and their elders strained without snapping familial bonds, and they carried with them into the twenties some late-Victorian tastes and biases.

Wilson had tried with considerable success to emancipate himself from the marks of his class and to acquaint himself with the America beyond the confines of Princeton. Thanks to his war experiences as a private and noncommissioned officer, he discarded the snobberies of his class and thereafter was attracted by the lives and culture of minority groups— Indians and Jews and other immigrant minorities. He would even claim in the sixties: "I seem nowadays to be obsessed with minorities, feeling that I belong to one myself." Yet what he said of his father (whom in his later years he came more and more to resemble) might have applied equally well to himself: "He was completely without snobbery of race or class—but though he dealt with people strictly on their merits, it was always to some extent *de haut en bas*." From his forays into the American hinterlands, Europe, Haiti, Israel, and Canada, Wilson amassed literary and linguistic treasure, new facts to bolster his relativistic outlook, new customs and ideas to mull over, new friends to correspond with, but the society he returned to was comparatively small and exclusive. It consisted of close friends (many of them women), classmates, poets, novelists, critics, scholars. He took to learned and witty people and quickened at the vibration of talent. He suffered in the company of bores more acutely than most. His idea of one kind of hell was the cocktail party, an occasion where civilized social intercourse gave way to gossip and jokes.

Cocktail parties belonged to the category of "idiotic trifling" he had once been given to, and early in the twenties, that "drunken siesta," he resolved to divide his time between work and disciplined dissipation. He was not the only one of his generation to take his drinking and fornications seriously, but a number of intimates and contemporaries had more trouble than Wilson did in rebounding from their moral, mental, and physical collapses. For these casualties, Wilson the exhorter and counselor of the literary fraternity had compassion and advice.

Friends in the doldrums or in deep depression got special messages full of understanding and encouragement. A tactful and tender letter he wrote to Dos Passos consoling him after the death of his wife is an elegy on "a whole life behind us, with many things that we could never have again." Fitzgerald "needs commemoration more than Joyce, because his contemporaries have done him less justice," Wilson writes to John Peale Bishop, and he summons Bishop to the sacred vocation: "I'm sorry you're feeling exhausted—but come! Somebody's got to survive and write."

He never lost this conviction about that artist's "obligation not to let the sick world down" and about the efficacy of work as an anodyne for the spirit. Many of his friends had suffered nervous collapses in the twenties—Zelda Fitzgerald and Phelps Putnam, to name only two—and the thirties were to take their literary toll. Wilson himself was, off and on, a victim of depressions. He had undergone "a sort of nervous breakdown" in 1929. It was with this experience in mind that he could write to Louise Bogan, herself then in a sanatorium, of his neurotic states when he found it impossible to be alone. Now, despite his gloomy moments, he thrives in solitude. But it is better to be alone outside a hospital than in it. Why doesn't she try "to give literary expression to your internal conflict and ranklings . . . Once you get the experience out of your system in a satisfactory literary form, you can thumb your nose at the world." Here, in brief, is his "wound and the bow" thesis: out of "the miseries of a writer's life" come "the glories of his work."

Every literary friend of Edmund Wilson probably received one or more admonishing letters on his or her novel or poems or essays; even an enthusiastic commendation was sure to contain at least a remark or two on an error in fact, a mistake in diction, or some other lapse in style or content. Wilson gladly learned, but he even more gladly taught. He never hesitated to inform, to correct, to set his correspondents straight. The more intimate the friendship, the more unabashedly critical he became, a measure of his paternal concern for the success and reputation of his friends. Of course it was they who requested his inspection, and one is more impressed, finally, by his generosity and kindness than by his severity. From his Princeton days on, "old Doc Wilson," as he sometimes called himself, dispensed advice to his literary patients, helped them obtain grants, worried over their marriages, and sent them detailed annotations of their novels and poems as well as encouraging them to be up and doing. His letters are peppered with observations on the technique of submitting manuscripts, on the art of book reviewing, on style, on dangerous literary influences, on the vagaries of editors ("unbusinesslike people who are subject to all kinds of worries, absentmindedness, metaphysical prejudices, partisan feeling, sinking spells, and whims").

Wilson's strictures on other people's writing were seldom *ad hominem*. When sensitive correspondents bristled at his blunt remarks, he seemed surprised, for he offered his literary judgments in the spirit of one technician to another and accepted criticism in turn without resentment. His candor may have exceeded his tact, but if he could not bring himself to soften his objections to what he considered obnoxious political or religious ideas, the target of a rough assault might be mollified by comradely expressions of esteem and an invitation to spend the weekend. For more than forty years he alternately praised and lambasted John Dos Passos in a series of letters remarkable both for their asperity and for their good humor. Wilson had been one of Dos Passos's warmest champions in the twenties and thirties, but even then, when he was more in sympathy with his politics than he was during Dos Passos's Goldwater period ("your article about the San Francisco convention sounded like a teenager squealing over the Beatles"), he kidded him for making American life unrealistically grim. Here was a novelist who enjoyed life and yet who considered it a duty to make all ideas appear phony and "all women obvious bitches." Every one of his characters seemed "to get a bad egg for breakfast." That particular kind of grumpiness and pessimism is rarely present in Wilson's letters.

Occasionally his efforts to enlighten were angrily rebuffed, as the long-drawn-out quarrel with a group of academicians mentioned in the letters will indicate. Wilson had no bias per se against academics or contempt for scholarship, but he did not try to hide his impatience with particular specimens of what his friend Mencken called the Professoriat. He challenged them on the ground that they were not scholarly enough and lacked taste and discrimination. They were too preoccupied, he felt, with the paraphernalia of research, and he had harsh things to say about the "pedantic and expensive editions" of American authors sponsored by the Modern Language Association. The rejection of his own project to get out "the American classics" in a series "well but not pretentiously edited" and "not impossibly priced" he attributed to the opportunists in the academic hierarchy who had come "to dominate the field of American literature." Wilson had the most cordial relations with a number of professors and students, it should be added, but he thought academic life, which demanded constant association with unformed minds' was "unnatural" and "embarrassing" for writers. His own brief adventures at teaching convinced him that "I might better do journalism after all, when I have to make money."

The problem of money is one of the leitmotivs in the Wilson correspondence, the problem of how to survive as a serious professional writer in a commercial society in which critical success does not necessarily enable a man to pay the rent. Wilson in his youth lived in comfortable surroundings. His family was not rich but was well enough off to pay for a privileged education and to furnish sufficient funds for modest traveling in America and abroad. A small legacy after his graduation gave him a margin of economic independence at a time when some of his gifted friends were reduced to doing hack work. In some respects, the twenties offered a favorable climate for the beginning writer, since a large number of publishers were competing for promising talent and the neophyte could survive on a small advance. But even then Wilson felt that publishers in New York were turning literature into a cloak and suit business "with its inevitable politics, combinations, incessant talking of shop, and general unfitting of its victims for any kind of activities other than their professional ones." His own dream of what then and thereafter constituted for him the desirable literary life never materialized.

Put in the simplest terms, this meant to be a literary editor and to write books. It meant working in the city and enjoying its amenities but with a pastoral retreat in the offing, perhaps in New England, where (he told Fitzgerald) "my ancestors served the altars of learning and committed murders in the name of God." Damned by dollars, Wilson developed a workable if not entirely satisfactory strategy for having at least a slice of his cake and eating it. He took on literary chores and stayed longer in the city than he cared to, in exchange for working holidays in rural Connecticut, the Cape, or Talcottville, where he could read and write the books that really interested him. From the twenties on, he rarely earned enough to build up a margin of security, but during the post-Depression years, as he watched younger writers—unsure of themselves and disinclined to swim against the current—sell their skills to Hollywood or the Luce publications or *Reader's Digest* or Washington, he ingeniously contrived to find outlets for his writing which would leave his values intact.

To keep himself afloat as a freelance writer, Wilson learned to drive hard bargains with publishers, most of whom he regarded as Henry Adams did Congressmen. He learned to husband his materials and not waste words. As a journalist facing deadlines, it was hard for him to find the leisure for what he called in a letter to John Dos Passos "long-range" writing—that is, writing that could only be done during periods of prolonged stability—and it was not easy to write even then. Every writer required his *recueillement* (a word that appears several times in his letters), his time of in-gathering and collecting. In order to earn his intervals of peaceful contemplation, Wilson had to do a good deal of "close-range" writing, or what he called, without apologies, "journalism."

All of his books, but especially his novels *I Thought of Daisy* and *Memoirs of Hecate County*, as well as nonfictional works like *Axel's Castle*, *To the Finland Station*, and *Patriotic Gore*, evolved through a similar intellectual process. First came the plan or outline of the work. Thereafter it unfolded in the form of notebook entries, letters, sketches, book reviews, and magazine articles. Emerson once described his habit of extracting passages from his letters and journals for his essays as "Boswell-izing" himself, but he did not have to publish his books in stages as Wilson did. Denied the time and money to write them without interruptions, Wilson had to compose them in segments ("dress rehearsals" was his name for them) and then to solder the prefabricated parts.

Wilson considered journalism a "serious profession" and one that involved "special problems" for the journalist, the chief of them being to get editors to pay him for what he wants to write. The view of Wilson as a mere popularizer and diluter of high culture betrays an ignorance of his intention and range of interests. In his capacity as literary editor, he had to review all manner of books. He managed, as he said of Poe, Shaw, and Eliot, "to be brilliant and arresting even about works of no interest," and, in the course of writing this kind of journalism, "to formulate general principles." Wilson objected to the cliché that he mediated "between artist and public." He preferred to think of himself as doing for important and sometimes difficult writers what Shaw did for Ibsen and Wagner: "to give popular accounts of them," he wrote, "will convince people to read them." He had a further intention as well: to give his readers an understanding of those writers he was recommending and to convey his own moral and artistic principles without being dull.

When Allen Tate, with whom he happily wrangled for decades, once accused him of "making art and science one" as a program for the "coming generation," he replied that both were "merely aids to getting by in the world. They harmonize or explain limited fields of experience and so comfort and reassure us and also, in proportion as they are original and profound, actually make it easier for humanity to live and improve itself. The end is not art or science but the survival and improvement of America." These words were written in 1931, a time when political issues preoccupied him, but almost anything he wrote before or thereafter called attention to some matter—historical, religious, scientific, psychological, as well as literary—that he deemed of social consequence.

The privilege of speaking his own mind and of being free to persuade his readers to accept his point of view was essential to him, and he insisted on reserving that right when he filled the book-reviewing slot on the *New Yorker* staff in 1943, although he was scarcely in a position to bargain. Before agreeing to take the job, he stipulated that the magazine would print what he wrote, "unless it chooses to suppress my articles or me altogether."

By this time he had mastered his own style of book reviewing, by turns magisterial, instructive, comic, and argumentative. His reviews and essays were neither impressionistic nor scholastic. They usually explained the author's general ideas, his point of view and temperament, the kind of effects he produced, and they gave evidence that the reviewer was familiar not only with the author's other works but also with the subject itself, since Wilson, for reasons already given, developed the practice of reviewing books having some relation to a subject he had once worked on or was currently getting up. During the literary wars of the twenties and thirties, he more usually than not delivered his blunt judgments on both literary and social matters as a party of one.

At the outset of his career, Wilson had sided with the "Younger" against the "Older Generation," without ascribing "his own private virtues and preferences to a whole movement," and fancied himself as satirist, entertainer, and moralist. He felt the nobility and appeal of Emerson and Thoreau, "real artists," he wrote to John Peale Bishop, who wonderfully conveyed "a sort of mystic exaltation of the spiritual life above the debasements of practical life." But he added that both Emerson and Thoreau overemphasized what a single person could do "merely by washing his hands of social obligations and practicing virtue by himself." In the twilight of the twenties he was ready to take an even stronger social line than he had before. The great writers he had been reading and interpreting —Yeats, Proust, Joyce, and Eliot—no longer served as useful guides for a disintegrating society: their heroes, as he put it, "never act on their fellows, their thoughts never pass into action"; they sacrifice the will for "lonely meditation." He could no longer tolerate this "resignationism" and was ready in 1930 to defend and encourage writers far less gifted than the men of genius he had discussed in *Axel's Castle:* he was trying to create "a social-idealistic literature." The trial and execution of Sacco and Vanzetti proved to be a turning point for Wilson as it was for many of his literary contemporaries. "It revealed," he wrote to John Peale Bishop, "the whole anatomy of American life, with all its classes, professions, and points of view and all their relations, and it raised almost every fundamental question of our political and social system. As Dos Passos said, it was, during the last days before the execution, as if, by some fairy-tale spell, all the different kinds of Americans, eminent and obscure, had suddenly, in a short burst of intensified life, been compelled to reveal their true characters in a heightened exaggerated form."

Wilson held on to his conviction that no humane society could stand upon rotten economic underpinnings, and rejecting the label of "liberal" (since liberals were neither a-political pragmatists nor adherents of principles they stuck to), he remained an unspecified radical independent for the rest of his life. As the country moved out of the Depression into war, his briefly held revolutionary expectations dwindled; by the mid-thirties he had already lost whatever hope he ever entertained in the possibility or the desirableness of a Communist system. Communists proved to be useful agitators for a time, he thought, but Communism itself had always seemed to him too foreign to make any headway with the optimistic, materialistic American public. He could celebrate Marx and Lenin but not their creepy perverters who had given Communism "some of the characteristics of a secular church" and completely detached themselves from the "humanistic tradition" out of which their masters came. Marx himself, Wilson decided, had unconsciously played the role of prophet, but it was strange and unpleasant to read his hagiographers—"almost as queer as reading the New Testament." The Communists worshipped the Dialectic "as a supernatural power which will bring them salvation if they trust it, without the necessity of thought or virtue on their part."

"Thought" or "virtue": neither word seemed to count for much among right- and left-wing zealots of the thirties. His own generation, Wilson reflected, had come of age in "one kind of world" and was now having "to adjust muscles socially, sexually, morally, etc., to another which is itself in a state of flux." The corruption and commercialism he had seen operating even during the comparatively innocent twenties had deepened in the thirties, taken on more sinister forms. The Republic of Letters, with its loyalties and comradeship, had fallen apart in a political atmosphere poisonous to art. Partisans of the left and right perfected their manipulative skills, engaged in vindictive campaigns of slander, and made political correctness the touchstone of approval. Authors peddling the current acceptable political line, Wilson thought, were likely to be the precursors "of some awful collectivist cant which will turn into official propaganda for a post-war state-socialist bureaucracy." He saw no political movement with which he cared to ally himself. Having acted "as a kind of liberal" by "bringing to the attention of the liberals things which they had been disregarding," he was now to cut himself off from programmatic politics altogether.

America's entrance into the Second World War did not tempt him to reconsider his decision. He found nothing morally or intellectually sanitizing about it and did not bother to hide his contempt for those who now condemned as "irresponsible" their once passionately held anti-war opinions. Needless to say, he was no less an anti-Fascist than they, nor was he a pacifist, but he refused to believe that Germany's defeat would leave the world much better off than it was before. Already he was formulating his bio-economic explanation for national aggression (men and movements may be "motivated by ideals and moralities," but wars are "battles for power" fought by men-animals); already he detected a war machinery at work beneath the camouflage of public rhetoric. The Cold War aftermath made the task of accommodating himself to the new America all the harder. Increasingly he deplored the glorifying of American tradition, a sign, he felt, "that the tradition may be dying—as Vergil and Horace celebrated the Roman ideas and virtues when Rome had just begun to decay." Anti-American propaganda, he wrote to Faulkner, was abetted by the national effort to combat it, and he wondered why a writer whose books were the best propaganda any nation could wish for allowed himself to be used in the national propaganda effort. "The American ideology is not to have any ideology."

Out of sorts with a country whose contemporary culture he found uncongenial and whose government made him feel unfree, Wilson spurned the chance to become a salesman of national culture or a "barker for Parnassus." He carried on in his independent and often irascible way.

But the Devil, as Wilson portrayed him in his fables, prepared other temptations for the artist-intellectual besides sips of power; he also offered him the narcotic of religion. Wilson did not have to rely upon his "principled obstinacy" (to use one of his sturdy phrases) to withstand that bait. Although no self-described atheist ever had so many Bibles on his bookshelves, he bridled when Allen Tate called him a Christian ("a malicious, libelous, and baseless charge"), scorned clergymen (with favored exceptions), and protested against the secular and spiritual impostures of organized churches. His anti-supernaturalist bias probably accounts for his resistance to most kinds of religious writing and to mystical experiences, gods, and creeds. People fell back on religion when they became discouraged about social improvements, he maintained, and lost their nerve. Like the narrator in *Memoirs of Hecate County*, with whom he must not be confused but whose history embodies some of Wilson's ideas and experiences, he adhered to his professional code in lieu of a religious one, to the "incorruptible line," to what the narrator calls "my old solitary self, the self for which I really lived and which kept up its austere virtue, the self which survived through these trashy years."

Grim and splenetic as Wilson can sound when he has the bit between his teeth, when he is defying the powers of heaven and earth and giving his readers a piece of his mind, the prevailing tone of his letters is cheerful, rational, and matter-of-fact. Critics who charged him with a total want of humor paid insufficient attention to his comic writing, which took the forms of burlesque, hoax, satire, and fantasy, and ranged from understatement to hyperbole. An unsolemn temperament is also reflected in his annual Christmas messages, his love of puppets, of conjuring (so full of beauty and poetic implications), and his fascination with magic, both white and black.

Readers of Wilson will recall the presence or immanence of ghosts, witches, and devils in his plays and fiction. He particularly enjoyed Richard Harris Barham's once popular *Ingoldsby Legends*, in which the jocose and the horrible most divertingly commingle, and discordant encounters occur between the representatives of heaven and hell. Since Wilson's eighteenth-century animus against "enthusiasms" and contempt for any sort of supernaturalism made him impervious to the occult, it might seem curious that the diabolic and the magical should fascinate him. To be sure, he treated the occult whimsically, but Wilson's future biographers may want to make something of the Poe-esque inclination. Whether these unearthly visitors emerged from the pit of Wilson's unconscious or were emblems of some social malevolence affecting America, it was almost as if the rejector of supernaturalism was letting it slip in through the back door of his imagination, or as if the spirit of his Mather ancestors was silently intruding. Ordinarily, the children of light in his fables (and they are few and far between) resist subterranean and terrestrial demons, but Wilson never minimizes the stiff price of rectitude.

Each of his books stakes out a Wilsonian position—for example, the importance of American literature; or defines a social evil; or argues the claims of non-American cultures and the defects of our own; or offers an opinion on the origins of war; or presents a dignified apologia for individualism and a warning against bureaucratic coerciveness. Each volume of miscellaneous writing contains a caveat against wordmongering and the immorality of opaque prose.

Predictably, the letters reveal this same concern for language. In giving one of his correspondents a "combing," he would couch his objections gently but not mince his words. The writer had an obligation to his readers. His business was to communicate his thoughts clearly and precisely, without sacrificing variety or sensibility. He ought to respect the language he uses and not set his reader's teeth on edge with fuzzy statements. To a correspondent whose sense of vocabulary and syntax struck him as unreliable, he recommended a dose of Macaulay or Poe or other writers with "clear and accurate expository styles." Watch how they "manage their sentences," he advised him, "and the terms they have evolved to convey their ideas." There was no better way of studying "the machinery" of style (the metaphor is revealing) than to write imitations. Worn-out phrases, solecisms, slovenly diction, "festooned abstractions"— all these disfigured meanings and were socially as well as aesthetically irresponsible. Like George Orwell, with whom he corresponded, Wilson equated debased language with social disease.

His penchant for concreteness and clarity lay behind his injunction to read foreign writers in the original, not through the blur of translation. He had no interest in Spanish, a language he could have easily learned, because he did not care for Spanish literature. German literature exerted a fitful attraction, and the paucity of references to German writers in the letters may simply reflect an inability to read German easily rather than a distaste for the literature itself. But Greek, Latin, French, Italian, Russian, Hebrew, and Hungarian opened fresh new territories to him and he regretted late in life that he was too old to start Chinese. Always "greedy for words," it relaxed him to learn new ones in a foreign tongue, even though he discovered as he got further into it that people said the same things in all languages. He took an almost sensual pleasure "in attacking a new language, especially if it has a strange alphabet whose barriers I find I can penetrate."

Language remained an escape and a challenge to him. As friends died off and he received unwanted attention from the Internal Revenue Service, his thoughts strayed to his childhood, before "the big moneymaking era." During the Depression, "even the tail end of the old culture and family life" seemed worth having; by the fifties he linked himself "to a past era from which I'm not sure I'm capable of emerging," the "frivolous twenties." Ten years later he found it "comfortable" to relapse in the post-war "American Renascence" when the country was less demoralized, and "restful" to read the memoirs of the Edwardian age.

Still, he pressed on with his work despite a cardiac condition, money problems, and the unsalubrious political climate. He planned new books and began to edit his notebooks for future publication. Periodically he complained, more ruefully than bitterly, that he was feeling "the onset of senility" and that the United States was getting him down. The letters of the early sixties contain several references to the Abominable Snowman, whom, were he young, he would like to search for in the primitive unsullied wilderness. He was incensed when the critics began to speak of him as mellowing. Meanwhile, no matter how ill or distracted he felt, he put in his daily quota of hours at his desk in Wellfleet or Talcottville.

Edmund Wilson, a serious professional writer, practiced what he believed. He gave to the profession of letters the dedication and responsibility encompassed by that word: he "professed" literature.

According to his literary creed, the imagination was to be placed at the service of society, the writer to be neither the cold abstract scientist nor the self-indulgent anarchist. The drift of Wilson's life was away from subjectivism and romanticism and toward the external world. Hence he rejected the suggestion made to him in the twenties by Christian Gauss that he write "a *confession d'un enfant du siècle*" as "repugnant to me" and strove "to become more objective instead of more and more personal."

This resolution may partly explain why he never became a cult figure or attracted the interest in academic sanctuaries that Eliot and Pound aroused. The young are not drawn to him today perhaps because he repressed his own romantic impulses and despised the current strains of "neophilia," because he was steeped in history and the literary past, and because he was anti-religious, though not indifferent to religion, and old-fashioned. He fought a number of battles with the Adversary in his various incarnations (or better, counterattacked him) without remarkable success. Politics failed him, but he fell back on the life of the social-minded artist without any public agonizing. He found no message in the annals of history to justify either the pessimist or the optimist. The honors he received were welcome when they took the form of money, but only art provided him an unassailable refuge. "Every work of art," the narrator in *Memoirs of Hecate County* declares, "is a trick by which the artist manipulates appearances so as to put over the illusion that experience has some sort of harmony and order and to make us forget that it's impossible to pluck billiard-balls out of the air."

The man who wrote those words was a performer of magic himself. He was also a producer of his own Punch and Judy shows. In one of his letters he observes that the "traditional Punch is jolly in the way he bursts into song after committing his crimes. In England, the male spectators, after seeing him dispose of his family, the landlord, the police, the hangman, the devil—all enemies or impediments to the ordinary man—used to want to shake his hand and offer him a drink."

Edmund Wilson, in his role of the American Mr. Punch, cracked the heads of his own devils—usually symbols of authority, ranging from Stalin to tax collectors—and tried to remove the mental impedimenta from the minds of his countrymen. Probably most of them would not have approved of his politics or his private life or religious opinions. But to the writers and readers he refreshed and delighted, to the recipients of his pungent, prickly, affectionate letters, he was the moral and intellectual conscience of his generation.

NOTE TO THE READER

It was Leon Edel who suggested that as Edmund's literary executor I could collect his letters more easily than others and that this would be of immense help in editing and annotating the Notebooks. Katharine White had given me the same advice soon after Edmund's death.

Most of these letters were written in longhand and have been transcribed either from original holographs or from photocopies. In the late twenties and early thirties, Edmund typed some of his correspondence with two fingers. He never dictated letters, and either wrote them out for the typist on a yellow legal pad or penciled a short reply on the letter to be answered.

Only two carbon copies of his own letters were found among Edmund's papers at Wellfleet, while a few others were among his papers at the Beinecke Library at Yale. As the uncollected correspondence began to pour in, it became apparent that more than enough was extant to prepare a volume of letters and that such a collection not only would be of value as a record but would complement and give background to the Notebooks.

At the outset it was decided that no love letters, family correspondence, and the like should be included; however, as will be seen, some of the letters cannot help but be personal, as they were written to close friends. The selection in this book reflects Edmund's primary concern with literature—and politics. "Heavens knows that, although my single aim has been literature," he wrote as early as 1917, "my great men have never been Pater and Symonds but Dante and Socrates and Voltaire, who can certainly not be said to have been indifferent to politics; and how should I remain *au-dessus de la mêlée?*"

If this volume has a certain biographical and narrative character and may constitute an epistolary autobiography, it is because the letters seemed to fall into place that way—into this pattern, rather than another. Editorial intrusions are kept to a minimum, so as to make this book entirely Edmund's.

Whenever possible, the recipient of a letter is introduced in Edmund's own words, by a short profile that prefaces a first important letter. This profile is not an attempt to emulate *Who's Who*, but rather to indicate Edmund's relationship to the person and his opinion of the writer's work; the comment sometimes dates from either a much earlier or a later period than the letter itself. The few footnotes needed to clarify the text are also, whenever possible, given in Edmund's words, as are the chronologies at the beginning of each decade. I tried to avoid bringing out the kind of book that Edmund described as "knee-deep or waist-deep or neck-deep in huge footnotes."

Edmund's instructions for the editing of his posthumous papers read: "I don't want him [the editor] to reproduce my contractions and ampersands, misspellings and faulty punctuations." All omissions are scrupulously indicated by ellipses. The many changes of address, which reveal so much about Edmund's way of living, are given in full, whereas the constant addresses, such as Wellfleet, Massachusetts, and Talcottville, New York, are indicated by town name only. Up to the time of his mother's death, many letters were written from Red Bank, New Jersey, and in the later years—when he made frequent trips to New York—from an office at *The New Yorker*. Series of letters written in the earlier days from *Vanity Fair* or *The New Republic* are prefaced by the publication's letterhead. These series often show Edmund as a literary editor: suggesting, soliciting, guiding, and encouraging contributors, and finally acknowledging an article and announcing the publication date.

Among the gaps in this selection are, unfortunately, letters to Dead Sea scrolls scholars, which could not be obtained, as well as some to English friends, "talking London gossip," which could not be found.

In his introduction to *The Shores of Light* Edmund wrote: "I have not arranged the pieces in strictly chronological order, but have sometimes grouped them in such a way as to put together pieces on the same subject or to bring out some special aspect of the period." Following this precedent —though the letters run chronologically, for the most part—it sometimes seemed advisable to bring in a letter or an excerpt from a letter out of chronology. It is hoped that these letters out of sequence, emphasizing an earlier idea or providing a retrospective comment, will elucidate a particular subject Edmund was curious about, or working on, and will lead the reader to realize the continuity of his interests over the years, of his enthusiasms, his likes and dislikes.

The dates in the section heads indicate the span in which the letters were written. The chronologies that introduce each decade carry the titles of Edmund's books in capital letters when they are juxtaposed to the years of first publication.

Passages relevant to the theme of this volume have been taken in some instances from very personal letters and from others of minor interest. The full text of these and other letters not included in this volume may someday find their place in a more scholarly and complete edition of all the correspondence.

ELENA WILSON
Wellfleet, Massachusetts

ACKNOWLEDGMENTS

To Edmund's friends, acquaintances, and correspondents who have helped me locate and obtain these letters, as well as to the libraries and collections where much of his correspondence has been deposited, I want to express my gratitude, as follows:

To the Amherst College Library and Ruth Limmer for letters to Louise Bogan; Valborg Anderson for letters to Margaret Marshall; Joseph Alsop, John E. Austin, Mrs. John Berryman and the University of Minnesota; the Honorable John Biggs, Fredson Bowers, Matthew J. Bruccoli, Mrs. James Branch Cabell, Morley Callaghan, Clelia Delafield Carey, David Chavchavadze, Loran and Mary Crosten, Lewis Dabney, Peter Davison, Barbara Deming; Babette Deutsch for letters to herself and Avrahm Yarmolinsky; Mrs. John Dos Passos and the University of Virginia; Joan Didion, Mrs. T. S. Eliot, Richard Ellmann; William Fenton and the Owen D. Young Library at St. Lawrence University; Tony Garrett, Oliver Gates; Maxwell Geismar and the Mugar Memorial Library at Boston University for letters to himself and Florine Katz; Celia Goodman for the important letters to herself and her sister Mamaine Koestler; Mrs. Chauncey Hackett, Sir Rupert Hart-Davis, Hazel Hawthorne; Mrs. Ernest Hemingway, Dr. Carlos Baker, and the John F. Kennedy Library for letters to Ernest Hemingway; Mrs. Frank Herzog, Paul Horgan, George Kline, Charlotte Kretzoi, Leonard Kriegel, Louis Kronenberger, Jacob Landau, Cecil Lang, Eugenie Lehovich, Anita Loos, Robert Lowell, Alison Lurie; Hugh MacLennan and the University of Calgary, Alberta; Mrs. Carey McWilliams for letters to Carey McWilliams and Elizabeth Huling; T. S. Matthews; Mary Meigs for important letters of the last twelve years; Nancy Milford for a letter to Zelda Fitzgerald; Arthur Mizener and the University of Delaware; Glyn Morris; Helen Muchnic for a correspondence of over thirty years; Vladimir and Vera Nabokov, Ada Nesbit, Blake Nevius; *The New Yorker*, William Shawn, and Katharine White for copies of correspondence to *New Yorker* editors; Ada Nisbet, Thomas F.

O'Donnell, Sonia Orwell, the Oxford University Press, S. J. Perelman, Stewart Perowne, Mario Praz, V. S. Pritchett; Jacqueline Rice for letters to Dawn Powell; Margaret Rullman, Arthur Schlesinger, Jr., Elizabeth Schouvalov, Marian Seldes, Wilfrid Sheed, Isaac Bashevis Singer, Francis Steegmuller, Frances Steloff, James Stern, Gleb Struve, Mrs. James Thurber, Eva and Philippe Thoby-Marcelin, Arlin Turner, John Wain, Dorothy Walsh, Robert Penn Warren, Thornton Wilder, Mrs. Albert Winham, and Susanna and Jonathan Wylie.

My thanks also go to Columbia University for letters to Bennett Cerf, F. W. Dupee, Jason Epstein, Gilbert Highet, W. W. Norton, and William Y. Tindall; the Cornell University Libraries for letters to Ford Madox Ford and Wyndham Lewis; the Houghton Library at Harvard University for letters to John Jay Chapman, E. E. Cummings, M. A. DeWolfe Howe, Robert Lowell, F. O. Matthiessen, and Alexander Woollcott; the Lilly Library at Indiana University for letters to Max Eastman and Upton Sinclair; the Library of Congress for letters to Huntington Cairns, Janet Flanner, and Felix Frankfurter; Malcolm Cowley and the Newberry Library, Chicago, for letters to him and *The New Republic*, and the same library for letters to Sherwood and Eleanor Anderson, Robert N. Coates, Floyd Dell, and Morton D. Zabel; the Berg Collection of the New York Public Library for letters to H. L. Mencken; the Princeton University Library for letters to John Peale Bishop, R. P. Blackmur, Whit Burnett, F. Scott Fitzgerald, Christian Gauss, Allen Tate, and one letter to John Dos Passos; the Smith College Library for Newton Arvin's letters; the Lockwood Memorial Library at the State University of New York at Buffalo for a letter to James Joyce; the State University of New York at Binghamton for letters to Padraic and Mary Colum; the Swarthmore College Peace Collections for letters to A. J. Muste; the University of California at Los Angeles for letters to Edouard Roditi and Cyril M. Schneider; the University of Edinburgh for two letters to Norman Kemp Smith; the Charles Patterson Van Pelt Library at the University of Pennsylvania for letters to Van Wyck Brooks, Theodore Dreiser, James T. Farrell, Waldo Frank, Rolfe Humphries, and Burton and Hazel Rascoe; the Humanities Research Center at the University of Texas at Austin for letters to Edward Dahlberg, Sir Compton Mackenzie, and L. A. G. Strong; Vassar College for a letter to William K. Rose; and special thanks to Donald Gallup of the Beinecke Rare Book and Manuscript Library at Yale University for many immediate answers to difficult queries and for the letters to Léonie Adams, Hamilton Basso, Alfred Bellinger, Kenneth Burke, Seward Collins, Stanley Dell, Muriel Draper, Alyse Gregory, Lincoln Kirstein, Jerome Mellquist, Marianne Moore, Max Nomad, Phelps Putnam, Gertrude Stein, Gilbert Troxell, and Elinor Wylie and William Rose Benét.

I thank Daniel Aaron for collecting and selecting many letters, for the many conversations which helped conceive this volume, and for constant advice; Leon Edel for reading the manuscript, many useful comments, and important letters to himself and Edna Kenton; Alfred Kazin for reading the manuscript, for his enthusiasm for Edmund's letters, and his approval of my unorthodox editing; Barbara Epstein for letters, her friendship for us, and constructive criticism; Bette Crouse Mele for letters and permission to reprint a part of her testimony from *The Indian Historian*; Yigael Yadin for permission to reprint his testimony from *The Listener*; my thanks to Robert Giroux and my gratitude to Roger and Dorothea Straus for their understanding of Edmund and their constant encouragement and help.

My thanks go to Lee Paskind for his translations from the Hebrew; to Elena Levin and Helen Muchnic for theirs from the Russian; to Lowell Edmunds for the Greek; and to Gyorgy Kepes for the Hungarian.

I thank Jonathan Aaron, who helped in the exciting task of selecting and listing; Geraldine Ramer and Jonathan Wylie for transcribing Edmund's difficult handwriting, for checking references, and for their patience with me; Timothy Walker Woodman for transcribing and typing; Sanford Schwartz, whose efficiency and taste helped pull the manuscript together; and Carmen Gomezplata and Patricia Strachan for months of work and objective criticism. I thank James Merrill and the Ingram-Merrill Foundation for their financial aid, and Helen Miranda Wilson for telling me I should take credit for what has been an exhilarating job.

ELENA WILSON

THE EARLY YEARS

I was born May 8, 1895, in Red Bank, New Jersey, and educated at the Hill School (class of 1912) and at Princeton (class of 1916). All four of my grandparents were born in New York State. Their families were all originally English, except my paternal grandfather's, which was originally Scotch-Irish. They had been living in New York and New England since the end of the sixteenth century, or thereabouts. My maternal grandfather belonged to a branch of the Mather family.

—To H. L. Mencken, 1923

1912

AND

PRINCETON

In the summers, I would visit the Bellingers in their house called Hilltop at Washington, Connecticut . . . Alfred and I, who had private jokes and exchanged epistles and verses, had an agreement that every year at Christmas each would send the other a book which the other would not otherwise be likely to read. Alfred later taught classics at Yale, and then became an authority on classical numismatics. He used to write excellent prose and verse.   (*A Prelude*)

To Alfred Bellinger   Wednesday [undated, 1912]

Dear Alfred: You made the stipulation that we should give entirely candid opinions of the interchanged books. If you want my candid opinion of *The Naulahka,** I must state that I think the best things about it are the chapter headings. Imagine my chagrin and disgust to discover that the hero was a brave, unfearing, honest, virile American youth who calls the heroine "little girl." This last item alone is enough to discourage me with almost any story. The heroine I found to be not «αἰνῶς ἀθανάτῃσι θεῇς εἰς ὦπα ἔοικεν»†—a type one meets in nearly every modern romance and which I have grown accustomed to, as one may grow accustomed to eating sugar, when there is nothing else in the house. No, this Kate Sheriff woman did not even have the privilege of good looks, for do not the authors refer repeatedly to her "plain, homely, features"? But, I forgot: you, of course, did not notice whether she was a pretty girl or not.

I was conscious of having met these two—also the female villain—in a

---

* A novel by Rudyard Kipling, written in collaboration with Wolcott Balestier.
† "In her countenance, she is marvellously like the immortal goddesses."
                                                              —*Iliad*, III, 158

good many other stories before. With such a pair for protagonists, no wonder the character interest of the tale became nil.

Mr. Wolcott Balestier—I take it that he wrote the Western parts, and the delicate love passages—writes with even less charm and grace than Mr. George Randolph Chester, whom I had supposed hitherto was the master of the business-letter school of fiction. Even Mr. Kipling seems to lose most of his charm, when writing in collaboration with his imaginative brother-in-law. In short, with the exception of two chapters which pleased me very much, *The Naulahka* seems to me to be only a tolerably interesting and fairly readable potboiler. Your enthusiasm about it surprises me.

I hope that you enjoy *Lavengro** as much as I did. I dare say you won't, out of spite. Everything is as merry as a marriage bell here. I have plunged into the sparkling waters of Shaw after my hard struggle to swim in the stagnant waters of Kipling and Balestier. Have also been reading James McNeill Whistler's *Gentle Art of Making Enemies*, by which I have learned how to be artistically snotty.   Yours as ever, Bunny

I am awaiting your critique of Borrow. Hurry up and finish the book.

To ALFRED BELLINGER   Friday [undated, 1912]

Dear Alfred: Excuse my not writing etc. etc. etc. I think you failed to appreciate *Lavengro* properly. Borrow's conceit and pedantry never irritate me, because he is so naïve about it. I think it is impossible for you to enjoy anything except works as noncommittal as Jane Austen and Gibbon. However, you said that you did enjoy *Lavengro* to a considerable extent, which I think it impossible for anyone not to do. Have you read *Romany Rye* yet?

Your charges against me in regard to *The Naulahka* are quite wrong. I don't think any of my statements are "wholly indefensible." As far as I can remember, the worst thing I said about it was that it had no character interest—a statement which needs no defense. I know at least two "Shaw-fed enthusiasts" who like the book. In fact, most people like it, it seems. Don't misunderstand me, I like a good story of adventure as well as any-one. I am as sensible to the thrills of *Treasure Island*, *Twenty Thousand Leagues under the Sea*, and *King Solomon's Mines* as anybody, but what I claim is that *The Naulahka* is not a good story of adventure. The only good thing in it isn't part of the adventure at all. The chapter in which the old Sultana—or whatever she is—persuades Kate to give up the hospital job and get married is a gem, and one of the most human things Kipling ever wrote, and well worth reading the book for—also the delightful

---

* George Borrow wrote *Lavengro* and *Romany Rye*.

4

chapter headings, which, between you and me, I don't believe to be real quotations at all, but I suspect that Rudyard wrote every one of them himself.

I have been reading various things this summer—Maeterlinck and Meredith chiefly. Your friend is quite right about the former, "he is too darn consummate," but Uncle George Meredith is a wonder. When I send you the second of our biannual books it will be *The Egoist*.

I have been doing lots of things this summer, and as I have taken up so much time with the Delights of Literature, and as I have written a letter just before this one giving a full account of myself, I shall spare a detailed description of what I have been doing. Suffice it, therefore, to say that I have been up in New York [Talcottville] for a long time (came back a week ago), where I enjoyed myself amain what with picnics and swimming and friends and relations and the charmingest girl that ever I laid eyes on, albeit 'twas she who jilted me on the Sixth-Form Dance last spring. Yet have I appointed to meet her at the Harvard–Princeton game this fall, when that I go down to Cambridge and stay overnight with Hugh Cole or Gussie Leroy, if they can give me shelter. I have to go down to Princeton the 18th, I believe.

. . . All your friends will soon be collegians, Alfred—and Gawsh! what tough rah-rah boys me and Larry'll be! I haven't written a word of prose or verse all summer, but I intend to try for *The Tiger* at Princeton. After I've made that, I'll have a shot at the *Lit.* and in time work around to *The News*. I do hope you'll make the Hill *Record* next year, Alfred! You've been trying so long and hard, it's high time they took you on. Remember me to your folks.　　　　　　　　　　　Yours respectfully, Bunny

SCHOOL AND COLLEGE FRIENDS

Morris Belknap		Yale
Alfred Raymond Bellinger	Hill School	Princeton
John Biggs		Princeton
John Peale Bishop		Princeton, *Nassau Lit.*
William Adams Brown	Hill School	Princeton
Sterling Carter		Princeton
C. Stanley Dell	Hill School	Princeton
John Dos Passos		*Harvard Lit.*
Walker Ellis	Hill School	Princeton
F. Scott Fitzgerald		Princeton
David Hamilton		Yale
Alexander L. McKaig		Princeton, *Nassau Lit.*
Laurence Noyes	Hill School	Yale
William Osborn		Princeton
E. E. Paramore, Jr.	Hill School	Yale

George Perkins	Princeton
Noel Robinson	Princeton
Gilbert Seldes	*Harvard Lit.*
Gilbert Troxell	Yale
Charles Rumford Walker	*Yale Lit.*
T. K. Whipple	Princeton,
	Nassau Lit.

To ALFRED BELLINGER   October 24, 1912
The Hill School   Princeton

Dear Alfred: Thank you exceedingly for the bound *Record*, with my name on the outside. I have been reading it over with considerable interest. Much of my last year's work seems already crude and silly, and I long to write better verse, and better prose, which I can do, for I have many ideas, if I would only cease idling my time doing trigonometry and going to the movies, and writing endless epistles to you . . .

The other day I was talking with Stan Dell about *The Record*, and its glorious past and uncertain future, and all the bright stars which once had shone in its pages. He told me many things that I didn't know before, and I gave him a résumé of last year's work. And I fell to meditating on the subject, and the gist of my meditation is embodied in the following advice (which is entirely needless). Although you may find that this year is a poor one for *The Record*, and travel sketches are ground out in abundance, and no one with any sort of talent appears, nevertheless, in the face of barrenness and jeers and complaints from the school, bring out the old magazine each month, and pull all the pep you've got into it to make it go, because someday in the future, when others are discovering the school, there will be "geniuses" as real as Walker [Ellis] and Stan [Dell] and the fellows who love *The Record* as much as yourself, who will enjoy the genial lively meetings and the lively quarrels and the dignity of seeing themselves in print, as much as we have done. It is your job to see that those who come after us get *The Record*, and I conjure you, by the memory of all those whom you have seen try for *The Record*, and make it and enjoy it and leave it, and all the jokes we have made, and the angry words we have exchanged, and the memories of yours that I know nothing about, and the memories of mine which you know nothing about, to stick to that job, for the sake of those who will be *The Record*, and have hilarious meetings—your institution—and have trouble with a too clever editor, and strive to make the board with breathless interest thinking it a supreme goal.

Amen, Amen, Yours ante-prandially, Bunny
Post-prandial P.S. I nearly missed supper writing this interminable thing.

·THE·RECORD·

·οὐδὲν· ἄνευ· πόνου·

VOL. XX.   MAY, 1911.   No. 7

Address all communications to Henry B. Gray, Jr., The Hill School, Pottstown, Pa.
Subscription, $2.00 per year of eight issues. Single copy, 25c.
THE RECORD is entered at the Post-Office at Pottstown, Pa., as second-class matter.

TABLE OF CONTENTS

Did you ever try deliberately writing an imitation of somebody? It makes you study the machinery of style and may be rather illuminating. (To Maxwell Geismar, 1942)

To Alfred Bellinger   April 22, 1913
                                                                              Princeton

Dear Alfred: On the Saturday of the present week, a small but intrepid band of pilgrims will be seen breasting the Hill; their voices will be joined in a resonant paean of victory; their appearance—dusty and maculate from the journey though it be—will betoken joyful spirits. They will be heard from afar off by Pottstown singing "We march, we march"—followed by the Hill School Hymns.

All this is by way of asking you to be sure and obtain our *five* suitcases from the Express office ere it closes. We must have decent garb, so we are sending our suitcases ahead. They will be addressed to *you*. Thursday afternoon we start forth. We shall wander through the beautiful countryside alive with the vernal breath and athrob with the myriad twittering of birds. We shall look upon the flowers of the meadows in their many-tinted glory. At every crossroads we shall stop and fish out the map and bicker about which is the shortest way to go. The first night we shall lie at Lambertville—that haven of semi-rustic location and thriving manufacturing on the banks of the noble Delaware. Then at some delightful old-fashioned hostelry we shall eat of the homely but satisfactory fare of the country and search out the local moving-picture show.

On the second day, when the rosy-fingered Aurora throws her pink cloak athwart the Heavens, we shall set out again; and, for a midday meal partaking of the homely but satisfying fare of the country, shall make progress as far as the town called Montgomery.

On the third day we shall proceed farther and, towns failing, sup mayhap with the hospitable farmer folk of the country, of whose homely but satisfying fare we shall partake. On this day Mr. Hinchman will have to be carried and Mr. Osborn restrained from endeavoring to reach the destination before noon. And finally we shall arrive at Pottstown in the manner described at the beginning of this letter. Hallelujah!

                                                    Yours till Saturday, Edmund Wilson, Jr.

To Alfred Bellinger   October 24, 1912
                                                                              Princeton

. . . I think I shall be able to get you a ticket, but the trouble is that you would have to sit in the Princeton cheering section, which I don't think is legal . . .

To Alfred Bellinger   November 4, 1912
                                                 Princeton

Dear Alfred: I have just finished a long letter in ink, and have decided to rest by writing one to you in pencil, meaning no offense. There's this about it, that I write fairly legibly in pencil . . .

I am just home from Cambridge where I had a very gay time what with one thing and what with another. Harvard is a helova place, and I wouldn't go to college there for money. There is no class spirit, no roughhouse—nothing but luxury. They have telephones in each room, and bathrooms adjoining, also private swimming pools, restaurants, etc. Hugh Cole and Ed Leroy are getting somewhat Harvardized already, but they treated us very well.

. . . Larry Noyes writes that all the Yale bunch are coming down here for The game. Thursday night I stayed in New York (before going down to Cambridge) and saw Shaw's new masterpiece, *Fanny's First Play*, which delighted me vastly, albeit not so much as *Milestones*,* and set me to think on many things, and to wonder how many of the audience understood that they were those very people which the author satirized in the play, and I marveled much at Mr. Shaw's so great wit and wisdom, for I know that he speaks the truth, and esteem him highly. Also meditating how that my friend Mr. Bellinger, the scrivener, would not like the play, and might even rage full force, as is his wont when he is angered, should he go to see *Fanny's First Play*. Yet would I rejoice to have him behold it, if only that I might wrangle with him about it. So home and to bed, and my cousin so deep in thought that he says scarce a word, and I also. (I don't know why I always adopt this Pepys' Diary style, when I begin to tell about a play. Pepys' Diary is a tome you should read.)

Cooper and Shea tell me that they have been up at school and that on account of the unsportsmanlike conduct of the Yale freshman team, many Hill students are changing to Princeton, which meseems a foolish reason to do a sensible thing, and I hope that you too may be induced to change your university . . .   Yours as ever, Bunny

To Alfred Bellinger   January 17, 1913
                                                 Princeton

. . . I commence my *Lit.* duties upon the appearance of the next number. I don't know what these duties may be, but suspect them to be made up to a large extent of loafing around the *Lit.* office . . .

---

* A play by Arnold Bennett written in collaboration with Edward Knoblock.

9

The
Nassau Literary
Magazine

Volume LXXI

APRIL 1915   MARCH 1916

FOUNDED BY THE CLASS OF 1842

Published by the Undergraduates of Princeton University

1916

To Alfred Bellinger   January 20, 1913
                                                          Princeton

. . . Your mother, as you may know, sent me a volume of Lady Gregory's plays, which I read with great delight. I am at present working away at George Meredith's letters, which are very interesting. One incident told therein surpasses any of the time-worn stories about Sordello, I think. It seems that a lunacy specialist wrote to Meredith and told him that the first chapter of *One of Our Conquerors* bore all the symptoms of incipient insanity. I shall write a review of *The Letters* for the *Lit.* Of course, I'll send you the number with my stuff in it, as soon as it comes out. The end of this week sometime. By the way, for heaven's sake, read *Pacchiarotto, and How He Worked in Distemper* by Robert Browning! Read it without delay . . .

To Alfred Bellinger   January 27, 1913
                                                          Princeton

. . . Monday—Up betimes and to Commons' where I do have a passing bad breakfast as ever and thence to McCosh Hall where I take an examination in the Science of Trigonometry, wherein, God help me!, I fear I did fail pitifully. To my rooms where I do find much mail, and one letter from Sir Laurence Noyes, the architect, which proves to be an unregulated composition running on for pages and pages with much nonsense and some news which I am glad to hear. Thence to Commons' again where all did talk of the examination, but My Lord Stanley Dell, who saith, "Why do we prate of this that is passed; it giveth me a megrim to think of it." Thence to my rooms where I do set out to write letters but Mr. William Osborn coming in doth exhort me to come walking with him and Sir Wilton Lloyd-Smith, which, although I had determined never to set foot out of door on such a drizzling, dark day, nevertheless I do, and we trudging through mud and rain, and I falling prone in a great stream whereat all do laugh, arrive at Rockyhill, a sorry hamlet, where, being hungry, we buy at the village store all manner of cake and biscuits which eating we become surfeited, and so walk home singing all the way, and passing merrily the time, what with rag, tag, and bobtail, till that I wonder how it is that on so cheerless a day, I may feel so carefree and joyous. When we reach the Colledge we buy some sandwiches, caring not to dine again at Commons'. So, donning dry clothese, to the rooms of Mr. Osborn and My Lord Lloyd-Smith, and, they building a roaring fire, we all do sit around it and eat, and I think that never was I so at peace with the world before. Mr. N. Robinson and Sir Stanley coming in, we do bid them not to break in upon the aesthetick spell, and they entreating us to go to the living-pictures but with no success, and so they leave us to muse by the hearth, and we do reminisce much and recall to each other times past when we were happy, and wondering how that the things which appeared to us of so great importance at school, have become little in our sight now, so that we do jest at them although we did view them so seriously. But we all unite in praising our school, but say that we saw it at its best. But the fire dying out, Sir Wilton and I to the post office where we do post letters and I a copy of my works to Mr. Bellinger . . . Thence to the rooms of Sir Stanley and Mr. Robinson and them we find reading—the former *Peer Gynt* and the latter *Tristram Shandy*, and both telling me what brave books they are, and I agreeing with both.

So home and to writing in my journal when there comes a knock at the door and I, thinking it to be the seller of food who comes the rounds nightly, do shout out, "Enter!" and then, "Sandwiches, apples, and pretzels!" very droll, but it proveth to be not the food-seller at all, but the coming editor of *The Nassau Literary Magazine*, Mr. Hunter, who, albeit astonished to be so accosted, maketh a call and praiseth my scrivening highly, and tells me of his publication's future, which I am glad to hear of. So, writing in my journal again, and bidding good-night to Mr. S. Carter, who retireth early ever, and, after reading in a book, to bed very well content . . .

To ALFRED BELLINGER   March 29, 1913
                                                               Princeton

. . . In my recent search for American literary art, I have discovered two masterpieces—Henry James's *The Turn of the Screw* and Edith Wharton's *Ethan Frome*—but I know that it is absolutely no use reporting discoveries in modern letters to you, be they ever so fine. Your oration on ancient and modern literature delighted me, but why, when you begin to feel a perfectly legitimate interest in recent literature, do you hasten to stultify yourself with some ancient rubbish? . . .

. . . Today I attended a meeting of the board of *The Nassau Literary Magazine*. The editor says to me, he says, "You write a one-act play for the next number, and I'll write another one, and we'll have a dramatic number." "All right," says I, so suppose I'll have to . . .

To ALFRED BELLINGER   September 30, 1913
                                                               Princeton

. . . I have been spending almost every evening during the last week in canvassing for the *Lit.*, which is one of the darnedest jobs I ever had —those blocks of freshman houses full of bleak, barren, dismal, dirty rooms where you find knots of freshmen gloomily discussing the probability of their being dismembered in the next mob, and convince them with great difficulty—since they have been fleeced for everything from shaving mugs to Tiger pictures—that it is an essential exhibition of college spirit to subscribe to the *Lit*. But there are campus amenities. Bates Hunter, the editor, and I are an uncommonly unhappy combination, because we haven't, either of us, an idea of orderly and businesslike procedure, so that we invariably leave part of the paraphernalia several rooms behind and have to return for it, fifty times a night, and because we are sometimes so overcome by the humor of the situation and the stereotyped quality of our remarks that we burst into open laughter, thereby convincing the wary freshman that he is the victim of some elaborate "horse" . . .

To Alfred Bellinger   October 23, 1913
                                                                  Princeton
Dear Alfred: To treat of the most vital matters first—it seems to me that your arguments to prove that Bennett's characters have no depth is applicable to many other novelists. Thackeray, for instance, and Hardy. The creative artist makes his characters, and succeeds in proportion as he makes you think them alive. Some excellent novelists actually not only indicate human depth but also explore them and bring forth authentic jewels. (But this kind of author is usually a poet—Browning is one of the best examples.) Other excellent novelists reproduce men faithfully from the outside. Thackeray is an extreme example. I think that Bennett created living characters, whose depths he suggested and understood although his exposition of them may appear sketchy and unpoetic to you. I can only say that I believe in them, and do not take exception to any of the things which you cite as particularly awful (I consider the last "fatuous half page" a stroke of genius—one of the most extraordinary in the book), and that I *do* think in those "complicated nothings." You say you don't and I say I do, and there we are, and we can't get any further. When did Bennett claim to "lay bare with entire completeness," etc.? I don't think we can expect any novelist to do anything of the kind.

In short, I accept these novels as valuable and beautiful impressions of life, although I don't pretend to Bennett's point of view any more than I do anybody else's. I don't attempt to defend his style, of course. I always objected to it violently, in fact. The things you say about it are true, and it is on account of these limitations of style that he is always obliged to stop outside the sanctum sanctorum and express himself rather inadequately, while Mr. Wells breaks the lock and enters. Meredith introduces himself politely and Hardy occasionally peeps through the keyhole.

However, since, although it is amusing to bicker about books, it doesn't get us anything, let us exchange life for literature during the remaining part of this letter.

The graduate school was opened formally yesterday. It was an occasion of great historical interest, an imposing sight and an opportunity to hear the foremost educators of the world speak. I was in New York at the time. Stan, Noel, R. P. Hinchman, and I went to see Shaw's *Caesar and Cleopatra* acted by Forbes-Robertson and his wife, which we enjoyed immensely. After some further dissipation I returned last night to this hard, hard life of monotonous routine.

I busy myself these days with reading for elaborate courses in English and French literature, writing Triangle Club songs with Sam Shoemaker —Gilbert and Sullivan have nothing on us—lucubrating for the *Lit.* . . . bicycling about the country . . .

Anon I shall have to attend Philosophy, so I shall stop after giving you an imitation of the Philosophy prof [Norman Kemp Smith], an individual with a curious accent, pointing to one of two things: (1) that he is a Scotchman who went to an English university; (2) that he is an Englishman who went to a Scotch university. But no! my time is short and phonetics, however elaborate, can hardly give you an idea of how he expounds his meandering little philosophical paradoxes. The other day in the midst of a beautiful disproof of the existence of sound, a lusty brass band came down the street and completely drowned out the lecture, to the infinite delight of the class.   Yours in all but literature, Bunny

To Alfred Bellinger   January 16, 1914
                                                               Princeton

Dear Alfred: I am glad you liked *Youth's Encounter* [Compton Mackenzie] so much.* Did you know that it is only the first volume of Michael's complete biography, the rest of which is to be published next year? The whole thing is to be called *Sinister Street*. Why *Sinister Street*, I wondered. The "motif of utter foulness" is one of the most uncanny things in the book; you feel that you are not walking on solid ground, that it may give way any moment and let you into the sewer. But I don't object to those parts where the author suddenly makes the infinitely beautiful disclose the infinitely vile, as in the convent episode and so forth, because I think it is more or less true in life, and has not been made to overbalance the pure human goodness of the greater portion of the book. Of course, with your ideas of fiction, this "is no argument" at all, so there we are!

Just at present I am very well occupied, but not getting as much done as I should like, for the days are drawing nigh when I shall say, "I have no pleasure in them," i.e., Exams. Last night I was laboring fiercely to finish a story, thinking to compete for the same prize I won last year. Teek Whipple came in and burst into roars of laughter at the sentence I had written, which was " 'My God, girl!' said the doctor. 'We don't wear

---

* See letters to Compton Mackenzie and Arthur Mizener, p. 562.

wigs in America,' " and really one can hardly blame him, because it is certainly a little startling, out of its context. He also told me that the members of the board cannot compete, so I gave up the story in disgust and we adjourned to Joe's to eat and discuss the Great Question, which is the complete renovation, rehabilitation, and resuscitation of the *Lit.* office, whose bare discolored walls and—and—well, really that's about all there has been to the *Lit.* office for years—have been an eyesore for all those who are anxious to have the place an Abode of Culture. So we decided to fix it up, and have been doing it for a week. It is the most humorous and amusing business I have had a hand in for some time. We began by buying a second-hand settle, which was placed in front of the ceiling-to-floor front windows so that the undergraduates could not see the editors taking tea; this shut out all the light, so Teek conceived the original idea of having windows cut in the back of the settle, which we have had done. Yesterday all the woodwork was repainted in dull black. The painter in his ardor painted a large portion of the floor and all the brickwork of the fireplace just to show there was no hard feeling, and now we all feel sensibly depressed when we go in, because it has all the atmosphere, as T. says, of a family vault. Now we are making haste to get gaily-colored hangings and rugs. All this in the face of the most complicated financial difficulties. This afternoon I am going to see the Curator about certain repairs which require his sanction. I'll have to negotiate this carefully, because you see we have been occupying the office from time immemorial rent-free, because "we don't make a cent out of the magazine," whereas nowadays the senior editors get a liberal rake-off of some hundreds every year. Also the light and heat bills have not been paid for forty years and have consequently mounted up a lot. Now if the Curator gets wind of the fact that we are affluent, there is no knowing what may happen. Here is a task indeed for a man of infinite tact! . . .

Yours always, Bunny

To ALFRED BELLINGER   February 13, 1914
                                                                Princeton

. . . Really we saw very little of you over your last flying visit. Also, you saw very little of us. But, nonetheless, though you see us but a few days, and though we drop all tasks and set ourselves to merrymaking for your pleasure, yet do you conclude, on this so slight evidence, that we are a new community of dilettanti and fritteurs away of time, squandering our golden youth on long rich meals, incursions into the country, amusing books, and frivolous conversation.

This is what you conclude, and I am anxious to be perfectly frank with you—we don't like it. Shall we, because we entertain you to our utmost, be contemned and condemned as idlers? A thousand times no! Neither shall I judge your Alma Mater by her appearance of inebriation on the eve of one of those great events—a football game. (Business of heaping coals on fire.)

. . . I am now going to don my cloak (once the property of an uncle who got it in its native land of Scotland), which makes me look a little like Tennyson, and sally forth into the lusty snowstorm now raging, to post this letter . . . Farewell, E.W., Jr.

To Alfred Bellinger   March 9, 1914
                                                                      Princeton

. . . There has been lots going on down here. Clubs have been and gone —for all except a trifling 100 sophomores, who are not considered as possible candidates for the private upper-class dining rooms. Stan, Noel, Arthur, and I went Charter—an excellent club. We had sworn to stick together, and did so although Stan and Arthur might have gone Cap and Gown, where More Gates and W. Lloyd-Smith are. I might have had a chance; the two last-mentioned gentlemen had put me through the sopho-more section, but the upperclassmen objected. You see, Cap and Gown insists on having people distinguished by some special ability, and if you haven't noticeable brains—a strong religious faith professed publicly in the sacred precincts of Murray Dodge will do as well. There is another way of getting in, too; that is, having a father or brother or whatnot who belonged to the club. So, you see, it is really made up of the most distinguished and admirable men in college, excepting, of course, those who were elected to Ivy, that glorious old organization, whose members we all respect; whose traditions we all revere. The traditions are father-or-brother-pull explained above, or what the newspapers call "great wealth." The members are two-thirds handsome blockheads. When the upperclassmen of this celebrated institution have elected to their midst the very pick of the sophomore class, they give a series of little parties to the new arrivals, in New York and Princeton, where a large part of the club makes itself as drunk as possible and entertains itself in other ways consistent with the fifty finest men in the university. While I am telling at such great length about these two old and honored clubs, I may as well mention the Cottage Club, hardly less so. This contains all the choice spirits who do not make Ivy and Cap and Gown, but this year something happened: some sad birds were elected and no other decent sophomores could be got to join. (Arthur turned down an invitation with no little nonchalance.) Altogether, you must understand, the election to one of the above clubs is a matter of great significance—or—to drop the ironical style—it is surprisingly evident that nothing of the club dope has any significance whatever. But what is still more surprising is the fact that everybody gets intensely worked up about it, everybody without exception. You would too. The upperclassmen

16

were vexed and amazed this year on account of the unprecedented way in which friends stuck together. Your sophomore would say, "I'll come, if you'll take so and so, too," instead of jumping at the honor of an invitation. This was partly due to the new system, tried for the first time this year, which postpones any club agitation until February, but it was largely due, I think, to the firmness and honesty of the class in general—although the juniors and seniors all cuss us out heartily as a class. Well, it was exciting and extremely interesting while it lasted . . .

In the summer of 1914, at the end of my sophomore year at college, I spent a summer in England, with four of my friends, Stanley Dell and Noel Robinson from Princeton and Larry Noyes and David Hamilton from Yale. (A Prelude)

To ALFRED BELLINGER   [undated, 1914]
                                              Bedford Hotel, Tavistock
"Go to," I said. "I will go up to London and see the play myself before it is taken off!" So I left the less Shavian members of the party and went up to London.

At Paddington I leapt into a cab, bade the cabman make haste, and promised him a shilling for his pains. Riding through London in a cab is the most perfect thing life has to offer. (And I say it who has tried all the pleasures of any number of continents; has rioted among the absinthe vapors of Montmartre, tried the terrors of Tibet, and fallen asleep over the gaming tables of Monte Carlo.) I am doubtful whether my ride could have been improved even by Dr. Johnson's second requisite for his ideal post chaise, which was, in my case, of course, lacking. Imagine my joy upon seeing Baker Street, the abode of Sherlock Holmes; Oxford Street, where De Quincey wandered in his squalid youth; and all the other places where all the other things happened!

Having deposited my luggage (a suitcase hopelessly disabled in early Pottstown days, and now further wrecked by continual overcramming, so that it incontinently burst asunder at unexpected times and I am obliged to glean a shirt from a station platform or gather a toothbrush from a city street) at the hotel, I rode to His Majesty's Theatre atop a varicolored bus, and purchased a ticket. Bookshops and Westminster Abbey next claimed my attention and the afternoon was passed with joy unbroken except by a Cockney who accosted me at Trafalgar Square and whined that he "'adn't the money to get back to Cardiff and was lyme, 'e couldn't work." I saw through the fellow instantly as an impostor and bade him begone. My cap (somewhat shrunken from the rains of the Lake Country), the shirt which I had borrowed from Davy Hamilton, and which had proved disparate to my figure, the necktie which I had borrowed from Larry

Noyes, and which proved to strike a jarring note with my complexion, and the other clothes which I had been wearing since I left America had evidently betrayed me as a provincial, so I hastened to a haberdasher's and persuaded an aged duke to sell me some modest articles of attire.

At supper I was initiated into the mysteries of English lemonade, which is known as "lemon squash." They bring you the ingredients and you mix them right before the audience. I sat alone in a very prominent place in the palatial dining room. I showed the ladies and gentlemen that I had nothing but a bottle of soda, a bowl of sugar, and a very little lemon juice at the bottom of a large glass. I poured the soda into the glass and then poised a tablespoonful of sugar. (The waiters hung breathless.) I introduced it into the mixture, and immediately there was a loud explosion, the lemonade ascended like a waterspout, and the table was flooded. The headwaiter himself rushed to my rescue. I haven't had so much fun since Chemistry 103.

After dinner I went to Shaw's *Pygmalion*, one of the best things he ever wrote, and the only one I have ever seen acted where the interest of the play centers more on the development of the characters than on the irony of the author.

The next day I decided to stay over the afternoon so that I could see the first public performance in England of Ibsen's *Ghosts*. It is a horrible thing and much more so for being wonderfully acted. The only time the audience laughed was when the curtain arose on the second act with the stage still gloomier than before and a character said, "Ah, today is comparatively bright."

I found there was no train to Devonshire (where I was to meet my companions) until midnight, so, feeling reckless, I went to two art exhibitions, bought a huge tome on Henry James, had a fearful debauch on the national beverage, and went to a "music 'all."

But, alas! the English train system is even worse than the Hartford–New Haven. I suffered until five in the morning in a third-class carriage; I found the inns at Exeter closed against me till I had wandered *hahlf ovah* the town and got two hours' sleep in a hotel whose night porter happened to be awake; I rushed off breakfastless to arrive in Ilfracombe at noon only to find that the rest of the party had gone on, and left a note for me to follow: I started hot in pursuit by means of a hired automobile, which broke down, so that I had to spend a large part of the journey leaning out to see if the wheel cap was safe, because, as the driver so justly said, "The wheel might fly off any moment"; and I finally found my friends eating a veal and ham pie at a place of refreshment. Our meeting was too touching to be adequately conveyed by words (as they say in *The Vicar of Wakefield*); I had had the time of my life, in short.

Pds 7 10s 6d. Ah, Paris! I shall have to walk the streets a very pauper.—

To Alfred Bellinger   November 20, 1914
                                                               Princeton

. . . As to Compton Mackenzie—I saw a letter from him sometime ago, and he certainly talked as if he was going to finish *Sinister Street*. Besides, I have since seen it announced for this fall in a publisher's catalogue. The English edition is published as *Sinister Street*, Vol. I, and contains a preface which throws some light on the title. "It has no reference," the author says, "to an heraldic euphemism, but is purely symbolic." *Carnival*, as you discovered, isn't nearly so good. *The Passionate Elopement*, I have never read: it is said to be very evidently modeled upon Meredith . . .

To Alfred Bellinger   December 5, 1914
                                                               Princeton

. . . I dare say that you have read the second volume of *Sinister Street* by this time. I have devoured most of it, and find it as wonderfully executed as the first part. As Michael grows older, however, it seems to me that the author allows the abundance of his material to swamp the thread of his theme; it can't cover some awful weaknesses. It appears that the point of the work is to lie in the hero's going into the Church. Where I am reading now, he is being conducted to it along very dubious paths. But I won't declare on its merits until I finish it. If this book is really the end: the reviews are full of rumors of more. By the way, if you want to read an excellent criticism of Mackenzie, and indeed all the modern people, get Henry James's last book, *Notes on the Novelists and Some Other Notes*, and look at the essay on "The New Novel." Aside from *Sinister Street*, I've been reading almost nothing but required Italian, Greek, and French, in the last of which, since I can read almost anything I like in the Honors' Course in Novels, not so ridiculously simple as it sounds, believe me! I'm going through Stendhal, and Gosh! as you would say, it makes Arnold Bennett look like *The Arabian Nights* . . .

To Alfred Bellinger   January 7, 1915
                                                               Princeton

. . . Arthur has just dropped in, while I was writing, to return Tolstoy's *Kreutzer Sonata*. I know a super-impressionistic fellow who was thrown off for five days, he said, by reading it: I am relieved to see Arthur as strong as ever.
    . . . write and tell me your opinion of *Marius*. Don't you think that the end, so strong in itself, is somehow weakened by Pater's telling of it? There is an effeminacy about his style that gets on my nerves, at times. Also, I think that the man's imagination, probably as a result of his experience doing the same thing, failed him very notably in this particular book, and we are not in the least thrilled by a change—the change from

paganism to Christianity—which must have been remarkably thrilling even within the strictly intellectual limits of Pater. Also, he often fussed with his words until they seemed to lose their meaning, and become simply printed things. I discover that I've written a rather Paterian sentence myself in this paragraph . . .

To ALFRED BELLINGER   February 22, 1915
                                                              Princeton
. . . I read in *The Prince*, this morning, that I am now the editor-in-chief of the *Lit.*, and I wish it were all over, because I can foresee that I shall have to summon whatever executive ability may lurk unsuspected within me . . .

To ALFRED BELLINGER   [undated, 1915]
                                                              Princeton
. . . I am sending you as much of my works as I can stand to have you read: namely, the three numbers of the *Lit.* issued since I have been editor, and *The Conning Tower* containing my incomparable Latin verses. Remember, even in reading such recent productions as these, that stuff published in a college magazine comes very quickly to look feeble and outmoded to its author . . .

To ALFRED BELLINGER   May 6, 1915
                                                              Princeton
. . . I'll take this opportunity to pronounce a pithy dictum upon *The Brothers Karamazov*, which I read last vacation . . .

In comment upon what I remember you to have said about this book, I think that it is indeed a satire, but a chiefly conscious one, upon the Russian people. As a picture of manners—one of the most valuable functions of the novel is recording manners—it is important and interesting. You said also, I think, that as a novel it is a "mess." Did you know that it was only the beginning of a longer work, designed, I imagine, to be something like Zola's *Rougon Macquart* series? Dostoevsky died before he finished it, and this, of course, must account for its strange inconclusiveness. An episode is closed, but the matter of first interest, the entanglement of ideas, never gets anywhere. You said, too, that it wasn't possible to consider any of the characters as sane. Well, many of them go through abnormal mental states, but it seems to me that they also remain intelligible and very recognizably human, and certainly show the hand of a great creative genius.

On the whole, in fact, I enjoyed it as much as any novel I've read this year. It kept me up late at night, in spite of its irrelevant *longueurs*—many of which, however, might have proved relevant, if Dostoevsky had ever carried out his plan. The episode about the precocious Russian boy, for example, was too elaborate and too amusing to have been merely a blind digression. The author combines the most naïve technique on record, I should say, with a treatment of his material which is anything but naïve. Even the speeches of the lawyers, for all their disproportionate and unconscionable length, have an ironic value somewhat similar to that of the ones in *The Ring and the Book*. In fact, the way he never ceases to discover interesting psychology in what might easily have been a common detective story is admirable. I applaud particularly the description of Dmitri's sensations upon being examined by the police at the tavern. However, I suspect that I enjoyed it all more than you did and I'm indebted to you for introducing me to Dostoevsky, whom I intend to investigate further . . .

Stanley Dell was one of Bunny's closest personal friends and they had been at the Hill School together. He had been handicapped by lack of vigorous health and had spent much time in Europe, where he had acquired a mastery of French and German such as few college graduates possess. Though he was the class poet, his interests were philosophical rather than literary, but he shared Bunny's wide background and wrote with a sense for literary nuances and a clarity that makes rereading his contribution to the *Lit.* after thirty years a pleasure. (Christian Gauss, "Edmund Wilson, the Campus and the Nassau 'Lit.,'" in *The Princeton University Library Chronicle*, 1944)

To Stanley Dell   August 29, 1915
                                        Hotel St. Francis, San Francisco
Dear Stan: We have had a long but interesting trip West by way of Canada. The West is a surprise and a shock: except for San Francisco and this part of California, all that we have seen is the most godforsaken even America can show. A Western city makes Trenton look like Athens, at first, until you discover that, whatever the harshness and crudity and desolation of country and city, the people are all much healthier and stronger than the people in the East. Nearly everybody, even in the worst towns, out here is in the bloom of health, whereas very few people you see on the street in New York, for instance, are.

And San Francisco is undoubtedly one of the most beautiful and attractive things in the country. I suppose it might be cloying if taken in too large quantities, but I think so probably because I am used to a state of bad weather and dull atmosphere. At any rate, they have woman suffrage. We took dinner a couple of nights ago with some Western relations. The women were all up on politics and busy about local affairs; they said that all the women in California were just as active, and while this is "almost certainly" an exaggeration, my observation of the way it works out here certainly confirms my conclusion . . .

I probably shall not be able to convince you of how good the Exposition is.* It was planned and executed under the direction of Jules Guerin, you know, and is architecturally so successful that it at once raises the question why, if American architects can build temporary buildings as good as this, can't they build permanent ones of the same kind. I went this afternoon to a concert at the Exposition, where Paderewski was playing, with a Western cousin who seems to understand all branches of art and she told me that the architects who did the buildings had been chiefly confined to erecting pretty bungalows and new banks and, when they had the opportunity of planning real temples and towns and fountains and gardens, even if only in pasteboard, as it were, let themselves go with a verve and taste which has produced such magnificent results that the city is seriously contemplating the preservation of some of the buildings for public purposes. There are panels by Frank Brangwyn, statues by everyone in the country who can sculpture, a huge gallery of chiefly American paintings, lots of trash, but some good stuff by Sargent, Pennell, and Whistler, and the whole, even to the rubbish cans, benches, and officials' costumes, planned and harmonized by Guerin. A great lesson should be learned from this Exposition! I look forward to the regeneration of America by means of architecture—or rather, I should, if I hadn't seen Winnipeg and Seattle first. Nothing can be done for places like that . . .

I have read most of the stuff I took with me; and have bought a lot more. The *Vie de Jésus* is a masterpiece, although I hardly think that Renan's *"charmant docteur"* displays much of the fierce enthusiasm with which I have always credited Christ. Mill's *Autobiography* is a strangely fascinating book; do read it . . .

Did you enjoy Emerson as much as I did? And what did you think of *The Brothers Karamazov?* But, what is more important, what are you doing and what do you intend to do? Write and let me know whether you are bound for the trenches or Princeton, N.J. I wish you were in San Francisco.

California, by the way, would be just as well suited for a honeymoon as Lake Como. It is the only place I have seen in the United States where romance seems pervasive and inevitable. The trouble is that you would have to pass through the Middle West on the way, and I wouldn't be sure of the felicity of any union inaugurated under those auspices. The children of such a union would be morose and deformed.

We are staying here about a week longer, then going for a few days to Los Angeles, and finally back East by way of Salt Lake City . . . Write occasionally, stating briefly but lucidly (a) your plans, (b) your opinions, and (c) your sensations.   Yours always, E.W.

---

* The Panama–Pacific International Exposition.

To Alfred Bellinger   September 2, 1915
                                                        San Francisco

. . . I am curious to know why you sent me *The Miracles of Antichrist.*
Did you think it had great literary excellence or profound thought or
what? I found it, on the whole, quite dull, with mildly amusing spots. As
for its thesis, that seems to me feeble and somewhat ridiculous. Socialism
is, of course, not a religion, but a political theory like another; it is not
supposed to be a substitute for Christianity. As a political theory it seems
to me that, far from being anti-Christian, it is more nearly compatible
with the Christian beliefs than any other political theory. And, as a matter
of fact, this is precisely what Miss Lagerlöf admits. It is, she says, coinci-
dent with Christianity, except in the matter of immortality and salvation
of the soul. But in what way does socialism interfere with this belief?
Assuming the truth of the doctrine (which is an important one to the
author, but to which I am indifferent), I do not see that socialism is likely
to interfere with it: I think few really religious people, however sincere
and absorbing may be their faith and interest in immortality, are likely
to claim that they are thereby exonerated from doing the best they can
find to do toward adjusting the society of the world in such a way as to
minimize the misery of their brother souls during their sojourn here. At
least, such a view seems to me unthinkably inhuman and a particularly
cruel perversion of the religious instinct. Unbelief may have followed
from socialism in Gaetano's case, but Miss Lagerlöf has no right to conclude that the two are essentially inseparable. Indeed, a man may be a
fervid socialist and a perfectly orthodox Christian at the same time (not
a Roman Catholic, I suppose; but is that important?). From the author's
point of view, no doubt, I am one of those "whose kingdom is truly of
this world"; from her point of view, I gladly accept it. But I protest
against the phrase as a singularly narrow piece of religious snobbishness
and heartily deny that the kingdom of the socialists or the French Revolutionists (whom Miss Lagerlöf takes pains to snub) is really of this world
at all. As I said, I am puzzled to know what recommended this book to
you . . .

Boswell I finished long ago, but have not written up, for obvious
reasons. Of course I don't think him an "utter ass," he was one of the
greatest artists of his time. He shows much of the special talent of the
novelist in writing biography. Macaulay, I think, calls him "[illegible]
vain, pushing, a snob, and a sot," and is completely unfair. Boswell was
not only an artist: he was a Scotch artist, which means that he was
governed by two things: a fascination in the glamour and charm of life,
and a rigid conscience in telling the strict truth about it. I wonder how
far he realized what a marvelous portrait he was painting of himself. His
Scotch honesty compelled him to tell the truth, even when his part was

a ludicrous or mean one. He was the true creative genius, which always feels more than it knows.

The book is one of the most thoroughly delightful I have ever read . . .

> Scott was sometimes called Fitz in college. I always called him that then, and for some time after we were out. (To Gilbert Seldes, 1963)
>
> "Shadows on Laurels" was the first thing of his I published when I was editor of the college magazine.   (To Charlotte Kretzoi, 1964)

To F. Scott Fitzgerald   August 28, 1915
San Francisco

Dear Fitz: I wrote a whole first act, lyrics and all; some of it was exquisitely humorous and some of it was very weak.* I sent it to Lane and told him to forward it to you, when he had finished with it, because I was too lazy to make another copy. He returned it to me with a long letter explaining that he liked it but that there were a number of important changes he wanted me to make. My impression was that he had failed to appreciate the exquisite humor of the exquisitely humorous parts but had fully appreciated the weakness of the weak parts. I received the package the night before I left for the West and didn't want to take it with me.

Lane wrote that he would send it to you, when he got it back the second time from me. I suppose the best thing I can do now is to write home for it to be sent now to you. I am sick of it myself. Perhaps you can infuse into it some of the fresh effervescence of youth for which you are so justly celebrated. The spontaneity of the libretto has suffered somewhat from the increasing bitterness and cynicism of my middle age.

Another thing. I thought until today that I was coming to St. Paul on my way East. Now I am almost sure it can't be done and so I shan't have an opportunity for talking it over personally with you until college opens. At any rate, I'll have the MS sent to you at once.   Yours etc. E.W.

To Alfred Bellinger   January 7, 1916
Princeton

. . . Why, with all the art and wisdom of the world at my disposal and a thousand times more to be done than I can ever hope to accomplish, do I sit before a page of Homer and play for minute after minute with half an eraser with a pin stuck through't. Calvin, I understand you; Jonathan Edwards, you are justified . . .

---

* " 'The Evil Eye' . . . Edmund Wilson, Jr., wrote the book and Scott Fitzgerald wrote the lyrics . . . for the elaborately costumed annual performance of the Triangle Club . . . It was a howling success."—Christian Gauss, "Edmund Wilson, the Campus and the Nassau 'Lit,' " in The Princeton University Library Chronicle, 1944.

Dear Alfred: I don't know when or where this letter will reach you. The only news I have had of you was from Larry, who said that you have been sent to Mexico with the Yale Battery. I hesitate to ask you to write me one of the many letters you owe me from a place where you will probably not have a chance to write very many letters; but since I am unlikely to see you this summer, unless the war is called off and you are allowed to come back, please send me some word of yourself either directly or through your mother. My address from September 1 will be 15 West Eighth Street, New York, the apartment Larry, Dave, Morris, and I are going to live in together. Of course, you must visit us there too, unless you should have to stay in Mexico the whole of your three years.

At any rate, wherever you are, you will have to listen to the biennial critique, which delivers itself and shall always deliver itself, independent of time, change, wars, and rumors of wars. (I hope we're not concerned with anything more than these last, in the present case.) I was fascinated by Trevelyan:* it is one of the most entertaining books I have read this year; the first volume is particularly good. I don't think there's much for me to say about Macaulay which wouldn't be evident to anyone else who read the book. He wasn't a complex or puzzling character; he was one of the most open, straightforward, and comprehensible literary men I have ever read about, and one of the most honest and admirable. He had one of those able, dogmatic, and stubborn minds of which Johnson was the great typical example in the eighteenth century and Chesterton a perhaps somewhat enfeebled one in our own, one of those essentially English minds which seem so difficult for Frenchmen to understand, which combine many good English qualities with some very bad ones. For Macaulay, with all his amiability and wide outlook, has a considerable share of English snobbishness, and moreover had never a doubt in his conviction that England was, as he says in one of his speeches, "the greatest, the first, and most highly civilized community that ever existed"!

Trevelyan is, of course, an excellent biographer, and he succeeds, just as Boswell did, in making an enthralling story out of a not particularly eventful life. He makes a fine and dignified figure of his subject, even though he is sometimes a little too pompous about it and lays on his admiration for his uncle a little too thick, stopping to go into sober ecstasies over fears and actions which would have been more impressive if they had been left without comment. But he does, as I said, do him justice, in a way that Macaulay seems especially to need nowadays, where it is the fashion to sneer at the great men of the last century. For we are

---

* *The Life and Letters of Lord Macaulay*, by his nephew, Sir George Otto Trevelyan.

struck not by Macaulay's superficiality and empty rhetoric—the academic stock phrases for him—but by his scrupulous thoroughness, his sound literary conscience, and his knowledge and acceptance of his own limitations.

But whatever *Lothair* is, it isn't English. The style is not English and the attitude is not English. That curiously bad style, which is far from being a pure style—Edmund Gosse calls it "Corinthian"—produces the same effect of not quite arriving which I have noticed in the writings of other Jews, who, however clever they may be, seem unable to write a really sound style. I have read that *Lothair* is the most carelessly written of Disraeli's books: the continual use of "rather" in the first part betrays the looseness of the amateur writer. But it has a kind of tinsel glitter which is often attractive.

Again, the magnificent episode in which Lothair is rescued by the Catholics from the battlefield and they pretend that he has been saved by the Virgin sounds far more like the irony of Voltaire and Anatole France than like the humor of Shakespeare and Dickens. At any rate, it is something detached, capable of keeping an imperturbable tone in the face of the ridiculous. The whole story, in fact, is told so detachedly that I was a little bewildered at first as to how much the author himself was meaning seriously. I decided, before I had finished, that he was taking none of it seriously.

Of course, I enjoyed it greatly, although I fell asleep over it more times than I ever remember to have done with any other book—perhaps because I read it under exhausting circumstances.

I congratulate you for having won the classics prize at Yale and also for making Bones . . . Good luck.   Yours always, E.W.

WORLD WAR I

I have never yet really felt it my duty to fight in this war, I consider myself well provided for in a branch of the service which commits me to nothing except a desire to repair damage and do something for my country—which I hope later to serve more effectively in other fields.

To ALFRED BELLINGER

July 29, 1916
Military Training Camps
U.S. Army, Plattsburgh, N.Y.

Dear Alfred: Charles Walker and I were going to write you a unique communication together . . . We set out to compose this thing, which was to have been a titanic satire on the army, last Sunday night, and went to dinner in town with the purpose of beginning it afterwards, but we fell in with an extraordinary man who had been playing great quantities of Wagner while he was waiting for a table and who, when we finally invited him to share our chops with us because he had played for us so long, entertained us all the rest of the evening, being then on the crest of the wave from something which he modestly described as "one high-ball." He was immensely interested in at least three things: wine, women, and classical music, and invited us first to have some beer and then to have some Meyerbeer; and this did not seem to him a jest, but a really felicitous and delightful harmony . . .

Meredith seems to be the safest thing I can send you and I intend to hand out Meredith novels to you to refresh you amid the dark stretches of "obscenity and lies" with which I generally seek to nourish you; this will allow your optimism an opportunity to repolish itself and your indignation to relax. I do not make sense of your reservations about Carinthia;* she has always been one of my favorites—perhaps my chief favorite—

---

* *The Amazing Marriage.*

heroine in fiction, and I think the apparent stupidity and naïveté which you seem to object to is quite in keeping and not repellent. I think you want Meredith to idealize her, whereas it is always just his point that you must take her as she is, but appreciate and admire her all the same, as you do with real people . . . This novel, which, as you probably know, was the last he ever completed—think of having written it at almost seventy! —contains a very clear presentation of some of his views of life; the main theme seems to be repeated with variations by the minor characters; as in all of Meredith's best, the characters come to represent very great things without losing individuality, and in Fleetwood's attitude toward life and Carinthia's, together with all that Henrietta and Gower Woodseer (did you know he was originally intended for Stevenson?) and the rest represent, I have always found meaning—which it is no use trying any longer to describe, except by mentioning that they have to do with the confusion of values in the society which we live in and what is really fine and worthwhile and what isn't. This is all vague and probably both obvious and uninteresting . . .

Also, I didn't mean that Disraeli was French, simply that he wasn't English. He was really of Italian and, further back, of Spanish extraction, I believe, and was to all intents and purposes, it seems to me, a continental Jew. At this point I will refrain from attempting to convey to you my impressions of the Jewish mind, which interests me as exemplified in Jewish writers and, just now, by a remarkably brilliant Jew named Sakolsky who is one of my tent mates. We began by disregarding him, as I, with a kind of instinctive snobbishness toward Jews, usually do, and have by this time come to regard him as the remarkable and amiable individual he is. He is an economist, an authority with railroads and apparently familiar with all the arts, and is capable of infuriating Mr. Sutton (Princeton '98) and me to frenzy even at the latest hours, when we are weariest, by saying subtly derogatory things about Princeton. Our tent is really a great bunch—though one of the men is, I think, the most perfect and invariable idiot I have ever known—and we begin to talk of having reunions in New York.

Well, as usual, this letter has been almost purely literary, and hasn't much to say about Plattsburgh, which I have enjoyed immensely . . . I cannot go into the question at length here and will gracefully dodge it by entertaining you with some aphorisms by Voltaire which I composed the other morning on a hike . . . Do write and come to visit me in New York and don't become atrophied by this damn military life any more than you can help.   Yours always, E.W.

"Le bienfait principal de la vie militaire, c'est de faire mieux goûter la civilisation."

"Le métier de forçat et le métier de soldat ne different qu'en un respect: celui-là rend sa liberté à l'Etat parcequ'il a tué, celui-çi pour qu'on l'instruit à tuer."*

To Alfred Bellinger   November 17, 1916
The Evening Sun, New York
. . . I am doing not very difficult work here—writing up little stories about people being almost killed under trucks, being fined for buying partridges, attempting suicide in hospitals, and things like that—or rather, rewriting most of them. The work is really quite varied, though, and so intermittent that I have a great deal of time to read and write in the office. And for this I receive $15 a week . . .

I became great friends with Mrs. Bellinger, Alfred Bellinger's mother . . .   (*A Prelude*)

To Mrs. Alfred Bellinger   August 14, 1917
The Evening Sun, New York
. . . There seems to be a chance that this unit I'm in may start this week, the last bulletin I had from Detroit sounded more authoritative than most of the others . . .
. . . and what I am going to do after the war is over we neither of us know: but we are convinced that what the world needs is a powerful publication of which we are the editors and owners . . .

To F. Scott Fitzgerald   October 7, 1917
Grosse Pointe Farms, Mich.
Dear Fitz: I am quite unable to tell you what effect the war at close quarters has on a person of my temperament: I have never got any nearer to it than the Detroit state fairgrounds, where I am associated in the errand of mercy with the sorriest company of yokels that ever qualified as skillful plumbers or, an even less considerable eminence, received A.B. degrees from the University of Michigan. I waited till the middle of August to be called into camp and have now waited till October for the unit to sail for France. The ordeal has, it is true, been somewhat mitigated by having David Hamilton with me (I am at present writing from his house) and another friend from Yale; but the latter has recently despaired of the hospital business and taken examinations for aviation and I have myself become so sterilized, suppressed, and blighted by two months of orderly, guard, and fatigue work that I am beginning to feel it wouldn't

---
* E.'s spelling.

take much to make me do the same thing. Where is the old esprit and verve? I sometimes think it was finally extinguished the night when you and I sat alone upon the darkened and deserted verandah of Cottage (its marble splendors more desolate untenanted than were ever the stinking halls of Commons when Princeton was alive) and let John Bishop take the shabby whoring of the Princeton streets for the royal harlotries of Rome and the Renaissance. Ah, how not only, to quote your friend, are the beautiful broken and the swiftest made slow, but the kindly made hard and the clever made dull! Seriously, I shall never forget that ghastly evening; I have never seen or heard from John and was consequently glad to get his poem, which is excellent, of course, except for the last stanza, which does seem to me inadequate. I like yours, too, although I didn't understand the two quoted lines in the last stanza, and ever since "Princeton: The Last Day," which, if it means what I think it does, possesses a depth and dignity of which I didn't suppose you capable, have thought you by way of becoming a genuine poet. If you have any more stuff of John's and your own, I wish you would send it along; my comrades of the unit make it seem to me incredible that I could ever have had friends who spent ecstatic hours pursuing the Beautiful. And if you have any news of Alec or Townsend, I should be exceedingly glad to hear it. You speak of Jack Newlin, but I have never heard nothing about him; has he been killed?

I'm inclined to agree with you about *The New Machiavelli* [H. G. Wells], at least so far as to admit that it is one of the best novels of the century. By the way, you should read James Joyce's *Portrait of the Artist as a Young Man*, which is probably another of the best novels of the century, and also an essay called "British Novelists, Ltd" by Mrs. [Katharine Fullerton] Gerould in the last *Yale Review*. I wonder what will happen to the *Lit*. Will it be compelled to subsist for a while as a memory merely on the strength of the brilliant past which you and John and Teek and I and the rest have just supplied? When I read a few fragments of platitude reprinted in *The Evening Post* from Mr. Hibben's* speech at the opening of the university I avert my inward gaze from a crippled Princeton which I have no more tears to weep and turn them back to the contemplation of a wretched world which, for all the men I may damage or repair in the service of the country, I know I can do little or nothing to correct and heal. Although the truth is I have almost forgotten about the war, since I have become a member of the army. It has reached such an impasse, since the rejection of the Pope's appeal, that it only exasperates one to try to figure a solution. And if my letter is arid it is only because I am arid myself at the moment as I hope never to be again; but still

---

* "The president of Princeton in my time was John Grier Hibben . . ."

remain, in the sacred name of the divine muses and the indissoluble bond
of our knocked-up alma mater,

> "Because her bells are clearer than the guns;
> Because her books are braver than the charge"

(to quote the lines of a great but temporarily neglected poet).

Yours for what you choose to consider the Celtic strain in us and
which, whatever it is, for all our laziness and ignorance, does separate
from the optimistic and sentimental mass of our countrymen, in company
with yourself,   Edmund Wilson, Jr.

You will pardon the effects of this vile stub pen.

To Stanley Dell   September 19, 1917
                                                    Grosse Pointe, Mich.

Dear Stan: We may arrive in New York any day and I shall certainly let
you know as soon as we do. The unit was all ready to leave tomorrow
morning, but was suddenly prevented by, it is said, some red tape connected with the typhoid inoculations. Camp has become unbearably dull.
I am sorry you didn't find much in my letters; but I have so few emotions susceptible of expression, except the ungenerous one of impatience
at my fellow workers on the errand of mercy, and this I have so vehemently
given vent to in letters to others that I have now scarcely a curse left to
communicate to you.

The only excitements I have had were furnished by the sudden marriages and engagements of my friends, but—and this is not said for
humorous effect—unlooked-for marriages now thrill me less than did once
the engagements I had expected . . .* Well, *pro deas nuptas, O Hymen
Hymenaee,†* as Catullus remarked on a famous occasion. While the rest of
you are getting married, I am only reading Catullus' wedding hymns on
the Detroit state fairgrounds. And, when I get married, there will be no
hymns, nay, not even the well-known wedding march from *Lohengrin*.
Like all the important events, happy or miserable, of my life, it will pass
without comments even from myself. Which of you has ever seen me
really cheerful or really gloomy, and known it? You will pardon this sort
of thing; but you have no idea how introspective one becomes during
guard duty on the long, cold autumn nights, sitting in the adjutant's tent,
companioned only by the bugs, or pacing the old familiar well-worn path
between the latrine and the camp gate. You have no idea, seriously, how
isolated and inward you become, surrounded by and dealing with people
with whom you cannot talk the real language, whose habits and manners
you detest, and with whom the only qualities which you have in common

---

* List of married friends omitted.
† E.'s spelling.

are the qualities which you would most willingly destroy forever. And yet *nihil humani mihi alienum est.* This is not the absence of charity on my part; it is only the reaction of intelligence.

The Hamiltons, among whom I now am, with Mary playing the phonograph for my delectation, represent the other pole from the class of society where men seem to be familiarized with the most obscene perversions and horrors of life from their earliest years and to spend a large part of their leisure conversing about them with unflagging delight. (I refer to the ordinary men of Base Hospital 36.) Like the Count's conception of Fanny in a play by a dramatist of whom you may have heard me speak [Shaw], one would say that the girls have "never seen an ugly sight or heard an ugly sound" in their lives. I spend two-thirds of the week cursing the results of American civilization (our commanding officer made a bitter jest the other day about the American troops bringing "syphilization" to [illegible]) as manifested in the unbeautiful and ungracious figures of my camp companions and the other third berating a group (exceptional in America, I admit) where the daughters know apparently literally nothing about anything except the pleasant, the gentle, and the nice. They are so pretty, so fine, and so ill educated; they know that woman's place is in the home and have no other desire or aim except to exhibit the domestic virtues. The age, the nation has passed them by; they are little girls at twenty. The truth is I have been greatly exacerbated, not only by the men in the unit, but also and most genuinely by the parade of drafted men which we yesterday led through the streets of Detroit. The crowds were incredible: the roofs were bristling with people and the roads were so full that four soldiers abreast could hardly get through and, to give them a free passage, the policemen had to shove them in, as if they were kneading dough. The women fought and called one another names. The boozy old men and decrepit prostitutes winked and attempted genial banter with us. In the open street the air was so foul with bad breaths and dirty clothes and bodies that the women fainted and those who had spent whole days, like myself, in the care of the latrine could admit they had had less unendurable ordeals. And there was no end of enthusiasm: clapping, fish-horns, "Hip, hip, hooray for Uncle Sam!" I could stand up against the condemnation of the crowd, but I cannot endure its compliments.

I find that I have written away most of my evening of leave and must bring this soliloquy to a close . . .   Yours for sweetness and light, EW

To Alfred Bellinger
October 30, 1917
A Canadian port

Dear Alfred: . . . We are on our way at last and I will spare the record of the cumulative horror and depression of my three weeks in Detroit.

Superficially, my case on board is not much better, because, through an unfortunate mistake which even our officers have been unable to remedy, the greater part of the unit (including myself) has been consigned to a filthy unventilated hold formerly used to contain the baggage of the passengers, which was stored away on tiers of racks. An open space in the center of the room was enforced by huge iron bars running vertically from ceiling to floor and supposed by the present unhappy tenants to have been erected for the purpose of preventing the escape of the bedbugs and rats (a purpose which has so far been startlingly successful). The whole place, in aspect and odor, reminds me of nothing I have ever seen before except the county jail at Freehold, New Jersey; but the jail was airier and infinitely better kept. (This is not a jest.) We are, of course, expected to sleep on the baggage racks, but, as no one could do this without suffocating during the night and having his body devoured by vermin, most of us either sleep on deck or double up with those of our friends who were fortunate enough to get staterooms in the steerage. And, all the time, I am told, there are staterooms vacant in the first and second class. But our commanding officer, who ranks all the others on the ship and has every desire to do his best for us, is powerless to change orders received from Washington, now that the ship has sailed.

In spite of all this, however, David and I are fairly happy at the prospect of seeing France and England again and at having just assisted at the organization of a unit magazine, for which I am to write the editorials . . . I am unbelievably glad to have something intelligent to do at last. Also, it gives me a pass to the second-class salon.

If you want to know why hospital orderlies have a bad reputation, it is at least partly because they are often recruited from the men who have bad records. I felt sometimes . . . that I had made a mistake in consigning myself to the society of a class of men who had neither the intelligence nor the initiative (though this is not true of all of them) to get commissions, as most of my friends were doing . . . but, after all, this hospital business has yet to be demonstrated to be a failure for me, as I have never yet really felt it my duty to fight in this war, I consider myself well provided for in a branch of the service which commits me to nothing except a desire to repair damage and do something for my country—which I hope later to serve more effectively in other fields. My only question has been whether I might not actually be doing myself a more fatal violence in engaging in a kind of work which would slowly destroy my energy and enthusiasm (ten weeks of hospital camp can seem as bad as that, I assure you) than in putting aside the mental attitude of my whole life and taking active duty in a conflict which I have never been able to look at with the same eyes as any of the combatants; but this question is silent just now and its reappearance and solution depend on how we fare in

33

France. All this is an attempt to answer some of the questions in your last letters . . .

We talk of the Dark Ages: yet the Dark Ages produced *The Divine Comedy*. What name will our children's children find for the ages which produced Dostoevsky and Dickens, Zola and Flaubert, and Arnold Bennett? Great in his field as I believe he is, I have never committed the absurdity of supposing that Shaw had a more justifiable place in the modern curriculum than Sophocles, because he has more vital things to tell the students. Or, if I am comparing two writers of different kinds, say rather Ibsen, about whose intermediate plays the things I have said in connection with Kipling are true. We have no longer the palaces of Oedipus and Agamemnon; we have only the country house of Rosmer and the common city dwelling of the Gablers.   Wilson

To F. Scott Fitzgerald   December 3, 1917
                                                            France
Dear Fitz: Your letter has just reached me; thank you for Townsend's letter; I can almost hear him talking. I should make haste to do anything in my power to dissuade John from calling his poems *Green Fruit*, but do not know his address, having heard nothing from him. I wish you would let me know where he is and whether he got his commission. Ask him to drop me a line.

I cannot even yet tell you much about war at close quarters, being only near enough to hear the guns, which do not sound as loud as thunder. We are stationed in what was once a popular summer resort* but has now been turned over to the American hospital service, which is going to turn the hotels into hospitals. It will be at least three months before they are ready to receive patients and I have decided, in the meantime, to resume the writing of my forthcoming books, war or no war. If I did not do this, I think I should die of my own futility and a growing conviction of the futility of prolonging the war; this last fostered lately by Lord Landsdowne's letter, Bernard Shaw's last public speech, the Russian armistice and the Italian defeat and, also on being nourished by [Romain] Rolland's *Au-dessus de la mêlée*, France's *L'Orme du mail*, and that fine series of ironies at the expense of the Franco-Prussian War: *Les Soirées de Médan*.

But the chief thing really is the terrible silence and weariness of this part of France. Our life here, with its round of marvelous French dinners at little cafés and of walks and bicycle rides to the ancient villages that are all around us, would be perfectly idyllic, if it were not for the fact that the unseen, unrealized reality of the war and one's own prolonged

---

* "We were stationed at Vittel in the Vosges . . ."   —*A Prelude*

inactivity makes it more ghastly than you can believe. Over such wine and food as this, we could once (Dave and I—and you and the rest, if you were here) have outworn and outdazzled the stars with the sparks of our jesting, but I feel that the door of the house of mirth and, in fact, of any normal occupation is shut till the war is over. Not that we don't hold revelry here of no mean order! David, a newspaperman from Harvard, an extremely amusing and nice artist, and myself are accustomed to consort together in the back rooms of cafés, restaurants, bistros, quinquettes, buvettes, and claquedents of every sort and drink with an enthusiasm verging on ferocity to the eternal damnation of the army. But all this is a revelry stunned and distraught, Christmas dinner among the convicts, the Black Mass performed by marionettes . . .

It somehow reassures me that you should be back at Princeton, as if, after all, the continuity of life there had not quite been broken up. Remember me to Gauss: I think of him often in France. In spite of the fact that I had been here before, years ago, it was chiefly because of what he had taught me that I felt so little a stranger when I arrived here a couple of weeks ago.   Yours always, Edmund Wilson, Jr.

To Stanley Dell   December 29, 1917
                                                                France

Dear Stan: Your last letter announced that your marriage was imminent and a clipping which Morris sends informs me that it has taken place. I have sent you a wedding present which, with the very limited range of shops here, is the most interesting I can do—though it is the kind of thing which, if I received it myself, I should not know exactly what to do with. It is made of the lace for which this part of France is more or less famous and I really think it is quite pretty. You might use it for an antimacassar or tablecloth—or a lunch cloth, if the lunch were small enough. At any rate, it has the merit of not being particularly useful and may be considered indefinitely as a *disponible*. The Dove of Peace will be found in the center of the design, inextricably entangled in the scrollery of intrigue and misunderstanding, in which the fleur-de-lis plays a prominent part— though I do think it would be more to the point if it were the thornbush of the English rose, growing with a splendid robustness but no training. I trust that, in thus pointing out the tragic symbolism of the design, I may succeed in partially comforting the perplexity which inevitably arises from an anomalous present like this.

I think that, for the remainder of this letter, I will confine myself to a description of my spiritual state rather than to a narration of the circumstances of my life. I may simply mention that I was originally interpreter at headquarters, whence I was transferred, at my own request, to the X-ray department; when I was transferred, much against my will, to the dental

35

department, because they needed somebody to talk French to the civilian patients. My job there is a sinecure; I light the fire in the morning and the rest of the day spend my time either in reading or talking to the dentist's assistant, arising from time to time to replenish the warm water pitcher . . .

At other times, I am horribly depressed by an all but compulsive skepticism. The illusions of nationalism, the private interests of politicians, and the ignorance and stupidity of most of the men who do the fighting make the ideals which are said to be the goals of this war seem as dubious as the ideals which we know to have proved false in earlier wars. The hospital business, besides, exposes so many of the wretched and ghastly ironies of war—men dying (in large numbers) through pneumonia and improper care, before they so much as see the front, and being buried perfunctorily before their families know they are dead (the news being communicated later "through military channels"), etc., etc.—that the cruelty of ineptitude and waste comes to seem in itself a heavy price, though I should be insincere to make it appear that the deaths of this "poor white trash" of the South and the rest made me feel half so bitter as the mere conscription or enlistment of any of my friends. In fact, in connection with the hospitals, I have felt little sadness or sympathy, having arrived, before I left America, at a kind of Nirvana of apathy and cynicism.

But, on rarer occasions, as when I read the fine speech of Wilson that you sent me or even when I am going through the piles of British propaganda with which Kemp Smith from London fortifies me by about every other mail, it occurs to me that I can hardly be described as exhausting my best energies, always inclined to be selfish and lazy, for the accomplishment of a purpose in which, as much as any political purpose, I believe and in the service of a leader whose political guidance, as much as any political guidance, I trust. I have applauded, when Georg Brandes said that "in our days, in all Europe, there was not a single statesman." Had there been one great statesman on each side, the world war would never have broken out . . . And now that the President of my own country is qualifying in that role and bringing all his wits to bear on the problem of creating order and honor in the chaos and shame of half the world I am prompted to ask myself if I am really proving equal to the occasion in the simple service of lighting the dentist's stove so that he can have the room warm while he fills some other officer's teeth . . .

I am too young to have made myself a place in the only field in which I have ever expected to win any distinction and the regime of the army seems to abort all my literary plans for the present. I should be more ashamed to have nothing, after the war, but "a soft complaint," as you suggest, than of any other kind of failure while the war is in progress; but heaven knows that, although my single aim has been literature, my great men have never been Pater and Symonds but Dante and Socrates and Voltaire, who can certainly not be said to have been indifferent to politics; and how should I remain *au-dessus de la mêlée* when better men have assumed burdens as dismal as any involved in modern warfare. Besides, I know now pretty thoroughly, I think, what the army means (the training of men for slaughter by means of conditions which are calculated to kill any quality which makes them gentle, intelligent, amiable, or happy) and I cannot pretend to be shocked by it any more, especially since I know also by this time that, in the history of humanity, liberty is commonly won by bloodshed and enlightenment paid for by prosecution and suffering. And when the facts do not simply affront me or give me nightmares and headaches, I find myself unable to say why I and mine should not come in for our share of the common misery. I cannot just now be a Sarpi or a Swift; I cannot even be a Norman Angell or a Bertrand Russell, though I would rather be either, I think, than the noblest soldier that ever wore medals. It is my lot to live in the Dark Ages of Nationalistic War which gave a few pointers in horror to the Dark Ages of Religious War and, since I find myself in a situation where I cannot make myself a public protest or follow that art which is more real to me than anything else in life, I sometimes think that, rather than endure and survive the political upheaval in demoralizing inertia, I might better be ready to extinguish myself in a political cause, to which, unhappily, my preoccupation with other things has never been able to make me quite indifferent. Let me have your opinion on this, if you understand it . . .   Yours always, E.W.

To Alfred Bellinger   January 29, 1918
                                                                      France

. . . I think I said in the letter I wrote from the boat that I could not believe in the cause of any of the belligerents; or something of that kind. I am now, however, entirely convinced of the justice and importance of America's cause; but it seems to me that the President is the keystone to the whole international situation now and that it is only to his idealism and good sense that we can look for an end to the war. From the viewpoint of those uncompromising statesmen, journalists, and ministers of the Gospel who want to see Germany annihilated and, if necessary, countless generations of young men who are not French or Italian, to say nothing of those who are, lay down their lives in the cause of Alsace-Lorraine and those parts of Austria that Italy wants, the peace which will come is bound to be patched up and unsatisfactory; from any rational point of view, it is bound to be a great victory for democracy and liberty. That victory has already taken place. Does your idea of the situation include no faith in President Wilson? no admiration for his leadership of the

37

diplomacy of the Allies? In spite of your reverence for established institutions merely *quo* established, you have really always been on the side of the angels. For all that you are so little easily susceptible to ideas, I have never since I have known you found you refusing the decent, the rational, the generous for the loud, the superficial, or the narrow . . .

To Alfred Bellinger   March 25, 1918
                                                                  France
. . . Your declaration of political faith really relieved my mind, though I still think that, as a raving-tearing idealist yourself and one who, whatever you may think, lives very largely through language—a very useful way to live; I live that way, too—you are a little unduly contemptuous about the idealism which, as you say, I so much admire, which has, at least, done more to bring the belligerents to a mutual understanding on war aims than any other single factor and without which, it seems to me, "the capacity of the American people for self-sacrifice" would be as little valuable as the capacity of the German people for self-sacrifice . . . After all, the question of France, Germany, America, Russia, Italy, England, etc., is the main thing and once an international league is formed among them, all the other matters which you mention might be adjusted more easily . . .

> He made us all want to write something in which every word, every cadence, every detail, would perform a definite function in producing an intense effect.   ("Christian Gauss as a Teacher of Literature," in *The Shores of Light, 1952*)

To Christian Gauss   March 30, 1918
                                                                  France
Dear Mr. Gauss: I have been getting the *Alumni Weekly* pretty regularly over here, but I have never yet seen any review of John Bishop's *Green Fruit*, a book of poems published in December . . . Every week I have expected an analysis from your hand beginning something like: "Mr. Bishop is one of those who have cried for madder music and for stronger wine. He has never committed the sin of being sad *'nel arce dolce che dal sol s'allegra'*: he has even, like the Chimaera, been seeking *des fleurs plus larges, des parfums nouveaux, des plaisirs inéprouvés*." I would even send you a review myself if I only had a copy of the book, which I have never yet seen. The *Weekly*, if it has failed to deal with John while allowing no sparrow to fall unnoticed, is, I think, gravely in error.

I thought of you the other day when I got hold of a volume of Browning in the Y.M.C.A. and observed with regret that the reaction which you may remember predicting had already begun to set in and that, while I still think the man a much more excellent artist than you do, I must nevertheless confess that such things as "Apparent Failure" are atrocious alike as truth and as art. This hasn't been the only time I've thought of you, though, because if I don't feel altogether a stranger here, it's not altogether to my having been here before that I owe it, but also, in large measure, to you.

I haven't had much chance to read but have got in some of Octave Mirbeau and Anatole France. Surely the *Histoire contemporaine* is one of the most brilliant novels of the time.

The German offensive is on and there is such a violent debate raging around me on the subject that I can't write intelligibly and will have to come to a close. Please remember me to Mrs. Gauss, Katherine, and the children, and please pardon this hasty and inadequate letter.

Yours as ever, Edmund Wilson, Jr.

To Gilbert Troxell   April 17, 1918
                                                              France

. . . I am writing in the laboratory surrounded by bottled bacteria and urine specimens; at my side a Danish friend of ours is reading Renan's *Les Apôtres* (the second volume of a great work which I especially recommend) . . . And, in the meantime, the war is in its most terrible and, we hope, its last throes . . .

To Gilbert Troxell   September 28, 1918
                                                               France

Dear Trixie: Your threat to stop writing makes me hasten to reply: I don't know what we should do without your wide-eyed bulletins; they mirror the sins and excesses of humanity in consternation mild and droll. Larry's [Noyes], on the other hand, have a smartness and sparkle which set yours off admirably. Between you, you keep us *en rapport* with metropolitan life, from which the echoes affected me at first almost to tears, but to which I have now become quite calloused and don't care how long I stay. In fact, I shouldn't mind staying several years, especially if the war should stop during the next. No doubt, the curious military rule that one must be mustered out in precisely the same place as he was mustered in may make this impossible, but otherwise you may not see me again till, middle-aged and slightly sad, like a Henry James hero, I return to America after long absence . . .

Thank you for telling me about [Compton] Mackenzie's latest confection; I shall send to London for it right away. I have already read some of Wyndham Lewis's stuff—he was the editor of *Blast*, the vorticist magazine of 1914—and nothing could induce me to attempt a novel by him. I saw the review in *The New Republic* and judge that, like his other writings, it is calculated only to set the teeth on edge. You must not suppose that I have a special taste for the *outré* and nauseating. It is rather that any color of heterodoxy or any description of sexual phenomena seems per se to outlaw a book for you. Now dismiss these prejudices, I pray you: clear your mind of cant. Remember that all life is the proper field of art and that men behave and feel in a variety of ways. I have, however, read a French novel that goes *Young Man** several better— Octave Mirbeau's *Sébastien Roch*. Joyce must have read it: it parallels his story so closely, Jesuit education and all, though the general effect of Mirbeau's book is quite different.†

Between two words in the last paragraph I went on night duty and it is now morning after the most hectic night I have known since I've been here. A lot of pneumonia cases came in, most of them delirious. I spent the night patrolling a hall in white cap and gown (supposed to protect against infection), to keep the wild men from jumping out the windows. One of them was evidently telling someone at home all about his initiation into the trenches; another was groaning, "Blood! Blood!"; but most of them merely touched lightly on a great number of different subjects. I kept awake by means of what Doc [Charles] Walker used to call "shrapnel-like thoughts" snatched from H. L. Mencken's *Damn!* (an excellent book which I commend to you; it is very short). I hope in time, however, to be out of this madhouse and in the Intelligence Section . . .

Between the last two paragraphs I have had a sound day's sleep. You should be able to realize my anxiety to keep in touch with you from the patience and ingenuity with which for three days now I have been snatching time for this letter from my too, too crowded life . . .

You do well to memorize Wordsworth as an antidote. What do you think of *Our Mutual Friend?* I always liked the Veneerings' dinner parties best, myself . . .   Yours always, E.W.

To Stanley Dell   May 19, 1918
                                                 France

. . . Bill Osborn was gassed with mustard gas together with a lot of his men; I cannot tell how badly from his letter, but it can't have been so badly as those of his regiment who recently arrived in this hospital, or he would say more about it . . . His letter is not comparable to those of C.D. and A.S. as a piece of carry-on! great-sport-this-army-life! literature, but it is a darn sight more typical of the point of view of the intelligent man of his generation . . .

---

* *Portrait of the Artist as a Young Man.*
† See letter to Richard Ellmann, p. 670.

. . . George Logan is recovering from spinal meningitis, contracted while he was training for an aviation commission . . .

. . . Do you realize that John Bishop published a book of poems last winter: *Green Fruit* . . . He is a first lieutenant of infantry now. Scott Fitzgerald is a second lieutenant!

To Alfred Bellinger   August 26, 1918
                                                                  France

. . . We are almost entirely evacuated now and I am working on my history again, but at the time of the great influx of wounded from Château-Thierry I spent my nights for a month dressing gas burns. I don't know either what sort of work I shall be doing, because Father is managing my transfer and says that he is unable to tell me what his Senator has in mind, "for reasons which," he incorrectly supposes, "may suggest themselves to me." It is so long since I have done any work requiring even moderate intelligence that I shall accept the humblest task with trepidation . . .

John looked the poet that he was. There was an air of distinction about all that he did. He came to Princeton with a more carefully thought out and more accomplished mastery of the technique of English verse than any other undergraduate of that talented group. Even as a freshman, John had a self-possession and self-mastery which gave him the poise and bearing of a young English lord. (Christian Gauss, in *The Princeton University Library Chronicle*, 1944)

To John Peale Bishop   January 22, 1919
                                              Intelligence Section GHQ AEF

Dear John: I have heard from you twice since you have been in France and have sent you one postal, from Germany, which I sent you when I thought I was never going to get away from there and which I'll wager a sonnet you never received. Yours of December 11 has only just come to hand and I hasten to reply that I, too, am thinking seriously of the university idea . . . For my own part, I should certainly choose the University of Paris, if it is possible to go there, and should avoid Oxford, which, I warn you, is, in spite of all its amenities, in many ways a deadly place. I should not expect to get much valuable instruction, in the event of my availing myself of this university scheme, knowing all too well how few the Gausses and Kemp Smiths are and how sterile most university teaching is—and it must be still worse since the war—but, if I went to Paris (or Bordeaux), I should at least expect to learn some French, and, in any case, anything would be a relief from the galling yoke of the army. I cannot, for various reasons, leave here at once, but I think that

41

our department may soon break up and, anyhow, I shall be pretty certain to make a heavy strike for the university in time. I shall pass on to you any dope I may get and I wish you would tell me about any steps you are taking. It would be worthwhile to spend a few months in Paris. Believe me, there is much to be learned, under any circumstances, in Paris. Before I pass on to a brief account of my own recent adventures, let me call your attention to the fact that *Qu'est ce que dites-vous* is impossible French. *Ça ne se dit pas!*

I have been at GHQ ever since last October, doing political intelligence, which is very interesting stuff, as stuff in the army goes, but which now, with everything else, has begun to flag, since the Armistice. I have been to Germany for about three weeks, where I had a rather extraordinary time with George Perkins (see accompanying poem, not in my best manner, perhaps)—you know, I suppose, that his wife is dead. I have, also, had quite a visit to Paris, where I saw Kent Colwall, more or less attached to the Peace Conference and full of diplomatic secrets of the highest importance, and Charley Bayley, who looks very queer in his French *aspirant*'s uniform. We had a number of parties together and your name was frequently mentioned and we sighed vainly to have you with us. Charley showed me a letter you had written him, full of plaintive bunk about how you didn't know whether you would ever write again. Never fear! you will write again. As you once told me, you couldn't stop if you tried. As Voltaire said of Rousseau: "Never did man use so much style to prove that he could no longer write." When you get back into a foulard tie, your fancy will exercise itself as vigorously as ever. Nobody can write in the army. I haven't written much, myself, but I have some excoriating literature sealed away in my mind. Let me know what you intend to do. Yours always, E.W.

To STANLEY DELL   February 5, 1919
                                                      France

Dear Stan: Your letter (undated) came today and I hasten to fortify your conviction by replying that I, too, intend to sit down and write as soon as I get out of this damn army. I have been worrying for some time now as to how I am going to earn an honest living when I get back and have about decided that I won't do so at all but, instead, will spend a life of simplicity, more or less poverty, and relentless application in the service of Apollo. In order to escape the worst consequences of the imminent Social Revolution, I shall declare myself a member of the "Intellectual Proletariat," invest none of my savings in stocks, and try to persuade the bourgeois by reason so that they will not be too rudely swept away. In some modest chamber off lower Fifth Avenue, I shall follow the bent of my humor, forswearing many of the vanities with which I wasted time in my early youth. Precisely what my arrangements will be, of course, I can't tell: I don't even know now whether the old apartment will be revived with the old personnel . . . The only kind of job which really appeals to me now is work on some liberal magazine or newspaper. I have met a number of men . . . who say the same thing, but where to find the liberal sheet? In America *The New Republic* has the field almost to itself, whereas in France almost anyone can start a newspaper with a little money and say what he pleases and be as *spirituel* as he pleases, because the advertising business hasn't eaten up journalism yet. But in America you have to have Capital; and if you have Capital you no longer have liberal views. A friend of mine here and I have sworn a solemn vow to return to the States and know no rest till we have made merciless war on everything represented by Dr. Henry van Dyke, Senator Lodge, and the Reverend Lyman Abbott (together with others whom my situation as a Soldier of Democracy makes it inadvisable for me to mention here), but the outlook for this sort of thing does not look encouraging. At any rate, I have made a number of Bolshevik friends to whom I shall look for companionship and support. Of our old crowd, you, I feel, were almost the only real Bolshevik in the bunch (not knocking the others), though Bill Osborn would probably have been one, if he hadn't been born at Garrison. I use Bolshevik, of course, in the sense you indicate and which is equally popular over here: the truth is, I regard Trotsky's class war as *funeste* as possible and only exceeded in blindness by the attitude of the people who say that "these Bolsheviks are absolutely crazy" and are very strong for taking a firm hand with them, sending more Allied troops into Russia (if they send any more, they'll have revolutions on their own hands), and generally suppressing them with gag and prison, forgetting how the enemies of the French Revolution harassed France into welding a great army and the persecutors of Christianity encouraged it when it was young by making martyrdom popular. They wonder what can drive people mad like this, without seeing that they are doing it themselves . . .

The most interesting encounter I have had was with George Perkins in Germany, when I was at Trèves and he at a little town down the Moselle, where he was almost the only American and entrusted with the function of A.D.D.C., that is: he had to stay there and dispose of American troops when they came, disarm the inhabitants, etc. He was staying with the Burgomaster and greatly endeared himself to the family, one of whom had but recently returned from a French prison camp, where he had been ever since August 1914. It was all terribly queer. I used to go out there in the evenings and we would have parties, with the younger members of the family in a little café*—and they were most amusing parties, very mixed,

---

* This café figures in E.'s war tale "Lieutenant Franklin," reprinted in *A Prelude*.

with the Burgomaster's little cousin in pigtails, who played the piano . . . with a vigorous technique, and George's right-hand man, a regular army private with a devastated nose. I was touched by George, who was isolated and lonely, it wasn't long after his wife's death, and some of the time, I gathered, in a rather awful state of mind. (Germany by itself now is enough to make anyone gloomy.) . . . I hope to see you before long, sometime during the summer, probably . . .   Yours always, Bunny

To CHRISTIAN GAUSS   July 5, 1919
                                                      Camp Mills, Long Island
. . . I just landed a few days ago and am going to be demobilized on the 9th. If you are at Princeton now or anywhere near New York, I should like to call on you . . .

To F. SCOTT FITZGERALD   August 9, 1919
                                                                    Red Bank
Dear Scott: I have heard various rumors about you since I have been back (I landed July 2), but can't seem to find out where you are now. I suppose you must be in St. Paul. I move up to the city tomorrow where I have an apartment (114 West Twelfth Street) with Larry Noyes and others. When you come to New York again, be sure to look me up and, in the meantime, drop me a line.

Stan Dell and I have conceived a literary project in which you might possibly help us. Our idea is to write a new *Soirées de Médan* on the American part in the war. The original *Soirées de Médan* was a set of short stories published after the Franco-Prussian War by a group of realistic writers headed by Zola (Zola, Maupassant, Huysmans, etc.). Our problem is to get enough other people to contribute besides ourselves, and I have written to John Bishop and a number of others. These stories don't all of them have to deal with the fighting proper, of course. One of the remarkable virtues of the *Soirées* was the fact that they dealt not only with the front but also with the mismanagement of the war by the government, the effect on the civilian population, and the stagnation of the troops behind the lines. You never got abroad, but *tant mieux!* let us have something about army life in the States during the war. I know that your line isn't the Zola–Maupassant genre, but I'm sure you ought to be able to produce something illuminating. No *Saturday Evening Post* stuff, understand! clear your mind of cant! brace up your artistic conscience, which was always the weakest part of your talent! forget for a moment the phosphorescences of the decaying Church of Rome! Banish whatever sentimentalities may still cling about you from college! Concentrate in one short story a world of tragedy, comedy, irony, and beauty!!! I await your manuscript with impatience.

I'm sorry to hear that you were disappointed about your novel; I should like to see it. And you must write another someday, in any case.

Yours always, Edmund Wilson, Jr.

To F. Scott Fitzgerald   August 14, 1919
[Postcard]   114 West Twelfth Street, N.Y.

I'm glad you've got a foothold with Scribner's. Don't worry about me: I'm not writing a novel, but I'm writing almost everything else, and getting some of it accepted. I hope your letter isn't a fair sample of your present literary methods: it looks like the attempt of a child of six to write F.P.A.'s [Franklin P. Adams] column. Send along your story, when you get to it.   E.W.

I don't think any of your titles are any good.

John Bishop hasn't arrived yet as far as I know.

To F. Scott Fitzgerald   November 21, 1919
114 West Twelfth Street, N.Y.

Dear Fitz: I have just read your novel with more delight than I can well tell you.* It ought to be a classic in a class with *The Young Visiters*.† Amory Blaine should rank with Mr. Salteena. It sounds like an exquisite burlesque of Compton Mackenzie with a pastiche of Wells thrown in at the end. I wish you hadn't chosen such bad masters as Mackenzie and the later Wells: your hero is an unreal imitation of Michael Fane, who was himself unreal and who was last seen in the role of the veriest cardboard best-seller hero being nursed back to life in the Balkans. Almost the only things of value to be learned from the Michael Fane books are pretty writing and clever dialogue and with both of these you have done very well. The descriptions in places are very nicely done and so is some of the college dialogue, which really catches the Princeton tone, though your hero as an intellectual is a fake of the first water and I read his views on art, politics, religion, and society with more riotous mirth than I should care to have you know. You handicap your story, for one thing, by making your hero go to the war and then completely leaving the war out. If you thought you couldn't deal with his military experiences, you shouldn't have had him go abroad at all. You make him do a lot of other things that the real Amory never did, such as getting on *The Prince* and playing on the football team, and thereby you produce an incredible monster, half romantic hero and half F. Scott Fitzgerald. This, of course,

---

* *This Side of Paradise.*
† A novel by Daisy Ashford, purporting to be written by a pre-adolescent English girl.

may be more evident to me than it would be to some reader who didn't know you, but I really think you should cultivate detachment and not allow yourself to drift into a state of mind where, as in the latter part of the book, you make Amory the hero of a series of dramatic encounters with all the naïve and romantic gusto of a small boy imagining himself as a brave hunter of Indians. The love affairs seem to me the soundest part of the book as fiction; the ones with Isabelle and Rosalind are the realest. I was, of course, infinitely entertained by the Princeton part: but you put in some very dubious things—the party at Asbury Park, for example, where they beat their way through the restaurants. If you tell me that you have seen this happen, I point to the incident in which the Burne brothers, who are presumably not supposed to be cads, are made to play an outrageous and impossible practical joke on the girl who comes down for the game. I was also very much shocked when poor old John Bishop's hair stands up on end at beholding the Devil.

I don't want to bludgeon you too brutally, however, for I think that some of the poems and descriptions are really exceedingly good. It would all be better if you would tighten up your artistic conscience and pay a little more attention to form. *Il faut faire quelque chose de vraiment beau, vous savez!* something which the world will not willingly let die! I feel called upon to give you this advice because I believe you might become a very popular trashy novelist without much difficulty.

The only first-rate novel recently produced in this genre is James Joyce's book and that is one of the best things in English because of its rigorous form and selection and its polished style and because the protagonist is presented with complete detachment, with the ugly sides of his life as accurately depicted as the inspired and beautiful ones. But what about the ugly and mean features of Amory's life! You make some feeble attempts to account for them in the beginning, but on the whole your hero is a kind of young god moving among demi-gods; the Amory I hear about in the book is not the Amory I knew at Princeton, nor at all like any genuine human being I ever saw. Well, I concede that it is much better to imagine even a more or less brummagem god and strike off from him a few authentic gleams of poetry and romance than to put together a perfectly convincing and mediocre man who never conveys to the reader a single thrill of the wonder of life, like Beresford's Jacob Stahl and a lot of other current heroes, but I do think the most telling poetry and romance may be achieved by keeping close to life and not making Scott Fitzgerald a sort of super-Michael Fane. Cultivate a universal irony and do read something other than contemporary British novelists: this history of a young man stuff has been run into the ground and has always seemed to me a bum art form, anyway, at least when, as in Beresford's or Mackenzie's case, it consists of dumping all one's youthful impressions

46

in the reader's lap, with a profound air of importance. You do the same thing: you tell the reader all sorts of stuff which has no bearing on your story and no other interest—that detail about how Amory's uncle gave him a cap, etc.

I really like the book, though; I enjoyed it enormously, and I shouldn't wonder if a good many other people would enjoy it, too. You have a knack of writing readably which is a great asset. Your style, by the way, has become much sounder than it used to be. Well, I hope to see you here soon. Thanks for the novel.   Yours always, Edmund Wilson, Jr.

INSCRIPTION on a copy of *This Side of Paradise*, published on April 20, 1920:

This "Exquisite burlesque of Compton McKenzie with the pastiche of Wells at the end" is presented as *toll* to Bunny Wilson

F. Scott Fitzgerald
March 20th, 1920

THE TWENTIES

It seems to me that there is a lot doing intellectually in America just now—America seems to be actually beginning to express herself in something like an idiom of her own.

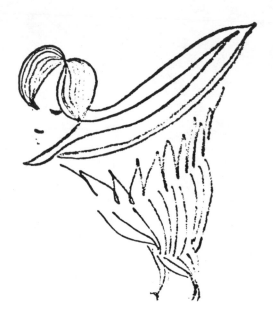

CHRONOLOGY

1920	*Vanity Fair*, on which I then had a job [January 26, 1920, to February 19, 1921].
1921	I have been hard at work on *The Undertaker's Garland*.
FEBRUARY	The great news is that I am going on *The New Republic* as managing editor.
MARCH	I have engaged passage for the old country.
JUNE	I arrived in Paris.
AUGUST	Haslemere, Surrey, England: *The Undertaker's Garland* has been accepted by Knopf.
	Venice, Florence, Paris.
1922	THE UNDERTAKER'S GARLAND
	Ted Paramore and I took an apartment at 777 Lexington Avenue.
MAY	John Bishop is getting married June 17.
JULY	I am back in the old madhouse *Vanity Fair* [July 10, 1922, to May 5, 1923, as managing editor].
1923	Married Mary Blair.
JANUARY	I am doing theaters for *The Dial*.
JUNE	My father died in May but left me nothing.
	Brookhaven, L.I.
SEPTEMBER	We have recently had a baby [Rosalind Baker Wilson, September 19, 1923].
DECEMBER	1 University Place: I have moved into a large corner room and bath two flights above Elinor Wylie.
1924	
MARCH	I have just come back from California . . . for the purpose of trying to induce Charlie Chaplin to act in the pantomime ballet which Leo Ornstein and I are

writing . . . I am going to write regularly for *The New Republic* again.

OCTOBER	*The Crime in the Whistler Room*, with Mary Blair, at the Provincetown Players, New York.
1925	3 North Washington Square, and Red Bank, N.J.
AUGUST	O'Neill's *Desire under the Elms*, which Mary Blair is in.
1926	DISCORDANT ENCOUNTERS
FEBRUARY	I am going down to New Orleans for a few weeks the first of March.
NOVEMBER	My present address is 224 West Thirteenth Street.
1927	*The New Republic*
JULY	Provincetown, Massachusetts: I have been living up here in the old Coast Guard station, fitted up as a house, in which O'Neill lived so many years.
1928	"A Short View of Proust," *The New Republic*.
APRIL	To Maxwell Perkins: Here are the first pages of my novel [*I Thought of Daisy*].
SEPTEMBER	I want to get away and go West the first of October. Here is an outline of the book I was talking to you about [*Axel's Castle*].
OCTOBER	Santa Barbara, California: I'll be back at *The New Republic* January 1.
1929	I THOUGHT OF DAISY; POETS, FAREWELL!
MARCH	Sanatorium, Clifton Springs, N.Y.: I had a sort of nervous breakdown about a month ago.
APRIL	*The New Republic*.
AUGUST	Dennis, Cape Cod, Massachusetts.
SEPTEMBER	*Axel's Castle* in *The New Republic*, September, October, November, December.

"VANITY FAIR" AND "THE NEW REPUBLIC"
1920–1921

To Christian Gauss   April 28, 1920
                                                          Vanity Fair
Dear Mr. Gauss: Fitz is in town, at the Hotel Commodore. I have just
had a telephone conversation with him. He said that he had left Princeton
in disgrace and was ashamed to go back, but when I told him we wanted
him for the dinner, he said that he would like to go down with John
[Peale Bishop] and me and come back immediately afterwards. I hounded
him about speaking and he protested that he couldn't speak except when
under the influence and that he didn't want to get drunk on this occasion.
I think he will be fairly tame, because he is going to leave Zelda at the
Commodore; I trust that she will seize the opportunity to run away with
the elevator boy or something.
    I have written to Kean Wallis, but not to Teek Whipple; I understood
that the committee would notify him. That's right, isn't it? John Bishop
says he will speak. Besides him and Fitz, Stanley Dell, Townsend Martin,
and Hardwick Nevin are surely coming.   Yours always, EW

To Stanley Dell   January 21, 1921
                                              136 West Sixteenth Street, N.Y.
Dear Stan: Deciding to give my evenings up to work (Edna [St. Vincent
Millay] having gone abroad) with the purpose of making a great deal of
money and escaping from this so-called country in the spring, I this week
planned out for myself a rigorous regime, including exercise every afternoon at the Yale Club and creative functionings every evening from nine
to twelve, together with intensive study of Hawthorne, on whom I am
going to do an article. I followed out this system with admirable consistency the first few days of the week, with the result that I soon fell ill

and have been obliged to take to my bed, with indigestion, a tumultuous headache, and general debility. I think it must have been the exercise that did for me: when I don't exercise I'm all right, and when I dissipate in the evenings I never have a headache. At any rate, I am taking advantage of this period of retreat (I am on indefinite furlough from the office) to give you of my news.

I have been hard at work on the March *Vanity Fair* (have you been getting *V.F.*, by the way?) and my "Emily in Hades."* It is these two really which have done me in. The latter has cost me more anguish than anything I have done for a year; I am at present rewriting it very laboriously. When it is finished, I want to send you and Marion a copy of it to see what you make of it.

I have really not much news. Roy Gamble, my old friend of the army, is staying here with us. He is at present dining with Dave [Hamilton]; I didn't feel equal to going there tonight: they keep all the windows shut and the steam heat going full tilt; when you have sunk into a heavy stupor, they bring the baby in for you to see.

The best book I have read lately, and one of the best of modern American novels, is Sinclair Lewis's *Main Street*. You and Marion must read it, if you haven't already done so. Lewis has caught the precise tone and mentality of the Middle West; I don't think I should have known how accurate it was if it hadn't been for the Detroiters I was imprisoned with in the army. The theme is much the same as that of *The Age of Innocence*. Think how many remarkable American books have been published in the last year—*Main Street, The Age of Innocence, The Ordeal of Mark Twain*, and Mencken's second series of *Prejudices*—and think how they were all of them written to tell what a terrible place America is. (I can think, at the moment, of only one great American book written to tell how somebody enjoyed America: Walt Whitman's *Leaves of Grass*.) It is rather tragic when you think of it, but actually I believe it is a cause for rejoicing: presumably, this devastating criticism of America is a prelude to its being made what the above authors want to see it become. On the other hand, of course, it may merely continue to get worse and worse. At any rate, I myself hope to sail for the Old Country (as I have hinted) in the spring: *The Bookman* has asked me to write for them and Walter Lippmann is enthusiastic about *The Undertaker*, which he wants to publish in *The New Republic*, and I am counting on these as sources of revenue. Another book you ought to read, by the way, is Zona Gale's *Miss Lulu Bett*. Omit, however, Floyd Dell's *Moon-Calf*, which is very poor.

---

* *The Undertaker's Garland.*

Well, I must get back to "Emily"—one of the most terrible nightmares ever written. I am in good form for it tonight: I have a head full of devils and noxious fumes. I am sick of the *Vanity Fair* office, which has now become a sort of madhouse, pervaded, as Frank Tuttle says, by "a sweet poison." John Bishop is in one of his periodical states of discouragement, pitifully protesting that his life will probably be a failure because the world no longer appreciates the only kind of thing he can do; he goes around reciting something which he says is the mad scene from *Bishop: A Tragedy*. One of the secretaries has had her heart broken and is in a comatose condition; the other, a nice little half-French girl who has been respectably brought up in Brooklyn, is in a continual state of rut, having reached the age for amour, and lays formidable siege to John from morning to night (having broken her teeth on me). Furthermore, the Well-Dressed Man has now become a member of the staff; he wears colored collars to match his shirts and nearly drives me insane; the clothes he recommends to our readers look like the ones worn by Mr. Salteena and Bernard Clark in *The Young Visiters* and often have to be suppressed by Crownie,* at my instigation, so that he (the Well-Dressed Man) is morose and peevish for days. Finally, Crownie himself is either ill or suffering from a badly adjusted love affair: he turns up every morning with ashen face and in a state of nervous collapse. Well, cheerio! I hope that you get away from the West at least as soon as I get away from America. Be sure to write me when possible. The fact that I haven't been very prompt about answering your letters implies no lack of merit in the manuscripts; it is simply because I have to spend so much time stalling off doing other things which I think I ought to do first, because they are less attractive. I am awfully glad to hear that you are writing; be sure to send me your things when you finish them. Convey to Marion all my compliments.   Yours always, EW.

To Stanley Dell   February 19, 1921
                                                    Vanity Fair

Dear Stan: The story is too long for *V.F.* (3,500 words, whereas our usual length is 2,000) and further handicapped by being fiction. Consequently, I have sent it with a note to Mencken. If he returns it, however, I'll press it on Crownie's attention. I think you had an awfully good idea; I am not sure that the treatment is just right, but don't know what suggestions I'd make about it. I am unscrupulously using your stamped envelope to send you the concluding narrative of *The Undertaker's Garland*. Give me the benefit of a frank and open criticism . . .

---

* Frank Crowninshield, editor of *Vanity Fair*.

The great news is that I am going on *The New Republic* Monday as managing editor. They offer me more money, more chance to write than I get here, and the prospect of becoming a regular editor some day. Lippmann got them to take me on. They are really in quite a bad way. The magazine has become so dull that the editors themselves say they are unable to read it and the subscribers are dying off like flies. The editors, who started out as gay young freethinkers, have become respectable to the point of stodginess. Lippmann is the livest of the lot. They are also very much at odds with each other. Each one has taken me aside and told me confidentially that the rest of the staff were timid old maids. They are taking me on because they think that the magazine needs younger men. (Merz has gone abroad; they seem to hold it against him that he acquired the *New Republic* manner so completely as to be indistinguishable from the others and have warned me solemnly that I mustn't get to write like Herbert Croly.) I have had a very amusing time lately being entertained by each one of the editors in turn. It is like being taken into Bones or the Masons or something. I find all the editors (except [Robert] Littell, whom I haven't met yet) curiously unattractive people, though some of them are genuinely learned and some of them are really clever. I dined last night with the Lippmanns and the Ordway Teads and was so depressed by the extreme conventionality and respectability of these eminent intellectuals that, after I left them, I fled to the Village and assisted at the latter phases of an ignoble studio party, where a mixed and ribald company were doing a little serious drinking. Really, nothing more correct could be imagined than the home life of the Lippmanns, and when I tell you that the Lippmanns regard the Crolys as old-fashioned and dull, you will be able to form some idea of what your poor old friend Dr. Wilson is going to be in for till July 1, when I shall take ship for the Old Country. It is all very interesting, nonetheless, and an excellent opportunity. When you become a regular editor of the N.R., you draw a large salary and never go near the office, but stay at home and write books. You can't lose, because the magazine is endowed. I'm going to do dramatic reviews and literary stuff. Read *The New Republic*.

. . . Well, I must stop, as I have to go out in a minute with Crownie, for what he describes as "a last supper." I am editing the MS of Fitz's new novel* and, though I thought it was rather silly at first, I find it developing a genuine emotional power which he has scarcely displayed before. I haven't finished it yet, though, so can't tell definitely. It is all about him and Zelda.   Yours always, E.W.

---

* *The Beautiful and Damned.*

The New
REPUBLIC
421 West 21ˢᵗ Street
New York City

I was always keenly aware that literature demands not only all one
can give it but also all one can get other people to give it.
(To T. S. Matthews, 1960)

To CHRISTIAN GAUSS   March 1, 1921
                                                        *The New Republic**

Dear Mr. Gauss: I was greatly reassured to get your letter and learn that
you were reconciled to your appearance in the Hall of Fame: I was afraid
that you might object to being written up in the *Vanity Fair* manner. But
you should have seen the caption before it was cut to fit the page!

I am doing here about the same work as I did on *Vanity Fair* (John
[Peale Bishop] having taken my place) but with more money and more
chance to write (for one thing, I am doing dramatic reviews). It is very
interesting and offers possibilities of more of a career than *Vanity Fair*
did.

The Undertaker's Garland has been delivered into the hands of the
publishers. Stan Dell has had a story accepted by Mencken for *The Smart
Set* and, I think, is quite encouraged by it. Fitz's new novel, which I have
been editing, is admirable, much the best thing he has done; it is all
about his married life.

I have engaged passage for the Old Country for the first of June and
hope that, sometime during the summer, I may have the privilege of
drinking a bottle of wine with you on the *Ile de France*. In the meantime,
could I come down to Princeton the Saturday after next? If you don't
want me at your house, I can always stay at the club. Remember me to
the rest of your family.   As always, EW

To STANLEY DELL   March 4, 1921

Dear Stan: It was Mencken I sent the story to and Nathan, when he
talked to me about it, said that Mencken liked it, so I don't think they can
have seen it before. I am awfully glad they took it. I wish you would
send me your Voltaire and Wilde article, if it's not too long for the
N.R., and also, if possible, write something else for us, not only because

---

* The letters in this section were written from *The New Republic*.

CHRISTIAN GAUSS

Because, as the first and chief builder of the Modern Language Department at Princeton, he has become one of the most important intellectual influences in the university; because he has filled the younger generation of Princeton writers with enthusiasm for French culture; and, finally, because he is everything that, according to Mencken, a college professor never is. —*Vanity Fair*, 1921

it would be pleasant to see you in print but also because they are at me for stuff by promising young writers and especially for stuff dealing with manners and morals—rather than with politics and economics. Your letter was very encouraging, except for the suggestion that you might have to stay out there longer than you expected; I am exceedingly glad that you are writing so much.

Thanks very much for the report on "Emily"; most of your points, I think, were well taken.

I am having a very pleasant time here: it is very like a club. The offices are two old houses almost in the river. There are no office hours, you come and go as you please; and lunch is served in a dining room at one. They entertain all the visiting celebrities and liberals, political and literary. As a rule, the visitor, if his views diverge from those of *The New Republic*, is fiercely challenged and made to defend his position against quite unfair odds. Alvin Johnson, by the way, is none other than our "laughing economist" of the Columbia summer school. He is a most curious and interesting man, of whom I shall some day tell you at length. He has reached a complete Nirvana of learning, wisdom, and detachment; he is the perfect skeptic and makes Mencken look like an evangelist.

Incidentally, I finished the article on Mencken a long time ago. *The New Republic* has offered to print part of it (it is very long), but I am trying to get somebody to accept it *in toto*.

I am reading Lytton Strachey's *Queen Victoria* in MS. We are going to run parts of it in the N.R. It is, of course, a masterpiece. The concluding scene is the finest piece of historic irony I have read since Renan.

Have you seen Gauss in *Vanity Fair*? I had a very funny letter from him about it. It has made him famous on the campus; the students are convinced, for the first time, that he must be a great man.

Well, let me hear from you soon again. Convey all my compliments to Marion, who has by no means kept her promise to write. There is so much that is amusing to tell, which loses its freshness when it is written. I wish that I could gossip with you.   Yours always, EW

To CHRISTIAN GAUSS   March 23, 1921

Dear Mr. Gauss: . . . I am anxious to produce interesting articles in order to convince the editor of *The New Republic* that I am a desirable editor. An article, introduced by me yesterday, on the morals of the younger generation (by Ted Paramore, of Yale) and asserting that the girls had become more human since they drank and smoked and that chastity was a "much overrated virtue," threw an editorial conference into such consternation that I am anxious to bring them a sober and unexceptionably balanced article to set their minds at rest again.

I wish you would change your mind about sailing in the spring: I should be glad of a companion to take the curse off the voyage.

Yours always, Edmund Wilson, Jr.

To CHRISTIAN GAUSS   April 18, 1921

Dear Mr. Gauss: . . . I am trying to get some Dante material into *The New Republic* and I wish you could do something later on—perhaps a review of a new book on Dante which is about to be published by Walter Arensberg, a minor poet. John Macy, the eminent left-wing socialist, is writing us an article on the *De Monarchia*.

Stan Dell's story appears in the new *Smart Set*. My little rhapsody on the eighteenth century is in this week's *New Republic*.

I do wish you would let me know if you are ever in New York because I would like to have you come to lunch at *The New Republic*—if you could stand it.   Yours in Christ, Edmund Wilson, Jr.

As for my ideas about the effects of American life on literature, I got most of them out of Brooks in the first place, the early Brooks of *The Ordeal of Mark Twain*.   (To Christian Gauss, 1950)

To VAN WYCK BROOKS   April 18, 1921
The Freeman

Dear Mr. Brooks: Could you possibly do an article or two for *The New Republic*? It has occurred to me that in the course of your researches into the genteel period of American literature you must have gathered a good deal of interesting information on the life and mind of that time which you did not put into your book on Mark Twain. It seems to me that there is a great need for some American to do for our own Victorian Age what Strachey has been doing for the English. You have certainly made a magnificent beginning in the Mark Twain, but I should think some of the minor figures would be worth doing—T. B. Aldrich or John Hay, for example.

I wish you could do a few portraits of this kind for us. Would you have time and be willing to?   Yours sincerely, Edmund Wilson, Jr.

A tameless critic not only of the national letters but of the whole tragi-comic spectacle of life in the Republic.   (*Vanity Fair*, 1921)

To H. L. MENCKEN   April 27, 1921

Dear Mr. Mencken: Have you seen the MS of the book which John Bishop and I recently submitted to Knopf? They told me that they were going to give it to you. If you have seen it, I wish you could let me know what you think we ought to do with it. Knopf has written suggesting that we remove a great deal of the poetry (which, I feel, would be a mistake) and submit it to him again in the fall. Do you think we could induce any other publisher to take it in its present form? I'm sorry to bother you about this but, if we could have your advice about it, we should know much better what to do. Incidentally, I suppose there is nothing in it that you could use in *The Smart Set*.   Yours sincerely, Edmund Wilson, Jr.

To H. L. MENCKEN   June 2, 1921

Dear Mr. Mencken: Thank you very much for your letter (and kind drinking invitation). I am sorry that my article had to be so short: I was unable to do more than touch upon your literary criticism, for example.*

I have just had a bawdy French postcard from Fitz, signed "Anatole France." I am going over myself for the summer the 11th of this month, and hope to give myself over to the composition of a novel.

Yours sincerely, Edmund Wilson, Jr.

To CHRISTIAN GAUSS   June 2, 1921

Dear Mr. Gauss: Thank you for your letter. I have had the grippe, but I am up again. I may come down this weekend if you can have me. I shall let you know definitely later. I want very much to see you before I go on the 11th, not to prove to you that the world is a dustbin, but for Consolation and Light, of which I am sorely in need.

Yours sincerely, Edmund Wilson, Jr.

---

* "H. L. Mencken," *The New Republic*, June 1, 1921.

EUROPE
1921

June 22, 1921
Mont-Thabor Hotel, Paris

Dear Fitz: I find no word from you at the American Express (though I got a postcard in America before I left), so am writing to find out where you are, etc. I arrived in Paris the day before yesterday and am not yet settled, so please write to me c/o Crédit Commercial de France, 22 Boulevard des Capucines. I'm very anxious to see you, when possible. If you are in Italy, I expect to go there sometime in August.

I may say in closing that the two great literary successes of the States since your departure are Don Stewart and myself. The first installment of Don Stewart's *History* arrived with a crash. Prodigious praise from F.P.A., Broun, Cabell, etc.—and he was finally summoned to the penetralia of *The Smart Set* and requested to write them an article on Yale. And as for myself, my Mencken article, completely rewritten from the version you saw, enabled me to leave *The New Republic* in an aurora borealis of glory. It brought me not only a letter from the Prophet himself—from the enthusiasm of which I am still recovering—but also complimentary communications from Van Wyck Brooks and Lawrence Gilman. *The Globe* wrote an editorial on it; one unknown person sent me an enormously long letter to prove that I was all wrong. I am doing all this boasting on behalf of Dr. Stewart and myself, frankly, to make you jealous. As you know, I have always regarded your great capacity for envy as the one unfortunate blemish in an otherwise consummately admirable character and I hope to cure you, as G. B. Shaw describes intelligent men, in *Back to Methuselah*, being cured of false ideas, by homeopathic doses of the disease. (This is both idiotic and dull, I'm afraid, but it's very late and I'm exhausted.)

By the way, Mencken summoned me to the sacred chamber of *The*

Smart Set the day you sailed, to talk to me about *The Undertaker's Garland*, and I greatly astounded Nathan by telling him that you were going abroad. He seemed a little crestfallen and I think he was sorry that you should have got off without patching up your quarrel. He told me that he was going to Europe himself and got your address from me, saying that he was going to look you up.

Scribner's passed *The Undertaker* up, with kind and noncommittal words. So we think we'll fall back on Knopf in the fall. Let me hear from you.   Yours for the shifting of the world's capital of culture
from Paris to New York, E.W.

To F. Scott Fitzgerald   July 5, 1921
                                                    16 rue du Four, Paris

Dear Scott: It was terrible that we didn't meet. I never knew you had been here until John Wyeth told me—I think, the day you left. But you should have left a note at the American Express. I called there, expecting something from you.

Your reaction to the Continent is only what most Americans go through when they come over for the first time as late in life as you. It is due, I suppose, first, to the fact that they can't understand the language and, consequently, assume both that there is nothing doing and that there is something inherently hateful about a people who, not being able to make themselves understood, present such a blank façade to a foreigner, and second, to the fact that, having been a part of one civilization all their lives, it is difficult for them to adjust themselves to another, whether superior or inferior, as it is for any other kind of animal to learn to live in a different environment. The lower animals frequently die, when transplanted; Fitzgerald denounces European civilization and returns at once to God's country. The truth is that you are so saturated with twentieth-century America, bad as well as good—you are so used to hotels, plumbing, drugstores, aesthetic ideals, and vast commercial prosperity of the country—that you can't appreciate those institutions of France, for example, which are really superior to American ones. If you had only given it a chance to sink in! I wish that I could have seen you and tried to induct you a little into the amenities of France. Paris seems to me an ideal place to live: it combines all the attractions and conveniences of a large city with all the freedom, beauty, and regard for the arts and pleasures of a place like Princeton. I find myself more contented and at ease here than anywhere else I know. Take my advice, cancel your passage and come to Paris for the summer! Settle down and learn French and apply a little French leisure and measure to that restless and jumpy nervous system. It would be a service to American letters: your novels would never be the same afterwards. That's one reason I came to France, by the way:

63

in America I feel so superior and culturally sophisticated in comparison to the rest of the intellectual and artistic life of the country that I am in danger of regarding my present attainments as an absolute standard and am obliged to save my soul by emigrating into a country which humiliates me intellectually and artistically by surrounding me with a solid perfection of a standard arrived at by way of Racine, Molière, La Bruyère, Pascal, Voltaire, Vigny, Renan, Taine, Flaubert, Maupassant, and Anatole France. I don't mean to say, of course, that I can actually do better work than anybody else in America; I simply mean that I feel as if I had higher critical standards and that, since in America all standards are let down, I am afraid mine will drop, too; it is too easy to be a highbrow or an artist in America these days; every American savant and artist should beware of falling a victim to the ease with which a traditionless and half-educated public (I mean the growing public for really good stuff) can be impressed, delighted, and satisfied; the Messrs. Mencken, Nathan, Cabell, Dreiser, Anderson, Lewis, Dell, Lippmann, Rosenfeld, Fitzgerald, etc., etc., should all beware of this; let them remember that, like John Stuart Mill, they all owe a good deal of their eminence "to the flatness of the surrounding country"! I do think seriously that there is a great hope for New York as a cultural center; it seems to me that there is a lot doing intellectually in America just now—America seems to be actually beginning to express herself in something like an idiom of her own. But, believe me, she has a long way to go. The commercialism and industrialism, with no older and more civilized civilization behind except one layer of eighteenth-century civilization on the East Coast, impose a terrific handicap upon any other sort of endeavor: the intellectual and aesthetic manifestations have to crowd their way up and out from between the crevices left by the factories, the office buildings, the apartment houses, and the banks; the country was simply not built for them and, if they escape with their lives, they can thank God, but would better not think they are 100 percent elect, attired in authentic and untarnished vestments of light, because they have obviously been stunted and deformed at birth and afterwards greatly battered and contaminated in their struggle to get out. Cabell seems to me a great instance of this: it is not the fact that he is a first-rate writer (I don't think, on the whole, that he is) which has won him the first place in public (enlightened public) estimation; it is the fact that he makes serious artistic pretensions and has labored long and conscientiously (and not altogether without success) to make them good. We haven't any Anatole France, or any of the classic literature which made Anatole France possible; consequently, Cabell looks good to us.

When I began this letter I intended to write only a page, but your strictures upon poor old France demanded a complete explanation of practically everything from the beginning of the world. I don't hope to persuade you to stay in Europe and I suppose you haven't time to come back to France. It's a great pity. (Have you ever tried the Paris–London airline, by the way? I think I shall, if I go to England.)

Mencken's letter went somewhat as follows (I haven't it with me):

> "Dear Mr. Wilson: It would be needless to thank you. No one has ever done me before on so lavish a scale, or with so persuasive an eloquence. A little more and you would have persuaded even me. But what engages me more particularly as a practical critic is the critical penetration of the second half of your article. Here, I think, you have told the truth. The beer cellar, these days, has become as impossible as the ivory tower. One is irresistibly impelled to rush out and crack a head or two—that is, to do something or other for the sake of common decency. God knows what can be done. But, at any rate, it is easier to do with such a fellow as you in the grandstand.
>
> "You must come down to Baltimore sometime. I pledge you in a large Humpen of malt. Yours sincerely, H. L. Mencken."

I am sending you *The Bookman*: I happen to have a copy.

Yours always, E.W.

To Walter Lippmann   June 29, 1921
                                                          Paris

Dear Mr. Lippmann: Thank you very much for your note about my Mencken article and please pardon me for not having acknowledged it before. I wanted to write you before I left, but got off in such a hurry that I didn't have time to. I think that the Mencken was really about the only absolutely first-class article I did for *The New Republic*. I am sorry that I wasn't able to do better, either with articles or ideas. I feel that, as editor, I fell very far short of what you said you wanted when you first discussed it with me. As far as articles go, I hope to send you some better ones this summer, now that I have unlimited time to write. In any case, I'm exceedingly grateful to you for getting me the chance to work on the N.R. I felt the cloud and the difficulties you described (and wish I could have done more to clear them up) but enjoyed the whole thing very much: it was certainly the most interesting job I have ever had. I don't know that I have anything to say about the N.R. that is worth saying. It seemed to me editorial power was very badly distributed: isn't it very clumsy to have so many editors, all with theoretically equal powers? I should think the machine would go more effectively if there weren't so many brakes being applied all the time. In most organizations, the departments are subordinate to the head. But I suppose this is all an old story to you and no doubt you

65

have arrived inevitably at the present arrangement for valid reasons and after having considered the matter much more thoroughly than I can do. It seemed to me also that there was a tendency to err in the direction of the safe and sane: I have heard objections, none of which seemed to me valid reasons for not publishing the articles, from Mr. Croly to something on the ground that it would offend the religious convictions of the readers, by Mr. Johnson to something on the ground that it lacked social perspective, by Mr. Littell to something on the ground that it was bad taste (something Mr. Hackett had written, which dealt with "sex"), and by yourself to something (William Hard's articles) on the ground that they tended to turn the labor situation into a melodrama (as they did, to be sure, but it seems to me that their imaginative and informative value outweighs this). My instinct is to feel that, even if a bolder and more ribald treatment of sex and religion, and even of politics, should lose *The New Republic* some of those Unitarian clergymen who, I am told, make up a large part of its subscribers, it would nonetheless bring the magazine readers of an even more important kind—though here again I may be wrong, and it may be that the N.R. has to be careful in this way in order to perform its function and hold its subscribers as a liberal political journal. In any case, please pardon this criticism, which, as I reread it, seems very obvious, gratuitous, and out of all proportion to any constructive influence I brought to bear on the magazine.

Please remember me to Mrs. Lippmann. I hope to see you if you come abroad . . . I hope you are getting on with your book. I am going to try to write a play this summer.　　　　Yours sincerely, Edmund Wilson, Jr.

To John Peale Bishop　　　　　　　　　　　　　　July 3, 1921
　　　　　　　　　　　　　　　　　　　　　　　　　　　　Paris

Dear John: Arriving about two weeks ago at the Gare du Nord, what was my astonishment to find myself met by a great delegation of *filles publiques* who demanded M. Bishop with eager girlish voices; I was much bewildered until a beautifully dressed old lady, of perfect dignity and manners (who was, as I afterwards found out, the doyenne of the profession), came forward and explained to me in excellent English that it had been understood in Paris that you were coming with me. When I explained that this was not the case, she could hardly conceal her emotion and from the rest of the delegation—who had been selected among much ill feeling as the most comely, the most impressive, and the most indefatigable of their craft—a great cry arose such as must go up when an ocean steamer is sinking. It seems that a new position, which I shall not attempt to explain here, had been named in your honor (*le soubresaut Bishop*). It was a heartbreaking scene. The committee decided on the spot that the whole profession should go into a period of fasting and mourning for four days—that is to say, every member should remain continent during that period—a decision which, when it was carried into effect, inflicted a veritable period of Lent upon the whole nation and will always remain a black period indeed in the memory of the *Patrie*. In fact, the government tried to prevent it, but without success.

I am enjoying myself here very much, though I haven't done much of anything yet but establish myself in a *pension*, run into a few friends, and go to the theater. I have, however, what it is the prime purpose of this letter to describe, seen Edna [St. Vincent Millay] a couple of times. I found her in a very first-rate hotel on the Left Bank and better dressed, I suppose, than she has ever been before in her life. You were right in guessing that she was well cared for as she had never been before. She also seems to be in very good health, the phase of being run down that Crownie hated has passed. But she looks older, more mature—at least she has on the occasions when I have seen her; she assured me that perhaps the next day she would be like a little girl again. She was very serious, earnest, and sincere about herself—inspired, I suppose, by my presence; no doubt, *ça passera*—and told me that she wanted to settle down to a new life: she was tired of breaking hearts and spreading havoc. She loved, she was very happy with her present lover, a big red-haired British journalist named Slocum, the Paris correspondent of the London *Herald* (a Labor paper), who had spent three years in France and had two teeth knocked out in the war. Unfortunately, he had a wife and three children at Saint-Cloud and a very cruel situation had arisen. She did not know whether he would get a divorce or not, but, if he did, she would marry him, go to England to live, and have children. She was very happy, she said. I am sorry to say that, when I first talked to her, I was inclined, with the memory of my own scars still giving out an occasional twinge, to jeer at her seriousness and be sarcastic at the expense of the pain she expressed at having wrecked another home; but I don't think this is the thing to do, because, after all, perhaps there is something in this idea and it is probably a good thing to encourage her. I thought I discovered signs that he watched her with a jealous eye and that my presence had had to be carefully explained to him —and also that she did not want me to know this. She looks well, as I say, and has a new distinction of dress, but she can no longer intoxicate me with her beauty or throw bombs into my soul; when I looked at her it was like staring into the center of an extinct volcano. She made me sad; it made me sad, curiously enough, that I had loved her so much once and now did not love her any longer. Actually, of course, I would not love her again for anything; I can think of few more terrible calamities; but I somehow felt that, impossible and imperfect as she is, some glamour and high passion had gone out of life when my love for her died. Well, these are old Dr. Wilson's last words on the chief maelstrom of his early years. Preserve them carefully, but do not publish them until all parties are dead. She asked about you and what your latest love affair was (I didn't go into it much, thinking you mightn't want the situation exposed) and wished you were there. She read me a long poem (rather good) that she had written and one or two short ones; she tells me that she has also done a short story and begun a novel (whose theme she is much disturbed to find anticipated by Cabell's "Taboo"). She had evidently prepared the *mise en scène* very carefully when she first received me: she had put on a serious black dress and was discovered sitting before her typewriter and a pile of manuscripts. And, as a matter of fact, I think she has been working more, perhaps, lately than she had when Crownie saw her.

. . . The Fitzgeralds have recently been here and tried to get hold of me, but, to my infinite regret, couldn't. I didn't know about it until after they had gone back to London. It seems they hate Europe and are planning to go back to America almost immediately. The story is that they were put out of a hotel because Zelda insisted upon tying the elevator—one of those little half-ass affairs that you run yourself—to the floor where she was living so that she would be sure to have it on hand when she had finished dressing for dinner.

Give my best to everybody in the office and tell [Jeanne] Ballot that I shall soon send her such a postcard as she requested. Don't repeat any of this stuff about Edna, or about my own reactions to her.

Yours always, E.W.

Edna St. Vincent Millay
1952–1953

To Floyd Dell*

June 12, 1952
Wellfleet

Dear Dell: Thank you for your letter. I am glad that you approved of my memoir of Edna. It was somewhat abridged in *The Nation* and really ended with a glimpse of you and her, which I got at second-hand, in the days before I knew her. I had been wondering whether you were going to write anything about her. I wish you would. She was, I think, one of the most interesting and extraordinary Americans of our time, and people who knew her ought to get that on record.   Yours sincerely, Edmund Wilson

---

* "Literary editor of *The Liberator* and now chiefly known as the author of *Moon-Calf*, his autobiographical novel of the adolescence of an idealist. Mr. Dell is too readily swayed by his political mind to be a pure critic, but is, nevertheless, one of the more acute among the younger arbiters of literary opinion."

—*Vanity Fair*, 1921

Edna St. Vincent Millay

Because she wrote her first and one of her most extraordinary poems, "Renascence," at the age of nineteen; because she is half Irish, half New England,
and has beautiful red hair; because she is a witty and charming prose writer
and is now engaged upon a novel; but chiefly because her lyric poems—combining austerity with emotional intensity—are among the best ever written by
an American. —*Vanity Fair*, 1923

First draft of a passage in *The Shores of Light,* sent to Floyd Dell: At the time I was writing this memoir, I happened one day, in the country, at Wellfleet on Cape Cod, where I live, to meet my neighbor from Truro, Phyllis Duganne. We talked about Edna Millay, and she told me of a memory she had of seeing her years ago in Greenwich Village running around the corner of Macdougal Street, flushed and laughing "like a nymph," with her shoulder-length hair swinging. Floyd Dell, also laughing, pursued her. Phyllis said she had always remembered this; and I leave this image here at the end to supplement my first-hand impression: a glimpse of Edna as the fleeing and challenging Daphne of her "Figs from Thistles" poem, from the time when I did not yet know her, when she had first come from Vassar to the Village.

To Floyd Dell   June 19, 1952
                                                                 Wellfleet

Dear Dell: . . . In connection with writing about Edna, everybody is up against the same problem. I saw Esther Adams last winter, and she told me that she wanted to write something, but couldn't decide how far she ought to go. I think she has about decided to put in everything but not necessarily publish it all. I thought at first that it would be impossible for me to produce anything publishable that would not be a fraud, and I have had it on my conscience that what I wrote falls so far short of the reality— which was once, in Edna's early phase, so much more amusing and romantic and, in her later years, so much more dreadful. Like you, I have had the idea of telling the whole story and burying it in a library, but I have not yet got to the point of doing so. I do think, however, that a record should be left, perhaps with the stipulation that the memoirs should not be pub- lished or circulated—until after a long interval, anyway—but merely used by responsible biographers. I feel that it is somehow important that she should eventually be shown as she was. The subject is fascinating and will unquestionably fascinate people in the future. I have read the proofs of the volume of her letters that is coming out in the fall and was more impressed than ever by the nobility and strength of her character. It is astonishing to find a contemporary literary woman writing hundreds of letters, to all kinds of people over a long period of years, with absolutely no gossip and no catty malice (though she had moments of indignation). Yet one cannot help becoming interested in—what did not much interest her—the per- sonalities and the human situations that gave her the themes for her poems. This correspondence is full of mysteries, and they will never be cleared up unless those who knew her well leave some testimony. It is not merely a question of gratifying curiosity about somebody's private affairs. The letters and records of writers of genius are one of the only ways we have of finding out how life was really lived in any given time or place . . .

                                            Yours sincerely, Edmund Wilson

To Floyd Dell   August 27, 1952
                                                    Talcottville

. . . I found both your memoir and the poems very moving. In the latter there are things that I didn't know—for example, that Inez Milholland had ever been an admiration of Edna's. I was glad to hear about her reciting poems to keep your morale up when the *Masses* trial was going on. About John Reed: I met her one day in a shoe-shining place on Twelfth Street— told her that I had just heard of his death. She was silent, and then said presently, "I'm mad at death!" The news stopped our conversation, yet I did not get the impression that she had known him particularly well . . .

To Floyd Dell   September 10, 1952
                                                        Wellfleet

Dear Dell: I imagine you are right about *Fatal Interview*—though I implied in my memoir that it was all about something or somebody in particular. Afterwards, Esther Adams told me that she had once asked Edna whom the sonnets were about, and she had answered, "What makes you think that they're all about the same person?" I was much interested in the Arthur Ficke poem, which I didn't know—also, in your poems in *May Days*. I suppose that a considerable collection could be made of the poems written about Edna. John Bishop did some very good ones. The *May Days* anthology is quite impressive, isn't it . . . Am going to send you a copy of my book of my old articles and new memoirs of the twenties and thirties, in which I've tried to give a panorama of the period.
                              Best regards, Edmund Wilson
    The quotation from Catullus shows that the poem I found her translating in 1948 was already much in her mind. The first of the quotations from Keats at the end illustrates the shift from *thou* to *you*. The third, fourth, and fifth quotations evidently apply to her own state of mind. The point of the second I do not understand. She has written them all down from memory, with variations on the original punctuation, and in the fifth has unconsciously changed *make* to *weave*.

To Floyd Dell   December 23, 1952
                                                        Princeton

. . . Here is my interpretation of "Shroud": the poet feels that her playing the harlot has alienated her lover, and that she has in some way—since she held the gate for them—facilitated his union with someone else . . .

To Floyd Dell   August 28, 1953
                                                    Talcottville

. . . Hearing from you has reminded me that I have not looked up the "Shroud" poem since you last wrote to me about it. Have just done so in the local library, and my present conclusion is that she happened to be wearing a black and red dress on the two different occasions and this seemed to her ironic. It may be that these were really circumstantial details . . .

To Floyd Dell   September 14, 1953
                                                                    Wellfleet
. . . You have certainly succeeded in making that poem mysterious—I had not paid much attention to it before . . . I am sure that she will eventually be revived and admired as she deserves . . .

England and Italy
1921

To Stanley Dell   August 16, 1921
                                                    Haslemere, Surrey, England
Dear Stan: I meant to write you before I left America, but left *The New Republic* only about a week before I sailed and had so much to do and was so much exhausted that I didn't get a chance to. As soon as I got aboard the boat I collapsed in a state of complete moral, physical, and mental bankruptcy and passed into a stupor in which all the events of my past life and the fundamental problems of the world passed before me. I recovered only after I had been some time in Paris. If you were with me, I should tell you the story of my life, but I cannot undertake it on paper. I do hope, however, that you may come to New York when I get back, as I expect to, in October.

Since I have been over here I have had a very pleasant time, but have not done much that is exciting (except attempt to go from Paris to London by one of the airlines and be stranded on the French coast when one of the engines stopped and the machine had to come down, thus giving old Dr. Wilson a bad quarter of an hour in the air). I have spent most of my time wandering around Paris, reading (notably Maupassant, whom I hadn't investigated much before) and redoing my old Y.M.C.A. story,* which I am converting into an entirely new and much more elaborate story by making it hinge upon the curious anecdote (about the girl who tried to seduce him) that John Amen told us last summer. I find that I return to fiction with renewed enthusiasm and (it seems to me) somewhat greater success. *The Undertaker's Garland*, by the way, has been accepted by Knopf for the fall on the condition that we cut out a little of the verse and substitute prose for it; he thinks that the proportion of prose to verse

___

* "Galahad."

72

ought to be more nearly equal. Mencken read it and wrote me a very appreciative letter about it and I afterwards had an amusing interview with him, in which he insisted that we ought to have something "very sardonic" in it—"the death of an Archbishop, for example." The Archbishop should be about to die, and reviewing his life in his mind, he should think: "Well, now I'm going to die, I wonder if it was all worth while: there was that girl I passed up back in the '00's . . . And then, all the weddings I've been to where I had to be kind of a kill-joy: I always had to leave as soon as the service was performed, so that the guests could begin to drink and enjoy themselves; I always had to go before the fun began . . . And now I've just read a book by Huxley that proves it's all been a mistake, so I'm going to hell anyway, and what was the use?" Or he's just read something that the Old Testament was written by Rabelais, that it was all a joke. "I think you have a good idea there," he said. "Here are two young men who have set out to spit in the eye of Death."

The Fitzgeralds, as you perhaps know, came to Europe last May on the $7,000 which Fitz got for his new novel from *The Metropolitan*. The astonishing (though, I suppose, natural) thing was that they hated Europe, especially the Continent, and started back home after staying not much more than a month. They had apparently become so accustomed to the luxurious appointment of the Ritz and the Plaza and the jazz of American life that Europe seemed to them too tame and too primitive to be taken seriously. I had a violent letter from Fitz in which he declared that the modern American was as far superior to the modern Frenchman as the modern Frenchman was superior to the Negro . . . *

. . . I am leaving tomorrow for Paris again, and expect to stay there for a short time and then go to Italy. I haven't the faintest idea what I am going to do when I get back to America: Croly promised to let me know about two months after I left whether the Privy Council, the Sanhedrin, of *The New Republic* was going to add me to its number, but I have heard nothing yet and am dubious about their decision, though Croly told me he would do everything he could to get me on. I have just had a note from Hackett announcing (with repressed elation) that Lippmann has left the N.R. to go on *The World* and, as he was the man who got me on originally and would, I should think, have been likely to support me, I rather expect that Hackett and Johnson will pass me up. My feelings about the N.R. are very mixed. It is a good place to be in many ways—particularly from the point of view of moving and leisure—but it is also very irritating in many ways and a chilly and unfriendly home for anybody but a respectable liberal of at least middle age. My affairs of the heart (confidential) are

---

* Two and a half pages describing a visit to Norman Kemp Smith are omitted, as they are repeated in the following letter to Christian Gauss.

badly entangled. I suppose it is old mother nature's revenge for my long period of freedom from these troubles that I should have spent this last year occupied with women at the expense of everything else; just now I am reduced to a state where I am anxious to find a modus vivendi which will enable me to live and let live. I really don't want to marry—but—but, I can't go into this subject here. I hope that you pray for my soul from time to time . . .   Yours always, EW

To GILBERT TROXELL   September 2, 1921
                                            Hotel Royal Danieli, Venice
Dear Trixie: . . . I share your enthusiasm for Jane Austen, though she and James Joyce have more in common than you seem to suppose. They share the almost unique distinction in English novels of having a sense of form. As for "restrained art," Joyce's *art* is surely restrained enough; it is his subject matter which you would outlaw. But this is an old dispute which we shall never come to the end of. By the way, I met people in Paris who knew Joyce, and you will be interested to hear that they regard him as full of old-fashioned prejudices. For example, he thinks it frightful for respectable young girls to use make-up. He is very simple and very serious and, as the result of having put furniture polish or something in his eyes, instead of eye lotion, some time ago, is obliged to spend so many days a week in a darkened room.

I am in Venice alone—a great mistake, because Venice is a sort of super summer resort, which ought to be enjoyed socially. I read Italian, write, and go in swimming at the Lido. I have been reading Leopardi's dialogues, which I recommend to you, not only on their merits (they are very amusing), but as a very clear easy Italian prose, if you are ever looking for any to read. I tremble to tackle D'Annunzio, who is quite hard, I believe. (Leopardi is pessimistic and atheistic, but I think you would enjoy him just the same: I recognize that your religion does not involve optimism.) From here I shall go to Florence and thence back to Paris and home (in October). I don't know what I'm going to do when I get back to America. I don't know what my connection with *The New Republic* will be and don't know whether our old ménage will ever recombine even in part. Think, Trixie, you may have slept for the last time in that ample but not too ample couch! You may have eaten your last Sunday breakfast with us, have worn out your last Sunday with the gossip of the university and the discussion of the eternal values (with interludes at the piano)! It is a profound and appalling thought, which I presumably can hardly bear—especially since I missed so many of those Sundays, owing to having gone to Red Bank. Perhaps, however, though I fear the irregularities of my behavior during the past year may have proved too much for Morris [Belknap], he and I might still struggle along in the

74

celibate consecration to the arts; it would be more seemly, I think, for the establishment to dwindle gradually. Then I shall die of a complicated life and Morris will die of a simple life internally complicated, nevertheless, and there will be only you left. Come, I pray you, once every fall, when the cold first thrills the air and the buses are full of eager young men awakened and keen for the winter, and standing under Washington Arch, the pivot of the sacred precinct, cross yourself and utter a prayer and then, proceeding in a solemn cortege of one, visit each of our habitations in turn (and in strict chronological order) and, standing before each house, recall for a moment its history: at Eighth Street, the coal grate, the inexpensive and faithful Chinaman, and me reading Homer promptly at nine o'clock every night; at Twelfth Street, David's marriage and our savage mockery of his wedding, Morris groaning at the oboe all day, the appearance of Pansy and Petunia; and at Sixteenth Street, the terrific debacle, the air charged with madness and storm, the human pianola below, the incurably bourgeois apartment, the restlessness and discontent, the divergence of habits and ideals! . . .

I shall now go out and hear the band play in the Piazza San Marco; I would give much for a familiar ear like your own.   Yours always, E.W.

To CHRISTIAN GAUSS   September 10, 1921
                                                            Florence

Dear Mr. Gauss: I have thought of you often here, surrounded as I am by the outward signs of the Dante celebration, the poet is being advertized and press-agented almost as if he were a presidential candidate. The rites themselves do not begin in Florence till about the 15th, but I expect to attend them and shall report to you on them later.

I have not done much of interest this summer, but have convalesced very pleasantly from my two years in New York. Almost the only human being I have seen has been Kemp Smith, whom I visited for about a week in England (at his sister-in-law's house in Surrey). Seeing him again was quite a shock, for I found him looking very badly and much nervously exhausted. I imagine, though he did not tell me so, that he had just been sick; at any rate, apparently the work at Edinburgh is too much for him; I gathered from talking with him that he would not be unwilling to go back to America in the course of time; he spoke, I think wistfully, of the sunny climate in contrast to the Scotch mists. I was really worried about him, not only from his appearance—he looks very gray and haggard and his eyes are bloodshot; all his old freshness and ruddiness was gone— but especially from the general tone of his talk; he spoke like someone who has been under a long strain and has been on the verge of a breakdown; he seemed full of strong fears about himself, about degenerating in middle age, etc. But the thing that shocked me most was the fact that

75

he seems to be becoming preoccupied by religious ideas and is even, unless I misinterpret his remarks on the subject, disposed to turn to Catholicism! He has come to believe in Providence and God and even talked seriously about the angels; he says that he has been forced to believe that there is a Providence taking care of things because it is intolerable, impossible to accept such an idea as that the fate of Europe after the war depended on Lloyd George. I think he took the war very hard and that the heavy work at Edinburgh on top of it was too much for him: Imagine me going to visit him in search of stoic strength and support, of which I was much in need, and then imagine the ghastly realization dawning, as Providence and the Catholic Church kept obtruding themselves into the conversation, that life had, for the moment anyway, proved too much for Kemp Smith. I challenged him directly one day about the religious business when, at the conclusion of an argument, he had said that what the world ought to have now was more religion (there is something in this, no doubt), by asking him what religion he thought was the solution; and was met by the laconic and mysterious answer: "Ah, well, that may appear in time!" I hope that my suspicions are insane that he has the intention of making public profession of the Catholic faith. It is not that I am a bigot to that extent, but that it somehow seems all wrong for Kemp Smith. It made my flesh creep to have him run down the Protestants, take angels for granted, and speak with an interest which seemed to me sinister of Newman's *Apologia*. I'm afraid I've drawn too gloomy a picture here and don't want to give an exaggerated impression; I had an extremely pleasant time with him: he had, of course, much that was interesting to say and with all of his old vigor and terseness; but it is quite clear that he is not very happy, and I wish as directly as possible that he could be induced to return to Princeton—else I am afraid we shall have him in a nervous breakdown or gathered in the Roman fold and on his way toward a Cardinal's hat. He asked after you and the rest of the family, of course, and wanted me to give you his best. I have told you about him at length because I was sure that it would interest you, but please don't tell people at large that I say he is developing Catholic leanings, etc., because I may misrepresent his views, about which I never dared press him much further. You know him much better than I do. What do you make of all this? I never realized till I saw him this summer how sensitive and high-strung he is.

I have recently been reading two favorite poets of yours and have been disappointed in both—Byron and Baudelaire. Both seem to me to have lost much of their force with time—Baudelaire to my surprise, for, never having read him except here and there, I expected great things of him. I don't know what it is you see in Byron—I don't think I ever heard you say—but I take it that it is general ideas and spirit about life, rather than *beaux vers*; but it seems to me that those ideas, though frequently true, and that spirit, though not without nobility, are both somewhat cheapened by being represented by Byron, who appears to my early twentieth-century eyes more a landmark in the thought of Europe than a genuine artist. As for Baudelaire, he does not seem to me, either, so good an artist as I had expected; is it merely because I happen to be out of key with him or simply that I find something rather arid and flat in his imagery and color? And then his everlasting remorse and outcry about sin seem to me to have very little reality. I have a feeling that he was rather bourgeois (spiritually, I mean) at bottom. There are certainly some fine things in him, particularly "L'Albatros" and "Don Juan aux Enfers," but here, too, I have a suspicion that there was an alloy of pose, of exaggeration, in his bitterness and pride. I have also been reading Leopardi's *Operette Morali*, which, on the whole, I prefer to either Byron or Baudelaire; they are certainly, in a sense, sounder literature, though the unrelieved tone of pessimism, without either gaiety or glowing passion to lighten or lift it, becomes, in the long run, rather oppressive. One feels that his indictments against life are pretty invalidated by the fact that he himself, subjected to abnormal privations and restrictions, has never really known its fullest, or even its ordinary capacities for enjoyment, satisfaction, etc. I disagree with the doctrine set forth in his *Dialogo di Torquato Tasso e del suo Genio famigliare*, and, it seems to me that I remember, on one occasion by you, that there is no such thing as happiness enjoyed and sufficient in the present. I find that the melancholy thing about happiness is not that it doesn't exist but that it doesn't last. But, God knows, as Oscar Wilde said about the revolutionists, "that I am with him in some ways."

I'm enjoying Florence extremely, though here all alone, and find I like it better than any other European city I know, except Paris. Venice I got rather fed up with after a week: it is too close, gaudy, and Byzantine for me; it should be John Bishop's city, not mine.

Please remember me to Mrs. Gauss and the children. I hope to see you all before long (I sail the 15th of October) . . . I tried to get you a picture postcard of Browning's palazzo at Venice. It seems to me that Browning was a better poet than Byron, anyway.   Yours always, Edmund Wilson, Jr.

To WALTER LIPPMANN   February 13, 1922
                                                      The Princeton Club
Dear Mr. Lippmann: I don't suppose there is any place on *The World*
now for a literary and dramatic critic? I have about come to the end of
my freelancing and should be glad of a job. I don't have much hope that
The World could use me, but you suggested this summer that I might
come to you about it. Could you drop me a line at 777 Lexington Avenue?

I'm glad to see that you're back and, I take it, doing the *World*
editorials.   Yours very sincerely, Edmund Wilson, Jr.

To STANLEY DELL   March 25, 1922
                                                 777 Lexington Avenue, N.Y.
Dear Stan: I have been on the point of writing you any number of times
but have always been so distressed at the prospect of giving an account
of my personal affairs that I have never succeeded. So forgive me if I
have nothing to say except that you will probably find me still single
when you come back. But with the resurgence of spring, the arrival in
town of the Fitzgeralds, the proof of *The Undertaker's Garland*, the
embarkation on a three-act comedy,* and the chances of a new job, I
have commenced to expand again.

In regard to the second of these events, we find them both somewhat
changed—particularly Zelda, who has become matronly and rather fat (about
which she is very sensitive) and is offended by the cynical indifference
of Fitz to the baby; much of her old jazz has evaporated; she seems quite
a different person from when he first married her and, as she becomes
more mellowed, I like her better. As for him, he looks like John Barrymore

---

* *The Crime in the Whistler Room.*

on the brink of the grave—chiefly, I guess, because he has just been sick—but also, somehow, more intelligent than he used to; his soul seems to have been somewhat scarified by his trip to Europe combined with the coming of the baby—two events which seem to have gone ill together. He has written a comedy, which he is trying to sell, and which he shouldn't have any difficulty in selling, I should think, from the fragments of it I have read—it is very funny.* He arrived this morning in a hansom, after an all-night party of some kind, and wanted to take me for a drive in the park.

This brings me to the tremendous burlesque (a play) which Ted Paramore and I are about to hurl together (we have a great idea of finishing it in a month and getting a little money out of it) and which will deal with the expedition to capture the glyptodon or plesiosaurus or whatever it is in Patagonia (you have doubtless read about it in the papers)—a theme which we conceive to have great comic possibilities. You see, for one thing, the president of the Anti-Evolution Society tries to crab the expedition. My story about John Amen's adventure I find myself unable to dispose of:† Mencken and Nathan said they would use it if I would change it, but, as they wanted me to eliminate the bedroom scene altogether, I refused. Burton Rascoe is trying to sell it for me to some Chicago magazine; both in subject and length I am afraid it is utterly unsalable except in book form. Rascoe tells me, by the way, that *The Smart Set* is the most prudish magazine in the country: it seems that Mencken has studied the anti-smut law so closely that he is now able to see how it could apply to almost anything and is consequently afraid of publishing anything; Rascoe told me some incredible changes he had made in manuscripts. Rascoe himself, by the way, is a most attractive fellow; I had never cared much for his criticism as I used to get odds and ends of it from the West, but since he has come East I have got to know him and found him one of the most agreeable and interesting people I have yet met in the journalistic business—he is one of the only ones who knows French and German very well and has genuine enthusiasm for them.

Of recent books, I have found Sherwood Anderson's *The Triumph of the Egg* about the best thing in current American fiction. You really must read it, if you haven't. It's not at all like *Main Street, Moon-Calf* et al.; Anderson has something quite different from the regular realistic formula. He has a seriousness about life and a gift for making a local story seem of universal significance that make me think he may be the best of this generation of American novelists. Just now I am reading *Civilization in America*, which I find much better than I had been led to believe. But

---

* *The Vegetable.*
† "Galahad."

these are about the only new books out of all that I have read for review, etc., that I have got much out of. There have been a number of good things in the theater: Connelly and Kaufman's *To the Ladies* is terribly funny and does something which, in the days of "It Pays to Advertise," etc., I had never thought to see on the American stage—it is a satire on business, with a solemn businessman and an adoring American magazine young employee made ridiculous as the chief characters. And *Back to Methuselah*, contrary to everybody's expectation, proved to be very attractive and, in parts, thrilling on the stage.

I hope you will not let my long silence prevent you from answering this letter promptly: if I have not written, it has not been because I have not thought of you, and I am eager for news of you. Do you expect to get East this spring?

To CHRISTIAN GAUSS   April 25, 1922
                                               777 Lexington Avenue, N.Y.
Dear Mr. Gauss: I read your article on [Alfred] Noyes with horror, consternation, and fear! Those excerpts from his latest book are the first mediocre poetry I have ever heard you praise. I think you must have believed in them through an act of faith for the purpose of making out a case. And I don't see why you should assume that the Carman–Noyes–Le Gallienne thing is the only authentic poetry of youth. Broken hearts —which presuppose a hunger for and belief in romance just as much as taking refuge in the Elizabethans—are surely youthful, too. You can't expect survivors of 1914–18 to have very much ho! for the open road about them or to romanticize about adventures and the wars of yester-year. It certainly seems to me that Sassoon's early poetry is youthful enough even from your point of view and that so was Rupert Brooke's and that of a number of other young men, bad and good, before the first fine flush of the war had been dimmed. If you dismiss this as "animalism" I don't see why youthful animalism isn't as youthful as anything else. I don't, to be sure, claim to have written any gladsome glamorous songs myself but I would protest on behalf of my colleagues that Fitz's early lyrics (inserted in *This Side of Paradise*) were full of youthful romance and that John, for all his early decadence, certainly struck a note of youth in such things as "Endymion in a Shack." As I say, I don't see why gaiety and rainbow horizons should be made the sole touchstones of youth anyway: adolescence and young manhood are a most painful parturition, the struggles of a drowning man who does not even know where the shore is. Someone wrote in *The Dial* a couple of years ago in an essay on Rimbaud that his experience as a teacher in observing adolescent young men had led him to believe that extreme disgust with life was a characteristic of the young. I know that when I was at Princeton during my

sophomore and junior year I used to be overwhelmed with a conviction that all life was dust and ashes as I have never been since; I used to feel as if I understood everything and nothing was any good. (Incidentally, I don't understand Noyes's story about Swift vindicating Newton: Swift did not believe in Newton and caricatured him savagely, whereas Voltaire admired him enormously and, whatever he may have said about his private life, surely does not deserve to be likened to a poisonous adder trying to sting a marble god. Still, perhaps I misunderstand the passage you quote from, not having seen the context.) I did like the Molière article, however; I thought it was fine. But didn't Arnold always used to include Molière among the great poets of the world?

I was awfully sorry you couldn't have lunch with me Saturday but hope to see you before long . . .

Yours for the open road and the rainbow horizon of dreams. By the way, I don't know how you have been deceived into thinking that Alfred Noyes is youthful: it is patently the poetry of middle age. Who else but a man who had lost his youth would strain so desperately after romance? Noyes does not understand the modern world well enough to know what its romance consists of and, supposing that life in Elizabethan times was more sugared and less shocking than life today, he invents for himself an Elizabethan Age which could never have existed and which the documents belie. Why, if Alfred Noyes had ever been swound! Yet was not Marlowe essentially youthful! (You deny it in your essay, I think —by implication at least), and was not precisely one of his symptoms that his soul was clouded by dark vapors? You cannot have ecstasy and divine vision without bitterness and despair, and both of these are the property of youth. Could any other but one who had understood what it was to bid the hills to fall and crush him that he might be rescued from the wrath of heaven ever have dreamed of women more lovely than the beauty of a thousand stars? What mere lighthearted wayfarer was ever really transfigured by joy? For the young are not always lighthearted; youth bears a heavy heart. The earth quakes beneath his tread; the stars are combined against him; he is the battleground for a menagerie which is ready to spring at his throat. And when in the midst of these disasters he finds a moment of calm or freedom, his heart goes up like a rocket to the farthest reaches of the sky. But is there any evidence on record that Mr. Noyes has ever harbored a menagerie? No more than there is that like a rocket he has ever touched the wonders of the sky. If you tell me that his early poems were written when he was actually young and are so, beyond dispute, youthful, I say, as you say of us, that he was prematurely middle-aged.   EW

I hope soon to get my revenge in a few hard words about Byron in a review I am to do of the new letters.

To H. L. MENCKEN   May 12, 1922
                                          777 Lexington Avenue, N.Y.
Dear Mr. Mencken: I haven't been able to think of any really good
subject for the kind of article you want. I can think of plenty of "assaults
on institutions held in universal respect," but the trouble is that I could
never make them run to two or three thousand, let alone five thousand
words. I suppose you couldn't use a set of perhaps three or four shorter
disquisitions—the trouble with this, I realize, is that it would tend to fall
into the *répétition générale* formula and would in any case load the
magazine with two sets of short essays. But how would you feel about an
imaginary dialogue?*—say between Van Wyck Brooks and Scott Fitzgerald
on the joylessness and lack of vitality in American life. It has just struck
me as ironic that while Fitz and Zelda were reveling nude in the orgies
of Westport (summer before last), Brooks in the same town, probably
without ever knowing they were there, should have been grinding out his
sober plaint against the sterile sobriety of the country. By the way, I don't
suppose the preface to *The Undertaker's Garland* would do for a leading
article? It could be used independently, I think, though, having been
written two years ago, some of its strictures are a little stale.

What was it you thought I might be able to do for the *Baltimore Sun*?
I have heard nothing from *The World*, found that somebody else already
had the *International Studio* job, and can't convince myself that I should
really fit in with Hapgood on *Hearst's*. I went around to see him a few
days after you told me about it and he said that what he wanted was
young men to heel the managing-editor job by doing articles on current
affairs, etc. The trouble is that what they want is romantic stuff such as
you get in its highest form in William Hard. In fact, it is 100 percent
boop-bumper as far as I can see. Not that I wouldn't be willing to be
managing editor if it were only a question of that, but I know that I could
never be a success writing their stuff. I'm very grateful to you just the
same for sending me around there. I may go out to Detroit in June with
Ted Paramore to see the A.F. of L. convention—usually a pretty dull
affair. Do you suppose *The Sun* could use a story on this?

By the way, why do you always use "jejune" as if it meant "juvenile"
or "callow"? This has been worrying me for years.
                                   Yours very sincerely, Edmund Wilson, Jr.

To STANLEY DELL   May 26, 1922
                                          777 Lexington Avenue, N.Y.
Dear Stan: . . . The chief news hereabouts is that John Bishop is going
to be married (June 17) and go abroad immediately afterwards. It is

---
* *Discordant Encounters.*

Margaret Hutchins, to whom he has been engaged off and on for a year. I regard it as more or less of a calamity, as she has always seemed to me a prime dumbbell, but I suppose it was inevitable. The suddenness of the whole thing—while Crownie is abroad—may make it necessary for me to go back to the old madhouse [Vanity Fair] and take his place till some new young man can be found to be groomed for managing editor. In any case, I hope to take over the book department he has been doing. The whole thing makes me sort of sick—in fact, after having dinner the other night with John, his fiancée, and her family, I came home and took to my bed—from which I have only just arisen after two days. It is true that I have been suffering from tonsillitis and intestinal disturbances, but contemplation of John's impending married life with a strong-willed, un-intelligent woman of passionate gentility and correctitude was what put the lid on me. She has a great deal of money, to be sure, and theoretically will enable John to serve the muses undisturbed by the necessity of earning a living, but actually I am afraid that she will set out to stifle poesy, and all the experience that goes to make it, with relentless jealousy. The worst of it all is that John isn't really in love with her and, I predict, won't be faithful to her ten minutes, whereas she is desperately in love with him.

I am sick of everything at the moment and have a great desire to escape to New England somewhere. I think I'll take a holiday to Provincetown until the Vanity Fair situation becomes clear. By the way, you must read Joyce's Ulysses, if you haven't already done so. You can get a copy from the Brick Row Book Shop (19 East 47th Street) for $25—730 enormous pages. It contains some of the most brilliant and some of the dreariest and dullest writing of the age, but has already been accepted as a sort of divine revelation by the intelligentsia—most of whom have not read it, as it is very hard to get and very long and unreadable in spots—and some of them have even expressed extreme indignation at hearing that I was going to review it for The New Republic:* "as if it were a book that you could review like any other book!" Still, Mrs. Bloom's soliloquy at the end is probably one of the most remarkable things of the kind ever written: I was greatly moved by it. Unfortunately, it has become the habit for people to skip through it as they do through Boccaccio or Rousseau's Confessions and there seems to be a generally prevalent impression that it is all some sort of obscene joke.

Now for heaven's sake let me hear from you and come back East as soon as possible. After John goes, if you are still away, I shall perish of spiritual inanition. Convey to Marion the recommendations of my pro-found esteem.   Yours always, EW

---

* The New Republic, July 5, 1922.

To F. Scott Fitzgerald   May 26, 1922
                                          777 Lexington Avenue, N.Y.
Dear Scott: I owe you a thousand apologies for not having answered your
letters before, but the Theatre Guild has been putting me off from week
to week almost ever since I gave them the play* and I have been waiting,
thinking always that the next week I'd be able to give you a definite
decision. The last date they fixed me was Thursday (yesterday) and when
I called them up today they gave me to understand that it was still being
read but that they would let me know immediately, etc. They are really,
however, considering it seriously: it takes them a long time to decide
partly because they have a sort of editorial board, each member of which,
apparently, has to read and vote on it.

So far as I am concerned, I think it is one of the best things you ever
wrote. I have read only the first version—I didn't take time to read the
second because the Theatre Guild insisted that they were in a great hurry
about it—so won't criticize it now at length. I thought the millionaire
episode, except the first scene, a little weak and the last act too palpably
padded. As for the battle scene, it was fine and you made a great mistake
in allowing them to kid you into removing it. The Guild thinks so, too,
and have expressed disappointment that it isn't in the revised version—so,
if they decide to take it, I think you ought to put it back. I should
suggest that you make the White House and battle the second act and
the millionaire and postman the third; this would do away with the necessity of stalling along at the beginning of the postman scene simply in order
to make it into a whole act. As I say, I think that the play as a whole is
marvelous—no doubt, the best American comedy ever written. I think you
have a much better grasp on your subject than you usually have—you
know what end and point you are working for, as isn't always the case
with you. If I were writing my *Bookman* article now, I'd have to do parts
of it in a different strain. I think you have a great gift for comic dialogue
—even if you never can resist a stupid gag—and should go on writing
plays. The Theatre Guild couldn't decide about the play at their meeting
for selecting the last play of the season and so—though why nobody knows
—fixed upon Arnold Bennett's *What the Public Wants*, which is now not
running a very successful course. By the way, the great question is, have
you read James Joyce's *Ulysses*? Because if you haven't, the resemblance
between the drunken-visions scene in it and your scene in the White
House must take its place as one of the great coincidences in literature.

As for gossip, the usual asslapping still goes on. *The Undertaker's
Garland* is nearly done, but, I suppose, will not be out till later. My
novelette, that *The Smart Set* found too obscene for them, will probably

---

* *The Vegetable.*

84

be published as a separate book. I dare say that by this time you have heard of John's impending marriage (to Margaret Hutchins, of course). I regard it as more or less of a calamity but I suppose it was inevitable. She will supply him with infinite money and leisure but, I fear, chloroform his intellect in the meantime. They are going abroad for a year almost immediately (they are to get married June 17). I think her a prime dumbbell with nothing much to distinguish her but an all too strong will which may lead John around by the balls. A sad, sad business! —unless it should turn out to be a very satisfactory arrangement. We have seen a lot of Dos Passos lately—he is extremely nice; he is writing a novel which, I gather from what he has told me, is about the devitalized gentility of modern Boston; he describes it as "a tragedy of impotence." Don Stewart has gone to France; I hope he gets a good screw there. Ted and I have written and rewritten the first act of our play and read it to Benchley and Mrs. Parker with more or less sincere enthusiasm on their part. We have only one copy of it or I'd send it to you. By the way, I don't suppose you read my great poem in *The Double Dealer*. I must send it to you, if you haven't. *The Beautiful and Damned* has had very interesting reviews—especially Mary Colum's in *The Freeman*.

If this letter is anything lacking in my usual wit and profundity, it is because I have been in bed most of the week with a combination of tonsillitis, general debility, intestinal disturbances, and malignant melancholia—the last superinduced by having dinner one night with John, his fiancée, and her family. I am faint and full of disgust with the city and think of fleeing to New England for a little country stuff (a desire which visits me only once every five years) and a chance for meditation and prayer.

Convey all my recommendations to Zelda, whose review of *The Damned* I thought fine and whose thing in *The Metropolitan* I liked less. Mary [Blair] tells me to tell you that the tickets to *The Hairy Ape* didn't cost anything and that it is perfectly all right. By the way, what has Harris had to say about your play; have you heard anything further from him? Farewell, farewell . . . I am growing weaker and weaker (having lived almost exclusively on orange juice and gargle for the last three days) and, if I do not break off soon, will fall forward unconscious into the typewriter and be ground to atoms by the relentless wheels . . . Farewell, farewell . . . If an old man's blessing can profit you anything, take it and fight the good fight . . . Every word that I write comes straight from the depths of an empty and unsteady stomach—it is written not in common ink but in my few poor last drops of gastric juice . . . Farewell . . . I go, I go to the high cold hills of New England—to that shore where the voice of the sea carries the heart with the urgency of its beat, where my ancestors served the altars of learning and committed murders in the name of God. My stomach is rotted with bad gin, my tonsils are riddled with ulcers, my soul is laid waste with contemplation of my own and others' sins—not against the Ten Commandments but against Honor, Justice, and Light! . . . Farewell! I fall like the fair statue of a god eaten out from within by marble maggots. Pray for my soul! EW

To F. Scott Fitzgerald   June 3, 1922
                                                      777 Lexington Avenue, N.Y.
Dear Scott: I'm sorry to say that I have just heard from the Theatre Guild to the effect that they have finally decided not to produce the play. There was apparently disagreement about it among the various members. Don't be downhearted, however. Mary Blair wants to take it—with your permission—to Frank Craven and Richard Bennett, both of whom she knows. I should think that you are practically sure of having it produced somehow. In the meantime, if I were you, I should certainly have it published. I am enormously honored to have your new book dedicated to me—if it is. You made an error in commiserating with me about my novelette, which I said *was*, not was not, going to be published. If Knopf doesn't do it, a Chicago firm has offered to—suggesting one of those editions where sixteen copies of this book have been done into print on hand-woven isinglass and the type shot from a gun—but I am against this.

You can get *Ulysses* for $25 from the Brick Row Book Shop, 19 East 47th Street, N.Y. So far as I know, this is the only place where you can get it, and they have only a few. See my review of it in a forthcoming *New Republic*. (See also my article on New Jersey in this week's *Nation*.)

I enclose a picture of John (from the *Daily News*) which tells the whole sad story in a coup d'oeil. I scarcely know whether I can summon cynicism enough to attend the wedding. Just at present I am about to leave town for New England—where I expect to make a tour of Boston, Concord, and Provincetown, investigating the Transcendentalists and other matters—coming back in time for the Princeton reunion and John's wedding (why don't you come on for these two occasions?). In July I'll probably have to go back on *Vanity Fair*—for a time, anyway—to take John's place. God help us all!   Your old college friend and sincere admirer, EW

To F. Scott Fitzgerald   June 20, 1922
                                                      777 Lexington Avenue, N.Y.
Dear Scott: We have given the play to Frank Craven, who promises to read it within the week. I wish you would write and let me know exactly what you are doing with it apart from this. Is your play broker still trying to do anything with it? Eugene O'Neill, whom I saw up at Provincetown, told me that Nathan had told him that he intended to take it to Hopkins when he had the revised version. Now, has Nathan taken it to Hopkins?

86

O'Neill thinks it would be a good idea to have Hopkins see it and says he will mention it to him. O'Neill, from what Nathan and I have told him, is very enthusiastic about it. He is an extraordinarily attractive fellow, by the way. I find with gratification that he regards *Anna Christie* as more or less junk and thinks it is a great joke that it won the Pulitzer Prize. His genius seems to be only just becoming properly articulate—in *The Hairy Ape*.

My tour of New England was a great success: I feel a bigger, better, and more wholesome man for it. I came back only just in time for John's wedding—the most amusing piece of buffoonery of the kind I have ever participated in. John was apparently scared into stupefaction and at the end of the ceremony was found to be standing on the bride's train, so that she couldn't leave the altar. His mother and sister were very skeptical and unreconciled about the whole business and, under the influence of champagne, became very plain-spoken. The bride's father, under the same influence, became amorous and tried to rape Elinor Wylie and Hazel Rascoe. The younger intellectuals formed a ring and danced round and round in the middle of the room to the jazz orchestra.

Well, uphold the Faith! Be strong. Quit you like men. Your friend [Thomas A.] Boyd hasn't turned up, but I'll put myself at his service when he does.

EW

To F. Scott Fitzgerald

July 31, 1922
Vanity Fair

Dear Scott: Craven sent back the play: he has written one for himself; and Winthrop Ames also has rejected it with soft words. Just now a man named Felton Elkins, who is very rich and has just started in on the producing business, has it; I am going to have lunch with him tomorrow and I understand he has read it and likes it, so will leave this letter open and add whatever may be of interest tomorrow. Tyler (producer of the Kaufman–Connelly comedies), Augustin Duncan (brother of Isadora and an excellent actor and director, who has just assumed the direction of the new Equity Players—what promises to be a very important enterprise), and Brock Pemberton (the young Algonquin Belasco who put over *Miss Lulu Bett*) have all expressed a desire to see the play: but do you want me to show them the present text or to send it back to you, after I get it from Elkins tomorrow, for the changes you have concocted—or will you send me a new copy of the second act? Also, what, if anything, has Hopkins done about it? I saw Helen Westley some time ago and she told me that she believed thoroughly in the play and was all for having the Theatre Guild produce it but that Philip Moeller had got cold feet when it came to the pinch and voted against it, though he liked it. She says that she thinks Lawrence Langner, at present abroad, will probably

champion it and that she would be glad to have it presented for consideration again in the fall when he gets back. She protested that she had roared
with laughter over the MS and assured me that that was an almost unheard
of thing for an actress to do.

John got off the other day and I am back in the old madhouse (V.F.).
It was all very affecting, nearly breaking Alec McKaig's and my hearts.
Just a few moments before the time of sailing a great and sudden storm
burst over the city as if in portent of some sinister and ominous event;
a child with a triple penis was prematurely born in Brooklyn, and a large
bright star in the form of the female genital was seen to hover over 53rd
St. and Sixth Ave. In the midst of these heroic thunders the fateful ship
left the dock and as soon as it had cleared the harbor the summer skies
cleared again—but a glamour was gone from the day; the sun lay more
heavily on the city.

Have you been reading the great controversy about the Younger Generation?*—carried on by Spingarn, Nock, Seldes, Rascoe, Rosenfeld, *The
New York Times*, and myself. It is weltering around in a great slough
of confusion, growing more and more hopeless all the time. Both sides
have revealed themselves—if we may judge by their utterances in the
debate—utterly incompetent to engage intelligently in the simplest sort
of controversy; it is all a great mess of misunderstandings and general
inability to deal accurately with ideas—accusations answered without being
read and explanations gone astray amid the "buzz" of the Algonquin (see
last week's *Freeman*), of insults, insinuations, recantations, and curses.
Instead of picking out the opponent's vulnerable spots and taking careful
aim at them, the combatants are in the habit of loading heavy artillery
pieces with nails, beer tops, old pairs of scissors, and fragments of broken
glass and firing them broadcast at the enemy. Everybody makes generaliza-
tions and every generalization is worse than the last; every member of
the Younger Generation identifies the Younger Generation with himself
and ascribes his own private virtues and preferences to a whole movement,
and the Older Generation does the same thing. I am sick of the whole
business and have just performed a great phlebotomy on Rosenfeld's
article for *Vanity Fair* on the subject, reducing it to three thousand words
from about a million.

I must cease: it's two in the morning and I get up every morning at
8:45 now, functioning on an efficiency basis for the first time in several
years . . .   Yours with kindest regards to the little woman. EW

I have seen Elkins and he feels just as I told you I did in connection
with the first draft—that it rather goes to pieces from the millionaire scene
on. I am absolutely convinced that the postman scene won't do as a whole

---

* "The Younger Generation," by J. E. Spingarn, in *The Freeman*.

act and should be a mere brief scene at the close, the first part of the third act being the last part of the dream. I really think it ought to be fixed up before circulating further—so I shall return the MS to you. Aside from this, Elkins's producing projects seem to be rather vague; he likes the play and says he would be glad to put it on if it is revised, but I have an idea that he may never get to the point of putting anything on.*

Elinor Wylie is, next to Edna Millay, probably the most remarkable of contemporary American women poets. Her first book, *Nets to Catch the Wind*, was awarded the Poetry Society's prize as the best first book of poems published in 1921. Her second volume, *Black Armour*, will be published in April. Mrs. Wylie's poetry gives the effect of bright metals and jewels melted by a single intense flame and poured molten into rigorous moulds which, when the fluid has cooled, stamp it with the hard mask of permanence. (*Vanity Fair*, 1923)

To Elinor Wylie   July 13, 1922
                                                                 Vanity Fair

Dear Elinor: Here is a proof of "Peregrine." The gray effect is going to be removed from behind the poem. Yes: I sent the Byron, etc. I have been reading Trelawny—which I think is wonderful.† In spite of all Mrs. Shelley's shortcomings, I feel that it is possible to blame her too harshly: after all, in spite of Shelley's humanitarianism, he must have been singularly inhuman in some ways, and surely Mary's yearnings for society were natural enough, if a little stodgy. No ordinary woman could be content in such abysmal isolation as she found herself obliged to live in.

John sailed at three this afternoon and at that hour exactly the elements, in a terrible compact, thundered an ominous farewell—or rather, less a farewell than a salvo for some approaching fate, the loud bellowing of doom that portends great peripeties of fortune. The sky was darkened for half an hour; the rain fell like a curtain of zinc; thunder detonated across the city with its elephantine quaking and in the lightning the giant buildings looked pallid and chill. In the lobby of the Algonquin walked the sheeted and gibbering dead; and a blinding meteorlike body of prodigious intensity and brilliance was seen to hover for half an hour above the junction of 53rd Street and Sixth Avenue. Then the sudden thunders abated and the city receded into torpor. But no longer the same as before —a gap had been riven in life. I miss him terribly: his going leaves me almost entirely to professional literary people, whom I find very unsatis-

---

* "I cannot remember anything about Scott Fitzgerald's reaction to the failure of *The Vegetable* to get to New York. He was highly critical of his own work and, I think, had ceased to believe in it."   —To Charlotte Kretzoi, 1964
† *Recollections of the Last Days of Shelley and Byron.*

factory in some ways. We have, however, planned to meet in a year or two and collaborate on another high fantasy—to outdazzle the first. In the meantime, pray for us both; let your prayers go up like bright diamonds, which, though they never bribe the Almighty, may at least scratch Him painfully in their flight.

Morton came in to *Vanity Fair* today for some captions to do, and as I was busy in Crownie's office at the time, I asked him to wait. Whether he had to catch a train or became panic-stricken through shyness I don't know, but when I came out he had disappeared. I hope he didn't think again that he was being high-hatted. I'll send him the pictures tomorrow. If he speaks of it, assure him that my intentions were extremely cordial and that I certainly thought he understood the situation.

Well, farewell for the moment. Let me hear from you from time to time. I hope that the novel goes well. I didn't like your T. S. Eliot thing in the last *Vanity Fair*—though Crownie thinks it is wonderful. It is almost the only one of your things I have not liked, but I won't be too harsh with it because I have fallen under the shadow of Eliot myself.

Yours amid the sadness of the world, EW

To Elinor Wylie   August 2, 1922
                                                  Vanity Fair

Dear Miss Wylie: Although I know it's wrong of me to write to you, I a perfect stranger, there's something inside of me that just had to come out and which says write, she will understand. My heart is flushed by your lovely poetry. It makes the sunshine a little brighter, the odors of eve somehow sweeter, but the nights, ah the nights, oh so restless. I lie and toss and think and burn and then you come, not in person of course, but "On the Nets of the Wind." My spiritual sister, my passionate playmate, my mental mother! What, oh what, do you look like? I have often pictured vainly the author of that lovely poem which begins "Avoid the lowing herd." Sometimes I see you thin as hope; again, full bosomed, waxing and waning like the moon.

As for me, what can I say? Unknown, unrecognized, I yet give forth that beauty which my saddened eyes can limn. Perhaps you have seen my poem "The Mill Stream" in the *Youth's Companion*, January 16, '22. Perhaps you did not realize it, but the verse which goes:

> "Oh mighty misty Mill Stream
> Pulse onward brave with joy
> Upon your shining bosom bear
> Like a beat my heart."

These words were written to you and your genius when I, too, tasted the future's wine.

90

But life, inscrutable, cruel, has set apart for me the humbler if more necessary tasks. But no more of that, I've never whined much and I never shall. It is a dim picture as I stand spade in hand, the ivy orator of my class at Buffkin. Why have I told you all this and laid bare my soul? I scarcely know. Will your heart beat a little faster knowing that your message has flown and nested in another's heart e'en though humble?

My P.O. address is National Wire Works, New Suffolk, N.Y.

With every good wish. Roscoe N. Wingo

To ELINOR WYLIE
[undated, 1922]
Vanity Fair

Lines inspired by the Voluptuous Pleasure Experienced in Writing the Letter Z with a Soft Pencil.

> An Aztec zinc adze for Mazzini,
>> With azaleas and zinnias, azure and glazed;
>> A kazoo intermezzo
>> Zoom-zoomed in Arezzo:
> The zanzare were dizzy, the zitherists dazed.
>> Zenobia, fezzed,
>> Guzzling Zuzus with zest,
> Was amazedly zézaying, Zut and Gadzooks!
> While, from Zeppelin razzias drowzy and lazy,
> The jazzing Tziganes of Fitzhugh Esterhazy
> But buzzed in gazebos to Bashibazonks.

Dear Elinor: This will give you an idea of the splendid intellectual and artistic form that I am in at present. I hope to see you soon and give you an opportunity of enjoying the inestimable treasures of my soul, of which the above is but a sample.

EW

To JOHN PEALE BISHOP
August 1, 1922
Vanity Fair

Dear John: I just received a letter from Knopf to the effect that our corrections had cost so much that they would have to charge us something like $48 for them—to be deducted from our royalties. You appear to have forgotten to supply them with a biography, so, as they have been clamoring for one, I have composed one myself which I hope does not omit any of your major claims to glory. The advertizing matter is being fomented and I feel at last as if the dawn were just on the point of breaking.

I was much impressed by the furious storm which burst upon the city just at the minute of your sailing and abated as suddenly about half an hour afterwards. Ominous and heroic thunders resounded across the city and one felt in the voice of the elements something fateful and definitive, as if an epoch had been ended, a drama brought to its close—or as if it signaled some august periphery in the ardors of a god. The sheeted and gibbering dead were seen to range between the Algonquin and the Yale Club and it was reported that on Brooklyn Heights a child with a triple penis was born; over the conjunction of 53rd Street and Sixth Avenue hovered a star of unheard-of brightness in the semblance of the female genital. And from one end of the city to the other rose the flutelike and heartbreaking cry of a thousand defeated virgins who had been saving for you the flower of their youth.

Since then, though a brightness be gone from the day, everything has gone on much the same. I discovered the key to the modern movement the other day, but will not disclose it to you here because I am on the point of writing a tremendous article about it. The controversy about the Younger Generation has reached almost incredible heights of ineptitude: Rascoe attacked [Albert Jay] Nock without having read his article, and Nock replied with an elaborate piece of sarcasm about the Younger Generation's being so muddleheaded that they couldn't even understand what they read—whereupon Rascoe published a statement to the effect that he had carefully told Nock about not reading his article and apologized in the Algonquin and that the Older Generation were so muddleheaded that they couldn't understand what was told them in plain words. Nock retorted that Rascoe had spoken so fast and the "buzz" of conversation at the Algonquin had been so loud that he hadn't understood what he had said but that he didn't see what business Rascoe had writing about his article without reading it anyhow. Now [Paul] Rosenfeld has attempted to meet all comers in the article which you appear to have ordered from him for *Vanity Fair* and which ran in its original form to some five or six thousand words. I performed a great phlebotomy on it, much to Rosenfeld's anguish, letting off several quarts of surplus metaphor, prophecy, Pythian rhapsody, outpourings about Stieglitz and nameless lymphatic humors. In it he hits out in all directions at once, furiously attempting to challenge, answer, and turn to scorn every word spoken for no matter what purpose by any of his opponents. The whole controversy is thus ending in a great whirlwind of mush which does but little credit to the intellectual powers of either the Younger or the Older Generation.

By the way, you are probably so far from these matters by this time that you will be able to summon them to your mind only with extreme reluctance and strain, but was there a set of *Spiegelmensch* settings which you had promised to use from Scheffauer and had you even gone so far as to pay for them? I seem to make this out from your correspondence but cannot find any such things in the office. I am sure that they were not among the Scheffauer material which I forwarded to Mencken. I may mention in passing that I have just been through the fetid catacombs where the poetry is kept and it seems to me that you have laid in some of the sorriest pipings that I ever saw. The most impressive spectacle is the old old verses which were already old when I first came—and the one about Geraldine Farrar that you and I parodied once. I have told Sew Collins that these MSS are to be carefully preserved but never on any account printed. One of the first things that happened, of course, was that Sew was given McMullin's "Fashions and Pleasures" to edit and that he edited it so vigorously that McMullin could hardly recognize his copy and flew into a great state of perturbation between anger and tears, which it took hours and hours of Crownie's most skillful illusionism to pacify.

Of the matter which we discussed at lunch the last time we were at the Yale Club I must wait until I can see you to give you an account. Hazel [Rascoe], I have reason to believe, was much impressed by you and after you had left, she tells me, dreamed of you three nights running. I am going to give her an advance copy of the *Garland* with the inscription of an appropriate gallantry, to which I shall sign your name as well as my own. But of all this we shall talk again, I trust, either over Château d'Yquem or over Lachryma Christi, in some villa open to the stars. Do you know Château d'Yquem? If you don't, as soon as you have read this letter, order a bottle at dinner. It is very expensive but the most wonderful wine I have ever tasted: it melts like some ardent vapor on the tongue and fills the mind with an ethereal ecstasy which is, nonetheless, of prodigious potency. One may commit I know not what divine follies as one floats in its iridescent cloud (Arthur Symons). It is late and I must go to bed now. Uphold the banner of the ideal! and be sure to begin to send out your poems to the magazines: Seldes says you promised to send *The Dial* some and then never did. If you like, I'll try to sell some to Crownie; I found one in the folder with the accepted stuff (that doesn't mean you've already sold it to him, does it?). It might be easier after the book has appeared and the whole American world shall have been set throbbing to a new rhythm by breath of your incomparable music. (Oh, by the way, Rascoe published my sketch of Strachey communing in sleep with the spirit of Queen Victoria and says he is going to publish some of the others!* I'll send you copies of any of yours that he may use.)

Yours in a fog of Vanity Fair exhaustion. E.W.

To John Peale Bishop   September 5, 1922
                                        Vanity Fair

Dear John: I have had three letters from you—the last from Vienna. The *Garland* will be out Friday; I have had printed copies for several weeks. I had them send you some, which should reach you about the same time as this letter. I also sent a copy to your mother and wrote her a letter

---

* In the *New York Tribune*.

explaining that I would send her more if she wanted them. Many of the presentation copies have been heard from. I enclose Cabell's letter. I take it that he will write you, as I think Dos Passos is doing also. Everyone seems to like it and, somewhat to my surprise, I think it will have a very brilliant-appearing press because Rascoe, Elinor Wylie, and Seldes will all be reviewing it. Fitz has offered to do it, too, but I don't think I'll urge him to; it rather bores me to have so many personal friends do it; I want to see what effect it will have upon a wholly disinterested mind. One disinterested mind has already been swept off its feet by it. William Benét, whose note on the subject I enclose, is reported by Elinor Wylie to be incoherent with enthusiasm. He is going to review it for *The Post* in addition to this comment in *The Lobby*. The whole incident has made me very uneasy about the literary quality of the book. Seldes, who is more critical, nonetheless puts us in a class with Eliot, Joyce, and Ben Hecht as leaders in the new something-or-other. He tried to explain it to me but I am not clear just what his idea is. I'll send you all the reviews in due course. You can send Knopf notes to go in your own presentation copies with directions as to whom to send them to.

I am much excited about Eliot's *The Waste Land*, which I have just read. I shall send you the proof I have if they will let me keep it. It will give you quite a thrill, I think; it is certainly his masterpiece so far. He supplements it with a set of notes almost as long as the poem itself, explaining the literary, historic, anthropological, metaphysical, and religious significances to be found in it; but the poem, as it appears to me from two or three cursory readings, is nothing more or less than a most distressingly moving account of Eliot's own agonized state of mind during the years which preceded his nervous breakdown. Never have the sufferings of the sensitive man in the modern city chained to some work he hates and crucified on the vulgarity of his surroundings been so vividly set forth. It is certainly a cry *de profundis* if ever there was one—almost the cry of a man on the verge of insanity. But I won't go on at length about it: you will soon see it. I shall send you some kind of a copy as soon as I can get one. I wish you were here to discuss it with me. Tell me if you agree with me that the beginning and the end are magnificent. I'm going to review it at length somewhere. By the way, I had a note from Sylvia Beach the other day stating that my review of *Ulysses* was read to Joyce— who was temporarily blind—and that he asked her to thank me for it, etc. Seldes is green with envy. I use it unjustifiably as a bludgeon to beat down people who disagree with me about the book.

This letter, which I am writing in the office while Mrs. Metcalfe discusses with me what pictures of Rudolph Valentino we shall run, will not, I am afraid, be a very toothsome affair, but I have the intention of embodying the latest intelligence upon my private life in a series of

94

sonnets which I shall send you from time to time—in the manner of Cino da Pistoia asking Dante for advice upon his love affairs.

Elinor Wylie is back, looking very healthy and robust, but no happier, I take it, than ever. Why don't you drop her a line? I think she is offended at not having heard from you. I am preparing to move downtown—perhaps into one of the apartments in the house where she is living—and live alone. My great ambition now is to buy a little house in the country whither I can retreat and derive strength from contact with the classics and the uninterrupted contemplation of my own thoughts. I am planning a prodigious prose work which shall contain all my ideas, experiences, and hallucinations for the last ten years. I hope you may enter now upon a period of extreme fecundity. I look forward with great eagerness to the Southern-grandmother thing. The publication of the *Garland* has had the immediate effect on me of egging me on to produce another book— and I hope it will have the same effect on you. All the old fakers are pursuing their respective lines of chicanery in about the same fashion as when you left. Miss Scherer says that she wants to send you more than love—explaining that she means that now that you are married, love has no value for you; Miss Ballot begs me to say that "though Mr. Collins is more witty and Mr. Wilson more erudite than you, neither is so handsome." I seemed to detect in your letter from Paris a note of acerbity and disgust aroused by the barnacles at the Rotonde. That was just how I felt last summer. You will find it quite a liberation and expansion of the soul to go from France to Italy or even, I should imagine, from Vienna to Italy. Tell me more of Pound. We recently had from him an ill-spelled, ill-written, ill-phrased, idiotic letter enclosing an incoherent and all but illegible article. He spoke of having seen you. If you see him again, don't encourage him to do any more articles for us.

I wish you would go to Florence, as I did last year about this time. I arrived there on a day of crystal fire just on the edge of autumn and coming out into that square along by the Uffizi Gallery heard the public band playing some gay piece of Italian trumpery and saw the pigeons riding the surf of sound on joyous and serene wings against the diamond light of the Paradiso—such a moment, in short, as Mr. T. S. Eliot would carry about with him for years as a fetish against Bleistein and Sweeney, as an indemnification for the horrors of Lloyd's Bank or whatever it is, but which I, since it had no moral significance for me, can do nothing more than utilize incidentally in a private letter like this. I hope, however, that you may experience such a moment and find it pregnant with inspirational ecstasy, that the lid of the soul may be lifted and the Muses upsurge in a chorus, mingling voices in divine song, drunken with the Tuscan light. With this high thought I shall leave you.

Yours for a work which the world will not willingly let die, EW

... My best to Margaret. I have had several meals with Esther Murphy*
—I gave her a copy of the *Garland* with a graceful and extravagant inscription as from both of us, which, together with the book, ravished her.

> The secretaries [at *Vanity Fair*] were very jolly, because Crowninshield,
> by exercising his charm for women, always kept them in good humor.
> Jeanne Ballot, of French origin though from Brooklyn, became in-
> dispensable to Crowninshield and still, since his death, works at *Vogue*.
> She was delightful and got along well with everybody.
> (*The Twenties: From Notebooks and Diaries of the Period*)

To Jeanne Ballot (Mrs. Albert E. Winham)   1947

... I have been going through all these old numbers, and it has brought
back putting them together in the *Vanity Fair* office. There was more
talent floating around in those days than there seems to be now—also,
women were prettier, though the costumes they wear in the pictures always
come to me as a shock. I had forgotten that the girls I admired were
dressed at the time like that, and I have the illusion that it is some sort
of deterioration that has happened to the pictures with time, like the
yellowing and crumpling of paper ...

To John Peale Bishop   September 22, 1922
                                                      Vanity Fair
Dear John: ... The only exciting recent event is the sudden arrival of
the Fitzgeralds, who decided that they could stand the Middle West no
longer and immediately came on. They are at present, of course, at the
Plaza but are going to get a house out at Rye and live East permanently.
The most extraordinary thing is that they are both in the most wonderful
form—partly owing to a summer in the country—and have resolved to
begin a new phase of their life. Fitz has not let anybody but me know
he is in the city and, though they have been here several days, they have
not had one drink! Both are wonderful-looking physically (Zelda has lost
her fat) and are functioning so rationally that I can hardly believe my
eyes. Fitz goes about soberly transacting his business and in the evenings
writes at his room in the hotel. I had a long conversation with him last
night and found him full of serious ideas about regulating his life. He
has hit upon a modus vivendi for preventing Zelda from absorbing all
his time, emotion, and seminal juice: they have made a compact for the
purpose of obviating the wasteful furies of jealousy, by which each is

---

* "... the sister of Scott's great friend, Gerald Murphy ..." She was later married
to John Strachey, and then to Chester Arthur, the son of President Arthur.

bound not to go out alone with another member of the other sex. I don't know how long it will last but I have never seen Fitz present a more dignified appearance than during this brief interregnum. I suppose that when the hyenas find out that he is in town they will all be on his neck— he has not even told Townsend and Alec. He is busy negotiating about his play.

As for the two ideas as to which you ask my counsel—I am dubious about the theological thing because it would require such enormous reading in so many dreary authors and, with the highest possible opinion of your abilities, I am inclined to doubt your endurance and your fitness to juggle surely with ideas of this sort. Besides, I don't think it would be worth the bother anyway. You could certainly do the Elizabethan thing very brilliantly, however. Still, parody is a genre of only secondary value at best. I am much more interested in the old Southern lady.

By the way, I have just had a letter from Joyce himself, this time, thanking me with an unaccustomed Old World courtesy for my articles on *Ulysses* and apologizing for not having written before—explaining that "circumstances of ill-health and travel" had been accountable for this "seeming discourtesy." Rascoe, under the pressure of public opinion and, I imagine, of editorial objection, has discontinued his *Diary*. I am glad because he quoted me so much and so inaccurately that it finally got on my nerves and I ceased to see him at all (though other causes contributed to this, too) for almost a month. I shall, however, get him to send you the old files. Don't, however, believe a word of it. In the long run, everybody began to give him the laugh about it and it is true that he wrote some of the most exquisitely silly things I have ever seen. Sherwood Anderson has suddenly arrived in town and decided to live here more or less permanently. I have seen him a number of times and think he is great. He has a very high opinion of you, he tells me. He described his new novel to me the other day—*Many Marriages*, which is to appear in *The Dial*—and it is one of the damnedest things ever written. It is a sort of wonderful erotic nightmare full of strange symbolic scenes reared on the old circus ground of American life. Eliot's poem is, however, the great knockout up to date. I have been reading the folklore book he claims he got it all out of—*From Ritual to Romance*, by Jessie L. Weston (the Cambridge Press, England)—and find it fascinating in the highest degree. You should really get it when you read the poem. It is a great mine of weird and interesting ideas, which you might be able to work yourself and which, in any case, throws an enormous amount of light on some of the more recondite workings of the mind of Europe. I'll send you the poem itself when I can get proofs again.

I took Elinor to the second night of the Greenwich Village Follies— having stimulated her to an unaccustomed thawing point with a bottle of port—and we had a grand party. The Follies themselves were wonderful—one of the best reviews I have ever seen. Bert Savoy was at his very best. When the young man asks her to come out for an automobile ride, she says: "Where are you going to take me? . . . Now where are you going to take me? . . . I won't go out on any automobile ride until I know where you're going to take me. . . . Remember, dearie, that you're dealing with an *old established firm!*"

Doesn't this make you homesick?   EW

To F. Scott Fitzgerald   November 6, 1922
                                                                   Vanity Fair

Dear Fitz: Egmont Arens, former art editor of *Vanity Fair*, is going to get out another number of his *Playboy*, which is to contain drawings and writings by all the more unruly native geniuses. We want you to come to a party given to discuss it this Wednesday night—to start from the Washington Square Book Shop on West Eighth Street between Fifth and Sixth at 6:30. Can't you come? Dos Passos, Sew Collins, Elinor Wylie, and others are going to be there. The idea is to make *Playboy* a sort of mouthpiece for all the bizarre and scurrilous things which people can't publish elsewhere. I wish you'd call me up as soon as you get this letter and let me know if you can come.   EW

To John Peale Bishop   November 29, 1922
                                                                   Vanity Fair

Dear John: I am sending, under separate cover, the Christmas *Bookman*, with a little squib by John Farrar about the *Garland*. I have just received your letter with Pound's gossip about Eliot in it, which I read with the greatest interest. He must be a dreary fellow. But I certainly think you have the wrong dope about the nightingale. In the room there is a painted panel with a forest glade on it and it reminds him for a moment of the "sylvan scene" in *Paradise Lost*—but *there*, he reflects, there was a nightingale singing (see Milton: Book III, I think), Philomela *there* could still tell how she had been outraged (violated) with a voice which, itself, was at least inviolable—but in *The Waste Land*, where the poet is living, his own soul, when it is violated, can no longer even tell its woe with inviolable voice. Nereus, the barbarous king, is not Eliot, but the things which are crucifying Eliot. For the passage which Eliot evidently had in mind when he wrote the nightingale part, see *Titus Andronicus*, act IV, scene i. See also for the bird crying "Tereu" further on in the poem Shakespeare's "Passionate Pilgrim." The quotation from *The Spanish Tragedy* is a miracle of ingenuity. You should really read the *Tragedy* itself (which, by the way, is excellent in spots) to find out about it. Old Hieronimo, when asked to give an entertainment by the murderers of his son (whom they *hanged*—the hanged God, etc.), replies, "Why then I'll fit you!" and proceeds to put in a drama à la the play in *Hamlet,* in which, under the pretext of the action, he actually kills all his enemies, who are also acting in it. The hanged son is kept behind a screen and at the climax revealed. The point about Phlebas, as Eliot indicates in his notes, is that he is, by Eliot's familiar trick, contrasted favorably with Mr. Eugenides. Both are merchants—but one is noble and the other ignoble. Eliot envies Phlebas because he died by water—whereas Eliot is dying of drought. I have done a long thing on it for *The Dial*—which see. Incidentally, for the god Hercules, which used partially to mystify us in Burbank, see *Antony and Cleopatra.* For the autobiographical significance of Tiresias' double sex, mentioned by Eliot in his notes, see the appendices of the Attis–Osiris volume of *The Golden Bough*—on the customs of the inhabitants of some savage islands or other. It is extremely interesting, explaining, as it does, what the primitive peoples did with their fairies. For the hyacinths which the girl carries in the remembered scene in the first part of *The Waste Land,* see the chapter on Hyacinth in the same volume—or section—of *The Golden Bough. The Golden Bough* elsewhere explains the mephitic river in the discarded poem of which I sent you a copy. What did you think of it, by the way? I liked the middle stanza. So much for Eliot. Of other matters, more anon. I have moved into a large corner room and bath two flights above Elinor at 1 University Place.

EW

To JOHN PEALE BISHOP   December 13, 1922
Vanity Fair

Dear John: I have sent you a copy of the new Yeats volume—most of which you have seen when it appeared in *The Dial,* etc., but which contains several admirable things—the "Black Centaur," for example—that are new to me. I have paid for this and your class dues—$5 and $6 respectively—out of the $17.50 we are paying you for the *Background of Flat Gold.* This leaves a balance which I shall keep against other debts and luxuries as they may arise.

"Allegra" is exquisite except for the "day shall have lacked due honor" line—which you evidently owe to Pound and which Eliot and I both think a little bogus. As for the other thing, it would be wonderful if it were not already an attempt to rewrite "La Figlia che Piange" by a man who has just read the Game of Chess episode in *The Waste Land.* I should suppress it, I think. Your Vienna thing has come out in *The New Republic* and I have forwarded the copy. Why don't you write some more of those things? I liked that one.

As for Eliot, I suspect you all in attempting to ascribe *all* the stanzas of the "Ode" to his marriage. The "mephitic river" is, as I said, a reference to *The Golden Bough*. I thought the "profusion of the calamus" was poetry, but perhaps it isn't. As for the "succuba eviscerate," that is evidently a description of the woman as she appears to him after the wedding night. "Succuba" is singular and "eviscerate" is an adjective. An eviscerated succuba—eviscerated on account of the bloody signs of deflowerment, etc.

I have been formulating some tremendous projects for my immediate future and shall presently impart them to you. In the meantime, be strong and for heaven's sake do read somebody besides Eliot for a little while—he is enslaving your style and your imagination. Thanks very much for your criticism of "Lesbia," which, however, I have revised since I sent it to you. Perhaps you are right and it is too long—but I don't think much of your sample of the style in which it ought to be rewritten. It is essentially in the style, tone, and rhythm of satiric verse—Swift, etc.—with the poignant things dropped as if casually by the way. In wanting me to redo it in the neo-William Morris style which you indicate, you misunderstand the *kind* of effect aimed at. You don't appreciate what can be done with a machinelike precision. See Housman's "Hell Gate" in his new book. However, I am not crazy about the poem. Well, dreario! avert not your eyes from Apollo nor undo too brusquely from your shoulders the white cincture of the muses, who dry up from the lack of stories in our desolate age.

EW

1923

One could give no idea of these extraordinary poems save by quoting
them in their entirety . . . Allen Tate . . . has become a great friend
of mine.   (To John Peale Bishop, 1928)

To ALLEN TATE   January 3, 1923
*Vanity Fair**

Dear Mr. Tate: I have been much interested in your poems—including
these, but I do think you are too much still under other people's influences—especially Eliot's and, it seems to me, in this case, E. E. Cummings's.
You certainly seem to have something of your own, however, which gives
your work felicity and strength apart from what you borrow. Thank you
very much for letting me see these. I look forward to something extraordinary from you. But do try to get out of the artistic clutches of T. S.
Eliot.   Yours very sincerely, Edmund Wilson, Jr.

To CHRISTIAN GAUSS   January 24, 1923

Dear Mr. Gauss: Thank you ever so much for your letter and please
pardon me for not acknowledging it sooner. I don't suppose you could
possibly come up to New York sometime soon for a little party. I should
like to take you to the Moscow Art Theatre, which is one of the most
extraordinary things I have ever seen on the stage and which I think you
ought to take in, if you can. I am doing theaters for *The Dial* now and
so get free tickets. If you will let me know when you can come next week
or the week after, I could arrange. They are doing Chekhov now—with
matinees Fridays. If you and Mrs. Gauss could both come, so much the
better.   Yours very sincerely, Edmund Wilson, Jr.
    P.S. In rereading the article you liked I discovered that I had stolen

---

* The following letters were written from *Vanity Fair*.

VANITY FAIR

19 West 44th St.   New York City

DRAMA LITERATURE ART MUSIC HUMOUR SPORTS

Published monthly by The Condé Nast Publications, Inc., 19 West 44th Street, New York. Condé Nast, President; Francis L. Wurzburg, Vice-President; W. E. Beckerle, Treasurer; M. E. Moore, Secretary; Philippe Ortiz, European Director, 2 rue Edouard VII, Paris. Subscription $3.00 a year in the United States and

Colonies, Mexico and Canada. $4.00 in Foreign Countries. Single copies 35c. Vanity Fair is entered as second class matter at the Post Office at Greenwich, Conn., and is also entered at the Post Office at New York, under the act of March 3, 1879. Printed in the U. S. A. Copyright 1923 by The Condé Nast Publications, Inc., Reg. U. S. Patent Office.

Frank Crowninshield—*Editor*
Edmund Wilson, Jr.—*Managing Editor*
Heyworth Campbell—*Art Director*

Cover Design—By Fish

JUNE, 1923

Volume 20   Number 4   *Subscribers are notified that no change of address can be effected in less than a month*   35c a copy $3.00 a year

one of my ideas from you—the one about Mencken's being the kind of satire proper to the American life which he is dealing with. I should have acknowledged my theft before—but it would keep me very busy if I attempted to acknowledge all the things I get from you. I am only anxious just now to lay in a new supply and would like to consult you professionally on many matters of literature and morals. Do come up and have dinner and let us go to the theater.

Yours always, Edmund Wilson, Jr.

To T. S. Eliot   January 24, 1923

Dear Mr. Eliot: Thank you very much for your letter. I am terribly sorry that the number containing your picture was already printed and on the newsstands before I had heard from you. I did say in the caption that you were the editor of *The Criterion* but I shan't do so again and shall try to prevent other people from doing so. I shall pass your picture on to *Vogue*, whose offices are next to ours.

Yours very sincerely, Edmund Wilson, Jr.

To T. S. Eliot   February 26, 1923

Dear Mr. Eliot: Thank you very much for sending the Wyndham Lewis drawing but it unfortunately proves to be too faint for us to reproduce.

I have just seen your thing on English prose in the *Nouvelle Revue Française* and I wish you could let us reprint it in *Vanity Fair*.* If you wrote it originally in English, couldn't you let us have the original text or, otherwise, either translate it or let us translate it? It is so admirable that I think it would be a great pity not to have it appear in English. We could pay you about $75.   Yours very sincerely, Edmund Wilson, Jr.

To T. S. Eliot   April 23, 1923

Dear Mr. Eliot: Thank you ever so much for the article. We shall make due acknowledgments to the *Nouvelle Revue Française*. I am enclosing a check for it.

We should be delighted to have the other articles too, and should pay for them at this rate. If they have to do with contemporary literature and affairs, we could certainly run them—so do send them to us as soon as they are written.†

---

* "Contemporary English Prose," *Vanity Fair*, July 1923.
† "A Preface to Modern Literature," *Vanity Fair*, November 1923.

Couldn't we run them simultaneously with the *Nouvelle Revue Française*, and perhaps, in this case, without acknowledgment.

Yours very sincerely, Edmund Wilson, Jr.

To T. S. Eliot   May 24, 1923

Dear Mr. Eliot: It is understood, of course, that we make no claim to the right of translating your articles into French.

We shall continue to acknowledge the original publication in the *Nouvelle Revue Française*, if you will send us the articles for the month after they have been published there.

The subject which you mention for your next article sounds excellent for us.

Thank you very much for your letter.

Yours very sincerely, Edmund Wilson, Jr.

Malcolm Cowley has come on *The New Republic* and is a great asset.
(To Allen Tate, 1929)

To Malcolm Cowley   March 27, 1923

Dear Mr. Cowley: . . . I wish you could send *Vanity Fair* a poem or two, if you have any that you think our readers would be capable of understanding. You are not sufficiently bizarre to warrant our exhibiting you on that ground alone and I should hesitate to publish in *Vanity Fair* some of the best of your poems which I have seen because they would be likely to puzzle people without amusing them as freaks. You understand that I am merely describing our peculiar editorial exigencies— personally, I like some of your least obvious things best. However, I'm sure you have something unmistakably effective and do let us have it.

Yours very sincerely, Edmund Wilson, Jr.

Because she is entitled to write both LL.D. and M.D. after her name; because she was instrumental in promoting the early fame of Matisse and Cézanne; because her Parisian salon is one of the most serious and interesting in the city of famous salons; and finally, because her experiments in style have already had an influence on the younger French writers.   *(Vanity Fair, 1922)*

To Gertrude Stein   June 6, 1923

Dear Miss Stein: Mr. Carl Van Vechten has sent me your Avery Hopwood thing, which I should like very much to use in *Vanity Fair*, but it is so much too long for us that it would have to be cut.

If you would be willing to have us do this, could you drop me a line and let me know also which of the Hopwood plays it is that you have rewritten. I think it might be interesting to run part of the text of the play opposite yours.

We have all enjoyed *Geography and Plays*—especially "Miss Furr and Miss Skeene," which we are running in the July number of *Vanity Fair* with the permission of the Four Seas.

I do hope you will let us use the Hopwood play.

Yours very sincerely, Edmund Wilson, Jr.

To F. Scott Fitzgerald   March 24, 1923

Dear Scott: Never mind about the house. We merely wanted it for a weekend or two, and as there are no servants or heat or anything, it would be too much trouble. You need not have been worried about crowding, however, as we intended to sleep in separate beds. I saw *The Adding Machine** the other night and the author has got some of your stuff in the first part—also in the general theme. The first half is excellent but it goes off before the end. You ought to see it when you get back. It seems incredible, in any case, that with it and Roger Bloomer on the stage, you can't get your thing produced. I enclose Burton Rascoe's report of a conversation with me, which speaks for itself. Ted Paramore and I have extracted almost as much amusement from it as from the original pleasantries. If Lardner ever sees his account of the fox story, I suppose it will be nuts to him. Love to Zelda.   EW

To John Peale Bishop   June 30, 1920 [1923]
Brookhaven, Long Island
Dear John: I must apologize for having delayed so long in thanking you and Margaret for the exquisite pastry forks, in the subtle colors of which, no less than in the delicacy of design, I detect the fine imperial eye of a flawless magician of taste. We have been living down here in the country since the middle of May and expect to stay on till fall.† Mrs. Chase has rented me her house, which is an enchanting little cottage situated in a remote region almost incredibly idyllic. We are embowered by the first light boscage of a wood which extends back from behind the house, and through the front yard runs a delightful brook, lush with iris and loud with frogs, which, though basically natural and rustic, has been embellished with just that touch of artificiality without which the most beautiful of natural objects must appear common, stupid, and gross. All sorts of agreeable birds and animals throng the ferny coverts about the

---

* Elmer Rice.
† E. was now married to Mary Blair.

house: in the morning the silvery voices of the birds tune an exquisite tangle of notes and in the evening little spiders invade the beds and forsaken and unhappy opossums crawl in under the house and die there, thus producing a horrible smell and making it necessary to hire a man to get them out. I have been reading, as you will readily guess, Virgil and would commend him to your attention. He was really one of the very great poets of Europe but has been spoiled for most people by being taught in school. It is easy for me to see, as I read him now, how he must have inspired Dante—his rigorous artistic conscience, his careful fitting of the manner to the matter, and his lifelong devotion to his craft. I recommend the *Eclogues*, if you haven't read them—also, Mackail's new little book on the subject. For the rest, I have written a large part of a play of which I have considerable hopes. I expect to finish it by September.*

As for gossip, there is so much to tell—though nothing of tremendous importance—that I can't face the problem of really bringing you up to date. Fitz and Zelda have struck their perfect milieu in the jazz society of Great Neck, where they inhabit a brand-new suburban house. Zelda plays golf, and Fitz is already acquiring pompous overtones of the successful American householder. They are still one of the most refreshing elements at large, however, and it would take me pages to do justice to their pranks. Elinor Wylie has gone to Peterboro with Bill [William Rose Benét], preparing (with a wry face) to marry him in the fall. Edna, as you doubtless know, won the Pulitzer Prize for Poetry and has bought an automobile with it. I had one magnificent evening with her in the spring during which all old quarrels were repaired; but during the summer she has been staying at Croton under auspices which I understand only imperfectly. She brought home from Europe with her a large handsome unattractive rich amiable discontented girl (Esther Root) who has attached herself to Edna and has been acting as a sort of combination nurse and social secretary. My impression is, however, that Edna is continually giving her the go-by and getting away, thus causing poor Esther great misery. But of Edna, as of all the others, I can give you no adequate account here. (By the way, when are you coming back? I hear rumors of January.) I bicycled over to Southampton yesterday and called on Esther Murphy, to whom I become more and more devoted; she sailed for Europe today. By the way, Mrs. Wharton has just left after a brief visit to America; the day she left she met Fitz in Scribner's and they had a rather surprising interview—surprising because he made a great hit with her. (His play is to be produced in the fall—though just how and when seems a little uncertain, as it seems somehow to be bound up with John Williams's moral disintegration.)

---

* *The Crime in the Whistler Room.*

Mary is working on a baby this summer and I hear rumors that you are expecting one, too. I am glad enough to have one, though all these bonds and responsibilities appall me sometimes. My father died in May but left me nothing, his will having been made ages ago. It is probable, however, that when the estate is settled, Mother may come through with something, in which case I have an elaborate plan of travel and literary production to pursue—though Mother's own plans of travel seem rather elaborate and there may not be very much in any case. My father's death gave me a sudden conviction of the shortness and unsatisfactoriness of life and partly perhaps as a result of that, partly on account of my tranquillity in the country, I have accomplished what is for me a good deal of writing. I have resolved furthermore when I waste time in the future to waste it only in dissipation, never in idiotic trifling. There is probably no other form of idling so profitable as dissipation. I feel that it was partly through an insufficient capacity for dissipation that my father suffered his melancholia; but at the same time he got more results with his nervous energy than I have yet got with mine, and it is high time for me to even the balance. With these inspiring thoughts I shall leave you. Mary sends her best to Margaret and you and thanks you enthusiastically for the present. Send me the record of your further travel and the latest intimations of the muses. Yours as ever, EW

Mrs. Colum, the wife of the Irish poet Padraic Colum . . . very interesting reviews, especially Mary Colum's in *The Freeman*.

To Mary Colum   July 1, 1923
                                            Brookhaven, Long Island

Dear Mrs. Colum: Mary Blair has read *The Dream Play* and is much interested in it and wants to know if you think it would be worthwhile for her to write [Rudolf] Kommer a letter and commend herself to his attention. Would you mind sending her his address if you have it and if you think there is any point in writing him? She would be very grateful if you would.

We are living here in a little house at the edge of a wood with a brook in the front yard. The whole place is incredibly idyllic, forming a delightfully pastoral arrangement embellished with just that touch of artificiality without which the most agreeable of natural objects must appear common, stupid, and gross. I have made a few simple experiments in magic but have so far not evoked anything serious, the utmost results of my efforts being but a few of the minor devils and one small cockatrice. I can, however, recommend the following magic ointments: (a) Eloosel'num, aconity, frondes populeae, the juice of water parsnip, and soot; (b) sium, Acarum vulgare, pentaphyllon, the blood of a flittermouse, solanum somniferum, and oleum. The first of these induces clairvoyance, bringing past and future events before the mind as if seen at a great distance and upside down; the second is for flying through the air but I have not as yet had much luck with it: I have found that taking it brings on an ague and the illusion of wandering in an arid plain—on one occasion I met an old man with a black face who spoke to me in a low growling voice, but most of what he said was unintelligible. I should be interested to see what effects you would get from it.

I hope you are well and enjoying Peterboro. Please give my best to Mr. Colum, and to Elinor Wylie and Bill Benét, when you see them. I don't suppose there is any chance of your being back in time to come down and see us here. If you should, we'd be delighted to have you.

Yours very sincerely, Edmund Wilson

To Christian Gauss   July 24, 1923
                                           Brookhaven, Long Island
Dear Mr. Gauss: I have been asked by Knopf to do a preface to a translation of Rousseau's *Confessions* which they are bringing out, and though I feel rather reluctant to write about a subject about which I really know as little as I do about Rousseau, I need the money and am going to do it. Now there is an anecdote about the *Confessions* which I remember your telling in one of your lectures but which I haven't been able to find in any biography I have consulted: it was about Rousseau's waylaying people on the street to explain his case to them and finally depositing the manuscript of the *Confessions* on the altar of some Paris church. I'd like to mention this and wish you would let me know where you found it—and what the exact facts of the story are. What is the best biography anyway? I have consulted Morley, Miss Macdonald, and Sainte-Beuve but can't seem to find anything exhaustive. I wish I had your little book; do you suppose Scribner's would carry it?

I hope that you and the rest of the family are well and are having a pleasant summer. I have done the greater part of my play and should have finished it by fall but I have been devoting so much time to it that I am now obliged to do a lot of journalism and pay my bills. We have been having a beautiful time down here—seeing nobody, making no excursions farther than the next town, and swimming and reading. We have been reading aloud lately from the wicked dramatists of the Restoration, for whom I have always had the greatest respect and whom I think it was not the least of Macaulay's sins that he brought into bad odor. When I go to New York nowadays I feel harassed and almost ask myself if it is possible for anybody to live there (live there and make a living) and produce anything serious at the same time. The tendency is for all writers to be driven the way of Heywood Broun—into an enormous mass production of diluted intellectual goods. I hope to see you again in a month or so. When do you go back to Princeton? I'll be awfully grateful if you can send me the dope on Rousseau soon because I have only a week to do the essay in. Yours always, Edmund Wilson

To CHRISTIAN GAUSS August 3, 1923
Brookhaven, Long Island
Dear Mr. Gauss: Thank you very much for your letter and for the book. I have already written a paragraph in which I called attention to the fact that the *Confessions* was the first great romantic autobiography and described the romantic shifting of the interest from objective ideas and works of art to the personal and internal life. Probably, though I did not attempt to develop your doctrine of personality, I got all this originally from you, but I hope that the little there is of it in my preface will not encroach on your book—in fact, I am sure it couldn't possibly do so. You really ought to write that book; I never remember to have read anything very satisfactory on the subject and I think that your whole idea of the significance of romanticism would be very illuminating to people in general. I was talking to [Paul] Rosenfeld the other day about his essay on Wagner, in which he tried to prove that the heroic characters of the *Ring* are really the figuring of the tremendous mechanical and industrial forces which were liberated in the nineteenth century, and I suggested that they really had less to do with mechanical power than with the old romanticism of the beginning of the century—Siegfried is surely a romantic who has read Nietzsche, and Walther in the *Meistersinger*, breaking in with his untamed warbling of spring breezes and mountain cascades and outraging and ultimately triumphing over the pedant Beckmesser, is a pure type of romantic hero. Rosenfeld, though he is extremely well read in both French and German literature, had apparently never considered the role of romanticism in emphasizing this importance of the individual, of the personality; and I'm sure I should probably never have done so either if it had not been for your teaching. He went straight and read Babbitt's book. Would that he had read yours. In rereading the *Confessions* and in reading the *Contrat social* for the first time, I was more impressed with Rousseau than I had ever been before; I seemed to feel a depth of sincerity and a breadth of intellectual beam which give him an extraordinary force and weight, for all his rhetoric and extravagance. In these things—though not in literary grace and skill—he certainly far outtops most of the disciples who have somewhat outdazzled his reputation since. I'll send you—with a good deal of diffidence—the volume with my preface when it is published; I am afraid that you will find that it testifies rather to my memory of your lectures than to my own familiarity with the subject. Love to all the family. Yours as ever, EW
Thanks again for all your trouble in sending me references, etc.

To H. L. Mencken   August 17, 1923
                                            15 Willow Street, Brooklyn
Dear Mr. Mencken: I have been thinking of writing a series of short
stories in the vein of the prose pieces in *The Undertaker's Garland* and of
the Y.M.C.A. thing* I sent you. Would *The Smart Set* be interested in
anything of this kind? There would be two or three army stories, perhaps—one about the American occupation of Germany after the Armi-
stice†—and a few about boarding school and college—but most of them
would have to do with New York—the whole to constitute a sort of
social criticism, a little in the vein of France's *Histoire contemporaine*. Do
you suppose that, if you liked the first two or three I sent you, you would
be willing to run a whole series, and if you did, how much would you
pay?—could you pay as much as $300 a story? If I had a reasonable
prospect of selling them and of getting enough for them to enable me to
spend as much time on them as I'd have to, I think I could produce
something quite amusing. How are you? Fitz is struggling with a new
novel and very low in his mind. John Bishop has become very fat and
pompous and writes me stilted letters from Italy on the satisfactions of
domestic life. I have just come to Brooklyn for a few weeks and my wife
and I have suffered a two-day collapse as a result of the execrable food,
the fumes from a nearby confectionary factory, and the demoralizing
effect of the inhabitants. Nonetheless, I shall have to be here for a little
while, so will you write me at the above address . . .
                                        Yours very sincerely, Edmund Wilson

To John Peale Bishop   September 6, 1923

Dear John: I was much delighted with your intelligence in re the Virgin.
As for Transcendentalism, I think your best bet would be to look up the
chapter about it in the *Cambridge History of American Literature* in the
Bibliothèque Nationale—which, though a little less easy to work with
than the New York Public Library, is nevertheless perfectly practicable.
You should also probably read, I think, at least the first series of Emerson's
Essays. Emerson and Thoreau were the real artists among the New England
group, and you are likely to underestimate both their intellectual abilities
and their style unless you actually read them. Emerson and the first and
last chapters of *Walden* still communicate very vividly the real exhilaration in the air of the time. It was a sort of mystic exaltation of the spiritual
life in the individual above the debasements of the practical life and the
complications of society. Much of it was vague and in the air and, as Gauss
said to me not long ago, it inclined to overemphasize the amount that the

---

* "Galahad."
† "Lieutenant Franklin."

individual could do by merely washing his hands of social obligation and practicing virtue by himself; but on the other hand it had, and even still has, a very genuine and noble appeal. Their point that all real distinction, achievement, and worth depend on what the individual can do in himself and by himself was a very valuable one at that time when the American landslide of nationalism had already begun (it is surprising, by the way, to see how much Thoreau's assault on American civilization sounds like that of Van Wyck Brooks or of some other young intellectual of today), and if they carried it to a positively unsocial attitude—Thoreau refused to vote and was put in jail for not paying his taxes, and Emerson had always been under the reproach of having remained lukewarm on Abolition— they displayed a great deal more intellectual seriousness in doing so than could have been easily found elsewhere in the U.S. of that time, even in the largely bourgeois and provincially "cultivated" society of rich merchants' families of Boston, against whom the Emersons, the Thoreaus, and the Margaret Fullers were really in bitter reaction (these Concord celebrities, you understand, are not to be confused with the Holmes, Longfellow, Whittier, Fields group). Old Bronson Alcott (Louisa's father) represented the more ridiculous and more [illegible] metaphysical side of the move- ment (though Esther Murphy admires him and will probably tell you a different story). Alcott, and even Emerson, when he becomes too much possessed by the "Over-Soul," is likely to get into the mystical, luminous, nebulous realms where "God is All" and "God is Love" where the Chris- tian Scientists, the Theosophists, and the New Thoughtists have taken up their abode—indeed, these movements are supposed to derive from Trans- cendentalism and to represent all that is left of it. Professor Reilly in the suppressed first edition of the last volume of the *Cambridge History* found that Mrs. Eddy got a lot of her stuff from Alcott and that *Science and Health* is little more than a dilution and confusion of Transcendentalist doctrine. The volume containing his essay ("American Religious Books," I think it—the chapter—was called) was suppressed by the craven and blackguardly Putnam at the protest of the Christian Science people and another, highly laudatory of Christian Science, published in its place; but if they have the original one at the Bibliothèque you should certainly look it up. I'm not really much of an authority on this subject and cannot help you very satisfactorily, I'm afraid . . .

I have not yet gone back to New York and, though I am thrilled, as always, by the awakening September activities of the town as their stirrings reach my seclusion, I shall probably not return to 1 University Place (where we are going to live this winter, having taken the greater part of a floor) for some little time. I am now making a final typewritten version of my play,* which is taking a lot of time, and sandwiching in the regular

* *The Crime in the Whistler Room.*

articles. My play I have shown to no one except Mary and haven't had enough outside criticism of it to be able to gauge its fate—it is unsatisfactory in many respects; my next one is going to be better (a play about Shelley and Byron; I have some wonderful ideas for this, which I wish I could discuss with you), and the next one—a full-length tragic portrait of the Puritan as Heroic Reformer (that is, the Bernard Shaw type, not the Anti-Vice Society kind)—better still.

Carl Van Vechten's *Blind Bow-Boy* is fairly agreeable—a much better work than I thought he could write. He told me, by the way, the other day that he never made the uncomplimentary animadversions about the *Garland* reported by Rascoe at all, but that Rascoe, who was in a state of pique with me at the time, had made them up himself and evaded responsibility for them by ascribing them to Van Vechten. A young man arrived from Boston the other day, with a letter of introduction to me—a former member of the *Atlantic Monthly* staff!—who said that he had read the *Garland* with enormous enthusiasm and wanted nothing better in coming to New York than to meet one of the authors. I expected he would ask me to get him a job or to review one of his own books—but he went back to Boston without having asked me for anything of any kind and I am compelled to suppose that his behavior was due to a genuine enthusiasm. The sales have been almost zero since Christmas; Knopf tells me that the difficulty has been to sell or advertize a book which does not fall into any obvious category. I have a feeling that when we have become more famous it will be reprinted and greatly admired. In the meantime, therefore, let us endeavor to surpass it. And with this inspiring, if harsh thought, I will leave you.   EW

To Christian Gauss   December 12, 1923
                                                          1 University Place, N.Y.
Dear Mr. Gauss: I'm awfully sorry you can't come up this week. If you should happen to be able to come up next, I wish you would let me know. The Russians [the Moscow Art Theatre], unfortunately, according to their present announcement, aren't going to be here after the first of the year. As for Symbolism, Eliot's *Waste Land* is full of Symbolism—though the symbols are not telescoped together quite so confusedly as in somebody like Mallarmé. But I should think that the passage about "Phlebas the Phoenician, a fortnight dead," or the passage about the Waste Land itself at the very beginning of the poem, would be good examples. An American poet who shows the influence of the French Symbolists throughout his work is Wallace Stevens, whose collected poems were published this fall by Knopf under the title *Harmonium*—he is really a very distinguished poet in a fairly small way. Of the extremely unintelligible modern Symbolists, Tristan Tzara in France and Gertrude Stein in English are, I

suppose, examples. In America, in general, I think, the Symbolistic tendency has been merged with the movement called Imagism, which was really nothing more or less than a kind of belated English Parnassianism—with the result that people like Stevens or Dos Passos, in his book of poems,* produce a mixture of the Symbolistic and metaphysical with the objective and hard.

I'll hope to see you in January, anyway—do be sure to let me know when you are coming up and I'll arrange to go, if not to the Russians, at least perhaps to the Swedish Ballet.   Yours as ever, Edmund Wilson

THE DIAL

SCOFIELD THAYER   GILBERT SELDES
Editor   *Managing Editor*

1923–1941

MEMORANDUM TO KENNETH BURKE   [undated, 1923]
The Dial†

Dear Burke: I have just had a letter from Seldes, who says that it is all right for me to take Virgil, and do the whole series if I want to. Will you either call me up or drop me a line, which I can get at the *Vanity Fair* office Saturday morning, as to what you think of the following suggestions:

July—*Through the Wheat*, by Thomas Boyd—2 pages (war novel published by Scribner's, which offers opportunity to discuss modern war fiction in general). Theater—3 pages.

August—*Virgil* (2 biographies)—perhaps 4 pages. Theater—2 pages.

Yours in haste, EW

To KENNETH BURKE   July 9, 1923
Brookhaven, Long Island

Dear Burke: If it is not too late—as I dare say it well may be—could you have them insert this paragraph just after the sentence about the Winter Garden, so as to make it a part of the first paragraph for *Helen of Troy*? If this is any trouble at all, never mind: send it back to me and I'll use it next time.

---

* *A Pushcart at the Curb.*

† In 1923, E. ran the theater section for *The Dial*; during the 1920's he continued to contribute articles and review books while writing regularly as an editor of *Vanity Fair* and *The New Republic*. He was also then published in *The Liberator*, the *Baltimore Evening Sun*, *Scribner's Magazine*, *Playboy*, *The Saturday Review of Literature*, *The Bookman*, and *The Literary Review*.

113

Here is also a piece of nonsense, which I wish you would bring to the attention of the proper authorities.

And believe me ever your servant, enthusiastic admirer, and grateful recipient of financial favors.   Edmund Wilson

To KENNETH BURKE   [undated, 1923]

Dear Burke: Here is a card from Seldes which explains about his articles. I'll send you a book review a little later. Virgil I'm afraid I'll have to defer for yet another month, but when it does come it is going to be stupefying. It might run into six pages—would this be too long?

Yours for a reintegrated Poland,* EW (still at Brookhaven, L.I.)

Glance at what I have to say about Josephson in this theater article. How do you stand about this semi-Dada point of view?

MEMORANDUM TO MARIANNE MOORE *or* ALYSE GREGORY
The Dial   [undated, 1923]

[Edwin Arlington] Robinson will follow by beginning of next week and will be about three pages, I think. The Renan thing, if I wrote it, would run, I should think, to about six. It could go that month, instead of a book review. I feel I have a special call to write this thing—but if you can't persuade Watson to print it, never mind, I can probably get somebody else to.   Yours delightfully, ENORMOUS WILSON

I should greatly appreciate it if you could persuade them to pay me fairly soon.

To ALYSE GREGORY   April 17, 1924
                                                    1 University Place, N.Y.
Dear Miss Gregory: Here are reviews of Ernest Hemingway's books and Seldes's *Seven Lively Arts*; in both cases, the authors sent me copies— so you do not need to send me the *Dial* copies . . . I hope the reviews are all right.   Yours very sincerely, Edmund Wilson

To ALYSE GREGORY   September 4, 1924

. . . I wish you would print my little notice of Hemingway's books some- time soon, if you are able to, so that he can get the benefit of it . . .

To ALYSE GREGORY   April 1, 1925
                                                3 North Washington Square, N.Y.
Dear Miss Gregory: Here are the Valéry article and the briefer mention of *The Grand Inquisitor*. In the article, I have mentioned the "Letter from

_____
* The United States was about to recognize Poland's boundaries.

114

Emilie Teste" as appearing in the same number as the article: if it does not, this ought to be corrected.* If these are satisfactory, I should be extremely grateful if *The Dial* could pay me for them this week—or whenever they can . . . I was sorry to miss you the other day at *The Dial* —I came in to see you but you had just left.

Yours very sincerely, Edmund Wilson

MEMORANDUM TO MARIANNE MOORE   [undated, 1925]

Dear Miss Moore: I was very sorry not to find you in. I thought that, as I had made a vow not to write anything more for *The Dial*, I ought to return these volumes of the Greece and Rome series, which I was to have reviewed in conjunction with some others which have not yet appeared. As a matter of fact, since I have already done two reviews of this series, it is probably just as well, if you give them any further notice, to have somebody else write about them. The volumes on individual authors—which are the only ones I have attempted to discuss—are, for the most part, not very interesting, as they usually confine themselves to a sketch of the history of the author's influence, without concerning themselves with criticism; and the others—on general subjects—ought to be dealt with by an expert. I hope to see you sometime soon.

Yours very sincerely, Edmund Wilson

TO ALYSE GREGORY   1941

Dear Miss Gregory: It was very pleasant to hear from you, to see your pretty and personal handwriting, which I remember well, to be reminded of the days when *The Dial* was flourishing . . . Do you ever get back to the U.S.? I wish you would let me know if you ever do. Of all the old *Dial* people, Scofield Thayer is in permanent eclipse as you probably know; Gilbert Seldes works for television and I never see him any more; Paul Rosenfeld I see quite often and he is still doing his musical criticism —unfortunately with no magazine that regularly publishes his work; Marianne Moore is now the idol of all the young women poets, who no longer follow Edna Millay; Kenneth Burke has divorced his wife and married her sister and now has two sets of children, who, when I last saw him, were living close together in Greenwich Village and between whom he was dividing his time—otherwise he seemed perfectly unchanged and he writes as obscurely as ever; Cummings has married a third wife, a former dress model and very pretty, with whom he seems to be happy— and is still turning out his poems; Dr. Watson I have heard nothing about since a movie he made about ten years ago.

---

* "A Letter from Madame Emilie Teste," by Paul Valéry, and "Paul Valéry," by Edmund Wilson, were published in *The Dial*, June 1925.

I live up here on Cape Cod and don't often get to New York nowadays. I have no connection with *The New Republic* any more—it has really gone to pot. The only literary magazine of any interest now in New York is *Partisan Review*. Do you ever see it? It is a queer mixture of near-Marxism and "advanced" writing more or less of the kind that used to be cultivated by *The Dial*.

Thank you for your letter and all good wishes.

Yours sincerely, Edmund Wilson

1924–1927

To John Peale Bishop   January 15, 1924
                                                        1 University Place, N.Y.
Dear John: You will pardon me for not having written in so long but
believe me it has not been through negligence but merely because I have
been waiting till I should have time to write properly and at length . . .
There is just a bare chance that I may get to Paris in the fall, or perhaps
before. I have written a great super-ballet of New York for the Swedish
Ballet*—a pantomime explained by movie captions and with a section of
movie film in the middle, for which Ornstein is composing the music and
in which we hope to get Chaplin to act. It is positively the most titanic
thing of the kind ever projected and will make the productions of Milhaud
and Cocteau sound like folk-song recitals. It is written for Chaplin, a
Negro comedian, and seventeen other characters, full orchestra, movie
machine, typewriters, radio, phonograph, riveter, electromagnet, alarm
clocks, telephone bells, and jazz band. They may send me out to the
Coast in a few days to try to persuade Chaplin to take part in it. If it
comes off—though it will probably start in America—they will later take
it to Paris and I might go over with them. In the meantime, I am trying
to get my play produced.† The Provincetown people have it now; they
have started up this winter with the most interesting season of their career
—Macgowan, Robert Edmond Jones, and O'Neill are doing it. Mary is
going to be in O'Neill's new play, which is about a white woman who
marries a Negro—Mary is going to be the white woman and we are both
expecting to be assassinated by the Ku Klux Klan.‡
    I won't begin to tell you all the gossip and scandal, but will attempt

---

* "Gilbert Seldes got me a job, when I was very hard up, as press agent for the
Swedish Ballet, which was visiting the United States."
                        —The Twenties: From Notebooks and Diaries of the Period
† The Crime in the Whistler Room.
‡ All God's Chillun Got Wings; the Negro was acted by Paul Robeson.

to sketch in some of the most salient recent events. Elinor [Wylie] is married, as I suppose you know, and lives in an agreeable American-Victorian interior on East Eighteenth Street, with Bill's little Victorian children. She has profited by it immensely, on the whole, I should say—looks better, behaves more calmly, and puts on flesh. I always felt that a solid base to function from was what she needed. I saw Edna the other day for the first time since her marriage. She summoned me around and I waited upon her in her little house in Bedford Street (buried in the bowels of the Village). The operation she had during the summer on her intestines—for congenital stoppages—was apparently really rather serious and she doesn't look terribly well yet. I found her drinking gin and reading William Morris on the top floor of her house, all alone and with really an air of having allowed herself at last to be attended to and put away and forbidden to see people. Her husband takes good care of her, and her lousy rout of followers has been banished. She is calmer than she used to be—and I really felt for a moment as if I were visiting a sort of voluntary prisoner who had crept away and given herself up to other people's kindness. Then she told me that she was about to start on a month's reading tour which, so far as I can find out, is to take in all the important cities east of Chicago! And she is going all alone. "I must keep clear of the people I know," she said, "in the cities that I visit"—but! she can never be caged for long, I know—never, never. I think the necessity for the question had something to do with her marriage and her partial helplessness since then with her withdrawal from the world.* Her husband came in before I left. He seemed a very nice honest fellow—he is a Dutch importer, you know, a little older than she and not, I think, overwhelmingly clever. She was at pains to tell me, as if she were on the defensive at having married a businessman, how irresponsible he really was—"just like me"—but I am sure he is the steadiest importer in the world. We are planning a grand party for her and you and me, detached from our respective husbands and wives, when you come back. She left today on her tour. I may close this department of my intelligence by noting that Raymond Holden has heroically left his wife and family and is now living in sin with Louise Bogan—a third lady poet of remarkable achievement who will merit your attention when you come back (she greatly admires your poetry). Raymond is trying to get a divorce and marry her. If he succeeds in doing so, all the remarkable women of the kind in New York will be married to amiable mediocrities. I do not know whether this is a very unfortunate thing or a very beneficial and reassuring one.

To go on to the Fitzgeralds, Scott's play went so badly on the road that it was taken off before it got to New York, thereby causing them a great

---

* Edna St. Vincent Millay had married Eugen Boissevain.

deal of chagrin. Since then, Fitz has entered upon a period of sobriety of unexampled duration, writing great quantities of short stories for the popular magazines. He is also doing a new novel. Esther Murphy, Seldes, Dos Passos, Mary, and I had Christmas dinner with them at Great Neck. I like Zelda better and better every year and they are among the only people now that I'm always glad to see. Alec [McKaig] and they are still at outs and I wish that, for heaven's sake, when you get back, you would try to reconcile them. I have attempted it in vain. It all dates from that terrible time they came to New York in March, I think, two years ago and stopped at the Plaza. Seldes and Dos Passos I have seen comparatively little—the latter hardly at all (he is living at a Yiddish boarding house in Rockaway Park and having his eyes treated—he is also, from the rumors I hear, experimenting with the amorous pastimes and entanglements from which he has withheld, I should say, all too long). Seldes, as you probably know, has left *The Dial* and is supporting himself chiefly, I think, with work for *Vanity Fair*. Burton [Rascoe] stews eternally in the same juice. Ted Paramore went out to the coast last spring and has never come back—nobody quite knows why. He is doing something or other in the movies at Hollywood. If I go out, I shall investigate. Mencken and Nathan have given up *The Smart Set* and published the first number of *The American Mercury*, which has had a colossal success and already run into a second edition. Ernest Boyd's article in it, "Aesthete: Model 1924," which contained hits at practically everybody except Malcolm Cowley, appeared to Cowley in the light of a direct personal attack upon him above everyone else—as a result of which he called Boyd up on the phone, called him foul and abusive names, and threatened him with physical violence—thereby terrifying Boyd very much. It was all very funny—I'll tell you about it sometime in detail. Cowley (on the strength of the passage about Proust, which was obviously perfectly innocent in intention) went around telling everybody that Boyd (who didn't know who Cowley was) had "called him a fairy," that he had offered to fight Boyd about it, that Boyd had refused and was therefore a coward; and Boyd went around, much agitated, telling people that if Cowley laid a finger on him, he would hand him over to the police, "like any common hooligan." I can't hand the *Broom* crowd very much: Cowley, I think, has some ability but is sort of an ass, and Josephson is an ass with practically no observable ability. Cummings, by the way, I understand, has come back to America, but I have not met him yet. I think that, after having been paid practically no attention to for many years, he is now rather in danger of being overrated. I see that you yourself are superintending a "Cummings number" of S4N;* but believe me, that young man is very half-baked

---

* S4N, a little magazine.

and needs correction rather than encouragement. He has a genuine lyric gift but apparently no judgment and, so far as I can see, is still in the sophomore stage. Wallace Stevens's book, on the other hand, I thought remarkably successful in a limited way. If you haven't seen it, I'll send it to you. Otherwise, I should say, *rien à signaler* in American letters. Except, I may add on second thought, Tom Beer's book on Stephen Crane, which you should certainly read.

Enclosed please find check for $4.70—your half of our latest royalties on the *Garland*. I hope you will give it to a fund for old and indigent authors. When you get back we might have dinner together twice a year and buy a bottle of Scotch with the royalties.

Alec McKaig is highly amusing and agreeable, though, as usual, always worrying and raging about something. You know, he has really changed extraordinarily with experience and time—even, I think, since you left America. And he is much more interesting since he has been in the theater than he used to be when he went in for business. His little Russian wench went West to the movies and married an utter bum—a veteran deadbeat of the theatrical business whom Mary tells me she has known for years. There is something rather odd and probably entertaining about the whole business which he will not divulge. Alec and Esther Murphy have effected a great rapprochement. Did a possible match between them ever occur to you? Alec, I am afraid, has too eager an eye for a snappy wench. Otherwise, I should think, they might go pretty well. By the way, I had no idea how sick you were this summer till Esther told me when she came back. You must have had a dreadful time and I hope that by now your widely admired form has regained its old resilience and amplitude. Let me hear from you soon and do forgive me for not having written before, but the arrival of the baby, the finishing of my play, then my work with the Swedish Ballet (for whom when they first arrived I did some publicity and other things), and later the distractions of the holidays and the composition and launching of my own ballet, have really kept me pretty busy, or at least in an occupied state of mind—you know what I mean—which made serious correspondence difficult.

Farewell: be strong in the faith; stand upon my second coming. Who knows but I may soon arrive among you? But if, as is more likely, I don't, I hope that you will soon be home.

I should advise your trying your next child in America (the land of astute gynecologists and adroit obstetricians).   As ever, EW

To Christian Gauss   March 3, 1924
                                                       New York
Dear Mr. Gauss: Will you be at home this weekend? I had some idea I might go down to Princeton. Would you be free at all Saturday night?

I have just come back from California, whither the manager of the Swedish Ballet paid my expenses for the purpose of trying to induce Charlie Chaplin to act in the pantomime ballet which Ornstein and I are writing. I failed to persuade him; but we are going to put on the ballet anyhow. Also, the Provincetown Players claim that they will do my play next season.

The result of my theatrical adventures, however, has been that I am now completely broke and under a great necessity of making money—till spring when I shall withdraw from this devil's caldron. I am going to write regularly for *The New Republic* again. It had also occurred to me that there might be a possibility of making a little money lecturing—as some of the New York literati do at the College of the City of New York and Columbia. I don't suppose that there would be any chance of doing anything of this kind at Princeton? I suggest it with extreme diffidence, as I really don't know enough about any subject to lecture on it and I have no reason to believe that I should be a good lecturer; but I have been impressed with the ease with which some of my confreres seem to pick up money in this way. I wish you would tell me whether you think there would be anything in it for me.

I have been rereading parts of Joyce's *Ulysses* and I am more than ever convinced of its importance. I do wish you would let me lend it to you: I'd like to talk to you about it. It is so long, though, that you oughtn't to attempt it unless you have time to go through it continuously. If you like, I will bring it down to you—or give it to you in the spring. I hope you are well and all over your trouble.   Yours as ever, Edmund Wilson

To F. Scott Fitzgerald   April 11, 1925
                                        3 North Washington Square, N.Y.
Dear Scott: Your book came yesterday and I read it last night.* It is undoubtedly in some ways the best thing you have done—the best planned, the best sustained, the best written. In fact, it amounts to a complete new departure in your work. The only bad feature of it is that the characters are mostly so unpleasant in themselves that the story becomes rather a bitter dose before one has finished with it. However, the fact that you are able to get away with it is the proof of its brilliance. It is full of all sorts of happy touches—in fact, all the touches are happy—there is not a hole in it anywhere. I congratulate you—you have succeeded here in doing most of the things that people have always scolded you for not doing. I wish, in your next, you would handle a more sympathetic theme. (Not that I don't admire Gatsby and see the point of the whole thing, but you will admit that it keeps us inside the hyena cage.) Rosenfeld has an essay

---

* *The Great Gatsby.*

about you in his new book, just out. I'll urge him to send you a copy if he hasn't done so, as he tells me you have sent him yours. Mary wants to send her best love to you both. I would give anything to have you here this spring. Let me hear from you—my best to Zelda. I hope she is over her peritonitis—she owes me a letter, if she is.   Yours as ever, EW

I particularly enjoyed the man who takes the oculist's advertisement for the eyes of God.

> Mr. Sinclair, who has been intimately associated for so many years with radical ideas and literature.
> (Review of *Mammonart*, in *The New Republic*, 1925)

To UPTON SINCLAIR   May 19, 1925
                                            3 North Washington Square, N.Y.
Dear Mr. Sinclair: Paul was a Roman citizen, to be sure, but a Jew of strictly Jewish stock, born in Asia Minor and writing Greek. Renan says he had no property but made all his living by his trade of "tent-maker" (*Les Apôtres*, chapter X). His family intended him for a rabbi and he became one of the leading zealots of the orthodox Jewish sect of the Pharisees, in which character he engaged in a vigorous campaign of persecuting the Christians—until his conversion on the road to Damascus. He was thus a renegade Jew rather than a renegade Roman gentleman. I can find no mention either in Renan or in the Encyclopaedia Britannica of his ever having been a tax collector. When you describe him as a Roman gentleman, it seems to me that you create a wrong impression: compare Paul to a genuine Roman gentleman—compare him to Gallio, before whom he appeared at Corinth: the difference is almost as striking as between Christ and Pilate, and the fact that Paul was technically a Roman citizen counts for nothing in his character or situation. He was a typically Jewish religious fanatic—preaching first the narrowest orthodoxy and afterwards a heresy. Wouldn't it be possible to find some better modern analogue for him than John Reed?   Yours very sincerely, Edmund Wilson

To STANLEY DELL   July 10, 1925
                                                          Red Bank
Dear Stan: I enjoyed "Malmanogus" very much. What most interested me from the literary point of view was that you seemed to have learned to do new things with your style, to have acquired new stops to your instrument, since the last things of yours I had seen . . .*

. . . As for disposing of it, it is a difficult length, and of rather a difficult kind, for a magazine. It might, however, be worthwhile to send it to the

---

* Two and a half pages of suggestions and criticism omitted.

Mercury and to *The Century*. I will send it to Mencken, if you are willing. On the other hand, I think that, if you have other short stories of a more conventional length, to do so would probably be to begin the wrong way around. I think you ought to get the other stories into shape and begin sending them out—start on the magazines I have suggested (if the others are anything like this one), to which might be added *Scribner's* (let me send the first one to Mencken, as I suggest). For hard cases, try the Franco-American magazine called *This Quarter* or T. S. Eliot's *Criterion*. Then, if you find a cordiality toward the short stories, take advantage of it for "Malmanogus." I advise you to do all this quite methodically and unperturbed by hope or fear—getting them in order one after the other and launching them. If you get one back two or three times so that it begins to look greasy and depressing, don't become discouraged about it, but get a fresh carbon copy at once and start it out again. I assume that you will probably get a bite before long, but even if you shouldn't, by the end of the year the editors will have become aware that there is a very accomplished young man out in New Mexico devoting himself to the art of literature with prodigious energy, and you will probably find yourself in correspondence with one or more of them. You will thus be able to calculate how to write a story which will fall inside the field which the given magazine considers itself to cultivate. You may think all this isn't worth the trouble—but you are scarcely in danger of becoming a magazine hack, which is the only danger, and I really believe that it is a good thing to send stories around (as I have been doing with some of mine for going on a decade now) because you find out certain things about your stuff from having it published that you don't in any other way. In a sense, you really begin for the first time to get a little interest on the energy you have loaned the muse, the writing by the mere fact of its being published and especially by the appreciation of people who don't know you personally gives you back in the form of confidence some of the strength you have put into it.

. . . Thanks ever so much for the Cocteau book, which I wanted particularly . . . There are several matters I should like to discuss with you but I shall not attempt to do so in this letter, which has already run to enormous length. Alfred Bellinger, whom I had not seen for years, turned up to my great surprise just before I came down here, on his way to Greece for a sabbatical year—and much more enlivened and affable than he appears to have been for some time . . .   As ever, EW

To Stanley Dell   August 6, 1925
                                                         Red Bank

Dear Stan: I am sending "Malmanogus" off to Mencken with the emendations. In thinking it over, I have come to the conclusion that what I really feel about it is that it is an attempt on the part of a Protestant, which I take you temperamentally to be, to write a Catholic myth. Not that I would discourage Protestants from exercising themselves in this way, but I believe their greatest successes have been achieved in other directions. As to mythology in general, I do believe that the European mythologies are particularly difficult for Americans to do anything with because they are obliged to find out about them from books instead of absorbing them in early youth from the air in which they have originally condensed. Mrs. Colum, the wife of the Irish poet, tells me that it is only when you see the Irish countryside that you realize how Irish folklore became possible, that the Irish light produces all sorts of effects of shadowiness and ambiguity which act on the imagination and which make it possible for one to believe that one sees almost anything—she told me that the servants in her father's house in the country talked about fairies as if they were perfectly actual facts of contemporary life. But in America we have no real folklore of our own: we have no contact with the Indian, and the early myths of our own civilization look very meager in Hawthorne and Irving, who, nonetheless, were particularly eager to make the best possible showing in this respect. And when the American writers come to deal with the richer material of European mythology, they show unmistakably, as I contend, that they are incapacitated for doing anything with it. Take Hawthorne's versions of the Greek legends, for example: I remember that when the *Tanglewood Tales* were given me as a child after I had read Kingsley's *Greek Heroes* (which, though rather Victorianized, is excellent) I was very much disappointed to find them so boring. And so far as I can remember, there has never been a single first-rate fairy tale (I mean dealing with the conventional figures of European folklore—not, like Rip Van Winkle, etc., indigenous legends) ever written by an American. Frank Stockton's are really admirable, I think, but they have none of the authentic glamour of myths—their success, in fact, depends precisely on the fact that Stockton is not trying, like Hawthorne and Irving, to fit out America with a needed mythology, but merely by writing about the fairies as soberly and dryly as he did about contemporary American life aiming at an effect of irony. We suffer in this connection from the double disability of being Americans and Puritans. That is to say, we not only found no mythology in the place we came to; we brought none with us from Europe. The English Puritans had already demonstrated that their temperaments were of a kind antagonistic to the spirit that makes myths: in spite of Bernard Shaw, I confess that I find Bunyan's Puritan mythology *très peu séduisante* and I think that one of the troubles with Milton (in *Paradise Lost* and *Regained*) is undoubtedly that the Puritan elements in him fought with and partly destroyed the classical and Catholic mythologies upon which he was trying to build. I hope I have now made it clear a priori once and for all that it is absolutely and forever impossible for an American to succeed with a myth and that I shall regard any further attempt of the kind on your part as an unpatriotic act, an affront to friendship, and a betrayal of literature! . . . I had started above to write about *Ulysses* under a mistaken impression of what you had said in that connection. As for the article you refer to, I meant to discuss in it something different from the mythology question—the attitude of *laudator temporis acti* and the tendency toward *pasticcio* on the part of modern writers which I can't help thinking is a sign of something wrong, if not with the writers, with society. As for the "American product," I did not mean to insist upon 100 percent American books: I agree with you that there has been a good deal of nonsense talked about this lately.

Desire under the Elms, which Mary is in, is running all summer, so that I am more or less tied down here with the baby. I have attempted to divert the monotony of my existence in the country by inviting members of my family and old friends of my youth to dinner. A good deal of Scotch makes this possible and even rather interesting—I have adopted a policy of making them drunk and provoking them to reveal themselves. Last night, I had with her husband a girl on whom I had a great crush when I was a boy, and whom I have not seen for it must be more than fifteen years. She turns out to be still quite attractive and has been on the stage. In the course of the conversation, it appeared that she and her husband were enthusiastic supporters (though not actual members) of the Ku Klux Klan and believed that it had saved the country in preventing Al Smith from becoming President—they think that neither Catholics nor Jews are "Americans." The Klan has a great hold on New Jersey. The result of living in New York is that you never meet the people who hold the boob opinions ridiculed there, and are very much surprised when you do. There is no doubt, however, that ordinary American country and small-town life—with its Fords, movies, real-estate developments, and little flappers with bobbed hair and "nude" stockings—is a much bigger and brighter thing than it was when I was a boy. It seems to me that it was inexpressibly dreary, ignorant, stagnant, and stuffy then. At that time, the Red Bank people never went to the shore: they had no cars to get there in; it was only the Sea Bright and Rumson people who went in swimming, and the women all wore dark bathing suits with skirts and stockings. Now the Red Bankers support a large bathing pavilion and I find the children and grandchildren of the grocers, the druggists, and the dry-goods merchants of my youth (most of them retired after selling out to chain stores) so smart and good-looking in white knickerbockers and bright one-piece bathing suits that I can hardly recognize them. I take it that a similar change is taking place everywhere else in America and I think it probably represents a real improvement in civilization.

Let me hear from you again. I'm glad you're coming East in the fall.

How do you find Santa Fe? Is it as interesting as it is represented by Austin, Lawrence, etc.? I saw Mrs. Gerould's article. I am always strongly disposed to disagree with anything she says but in this case have a rather antipathetic reaction to the opposition, too. I have never read any of Lawrence's books but met him once in New York. What do you think of his novels? Are they worth reading? I have an idea that Norman Douglas got his number in that pamphlet about him apropos of Maurice Magnus. Isn't he one of those inferiority-complex romantics (like Wells) of whom Rousseau was the archetype?   Yours as ever, EW

To Stanley Dell   August 27, 1925
                                                          Red Bank

Dear Stan: If I were you, I should send "Malmanogus" to *Harper's*, which seems to be starting out on a new policy (see the last number). I don't know anybody there, but I think it would be worth trying. *The Century*, which I suggested at first, seems to be on the point of collapsing—as the great uplift editor Glenn Frank has been "called" to the presidency of Wisconsin University: I understand that they are not buying any more fiction. If you get it back from *Harper's*, I should try *The Dial*—or perhaps try *The Dial* first. Scofield Thayer has gone abroad and Marianne Moore is now managing editor there: send it to her personally (Miss Marianne Moore) and say that I suggested they might be interested in it. I don't think they will take it, as they rarely take stories by Americans, though they print compositions of great length by Germans, Russians, Hungarians, and Poles; but you will find, I think, that she will read it with the greatest care and write you a curiously worded but intelligent note about it. This is at least an improvement over the old regime at *The Dial*, when, so far as I could see, the contributions were never read, the editors were never in the office, and the magazine knocked itself together every month without human intervention except on the part of the proofreaders and stenographers. Marianne Moore is really awfully nice and very intelligent; but I am afraid that her co-editor Watson will prevent her from making the magazine any different from what it was before. I think, however, that you ought to make a practice of sending things to them.

My observations on mythology, etc., weren't meant seriously for an a priori theory but were the result of a sentiment arising from reading your works and those of the other illustrious authors named, as well as from my own experience. There is a truth contained in them, I am sure, but I won't press the matter. I think the Italian-American subject sounds excellent—but perhaps the grocer would better remain unwritten, as it sounds like one of those excruciating indulgences of self-torture to which our Puritan temperament runs. You ought to be able to sell the novel to a publisher, I should think—getting novels published seems to be much easier than anything else. New York is full of publishers and many of the old publishers have adopted new policies and are all on the lookout for first novels by promising young novelists, which they will take a chance on—even when they are inferior—though they are afraid of short stories, poems, essays, etc., by unknown writers.

I get disgusted in some ways with the literary people in New York. What one misses are men who occupy themselves with literature without turning it into a business—I mean, a business like the cloak and suit business, with its inevitable politics, combinations, incessant talking of shop, and general unfitting of its victims for any kind of activities other than their professional ones. This is usually the result of necessity, however: in order to avoid it one seems to have to have at least a partial financial independence. Seldes and Rascoe, for example, who are both men of unusual abilities, have to spend so much thought and energy on earning a living that their minds are rarely free for anything else. John Bishop was designed by nature and training for the career of a gentleman pursuing literature disinterestedly; but has suffered various casualties as the result of not having money enough to carry it out—the latest of which is being reduced to writing movie captions, an occupation which pays pretty well but seems to have a demoralizing effect. Paul Rosenfeld, who is the heir of rich German-Jewish brewers, has been able to maintain his leisure and independence as well as anybody I know—but unfortunately, as the years of Prohibition have worn on, his dividends have been steadily decreasing and, since I have known him, I have seen him obliged to give up many things which he was once able to do, and reduced to anxiety about selling his critical articles. At any rate, the moral is simply that, when your health permits, I wish you would come and live near New York at least—which I dare say you never will. I hope you will bear with these rambling letters—they are the product of the unpeopled solitude in which I live. Having, as a rule, no one to talk to at the highball hour, I have formed the habit of pouring it all into my correspondence to avoid the necessity of talking to myself.   Yours as ever, EW

To MALCOLM COWLEY   August 21, 1925
                                                          Red Bank
. . . I am contemplating myself experimenting in a vein so journalistic and optimistic that admirers of Eliot will never speak to me again . . .

To ALLEN TATE   December 11, 1925
                                       3 North Washington Square, N.Y.
Dear Tate: I am awfully sorry not to have had a chance to see you before you left. I was just on the point of trying to get hold of you when I got your letter. I had so much work to do last month that I spent most of

the time at a friend's apartment uptown, where I was able to be uninterrupted, and didn't see anybody; then I got sick and went to the country for a week. I wish you would let me know if you are ever in town: I shall be here from now on. Thank you very much for inviting me to come to see you! I'd like to very much, but don't see any prospect of being able to do so in the immediate future, as I have to go down to Red Bank to see my mother every weekend. I am returning these manuscripts of your poems, as you told me you wanted them. In rereading them, I like them even better than I did before. In my opinion, "Mr. Pope" and the "Death of Little Boys" are the best of these: they are fascinating and not like anything by anybody else. I don't agree with you, if you told me, as I seem to remember, that the "Duchess of Malfi" is one of your favorites: this and "Bored to Choresis" seem to me too suggestive of a certain vein of Pound's, a vein that I don't care much for—the combination of pedantic words and deliberately rough versification. Your own particular language appears in them, too, of course but to better advantage, I think, in the others I speak of. You have a very curious quality, not only a gift of imagery but a beauty and a "strangeness" which make me willing to bet on your future. I prefer your best things to anything of Wallace Stevens, to whom you have some points of resemblance. I saw Mark Van Doren the other day and he told me he had the manuscript of your book. I suggested trying the Boni brothers with it and will take it around to them, if you are willing. In my opinion, there is quite a good deal of American poetry which ought to be published: yourself, Cowley, and a man named Phelps Putnam, notably. Perhaps Hart Crane, who seems to be admired by a great many people, though I have not cared much for the poems of his I have seen, would be another. Perhaps Rolfe Humphries, who has the manuscript of a book, would be another. And your friend Miss Gottschalk? I should also like to see John Bishop preserve some of his old poems and find himself stimulated to produce something new. I would also be glad, I may add, to get my own poems published. I believe I will ask Boni if he could be interested in a series of new poets. I doubt if he would be, but it's not inconceivable that somebody might be—Jacobs, who published Cummings, for example. What would you think of some concerted action of this sort? I think you've done well to go to the country—I hope you'll be able to do some new work there. Be sure to let me know if you come in and have any time to spare. I hope that your family are well.

Yours as ever, Edmund Wilson

To Christian Gauss   February 23, 1926
3 North Washington Square, N.Y.
Dear Mr. Gauss: I was very much relieved to hear that you had refused the Oregon thing. I have been intending to come down to Princeton but

haven't been able to and am now planning to go down to New Orleans for a few weeks the first of March. I hope to see you soon after I get back. Hemingway has been in town for a few days—has now gone back to France. He reports that the Fitzgeralds are in good condition, have withdrawn from Paris, and that Scott is working on a new novel.* Scribner's is going to publish Hemingway in the future. I read his book the other day and I thought it was awfully good. Did you tell me you didn't like his writings? I wish you would look into *In Our Time* sometime. I am enclosing some choice *New Republic* articles, including one with some profound observations on Ibsen, of whom I become more and more convinced that you take a wrong view, and another which is intended to convey an idea of why New Yorkers try to leave home for Louisiana. Please remember me to Mrs. Gauss. I am so glad you are going to stay in the East. Indeed, I should have felt that, if you had gone, one of the heroic supports of Eastern civilization had been knocked out.

Yours as ever, Edmund Wilson

To ALLEN TATE   February 24, 1926
                                                          New York

Dear Tate: The advertizing man at *The New Republic* says that they have never been able to do anything with books of poetry, but would be glad to see the proposed volumes *after* they were published, etc. I don't believe that even then they could be induced to carry them with their subscriptions. I have also discussed the question both of a series and of your poems separately with Boni, but with absolutely no success. The trouble is that the little publishers can't afford to bring out things that they think there is no chance of a large sale on and the big publishers, who could afford to, are too stupid to know that a manuscript like yours ought to be published. I am, however, going to take your MS to Scribner's this afternoon—I know some people there—though I haven't much hopes of them (as they don't bring out much poetry). I shall direct them to send the MS straight back to you and I should then try to interest Jacobs in it or perhaps Warshow. Or take it to [Henry Seidel] Canby of *The Saturday Review*, who is one of the advisers of Harper's. If you don't know him, say that I suggested they might be interested in it. I am going down to New Orleans for a few weeks the first of March but expect to be back the end of the month. Let me know what happens. I have become very cynical about publishers—from long experience of them—and, so far as I can see, Warshow is rather more cautious, instead of more generous, than the average. I should, however, as I say, try to interest him in your work on the strength of the Novine's willingness to carry it or on its own

---

* *Tender Is the Night.*

merits. I am writing him about *The New Republic*. Don't despair of getting the book published but keep on submitting it indefinitely—you will surely get it published eventually.

Liveright is another possibility—sometime when he is feeling a little more prosperous than he seems to be just at present. I hope to see you when I get back.   Yours as ever, Edmund Wilson

To SHERWOOD ANDERSON   April 10, 1926
                                                              New York

Dear Anderson: This is just a note to tell you to shake that thing! I saw the *Cahier du Mois* devoted to you in Brentano's today and sent it to you, thinking you had said you hadn't seen it. I am also enclosing an article by Mrs. Colum with something about you in it. I hope you have been enjoying good weather since I left New Orleans: I found it almost as cold and bleak here as when I went. The New Yorkers look very dull and dehumanized after the Orleanians: I thought it might be merely my own distemper that made me think so when I left; but, coming back in improved humor and greater calm of mind, I see that it is the truth. I have had hopes of New York, since the war, becoming one of the greatest centers of civilization, but I don't know how there can be a city of real creative importance when the people enjoy themselves so little. I have found everybody here with their spirits under the same old perpetual eclipse, or semi-eclipse, imperfectly relieved by hard liquor. Please remember me to Mrs. Anderson and to your brother: you were so kind to me when I was in New Orleans—if I hadn't found you when I went down there, I probably wouldn't have such a high opinion of the place. By the way, when we reorganize the United States along monarchical lines, perhaps we'd better transfer the capital to New Orleans and make it the center of culture and fashion. I hope you will offer up a prayer for me when you go to the old beer saloon.   Yours as ever, Edmund Wilson

To MAXWELL GEISMAR   1942

. . . About Anderson: I've been impressed by his autobiography too. How middle-class he makes Sinclair Lewis and a lot of other people look! For him the inhabitants of a little Ohio town were just as important and on just the same level as the people with names that he afterwards met in Chicago and New York. He and Dreiser were, in my opinion, the only really first-rate men who came out of the Middle West in that period. I liked him very much personally—will tell you about him when I see you. He was not irritating at all personally, but one of the most agreeable men I have ever known. It is only in his writing that he is sometimes irritating. Personally, he had a humorous racy quality that was very

Southwestern and that hardly ever got into what he wrote. He had a kind of reverence for literature which made him a little stilted in a peculiar way when he "took pen in hand," in the old phrase that is very appropriate to his attitude. His conversations, for example, never sound like real Americans talking; but when he told you stories, it was as good as *Huckleberry Finn* . . .

To ELINOR WYLIE   July 5, 1926
                                                    New York

Dear Elinor: I hope you will forgive me for not having written to you before, but my existence since you left has been one long series of disasters which have prevented my doing anything. I had a week or two of perfect tranquillity at Bank Street—which I greatly enjoyed and consider about the best place to work I have ever had—but immediately thereafter everything began to disintegrate . . . I have not been very much at Bank Street and everything is exactly as you left it, with the exception of the lamp shade behind the sofa, which I broke one night by sitting down suddenly on the sofa and hitting my head against it. I am terribly sorry and am doing my best to get you a new one like it. I hope that it was not something particularly precious and irreplaceable. Marjorie disappeared about two weeks after you left and has never been seen since: somebody else whom she worked for called me up to find out whether I had heard from her and told me that Marjorie had sent her word that she had sprained her ankle. I have, however, had other people in to clean and the apartment is in excellent condition. I take it that Bill will be back sometime this week and I will remove such of my things as are left. Dos Passos had dinner with me one night and we both sat around and said what a swell person you were. I thought he was in unusually good form. Except for him, I don't think I have seen anybody you know. I hear that the Bishops are going abroad to stay indefinitely, but I haven't seen them since your sailing. The weather still remains like early spring and July is coyly going in for cold April mornings and gusts of March wind. I found a little fiend in your bathroom, who made me feel very self-conscious until I finally caught him and put him out. As you know, I am far from objecting to them on principle, but I didn't like the way this one behaved. My opinion is that Marjorie is a fiend and that when she disappeared she took this modified form, in order to remain in the apartment unnoticed. It is also my opinion that a poltergeist broke the lamp, as I only hit it lightly with the back of my head and it fell broken almost exactly in half: it was evidently a practical joke of some kind. Some of the presences there were in the habit of playing a delightful little waltz—always the same one—of the vintage of 1870 at about five o'clock in the afternoon, while I was taking a bath and getting ready to go out, and I found this very agreeable. Did you ever observe that phenomenon? I think that the few spirits you left behind, though perhaps a little mischievous and licentious, are not really bad at heart, or are perhaps too feeble to do much harm, if they wanted to. I watched in vain for your big hobgoblin, Buster, but I suppose you have taken him with you. I have devoted some attention to your astrological library, but have not had much success in working the charms. I have experimented a little with the love philters, but have finally come to the conclusion that perhaps Scotch is better, after all. The little fiend I spoke of offered to supply me with something of fabulous efficacy in this line if I would let him stay in the apartment—he put his cold little claw on my hand and said, "Meestah Weelsong, I weel breen' you a pheeltah what weel inflamm a mahble spheenx." But I told him I was not interested in sphinxes, though I confess the idea has lingered in my mind and has a certain morbid interest. I did not want him around and had no confidence in his philters.

I hope you are having a good time. I wish you would drop me a line when you can.   Best love, Bunny

I saw an old New Orleans friend of mine—Hamilton Basso.
(To John Peale Bishop, 1934)

To Hamilton Basso   January 25, 1927

Dear Ham: I had just started to write you when I got your letter. I asked Albert Boni about your book the other day and he told me that he would read it again immediately, and then show it to Charles [Boni], and that they would decide about it. He was going abroad in a few days, however, and has now gone off without attending to it. He is to be gone six weeks. In the meantime, I have spoken to Charles about it and he says he will look the manuscript up right away. It's Albert, however, who makes the real decisions, so I'm afraid you can't expect much action till he comes back. When he does, I'll bring the matter to his attention again.

I wish I could come to New Orleans in February, but I don't see how I possibly can. Lovett has gone to Chicago for three months and I have to attend to the book department while he is away. Besides, I haven't got the money. If, however, by some miracle, I should be able to get away—after the first of April—I'll let you know. By the way, if you have any ideas which you think would do for *The New Republic*, write me about them or send what you have written. Lyle Saxon has done a long thing about his voodoo party which is excellent. I took Lyle to the dress rehearsal of an Expressionist play—the worst I ever saw—the other night, and we spent rather a sane evening till, afterwards, when I took him to the house of some drinking friends of mine—from which, however, he withdrew at an untimely early hour as a result of his old Southern gentleman bladder trouble, a situation which, I am ashamed to say, I was too stupid to grasp at the time.

Since you asked, my book has appeared—and a wretched-looking volume it is.* The cover looks like a strip of bathroom linoleum seen through the eyes of somebody who has just gone to get the Bromo Seltzer, and the pages are printed on paper something like that used in patent-medicine almanacs. There are also a good many misprints, repeated lines, etc., which give a smart modern effect something like Gertrude Stein. The contents, however, I needn't say, are A number 1 in every way and can be recommended to any lover of literature for a hearty laugh.

Let me hear from you from time to time. I can see how New Orleans would get on your nerves, but would give anything to be able to go there now myself. Please remember me to anybody you see whom I know. Don't fail to keep on writing.   Yours as ever, Edmund Wilson

. . . an English friend then studying at Harvard Law School.
(*The Twenties: From Notebooks and Diaries of the Period*)

To Sylvester Gates   April 6, 1927
                                                    The New Republic

Dear Gates: Here is the five dollars I still owe you. Thank you ever so much. I had an awfully good time in Boston, but am afraid I kept you up too late the last night I was there and remember reading you Emerson's poems with all the fluency and charm of a drowning man gasping and gulping for breath. You seem to have the effect on me of encouraging, by your polite interest, a certain vein of reminiscence and commentary which I don't ordinarily get much of a chance to indulge, for lack of an audience—and I fear that if I saw you continually, I should rapidly become buttered on both sides. I hope you're not doing too much sinking in your solitary drinking chamber. I had another rather amusing run-in with the old man who put you out that night, when I got back from Cambridge Sunday. I hope you'll get to New York at Easter, so that we can have some sort of party. There are several people and things I should like to have you see.   Yours as ever, Edmund Wilson

To Seward Collins   June 19, 1927
The Bookman   Red Bank

Dear Sew: I regret to say that I have recently examined the poem you refer to and that it is useless. I hope to send you something else, however, in the course of time. Good luck! I expect you and Burton [Rascoe] to

---

* *Discordant Encounters.*

133

turn out the most interesting literary magazine ever seen on this continent. I'm on my vacation now and am leaving for Cape Cod tomorrow, where I'm going to try to find a place to live. I hope to see you in the fall.

As ever, Edmund Wilson

> . . . as a romantic personality of the twenties, Phelps Putnam seemed almost comparable in his day, in the minds of those who knew and read him, to Scott Fitzgerald, Ernest Hemingway, and Edna Millay. (Foreword to *The Collected Poems of H. Phelps Putnam*, 1971)

To Phelps Putnam
July 13, 1927
Peaked Hill Bar, Provincetown, Mass.

Dear Phelps: I've just been reading your book in the proofs—a copy of which has been sent to Herbert Gorman, who is staying with me here—and, in my opinion, sir, you have knocked off one of the best books of English poetry of the time. I realized that I hadn't half appreciated and understood it in manuscript—partly because I didn't have a chance to read it as a whole—as which it is most effective and I hope will plant you firmly at the top of the profession, where you belong. Well as I already knew the separate pieces, I haven't enjoyed a book of verse so much since it would be hard to say who and I expect to read it often again.

I was able to get O'Neill's Coast Guard station, after all, up here—which is a swell place to live—nothing but ships, sea, sand, lighthouses, etc. Why don't you come up and see me sometime? There is plenty of room. I like it up here so much and have been accomplishing so much work (having just finished a play) that I think seriously of spending next winter here (not on the coast, but in town), with the purpose of producing enough high-grade literature to make it possible for me to enjoy the fleshpots of New York with a full purse and a clear conscience. Drop me a line and let me know about your movements. I expect to be passing through Boston again about August 1 and will hope to see you then anyway.

As ever, Bunny Wilson

To Christian Gauss
July 30, 1927

. . . I have been living up here in the old Coast Guard station, fitted up as a house, in which O'Neill lived so many years. It is great fun—like being in the middle of the Atlantic . . .

To Seward Collins
August 21, 1927
Provincetown

Dear Sew: Won't you *please* send me some news of my play manuscript. When I read about your adventures in Boston, I telegraphed asking you to come up here, but got the telegram back from the Bellevue. Dos Passos wired me yesterday to come to Boston and assist in the demonstration,[*] but I can't—wish I could and am eager to hear what happened to you. I expect to be back the first of October and may then have some weighty matter to discuss with you.   As ever, Bunny Wilson

> Her name is Hazel Ufford . . . She is a girl who lived near me last summer, when I was living in O'Neill's old Coast Guard station near Provincetown. She is very young and very pretty, and she has quite a remarkable literary gift, as yet in rather an immature state.
> (To John Peale Bishop, 1928)

To HAZEL UFFORD [HAZEL HAWTHORNE WERNER]   November 12, 1927
Red Bank

Dear Hazel: Thank you ever so much for your sweet letter. Your observations about the jelly and the autumn colors—also the opalescent cabbages —are so good that I should steal them, if I didn't remember that you were in the literary business yourself. I haven't done anything exciting since I have been back but have been leading almost as solitary a life as at Peaked Hill, going nowhere and working on the book that I began up there almost all the time that I am not at *The New Republic* . . . I have read nothing very thrilling with the exception of E. E. Cummings's *Him*, a long play which hasn't been, and no doubt can't be, produced, but which has appeared in book form. It is a mess as a whole, but the best parts of it are wonderful. I began this letter, as you see, more than two weeks ago, but wasn't able to finish it at the time, and immediately thereafter had so much to do on a very long thing about the Woodrow Wilson biography for *The New Republic* and was then put out of commission by an attack of grippe, from which I'm only just coming to life, that I haven't been able to get back to it before now (November 27). I was worried at the time of the flood, for fear you might have been in it, but from what I hear, it appears that Tynesboro is well out of the way. I still think New York is an awful place to live, and am at present scheming to find a way for getting out for part of the winter—have even thought seriously of going up to Provincetown again . . .

I have just been reading the centenary edition of Blake—complete works in one volume of more than a thousand pages. It is most interesting—all kinds of queer things in it I never knew he had written. Besides, I had never read him steadily before and find him even more remarkable than I had thought. Though I had often thought lately in New York of

> "I wander through each dirty street,
> Near where the dirty Thames does flow,
> And mark in every face I meet
> Marks of weakness, marks of woe," etc.

_____
[*] In behalf of Sacco and Vanzetti.

By the way, have you seen the Christmas number of *McCall's* with poems on the Nativity by all the poets—Elinor Wylie, Robinson, Edna Millay, Dorothy Parker, etc.? Some of them are pretty good. Give my best regards to Roger. I don't approve of his insistence on studying English rather than some foreign literature—but I do think it is a very good idea to do all your work at college on one subject, instead of half a dozen, as is usual—and so am with him, as far as that goes. Tell Duff that it often gives me great comfort and reassurance to think of him carrying on Christ's work in the North. In New York, the common substitutes for religion are psychoanalysis, the Gurdjieff Institute, H. L. Mencken, and bad alcohol—and I haven't met an intelligent clergyman, so far as I can remember, since I have been there. Well, best luck to both of you—I hope that you are happy and not leading the village boys and girls astray with cigarettes and hard cider. Let me hear from you again, when you can—I was awfully glad to get your letter.   Yours as ever, Edmund

To Sylvester Gates   December 26, 1927
                                                Red Bank

Dear Gates: I was very glad to hear from you and send all my felicitations on your engagement. I've enjoyed Siepmann very much—have had a good deal of fun with him—though, I fear, as you suggest, that he is bent on becoming another Noel Coward. If he is, however, New York is just the place to do it. Whenever he feels that anything has been put over on him, he always smiles ironically and says: "Ah, you Americans, you're so very quick!"—or "well-informed," or whatever. We spent quite an amusing night in an old downtown saloon (run by Tammany) last Friday—and I heard him murmuring, "Ah, you Americans!" to the barflies and thugs from time to time. I didn't mean that he's not appreciative and amiable— on the contrary, he is extremely. I'm sorry that I didn't get a chance to see Anthony Asquith until just before he left.

I'm slightly sick from Christmas and from New York, but I have a sort of leave of absence from *The New Republic* for a few weeks, and I think I'll go down to Atlantic City and work on a sort of novel I've been writing. I've just been reading the new volumes of Proust and think they're highly satisfactory—the last pages, especially, are wonderful and very moving in a curious way. I was a little disgusted at first by Charlus's big masochistic scene, but thought that what Proust succeeded in doing with it was quite remarkable. I've also read Gide's *Faux-Monnayeurs* lately, but, when all is said and done, can't help considering it more or less of a washout. I feel that Gide, by all sorts of hocus-pocus, has succeeded in kidding himself and his admirers into thinking it is a masterpiece. In the *Journal des Faux-Monnayeurs* he has published, the only influence he does not mention is Dostoevsky, of whom the whole thing is obviously an imitation.

Gide is the fairies' Dostoevsky—or would be, if he were not a Presbyterian minister. What do you think of it? Have you read it? It is having a great success over here in a translation.

I haven't much news—until the last week or so, I haven't gone anywhere or seen anybody this year . . . The Sacco–Vanzetti tragedy made a profound impression on everybody—with distinct effects on the literary people in certain quarters. Croly wants me to write a history of it (the case), and I may begin on it in the spring. (In the meantime, please don't mention this.) I wish I could go to England, but am afraid I shan't be able to for some time. When I do go abroad again, I want to be able to stay for a year or so. I wish you would come back to New York (which I feel you never did properly). I have missed you this winter.

Yours as ever, Edmund Wilson

The New
REPUBLIC
421 West 21st Street
NewYork City

1926–1928

A poet with a real gift for language, for a melting music a little like Shelley's . . . but he never seems to know when he is writing badly and when he is writing well. (*The Shores of Light*, 1924)

To E. E. Cummings
October 11, 1926
The New Republic*

Dear Cummings: They are very much interested in the Wills–Sharkey idea, but as they have never seen any of your prose, are not prepared to order the article. Would you be willing to do it on the chance of their taking it? The chance is pretty good, I think. If possible, they would like to have it Thursday so that it could get into next week's magazine. Could you do it by then?

I will come around to see you about it about Thursday noon.

Yours as ever, EW

To John Peale Bishop
November 1, 1926

Dear John: . . . I am trying to get some articles for *The New Republic* and wish you would let me know if you have any subjects in mind which you would like to write about. (We could pay only $50 for a page of 1,200 words.) Mr. Croly liked your thing about Vienna so much that you

---

* The letters in this section were written from *The New Republic*.

wrote when you were abroad before that I think he would be very glad to get anything from you. So that if you have anything I wish you would send it along. If you can let me know the subject beforehand in order that I may get it approved by *The New Republic*, then I can order the article from you. Will you drop me a line about this?

Never mind about the Valéry. Under those circumstances I could not afford to read him now. I will write you a letter later.

Yours as ever, Edmund

I have moved and my present address is 224 West Thirteenth Street. I have a part-time job here now and altogether am doing rather well. Elinor is back—she seems to have had a great success in England. So are the Seldeses. What has happened to your book? I am writing a play. I miss you very much and wish I could discuss Proust with you since I have read him up to date. To say nothing of this vale of tears, where, as Dr. Johnson remarked on a celebrated occasion, "much is to be suffered and little known." Though, I confess, at the present moment, I seem to be suffering a little less and feeling that I know a little more than is always the case with me.

EW

To Malcolm Cowley   November 27, 1926

Dear Cowley: By all means, go ahead and do a portrait. I can't order it but they have always been particularly fond of portraits here and are very favorably disposed. I wish you would send me the translation of the whole *Crise de l'esprit* series.* It doesn't make any difference about their having been published in *The Athenaeum*, and I really think the letters would be better than the lecture. I'll let you know about the French poetry later. I like it, but don't know how Lovett will feel about printing it. It's hard to get in a long literary essay which is not hung on some recent book, or, like the Valéry, on some particular brilliant writer.

Yours very sincerely, Edmund Wilson

I have written a long thing on Poe which may come out next week. I hope I haven't stolen your thunder—as I should never have thought of writing it, if it hadn't been for that conversation with you. It is long, but, nonetheless, incomplete. I discovered that, after attacking Mr. [Joseph Wood] Krutch through 4,000 words, I have entirely forgotten myself to state at any point that Poe was a good writer.

Yours for the Poe Society, EW

---

* Paul Valéry.

139

... absurd and insufferable though he often was, he was one of the foundation stones of my generation.   (Notebooks of the sixties)

To ERNEST HEMINGWAY   January 7, 1927

Dear Hemingway: I think your book is a knockout—perhaps the best piece of fiction that any American of this new crop has done.* Croly, the editor of *The New Republic*, has also been extremely interested in it and has even written an editorial about it, which I am enclosing. We wish you would do something for *The New Republic*. Won't you send me something which you have on hand that you think there is even a remote chance of our being able to use?

How are you? When are you coming back to America? I am anxious to see you.   Yours as ever, Edmund Wilson

To ERNEST HEMINGWAY   May 4, 1927

Dear Hemingway: Your Italian sketches are fine. They have been received with enthusiasm in the office and will appear this week, I think.

I liked the stories in *Scribner's* very much, especially the one about the Italian major. I like "The Killers" too, but I thought you gave the thugs a line of banter which sounded a little too much like the hero of your novel and his friend on their fishing trip—that is to say, a little too sophisticated.

I have seen the Fitzgeralds. They have bought a large house containing twenty rooms, at a place called Brandywine Hundred, near Wilmington, Delaware. They are contemplating some prodigious parties. I wish that you were over here and were able to attend them.

What with the Literary Guild and other things, the Van Doren trust is practically controlling the literature over here. A thick crust is forming over literature, and I think it is your duty to come back to your homeland and help to break it up.

By the way, do send anything more that you have or that you should happen to write in the future, that you think we could use.

                                    Yours as ever, Edmund Wilson

To ERNEST HEMINGWAY   May 18, 1927

Dear Hemingway: Gauss of Princeton was telling me the other day that you used to know Mussolini in the *Avanti* days and that you had rather an amusing story about seeing him after he reached his present eminence. Have you ever had the idea of writing anything about him?

---

* *The Sun Also Rises.*

140

I wish you could do us a sketch of him—a short story or whatever you please.

Your Italian sketches have appeared, and I suppose by this time you have received a copy.   Yours as ever, Edmund Wilson*

He has some excellent unpublished poems. I'm running a group by him in the sup.   (To John Peale Bishop, 1941)

To Rolfe Humphries   November 3, 1927

Dear Rolfe: Thank you for your letter. Lovett suggests your doing the *Julius Caesar* in five or six hundred words but says that he doesn't think the book is important and can't engage to take it if he doesn't think the review interesting. Would you undertake it on those terms? I hope you will. I don't suppose there would be material for a long special article in it.

It's been suggested here that it would be a good thing to have some sporting articles—on baseball, etc.—by you.† Your article on the fight film has made a great hit with the editors. I didn't know they were dropping the subtitle but I think they did right in doing so, because it wouldn't have meant anything to anybody; it would in fact have puzzled people. I can't help the fact that you are self-conscious about writing literary articles.

I was much delighted by the elegiacs. My only criticism would be that describing the nettles as *glaucus* makes it appear that that was their natural color, when they should really owe their color to the moonlight. The *surdi murmuribus* is a particularly happy stroke. Couldn't something, however, be done with Joyce's repetitions such as *falls softly, softly falling,* on the principle of some of those *pathetic iterations* in Latin poetry such as *illa Lesbia, Lesbia illa* or that line toward the end of the fourth Georgic, *Te veniente die, te decedente canebat*? Why don't you let us run the verses in our correspondence department with a little note from you explaining that you have put Joyce's poem into Latin, the way they do in the English magazines? I think it would be rather amusing.

In any case, do think seriously about sending us some more special articles.   Yours as ever, Edmund Wilson

Can *pullus* be used of people? Would *pullus amor* make a Roman laugh?

---

* "I wrote a review of *in our time* [title of first version Hemingway submitted was lower-cased] and *Three Stories* which appeared in the *Dial* of October 1924 . . . I have learned . . . that my review of *In Our Time* was not the first. An earlier one, signed M.R., had appeared in Paris in the April 1924 issue of *the transatlantic review.*"   —*The Shores of Light*
† Rolfe Humphries had been athletic coach in a boys' school.

Professor Nevins has produced an attractive book—well written, accurate, consecutive, beautifully proportioned, and disciplined by a detachment as far from the silly irony that has lately become the fashion as it is from the injudicious impulse to magnify or rehabilitate of the fanatical enthusiast . . . (Review of *Frémont: The West's Greatest Adventurer,* in *The Shores of Light,* 1928)

The difference between him and me is that Nevins enthusiastically approves of everything the U.S. has done since [the Civil War] in the way of intervention and expansion.

(To Arthur Schlesinger, Jr., 1958)

To ALLAN NEVINS   March 5, 1928
The Saturday Review of Literature
Dear Mr. Nevins: Would there be any chance of getting you to review for *The New Republic* Stanley Vestal's book on Kit Carson? I have just been reading your biography of Frémont with great interest and admiration.   Yours sincerely, Edmund Wilson

To ALLAN NEVINS   March 16, 1928

Dear Mr. Nevins: I am so glad you will do the Kit Carson. I was wondering whether you would care also to review a biography of Stonewall Jackson, by Allen Tate. I have the page proofs here and will send them to you, if you don't mind reading the book in this form. If you do, we will wait until the volume arrives.   Yours sincerely, Edmund Wilson

To ALLAN NEVINS   April 2, 1928

Dear Mr. Nevins: Thank you very much for your Kit Carson review. I am sorry you can't do the Stonewall Jackson, but hope to be able to get you to do something else later.   Yours very sincerely, Edmund Wilson

To PHELPS PUTNAM   March 23, 1928

Dear Phelps: I made out a long list of people to send copies of the literary supplement to, and I probably put your name on the list. Thank you very much for your appreciation of the Proust, which, however, ought to have been much longer and much better and which someday, I hope, will be.*

I was wondering what had become of you. I have only just succeeded in getting a copy of your book to send to Scott Fitzgerald, after innumerable unsuccessful attempts at many bookstores. The trouble is that it is out of stock at the publisher's. How does this happen? Can't you get Johnny Farrar to print a new edition?

I have just had a most amusing correspondence with Louis Untermeyer,

---

* "A Short View of Proust," *The New Republic,* March 21, 1928.

who began by accusing me of doing the poets of the *American Miscellany* an injustice, in order to persecute him, and has ended by begging me with tears in his eyes to take over the *Miscellany* myself, alleging that he feels grateful to me for the "purely sentimental reason" (What does this mean?) that it was I who in one of my articles first called his attention to your poetry.

I hope you will be coming on soon. I want to see you. I had forgotten that you were suffering from the same malady as Proust, and I heartily hope that you will never read much about him or we shall have you in a cork-lined chamber with all the windows closed, writing by an electric light. Yours as ever, Edmund Wilson

Good luck with your poem—though I sympathize with your difficulties in writing with a time limit.

To Malcolm Cowley   February 2, 1928

Dear Malcolm: I can't remember precisely what you said about reviewing books, and I forgot to ask you last night. Did you say that you were too busy to do anything now, and if so, when would you be able to?

I have a new collection of essays here by Aldous Huxley called *Proper Studies*. They are not literary, but political, social, and so forth. Would you care anything about them? I don't know how Aldous Huxley affects you, but he bores me to death, and I think he is probably the most overrated modern writer. Yours as ever, Edmund Wilson

Also, how about doing something with [William] Beebe? I have his last two books, *The Arcturus Adventure* and *Pheasant Jungles*, but have never written about them and will hand them over to you, if you will write something. Couldn't you do it for the spring literary supplement, about March?

To Malcolm Cowley   March 21, 1928

. . . In the confusion yesterday, I forgot to ask you about the Beebe article, which, of course, is at present the thing I am most anxious to have you write. Could you possibly do it right away before anything else, and would you like to have me send you copies of *Pheasant Jungles* and *The Arcturus Adventure*? I do hope you can and that you will let me know right away . . .

To Malcolm Cowley   March 26, 1928

Dear Malcolm: I think that your little "Style and Fashion" review is more or less a masterpiece in its way. Your capacity for doing these trivial things well is astonishing.

I will send you the Beebe books as soon as I can, and I think it would be an excellent idea to have the article for the next literary supplement, the material for which has to be in the office by April 25. I am trying to make these literary supplements all-star affairs. By the way, we are in the market for all kinds of special sketches, satires, and whatnot . . . I wish when you get a chance you would try your hand at something of this kind. The more amusing, the better.   Yours as ever, Edmund Wilson

To Malcolm Cowley   April 2, 1928

. . . I am having the Beebe books sent you. I hope you can let me have the article by April 23, and I wish you would let me know in advance how long you want to make it. Also, would you care to do Sinclair Lewis's new book, *The Man Who Knew Coolidge*? I wish you would, because I think it is probably the sort of thing you could polish off very pungently . . .

To Malcolm Cowley   April 13, 1928

. . . The Sinclair Lewis is going in this week . . . The Beebe article we ought to have very soon now—next week, if possible. I have just got an announcement of a new book called *In the Beginning*, by Norman Douglas, and I should like to get somebody to do a leading review which might also perhaps be something in the nature of a general consideration of Douglas. Would you care to undertake this? I have never read Douglas much myself, but I have an idea that there is probably more to be said about him than anybody has yet said . . .

To Malcolm Cowley   April 27, 1928

. . . Thank you very much for the Beebe review, which is first-rate. You are excellent on Beebe's style—a matter which has never received any attention—and, in fact, on the whole subject. Do you think the last sentence is pointed enough? Perhaps it is, but I was afraid that the ordinary reader mightn't understand what you meant. See what you think when you read it in the proof. Would it be possible to ask, in so many words, what precisely is Mr. Beebe's contribution (beyond his monograph on pheasants) to scientific thought? I will try to have you paid right away . . .

To Malcolm Cowley   August 29, 1929

. . . The fall books are beginning to come in, and if you say so, I'll send you some. Would you care about *Steppenwolf* by Hermann Hesse or *Gold Coast Customs* by Edith Sitwell, for example?

Dear Allen: Thank you for giving attention to all those things. I should never think, myself, of printing a note to a signed article to indicate that the editor did not share the contributor's views, but Croly makes it a matter of principle to do this—he has done it before in those political matters where his convictions have really the character of religious faith. It is not in the least a matter of caution with him—as in the case of the magazine, I forget which, that published an interview with Mencken, in which he said that he believed an injustice had been committed in the case of Sacco and Vanzetti, and then explained (the editors of the magazine did) in an editorial in the same issue that they thought he was going much too far: with Croly, it is a matter of piety.

. . . I had to miss Monday at the office and have consequently decided not to knock off till next week. If you get a chance, come in someday. You're very kind to express a wish to see my book, and I'm astonished that you should do so, as there is nothing I hate worse myself than to be asked to look at uncompleted prose works in manuscript—so that I'm also reluctant to show my own before they're finished. When I've written the book all through, I'll have to go over it all again, and I expect—I hope— that then, for the first time, the electric lights will really be turned on.

As ever, EW

To Walter Lippmann   February 29, 1928
The World

Dear Lippmann: I like and admire George Nathan, but I was rather glad to see you take a crack at him in *Vanity Fair*. I suppose that Nathan's opinions on politics are merely a shadow of Mencken's and that Mencken is the real enemy in this regard, but I think it is a good thing to have somebody take a stand against the point of view expressed in the passage you quoted. I feel very strongly myself that America has been unfortunate since the war in being obliged to take over all the indifferentism and defeatism of Europe, and that it is high time we set out ourselves to supply some sensible ideas about society and life in general. Dos Passos, one of the only young American writers who has been carrying on ever since the war and who has been unaffected by the European malady that I speak of above, was saying to me the other day that he thought the indifference to politics on the part of the literary and artistic people in New York was extremely sinister, because it was merely the first step in a process which subsequently involved the discarding of almost every other sort of interest, too, so that there was nothing left except a nonsensical Algonquin joke or an arid poem. I seem to see signs of a rally against all that state of mind which has been one of the causes for the eminence of Nathan and certain other people.

As you are working constantly in the political field, you are perhaps not aware of the extent of the detachment of literature, since the war, from all sorts of public affairs and social questions, but I think that in pillorying that particular opinion of Nathan's you have said something very much to the point for literary people in general.

Yours very sincerely, Edmund Wilson

"I THOUGHT OF DAISY" AND "AXEL'S CASTLE"
1928

It must be good because Max Perkins thinks so highly of it . . .
(To Florine Katz, 1941)

To Maxwell Perkins   April 9, 1928
Charles Scribner's Sons   *The New Republic*

Dear Perkins: Here are the first pages of my novel.* I am a little reluctant
to have it printed even as a dummy in this form, because I shall have to
revise it, but I suppose it won't fall into the hands of anybody but book
dealers. As for the title, I have never yet been able to think of one that is
satisfactory. I want to have the name Daisy appear in the title, but that
won't do by itself, and I can't think of any happy phrase. I have been
hoping that the last part of the book, where I state the subject more
explicitly, might supply me with one. Do you want me then to suggest a
tentative one? When I have finished the section that I am working on,
which is the longest and most difficult, I shall be able to let you know
more definitely when I can expect to have the whole book finished.

Yours very sincerely, Edmund Wilson

I don't think that any of these   *Daisy: Five Poses*
is very much good, unless per-   *The Daisy Symphony*
haps the last which I've just   *Daisy: A Symphonic Poem*
thought of. How does it strike   *Daisy and Rita*
you?   *I Thought of Daisy*

To Maxwell Perkins   April 30, 1928
                                                         The New Republic
Dear Perkins: I have just received a radiogram from Heinemann which
says that they would like to see my novel. I am not clear as to what I

---

* *I Thought of Daisy.*

should do about this. Is the publication of a book in England ordinarily undertaken by the author or by the American publisher? What do you advise me to tell them? . . .

My own book is coming along well. I think the title I suggested is a good one—that is, when people have read the book they will find that it is appropriate, significant, etc. The only trouble about it is that it sounds a little silly and might mislead people who would buy the novel, thinking it was a piece of light fiction, and then be disappointed to have unloaded on them a lot of heavy rumination on life and literature.

Yours very sincerely, Edmund Wilson

To Maxwell Perkins   June 9, 1928
                                                           Red Bank

Dear Perkins: Thank you very much for asking me to lunch. I'm afraid, however, that I can't come, because I shall have to go back to the *New Republic* office next week, and Wednesday is precisely one of the only days which I can get entirely off and when I come down to the country here to work. I have vowed to go nowhere and do nothing till I have finished this confounded book. I have been away from *The New Republic* on a vacation for two weeks and have accomplished a good deal, but don't see how I can have the whole thing finished, including revising the whole manuscript and having it read by certain people whom I want to have see it before it is even set up, before another two months. In any case, I shall send you the part I am working on now as soon as I have finished it and have had it retyped—that is, I hope, sometime the beginning of the week after next. With the parts you have seen, it will represent about two-thirds of the whole book. I am sorry to take so long over it, but it is the sort of thing that has to come off completely or it is likely to be impossible. I mean that, from beginning to end, I have made characters, incidents, and situations subordinate to a set of ideas about life and literature, and unless the ideas are really put over, unless they are made interesting enough to compensate the reader for what he is missing in action and motion, for what he ordinarily gets in a novel, the whole performance will fail. You will see what I mean when I send you the part I have been writing . . .   Yours very sincerely, Edmund Wilson

To Maxwell Perkins   September 12, 1928
                                                           Red Bank

Dear Perkins: Here is an outline of the book I was talking to you about.*
I want to get away and go West, if possible, the first of October, so that anything I might be able to raise on it, I should be glad to get before then.

---

* *Axel's Castle.*

I am going to be in town off and on the rest of this week, and I was wondering whether Molly Colum and you and I couldn't have dinner some night—I think that any night except Thursday would be all right for me. You can reach me at *The New Republic*—if I'm not there, just leave word for me to call you.   Yours very sincerely, Edmund Wilson

To Maxwell Perkins   [undated]

Dear Perkins: Here is a description of the book of literary criticism of which I was telling you:

The book is to deal only with a certain aspect of modern literature and a certain group of writers. The first chapter will be introductory: it will deal with the French movement of Symbolism at the end of the last century. All the writers whom I propose to discuss—though it is not always recognized—arose directly out of that movement; and it is impossible to understand them without understanding the theory of Symbolism, which was fully formulated at that time and which has only since been applied on a larger scale.

My idea is that European literature has been vibrating for two or three centuries now between what we ordinarily describe as scientific ideas and what we may roughly call poetry, using *poetry* in a wide sense to cover prose as well as verse. The Romantic movement of the beginning of the nineteenth century was, among other things, a reaction against a kind of literature—such as the poetry of Pope—which had been deeply affected by the mechanistic ideas of seventeenth- and eighteenth-century physics. The Romantics succeeded in swinging literature back in the other direction, and they swung it too far. Presently, mechanistic ideas were given a new impetus from biology, evolution, etc.: the pendulum swung in the other direction and, in highly developed naturalistic artists like Flaubert and Ibsen, you got something that really corresponded to the neo-classicism of Pope. Naturalism (what we loosely call "realism") eventually became, however, what eighteenth-century neo-classicism had been, a menace to literature: by its ideal of scientific documentation, it was tending to banish the imagination. Symbolism was a second swing of the pendulum in the same direction as Romanticism: we have now arrived with this second movement just about where they were with Romanticism a hundred years ago.

In the chapters that follow, I propose to discuss six writers whom I regard as the outstanding figures, in French and English, of this movement: W. B. Yeats; Paul Valéry; T. S. Eliot; Marcel Proust; James Joyce; and Gertrude Stein. Of these, Yeats is closest to conventional literature, and Gertrude Stein furthest away. I shall devote a chapter to each of these; and those chapters will be an attempt to give complete and intelligible accounts of what those writers are all about. The kind of thing I want to do may be seen from my article on Proust in *The New Republic* (of which I enclose a copy), which will be the basis of my chapter on Proust. I want to do something, the same kind of thing—though I don't mean I can do it as well!—for those writers that Shaw did for Ibsen and Wagner in his younger days. I want to give popular accounts of them which will convince people of their importance and persuade people to read them. I shall leave further general ideas to a final chapter.

The final chapter will contain a discussion of the difference between the literary generation of before the war and the generation since the war. Yeats and Shaw, who went such different ways after coming to the modern world from Dublin, offer an excellent opportunity for contrast (there is not so much difference in their ages, but that, of course, is not the point: Yeats has had an importance and an influence since the war far beyond anything he ever had before). And Paul Valéry and Anatole France offer an even better opportunity—especially as Valéry succeeded to France's chair in the French Academy, and said some very damaging things about his predecessor in a speech which was supposed to be in praise of him.

This was really, for literature, a very dramatic and important occasion, and shows the whole situation more clearly than any other single incident has done: Valéry tells, in his address of reception, in no uncertain language, how, when he himself had first come upon the literary scene, he had belonged to the party of the Symbolists, whom France had treated with scorn; now, with his own accession to the Academy, Symbolism, he triumphantly lets us know, has won the day!

The difference between these two generations—Shaw and France on the one hand, and Yeats and Valéry on the other—is, as I have suggested, that the earlier group were deeply influenced by the materialistic and mechanistic ideas of science, and that, partly as a consequence of this, they occupied themselves with public affairs in a way that their successors scorn. The generation since the war go in for introspection: they study themselves, not other people: all the treasures, from their point of view, are to be found in solitary contemplation, not in any effort to grapple with the problems of the general life.

Now I consider three of these writers—Yeats, Proust, and Joyce—among the greatest in modern literature, and even now, not half enough appreciated. And I consider the others—even Gertrude Stein, in her early fiction —very fine. And I believe that there is a good deal of justice in their criticism of the group before them—I believe that such a reaction was inevitable. But they are themselves, it becomes more and more plain, open to serious criticism. In every one of them, the emphasis on contemplation, on the study of the individual soul—or rather, the individual mind, as in Valéry's case, the individual temperament, as in Proust's, the individual "stream of consciousness," as in Joyce—has led to a kind of resignationism in regard to the world at large, in fact, to that discouragement of the will of which Yeats is always talking (I mean that he actually advocates discouraging the will in order to cultivate the fruits of lonely meditation). The heroes of these writers never act on their fellows, their thoughts never pass into action.

This is partly, I believe, the effect of the war, either acting directly on the writers themselves or acting on the literary public who, after the war, began to interest themselves in writers who had interested them less before, but who now seemed more congenial to the post-war state of mind. This raises general political and social questions, which I propose to touch on at the end of the book. I believe that any literary movement which tends so to paralyze the will, to discourage literature from entering into action, has a very serious weakness; and I think that the time has now about come for a reaction against it. The disillusion and resignationism of contemporary European literature is principally the result of the exhaustion which has followed the war; and we in America, in taking from Europe, as we have almost always hitherto taken, our literary standards and technique, have taken also, with the most recent consignments of artistic goods from Europe, a sea of attitudes and ideas (I mean that the literary people have) which have absolutely nothing to do with the present realities of American life and which are largely inappropriate for us. I believe—or rather, I hope—that the reaction of which I speak may come first in the United States. I seem to see certain signs of it: in another generation or two, we may be leading the world intellectually. I feel that Europe is coming now to look to us for leaders while we are still respectfully accepting whatever they send us. I don't expect to wave Old Glory quite as openly as this, but I want to make this point at the end.

Edmund Wilson

To Malcolm Cowley   September 17, 1928

. . . I am about to embark on a book of modern literature, and I wanted to have a chapter on Valéry. Have you, by any chance, got a copy of the originals of those articles of his which you translated for the *Herald Tribune*? If you have, I wish you would lend them to me, as I didn't read them when they came out except in spots, and suppose I ought really to read the originals . . .

To Maxwell Perkins   October 5, 1928
Gold Coast Limited, Union Pacific System
Dear Perkins: Please forgive me for not having thanked you for the check before I left New York. I expected to come into the office to see you the

day before I left, but had so much to do between New York and Red Bank that I didn't get a chance. I wanted to start West right away, because I had to give up my New York apartment the first of October, and had engaged a place in California. I still have some more work to do on *Daisy*, but will send it to you soon. I have rewritten it so completely that I shall have to get it typed again. Parts of it, you will find, are totally different, and I hope the whole thing is much improved. I'll send you the other book in installments, as I write it, if you like, as I did with *Daisy*. You have been very kind to help me out, and I hope I haven't imposed on you. I expect to be back by Christmas, and shall hope to see you then. I hope that this letter, which is being written on a rough roadbed, isn't illegible. Yours very sincerely, Edmund Wilson

To Maxwell Perkins   November 19, 1928
                                                    Santa Barbara, Calif.

Dear Perkins: I was just going to write you when I got your letter. I have spent most of my time since I have been out here rewriting *Daisy*. There is now scarcely one word of the manuscript you saw left standing on another. When I set myself to put it in final order, I was sorry that you should have had to read what was really still a pretty rough draft, in which I had hardly done more than assemble the material and had entirely failed, it seemed to me, to hit most of the nails on the head. I have been rewriting it from beginning to end, and have still about a fifth to do. I expect to finish it during the next ten days, but after that, shall have to have it all typed and correct the new typed copy. I'll send it to you as soon as it's done, but would like to have a chance, if possible, to discuss it with you and others before it is set up. I'll be back in New York by Christmas. Could you hold it till then, or would this be too late? I'm sorry to have delayed *Daisy* so long, but have been sandwiching in work on the other book with it. The other book, being literary criticism, is easier to do and in the nature of a relief from *Daisy*, which has cost me more trouble to rewrite than it did when I wrote it the first time, and, in long stretches, gets on my nerves: you'll see, however, that it's vastly improved. I'll have a substantial section of the other book by the time I go back to New York, and should easily finish it by spring . . . I had a telegram from Scott the other day, forwarded from *The New Republic*, inviting me to visit them for the Yale game. I suppose he had simply forgotten that you had told him I was out here. He also offers to review *Daisy* very favorably in some conspicuous place! (He hasn't read it yet, of course.)

                                                    Yours as ever, Edmund Wilson

I have a little house here on the beach and have done nothing but read, write, and swim. The weather is beautiful and all the days are exactly alike. The calm Pacific spaces are excellent for work. I always feel stampeded in New York. But if you stayed out here very long, you would probably cease to write anything, because you would cease to think—it isn't necessary out here and the natives regard it as morbid.

To JOHN PEALE BISHOP   October 17, 1928
                                                              Santa Barbara

Dear John: Léonie Adams has won one of the Guggenheim fellowships and is now in Europe.* I do wish, if it's possible for you, you'd look her up when she is in Paris. I have seen a good deal of her in the last winter and have found her by far one of the most interesting girls in New York. She is a little shy at first, but extremely intelligent and amusing when you get to know her. She is not at all good at pushing herself and making herself known in literary circles, so I have been particularly anxious to have people look her up abroad. She is going from London to Paris, she writes me, about the first of November.

I have come out here to the great Pacific spaces on a vacation from New York, which I am getting so that I can't stand. I've got a little house on the beach and do nothing much but swim, read, and write—it's rather like the Riviera. I'm rewriting my novel, which I hope to have out by February. They tell me that you have written a story which is more or less of a masterpiece, but of difficult length. If I were you, if other resources fail, I'd send it to *The American Caravan*, which pays pretty well, you know. What else are you up to? And how about coming back sometime soon to the old city that has no heart? I've got to go back myself the first of January. I had an awfully good time with Phelps Putnam just before I came out here—he has come to live in New York and has just written a wonderful poem. And I have been thinking often, since I saw him (he is just on from Boston and hasn't been Manhattanized yet), of the days when you used to live in Townsend Martin's apartment. It seems ridiculous, when one remembers all the really first-rate ability which is isolated and chilled in New York, that some more profitable kind of intercourse couldn't be cultivated. For my own part, I have uprooted myself from the Village and am going to attempt, when I go back, to live under more human conditions. I have various projects, but won't rehearse them here. Do let me hear from you (better address care of *New Republic*); the only news I have had of you lately has been by way of Howard Cox.

I hope that your family are all well. Give my best to Margaret. Do look up Léonie, if you can. Her address is the Guaranty Trust Co.

As ever, Bunny Wilson

Have you seen Edna's new book†—I think the best things in it are

---

* Léonie Adams's first book of poems, *Those Not Elect*, had been published in 1925.
† *The Buck in the Snow.*

wonderful. Her muse came to lately with a bang and she has already written almost enough for another book.

By the way, Allen Tate got another of the Guggenheim fellowships and will soon be in Paris, too. I forget whether you have ever met him, but I saw him just before I left New York and he expressed a desire to see you. I can't remember whether I gave him your address—though I think I did—but his is the American Express. He has become a great friend of mine, and is a fellow countryman of yours. He has just published an unreconstructed biography of Stonewall Jackson.

To John Peale Bishop   October 22, 1928
                                                              Santa Barbara

Dear John: I got your letter just after I had already written you at some length in a letter I sent Léonie Adams, who is now abroad, to present her to you. I was delighted to hear from you—it is good news that you've undertaken the book about the South. I grow more interested myself in American affairs every year, and have come to the conclusion that the United States is probably now the most interesting part of the Western world—could hold forth on the subject at length, but shan't attempt it in a letter. I hope to say something about it in a book which I am to start on when I have finished with this novel. A book on the Sacco–Vanzetti affair would have furnished an excellent opportunity. I shall probably never undertake it—not, as you suggest, because I might be better employed—but because I had no first-hand knowledge of or participation in it while it was going on, and also because I am so lazy about matters demanding research. I can see by the way you write about it that you were too far away at the time to appreciate properly either its importance or its interest. It revealed the whole anatomy of American life, with all its classes, professions, and points of view, and all their relations, and it raised almost every fundamental question of our political and social system. It did this, furthermore, in an unexpectedly dramatic fashion. As Dos Passos said, it was, during the last days before the executions, as if, by some fairy-tale spell, all the different kinds of Americans, eminent and obscure, had suddenly, in a short sudden burst of intensified life, been compelled to reveal their true characters in a heightened exaggerated form. Edna has a set of poems* in her new book about it, by the way—she went on to Boston and demonstrated, you know.

I'm sorry to hear that you've been feeling depressed, but I don't wonder that you are. What on earth you want to live in France for, I can't imagine. I should think, if it's a question of living cheaply in the country, that you could do equally well over here. I have, however, little appetite for Europe

---

* "Justice Denied in Massachusetts."

154

now myself, but enjoy extremely traveling in America—and even the scenery and the life of the part of New Jersey that I come from, which used once to bore me to desperation, seem now of absorbing interest to me. At one time in my life, I shouldn't have been even able to imagine this— and, of course, there is no reason for assuming that what is true of oneself today will indefinitely remain so. But I have been moved to these reflections by your saying that you find your own mind, in Europe, is beginning to turn to America . . .   As ever, EW

To Elinor Wylie   November 19, 1928
                                                                  Santa Barbara

Dear Elinor: I was so terribly sorry to hear about your accident and so glad to get a letter from you today. I had never seen the newspaper story, however, and first heard about it from Dorothy Parker, who gave me a less sensational and more nearly correct account of it—she had seen someone who had seen you. I was reassured by Bill's statement in *The Saturday Review*, but have been horribly distressed to think about you. I have thought about you often out here, and wondered whether you had come back yet.

I have been out here since the first of October and am going to stay until just before Christmas—shall be back in New York by Christmas. I have taken a little cottage on the beach and have been rewriting my novel, which is to come out in the spring. I am also preparing to expose myself to the poets whom I have so long been harassing, by publishing a book of poems. And I am also working on a book on modern literature. I have done nothing out here but read, write, and swim. The weather is beautiful and the scenery is beautiful, and all the days are exactly alike—and I expect that by the time I go back I'll be eager for a spell of good old-fashioned grippy New York weather. Though, if I didn't have to go back to do my six months on *The New Republic*, beginning the first of January, I'd probably have Rosalind come out and stay on all winter—it's so much easier to work among the great Pacific spaces. This is an exceptionally dull letter, I see—but that is how California affects you. It's easy to work, but if you stayed out here long enough, you'd probably cease to think, as most of the inhabitants have. So I look forward with eagerness, and even with avidity, to seeing you in December. I'm awfully anxious to read your poems. I haven't seen any of them in *The New Republic* yet. Let's inaugurate the New Year by a spirited dinner together sometime as soon as possible after we both get back.*   Yours as ever—that is, with all affection and admiration, as always for the last seven years, Bunny

---

* Elinor Wylie died on December 16, 1928.

ELINOR WYLIE

To William Rose Benét   December 21, 1928
                                              Sunset Limited

Dear Bill: I heard about Elinor just before I left California. Mary telegraphed me and has asked me to write you for her, as well as for me. It is
hard for me to write or even to think about it now, and I know that you
will not want to hear much—but I wanted you to know of the sympathy
and distress I feel for you when I realize what a hole has been made in
my own life. My only consolation is remembering that the last letter I
received from Elinor—written from England, after her accident—was the
happiest I had ever had from her. She told me that she had never enjoyed
life more and that she had never taken more satisfaction in her poetry.
She said that she was coming back in December, and I realized out there
in California that seeing you and her again was one of the few things which
could make me glad to get back to New York. But it's better to be cut off
at the height of life with the head and heart full than to die as most
people die. In Elinor's case, it leaves the impression undimmed of her
almost supernatural brilliance and energy—it is like the sudden extinction
of a sun, which has never been seen to cool—and there is something almost
supernatural, too, about such a death, because it is not accompanied by
any sign of weakness or decay. Please forgive the illegibility of this letter,
which is written on a jolting train—and forgive my clumsy expression of
my sympathy in a loss of which it will never be easy for me to write and
of which it is peculiarly difficult just now, when my mind refuses to
accept it and I have several times found myself thinking of her, as if I
should see her when I got back. Such reality as this, such reality as Elinor
had, is given to few human beings, and death has no power over it, for
it endures in her and our minds, continuing to give us life, as few of the
living do. You are fortunate in this, that you had more of it than anyone
else. I sometimes envied you when Elinor was alive, and in spite of the
grief you must now be in and the bleakness you must be feeling, I do
so even now.   Yours always, Bunny Wilson

To ALLEN TATE
Paris, France

January 10, 1929
The New Republic

Dear Allen: I read your article in *The Bookman* last night, and, though I may be affected by your complimentary reference to me, I thought that it was as good as the Emily Dickinson; that is to say, one of your very best.* I got back to the East Christmas and am back at *The New Republic* again. I am sending you John Gould Fletcher's *John Smith* and also a book on Andrew Jackson which has just come out. As they have got to go back and forth across the sea, I hope that you will do them as promptly as possible.

Perhaps you have heard that Croly had a bad paralytic stroke. He is pretty well incapacitated—for the present anyway. This and Elinor Wylie's death and other things make me feel as if I had been away from New York for a thousand years.

I was glad to leave California because there is a sort of insipidity about everything there, in spite of the superficial brilliance—that is, the brightness and coloring of both man and nature—which ends by taking the savor out of life. I came back by way of New Orleans and spent an evening there which in some ways was worth the whole of Los Angeles. On the train as I was coming into Louisiana the dismal sticks of the Southern swamps tattered with Florida moss, so melancholy and themselves so monotonous, seemed to me a cheering sight after the sunshine of California. I am not joking. My heart was actually cheered by the Louisiana landscapes again. I believe that the point is that a very bright dry air in which everything is seen too clearly rather discourages the spirit, whereas mists and clouded skies have the effect of nourishing it. I could go on like this for hours, but will hold the rest of my traveler's observations until I see you again.

---

* "Edmund Wilson has written some of the most accomplished poetry of our time . . ."

—Allen Tate, "American Poetry Since 1920," *The Bookman*, January 1929

You are right about the Dostoevsky that you read in *The New Republic*. It is a dramatic monologue from my novel and is explained by the situation of the character who is supposed to be having those ideas. It is counterbalanced and counteracted by other parts of the book. It is much better in the book. What you read in *The New Republic* was merely pieced together to make an article. I finally got my novel off to the publishers last Monday, and I have gotten started on a book of literary criticism. I have been working also on my poems and, encouraged by your appreciation, I hope to get them together in a volume soon.

I shall try to send you some books that I think will interest you. Hergesheimer is bringing out a novel on the Civil War this spring which has the lovely title *Swords and Roses* . . . Lovett tells me that the number of books published this fall and winter was so tremendous that the market was finally oversupplied, with the result that the publishers lost money and are now frightened, so that they are announcing very few books for this spring. There is certainly very little coming into the office just now. The same thing has happened in the theater.

I just received a letter from Léonie this morning. I am glad that you have all been together and sometimes long to be with you.

Yours as ever, Edmund

To MAXWELL PERKINS   February 15, 1929
                          The Clifton Springs Sanitarium and Clinic
                                                  Clifton Springs, N.Y.
Dear Perkins: I am so terribly sorry to have delayed so long in sending you the manuscript,* but one of the people I sent it to was ill and kept it for weeks, and in the meantime I had a sort of nervous breakdown myself. Is it too late now to bring it out this spring? I hope not. I'll try to get it to you within a week. I am going to make a few last changes on it up here. Won't you drop me a line at this address? I hope my delay hasn't put you out, but it was unavoidable.   As ever, Edmund Wilson

To CHRISTIAN GAUSS   February 16, 1929
                                                       Clifton Springs
Dear Mr. Gauss: I came back from California in excellent form but, soon after arriving in New York, passed into a nervous decline and have been sent to this sanatorium—not, I hope, for long.

I'll be glad to judge the essay contest. Perhaps I can come down to Princeton for the purpose.

I have finished my novel and have been working on a book on modern literature, which I want, with your permission, to dedicate to you.†

---

* *I Thought of Daisy.*
† *Axel's Castle.*

Please forgive this meager letter, which I am writing in bed. I hope to have a chance soon to talk to you at length. Give my love to all the family.   As ever, Bunny Wilson

To Seward Collins   February 18, 1929
The Bookman   Clifton Springs

Dear Seward: Will you please be sure to send me proof on that poem of mine you have. I am rewriting it and improving it. Am enjoying a brief nervous breakdown up here, but expect to be back before long.

                                                   As ever, Bunny Wilson

To Maxwell Perkins   [undated]
                                                     Clifton Springs
Dear Perkins: Here it is at last. I wish you would have them send me two proofs. Call up *The New Republic*, when the proof is ready, and they will tell you where I am. I'm sorry to have had to delay it so long. Thank you for your letter, and for your sympathy and kindness through the whole affair.   As ever, Edmund Wilson

To Maxwell Perkins   February 23, 1929
                                                     Clifton Springs
Dear Perkins: I have been occupying myself up here getting my poetical works into shape,* and am going to have them typed next week. I should like to submit them to Scribner's, though I should like, if possible, to get them published this spring and off my hands, and I suppose you will hardly be wanting to bring out another book by me so soon . . . I hope to be out of this lazar-house by the middle of next week, and will show the manuscript to you then, if you want to see it. In the meantime, however, I wish you would drop me a line and let me know whether publishing them this spring would be out of the question, anyway.

I'll correct the proofs on *Daisy* as soon as you can send them to me . . .
                                                   As ever, Edmund Wilson

To Maxwell Perkins   March 4, 1929
                                                     Clifton Springs
Dear Perkins: Here are the poems, such as they are. Don't hesitate to tell me, if you think that there is too little to them, or that some of them are objectionable from the publisher's point of view. At one time, I had the idea that the little play of which I gave you the manuscript sometime ago—*Osbert's Career, or the Poet's Progress*—might be combined in a

---

* *Poets, Farewell!*

volume with them, but I suppose this would make the book too mixed, wouldn't it?

I'm leaving here Wednesday night and will be back in New York Thursday. I'll be staying at my wife's apartment, 14 East Ninth Street (c/o Miss Mary Blair). I forgot about the contract for *Daisy* and left it at the *New Republic* office, but will attend to it when I get back.

I have fixed up the first chapter of my book of literary criticism as an article for the spring literary number of *The New Republic*. I'll have them send you a copy. I'm afraid it is rather dull, but that is partly because I had to cover so much literary history in a short space.

As ever, Edmund Wilson

What do you think of the taste of the last line of the poem called "Americanization"? I think it would probably be better to leave it off.

To Gilbert Seldes   March 6, 1929
Clifton Springs

Dear Gilbert: You were kind beyond words to write me. I have been a sorry case, and your letters cheered me up. I've been in this godforsaken sanatorium for three weeks, but am going back to New York tonight. I'd love to come to Bermuda, and will write you about it later. If I'm well enough, I ought to stay in New York and work on the N.R., and in any case I'll have to be there to correct proof on my book. Yes, some of those things in *The New Republic* were adapted from the book—and there is another long one coming—but don't bother with it in its *New Republic* form, if in any form.*

I did finally get the copy of your own book, and am ashamed never yet to have thanked you for it. I haven't read it, because I have been confining my reading pretty rigorously to the field of a book of literary criticism which I am writing and of which the first chapter—fairly dull, I fear—will burst upon you in the spring literary number. I put it aside, with other books on American subjects, which I hope to attack presently.

Give my best love to Alice, and thanks again for your invitation. More on the subject anon.   As ever, Edmund Wilson

By the way, did you get the Henry James book all right? I take it you did. I was sorry to return it in that unceremonious fashion, but was terribly rushed when I was trying to get off to California and didn't have any place to put all my stuff.

Your *Jimmy Durante* was excellent on a difficult subject, where many have failed—one of your best in this kind.

---

* *I Thought of Daisy.*

The New
REPUBLIC
421 West 21st Street
NewYork City

1929

To Allen Tate   March 21, 1929
*The New Republic**

Dear Allen: Thank you very much for the Malcolm Cowley review, which gives an excellent account of him. I have seen him several times lately and have been through the manuscript myself. It is certainly a very sound and distinguished piece of work.† The book is not coming out until June or July, and the review will be run then.

I had a sort of nervous breakdown about a month ago and was in a sanatorium, but am back now and well again. While I was away, I got my poetical works in order. I sent a copy of the manuscript to Léonie Adams, and should be glad to have you see it. I followed a piece of advice she gave me about the poem called "American Masterpieces," and have considerably improved it thereby, I think. I am going to add a few more poems so that the manuscript will not be quite so slight as it appears.

I saw Phelps Putnam last night, and he showed me a note from you in which you propose a religion of confusion, in which I shall play the part of St. Augustine. It is true that I have recently contemplated a crusade against certain formidable heresies. Unfortunately, I collapsed and sank like a stone just on the point of delivering my message, but I still hope to get it out. I am sending you some copies of articles which I wrote after I got back from California and which were intended to contribute to the setting forth of a point of view. Not that they are particularly well written.

---

* The letters in this section were written from *The New Republic*.
† *Blue Juniata* by Malcolm Cowley.

Next week I am going to return to it unless the gods have any more practical jokes in store for me. As ever, Edmund Wilson

To R. P. BLACKMUR   April 15, 1929
The Hound and Horn
Dear Mr. Blackmur: Thank you very much for asking me to contribute to *The Hound and Horn*. I do know the magazine, and have read it with great interest, and I am sorry that I have so much to do just now that I cannot undertake the article you suggest, or in fact, anything outside of my regular *New Republic* work.

A subject which seems to me as interesting, by the way, as the one you propose is the contribution to French Symbolism of the two American poets Francis Vielé-Griffin and Stuart Merrill, who lived in France and wrote French. For some reason this subject seems to have been entirely neglected by American criticism, and yet an American critic would be the only kind of critic who could deal with it adequately. The opinions of the French on Vielé-Griffin and his work, which had quite an important influence, are especially curious and interesting. The subject really ought to be dealt with in connection with American literature as well as in connection with French.   Yours sincerely, Edmund Wilson

To ALLEN TATE   April 17, 1929

Dear Allen: I am sending you Hergesheimer's book of historical sketches of the old South. I hope you can do it—if possible soon. If you can't, let me know right away.

I lost the threads of my correspondence during my illness, and have never yet written you about your poem, which I think is excellent and as good as the best things of the kind in your book. But I think that your instinct is probably right when, as you say, you feel that you ought to be doing something of a different kind—not that I mean that this poem is one too many of this kind, but,—it is simply what you say yourself which has made me think of this—that I feel that you may be counted on, and that you count upon yourself, not to do too many of anything. There is a kind of poet who does the kind of thing he is sure of being able to do so many times that it finally fails to attract interest and, in fact, actually loses its value—Verlaine, for example.

As for what you say about the American situation, it makes me think that I have, perhaps, seemed to exaggerate the difference between Europe and America or, rather, the importance which I put upon it. The prime thing to remember from my point of view is that all humanity is in the same boat and that all these problems ought to be thought out without too much regard for local habits and traditions. I believe that, as a Southerner, you exaggerate to some extent the importance of certain aspects of the American past. The United States carried over, especially in the South, an unbroken European tradition, but at the same time they made a new departure. I have kidded the Southern point of view a little in my review of Eliot. I don't accuse you of indulging, yourself, in any such fantasy as I have described there, but I think that most intelligent Southerners at least tend to do so. Everybody nowadays tends to do something of the kind, but I believe we probably ought to try not to depend upon these fantasies too much. But I must pull myself up. I will send you some more of my writings on the subject, though don't bother to read them if you are better employed.

Léonie got the flu when she first came back, and was quite ill, but she is all right now and has gone down into the country to see her family. She says that she is going back to Paris.　　　　Yours as ever, Edmund

To Allen Tate　　　　　　　　　　　　　　　　　　May 20, 1929

Dear Allen: I was awfully sorry to hear that you had been sick, and I hope you are well now. Checks for both of your reviews have been put through. The Hergesheimer one is first-rate, I think.

As for the American problem, "American consciousness" is a phrase which you seem to have invented yourself, and doesn't quite express what I mean. Of course everybody, as you say, has to have something to lean on outside himself, but my point about the "fantasies" I was discussing was that they had been allowed to become a means of getting away from the probabilities of the future. I always distrust the *laudator temporis acti* when he seems to have no hope or faith in the future, and the American social revolutionaries who look forward to a clean sweep of American bourgeois civilization seem to me in the same class as the peoples whose eyes are turned toward the past, because they are looking forward to something which seems to be extremely unlikely, if not impossible. I think it is true, as you say, that the only thing possible in the present situation is for the individual to save his own integrity. As a matter of fact, this has always been true in America—in the North, at least—but I begin to wonder whether the time hasn't arrived for the intellectuals, etc., to identify themselves a little more with the general life of the country. This is pretty difficult, God knows, and it may be that the United States will develop into a great imperialistic power with all its artists, critics, and philosophers as ineffective and as easily extinguished as the German ones were in 1914. But this is a gloomy vision, and I do not want to see it become actual. The people with social-revolutionary leanings like Dos Passos and Rob Wolf* talk as if they did. I did not think that you, on the basis of your

* Robert Wolf was a contributing editor to *The New Masses*.

writings, could be convicted of the kind of point of view in respect to the old South which I was talking about in the Eliot article. Otherwise I should have named you. But I have met a number of Southerners, even among the ablest, who have seemed to me to have their eyes turned backward in this way, and I am sure you must have had such moods and moments yourself, though you are now distinguished from many of your fellow Southerners and from most Americans of all kinds by your curiosity about and interest in the whole country and in the world in general. I have leaned heavily on backward-looking fantasies myself in my time, and will sometime describe them to you. Naturally we fortify our own souls by looking backward, but it is surely mistaken to talk as some people do, as if the future were to contain the realization of some ideal conditions of the past, or as if the future could never, under any circumstances, come up to the past.

I saw Raymond [Holden] and Louise [Bogan] the other night for the first time since last summer. Raymond has had an appendicitis and has been quite sick. Louise has been working on her book of poems, which is coming out in the fall. She looks fine and is all full of Thoreau. I had a party last Saturday night to which they came along with the Humphrieses and some other people. About midnight the guests began very slowly breaking phonograph records over each other's heads. It was like a slowed-up moving picture. I don't know what the significance of this is.

Yours as ever, Edmund

To John Peale Bishop   August 7, 1929

Dear John: I'm sorry to have delayed so long in answering your letter, but it hasn't been on account of indifference, as I have been occupying myself precisely with you in a poem I have been writing for my book of verse. It is the last poem in the book, and constitutes at once a salutation, a reproach, and an exhortation. I was going to send it to you, but think now that it will be better to send you proofs of the whole book, as that poem is related to a series. I wish you'd read the whole thing and send me any suggestions that occur to you, if possible soon enough so that I can have the benefit of them before I have to send back the proofs. Would that I had had your advice in composing them! The proofs will be ready in two or three weeks. I've sent you a copy of my novel, such as it is. I'm working now on a book of criticism and, after that, am going to get together a book of short stories. I'm trying to cash in on my miscellaneous literary material of the last ten years. The truth is that during those years there has been comparatively little I have written that has really been brought properly to completion, and a couple of years ago I set to work on my articles, verses, short stories, sketches, notebooks, etc., to try to get something more solid out of them. I am pretty stale on a good deal of it, but wanted to get it into decent shape and get it off my hands, along with all the interest, ideas, and emotions mixed up with it. I speak of this because I have a feeling that you ought to do the same thing— you have been producing all kinds of material now over as long a period as I, and I believe now that the principal reason why you haven't so far got it into more satisfactory shape is that you haven't been over here to be encouraged and spurred on by association with your fellow writers and —what is perhaps most important of all—to market your own productions. You would probably have sold your novel long ago, if you had been here on the spot to discuss it with publishers and friends. And you should certainly be able to do something with your Southern stories—the one that you sent Scribner's made a great impression on Max Perkins and the others. Furthermore, you should certainly get out a book of poems—I ran into an old copy of *The Measure* the other day with your "Speaking of Poetry" in it and it seemed to me perfectly incredible that you should have vanished from the poetic scene while Archie MacLeish flourished like a green bay tree! If you could come over for six months, I'm sure you'd be able to accomplish a great deal more than you can do in your present situation in France. You could certainly do some article writing— Mary tells me you are doing articles for the *Ladies' Home Journal*—and you could probably make some connections with a publisher, perhaps even get an advance which would enable you to sit down and write. You certainly wouldn't have all the comforts of your present home, but you would probably have more satisfaction of the mind and imagination. If you want a place to stay in New York, I may be able to put you up—I don't know now precisely how I am going to be living. Please forgive all this good advice if it has no real application, but from what Margaret told me and from your last letter, I thought you were in some perplexity, and wanted to give you the benefits of such lights as I could supply. I have an idea that, aside from the practical uses of being over here, you probably ought to get away from your family for a while—they could surely spare you for a few months. I believe that almost all writers require intervals of complete detachment from responsibility and family relations— I certainly do, at any rate, and find sometimes that my mind begins to function twice as vividly and energetically when I have detached myself from some familiar situation which has been growing up around me and into which I have been growing.

I have just come back from my vacation—have been visiting Raymond Holden and Louise Bogan in the country, and have been up on Cape Cod with Rosalind. I'm going up to see the Cummingses in New Hampshire this weekend, and hope to hear news of you. I saw Edna the other day—she is writing a sequence of thirty sonnets called *Epitaph for the Race of Man*, which seemed to me, perhaps, from what I saw of them, in some ways to surpass anything she had yet done. Dos Passos has broken with the social-revolutionary New Playwrights group, which I think is an excellent thing; they apparently kept trying to high-hat him by giving him to understand that *Airways* was insufficiently social-revolutionary, while he on his part had certainly made a supreme effort to be as social-revolutionary as possible!—and he is now working on a gigantic novel, dealing with the Americanization of the Western world and to appear in three parts, laid respectively in Mexico City, Paris, and New York.* *The Dial* and *The Little Review* have gone out of existence, as I suppose you know. I felt rather sad at their passing—it reminded me of the first more or less exciting days in New York after the war.

As for my going to Europe, I'd like to, but can't. I have often longed for Paris lately, but don't see any prospect of getting away for some time—the principal reason is that I can't afford to. I do cherish dreams, however, of getting off for a month or two next spring. Give my best to Margaret —I enjoyed seeing her very much in New York. And let me hear from you again soon—what have you done with your musical comedy? I'd like to see it.   As ever, Edmund

To Allen Tate   August 13, 1929

Dear Allen: I was terribly sorry to hear about your mother's death. I should think it would be particularly shocking and distressing to have one's family die when one was away . . .

As for my review of Lippmann, what on earth have I done to earn this terrific rebuke for falling for the false pretenses of science? I have known all that for years and frequently expressed the same opinions. Science is, of course, only one of the modes of human thought, and has the same sort of weaknesses—as well as the same sort of triumphs—as all the others. I certainly cherish no nineteenth-century ideas about the "truth" of science as opposed to the "truth" of metaphysics, art, etc. It is simply that I believe that religion—that is, in the sense of a church—has become impossible. When Lippmann was talking about the "mature man," by the way, he was not talking about throwing off the beliefs of adolescence, as you say, but of something quite different. As a matter of fact, your idea of maturity, as you state it in your letter, seems about to coincide with his.

I am working now on a book on certain aspects of modern literature—the growth of Symbolism and its flowering in Yeats, Valéry, Eliot, Proust, and Gertrude Stein—and I am not going to write on any other subject for *The New Republic* until I have finished it. In my recent articles I have raised more issues than I am capable of dealing with—now at any

---

* *U.S.A.*

rate—and I am going to clear up that particular corner before proceeding further.

I have just been up to see Cummings and his wife in New Hampshire. He has been sober for weeks, and I found him more interesting and satisfactory to talk to than I ever had before. He certainly has the most extraordinary point of view. It is 100 percent romantic. The individual is the only thing that matters, and only the gifted individual—in fact, only the poet and artist. The rest of the world is of no importance and has to take the consequences. He keeps protesting his lack of interest in anything outside the world of his own sensations and emotions, but at the same time he has a much keener sense than most people of what is going on in the world and is at bottom apparently perpetually worried by his relation to it. I don't know whether the type of pure romantic can survive much longer, though perhaps I think this merely because the romantic in myself has recently been giving up the ghost.   Yours as ever, Edmund

He never gets full credit now for all he did in the twenties and before. In his best days, he was worth a dozen of the so-called New Critics.
                                                            (To Hazel Rascoe, 1957)

To Burton Rascoe   September 6, 1929

Dear Burton: I am terribly sorry to hear that you have been so sick, and hope you will soon be all right. For heaven's sake don't worry about that review.   As ever, Bunny Wilson

Here is a literary anecdote to divert your bed of illness. It seems that Hemingway's novel, in its serial form, had to be expurgated for the readers of *Scribner's Magazine*. And when Maxwell Perkins came to go through the manuscript, he found three words which he was doubtful about printing even in the book. The words were *balls*, *shit*, and *cocksucker*. So he had a solemn conference on the subject with old Mr. Charles Scribner. The first two words were discussed, and it was decided to suppress them, but when Perkins came to the third—which he thought Mr. Scribner had probably never heard—he couldn't get it out, and wrote it down on a piece of paper. Old Mr. Scribner put on his pince-nez and considered it with serious attention—then said, "Perkins, do you think that Hemingway would respect you, if he knew that you were unable to say that word, but had to write it out?" Perkins was so flustered by the incident that he forgot and left the memorandum pad with *cocksucker* on it on a bracket in his office, where it was just on the level of the eyes of anybody who came in. He didn't discover it until just before he left in the afternoon—

by which time it had thrown the whole Scribner's office into a state of acute embarrassment, deep mental and moral distress, and troubling mystification.

To Burton Rascoe   September 23, 1929

Dear Burton: I don't know why you were visited by all those misgivings about your article. I don't think it sounds in the least unamiable, and it is the only real overhauling which [George] Nathan has had. I think that his insolence has intimidated people, so that they have been afraid to point out how badly he writes and thinks a good deal of the time. Either that, or we are all so used to reading him that as soon as we take up something he has written, we pass into a state of mind where we are unconscious of defects which we should never forgive another writer. What happens when you begin to take him apart—that is, in his *Monks Are Monks* vein—is terrible. Also, your review is extremely funny. Thank you very much.

As ever, Bunny

To Burton Rascoe   September 30, 1929

Dear Burton: It is my earnest intention this season to try to make the literary part of *The New Republic* more interesting. Would there be any chance of getting you to do long reviews for us fairly regularly? We are supposed to have a rule that we cannot print reviews by writers who are reviewing the same book elsewhere—so that we ought to have books which you are not discussing in *Arts and Decorations* or *Plain Talk*. But mightn't there be a good many subjects that would interest you outside the books that you deal with in these regular departments? In the case of a book or an author, for example, that you might want to write something *un peu approfondi* about, aside from the obvious immediate interest of the book? You know as much about what is coming out as I do, so I won't suggest anything in particular. How about that series in which Rosenfeld's book occurs? Would you care to do it as a whole? Perhaps it is not a very promising subject. Of course, we can't pay you anything like your regular prices, but I am anxious to get reviews written by writers rather than the kind of thing that we have all too often been filling up with, and hoped you might do us something occasionally, if not regularly.

I hope you are well again by this time. By the way, Tom Matthews and I spent half an hour's serious thought in a search for injurious adjectives to enrich that paragraph in your Nathan review. I hope that we haven't made you say anything that you would not be willing to have said.

Yours as ever, EW

To Burton Rascoe   October 23, 1929

. . . In the meantime, what about the new Oxford dictionary? I understand that it is full of Americanisms, and I think the subject certainly ought to be written about . . .

To R. P. Blackmur   November 14, 1929

Dear Mr. Blackmur: Thank you for fixing up the review, which is now much clearer. As for your reviewing the same book elsewhere, that is all right so far as we are concerned, as long as our review appears first. We have a rule that we must not print reviews by writers who have already reviewed the same books elsewhere. I'll arrange to have your review of Dobrée appear as soon as possible, and I hope you won't let the *Herald Tribune* publish your second review until ours has come out. I am sending you the Huxley book.

I should like to make a suggestion to you about book reviewing generally. Don't suppose that I mean you to take it seriously if it runs contrary to your principles and tastes, because it is really impossible for one writer to tell another writer how to do anything. The only thing that he can tell him is how he would do it himself. But it seems to me that the kind of philosophic criticism now in vogue has certain weaknesses which appear especially when the critic is discussing a particular writer or a particular book. There is a tendency nowadays to discuss literature entirely in abstract terms, either philosophic or psychological or, as in the case of Herbert Read, in terms of a sort of literary scholasticism which limits itself to putting things into categories. It is true, of course, that when people write psychology or metaphysics they are not concerned with producing portraits of particular human beings but with discussing general principles; and there is a philosophy and psychology of books from the point of view of which it is possible and proper to treat them in the same way. At the same time, I feel that modern literary criticism is rather suffering from the predominance of this kind of thing, and that it may be particularly unfortunate in book reviewing. The reader more or less expects the book reviewer to tell him what the book is like—that is to say, how it is written, what sort of temperament the author has, and what sort of effects he produces. There has lately been such a reaction against the impressionistic criticism of the day before yesterday that there is a tendency entirely to eliminate any intimation of what the work under consideration looks, sounds, feels, or smells like. I think that the example of Eliot has been partly the cause of this, but it has been his disciples, and not himself, who have carried this tendency to extremes. You will observe that Eliot, though his style is so precise and dry, does, nonetheless, as a rule, convey vividly the special quality of genius of the author he is writing about. He may not take more than a phrase or two to do this, but he does it with marvelous accuracy, and when he does it, he is, in his laconic way, being as impressionistic as Arthur Symons in his effusive one—as, for example, when Eliot speaks of the "mossiness" of Mallarmé or the "terrible clairvoyance" of Shakespeare. I don't mean, of course, that the literary critic ought to slight his subject's general ideas: on the contrary, the trouble with most of our American literary journalism is precisely that the literary critic usually doesn't make any effort to understand the writer's point of view. But I do think that in ordinary reviewing, the two things ought to be better balanced than they usually are.

I have written you at such length on the subject because I have thought that *The Hound and Horn* was a good deal infected by the tendency to be too abstract. And I hope that, in reviewing for us, you would tell a little more about the author's style, about his "atmosphere" and personality, than the critics on *The Hound and Horn, The Criterion*, and other magazines of the kind, often do. I am going to send these suggestions to several others of our reviewers as well. I hope you will forgive me for holding forth to you at such great length, but I know that you are a poet as well as a critic, and I should be glad to see the poet's sensibility as well as the critic's intellect manifest itself in your reviews.

Yours sincerely, Edmund Wilson

To R. P. BLACKMUR   December 9, 1929

Dear Mr. Blackmur: I am sorry not to have written you before, but I have been so busy with a new literary supplement that I have had to neglect other things.

I like your review on Aldous Huxley very much, and I entirely agree with you about him. He seems to me to be probably the most overrated modern writer. He is not an artist and he is not particularly intelligent.

At the end of your second paragraph you say, "to air himself of what comes most persistently to his mind," when I think you ought to say, "air his views upon," etc. Why not drop the whole of that last sentence out, anyway? Would you mind? I don't know that your analogy with the man who talks about the stock market is quite happy, because, after all, what one objects to is not that Huxley talks about some subject with which he is preoccupied, but that he talks badly about it.

I had Aiken's poems sent to you some days ago. I think that the review ought to be about a page—that is, about twelve hundred words—or it could run a little over that if you have more to say.

Yours sincerely, Edmund Wilson

To R. P. BLACKMUR   December 13, 1929

. . . I am sure there is a great deal to be said about Aiken's poetry which
has never been said. I was interested in what you told me in your letter
about the "Electra" poem . . .

To R. P. BLACKMUR   December 23, 1929

Dear Mr. Blackmur: Thank you very much for the Aiken review, which
is the most *approfondi* that I have seen. I think I can run it without cuts.
I have made one or two small changes where I thought you had expressed
yourself a little awkwardly. The phrases I have substituted, however, are
pretty banal, so I hope you will change them to something better, if you
object to them.
      All the compliments of the season. I applaud your supporting [D. H.]
Lawrence, but fear that in Boston it will be vain.
                                    Yours very sincerely, Edmund Wilson
      On your first page, you say that Dante, Swinburne, and Shelley are all
alike, in the same way that Aiken is. I think that this is true of Swinburne
and Shelley, but not of Dante. Did you read him in translation? A translation might make him sound all alike, but really it seems to me that he has
tremendous variety—for one thing, all the people speak in character and
more or less differently in the *Divine Comedy*—perhaps you were thinking
of the *Vita Nuova*.

To LOUIS ZUKOFSKY   December 11, 1929

Dear Mr. Zukofsky: Thank you very much for letting us see this essay
on Pound. I have read it with interest, but I think it is a little too
specialized, a little too technical, for us. It is the sort of thing which really
ought to appear in some poets' magazine.
      I do not think I have ever seen anything else which went so deeply
into Pound's method, but in general, in *The New Republic*, when we
want to discuss questions of literary method we have to combine with
them other sources of interest, in order to make them go down with the
ordinary reader!   Yours sincerely, Edmund Wilson

"I Thought of Daisy"

To HAMILTON BASSO   May 9, 1929

Dear Ham: I was just thinking about you, and was glad to get your
letter. I have just called up the Guggenheim Foundation and learned

that the applications are to be available sometime this month—I told them to send one to you. If you win it, you get the money in March of next year.

I'm glad to hear that your book is in type. I took so long over the proof of my own that it's too late to bring it out this spring and it will have to be held over till fall. I've got a book of poems, if you'd call them poems, coming out then, too.

I wish I could go to New Orleans, but I've been out of the office a month, and have got to stay on the job for a while. Paul Rosenfeld told me about Sherwood, but not much—I didn't see him when he was in New York.

I'm delighted to hear about your getting married, should like to see your fiancée, as I have the greatest confidence in your taste.

Don't buy my novel, I'll send you a copy. I was rereading *The Great Gatsby* last night, after I had been going through my page proofs, and thinking with depression how much better Scott Fitzgerald's prose and dramatic sense were than mine. If I'd only been able to give my book the vividness and excitement, and the technical accuracy, of his! Have you ever read *Gatsby*? I think it's one of the best novels that any American of his age has done. Of course, he'd had to pass through several immature and amateurish phases before he arrived at that one, and writing, like everything else, is partly a matter of expertness—so I'm glad to hear you're launched on a second novel—good luck to you! Keep at it, in spite of hell!   As ever, EW

To Christian Gauss   August 13, 1929

. . . Thank you very much for writing me about *Daisy*, and for the kind things you say. I am glad you liked the part about New York Harbor, which I rewrote more times than anything else in the book. I repeated *slug* purposely, because I wanted to make it appear that the hotel and the Statue of Liberty were reduced by the August day to the same sort of aspect. It was part of my policy of making great things seem prosaic in that part of the book. Still, you may be right about it. As for my pessimistic description of the birth of literature, it was not intended as my own serious opinion. It was supposed, like all the other opinions in the book, to be relative to the special situation and state of mind of the hero . . .

To Maxwell Perkins   October 3, 1929

. . . I am sending you this review of Burton Rascoe's because I thought that, in the event of your doing any more advertizing of *Daisy*, you might get something a little more enticing out of it than the quotation from the *New York Sun* which you are using in the current advertizement, and which, it seems to me, is calculated rather to discourage than to stimulate the reader. I also wish you would have them take out the Jr., as I have not been Edmund Wilson, Jr., for many years . . .

To John Peale Bishop   October 4, 1929

Dear John: I was very much pleased by your letter about *Daisy*—more pleased than by perhaps anything else which has been said about it. You have understood the situation in regard to Rita exactly—there were two things about it: in the first place, I couldn't give the early affair its true value, because if I had done so, it would have eclipsed in interest the part about Daisy at the end and brought about an anticlimax (the book was originally imagined from the Daisy end of it); and then, it was also true that, once having written more or less real descriptions of Edna, I became self-conscious and began to handle the subject gingerly. The book was somewhat artificially conceived in the first place—that is, it was to be a pattern of ideas and all to take place, as to a great extent it does, on the plane of the intelligence—and when I came to write the actual story, this had the effect of involving me in a certain amount of falsified psychology. I rewrote it to take this curse off it, but a certain amount of it was inherent in the thing which I was attempting to do.

Scribner's insisted on having my page proofs (on my book of verse) back at once, so I couldn't send them to you, as I had wanted to do. I expect to have copies of the book in a few days and will send you one.

I was very much relieved and cheered to hear that you are coming back. The *Ladies' Home Journal* articles are an excellent idea—and why couldn't you get out a book of them afterwards? I know that you've been going through a hard period—I have, too, and am just struggling out of it. I'm trying to put my own affairs on a new basis—of which I'll write you at more length later—and have had to go through a good deal that was emotionally harrowing, financially embarrassing, and nervously devastating! I suppose that you and I have both got to the time of life where one has to take pretty desperate action or be choked in one's own toils—and *tanto è amara, che poco è più morte!*

As ever, EW

To Allen Tate   October 11, 1929

. . . I am glad that you liked my book, and I am grateful for your insight into the design. I should like to discuss it with you sometime. I fear, however, that when you have gotten beyond the third volume of Proust, you will see that I have borrowed more from him technically than you suppose. Proust is the real inventor of the alternation between revery and narrative, but the narrative part really doesn't begin until the

Guermantes volumes. Proust's technical design in his novel is masterly but it really doesn't begin to appear until you have gotten quite far into it. He, too, writes essays on his characters and has different parts of the story dominated by key characters . . .

Also, if you get to Los Angeles, be sure to look up a young lawyer who writes—did one of those books on Ambrose Bierce—Carey McWilliams.   (To Burton Rascoe, 1931)

To Carey McWilliams   October 18, 1929

Dear Mr. McWilliams: I am sorry that I did not get a chance to see you when you were in New York. I was so rushed with the fall book supplement that I was delayed with a great many things.

In answer to your questions, I have published the following books: *The Undertaker's Garland* (Knopf), written in collaboration with John Peale Bishop; *Discordant Encounters* (A. and C. Boni); *I Thought of Daisy* (Scribner's); and a book of poems, *Poets, Farewell!*, which is just out this week, also published by Scribner's. Just now I am writing a book on modern literature, which will be out in the spring. My articles, which are appearing in *The New Republic* now, were written as part of this book, though they will appear there in an extended and emended form. In regard to *Daisy*, I had intended to have the points of view partly dependent on the hero's personal situation. There are five different points of view—a different one in each section. In each case, except the third, and even here Larry Mickler is a sort of key character, the hero's ideas are being influenced by the ideas of another and stronger personality—a different one in each case. But, at the same time, in each of the sections, a good deal of what he thinks—what he thinks he is taking over from these other personalities—is really determined by his personal situation in relation to Rita. I began *Daisy* two summers ago and was writing on it for about two years. As for the period it is supposed to cover, I have falsified my chronology a good deal. The actual action of the book covers only a little more than two years, and I have telescoped into this short period social changes which actually took a much longer time, and psychological changes in the hero which probably would have taken a longer time. The part about the demons was taken from an old *New Republic* article written several years ago. The whole novel was written recently, although I laid under contribution articles, sketches, and notes which had been written at various times during the last ten years. I am sorry that you thought the last section inadequate, because I had hoped to make it the most effective one. It was really the point of departure in writing the book. It was the part which I had imagined first. You speak of the "new

Pete." There is not supposed to be any change in Pete's character. He is presumably just as bad as ever, and will probably do just as badly in Boston as anywhere else. The character of the professor was a composite of several men I have known. His point of view and his general ideas, as well as something of his personality, were taken from A. N. Whitehead, the English philosopher and mathematician, now at Harvard. If you have not read him, I strongly recommend him to you. Probably the best book to begin on is *Science and the Modern World*, though a more recently published book, *The Aims of Education*, is perhaps easier reading and shows him at his most stimulating.

"Galahad" was not intended as a fragment. It was a story which I wrote sometime ago. It has nothing to do with the present novel. The man in the novel is not to be identified with me. He is definitely conceived as a character, and his experience does not parallel mine at all. Neither does that of the boy in "Galahad." I myself have never had any intention of writing a novel about my early life or about the early life of the man in *Daisy*. "Galahad" was based on an experience of a friend of mine about which he once told me, and the remark of the character in the book that he had had a rotten time at school and had always wanted to write a novel about it is something that I once heard another man I know say. The man in my book is the kind of fellow who would have had a rotten time at most boarding schools. It would have rankled with him, and he would have cherished the idea of writing a novel about it. When he fell in love with Rita and began to talk to her intimately, one of the first things he would have done would have been to tell her about all the things that had hurt him in the past, the memory of which he had never been able to get rid of by expressing himself fully about them. I myself had a very good time at boarding school. The general conclusions which you draw from *Daisy* are the kind, it seems to me, that I wanted to have drawn. There is supposed to be a good deal implicit in the apparent banality of the last section. The point is that Daisy is supposed to represent ordinary human life undirected by special ideas. The hero comes close to her for the first time: the end is intended as a sort of descent to "the C major of this life," to which, however, the hero is now able to bring the wisdom of his previous experience. At the same time, the last section represents a point of view bound up with a special mood and situation, like all the others. You are not to suppose that the man who is telling the story will always see things precisely the way he did that particular afternoon and evening.

Thank you very much for taking such an interest in my book, and for undertaking to write an article about me—something which has never occurred before. I hope you will send me a copy of it . . .

Yours very sincerely, Edmund Wilson

To L. A. G. STRONG   October 23, 1929

Dear Mr. Strong: You were very kind to write me. I was very much
surprised and pleased by your having liked my articles to that extent. The
series I am writing now for *The New Republic* is intended for a book,*
and the articles in their present form are rather unsatisfactory because my
space in *The New Republic* is limited.

Thank you very much for your elucidation of Yeats's point of view. I
cannot help feeling, however, that there is some ambiguity in his own
mind, because he appears occasionally to express dissatisfaction with his
own point of view. On the other hand, it may, of course, be that I have
read this dissatisfaction into him. At any rate, I have found him a very
difficult subject to treat critically. Thank you again for your letter.

Yours sincerely, Edmund Wilson

To CHRISTIAN GAUSS   November 12, 1929

Dear Mr. Gauss: Thank you very much for taking the trouble to write
me at length† about my book, and for the kind things you say about it.†
I did not mean to put a task on you. I didn't expect to have those last
poems understood particularly except by the people they were addressed
to—not, however, that I think poetry ought to be obscured through being
too personal. Those long lines at the beginning of the sestets of the sonnets
are really not alexandrines, but pentameter with a lot of anapaest substituted for iambs. The idea was to start the sestets off with a new impetus—
to swell the strain a little.

As for the *New Republic* articles, I would just as soon you didn't read
them in the version they have been appearing in in the paper. I am going
to revise them completely and expand them considerably, and I thought
that, as I want to dedicate the book to you, I should like to have you go
through the proofs, if you can. That should be sometime in February. So
please don't bother with the articles. Thanks ever so much for telling me
about the lines from Musset. I was quoting them from memory and
thought they looked suspicious at the time. I have made a number of
other mistakes, too. I shall certainly come down to Princeton sometime
after the Yale game in the hope of getting a chance to talk to you about
these literary matters and others.

As for a *confession d'un enfant du siècle*, I fear that I shall never write
one. That kind of thing is really repugnant to me, and I expect to become
more and more objective instead of more and more personal. Incidentally,

---

* *Axel's Castle.*
† *Poets, Farewell!*

the diet of Symbolism, early and recent, which I have lately been con-
suming, has had the effect in the long run of wearying and almost disgusting me with this kind of subjective literature. I have a feeling that it
has about run its course, and hope to see its discoveries in psychology and
language taken over by some different artistic tendency.   As ever, EW

To KATHARINE WHITE   December 9, 1929
The New Yorker
Dear Mrs. White: I should be very glad to write for *The New Yorker*, but
it is, unfortunately, impossible for me to do any work for anybody but
The New Republic. The point is that I am always writing books, and that
in order to give *The New Republic* enough copy I have to publish anything utilizable from these books in it—a good deal of *Daisy* came out in
it—and whatever journalism I am able to do besides, I owe to them, too.
I never have time enough to do my regular work nowadays.

   I am glad you like *Daisy*. And thank you for asking me to write for
The New Yorker. There is no magazine I would rather contribute to.
I read it every week with delight.   Sincerely yours, Edmund Wilson

To BURTON RASCOE   November 15, 1929

. . . I hope that you weren't hit by the stock-market disaster. I haven't
heard anything from you, and hope that this is not the reason . . .

JAMES JOYCE
1925–1965

You must read Joyce's *Ulysses*, if you haven't already done so. You can get a copy from the Brick Row Book Shop for $25—730 enormous pages . . .   (To Stanley Dell, 1922)

To CHRISTIAN GAUSS   November 10, 1925
                                    3 North Washington Square, N.Y.

Dear Mr. Gauss: I am enclosing some propaganda in connection with *Ulysses*—also a note on what we were discussing the other night. Forgive my persistence, but I feel very strongly that your indifference to and mis-understanding of Joyce amounts to an international calamity in the world of literature! I hope to see you before long and discuss this and other matters. Do let me know when you come to New York, if you have time to do anything. I don't suppose you could possibly come up this weekend. I usually have to go to Red Bank over Sunday but I am going to be here this week. Please remember me to Mrs. Gauss, who is much too kind to take me in as she does. I wish you both could come up and go to the theater with us some night. If you like, we could have a little party with the Bishops and any specimen intellectuals that you would be curious to meet. We should try to keep them in hand, so that they would not do anything savage during the evening—as they seem to be becoming more and more volatile, licentious, quarrelsome, and alcoholic.

                                        Yours as ever, EW

To JAMES JOYCE   July 23, 1928
c/o Miss Sylvia Beach, Shakespeare & Co.
8 rue de l'Odéon, Paris, France

My dear Mr. Joyce: You were kind enough to write me several years ago about an article of mine on *Ulysses*. I want to have a chapter on you in a book on modern literature which I am planning, and I wondered whether

Man Ray

JAMES JOYCE

Because he is the author of one of the supremely beautiful lyrics in English poetry; because he has devoted himself more rigorously to the novel as a literary form than anyone since Flaubert, not even excepting Henry James; and finally because Valéry Larbaud calls *Ulysses* the only epic of our time, and says that with it "Ireland makes a sensational re-entry into high European literature."
—*Vanity Fair*, 1922

you would be willing to let me see your outline of *Ulysses*.* I suppose that you would not object to my drawing on this outline in writing about the book. Herbert Gorman and Valéry Larbaud have already published articles based on information derived from the outline, but would you object to having it published in full, and, if you would, how much of its contents would you be willing to have made known?

I should also like, if possible, to be able to include some notice of your new book which has been coming out in *transition*.† It has been announced for publication by an American publisher, and I was wondering whether there was any chance of its being out by the first of next year. The publishers tell me that they have been given no definite date. I hope you will forgive me for troubling you about all this.

Yours sincerely, Edmund Wilson

EXACT COPY of dictated, handwritten answer on bottom and back of above letter: *Empêché d'écrire. S'adresser à M. Gorman. Le plan d'Ulisse était donné en voie amicale à des amis, et ne doit pas être reproduit en entier. Mr. Joyce n'a pas de contrat pour "Work in Progress" pour l'Amérique sauf le petit fragment: (quelques centaines d'exemplaires) Alp.‡ Il ignore les publications dont Mr. Wilson parle.§*

He is certainly one of the best, if not the best, of the young critics.
(To John Peale Bishop, 1941)

To HARRY LEVIN   October 31, 1939
Truro Center, Mass.

Dear Levin: I thought your Joyce review was excellent—even brilliant.||
But though the embroidery is certainly beautiful and the first thing you notice and appreciate, I don't think Joyce is really at all frivolous. Underneath there is a masterly grasp of fundamental psychological processes. He is unconventional from the point of view of most serious modern literature in making these things humorous; but it seems to me that he has really gone beyond Proust, Mann, Lawrence, et al., in weaving the kind of themes which they deal with in a more agonized or grandiose way into the homely warp and woof of an ordinary night's sleep. I have always thought that his psychological researches were the most interesting of our

---

* "Joyce has drawn up an outline of his novel, of which he has allowed certain of his commentators to avail themselves."   —*Axel's Castle*
† "Joyce has allowed it to be published separately in a little book called *Anna Livia Plurabelle* . . . one of the most remarkable parts of *Finnegans Wake*."
—*Axel's Castle*

‡ *Anna Livia Plurabelle.*
§ See p. 459.
|| "On First Looking into *Finnegans Wake*."

time in literature, and in a way the most scientific because he analyzes the human consciousness into a thousand combinations and nuances and yet always leaves it organic.   Sincerely, Edmund Wilson

To HARRY LEVIN   November 29, 1939
                                                             Truro Center
Dear Levin: Thank you for *New Directions*. This piece of yours really adds a lot to the understanding of the subject. I don't, as you know, agree with you about the nullity of what Joyce has to say, but I think that a good deal of the criticism proper is excellent, too. In fact, these articles of yours seem to me among the few really good things that have been written about Joyce. I hope you'll be doing more criticism. By the way, "Work in Progress" was not Joyce's own name for his work, but the regular head used by those Paris magazines for an untitled fragment of the work of any book.   Sincerely, Edmund Wilson
   It seems that Van Houten's is a kind of chocolate advertized all over Dublin.

To LOUISE BOGAN   [undated, ? 1938–1939]

The breast kind of breath-and-busser leper[1] in recknowledgements of ex-panse of hespertalentry with limpid nympid aquatic sports acomfied by light dry slowturn and whitey aspyreglass[2] fingers as well as a volley volka distilluted for tsarskoye sellout and syrup of cherry bandy (children cry for their paregorgeup) at a chaste little café stable amidst old bureaux and beauzos in the battic[3] with a companion intrinsically brillious if a tiny-in-tongue-sick balbutious[4] would be pronto-promto dispatchal of mappal of Dublin the dump together with young Critipher Ichorword's sly silkspoken shy autobuggerphy (there was sleek-un Steamin Slender and likely Lewis MacNice and Seedy Louis the Gooise and don't be forgetting old W.H. Odd-un the most glorious of the grope What hope! They live in despair without dope.) Yrs Jails Juice
   1. Hold that female! She swiped the bishop's scandaltricks.
   2. Don't look now but isn't prat the pink?
   3. Humph I snuff duff.
   4. The ambulance ding ding!

To WILLIAM Y. TINDALL   February 6, 1940
                                                             Truro Center
Dear Professor Tindall: I want to lecture at Columbia (if this doesn't conflict with your other plans) on James Joyce's *Finnegans Wake* (which will involve a consideration of Joyce's work in general). The book, as you no doubt know, presents peculiar difficulties, and it might be a good idea if certain passages from it could be mimeographed and given to the mem-

bers of the class, so that they could have them before their eyes. Would this be practical? I should also like to have them listen to Joyce's reading of a section of the book on a phonograph record. I can supply the record if it would be possible to get a big victrola for the classroom.

The books you ought to have on call are all the books of Joyce (including his *complete* collected poems—which you can get from the Gotham Book Mart, 51 West 47th Street); *Our Exagmination* (New Directions, Norfolk, Connecticut); Herbert Gorman's biography of Joyce; *James Joyce and the Making of Ulysses*, by Frank Budgen (Gotham Book Mart can supply); Harry Levin's book on Joyce (if it is out by that time—also published by New Directions); *The Literary Mind*, by Max Eastman, which has some material on Joyce (Scribner's).

Yours sincerely, Edmund Wilson

To WILLIAM Y. TINDALL   August 25, 1941
Wellfleet, Mass.

Dear Tindall: I thought you might like to have these corrections for *Finnegans Wake*. I made them from Joyce's copy and sent it back before I had checked them. You will see that there are some mistakes—some but not all of them corrected here. The others can be easily straightened out. You can keep this copy, as I have several.

It was nice to see you at Columbia. Please remember me to Mrs. Tindall.   Yours sincerely, Edmund Wilson

To WILLIAM Y. TINDALL   September 17, 1941

Dear Tindall: I saw the Colums the other day, and they say that 1132 can't be Earwicker's street address, because the numbers don't run that high in Dublin; but that it is the date of the Anglo-Norman invasion of Ireland. The date of the Battle of Clontarf, 1014, also figures: it is the telephone number of the pub. It seems that the Chapelizod central is Clontarf. This last came direct from Joyce.

Yours sincerely, Edmund Wilson

To FRANCES STELOFF   1940
The Gotham Book Mart
. . . I suppose that that other phonograph record that Joyce made from *Ulysses* is unobtainable or worth its weight in radium? . . .

To MAXWELL GEISMAR   August 29, 1941
Wellfleet

Dear Max: Thank you for your letter. I've been thinking about the general anti-woman tendency in modern fiction. As you say, it's a large subject, and I don't know yet precisely what I think about it. I've just realized that the antagonism is in Joyce, too. That's one reason women don't like him. He glorifies them, but, from their point of view, in the wrong way. There's a fundamental slight involved, which he's trying to make up for (by giving Molly Bloom and Maggy Earwicker the last word). The key to this aspect of Joyce is in his play, *Exiles*, which I've been looking into again . . .   As ever, Edmund Wilson

. . . and I have also had the advantage of discussions with Mr. Thornton Wilder, who has explored the book more thoroughly than anyone else I have heard of.
("The Dream of H. C. Earwicker," *The Wound and the Bow*)

·To Thornton Wilder   June 20, 1940
                                                        Wellfleet
Dear Wilder: I was very much interested in your letter, but I think you're exaggerating the importance of the anal element—which has always been present in Joyce (Bloom's preoccupation with Molly Bloom's rear). Don't you think, after all, that he means to present it as merely mixed up with all the other elements of the human situation? I think you're probably right about AACB (though this would be only one aspect of 1132—I agreed with your earlier idea that it represented the Earwicker family, and this seems to me the fundamental symbol). But I'm not so sure about *the keys to my heart*, or the *Arkglow's seafire*—why should some of it go according to Grimm's law, and some not, and why should *K* be used twice? Nor does it seem to me quite legitimate to get *arse* out of *heart*. Have you ever read any of those books about Baconian ciphers in Shakespeare? Those theories can sometimes be made to seem quite plausible. And I once examined a book of Walter Arensberg which attempted to show by anagrams that Dante had an Oedipus complex. One of his points was that the recurrence of the word *Poi* at the beginning of lines in the *Divina Commedia* was dictated by the requirements of the cipher. After all, there are only a very limited number of letters in the alphabet, and the combinations in any one language are limited—certain combinations are bound to recur. If you read the words backward, you can make them recur more often; if you bring in Grimm's law, you can make them recur oftener still. You say yourself that you can do more or less the same thing by applying the same method to the *Boston Transcript*.

I still feel that the central thing in *Finnegans Wake* is the family situation, which is to be regarded as one of a series of such situations presented in Joyce's books. This is really, it seems to me, the thing that ought to be fully worked out. If you go through the book from *this* point of view, you will find it in almost every paragraph—and there is some kind of a little imbroglio (about the letter and the woman who wrote it) that has never been disentangled.

I've looked for the deadly sins in *Anna Livia Plurabelle*—but can't seem to find them. Where do they begin?

I found *Our Town* up here at the newsstand in that cheap edition the other day, and read it—it still seemed to me awfully good. It's certainly one of the few really first-rate American plays. You were going to send me *The Merchant of Yonkers*, which I haven't seen.

I do hope you turn up here later. There are a number of things I'd like to talk to you about. For one thing, I'm going to be back on *The New Republic*, for a few months anyway, in the fall, and was hoping I could get you to write something about *F.W.* for it.

Cordially, Edmund Wilson

To Mary Meigs   1965

. . . About *Ulysses:* It is certainly true that parts of it—especially toward the end—are just incredibly dull. It is better when you reread it a chapter at a time: particularly the opening chapters, the Walpurgisnacht in the brothel (the real climax of the story), and Mrs. Bloom at the end. But a good deal of Bloom's peregrinations are also very good: the funeral and the scene in the bar. The trouble with Joyce is that he has so little sense of the reader's capacity for sustained attention. He is always likely to go on too long . . .

7

THE THIRTIES

Marxism never had the effect of destroying my belief in literature. All through the thirties I was defending literature.

CHRONOLOGY

1930	*The New Republic.*
APRIL	I have gotten married to a girl named Margaret Canby.
MAY	Croly died about a week ago.
	Politically I am going further and further to the left.
JULY	Provincetown: I expect to stay until the first of October.
NOVEMBER	*The New Republic:* Correcting proof on my literary book.
1931	AXEL'S CASTLE
FEBRUARY	*The New Republic.*
MAY	I'm trying a book . . . more or less journalistic in shape [*The American Jitters*].
JUNE	Miners' strike, West Virginia.
JULY	Bland, New Mexico.
	My address after August 1 will be 7 Lingate Lane, Santa Barbara, California.
DECEMBER	Provincetown.
1932	THE AMERICAN JITTERS
FEBRUARY	Harlan, Kentucky.
AUGUST	Provincetown: Struggling with a play [*Beppo and Beth*].
OCTOBER	The death of my wife.
1933	*The New Republic.*
	314 East 53rd Street, New York: I am living in my little house . . . It was next door to a similar house in which Muriel Draper lived.
1934	"The Ambiguity of Henry James," in *The Hound and Horn.*
MARCH	Engaged on some essays . . . Vico to Marx.

JULY	Provincetown: First chapters of *To the Finland Station* in *The New Republic*.
AUGUST	Thinking of applying for a Guggenheim to go to Russia.
1935 MAY– OCTOBER	314 East 53rd Street, New York. Russia.
1936	TRAVELS IN TWO DEMOCRACIES
AUGUST	My plan is to arrive in Provincetown August 1 [571 Commercial Street].
OCTOBER	Trees, R.F.D. 1, Stamford, Connecticut: A place I've taken outside Stamford [the house belonged to Margaret de Silva].
NOVEMBER	*The New Republic:* Going to be a regular contributor.
1937	THIS ROOM AND THIS GIN AND THESE SANDWICHES: *Three Plays** *To the Finland Station* in *The New Republic*. Stamford: I hardly ever go to New York and am as rural as any agrarian.
1938	THE TRIPLE THINKERS†
APRIL	I'm married to a girl named Mary McCarthy.
DECEMBER	The baby arrived Christmas day, a boy [Reuel Kimball Wilson].
MAY	To W. W. Norton: The book I propose to write is to be hung on the Philoctetes myth [*The Wound and the Bow*].
1939	
FEBRUARY	The University of Chicago has offered me $1,200 to go out there for ten weeks . . . we're going on the first of June.
OCTOBER	Truro Center, Massachusetts: We came up here from the West and hope to stay here more or less permanently.

---

* *The Crime in the Whistler Room* / *A Winter in Beech Street* (later retitled *This Room and This Gin and These Sandwiches*) / *Beppo and Beth*.
† *The Triple Thinkers* (First edition, 1938): Mr. More and the Mithraic Bull / Is Verse a Dying Technique? / In Honor of Pushkin / A. E. Housman / The Politics of Flaubert / The Ambiguity of Henry James / John Jay Chapman / The Satire of Samuel Butler / Bernard Shaw at Eighty / Marxism and Literature.

1930–1931

January 15, 1930
                                                    Riverton, Conn.

Dear John: I've come up here to get away from New York and do some work. I usually begin to crack with the strain in the city after the holidays. I saw Esther [Murphy] and Allen Tate before I left, and they gave me good reports of you; Allen said you might be coming back in the spring— I hope it's true. He was very much impressed by your recent poems and stories—I wish you would send me copies of the former—it's so long since I've seen anything from your hand. And why don't you send the stories to *Scribner's*, which now has a new editor (old Robert Bridges having retired), a young man named Dashiell, who is very anxious to get new writers for it. Max Perkins was talking to me, when I last saw him, of the possibility of encouraging short fiction of the type that is shorter than a novel but longer than a short story, as I take it your stories are. He said that he thought *Scribner's Magazine* might make a practice of running them. Why don't you send some of your stories to him? Also, have you ever tried *The American Caravan*? I should think it would be a good place for either your stories or your poems—send manuscripts to Paul Rosenfeld, 77 Irving Place. I know that he was enthusiastic about the one that he saw. I do think, however, that the thing to do is to come over and transact your business face to face.

Thank you very much for your letter about my poems—I agree with you that they too often don't emerge from the private situations that gave rise to them. I wish that you, just for fun, would try a version of the Petronius poem yourself; I was conscious of paring it down too much and making it too dry—especially in reducing the enumeration of sounds, of dogs, birds, men, etc., which were silent while the poet was taking his nocturnal walk and by mentioning which he gives an effect of the small hours much as I don't reproduce in my translation.

This place up here is quite wonderful—I had never been here and

didn't expect much, but found a splendid inn on the old Albany Post Road and in continuous use for a hundred and thirty years, but with all modern improvements, steam heat, etc., and an excellent bar serving applejack. There is a fine New England river, with a succession of falls, flowing past the door, with all sorts of New England white houses, wood roads that follow the river and the dark foothills of the Berkshires. It's a great relief to get away from New York, where it always becomes more and more impossible for me to accomplish anything about this time of the year—though I have ended by getting pretty well broken in to it and enjoying it more or less continuously. I believe that it has as great a variety of interest as any city in the world—you can pass so rapidly from one kind of thing to another.

Sew Collins, who, as I suppose you know, now owns and edits *The Bookman*, has taken up with the Humanists—Paul Elmer More, Irving Babbitt et al.—who are organizing what they evidently believe to be nothing short of a countrywide intellectual movement. Your old towns-fellow, Bob Shafer, has recently stepped into the breach to defend More against Allen Tate. He is falling foul of everybody of his own generation, charging them with romanticism, impressionism, Bohemianism, and all the stock crimes which More and Babbitt, looking out, at the beginning of the century, from their academic shelters, supposed people who produced literature to be guilty of. He has buried us all alive in an article in the January number. I don't take any stock in Humanism nor believe that the new realists will get very far with it, but there is this natural explanation of the present flaring up of interest in it, that all the intellectual tendencies —liberalism, delayed romanticism, etc.—of the period immediately after the war have completely evaporated, or, rather, have been developed into systems, so that the doctrine of Babbitt and More (they are quite impressive in some ways when you come to read them) looms as the only systematic attempt in sight to deal with large political, social, moral, and aesthetic questions, in relation to each other, in a monumental and logical way. I think that their system is going to sink through its preoccupation with American small-town morality of the day before yesterday, its little sympathy with and insight into humanity, and its incomprehension of art; but it, after all, given its assumptions, makes sense—which comparatively few other things do just at present. I believe that the only valid rival system over here would come from the Bernard Shaw–Dos Passos point of view—though it is hard to apply to the United States any of the forms of European socialist or Communist theory, and hard to formulate any original theory to a generally prosperous and contented, all-bourgeois half-a-continent who know how to read and write but are not at all susceptible to ideas. Still, it may be merely that the intellectuals themselves are not sufficiently susceptible to ideas, and haven't the courage and the brains to articulate the point of view which would meet the situation. I dare say these questions lie somewhat outside your interests, but wish I could talk to you about them just the same—have been writing this letter on the remains of a bottle of applejack and wish you were here to share it with me. Let me hear from you now and again, and come over when the opportunity presents . . .

As ever, EW

EDITORS
HERBERT CROLY
BRUCE BLIVEN
ROBERT MORSS LOVETT
GEORGE SOULE
EDMUND WILSON
STARK YOUNG
T. S. MATTHEWS, ASST.

The New
REPUBLIC
421 West 21# Street
New York City

HERBERT CROLY
PRESIDENT
DANIEL MEBANE
TREASURER
———
CABLE ADDRESS
NEWREPUB

To Carey McWilliams

February 5, 1930
*The New Republic**

Dear Mr. McWilliams: Thank you ever so much for your article. It has pleased me very much—I never expected to see anything so elaborate on the subject. I agree with you about my articles on movies and allied subjects, and often wake up in the middle of the night to think of them with horror—especially one that I wrote on Lon Chaney some years ago. You were right about my having gotten the first line of my first poem from Ezra Pound. I always had an uneasy suspicion that I had cribbed it from somewhere, but thought it was from Waller's "Go lovely rose! Tell her that wastes her time and me." Now I see, however, that I was merely imitating Pound's imitation of that poem. I had known it well at one time, then forgotten it. On the other hand, the line you speak of in the next to last poem in the book was repeated on purpose. There are other similarities of phrase between this poem and the first poem of the series. These five are all supposed to go together and to develop the same set of feelings and ideas, but I realize that the connection is sometimes rather obscure. In regard to the Proust article, you are mistaken about my having said that he had never published anything before his novel. On the contrary, I noted that he had published one book before that, *Les Plaisirs et les jours.* I have a discussion of it in this week's *New Republic.* This new essay and the old one are to go together to make a chapter of my book.

I am sending back the books, duly inscribed. I have really been quite overcome by your appreciation, as I don't think very highly of a good deal of the work I have done for *The New Republic,* and was quite dismayed at your remembering and quoting my old articles, most of which I think would be well forgotten.

---

* The following letters were written from *The New Republic.*

By the way, I am sorry that you don't think highly of *Discordant Encounters*, because *The Crime in the Whistler Room*, in spite of a good many things that are obviously wrong with it, is really my favorite production, and my principal ambition for the immediate future is to write more plays.   Yours very sincerely, Edmund Wilson

> Muriel Draper seemed old-fashioned like John Bishop, embedded in the nineties, obsolete, though still with the something, the real courage, imagination, wit, which made her likable and interesting.
>   (Notebooks of the thirties)

To MURIEL DRAPER   March 17, 1930

Dear Muriel: I'm sorry that we didn't get there Saturday night—the whole Cummings–Orage imbroglio seemed to be too much for us—especially as the Cummingses had already arranged to do something else; if you sent Cummings a telegram, he never got it. I hope you will forgive me for being so rude the other evening—and believe me that I enjoy your parties more than anybody else's in New York, and never stay away without a reluctance which lends bitterness to my obstinacy.

                                   As ever, Bunny Wilson

To UPTON SINCLAIR   March 25, 1930

Dear Sinclair: I do enjoy your arguments, and don't think you have anything in common with Babbitt and More except the tendency I mentioned. I read *Mammonart* when it came out and reviewed it in *The New Republic*, making the same point. I'll look up the reference you mention. The humanistic business would be an excellent subject for your type of criticism, I should think, because precisely one of the things that make it hollow is the fact that it is an attempt to write literary history in a vacuum, with the social and economic background left out.

                                   Yours sincerely, Edmund Wilson

To BURTON RASCOE   April 8, 1930

Dear Burton: I have read this with vast entertainment, but we have already run so much about Humanism that we have decided never to print another word about it. My own feeling is that Humanism is now a flattened corpse over which the whole army of American intelligence has passed, and that it might as well be left for dead.   As ever, EW

I understand that Seward Collins has all the articles on Humanism piled up on his desk, and that he is going to address himself to them all systematically.

April 25, 1930

Dear Blackmur: Thank you very much for the Cowper and Baudelaire reviews, which, from the point of view of what you say, seem to me admirable. I do feel, however, that you have never quite mastered a satisfactory expository style. I believe that the principal trouble is that you attempt to be too terse. Terseness is an excellent quality, but there are very few people who can do it in this sort of thing, and it may be said that, in general, reviewing is not the place for it. I wish that you would take more words and say what you mean more exactly. I think that you often take short cuts in expression when you ought to be a little more patient. I wish you would revise these reviews from this point of view. I have made some notes in the margins.

Aside from this criticism, I like these reviews, especially the first paragraph of the Cowper. It seems to me that in the second you have given quite a brilliant brief portrait of him. You have certainly been heroic in reading through *The Task*. I have never been able to understand what there was supposed to be in Cowper. He has always put me to sleep, and I sympathize profoundly with your first sentence.

Yours sincerely, Edmund Wilson

To ALLEN TATE   May 28, 1930

Dear Allen: I have not answered your letters before because I have been away. I have gotten married to a girl named Margaret Canby from California, and we went to Washington on our wedding trip. I don't know whether I told you about this before you left. I was sorry not to come to your party that night. I understand that it was a tremendous affair. I have written to Harcourt about Katherine Anne Porter. I didn't know that she was in such a bad way and was distressed to hear about it.

Croly died about a week ago, as I suppose you have heard, and it has left us all feeling very blank. I don't know precisely what I am going to do in the future. I may resign from the book department here and follow your example by going to the country to live for a while. I am working on my literary book now and improving it considerably, I think.

Washington is a charming city. Its nearness to the South makes it so, but I was depressed by the political side. I sat in at the Senate hearings on the Naval Treaty. Politically I am going further and further to the left all the time and have moments of trying to become converted to American Communism in the same way that Eliot makes an effort to become converted to Anglo-Catholicism. It is not that Communism in itself isn't all right, but that all that sort of thing in America seems even more unrelated to real life than Catholicism does in England. By the way, have you read

Eliot's "Ash Wednesday"? It has some very fine things in it, but is way behind *The Waste Land*, according to me. I don't like his literary religious imagery and much prefer the imagery of *The Waste Land* picked up in the London streets . . .

As ever, Edmund

To Arthur Schlesinger, Jr.   1964

. . . I suppose that you have gone into the question of the relations between T.R. and Croly and have good authority for your statement that the former influenced the latter more than the other way around. I remember Croly's telling me that *The Promise* had influenced T.R. at the time he was creating the Progressive Party. He gave me an account of Roosevelt as he used to see him at Oyster Bay. He said that he talked in private like the well-educated man of the world he was, but that as soon as any agent of publicity appeared, he would go into his public act and talk like a demagogue. (Stephen Spender told me something similar about a conversation with Hemingway in Spain. He, Hemingway, was perfectly serious and natural when he talked about Stendhal and other literary matters, but switched into his bogus public character the moment there was publicity in the offing. In both cases, of course, they were trying to live up to the myth of the two-fisted American man of action.) . . .

Croly told me, when I was writing about Chapman, that the latter's *Causes and Consequences* had made a great impression on him.

. . . One thing you don't mention . . . is Croly's firm rejection of socialism, his refusal to entertain the idea that any kind of real class conflict could occur in the United States. This was brought home to me for the first time when he came back from a Pacific conference after the Sacco–Vanzetti crisis of the summer of '27. We had been handling this without Herbert's supervision, and—though goodness knows we had hardly been incendiary—he thought that we had gone much too far. Bob Lovett and he were old colleagues and friends, but their temperaments were very different and they went at things from entirely different points of view, and during Croly's absence Lovett had had his head, and as always had been outspoken and provocative. I had written an editorial paragraph in which I had raised the class issue, and Herbert, on his return, admonished me that the class conflict had had nothing to do with the verdict. I believe that it was from this moment that I realized that he and I could not really agree about such matters (I had always had at the back of my mind the *Fabian Essays* and the Russian Revolution) and that I began to gravitate toward the socialist left. Hitherto I had rather cannily been confining myself to the cultural end of the paper. I had never at that time read *The Promise*, so I never foresaw objections when an occasional review ran counter to Herbert's version of American history. When this happened—as it did when Allen Tate once wrote something heretical about the Civil War—he would insist on my running a note explaining that the opinions expressed were not those of the editors. I never read *The Promise* till after his death, when I wanted to reorient the magazine and began for the first time to write regular articles on politics and labor. These could hardly have been published while Herbert lived. Everything had had to be kept within the frame of the philosophy of *The Promise*, and he shrank from making issues over current events. He was always, as you say, generalizing in terms of abstractions—a kind of writing which I can't help disliking—I disliked it even more in John Dewey, whom I sometimes had to rewrite!—since I am myself very concrete-minded. Yet it seems to me that Croly was one of the most admirable men I have ever known. In spite of what I have said above, he was never dogmatic and never incoherent, always modest about his own limitations, and very appreciative of what other people could do. I suppose that I sensed very early that there was a body of doctrine there, and managed to keep out of its way. Later I grasped the fact that though *The New Republic* had started out with a theoretical equality among the editors, so that each, as in the Polish Assembly of Nobles, had a *liberum veto* and could kill by his one individual vote any measure that everybody else had approved, Herbert Croly—I am sure, without knowing what he was doing—eliminated everybody whom he could not dominate (Lovett became only a contributing editor) or who, like the slippery Alvin Johnson, could always more or less cynically evade him. Stark Young—an unreconstructed Southerner, who agreed with the N.R., politically and socially, about nothing the paper stood for—and Phil and Bob Littell (Phil Littell was the inventor of the phrase "Crolier than thou") and I simply kept to our end of the paper and thought we were lucky enough to have the freedom and the pay we did. Francis Hackett, a militant Irishman, who persistently but no more or less ineffectively attempted to plug his cause on the political side of the paper, used to say that Herbert was like the Great Boyg in *Peer Gynt*: "You can't go through, you have to go around."

Sometime remind me to tell you about Croly's relations with Lippmann . . .

To CHRISTIAN GAUSS   June 30, 1930

Dear Mr. Gauss: I have read this Flaubert article with the greatest interest, and I send it back with the greatest reluctance. So far as my experience goes, it is far the best thing on Flaubert in English. Unfortunately, it is the kind of thing that it is impossible for us to use. The trouble is that we can't run so long an article on somebody so long dead as Flaubert. It is the kind of thing which would be more suitable for a magazine like *The Bookman*. We have to stick pretty closely to contemporaries, unless there is a centenary, or something, or unless the subject has some special relevance to something contemporary. As I say, I hate to pass it up, because I think it is one of your very best pieces of critical writing.

We are leaving this afternoon for Provincetown, where I expect to stay until the first of October. I am still struggling with the manuscript of my book—having a terrible time finding a good name for it. I wish I could get something appropriate out of Mallarmé or one of those poets, but I have never yet struck anything. If you should happen to run into anything happy, I wish you would let me know. I want to have some fairly attractive or striking title which won't sound too much like the ordinary book of literary essays. I hope you have a restful summer.

As ever, Bunny Wilson

To Allen Tate   July 26, 1930
Peaked Hill Bar, Provincetown
Dear Allen: I'm up here in the O'Neill place, where I came before, three summers ago—the tip of Massachusetts, where the essence of New England is concentrated and even in some ways at its most attractive, the seafaring side of it. You ought to come up here sometime and examine it. I'd invite you if you weren't miles away. If you should by any chance come north, be sure to let me know. I've got Margaret and Rosalind and my stepson (twelve years old) here—the latter full of Wild West ideas which have nothing in common with mine at his age (I'm not sure I had the best of it, though!). I'm still working on my book made out of the N.R. articles— a good deal of the stuff seems to me pretty bad now that I get away with it and examine it. I've ended by writing a lot of new material which goes into the aesthetic ideas of Valéry and Eliot in a much more thoroughgoing fashion—if I keep on, I'll publish an original aesthetic theorem and leave out all mention of the subjects I started with. Dos Passos is up here— he has married, bought a little farm in Truro, and decided that he is a "middle-class liberal." He and I have been trying to decide precisely what that means—some of the fruits of our deliberations may appear in the N.R. Dos has finally come to the conclusion that, since the Communist Party with its pedantic Marxism is impossible, the thing to do is to persuade some radical millionaire to hire an Ed Bernays or Ivy Lee to use American publicity methods to convert the Americans to Communism. It is interesting to contemplate the kind of Communism this would produce . . .

I have just had the distressing news that Zelda Fitzgerald has gone insane and is in a sanatorium—I hope it isn't as bad as that. John writes me that he will be over during the summer—first going South, then coming back to N.Y. in early September. You might get him to stop off on the way. Thanks for asking us down—I hope certainly to make it in the course of time, but in the meantime I hope you'll be coming to New York.

I'm going to stay up here till the first of October anyway—maybe longer. I dare say you have heard that the N.R. is going on—presumably reorganized and reoriented; it is going to be interesting to see what turn, if any, it takes. By the way, it has lately been arranged that the staff are to be allowed a certain number of subscriptions to give away to their friends, so I have been having it sent to you. If it doesn't reach you, let me know—that is, if you care about getting it. My best to Caroline and Nancy.   As ever, Edmund

To Alfred Kazin   1965

Dear Alfred: I have just read your book with much interest.* You made connections with the intellectual left in New York just the moment after I had quitted it, and I am glad to get your impressions. As a neophyte, just starting out, you gave certain people more attention than I did and throw light for me on men that I did not know well such as Calverton and Sidney Hook. You are extremely good on Saroyan, whom you understand better than I could. These are real portraits, not simply reminiscences. (Why do you describe Max Nomad without naming him?) The best pages in the book, however—and among the best you have written—are those on your mother and your cousin Sophie.

In the chapter about Provincetown, I think that you are sometimes inaccurate. The piles of the old wharf on which the Provincetown Players started were just behind Dos Passos's house, and O'Neill never lived in a "beach hut" on the dunes. He lived at first in one of the studios above John Francis's store; then in an old Coast Guard station which had been magnificently equipped by the Lewisohns and decorated by Robert Edmond Jones. It even had a bathroom. Mabel Dodge at one time lived in it, and I spent two summers there. I was in Provincetown in the January when it was washed out to sea in a storm. It is Peaked *Hill*, not Peaked *Hills* . . . Finally, the assassin of Trotsky murdered him not with a *pickax* but an *ice axe* of the kind used by mountaineers. A pickax is an instrument for breaking ground, which he could hardly have concealed about his person. You have this also in *Contemporaries* . . .

By the way, that was an excellent piece on the Brooklyn Bridge—you ought to reprint it later . . .   As ever, Edmund

To Maxwell Perkins   [undated, 1930]
                                                                  Provincetown
Dear Max: What do you think of *Axel's Castle: A Study in Contemporary Literature*? I don't know whether you saw the last of my chapters when

---

* *Starting Out in the Thirties.*

it came out in *The New Republic*. Axel is the hero of a play by Villiers de l'Isle-Adam, who typifies the kind of thing I am dealing with in the book—the point is that his castle represents the imagination, which he didn't want to get out of to participate in reality. I wish you would let me know whether you think this is satisfactory—if so, you can announce it—it seems to me pretty good. I have been very much worried by reports that Zelda Fitzgerald has gone off her head and is in a sanatorium—I wish you would let me know if you know anything about it. I wish something could be done about them—I have a feeling they never see anybody with any sense. I have written a lot of new stuff in my work, but it will soon be done now.   As ever, E. Wilson

To MAXWELL PERKINS   August 8, 1930
                                                          Provincetown
Dear Max: I don't know precisely what Zelda's condition is, but have written her a letter which I want to send to Scott, to give her, if he thinks proper. Will you forward it to him?

I'm still strong for my title, in spite of the arguments you urge. It seems to me that it is much more likely to appeal to the reader's imagination than the titles of most books of literary criticism, and I should think that if it were followed in the advertisements and on the jacket by the subtitle, "A Study in Contemporary Literature," and if it were plainly indicated that the book contained essays on Joyce, Proust, etc., the character of the contents would be unmistakable. A title like *The Golden Day* or *The Sacred Wood* or *Unicorns* or *Peacocks and Ivory*—all of them good, it seems to me—would be open to the same objections you make—or *The Cutting of an Agate* or *Sesame and Lilies* or *The New Laocoön*—or the old *Laocoön*. I am having my MS completely retyped—a good deal of it is entirely new. I have still three more chapters to do, but I expect surely to be able to finish it by the first of September. I suppose that it will be impossible now to publish it before spring.

Would there be any chance of your being able to come up here and see us? With your wife and one or more little girls, if they wanted to come . . . I suppose you've probably got them all sent to the country somewhere already, however. It's really swell up here from the point of view of beach and bathing—we're right on the end of the Cape among the sand dunes with the whole shore to ourselves . . .

                                                  As ever, Edmund Wilson

To F. SCOTT FITZGERALD   August 8, 1930
                                                          Provincetown
Dear Scott: I have just heard from Max Perkins about Zelda's illness. From what he has written me, I can't tell precisely what has happened,

but I know from my own experience that these breakdowns where people seem to go off their heads aren't necessarily serious, and as people in that condition are extremely sensitive to suggestion, I thought it might be worthwhile to write her—use your own discretion about giving her the letter.

I've often thought about you both—you must be having an awful time now. I wish there were something I could do—if there should be, you must let me know. I've missed you and Zelda these last years more than any other friends and wish you didn't insist upon living abroad, which I'm convinced is a great mistake for American writers, hard as America can be to live in.

I got married last February to a girl named Margaret Canby (she was formerly married to a cousin of Henry Seidel). I've known her for years— knew her first through Ted Paramore; she comes from California. Mary is married again, too. We're up here in O'Neill's old place, where I came before, three summers ago . . . I'm thinking of spending part of the winter up here, in Provincetown, at least to get away from New York. Dos is married, as you know, and has bought a little farm over at Truro in a lonely and rather somber little hollow where the occasional booming of bitterns is the only sound to be heard. He is becoming more and more of a respectable householder every day and has decided that he is "a middle-class liberal."

I hope things may be going better with Zelda by this time. Don't let the neurologists depress you—the old-fashioned neurologist can be the most funereal and unnerving type in the world. If Zelda is in Switzerland, I shouldn't hesitate to go to Jung at Zurich about her. He got Stan Dell out of a sad condition a year or two ago, and everybody who has had anything to do with him seems to swear by him.   As ever: Bunny Wilson

To MAXWELL PERKINS   September 1, 1930
                                                      Provincetown
. . . I said that I'd be glad to do the Hemingway introduction.* I'm going to New York for a few days next week and will talk to you about it then, so don't bother to send the book up here. Thanks for the royalty report, with its sad story . . .

To CHRISTIAN GAUSS   November 10, 1930
                                                 The New Republic†
Dear Mr. Gauss: Thank you very much for the book and the inscription.‡ I have been reading the book with great enjoyment—had already

---

* *In Our Time,* 1930 ed.
† The following letters were written from *The New Republic.*
‡ *Life in College.*

seen some of it in *The Saturday Evening Post*. I want to talk to you about it when I see you. The whole American college business somehow depresses me now, and the account of things that you give doesn't reassure me. I sympathized with what you said about the football riot. If the students had been Communists they would now be either in the hospital or in jail. But then, after all, they aren't to blame for a system which deliberately keeps them immature and irresponsible till they are past twenty.

I am correcting proof on my literary book now. I thought I would wait to send it to you till the page proof came, so that you could see it in better shape . . .   As ever, Bunny Wilson

To CHRISTIAN GAUSS   December 9, 1930

Dear Mr. Gauss: Thank you ever so much for going through the proofs and writing me at length about them. I am sending you the rest of them herewith. I have got a subtitle: "A Study in the Literature of 1870–1930." What do you think of this? It doesn't sound quite right to me. I feel that "literature" needs some qualifying word. As for Rimbaud, I left him out at the beginning because he is in some ways fundamentally different from the other Symbolists and I wanted to have him at the end to point a moral. My idea was to begin the book with Mallarmé and end it with Rimbaud. (I mention Rimbaud in the introduction.) As a matter of fact, I don't discuss any of the Symbolists at length in the first chapter, except Mallarmé. I take up Corbière and Laforgue in connection with Eliot, Ducasse in connection with the Dadaists, and use Villiers and Rimbaud together at the very end for a contrast. I thought that it was better to introduce them like this in connection with the various aspects of the movement which they influenced than all at once at the beginning. I touch on Verlaine in connection with Rimbaud. You caught several mistakes on the proof which had escaped me. Thank you ever so much for taking the trouble over it. As I reread the book in proof it seems to me terribly heavily written.   As ever, EW

I think that it is true that Symbolism has pretty well run its course, but my conclusions about this, at the end, as you will see, are really not pessimistic.

John Dewey is doing your college book for us.

To CHRISTIAN GAUSS   December 19, 1930

Dear Mr. Gauss: I think that you are much too kind about my book. It probably ought to have a wider scope. Since it has been set up, I have thought of further applications of the same ideas. Some of the things you caught in the proof I had already mended, and I'll try to correct the others. That impossible sentence in the Proust had been printed wrongly. I am enclosing the dedication. Would you mind sending it back, as it is the only proof I have, and it has to be returned to the printer? I don't know whether what I say about "my idea of what literary criticism ought to be" sounds as if I thought that was the only kind of literary criticism. There is the philosophical kind too, of course. But it happened that the more or less historical kind has always been the kind I wanted to write . . .

As ever, Bunny W.

To John Peale Bishop   February 2, 1931

Dear John: I have just heard from Scribner's that you won the prize.* I can't tell you how delighted I am. It is the greatest piece of good news that I have heard in many a year. The judges, from what I hear, were unanimous.

The winter here has been pretty gloomy, but extremely interesting from certain points of view. I have a feeling that the United States is going through a profound psychological change, that the moneymaking ideal is about played out and the country ripe for something new. I have been doing a lot of reporting in *The New Republic* of events that have taken place this winter, and am going to make a book of them. Expect to get off this week on a trip to Detroit and the South. We hope to go to Mexico in the spring when I get done with this.

I am glad you liked my burlesque. It was composed spontaneously while lying in bed one night—as a result of my years with the *New Republic* book department. I am extremely glad to be out of it, and Malcolm Cowley is now quietly going to sleep in it.

I hope you won't spend all of your money on your trip to Greece, but will save a little for a passage to your native shores. In any case, your getting it has given me much joy.   As ever, Bunny

I have sent you a copy of my new book, "Asshole's Cactus." Look forward eagerly to reading yours—of which I saw the proofs in Scribner's the other day.

To R. P. Blackmur   February 25, 1931

Dear Blackmur: If I were you, before bothering with an agent I'd send the play to Harold Clurman, c/o The Theatre Guild. Mention that I suggested he might be interested in seeing it. Then, if he sends it back, send it to James Light, c/o Jed Harris, saying the same thing. Though I believe that you probably ought to try Arthur Hopkins in between. You

---

* *Many Thousands Gone.*

might ask Clurman for his frank advice about it. He is one of the really intelligent people in the theater, and I think he would be glad to help you if he can.

Thanks for what you say about my stuff. As for Symbolism, it is a misleading word, but it seemed to me the only word there was. The kind of Symbolism I am writing about has practically nothing to do with the conventional kind, and nothing whatever to do with the allegory in *Ulysses*. Joyce is related to the Symbolists in a different way. I tried to make this clear in the first chapter. Have you ever read much of the French criticism on the subject? It is really true that Symbolism in France involved all the elements I say. The whole disquisition on what literature ought to be, in the last part of Proust's novel, is an exposition of the Symbolist point of view. The point about the piece of writing that the narrator showed M. de Norpois in one of the earlier volumes is that it was more or less in the Symbolist vein. This was a great issue at the time, and that is the reason Norpois gets so proud and stiff as soon as he reads it. The important thing is to clear one's mind of the ordinary English connotations of the word Symbolism. I am sorry that this is hard to do. There have been a great many complaints about the inappropriateness of the Symbolists calling themselves Symbolists even in France, but I didn't know how else to go about discussing it.

As for politics, I wish that I knew of some promising movement or program for action, but I don't, and all that we write in *The New Republic* is still almost as much in the domain of pure literature as the productions of the Symbolist poets.   Yours very sincerely, Edmund Wilson

Louise Bogan—a third lady poet of remarkable achievement . . .
(To John Peale Bishop, 1924)

To LOUISE BOGAN   April 1931

Dear Louise: I'm terribly sorry you've been in a bad state—I sympathize profoundly, having been there myself. But it is an excellent thing to go to bed on these occasions, and McKinney is really an awfully good man. Remember me to him.

I'm sorry that I haven't seen more of you and that we haven't had more chance to talk lately. My affection and admiration for you are deep— have been from way back, as you know. You are one of the people that I value most and count most on. I didn't realize how upset you were lately, though I suppose I ought to have. I always think of you as fundamentally such a strong and wise individual that I discount your anxieties and things.

These are times of pretty severe strain for anybody, to lapse into a vein

LOUISE BOGAN

Louise Bogan, already well known in anthologies and magazines, is publishing her first book this fall, *Body of This Death*. Her poems vibrate like tense plucked cello strings; she is one of our first writers of lyric verse.

—*Vanity Fair*, 1923

of editorial generalization. Everything is changing so fast and we are all more or less in a position of having been brought up in one kind of world and having to adjust muscles, socially, sexually, morally, etc., to another which is itself in a state of flux. Still, we have to carry on, and people like you with remarkable abilities, even though they're more highly organized nervously than other people, are under a peculiar obligation not to let this sick society down. We have to take life—society and human relations— more or less as we find them—and there is no doubt that they leave much to be desired. The only thing that we can really make is our work. And deliberate work of the mind, imagination, and hand, done, as Nietzsche said, "notwithstanding," in the long run remakes the world.

I don't know if these edifying remarks may not be entirely beside the point in your case. If they are, please forgive them. I am appending a little poem in a different vein, which, however, points the same high moral.*

Margaret is writing you. We called you up on the phone a lot of times before we knew where you were and never could get an answer at the apartment. We'll come up to see you as soon as you can see people.

In the meantime, my dear, my best sympathy and love are radiating at a high rate of vibration in the direction of the neurological.   Edmund

By the way, here is the title of my forthcoming book:

Jitters of 1930–31
A Record of Happenings between October and March
with some records on American Idealism

What do you think of it?†

To Louise Bogan   May 4, 1931

Dear Louise: Swift's poems can't be bought in New York; so I am sending you mine—also rather a good little book on him by Leslie Stephen, Virginia Woolf's papa. I hope reading him and reading about him will have the same effect on you it always has on me—that of making one react in the direction of thinking that, after all, one isn't so badly off as that and that, compared to what Swift thought about it, the world is really a delightful place.   Love, Pollyano, The Glad Boy

To Christian Gauss   May 16, 1931

Dear Mr. Gauss: I am getting out a more or less journalistic book made up of accounts of miscellaneous events between last fall and this spring.

The winter before last, however, I wrote down an account of our call on

---

* "The Extravert of Walden Pond," printed in *Note-Books of Night*.
† *The American Jitters.*

Paul Elmer More one weekend, and I thought that I would put it in with the rest as a specimen of the contemporary literary and intellectual life. Would you mind looking at it? I want to be sure in the first place that it is accurate, and in the second, that it won't be embarrassing to you. If there is anything that is embarrassing, I will take it out. I haven't revised this manuscript at all, because I wanted to let you read it first. There is a good deal still to be done on it in the way of rewriting, so don't bother about bad style, of which there is a good deal.

Have you seen John Bishop's book? Some of the stories are darn good. He seems to be coming to life—has been sending over some new poems.

As ever, Bunny W.

If you don't want to figure by name in this way at all, I could give everybody fictitious names and otherwise disguise it.

To CHRISTIAN GAUSS   May 25, 1931

Dear Mr. Gauss: I think you are right. It's a mistake to publish personal stuff of this kind. I must protest, however, that I wasn't in the least conscious of trying to roast More, represent him as a stuffed shirt—even thought I was giving an attractive picture of him and correcting past asperities. But I suppose my satiric bent got the better of me.*

I don't know when Chaplin is coming back—he is extremely sensitive and intelligent, and interesting to talk to. John Barrymore rarely leaves the Coast nowadays. I have some ideas about him—he seems to me a perfect example of the genuinely gifted man who never matures in America. Good as he is, he has always seemed to me to have no serious interest whatever. See his last picture, *Svengali*, which is amusing but basically silly. And I never could see that his Shakespearean roles were much different. I don't think he had a strong actor's vocation in the first place— merely went into the theater because it was the family business. And the theater that he went into was one that doesn't know what to do with the good people it has at its command. I think Barrymore a much more typically American phenomenon than Chaplin.

Thanks for your trouble and advice about my manuscript.

As ever, EW

To JOHN PEALE BISHOP   May 12, 1931

Dear John: Thanks ever so much for the book. I've just finished reading it. Your letter came this morning. Of the stories I hadn't read, I particularly like "The Cellar" and "Young Desire and Death." It seems to me that

---

* "Mr. More and the Mithraic Bull," in *The Triple Thinkers*.

you've made *Many Thousands Gone* much plainer. I congratulate you on the book—I've had great pleasure reading it. Besides the distinction, music, and charm that all your writing has, there is thought and structure in the stories which I don't remember in any of your other prose. The only thing I'd complain about is that they're a little dim with distance (though not always: the descriptions of the cellar and the summer afternoon in "The Cellar," for example, are vividly evocative). Good as these stories are, you must have much more than this in you. You told me when you were over here that you did a good deal of doubting your own abilities—but if you do, you're crazy. You've got the magic touch that very few writers have, and you certainly ought to take it pretty seriously.

I look forward to your poems. Will you bring them out in the fall? Did you get my note asking whether we could use the "Ode"?

By the way, did you intend to have a single figure of Southern womanhood who dwindles through a series of different individuals from the first story to the last? That was the impression I got, and whether it was intentional or not, the result is artistically effective.

I'm trying to get a book of my own—more or less journalistic—in shape to get it out in August. It's an attempt to show what's been happening in America during the last winter—but doesn't begin to do the subject justice, as some of the most important sides of life are left out. I have a strong conviction that this is a crucial time for the United States. Will send it to you.   As ever, EW

To Maxwell Perkins   July 1, 1931
                                        John Boyd's Ranch, Bland, N.M.
Dear Max: Thanks ever so much for depositing the money. I'm sorry I didn't get a chance to see you before I left.

This country out here is one of the greatest things I have ever seen and I can strongly recommend this ranch, which is not a fancy dude ranch but very plain and cheap—$32 a week per person, which includes everything, meals, horses, etc. It is way up in the mountains, 8,000 feet above seal level. We haven't been around much yet, but there is a great variety of landscape and interest in the country. We went over to Bland (the nearest post office) yesterday—it used to be a gold town of 15,000 people and now there are only eight or ten, including two aged prospectors who have never been able to tear themselves away. The mountains here are inhabited by bears, mountain lions, wildcats, wolves, coyotes, and deer, but I haven't seen any of these animals yet. There are communistic Indian villages, said to be models of good government, which I am anxious to investigate. The landscapes and forests are unlike anything I have ever seen and are probably equal to anything in the world. New Mexico is the best possible antidote to New York.

What is the deadline on my book in order to bring it out in the fall—
which I want to be sure to do? The first of September?

As ever, Edmund Wilson

To Maxwell Perkins   July 21, 1931
                                                              Bland, N.M.
Dear Max: I just got your letter. Would you object to putting the book
over to February? The more I work on it, the more ambitious ideas I have
about it—and I think it would be a good idea to have it cover exactly a
year—from October to October. I'm anxious to get as many things into it
as possible. In its way, it is a sort of history, and I don't believe its value
will be spoiled by the fact that, when it appears, some of the events it
tells about will be more than a year old.

I have a good deal improved the Ford article, I think, in rewriting it
for the book—also the other thing which is to come out in *Scribner's;* I
wish they could have had them in this form.

I haven't been able to think of any better name, which is why I haven't
answered your telegram.

This is one of the swellest parts of the country I have ever been in—
something like the Adirondacks or New Hampshire, but less somber and
grim and much more fun. We spent a week in Santa Fe and Taos and,
though they are both immensely attractive towns, have about the worst
set of artists and writers to be found anywhere, as they most of them have
or have had t.b. in addition to their artistic disabilities.

. . . I want to do, besides New Mexico, something about Boulder Dam
and Hollywood—also, if the publication of the book can be put over, to
try to do something with Chicago on the way back; I'm coming back from
the West the first of October. If any English reviews of *Axel's Castle* come
in, I wish you'd send them out to me. I understand it got panned in the
English *Bookman.*   As ever, E. Wilson

To Christian Gauss   July 31, 1931
                                                              Bland, N.M.
Dear Mr. Gauss: . . . We're up in the Jemez Mountains—the most beautiful mountain country I have ever seen . . . Also a most extraordinary
population of rich people, writers and artists who pose as Indians, cow-
boys, prospectors, desperadoes, Mexicans, and other nearly extinct species.
All bearing out my theory about Rimbaud!

. . . I expect to be back in the East about the first of October, but not
for long, I hope, in New York—am resigning as an editor of *The New
Republic* and am going to try to get more writing done.

I've been reading the Beards' *The Rise of American Civilization* and
am very much impressed by it. Have you read it? It throws more light for

me on affairs in the United States than any other history I have ever read. I came out here by way of Virginia, West Virginia, Tennessee, and Missouri, stopping off for various stories—and America certainly seemed a wonderful country. Its present sour situation is ridiculous.

I read Marx last winter, and so far as I can see, his prophecy is now being fulfilled and he ought to be turning in his grave with glee: combined overproduction and destitution, the complete divorce between the country and the city, with the people in the cities cut off from the earth and physically and spiritually enfeebled and the people in the country not able to make a living, and the concentration of money and means of production in a very few hands, with more and more of the rest of the people finding themselves dispossessed.

Yours for the parliament of men and federation of the world! Best love to Mrs. Gauss. I hope to see you both in the fall.   Bunny Wilson

To Allen Tate   July 20, 1931
                                                          Bland, N.M.

Dear Allen: I got *The Hound and Horn* with your review when I was over at Santa Fe the other day and it seems to me that you have misunderstood some of my ideas. My remarks about making art and science one were not intended as "a program for the coming generation" but as an extremely remote prophecy. The point that I am trying to make when I talk in this vein is that art and science both are merely aids to getting by in the world. They harmonize or explain limited fields of experience and so comfort and reassure us and also, in proportion as they are original and profound, actually make it easier for humanity to live and improve itself. The end is not art or science but the survival and improvement of humanity. So that it seems likely that the time will come eventually when the artistic and scientific masterpiece will be not a theory or a book but human life itself. As I've told you, I believe in progress like the Abbé de Saint-Pierre—except that I don't think it goes quite so fast as the eighteenth-century people did when they didn't foresee that mechanical inventions were not immediately going to be used to improve the general human condition but were also on the way going to be used for the exploitation of one class by another. But I expect the human generations of the future to be as superior to ourselves in education, in the mastery of techniques, in the comprehensiveness of their mental range, and in their capacity for organized cooperation as we are to the prehistoric cliff dwellers whose caves I went over to see in the Frijoles Canyon yesterday. (I've expressed myself on this subject before: in the third section of *Daisy*, where the hero, seeing science and art as techniques for getting by, gets profoundly pessimistic about them, as anybody must do who can't hope anything for humanity in general—though at the end, becoming more hopeful, he embraces art as a useful trade like carpentry; also, see the end of my Beebe–Iguana dialogue.)

As for the "coming generation," I tried to make clear that what I expected to happen was what in fact was already happening when I wrote: a combination of Symbolism and naturalism. Joyce had already effected this and all the people who stem from him—as well as a good many others—continue it: Expressionism, the later O'Neill, Dos Passos, the Dadaists in their later manifestations; Thomas Wolfe, I suppose; and your countryman William Faulkner is an example of that, isn't he?

"Symbolism and naturalism" is not the same thing as saying "art and science." Symbolism was the atmospheric or arty side of art and naturalism the factual side, which got divorced from each other during the nineteenth century and, in my opinion, ought to be wedded again. What is at the bottom of my own attitude about this, in contrast to yours, is the fact that I am enough older than you to have been brought up on a literature which did mix these two elements in better proportions than the literature of after the war, which was what you were reading when you were in college and which still seems to you the normal thing. It seems abnormal to me and that is the reason I take the point of view I do in *Axel's Castle;* I'm looking back to Shaw, Wells, Bennett, France, Flaubert, Dostoevsky, Ibsen, Renan, et al. You call some of these people propagandists, but I don't see how you could if you had read them—which I bet you haven't— if by propaganda you mean the kind of thing which is put out by governments, political parties, etc. If by propaganda you mean, on the other hand, merely attempts to persuade people of one's point of view or particular way of seeing things, every writer is a propagandist.

Science and art, as conventionally practiced, require different techniques, granted—but except when one is under the influence of people like Eliot, they do not seem so different as you seem to suppose. The great scientists have been occupied with values—it is only their vulgar followers who think they are not. If scientists like Descartes, Newton, Einstein, Darwin, and Freud don't "look deeply into experience," what do they do? They have imaginations as powerful as any poet's, and some of them were first-rate writers as well. How do you draw the line between *Walden* and *The Voyage of the Beagle?* The product of the scientific imagination is a new vision of relations—like that of the artistic imagination. You are still, I think, too much impressed with the dicta on this subject of the Aquinas of *The Criterion,* who has an obvious interest nowadays in disparaging scientific revelation in order to fortify religious revelation—though in an earlier essay, I think in *The Sacred Wood,* he made some admirable remarks about there being only one kind of intelligence and that the scientific intelligence. At that time, he talked about Remy de Gourmont as the most comprehensive critic since Aristotle or something of the sort—

though Gourmont had never done, so far as I know, any more first-hand scientific research than H. G. Wells, at whom Eliot now scoffs, and had, if anything, even more secular views.

Another thing: there is a fundamental difference between what Milton did and what Valéry does. Accepting your idea about the poet's applying a system, Milton had a particular system—whereas Valéry has merely the abstract idea of a system, any system.

In the meantime, without being aware of it, I have been revenging myself, as you may have seen, by misrepresenting you, as you will doubtless think, in *The New Republic*. The article is in bad condition because they didn't wait for my corrections and only put in a few of them at the last moment.

We've been out on this ranch since June—marvelous country and very interesting, but more or less of a museum now. Are going on to California next week . . .

I saw Phelps Putnam in Santa Fe, where he is living in style with Cutting, the liberal New Mexico Senator. Since he was in Clarkesville, one of his principal amusements is reciting his own poetry with a Tennessee accent.   . . . Edmund

To ALLEN TATE   August 16, 1931
                                          7 Lingate Lane, Santa Barbara, Calif.
Dear Allen: In reading your letters, I feel more and more that you get me all wrong. But will leave it to my forthcoming book to straighten things out, if that is possible. This stuff I am writing for the N.R. will make more sense when it is put together and in a different form . . .

As for human history in general, I've never been able to see how anyone who is not a sincere Christian or a believer in some other religious faith can escape assuming that humanity builds better and makes more sense as it gets along. If you can believe that there is another world and that everything that happens on earth has its only significance there—and at the same time (what has often gone with it), as the seventeenth-century classicists did, that the perfect works of literature, art, etc., have all been produced in the past, so that the best we of the present can do is imitate them (and I suspect you of a form of this: trying to keep things in scholastic categories, based on obsolete distinctions)—if you really believe this, then you don't have to believe in progress. Otherwise, I don't see how you can get out of it. What about the cave men?—don't you think our society with all its faults is an improvement on theirs? Not that I could prove it was to anybody who didn't think so, but that is the faith on which my own ideas are based. And I can't see that people who don't think so and are not religious are ever able to give life any meaning at all.

In regard to your snootiness about science, I remember talking with you once about the snootiness of the humanists when confronted with poetry like Baudelaire's: we agreed that the beauty and the discipline of even a poem which expressed a perverse moral involved moral values to a high degree. What about the physicist's formulas, then? Isn't the same thing true of them? It seems to me that you talk about science just as the humanists talk about poetry.

My thing in the N.R., by the way, wasn't intended to be so satirical as you apparently think and, to anybody else but you touchy Nashville guys, sounds extremely sympathetic.* You people certainly take the Southern Cross. Did or did not you and John Ransom and Davidson have the abominable manners to sit around and entertain Raymond and Louise and me with a prolonged headshaking and jeering over an unfortunate Northerner who had presumed to come South and try to edit a paper, and with a sour account of other Northerners who had had the effrontery to try to hunt foxes in Tennessee? And then you raise the roof when I kid you a little about General Bragg!

Thanks for Red Warren's address—I hope to get to San Francisco and will certainly look him up. I don't get the same kick out of Southern California this time that I have before—it is beautiful like the Riviera and full of felicity after a fashion, but it seems to me now a great empty goofy place . . .

As ever, Edmund

To E. E. Cummings
[Postcard]

August 20, 1931
Santa Barbara

This will give you an idea of Mrs. Oakleigh Thorne's garden vista. We think of you often—are eager to hear about Cummings's adventures in Russia—understand that there has been a slight capitalistic relapse since his visit. We had a very good time at a ranch in New Mexico and are now in Santa Barbara, Cal., where the sun shines like a fool every day and every blue wave lisps, Thunkitht California—we miss those big Atlantic storms.

Bunny and Margaret

To Maxwell Perkins

September 8, 1931
Santa Barbara

Dear Max: When my royalty report is ready, which I hope will soon be the case, I wish they'd send the check straight to Red Bank, Second National Bank and Trust Company, instead of out here.

I've just come back from Hollywood and Los Angeles—they are interesting but absolutely balmy and really pretty awful. I went to see Upton

---

* "Tennessee Agrarians," in The American Jitters.

214

Sinclair and found him full of gloomy predictions—he says that if Germany goes Communist before Russia gets into her stride, the American bankers will loan France money to fight her and by monopolizing the radio launch America on a war to save Christianity, with a propaganda of Communist atrocities in Germany and bleeding Lithuania—labor leaders will immediately be jailed and radicals will be reduced to grease spots . . .

As ever, Bunny Wilson

To BURTON RASCOE   October 2, 1931
                                                   Santa Barbara

Dear Burton: I'm terribly sorry you've been having such a bad time. What has been the matter? . . .

I suppose you have seen how Malcolm [Cowley] lays you under contribution in his last installment. I think his stuff is awfully good, though I take exception a little to the tone of a mellow old man of letters reviewing the indiscretions of his youth from a distance of many decades. Still, I suppose I did something of the same thing in *Daisy*—and Mumford in his reminiscences of *The Dial* and *The Seven Arts* sounds as if he were summing up the generation of 1830. I suppose all these premature memoirs on the part of the comparatively young mean that something has really come to an end for them and that they are merely cleaning it out of their systems.

I have had a very good time this summer—have ranged around considerably and seen a good many singular happenings.

. . . Hope you will soon be all right. I hadn't known, either, about your father's death—you have certainly had a dose of trouble. Your father's death makes a big psychological difference to you, I think—robs you of something and gives you something new at the same time—at least it did in my case.   As ever, Bunny W.

The only thing I am writing about Hollywood is about the film that Eisenstein is making in Mexico, instigated and financed by Upton Sinclair, and I wanted to include that in my *Jitters* book . . .*

---

* "Serge Eisenstein arrived in Hollywood in the spring of 1930. He had signed a contract with Jesse M. Lasky . . . for Paramount . . . The kind of thing that the Paramount producers tried to get Eisenstein to do he stubbornly refused to do . . . The producers were so anxious to get rid of him that they bought him his ticket back to Russia . . . for the moment his contract ran out. His passport was to expire with the contract . . . Eisenstein went to Upton Sinclair, who lives in Pasadena . . . He got Eisenstein's passport slightly extended and he appealed for funds to some of the radical millionaires who flourish so oddly in Southern California . . . He got off to Mexico with his cameraman and scenario man . . ."
—*The American Jitters*, 1932

". . . this potentially great picture . . . *Que Viva Mexico!*—as Eisenstein was going to call it . . ."   —*The American Earthquake*, 1957

December 9, 1931
                                                        Provincetown

Dear Sinclair: I'm sorry that Mrs. Elmhirst's committee didn't come
through (it's a fund left by Willard Straight). But I've just heard from
Gilbert Seldes that he thinks it may be possible to get something from
J. S. Watson, the former editor and owner of *The Dial*, who has money
and is much interested in the movies. He is writing him, but wants to
know precisely what the terms are. I have sent your letter on to Miss
Bogue and have forgotten exactly what you said about it, so would you
mind writing to Seldes? He is very much interested and I should think
would be able to help. He is anxious to see the film, so I hope you will
have your brother-in-law get in touch with him if he comes on. His address
is 10 Henderson Place.

Thank you very much for your letters and enclosures. I'm glad you
approved of my Lippmann letter. I should also have thanked you and
Mrs. Sinclair before now for all your kindness in California. My visits to
Pasadena were among the bright spots of my stay out there—otherwise
enervating and dull. I don't know how you stand up against it!

By the way, did you see Eisenstein's protest against my article in *The
New Republic*? I don't suppose he's really miffed about it, is he? I took
it that he merely didn't want it thought that he'd been complaining about
the Soviets or that he was enjoying himself in Mexico more than at home.

Please give my best regards to Mrs. Sinclair.

                                        Yours very sincerely, Edmund Wilson

"THE AMERICAN JITTERS"
1931–1932

To Sherwood Anderson   June 24, 1931

Dear Sherwood: I found the [Frank] Keeney union* on the verge of a strike. The Musteites *are* a little bit like Y.M.C.A. secretaries, as you say, but they evidently have a lot of courage. I attended one meeting called by the Lewis organization,† where half the audience were Keeney adherents, and the two factions walked around each other like dogs getting ready to fight.

From there I went to Chattanooga, one of America's most horrible towns, what with the niggers and the mills. I discovered to my surprise that the Communists were having considerable success there. For the niggers, Communism is a new and exciting kind of revivalism. People were beginning to get worried about it, and I confess if I were a white there, outnumbered six to one by Negroes, I don't think I'd encourage the Communists. The Scottsboro case‡ is full of interesting features, but everybody has done so much lying that it is hard to get to the bottom of it. The double defense§ makes things harder—not only are the two lawyers estranged by the different organizations which are retaining them, but they ran against each other for the nomination for attorney general in

---

* "Frank Keeney's independent union . . . stands . . . between the Communists, on the one hand, and the corrupt A.F. of L., on the other, as a spontaneous native labor movement . . ."   —*The American Earthquake*
† John L. Lewis's United Mine Workers of America.
‡ "Scottsboro is a small town, and the people there have little excitement: it was a long time since anything had come their way so sensational as nine niggers accused of rape of . . . two white girls from Huntsville, Alabama . . . both had apparently from an early age been practicing prostitution . . . They are alleged to have lived indifferently among Negroes and whites . . ."   —*The American Earthquake*
§ The defense was split between the NAACP and the Communist organization, the International Labor Defense.

the last Democratic primaries. The I.L.D. man is a foxy and amusing old bird, half liberal, half cynical, who regaled me with all the local scandal. He and his son are both in politics and depend a good deal on the Negro vote: he doesn't know anything about what the Communists are doing, he claims, and denies there are any in town.

I had a most enjoyable visit at Marion—was glad to find you going strong. Most of the writers have been dopeless, despondent, and drunken lately—worse than the bond salesmen and brokers.

Am between St. Louis and Kansas City en route to Albuquerque—and have just been passing along the wide Mizzoura. What a wonderful country this would be if only the people got some good out of it.

Good luck with your novel—which I'm anxious to read . . .

As ever, EW

I really think that Keeney and his lieutenants are more valuable radicals than most of the Communists. Maybe they will be Communists in time.

Edmund Wilson

To John Dos Passos   June 24, 1931

Dear Dos: I found Sherwood Anderson all full of Communism. He doesn't know much about it, but the idea has given him a powerful afflatus. He has a new girl, a radical Y.W.C.A. secretary, who took him around to the mills. He is writing a novel with a Communist hero and I have never seen him so much aroused.

I spent five days in West Virginia. The situation in the coal fields is probably the most exciting anywhere on the industrial scene. The Communists are raising hell in Ohio and Pennsylvania, and in Harlan County, Kentucky, the operators have brought in the militia and are only holding the lid on by means of a reign of terror. Between the two, in the Kanawha Valley, secessionists from the Lewis organization have organized what seems to be a pretty strong independent union. [A. J.] Muste has sent them some Brookwoodites—the Brookwoodites are quite unlike Communists and superficially rather like Red Cross workers or young radical professors, but, without being particularly militant, they seem to have a lot of backbone—it takes a good deal of courage to go into that country, where shootings frequently occur and where just at present the atmosphere is full of uncertainty and suspicion, what with the authorities, the Communists, and the A. F. of L. Lately, the neighborhood of Charleston has been infested with phony miners who try to get the Musteites to supply them with Communist literature—greatly to the latter's disgust. This West Virginia Miners' Union is apparently about to call a strike and it will be worth watching as a 100 percent American non-A.F. of L. radical venture. The three leaders of the union—the former miners and union organizers, not

JOHN DOS PASSOS

I first became acquainted in the Harvard *Lit.* with the names
of Gilbert Seldes and John Dos Passos.   —*A Prelude*

He is perhaps the first really important writer to have succeeded in using colloquial American for a novel of the
highest artistic seriousness.
—*Review of* The 42nd Parallel, *in* The New Republic, 1930

the Musteites—struck me as very sound types. They are genuine native leaders, were born there and command confidence and enthusiasm—Frank Keeney, the president, was the district head at the time of the 1920 armed march—and are old socialists, who got discouraged when Debs was jailed during the war but who still hang on to their fundamental radical convictions. The Lewis organization apparently let the Kentucky miners down, were partly responsible for bringing in the militia and handing the miners over to the operators bound hand and foot. And they are now active in West Virginia, where they have just made an agreement with some of the Northern operators for wages way below non-union rates. I attended a meeting called by the Lewis people at which half the audience were Keeney adherents and at which the different elements were so much preoccupied with watching each other and searching each other for weapons that the speakers hardly got any attention.

My next stop was Chattanooga, what with the niggers and the mills one of the most squalid towns I have ever been in. The Scottsboro case has set the town agog, insofar as Southerners of that kind can be set agog. I was somewhat surprised to find that the Communists, even on the admission of the respectability-loving Negroes, have been having a good deal of success. There are lots of Negroes laid off from the mills and Communism presents itself as a new and stimulating kind of revivalism. The Scottsboro case itself is very difficult to unravel, because there is not only a defense and a prosecution but a double defense with the two lawyers very hostile to each other—they competed for the attorney-general nomination in the last Democratic primaries. It's an extremely interesting case, however—on account of the Communist element something new, I suppose, in the South. I confess that if I were a white in a Southern city like Chattanooga, outnumbered six to one by Negroes and with the Negroes enslaved to the mills and making a sea of squalor all around and shooting each other and cutting each other's throats at the rate of about one death a day, I shouldn't be very blithe about encouraging Communist propaganda.

. . . Give my love to everybody . . . Tell Katy that I am going hither and yon and quietly sowing the seeds of perversity.   As ever, EW

To ALLEN TATE   August 16, 1931
                                                        Santa Barbara
. . . The point is that it seems to me that the world is in for a big struggle between capitalism and Communism. America is just beginning to be affected—having, according to me, definitely come to the end of her period of capitalist expansion—and I am trying to write a sort of fragmentary history of what is happening here—events during a year of the Depression.

In regard to the agrarians (it is true that I haven't done any more than look through the symposium), it seems to me that the farmers are as much at the mercy of the capitalist system as anybody else. The issue is not between industrialism and agriculture but between anarchic private enterprise and profit and socialism. An I.W.W. that I saw at the Boulder Dam strike was telling me about a conversation he had had with a farmer: he (the I.W.W.) had said to him, "When the fight comes, I'll at least know which side I'm on and how to act" (the farmer had been sniffing at industrial work compared to farming) "—whereas you won't know whether your solidarity lies with the farm hands who work for you or the banker who holds the mortgage on your farm." According to Beard, the South had already been corrupted by capitalist enterprise on the part of the cotton planters as distinguished from the planters of tobacco, indigo, etc., before the Civil War. What I don't see about the agrarians' point of view is how they are going to carry out their program without meeting the issues created by the social-economic machine which now controls a large part of the world and the whole of America. And how does agrarianism take care of such a situation as the one which has followed on the Scottsboro trials in Chattanooga and Alabama? (I have an article about it which is probably out by this time.)

To John Dos Passos   February 29, 1932

Dear Dos: What happened in Kentucky was just about what you would expect. The liberal-radicals had a wild time between the Communists on one side and the infuriated Kentuckians on the other. When we first started off on the train, those of us who recognized the vein were made very uneasy when Charley Walker's mouth opened and a couple of columns of the *Daily Worker* poured forth, and when we got down there we discovered that they had already been circulated in a handbill announcing that the "Solidarity Delegation" was arriving in Pineville to hold a mass demonstration around the courthouse and demand the release of the political prisoners. As a result, they had the courthouse fortified with machine guns. The delegation were mostly in favor of negotiating in an orderly way with the authorities, but the Communists stuck to their own ideas of the program. We would make them promise to leave the talking to us and refrain from provocative speeches and they would always cheerfully assent but then, as soon as there was an audience, go ahead and make the speeches—while the liberals climbed down from the truck and went to look into conditions in the miners' homes.

The final result of this dual policy was that Harold Hickerson and one of the Communist girls got arrested for making inflammatory speeches while Waldo, Malcolm, and I were trying to get permission to speak from the authorities. In the evening, we went over and called on the people in jail. This, coming on top of the handbill, caused a rumor that we were preparing a jail break, and a guard of deputies was put on the jail. This may have been the reason they ran us out—though they may have been planning to, anyway. At any rate, that night they came to the hotel and got us and took us in cars to the state line. There they turned off all the lights and slugged Waldo Frank and Allen Taub, the I.L.D. lawyer, in the head—evidently with the butts of guns. Waldo, who was chairman of the committee, played his role with great sang-froid and tact.

The whole thing was very interesting for us—though I don't know that it did much for the miners. One of the organizers was shot that day—the governor called out troops to keep people from attending his funeral—and another was badly beaten up. I came back convinced that if the literati want to engage in radical activities, they ought to organize or something independently—so that they can back other people besides the comrades and so that the comrades can't play them for suckers.   . . . As ever, EW

To Theodore Dreiser   May 2, 1932
                                                52 West 58th Street, N.Y.
Dear Mr. Dreiser: Lewis Mumford, Waldo Frank, Dos Passos, Sherwood Anderson, and I have signed this manifesto (composed by ourselves without the collaboration or knowledge of the Communists). We have sent it also to Paul Green, Edna Millay, Van Wyck Brooks, and yourself. I sent you a copy of it sometime ago at an address where it may not have reached you—I have just been told that you are at the Ansonia. We hope you'll be willing to sign it.   Yours sincerely, Edmund Wilson

MANIFESTO

1. The present crisis of the world—and specifically of the United States—is something more than a mere crisis of politics or economics; and it will not pass with the depression. It is a crisis of human culture. What faces us today is the imperative need for new social forms, new values, a new human order.
2. Of this crisis, however, the economic chaos is the crucial symbol. The need of a new economy in which men and nations can live and build and grow is the focal point of the human crisis.
    a. The present economic system is based on the subordination of human values to motives of anarchic self-assertion.
    b. It depends on the exploitation of the many for the profit of the few.
    c. It encourages a leadership of cunning and greed.
    d. It encourages in the nations the same anti-social motives as in individual men.
    e. It neglects or makes eccentric to the main stream of life these creative impulses which are as fundamental in all men as the impulse toward acquisition.

222

3. The need of human growth is, therefore, inextricable from the need of a new social-economic order.
4. We subscribe to certain lines of action as immediately urgent:
   a. The ruling castes, hopelessly corrupted by the very conditions of their emergence, must be expelled from their present position.
   b. A temporary dictatorship of the class-conscious workers must be set up, as the necessary instrument for abolishing all classes based on material wealth.
   c. A new order must be established, as swiftly as can be, in which economic rivalry and private profit are barred; and in which competition will be lifted from the animal plane of acquisition to the human plane of cultural creation.
5. This revolution must not be understood as simply a revolt against the economic chaos of today. It is an immediate organ of creation. We believe that in imaginative works, in philosophic thought, in concrete activities and groups, the nucleus and the framework of the new society must be created *now*.
6. Wherefore, in our function as writers:
   a. We declare ourselves supporters of the social-economic revolution— such revolution being an immediate step toward the creation in the United States of a new human culture based on common material possession, which shall release the energies of man to spiritual and intellectual endeavor.
   b. We recognize the fundamental identity of our interests with those of the workers and farmers of the nation.
   c. We call on our fellow writers, artists, teachers, scholars, engineers, and intellectuals of every kind, to identify their cause with that of the workers, in whose ultimate capacity to rise and to rule rests the destiny of America and mankind.

As for Waldo Frank, he writes in a style—to me, never quite satisfactory—that combines James Joyce with the Hebrew prophets. At his best, he touches tragedy and, at his worst, he embraces melodrama.   (*The Shores of Light*, 1926)

To Waldo Frank   June 17, 1932
                                                          52 West 58th Street, N.Y.
Dear Waldo: I have been having long debates with Dos Passos about our manifesto. He feels very strongly that, in spite of our efforts to keep clear of the Communist formulas, we have followed them too closely. He points out that these formulas don't allow for the immense proportion of white-collar workers in America, without whose support a revolution could

hardly be pulled off—one ought to emphasize the identity of interests of the petty bourgeois with the proletariat rather than the possible class dictatorship of the proletariat over the bourgeoisie. He also thinks that we ought to take pains to translate the whole thing into language familiar to the average American—"plutocracy," "money-power," "democracy," etc. I think there is a good deal in both these contentions. I believe that if our manifesto were written more along these lines, we should have more chance of getting people like Brooks and Sinclair Lewis to sign it. Dos has tried in the enclosed draft to state the case in this way. As he has done it, it is incomplete and lacks concision; but what would you think of rewriting the manifesto and handling it more like this? Dos's idea is that we could call it "An Appeal to Desk Workers." I'm enclosing a letter from Dreiser. I hope you're getting along with your novel.   As ever, Edmund

I don't think it does any harm to delay the manifesto. Perhaps the most effective time to publish it would be not long before the elections—as a gesture of dissociation from regular politics.

To Waldo Frank   August 10, 1932
                                        571 Commercial Street, Provincetown
Dear Waldo: . . . My point of view about our manifesto was that I was perfectly willing to sign it as we agreed but that I thought it was an object to get as many people as possible and I was impressed by some of the points that Dos Passos raised. Since then, Dreiser has published a statement of his own and the Communists have asked people to contribute statements about the election to a pamphlet they are planning to publish. It has occurred to me that this pamphlet might serve the purpose of our manifesto—that each could contribute his own manifesto and that if it is sent around in such a way as to get publicity it might have the same effect (if any). There are other things to consider about it, however, and I'd like to have a chance to discuss the whole matter with you . . .

I see by the paper today that you went on that delegation to Hoover and met with the regulation reception. I went on one of those expeditions a couple of springs ago—they are entirely depressing, but this one of yours was worth doing, I think; the protest you drew up seems to have gotten full publicity in the *Times*. Hoover is one of the worst, if not the worst, we have ever had in the White House: like the man in Robert Frost's poem who worked so hard over his walls, "he walks in darkness"—seems something hardly human which has emanated from the primary sordid substratum of the life of the commercial-industrial era, an amoeba with nothing but self-nourishing and self-protective instincts. The affair of the veterans made me feel sick with indignation which had no comeback, and now the account of your expedition has affected me the same way.
                                        . . . As ever, Edmund Wilson

PROVINCETOWN AND NEW YORK

1932–1933

To ALLEN TATE   March 22, 1932
                                                    52 West 58th Street, N.Y.

Dear Allen: Thanks ever so much for the poems, which I've been reading with great enjoyment. I'm not sure I don't like the "Emblems" best, though "Alice" is one of your best examples of your peculiar imagination and the sonnets of your language. I've sent you a copy of my own book, in which I've tried to improve my remarks about the agrarians.

I was sorry to hear that you'd been sick and hope you're all right. When are you coming to New York? Life and people here seem to me to have gotten much more interesting since the Depression. They grow more amiable and have more ideas in proportion as they have less money or less hopes of making it in large quantities. Compared to what it was, the intellectual world is seething. For myself, I am composing a play and in my spare time working quietly at the revolution, of which I will doubtless be one of the first victims.

Raymond and Louise seem to have been having rather a bad time during the last year, but Louise is in fine shape now, better than I have seen her for years. Malcolm, as I suppose you know, embroiled himself in all kinds of controversy with [Gorham] Munson over what Joe Gould calls his "Up from Slavery" articles. I thought that Munson did have some cause for complaint but the controversy certainly got progressively on a lower and lower plane, especially when it became a question between Munson and Matty Josephson as to which was the other's disciple. Joe Gould's comment on this was, "I think I can claim Josephson as my disciple!" Munson has now come out in *The Modern Quarterly* with the discovery that, though a good Humanist can have nothing to do with Rousseau, there is nothing to prevent him from being a Marxist—one of the most remarkable positions ever sustained.

Give my love to Caroline.* Congratulations on her getting the Guggenheim—where are you going to go? It's all too long since I've seen you.

. . . Edmund

To CHRISTIAN GAUSS
April 5, 1932
52 West 58th Street, N.Y.

Dear Christian: . . . I want to talk to you about a lot of things—Flaubert among them; I'm going to rewrite that *Herald Tribune* article for a book and want to be better posted on his life than I was when I wrote it. You haven't that book of memoirs by Maxime Du Camp, have you? I reread your introduction to *Madame Bovary* with much instruction . . .

As ever, Bunny W.

To RAYMOND HOLDEN†
August 12, 1932
Provincetown

Dear Raymond: How about coming up here? I can't figure out exactly how much it would cost to live. I pay the Portuguese girl $8 a week, but would have to pay her more, of course. She only gets us lunch and cleans up as it is, but could get all the meals. If you live on fish, the food is not awfully expensive. The house is most attractive—right on the harbor—swimming off the back porch. The simplest and cheapest way to get up here is to take the Boston boat (Eastern Steamship Co.) which leaves about five—then, when you get in at Boston in the morning, the Provincetown boat is only a few blocks away. Boston boat about $6.50 plus about $2.50 for stateroom; Provincetown boat, $1.75. Let me hear from you immediately in regard to this matter! EW

You could have the two bedrooms and bath on the bottom floor. You needn't pay me any rent.

To JOHN PEALE BISHOP
September 20, 1932
Provincetown

Dear John: I like these poems very much—they are better, I think, than the other recent stuff which you'd written when I saw you last fall—particularly "Easter Morning," "Perspectives Are Precipices," and "My Grandfather Kept Peacocks"—though I don't quite get the Eliot–Webster passage (a shade too much so, I think) in the middle section of "Easter Morning." I think you've arrived at something new and very good in the rather gray style with its close writing and vivid original images. I'm sending them on to Ridgely Torrence—he was saying the other day that you'd have a most remarkable book if it was all made up of your best. By the way, is the end of "Aliens" all right? It reads:

---

* Allen Tate was married to Caroline Gordon, the novelist.
† Raymond Holden was married to Louise Bogan.

"The direction
Is not know whither all these planets go."

As for Marxism, etc., it seems to me that like most people who haven't looked into it, you really don't understand the point of view, and I strongly recommend to you the works of Marx himself, Lenin, and Trotsky. I can assure you that you'll find them good reading. Be sure to read Trotsky's *Literature and Revolution,* an extraordinary and unique piece of literary criticism. A good way to begin is probably with the *Communist Manifesto* and Marx's *Eighteenth Brumaire of Louis Bonaparte.* If you can't swallow the abstract parts of *Das Kapital* (there is an excellent new translation in Everyman's), at least read the historical. The point is that the literature of Marxism is not really a body of dogma (you know that Marx said he was no Marxist and that Trotsky's writings have been suppressed by Stalin), though Communism itself—the Third International, that is—has some of the characteristics of a secular church: it corresponds more or less to the literature of the Enlightenment before the French and American Revolutions, and people of our own time can no more afford to be ignorant of it than people of the eighteenth century could of Voltaire and Montesquieu and Rousseau.

Yes, I have read Stavrogin's confession and think that great damage was done to the book when Dostoevsky was forced to leave it out. I haven't read Cino da Pistoia's poem, but will look it up and do so.

I've been struggling with a play,* which is now nearly done, and after that am going to do some more reporting and another play. I've been up here in Provincetown for a couple of months, but am going back to New York next week—can be reached through *The New Republic.* I hope you'll be coming back. I've been leading a very quiet life here with Rosalind, now old enough to be an interesting companion (Margaret is out in California with her kid)—reading, writing, swimming, and very little whoopee, though the eclipse was a great social occasion, also a wonderful spectacle (this was one of the places up here where it was total). Did you ever see one? It is something like one of your later poems. In mid-afternoon, as the sun becomes obscured, an ashen color rises from the horizon, then a sort of blank uniform twilight falls, the sea has become gray-blue and the sea birds fly low as if they were going home for the night—then a sudden great bright bead of white light blazes out just below and to one side as the mask of the moon moves past—you have a strange feeling of joy and relief—everybody goes for a swim and a drink. We watched it from the Truro hills beside one of those big old wooden churches, where you could see the sea on both sides. Do you remember coming up here to see Edna? You ought to come up again sometime when you get back. The Provincetown harbor is marvelous.

---

* *Beppo and Beth.*

Well, "the stars move still, time runs, the clock will strike." (I refer to the world in general.)

Give my best to Margaret—I hope the children are flourishing.

As ever, Edmund

I thought MacLeish's *Conquistador* was lousy and regret to detect traces of it in "The Return"—otherwise excellent. It *is* very much like Chirico, but that's all right—quite a feat. The opening and the last two stanzas are fine—Archie only gets in with "the old sea-fights, the soldiers' names and sculptors' "—couldn't you do something about this? Also, the sad old Anglo-Catholic rememberer of eyes that a little while outlast the dream, in lines 3 and 4 of stanza 6. But the next two stanzas, as I say, are marvelous! Only call attention to these reminiscences, thinking you'd want to weed them out.

Mr. Hueffer's *transatlantic review*—a kind of badge for all that is freshest and most interesting in contemporary writing . . . Ford Madox Ford, who changed his family name from Hueffer.

(*The Shores of Light*, 1924)

To Ford Madox Ford

October 13, 1932
The New Republic

Dear Ford: Thank you for asking me to contribute to the Pound pamphlet. I intended to, but haven't been able to, first on account of a long piece of work I had to finish, and then the death of my wife. I am told now that the *Cantos** are just about to be published, so I suppose it is too late. I should have been glad to pay my respects to Pound, who meant a great deal to the writers of my generation in America. In spite of his expatriation, which I deplored, and the rather meager and bookish fare with which his poetry always seemed to me to be nourished, he was one of the few American writers of his time who represented genuinely high standards and never let us down.

How are you? Remember me to the Tates if you see them.

Yours sincerely, Edmund Wilson

To F. Scott Fitzgerald

November 7, 1932
Red Bank

Dear Scott: Thanks ever so much for asking me to Baltimore. I've been wanting very much to see you and Zelda and have been on the verge of writing you. I'm afraid I can't make it, though, till later. I'm going West on a reporting trip the end of this week, but will be back before Christmas and would love to come sometime in January, say, if you can have me. Is there any chance of your coming to New York?—one of the most dismal

* Pound's *A Draft of XXX Cantos*.

places ever known now, but with no temptation any more to disorganizing debauchery.

I thought your story in *The Mercury* was swell—wish you would do something more about Hollywood, which everybody who knows anything about it is either scared or bribed not to tell about or have convinced themselves is all right. I've only just started Zelda's novel.* I thought Hemingway's bullfighting book was pretty maudlin—the only thing of his I haven't liked.† My feeling was that, though bullfighting was probably a good clean sport, H. had made it disgusting. Best love to Zelda. Hope to see you soon.   As ever, Bunny W.

To CHRISTIAN GAUSS   November 7, 1932
                                                          Red Bank

. . . I've been reading Michelet's history again lately, after dropping it years ago after the Saint Bartholomew's massacre. It made a great impression on me at the time of the war and still seems to me one of the most satisfactory books I ever read—I wonder people don't make more fuss about it nowadays. Let's hope we're not going to have the period of the religious wars duplicated in a struggle between capitalism and Communism. I see some striking resemblances! . . .

To F. SCOTT FITZGERALD   March 26, 1933
                                                314 East 53rd Street, N.Y.

Dear Scott: The Red Bank bank has folded up with a loud crash, so you will have gotten back the check I gave you. Here is the currency.

I've sent back *Sanctuary* through *The New Republic*. I thought it was pretty good. He [William Faulkner] certainly has a compelling imagination, and I thought the whole fable very well conceived, though sloppily executed stylistically and technically.

When are you coming to New York? Looking back on our conversations, I'd like to enlarge on certain points.   Bunny

The moralist in Paul Elmer More, who had always been at war with the poet . . .
        ("Mr. More and the Mithraic Bull," *The New Republic*, 1937)

To PAUL ELMER MORE   April 22, 1933
                                                314 East 53rd Street, N.Y.

Dear Mr. More: I have read your essay on Proust with great interest. You have more real insight into Proust than most of his sympathetic critics—have handled the fundamentals of his emotional situation as perhaps

---

* *Save Me the Waltz.*
† *Death in the Afternoon.*

229

nobody else—in English, at any rate—has done. I wanted, however, to call your attention—in case you should be reprinting it in a book—to the fact that you have made me in one instance say the opposite of what I meant. It was Marx's own predictions and not those of his opponents which were based "only on an assumption of the incurable swinishness and inertia of human nature." The liberals whom *The New Republic* represented had never been willing to accept Marx's assumption that the owning class under capitalism must eventually become incapable of running the industrial system—they used to talk about American capitalism gradually "socializing itself." The point I was trying to make—not writing at that time as a Marxist—was that the liberal bourgeoisie had better bestir itself if they didn't want the Marxist catastrophe to occur. Today I should say in the light of events that Marx's prophecies were correct and that our own ruling class has proved as incapable as any in the past of resisting the temptations to inertia and greed to which their money and power have exposed them. Yours sincerely, Edmund Wilson

To John Dos Passos   May 11, 1933
                                                              314 East 53rd Street, N.Y.
Dear Dos: I am sorry the Proustian fumigations haven't done all that I had hoped of them, but have sent you another slightly different prescription from the same pharmacopoeia. (I also had [Nathanael] West send you *Miss Lonelyhearts*—did you get it?)

Griffin [Barry] and I are quietly working along here toward a better understanding between classes and nations, but with results increasingly disappointing. We are expecting to have all our children here presently and think seriously of turning the place into a home for unmarried fathers—one of the most pathetic and helpless types produced by our modern civilization and one for whom society has as yet done nothing to provide . . .

I heard Eliot read his poems the other night. He did them extremely well—contrary to my expectation. He is an actor and really put on a better show than Shaw. I suppose that a kind of dramatic resonance he has is one of the things that have made his stuff carry so. He gives you the creeps a little at first because he is such a completely artificial, or rather, self-invented character—speaking English with a most careful English accent as if it were a foreign language which he had learned extremely well—but he has done such a perfect job with himself that you end by admiring him.

I saw Mary [Heaton] Vorse on her way through en route to Germany and she gave me to understand that the people in Provincetown were in such a state that Hitler seemed a relaxation . . . About the Rockefellers and [Diego] Rivera: I saw the mural just before they pulled it and he was just painting in portraits of [Jay] Lovestone and his chief lieutenant, who were to figure as the Communist heroes. This pleased nobody except Lovestone.

. . . Our back yard is getting quite inviting. Some little yellow flowers have come out and Tom has painted the iron furniture green. Muriel Draper is doing some landscape gardening which I don't understand and doubt whether she does either. Do come on and let us entertain you in the back yard.   As ever, Bunny W.

To BENNETT CERF   September 28, 1933
Random House   314 East 53rd St., N.Y.

. . . I wish, by the way, that the Modern Library could bring out Malraux's *Les Conquérants*, which was published in translation by Harcourt as *The Conquerors* and fell flat. Malraux's last book has been a sensation in France and I shouldn't wonder if he turned out to be the next great French novelist. I should think something could still be done with *Les Conquérants*, which is a hair-raising story of the Chinese Revolution . . .

To F. SCOTT FITZGERALD   October 21, 1933
                                             314 East 53rd Street, N.Y.
Dear Scott: I liked your thing about Lardner and was glad you did it for the *N.R.* The only thing I objected to in the last paragraph was the "great and good American," which didn't seem to meet the case exactly. Am delighted to hear about your book. I have just read Hemingway's new short stories,* and though the best of them are excellent, now is your time to creep up on him. John Bishop is here—in pretty good form, I thought, when I saw him. I haven't seen his book of poems yet. Margaret has got him planted out at Westport, which has been obsolete ever since you left. I am living in my little house here—a different kind of life from anything I have ever had in New York before—no neighborhood I know, no telephone, no doorman, no people all around in other apartments—I enjoy it. Best love to Zelda. When are you coming to N.Y.?
                                             As ever, Bunny

To F. SCOTT FITZGERALD   November 4, 1933
                                             314 East 53rd Street, N.Y.
Dear Scott: I thought that "great and good American" sounded like a political speech. Besides, Lardner, though a first-rate writer, wasn't exactly great, was he?—and, though personally likable, his chief claim to distinction was a gift for Swiftian satire based on hate. He always seemed to me to be desperately irked by his family, his associates, and himself. I'm sorry I missed seeing Zelda when she was here. Saw John Bishop a

* *Winner Take Nothing.*

couple days ago. His book of poems is quite impressive. Have you seen it? Now is your time to creep up on Hemingway.   As ever, EW

To Louise Bogan   November 22, 1933
                                                            314 East 53rd Street, N.Y.
Dear Louise: I was very much dismayed to hear of your claustration, as I had been counting on our German evenings and made repeated efforts to get hold of you before I learned that you had gone away. Do try to get things straightened out and get back. We miss you terribly. Rolfe Humphries and I had a discussion of your abilities the other night that lasted for hours—he puts you way above Edna Millay, which I demurred to at first, but when he challenged me to go through her books poem by poem and then consider yours, I was almost convinced. You are always a first-rate artist and it is a calamity for you to be languishing like this (if you are languishing). I don't know what else to say to you, because though I know what frightful difficulties you are in and deeply sympathize with you, it is the kind of thing one can't discuss by correspondence.

. . . I have succeeded in getting an advance from Harcourt, so I am feeling a little more stable . . .

Do some writing while you are in there and get out as soon as you can. The world needs, awaits, and will reward you. Let me hear from you in the meantime.   Love, Edmund

To Phelps Putnam   November 23, 1933
                                                            314 East 53rd Street, N.Y.
Dear Phelps: . . . I'm living here in a little house which I get for $60 a month. It is no palace but at least a house after years of living in apartments. It is way over on the East Side, almost on the river, and I live here what amounts in New York to the life of a recluse, alone, with only a faithful blackamoor to tend me.

I'm glad you liked my articles about Marx, etc.—I'm going to rewrite it later on for a book, I think. I've been made not a little uneasy by the activities of the Marxist literary guys; I think that the soul of the late Irving Babbitt has entered into Granville Hicks. Also, I find that I am continually being attacked for views which I have never expressed or held.

Good luck with your poem. I saw Eliot when he was over here and was glad to discover that he admired your poetry and thought Archie MacLeish's lousy.

I have no particular recent news—am working here on various literary undertakings, which, if God spares me, will see the light in time.

Please pay my respects to your new wife, whom I hope to see when you come back—and take care of yourself.   As ever, Bunny W.

To F. Scott Fitzgerald   December 4, 1933
                                            314 East 53rd Street, N.Y.
Dear Scott: I'm sorry about the other day, but you are sometimes a hard
guy to get along with and I'm told I'm not wonderful in this respect
either. What I object to is precisely the "scholar and vulgarian," "you
helped me more than I helped you" business. I know that this isn't entirely a role you've foisted on me: I've partly created it myself. But don't
you think at our present time of life we might dispense with this high-
school (Princeton University) stuff? I've certainly laid you under contribution in the past in the concoction of my literary personae and I don't
blame you or object a bit if you do the same with me. But just don't make
yourself disagreeable about it after asking me to lunch, you mug, if you
expect me to eat any with you.
    Hope you're recuperating in Bermuda. I'm looking forward to your
book. Love to Zelda.   As ever, Bunny

To Arthur Mizener*   1949

. . . The only one of these excerpts from my letters to Scott that I don't
care to have printed is the one that begins, "I'm sorry about the other
day"—which requires too much explanation. I had been seeing him during those years only at long intervals and we were rather out of joint with
one another. We had both been having our troubles and were touchy. The
incident mentioned here was due to a misunderstanding on my part, but
it had been brought on by Scott's habit of needling his friends when he
had passed a certain point of alcoholic consumption. On previous occasions when I had seen him he had presented me with writings of his,
pointing out passages, sometimes highly invidious, which he would tell
me were based on me. On this occasion, he wrote me to clear the situation
up and afterwards came round to see me in New York to be sure things
were all right between us. But he handled it with his usual lack of tact,
and I received him rather coldly . . .

To Arthur Mizener   1950

. . . Scott did not "quarrel with me viciously." He did not quarrel at all.
I became offended and walked out. My letter to him may sound vicious,
but there was nothing of the kind on his side. This whole thing was due
to a misunderstanding on my part, my own self-confidence at the time
being probably in as bad shape as his. What had led up to the incident

---

* In 1944 *The Princeton University Library Chronicle* published "Edmund Wilson:
A Checklist" by Arthur Mizener, at which time E. wrote him: ". . . looking at
the bibliography, have been very much impressed, not by my output, but by your
patience and industry. It will be immensely useful to me, if not to anyone else."

was his habit of needling one—which he would alternate with an admiration even more annoying. John Bishop told me that he did this with him, and I have seen him do it with Hemingway . . .*

To Louise Bogan   December 12, 1933
                                                   314 East 53rd Street, N.Y.
Dear Louise: I have wanted to come out to see you, but it is pretty hard just at present, as I have an immense amount of work to do here and have to go down to Red Bank every weekend. I've read a number of books lately which you might be interested in: Auden's *The Orators, The Dance of Death*, and *Poems*; Spender's *Poems*; Eliot's *The Use of Poetry*; John Bishop's *Poems*. I have them all here, and if you would like to read any or all of them, will send them to you (mail them back, though, will you, when you're done with them). I don't think so terribly much of Spender on the evidence of this book—it is a little on the clever-undergraduate side; but Auden seems to me really good. I think you said you'd read his poems and didn't think very highly of them; but *The Orators* and *The Dance of Death* are more interesting. Have you read any of the novels of an Anglo-Irish woman named Elizabeth Bowen? I saw her when she was here and liked her—haven't read any of her stuff. Dorothy Parker's new book has seemed to me amazingly good, particularly the last story. You should read it, if you haven't—I'll send you my borrowed copy, if you'll promise to send it back. I hope you're accomplishing something yourself. Those are just the conditions for high endeavor. I'm leading a pretty austere life myself, having squandered most of my advance from Harcourt and being broke again. I live here, tended by Hatty, reading and writing, rarely seeing anybody, and some days hardly going out of the house. When I was in a neurotic state myself, I used to think it was impossible to be alone; but now, though I sometimes get gloomy, I seem to thrive on it—there is nothing like it for literary composition. And it can be done more agreeably outside a sanatorium. I miss our evenings on Lexington Ave.—have not been around there since you left. Why don't you write a *confession d'un enfant du siècle?*—maybe Auden's *Orators* would give you a cue. What you really ought to do, I should think, is to give literary expression to your internal conflicts and ranklings. You haven't really done this for a long time, have you? Once you get experience out of your system in a satisfactory literary form, you can thumb your nose at the world. In any case, get out of there as soon as you can—the world needs you, and you, it.   Love, Edmund

_____

* "I'll be glad to read the MS [*The Far Side of Paradise: A Biography of F. Scott Fitzgerald*]."
                                                   —To Arthur Mizener, 1950

"THE AMBIGUITY OF HENRY JAMES"

AND

JOHN JAY CHAPMAN

1925–1959

To Louise Bogan   April 9, 1934
                                        314 East 53rd Street, N.Y.
Dear Louise: I was glad to get your note—sorry to have missed you every time you've been here. When are you coming back for good? I'm anxious to begin our German course—recently bought a fine set of Heine at a bargain sale at Brentano's, in preparation. I think that a certain number of regular German sessions a week would be an excellent thing for you. Have you seen these little evanescent poems of Eliot's? Some don't like them, but they seem to me exquisite . . . I've been reading great quantities of history and philosophy of history in preparation for writing a momentous essay on the subject. I am also very good on Henry James in *The Hound and Horn*, of which I'll have Kirstein send you a copy.

                        Love—hope to see you very soon. Edmund

To Lincoln Kirstein   February 15, 1934
The Hound and Horn   314 East 53rd Street, N.Y.

Dear Kirstein: Maybe I can get out some of *The Turn of the Screw* when I go through it in the proofs. Could you possibly pay me for the article now, by the way? I'd be very grateful if you could.

                        Yours sincerely, Edmund Wilson

To Lincoln Kirstein   [undated]

Dear Kirstein: This has turned out longer and more elaborate than I had intended—due partly to my having become embarked on a retelling of *The Turn of the Screw*. I thought, however, that this might be worth-while, as the case for this interpretation has never, so far as I know, appeared in print. Let me know if it is all right.   EW

Perhaps a better title would be simply "The Ambiguity of Henry James."

To Edna Kenton   1925

Dear Miss Kenton: I have read your review of [Van Wyck] Brooks's Henry James* with the greatest gratification. I called attention to these falsified quotations in a review of my own but hadn't the space or the thorough knowledge of James to make out a very impressive case; and everyone else seems to have taken the book in perfectly good faith. I do not know if you live in New York, but if you are within reach and not too busy and if it wouldn't bore you, I should like very much to have an opportunity of talking with you sometime about James. I have contem-plated writing something about him myself.

Yours sincerely, Edmund Wilson

To Edna Kenton   1925

Dear Miss Kenton: I read your article last night and went through *The Turn of the Screw* and I believe you are right—though I don't think, as you seem to do, that both the ghosts and the children are imaginary. I think we must accept the children as real. The point then would be that, though they have actually been exposed to rather bad influences in the groom and the former governess, whom, I take it, we must accept as having existed, too, it is the new governess who makes the real trouble. She has been fluttered by the uncle; but isn't it the boy that she really falls in love with? Isn't that the reason she insists on keeping him in the country when he really wants to be sent to school, and isn't she so willing to send Flora away so that she can be alone with him? She has made the little girl ill and when she has the boy to herself she scares him to death. This theory would be borne out by James's treatment of Olive Chancellor in *The Bostonians:* you remember he makes her misunder-stand her real motives throughout: like the governess, she is full of re-pressed sexual impulses which first make her invite Basil Ranson to Boston (remember her embarrassment when she first meets him) and then cause her to fix on Verena Tarrant—alleging, in both cases, extremely high-minded and entirely false reasons. Ezra Pound once described *The*

---

* *Pilgrimage of Henry James.*

236

Turn of the Screw as "a Freudian affair." The only interpretation which would make it "Freudian" is the one that you have suggested; so this theory has evidently occurred to other people, too.

In any case, if you are right, your explanation tends to bear out my own theory of *The Sacred Fount* (which was written at about the same time as *The Turn of the Screw*). *The Sacred Fount* is always put forward as an example of James's decaying faculties because the man who is supposed to be telling the story behaves so objectionably and comes to such preposterous conclusions about the other people; and if we believe that James's point of view is identical with that of the character, I think it is hard not to admit this. Isn't, however, the point of *The Sacred Fount* perhaps to be understood only in connection with the character of the narrator? The relations which he thinks he has worked out are as much products of his own imagination as the ghosts of the governess. The joke is at his expense—as it is plainly at the expense of that teller of his own story, the hero of *The Aspern Papers*, who, like the man in *The Sacred Fount*, has set out to find out a secret which he has no business to know and the point of whose story is that he is in the end put in an odious light. When I first began *The Sacred Fount*, I remember that from the first chapter in the railway carriage I got the impression that it was Long and Mrs. Brissenden who were interested in each other. Isn't this what James wants to suggest to his reader without allowing the narrator to suspect? The narrator is rather a fatuous gossip who indulges in a great deal of curiosity about his neighbors' affairs without ever doing anything interesting himself or indeed ever coming close enough to other people really to understand them (see how James makes him check his friendly sympathy and pity for Mrs. Server with a perfectly cold and indecent desire to get her secret out of her—in chapter VIII, I think). The truth is simply that Long and Mrs. Brissenden are having a love affair and are happy on this account; Brissenden and Mrs. Server are unhappy because they know about it. When the narrator tells Mrs. Brissenden, in the course of his conversation with her as they are walking about the grounds, that he suspects Long must be in love with someone, she tries to throw him off the track by misdirecting his suspicions toward the first woman they run into, who happens to be Mrs. Server. The narrator then elaborates an ingenious but wholly fantastic theory about what is going on and observes the others diligently in order to find evidence for it. He observes them so diligently, however, that he succeeds in finding evidence of the truth—that Mrs. Brissenden and Long are interested in each other —which he supposes to represent a change in the situation, whereas it has been the case all along. When she realizes that he has got on the right track, she sends for him and endeavors to put him to rout once and for all. In the meantime, Mrs. Server has been drawn to Brissenden

—evidently because he, like her, is a sufferer; and Mrs. Server, realizing that the narrator has already begun to notice this, too, and that he will no longer be able to believe that there is a love affair still going on between Mrs. Server and Long, hastens to assure him (to direct his attention from herself) that the real woman is Lady John. "The Sacred Fount" is love and Mrs. Brissenden has the strength derived from it, which enables her to triumph over the parlor detective who has been prying on them, in spite of all his astuteness and the fact that he knows at bottom she is lying. Even if his original theory is supposed to be the right one, this explanation of the end, when the combinations would have altered, would still hold good; and the moral defeat of the narrator still be considerable (see the last sentence of the story).

I wish you would consider *The Sacred Fount* sometime from this point of view and tell me what you think. If you think James sufficiently clever and sufficiently ironic to intend *The Turn of the Screw* in the way you say, I really think you ought at least to consider the problem of accounting humanly for *The Sacred Fount*. There is a lot more to say about all this, of course, and I hope we can discuss it again sometime soon, if this letter hasn't been too much already. Thanks ever so much for your article, which I will stop in at the library someday soon and give you back.   Yours for justice to the Master! Edmund Wilson

To Morton D. Zabel   [undated]

... I'm glad to see you revive "In the Cage," a favorite of mine. But isn't the title one of those Jamesian reversible things, like the title of "The Liar"? It turns out that the little telegraph girl is relatively free, and it is the swell she admires who is "in the cage" . . .

Since writing this last night, I have reread "The Jolly Corner." What Stovall says about it is so silly that I wonder you notice it at all. There is only one ghost, not two, and the American alter ego has lost his fingers—partly his sight in the Civil War, then been further brutalized by realizing his possibilities as a tycoon of big finance or business. Stovall's idea is ridiculous that Brydon was ever a big-game hunter. The references to hunting show that he has had no first-hand experience of it . . .

To Morton D. Zabel   [undated?, 1957–1958]

... My own theory about "In the Cage" is that Lady Brad was sending Captain E. the winner's name in a fixed horse race. It is a wonderful story anyway . . .

238

To Morton D. Zabel   July 19, 1938

. . . About Henry James, I've always felt that the psychological alterna-
tives which grew on him were an inferior substitute for presenting things
directly. It seems to me that it's only good when he's rendering direct
experience impressionistically—as in his autobiographical volumes, which
is something rather different. I've just had confirmation of the *Kinderschänder* theory about him in remembering that *The Other House*,
in which a little girl is actually murdered, belongs to the same period as
The Turn of the Screw and *What Maisie Knew*. It must be a combination (narcissistic) of love for his younger and innocent self and a desire
to destroy it and grow up. I suppose he relapses frankly into this narcissism
in *A Small Boy and Others* . . .

To James Thurber   1959

Dear Jim: You must have the first edition of *The Triple Thinkers*, published by Harcourt, Brace. I remember now that it was in the reprint
(Oxford) that I gave the reference to the Kenton article: *The Arts*,
November, 1924. The Demuth illustrations are included in the same
number of the magazine in which the Kenton article appears.

In connection with the *Screw*, read "The Liar," included in the same
volume in the New York edition. The idea is very much the same. The
real liar turns out to be not the man that the narrator is writing about—a
harmless pathological liar, whose romances nobody believes—but the
narrator himself, who, from jealousy, tries to misrepresent the other man.

The TV version of the *Screw* attempted to have it both ways. They
didn't use the Britten score but had a kind of imitation of it. You can
get the Britten opera on records, and it is well worth hearing.

I suppose you got the Houdini book that I sent back to you. I enjoyed
it very much.

It seems, by the way, that Henry James had seen quite a good deal of
psychiatrists in connection with his sister Alice. I suppose that Alice and
her ailments are also behind the Milly Theale situation.

                                              Regards as ever, Edmund W

                          John Jay Chapman
                             1927–1937

To Seward Collins   1927

. . . I've just made a great literary discovery, by the way—John Jay Chapman.
When I was on *Vanity Fair* and used to meet him at the Coffee

House, I used to take it for granted that he was just a dreary old man. Now that I have been reading his books, I realize that he was one of the best writers and one of the most intelligent Americans of his generation. He has always been able and content to remain a little of an amateur—otherwise, I believe, he might have been a real leader of thought, and perhaps have helped American literature to get over a little more easily and gracefully the great earthquake crevice between Paul Elmer More and Mencken. Ask Burton [Rascoe] if he has ever read Chapman . . .

To JOHN JAY CHAPMAN   May 23, 1929

My dear Mr. Chapman: Thank you very much for your letters. I am sorry that, through a mistake of the printers, a sentence at the top of page 32, which should have been my introduction to the quotation that followed, was run as if it were something which you had written. I have corrected the mistake in this week's number.

In regard to the Catholic Church, I did not mean that no such issue existed, but that I thought you had exaggerated its importance. I know that this issue does exist, but I don't happen to have run across it very often, and I therefore perhaps underestimate its importance. What especially made me feel that you overestimated it was your letter about Al Smith. I could not believe that his statement was "disingenuous," as you did. I thought that he was an honest and independent man who meant what he said and would do his best to live up to his promises. I happened to be traveling through the West just before the election, and I comparatively rarely heard the Catholic question invoked on the part of people who were voting for Hoover, but all the solidarity of the businessmen seemed to be against Smith. They were afraid that he would not put business interests before everything else; and this business solidarity seems to me far more formidable than the solidarity of the Roman Catholics.

My article, as I reread it, seems to me very inadequate, and I wish, among other things, that I could have talked more about your literary criticism.   Yours very sincerely, Edmund Wilson

To JOHN J. CHAPMAN   September 8, 1931
                                                   Santa Barbara
Dear Mr. Chapman: I have just read your book with great enjoyment and written something about it for The New Republic. I'm glad you wrote me about it.

I always sympathize with your onslaughts on the scholars—though I do think that in your first chapter you are a little too sweeping. There are

240

Pirie MacDonald/Houghton Mifflin Company

JOHN JAY CHAPMAN

It got me started reading John Jay Chapman and I am astonished to find how good he is—that Emerson book is certainly one of the best volumes of literary criticism ever produced by an American.   —To Christian Gauss, 1927

surely cases of accurate scholars who are imaginative, too. A. E. Housman, for example. You know that in several cases his proposed readings were justified by texts afterwards found. And his emendations of the Latin poets spring from a kind of divination that only a poet could have. Did you ever read the preface to the first volume of his text of Manilius?—it is a fascinating production. It also contains a fine Latin poem by him.

One gold brick I believe the scholars have put over on you. I think that you have been misled by Jebb about Antigone. So far as I have ever been able to see, all that about Antigone's crying out the name of Haemon is a pure invention of his. In the original text it is only Ismene who is concerned about Haemon. Antigone is interested only in her brother and never thinks about her fiancé or makes any attempt to see him. Jebb's assignment of certain lines to Antigone is based wholly on his feeling that Antigone *ought* to have something to say about Haemon. His emendations are very implausible because they break up the one-line dialogue. Also, there is no textual reason whatever for outlawing the famous passage about dying for a brother but not a lover, etc., which Sophocles evidently intended. Goethe hadn't been able to understand it and Jebb set out to make the play more acceptable from the nineteenth-century point of view. See how closely certain features of the Electra parallel the Antigone—the contrast between the sisters, for example—and how Sophocles has failed to provide Electra with a husband where Euripides did. Evidently he had a special sympathy for these fierce virgins.

I hope that we can have lunch together sometime in the fall when I get back to New York and you are in town, and discuss these matters.

Your Lucian book makes me want to read him. I agree that Plato is buttered on both sides. No doubt there is a lot to be said about him that has never been said—or at least that I have never seen said. It is interesting to compare Plato's "sublimation" of love with Dante's. They can be made to sound alike, but they are really very different—and the difference is certainly partly the difference in sex between Socrates and Beatrice. The type of Socrates in Dante is Ser Brunetto and he is condemned to the sterile plain.   Yours very sincerely, Edmund Wilson

To Malcolm Cowley   1934

. . . John Jay Chapman died sometime last fall or winter—it's too late to do anything in the nature of a notice now. I shouldn't want to myself anyway, as I've already written so much in the N.R. about him. Did Van Doren include him in his prose anthology, by the way? If he didn't, it's a scandal . . .

. . . Another book I might be interested in is DeWolfe Howe's book
on John Jay Chapman . . .

To Mark DeWolfe Howe   1937

. . . I thought that you did an extremely good job with your book. The
only thing I regretted was that the publishers had you cut it down. I
am very curious to see whether Chapman is remembered and read. I
believe that I could read volumes of his letters myself. He must be the
best letter writer we have ever had . . .

1934

AND

"TO THE FINLAND STATION"

To Gertrude Stein   March 4, 1934
                                              314 East 53rd Street, N.Y.
My dear Miss Stein: I should have thanked you before for the books
you have sent me—which I was very glad to have. It was interesting to
see *The Making of Americans* in French—Bernard Faÿ made a very good
job of it.

I went to *Four Saints* the other night, and it seemed to me to be much
the best thing I had seen in the theater this season. The Negroes do it
beautifully—they feel and enjoy your words, which come with a strange
naturalness from them. It's a pity you're not here to see it. I think it's
likely to have quite a run. I'm enclosing the *New Republic* reviews on
the chance that you haven't seen them.   Yours sincerely, Edmund Wilson

To Maxwell Perkins   March 12, 1934
                                              314 East 53rd Street, N.Y.
Dear Max: There is a man named Nathanael West who wrote a book
called *Miss Lonelyhearts* which I thought was extremely good. He has
written another book now which he says he can't get anybody to publish.* I thought you might be interested in it and have told him to get
in touch with you.   Sincerely, Edmund Wilson

To Cyril M. Schneider   1952

Dear Mr. Schneider: I knew Nathanael West, but not intimately, and I
doubt whether I could tell you anything you don't know about him, if

---

* *A Cool Million.*

you are working on him. I suppose that you are in touch with his sister Mrs. Perelman. What I have written about his work is in my book *Classics and Commercials*. I never heard him talk much about writing, except to tell me how much work he had put in on *Miss Lonelyhearts*, which was rewritten and polished innumerable times. Of course you know that he had been in Paris and was influenced by the Surrealists. It used to amuse me to look at Max Ernst's books of scrambled illustrations, which he had in his apartment in the hotel of which he was manager. You might take a look at these—I can't remember their names, but one of them was called something like *Rêve d'une jeune fille*. He also used to show me his gun, of which he was very proud, but I had a feeling that his hunting was largely a following of the Hemingway fashion. He told me once about shooting a bear in the Adirondacks, but said that the bear was a poor specimen, and the effect of the story was to make me feel sorry for the bear. He had a sad quiet Jewish humor, and the quality of his imagination was, I think, both Russian and Jewish. There was something of Chagall about him and even something of Gogol. He was well dressed and good-looking and had an extremely pretty girl friend who was a model. I liked him personally as well as admiring his work, and felt very badly about his death.

Yours sincerely, Edmund Wilson

To CHRISTIAN GAUSS
April 23, 1934
Washington, D.C.

Dear Christian: . . . Thanks ever so much for your book, which came just as I was leaving—and for the inscription, which touched me very much, as I had always supposed that the help and encouragement were all the other way. As for my verses, they were not supposed to be a speech which I was putting into your mouth—I wasn't aiming at your "Decline of Religion" article—I don't think I even knew about it. The quotations mostly dated from my prep-school days. I went to Hill, which was at that time dominated by the headmaster's evangelical wife and great play was made with the religious passages of Tennyson and Browning, some of which we had to memorize.

I have been having a very interesting time here . . . I know a number of people in the Administration from my *New Republic* days, and so have been able to hear something of what is going on at first hand. Washington seems much more intelligent and cheerful than under any recent Administration, but as one lady said to me, it is "pure Chekhov"—where the Ohio gang played poker, the brain trustees get together and talk. Nothing really makes much sense, because Roosevelt has no real policy . . .

As ever, Bunny W.

To Christian Gauss   March 19, 1934

. . . I'm engaged on some essays on the evolution of the idea of history
from Vico to Marx and after—and I'd like very much to get your advice
on them. There's an awful lot of work to do on it, however, and I shan't
have them in any kind of shape for a long time . . .

To George Soule   July 11, 1934
The New Republic   Provincetown

Dear George: Malcolm suggested to me sometime ago that I write for
the N.R. on the basis of being paid at half my old rates, the other half
being charged against my debt. If this is still agreeable to you, I propose
the following arrangement. Pay me on that basis for the two articles of
mine you have just published—my old rates were 4¢ a word for regular
stuff, 2¢ for book reviews. Then I could send you a series of articles out
of a book I am writing.
   The book deals with the development of the modern conception of
history from the first attempts to apply scientific methods to the study of
human affairs in the past (beginning of the eighteenth century) to the
recent more or less successful effort to determine the course of events in
the present through a technique based on this study (the Russian Revolution and after). I have one large section in a state where I could begin
sending you installments of it immediately. It deals with Vico, Michelet,
Renan, and Taine and the tradition of the French Revolution generally.
I figure it will come to something like 15,000 words, which would make
four or five articles that you could use during the summer. The section
after that will deal with Marx and Engels (Hegel and Proudhon, etc.),
and the third section with the Russians. My idea is not to write a complete
account, but to present the development of the organic conception and
scientific study of history through a number of key figures, with the
background amply filled in. It is worth doing, I think, because Marxism
tends to get dissociated from the French revolutionary tradition it grew
out of and we tend to look back at the French tradition through its later
and less revolutionary, more disillusioned, representatives. The ordinary
academic discussion of this subject, furthermore, always stops and makes
a big detour when it comes to Marx and Engels, so that it leaves out most
of what has happened since—and the socialists stop with Marx and Engels,
and the Communists with Lenin, or rather with Stalin's version of Lenin-
ism. I calculate that, even paying me at this half rate, most of my debt
would be wiped out if you used a large part of the book (the title is to

246

be *To the Finland Station,* and this might be run as a general title to
the series). The three sections would come with fairly long spaces in-
between, so that your readers wouldn't be overwhelmed by it.

Yours sincerely, Edmund Wilson

To GEORGE SOULE   July 28, 1934
                                             Provincetown

Dear George: . . . This is the first section, which is hung on Michelet;
the second section is hung on Marx and Engels; and the third on Lenin
and Trotsky. The subheads of this first part are as follows:
  1. Michelet Discovers Vico
  2. Michelet and the Middle Ages
  3. Michelet and the Revolution
  4. Michelet Tries to Live His History
  5. Michelet between Nationalism and Socialism
  6. Decline of the Revolutionary Tradition: Renan and Taine
  7. Decline of the Revolutionary Tradition: Anatole France
I know that the handling of essays as long as this presents difficulties
to *The New Republic*—though the whole thing oughtn't to fill as much
space as the essays that went into *Axel's Castle.* A few sections, such as
the one on Anatole France, which will follow pretty closely a *New Republic* article, might be abbreviated or omitted. This section, if you
thought you could use so much, could be covered in four installments, as
follows: 1 and 2; 3; 4 and 5; 6. I think that the general title ought to be
given somewhere, with an explanation that more is coming, so that the
readers would know where they were headed. The next large section
(Marx and Engels) wouldn't be ready for some time (sometime in the
fall), so that there would be fairly long intervals between them. I suppose you wouldn't want to get out three supplements, each containing a
section, at intervals . . .   Yours sincerely, Edmund

To GEORGE SOULE   August 10, 1934
                                             Provincetown

. . . I'd like to know precisely when and how you're going to run it, so
that I can get the last installment to you in time. I am . . . enclosing a
memorandum for the advertizing department. I don't know precisely
what you are going to do about the heads on each installment. Perhaps
To the Finland Station: I, with the subheads as I have them, would be
all right (I think these ought to be run in the paragraph, as I have them,
to save space—if it's impossible to get a big initial in italics, they might
be put in caps and small caps). I think this would be better than

247

"Michelet: I," "Michelet: II," etc.—it is important to keep before the readers' minds that I am driving at something in particular; otherwise, they may be puzzled at the beginning at my devoting so much space to Michelet . . .

To Christian Gauss   August 31, 1934
                                                Provincetown
Dear Christian: . . . I thought that *To the Finland Station* was a good title, because the Finland Station in St. Petersburg was where Lenin arrived when he got back from exile. Have you read any accounts of the extraordinary scene that occurred? It marked dramatically the first occasion that a trained Marxist had been able to come in and take hold of a major crisis. I was going to have a subtitle: An Essay on the Writing and Acting of History.

In regard to romanticism, wasn't it merely one of the phases of the individualistic and rebelling middle class? It was from his revolutionary tradition that Michelet got that impulse. The romanticism which as a young man he was trying to steer clear of was the indulgence of the imagination and the emotions for their own sake—what artists and poets tended to do when the purposes of the Revolution seemed frustrated. The great phenomenon behind both these tendencies is the rise of the bourgeoisie: Protestantism in religion, revolutionary idealism in politics, romanticism in poetry, and laissez faire in economics all have their roots in this. In regard to Byron and Shelley, why do you think I don't give them credit? I just haven't had occasion to write about them.

I don't know precisely what you mean about Taine and his *petit fait significatif*. It seems to me that what made them significant to him was the fact that they suited his thesis. You have only to look back after reading *L'Ancien Régime*, for example, and think how many significant facts, big and little, he has left out. He does establish some things solidly, but establishes only what fits his system; and the whole picture, as well as the reality, suffers, it seems to me, from his excessive classification.

Do you happen to remember what it was that Renan ran for in 1869? "*Lors des élections de 1869,*" he says, "*je m'offris aux suffrages de mes concitoyens . . .*" The Senate? I can't seem to find it in anything up here. Also, I remember your repeating to me several years ago a phrase of Anatole France—something to the effect that the only things we could count on in the world were the relativity of phenomena and the succession of appearances. Do you happen to know the precise words and where they occur?

You have been very good to take so much trouble and I hope to profit by your suggestions. Please thank Alice for her appreciative postscript. I hope you are all well.   As ever, EW

. . . About Michelet, my problem in the first section of the *Finland Station* is to present the non-Marxist French Revolutionary bourgeois writers from the point of view of my own Marxist lights and yet give an illusion of how the world looked to them and what they thought they were doing —so that I don't overtly bring the Marxist analysis to bear at all except when it is absolutely necessary. Marx's discoveries are precisely a part of my story, and I mustn't give them away any more than I can help before I come to them. I try to indicate, without stating too explicitly, that the Paris Commune was a pivotal point in the intellectual careers of all the people whom I treat in this first section, because they were all trying to get away from it. Later I show explicitly how it was to become the pivotal point in the opposite way of the thinking and practice of the Marxists. This whole first part will fall into a different perspective when the reader gets to what follows . . .

To Christian Gauss   October 21, 1934
                                                                          Provincetown

Dear Christian: Thank you very much for your letters and for your trouble about my articles. About Renan and Taine, I am going to improve them when I rewrite them—I hadn't gotten them up as thoroughly as Michelet. But I can't give them much more space. The point is that what I am writing is not a literary history or even a history of the study of history. If it were, the relative amount of space given to the different men would be quite different—in fact, the selection of Michelet, Renan, et al., to start off a book on this subject is in itself more or less arbitrary. My treatment of these French writers will have to justify itself artistically in relation to the whole scheme. The purpose of this first section is to show the dying out of the bourgeois revolutionary tradition as a prelude to presenting the rise of Marxism; and one of the things I want to do, in dealing with Renan, Taine, etc., is to disarm the bourgeois liberal reader's objections to the Marxists by reviewing the various liberal attitudes—and pessimistic attitudes—exemplified by these French writers and stated as eloquently as they can be stated, all attitudes which are still current today—and by showing their relation to social class and to fear of socialism. It seems to me that the effect of the Commune on the thought of such men as Renan and Taine cannot be overestimated. It is very curious to read the bourgeois writers of this kind, or even a bourgeois encyclopedia, and then to read the Marxists. With the former, the Commune is a scandal that they are trying to keep out of their picture of the world; with the latter, it is (before the Russian Revolution) the pivotal event on which their historical thinking turns. I didn't mean to denigrate R. and T. or to imply, as you say, that they were not "honest men." I tried to make it plain that they were. I admire them both—though I will confess to getting a little out of patience with Taine on the origins of contemporary France this summer. It is true, of course, that this shows him at his worst. But even when I went back and reread some of *The History of English Literature*—which fascinated me when I first read it (at a very early age: it must have been the first criticism I ever read and I owe a lot to Taine)—I was surprised to find how Victorian it seemed. Michelet does not seem Victorian. Renan, whom I read during the war with enthusiasm, seemed a little sickly when I went back to him. (By the way, do you feel any discrepancy between Alfred de Musset's own writings and Taine's description of him? I have never read anything by him that gave me quite the effect of Taine's picture. His fault has always seemed to me to be to tend toward a sort of insipidity.)

As for France's passage about the relativity of things, etc., I looked it up and what he says is that he believes "at least" in them, not "only." He is really repudiating extreme skepticism, affirming that he *does* believe in acting as if the world were logical and real; and I think that by "relativity" he may really mean the "relationships" of things and that I may have made an improper use of the passage.

I'm leading an incredibly dreary life up here, as all but four or five of the people I see have left town and I don't see much of them; but am otherwise having rather a satisfactory time. Having been behind my literary schedule for years, I'm gradually catching up to it.   As ever, EW

To CHRISTIAN GAUSS   August 13, 1934
                                                          Provincetown
. . . I've been feeling definitely middle-aged lately, am moving on toward forty and celebrated my thirty-ninth birthday by getting a nose infection which afterwards permeated my whole system and seemed to me to give premonitions of my approaching dissolution. It has practically cleared up; but my state of mind seems to me to have passed the great climacteric. It is rather pleasant, as it involves one's no longer feeling under the necessity of doing a lot of things—because either you have already done them and have gotten out of them all that there is in them for you or you have discovered that you can't do them and might as well stop trying.

I've been learning German, the lack of which has always been a gap in my education. It seems to me a wonderful language—though I don't agree with Matthew Arnold's scorn of French poetry, the language in German poetry does have a freshness and relief after French, due to the words' being closer to their origins and not having been rubbed down

250

by long currency. That early-nineteenth-century period in Germany is really hard to match for creative vigor; but I suppose their very closeness to barbarism, without any Latin admixture such as the English have had, is what has made them so fatally susceptible to all the absurdities of German imperialism and Hitlerism . . .

To LOUISE BOGAN   August 20, 1934
                                                       Provincetown
*Wundersusses Nachtigall!** Here is the five which I *geborgt*—I'm sorry to have been so long in sending it. Also about the clothes, which I'd forgotten, but have now gotten off. There is absolutely no news with me— my boils seem to be finally fading away. I'm pursuing the same simple and intensively literary life as when you were here. It's too bad we dropped Heine just at the point we did—I have read quite a little more of it, and that poem about her borrowing his money, which was the last we read, is the beginning of his new characteristically ironic vein—the best of them are marvelous, and it's too bad we weren't able to read them together . . . Matty Josephson has been up here for a few days, rendered surprisingly agreeable and entertaining by his Guggenheim trip—he regaled us with such lively news of Russia, France, and Spain that it made me decide to apply for a Guggenheim myself this year. I'm glad to hear that you've been enjoying yourself in New York . . .
                                                       Love, Edmund

To MALCOLM COWLEY   August 4, 1934
                                                       Provincetown
. . . Dos has gone out to Hollywood to do Spanish background, at a huge salary, for Marlene Dietrich. He writes back that he hates it, but what a break! . . .

To F. SCOTT FITZGERALD   September 11, 1934
                                                       Provincetown
Dear Scott: I'm glad you liked my stuff in *The New Republic*. It will be better when I've redone it for a book. Yes: Michelet seems to have been the first great master of the social-relativity idea. People don't realize how much Proust and a lot of other writers got from him.

I've just come back today from a visit to John Bishop, who is staying down the Cape at South Harwich. In spite of my usual fits of exasperation with Margaret, I enjoyed seeing John extremely. When Margaret is around, they talk about nothing else but fine food—how, even though the stock of the local grocers is so limited, you can have all the rare old

---

* E.'s spelling.

dishes if you send away for the things. But when you get John alone, he reverts to literature and art and is really awfully good on them. I had forgotten how good he was—and he seemed to me particularly stimulating after Provincetown, which, though it has kept up quite a noble standard at times in the past, has now sunk to a level of incredible intellectual sterility. Even Dos is out in Hollywood, turning Pierre Louÿs into a picture for von Sternberg.

Love to Zelda—I hope she is better.   As ever, Bunny

To JOHN PEALE BISHOP   December 4, 1934
                                                            Red Bank

Dear John: I'm sorry to have delayed in answering your letter—I got it just before I left Provincetown, had a lot of things to do when I first got to New York, and then came down with the grippe—am writing this in bed. I'll write Lyle Saxon and John McClure to look you up. Lyle, if he is not up the river at Baton Rouge, knows everybody and I think you will enjoy him. Grace King's short history of New Orleans is worth reading and she is worth meeting, if she is not dead, as I seem to remember she is. You ought to read Cable, too, if you haven't—read "The Story of Bras-Coupé" in *The Grandissimes;* especially, in connection with New Orleans, a book called *Strange True Stories of Louisiana*, which, however, is rather hard to get—Lyle Saxon lent it to me. You ought to go down to Grand Isle sometime in the little steamboat.

I have no news, have been down here a good deal of the time since I came back from Provincetown. If I come to in time and succeed in getting some magazine to put up the fare, I may get off to the big Zuñi Indian dance.

I saw an old New Orleans friend of mine, Hamilton Basso, in New York the other day and he told me that he believed the literary life of the French Quarter had largely dwindled away since I was down there. But I believe you will meet many entertaining people. . . .

As ever, Bunny

To PHELPS PUTNAM   December 4, 1934
                                                            Red Bank

Dear Phelps: I was extremely glad to get your long letter—I seem to be seeing very few of my old friends nowadays, and it was cheering to hear from you. I came back last month from Provincetown, where I had spent five months living a very solitary life . . . I've applied for a Guggenheim myself, and if I get one, shall go to Russia, but want to come home by way of the Mediterranean, and there might be a chance I'd be somewhere near you—so keep me posted on your whereabouts . . . The Walkers are back from Russia, but I haven't seen them yet.

As for literature, I didn't think Scott's novel* quite as bad as you seem to: the characters and the story are cockeyed, but I thought he got something real out of the marriage relationship—a kind of situation which in less aggravated forms is not uncommon among people of that kind nowadays. He claims to have improved it a lot in rewriting it for the book. Have you heard about the young guy named Paul Engle from the West who has been setting the front page of the *Times Book Review* section and other similar places all agog? I wasn't so much surprised when Archie MacLeish vulgarized Eliot and Pound enough to get himself the Pulitzer Prize, but I never expected to see the day when they would be practically hooked up with Edwin Markham and James Whitcomb Riley. As for Archie himself, after repeatedly declaring his belief in the duty of the artist to stand clear from politics, etc., he has not been able to restrain himself from sticking his finger uneasily into almost every political pie that seemed respectable enough and was not long ago delivering after-dinner speeches on Major Douglas's Social Credit. A young Yale [Harvard] boy named James Agee, though, sponsored by Archie, has done some quite fine and original lyrics in a book which the Yale Press has brought out.†

I'm sorry that you've been suffering from asthma and hope you'll be getting to your poem. I've had a slight relapse into verse myself lately and am thinking of bringing out a book called *Wilson's Night Thoughts* someday. The stuff in *The New Republic* will make some sense when it comes out in a book.   As ever, Bunny W.

Muriel Draper is in Russia. I *have* been suffering from uncomfortable health, but with opposite effects from those of yours . . . While physically able, I could drink or do the other things which have sometimes in the past taken me away from my work—there was practically nothing I *could* do but work, and I was quite surprised at the amount of writing I produced *tant en vers qu'en prose*; reading some of it over, I doubt whether I should have produced quite so much. However, my maladies seem to be waning, so I shan't be tempted to overdo it again.

To Malcolm Cowley   1951

Dear Malcolm: I was interested in this introduction.‡ I have never really read *Tender Is the Night*, since it first came out in *Scribner's*—though Scott told me that he thought he had much improved it when he revised it for the book. Maybe I'll read this new edition. Do have them send me a copy. Scribner's proofreading (in our time) has always been terrible.

---

* *Tender Is the Night.*
† *Permit Me Voyage.*
‡ Malcolm Cowley's introduction to a new edition of *Tender Is the Night.*

When they republished *Paradise* lately, they left some of the misspellings of the original edition. Max Perkins couldn't spell himself and couldn't be made to take proofreading seriously.

I have always felt that the weakness of *Tender Is the Night* was that Scott, when he wrote the first part, was thinking only about Gerald Murphy and had no idea that Dick Diver was a brilliant psychiatrist. It is hard to believe in him as a scientist—and also, I think, hard to believe that such a man as Scott tries later to imagine should eventually have sunk into obscurity instead of becoming a successful doctor with a fashionable practice in New York or attached to an expensive sanatorium. Except for the movies, Scott never had any kind of organized professional life. It is, of course, a remarkable book just the same . . .

As ever, Edmund

1935

To John Dos Passos

January 11, 1935
314 East 53rd Street, N.Y.

Dear Dos: . . . In regard to Russia, it seems to me a mistake to form any too definite opinion because we really know nothing about it. I don't see any reason to disbelieve that they had a counterrevolutionary conspiracy backed by Germany on their hands, as they say they had. Not long ago the Germans were trying to get at them through the Ukraine. The story is, as you've probably heard, that they didn't want to publish the details for fear of getting into war with Germany. It is surely a mistake, as Lovett said the other day, to assume that the victims were innocent because there were so many of them. I regret that Stalin should have thought it necessary to involve his political opponents in it; but the way they handle those things in Russia has been familiar ever since the Trotsky split. That is largely Russia, which can't be expected to undergo a complete cultural transformation from the Russia of the Tsars in the short time since the Revolution. It is also, as you say, partly Bonapartism. Revolutions, which bring forth great statesmen, are almost always followed by bureaucracies and "strong men," who come to be a force of inertia that has to be opposed in the interests of progress. And Stalin, however much he may want to maintain his power, is certainly a good deal different from Napoleon. Stalin is a convinced Marxist and old Bolshevik; Napoleon cared nothing about the principles of the French Revolution and betrayed it. Also, he had megalomaniac imperialist ambitions which one can hardly imagine Stalin entertaining. Stalin, whatever his limitations, is still working for socialism in Russia. He and his regime are not interesting in the same way that Lenin and Trotsky were; but I don't think you ought to say, as you do, that a country which is still trying to put socialism into practice has ceased to be politically interesting. I have lately been goaded, I find, to put the emphasis on the other side from you by my encounters with the intelligentsia. When I got back and began to see them, I found Russia usually the chief topic of conversation and most people filled with indecent delight at the idea of getting something serious on the Soviets. Ben Stolberg is having the time of his life raving to Louis Adamic, Bill Woodward, et al., about the iniquities and bankruptcy of Russia. On these occasions I found that I was almost driven into talking like a loyal Stalinist. One doesn't want to give aid and comfort to people who have hopped on the shootings in Russia as a means of discrediting socialism.

Aside from this, you are right, of course, in saying that Americans who are in favor of socialism oughtn't to try to import the methods of the Russians. I have very little knowledge of how they actually manage things in Russia, but I should think we were probably much better fitted than the Russians to handle the problems of socialism, once the idea had been accepted. Do you mean that you think it can be put over without a general breakdown of our present institutions? I can just barely imagine this happening since Upton Sinclair nearly got elected, but it is hard to imagine its happening without a certain amount of civil war. I don't think, though, that you ought to lump England and the United States together, and the present with the past, as "Anglo-Saxon institutions." I don't know what institutions you mean. In many respects, we are closer to other countries than to England.

I haven't much news. The Trotskyites and Musteites have merged as the Workers' Party of the United States. Sidney Hillman has been so much outraged about Leo Wolman's behavior in Detroit that he is no longer on speaking terms with him, and Leo feels very badly and apologetic. Esther Strachey seems to have gone in for Utopianism. Seward Collins has gone in for psychic research and receives many messages from the other world. Thornton Wilder has taken up the challenge flung down by Mike Gold and written the best book of his life.* I wish you would overcome your prejudice against him and read it. Muriel Draper is teaching English in Moscow and seems to be having a very good time. Bob Lovett has got backing to start a weekly newspaper in Chicago, printing the facts not published in the other papers, and is looking for an editor. I suggested Blankenhorn. I have applied for a Guggenheim, alleging that I want to work in the Marx–Engels Institute in Moscow; if I get it, I'll go over in February or March—though I confess that recent events have inspired me with some misgivings. The boys over here seem to suspect me of being attainted with Trotskyism; and I see that a number of people were thrown out of the Marx–Engels Institute lately for "ideological perversion," a sin of which I am as likely as not guilty. I've just read William Saroyan's book and was surprised, after what I had

---

* *Heaven's My Destination.*

heard about it, that it should be so good.* He has a curious kind of rarefied poetry, very precisely expressed, quite different from anybody else; though there is a certain amount of second-hand Hemingway and Anderson, I think he is good. Have you read him? Can't you persuade Hemingway not to indulge in any more performances like his last in *Esquire*? I called on Gertrude Stein and Miss Toklas the other day. I like Gertrude Stein and found her stimulating to talk to; but the whole setup is rather creepy and I don't think I could ever become a habitué. It is the most complete example of human symbiosis I have ever seen. The Shays, Bill Smith, and myself are getting along very pleasantly in this house. I don't much like living in New York, though, any more and have been getting away as much as I could.

Give my love to Katy—and let me hear about your adventures.

As ever, EW

To JOHN DOS PASSOS

January 31, 1935
314 East 53rd Street, N.Y.

Don't agitate me, comrade, I'm with you—at least on what I take to be your main contentions. Though it does seem to me that in your present state of mind you tend to talk as if you were ready to throw the baby out with the bath. Surely it's entirely unnecessary to worry about the possibility of a Stalin regime in America. I can't imagine an American Stalin. You talk as if there were a real choice between Henry Ford on the one hand and Browder, Bob Minor and Company on the other; but who outside the Communists themselves has ever seriously entertained the idea that these individuals would ever lead a national movement? At the same time, you ought to give the Communists, with all their shortcomings, credit for playing a valuable role as agitators. It seems to me that during these recent years their influence has been felt through the whole length of American politics. They have put fundamental questions up to the rest of the world and have worried people into trying to find answers. You speak disapprovingly of intellectuals, theories, etc.; but aren't you giving evidence, in your present disillusion about the Communists and Russia, of having cherished a typical intellectual illusion? I don't think you ought to be so shocked at discovering that political movements are failing in practice to live up to their pretensions. They never have, and when the whole world is socialist, will continue to fail to do so. I don't think you ought to let yourself be driven into Marxophobia by the present literary popularity of Marxism—which I suspect is what has been taking place with you.

I saw the Walkers the other night for the first time in a year. At first

---

* *The Daring Young Man on the Flying Trapeze.*

I was rather relieved to discover that their Communist orthodoxy had abated; but presently it appeared that they had gone in for the Trotsky–Muste party in the same spirit, swallowing Trotsky hook, line, and sinker. They refer to him affectionately as "the old man" and, if you express any doubts about his political future, behave very much as they used to behave about the regular comrades. They are even more outraged than you are about the Russian executions and Adelaide has sent me clippings (which I pass on to you) to demonstrate the idiocy of the *Daily Worker*. They have taken part in a split in the National Committee and with others are resigning from it. I shouldn't wonder if their change of opinions were reflected in a change of policy in the Theatre Union—I hope so.

I've seen a number of shows of various kinds, all of them disappointing (including the Theatre Union's *Sailors of Cattaro*)—with the exception of Noel Coward's *Point Valaine*, which is the best thing of his I've ever seen. It's of no real importance, but stands out from the rest of the current theater as something written and produced by somebody who still likes the theater and who has been able to induce the actors to impersonate the characters in the play. These are rudimentary merits, but now rare. Noel Coward is really all there is left of the English theater.

I saw Malcolm the other day, and I'm certain that this indiscretion with your letter was simply due to his characteristic tactlessness and not to any political motive, as you seem to think. He wanted to get something about the exhibition into print as quickly as possible and says that it seemed impossible to get it written about in any other way. It's true that since Croly's death they have been implacably opposed to printing anything about the arts. They took advantage of Bliven's absence abroad to put an end to a verbal arrangement which Bliven had made with Paul Rosenfeld to write a monthly or biweekly article on music, so now music is out.

I've been leading a pretty quiet life—everything is going along painlessly here. I'm in the midst of Marx and Engels—the next installment of my *New Republic* stuff. The closer you get to it, the better it seems. Heine's satirical poetry, written under the influence of Marx, is the best verse of the kind I have ever seen—and a kind of thing that would be welcome now rather than the bogus proletarian poetry written in T. S. Eliot's meters. But it came out of a world (before 1848) that was less sick, had much more spirit. The members of the romantic intellectual generation who did not die off with their personal disappointments like Byron, Shelley, Musset, et al., but lived to expand the romantic emotions into something larger, are the most impressive writers of the nineteenth century. Marx belonged to this class: one romantic early poem of his I have read has the whole moral attitude of his subsequent career in it. It was Marxism that was the real second blooming of the Enlightenment and it has still great vitality today. It may be, as you say, that political salvation will have to come now from outside Marxism proper; I don't see, however, that the events in Germany, Austria, and Spain necessarily prove this: the Marxist answer is that the objective conditions weren't ripe, and that, as Trotsky says, no society can go till it has exhausted all its possibilities. There is more of an explanation, it seems to me, from the point of view of the uncongeniality of certain national psychologies to Marxism. Marx, when he was working with the First International, for example, seems never really to have reached much of an understanding with the English working-class movement, whereas the Russian, against whom at that time he had a violent prejudice, seized upon *Das Kapital* at once and gave him some of his first and most enthusiastic followers. Marx is, however, congenial to the Germans, and I shouldn't be at all surprised at an eventual socialist revolution there conducted in terms of Marxist formulas. Why not? They have had the biggest Communist Party outside Russia and a more important Communist opposition (I mean opposition to the official Communist policies) than any other country. But we live in a world now which has been profoundly permeated with Marxism— Washington as well as Moscow (since Tugwell went to Russia, took his cue from the Five-Year Plan, etc.). What is needed is to see Marx and Lenin as a part of the humanistic tradition which they came out of. You know that Marx said: "As for me, I'm not a Marxist."

I'm glad to hear you're both in good health now. Love to Katy. Yes: I wish you would give me some letters to Russia, if I get there. The Walkers had been in Russia and Germany since I'd seen them and were very interesting on the subject. They say that they got the impression in Germany that the industrials were now running things more or less openly without paying much attention to Hitler and his friends, on whom they were quietly bringing pressure to pipe down.　　　As ever, EW

To John Dos Passos　　　　　　　　　　February 26, 1935
　　　　　　　　　　　　　　　　　314 East 53rd Street, N.Y.
Dear Dos: I suppose the great contemporary book on the English Revolution is Clarendon's *History of the Great Rebellion*. I have never read it and don't know much about the period—had been thinking of attacking Carlyle myself.

I have nothing in particular to report, having spent most of the usual dreary New York February alternating between the dentist's and the Public Library . . .

I saw the new Shaw play* the other night, and, though I have stood up for the old man's later works, I was forced to admit that his hand was faltering. It is like *Back to Methuselah*, but worse . . .

I picked up an English edition of your *Orient Express* the other day

---

* *The Simpleton of the Unexpected Isles.*

and was going to read it to take my mind off Marx and Engels before going to sleep at night, as I've been inventing German irregular verbs in my sleep lately, but became so fascinated with your caravan trip that I sat up till the milkman came around. I suppose it was the English publisher who presented you with those petrol-tins and goods-waggons.

I came to realize recently that Rosalind, who goes to Sunday school for social reasons, had learned nothing about the Bible there, so I have set out to read the New Testament to her. I've explained to her that there were inconsistencies in it and that the miracles are probably not true, but she has subjected me to such a searching cross-examination about it, pointed out so many serious discrepancies, that I've been almost forced to conclude that Dr. Smith was right about J.C. In any case, I don't see how it was possible to put the New Testament over on children for so many generations. The most serious thing is not the mere variations in the different Gospel accounts, but the contradictory feelings and ideas ascribed to Christ within a few verses. I began by trying to put her on her guard against the obvious impossibilities and then began to be afraid that the central ideas of Christianity wouldn't come through for her at all. The growth of Christianity looks very strange when you read the New Testament again and look back on it today. But I've also been impressed, in reading about socialism from its beginnings, by the instinct to create religions which survived even after Christianity had fallen into discredit among the enlightened. Saint-Simon, after the French Revolution, agreed with writers like Joseph de Maistre that what people needed was religion; but he rejected Maistre's Catholic Church. But then, when Saint-Simon himself was dead, his followers based a cult on him, making use of a hierarchical machinery he had indicated. I have just been looking at a picture of one of them with a sign on his chest which says "Le Père." The same kind of thing really happened to Marx. He was against religion, but had the prophet's vocation; and unconsciously he played the role to perfection. That his beard was not grown for nothing is shown by his extreme sadness at being obliged to cut it off in his old age and his having a last photograph taken first. And reading Marx and reading about him, after one has heard a good deal of the doctrine and the legend, is almost as queer as reading the New Testament. Of course we have never really yet had a world without religion—or any part of the world. It's something, however, that ought to be aimed at.

By the way, it is being rumored that you are "rubbing your belly" and saying that "the good old Republican Party is good enough for you." Maybe you ought to make a statement of your present position.

Well, it seems to be snowing or hailing again outside. This has been a pretty dull winter on the whole and you have missed nothing by being away . . .   EW

To John Peale Bishop   April 25, 1935
                                                          Red Bank

Dear John: I've just read *Act of Darkness* with great interest, but some disappointment before I'd finished it. It's the only thing of yours that I remember that seemed to me to be carelessly executed. I believe you ought to have spent another year on it.

I began by being enchanted by your evocation of the American small-town-and-country life of thirty years ago. What you describe in West Virginia is very like what I remember myself up here, and I have never read any book which brought me back as yours did into that world of large old houses away in the woods and fields or in little countrified towns where rather a high degree of civilization flourished against a background of pleasant wildness. I had been thinking a lot lately about this life, which as a boy after a certain age I was anxious to get away from, and it seems to me that there was much in it that was valuable (see enclosed poem) which has gone and has never yet been replaced by anything else equally sound and human. Of course, by the time you and I came along, it was breaking up or in a state of decay and the people, as you represent them (they were under a more immediate pressure from the big money-making era in the North than in the South, but the effect, as I remember the country life here, was not so different as I might have supposed), were getting neurotic or withering up; and it seemed to me later that the new and bright and more or less generally suburbanized life of the Boom was much better for people and that more people got something out of it, than the in some ways rather dreary life of my boyhood. This was true, I believe, in the towns around here; but I come to feel more and more as I grow older that even the tail end of the old culture and family life, which was all we really got, was worth having. And when I started reading your book, I found myself entering the houses you described as if they were houses that I had known myself. I remember perfectly that picture of Charlotte Corday in prison in some relative's house that I used to visit (in upstate New York, I think). The scene that I liked best in the whole book and which seems to me the most successful is the scene where the boy goes to his grandfather's, when the latter tries to tell him the facts of life. (I was going back after the same sort of thing in this poem.)

You do succeed in getting all this over; but it does seem to me that you neglected your style. I have always thought your prose was good, but it seemed to me in reading *Act of Darkness* that perhaps your very mastery of verse technique had sometimes gotten in your way. "Then a slot clicked, there was only a sound in the piano of slidings": maybe this is all right, but there were other things of the kind that seemed to me wrong. Then I believe you give a false air of solemnity to certain passages: "I paid the admission for both. The air inside was dark and leaned

261

with smoky faces. We sat forward on thin wooden benches. The dirt of the field was under our feet." Why not "We sat forward on thin wooden benches, with the dirt of the field under our feet"? You tend to do this kind of thing so much that when a real moment of solemnity or tension arrives the reader does not know whether or not to expect anything special. The thing which upset me most was your habit of beginning your sentences with adjectives or participles which don't modify anything that follows: "Wilted in his linen suit, his black tie was crossed on a glazed shirt front." What you ought to say is "Wilted in his linen suit, the minister sank into a chair"—or something of the kind. A few pages on: "Charlie had put on a shepherd's plaid coat to come to the table, old and small for him." I thought at first it was the table that was old and small for him.

As for the subject, it is splendid. But why on earth do you make those occasional excursions into the minds of other characters than the boy when all the rest is seen only through his eyes? Or if you are going to tell us about the other people, why don't you tell us more? I felt that I only half knew Charlie and didn't understand Virginia at all. The whole trial business seems to me a mistake: I can't believe that such a woman would have brought charges against him. Also, it may be that I don't understand what you are getting at, but I don't see why you have him insist on the stand that it was she who took advantage of him. If he had wanted to assert himself against the whole sterile and women-dominated setup, I should think it would have been better if he had stuck to his point: it would have antagonized the jury just as much. And what is the upshot of the whole thing for him? You never tell us. The effect on the life of the boy, the whole idea of the relationship with the boy, is finely conceived, though I kept expecting more—expected, for example, that the boy would give the miscreant hired man the kick that Charlie had told him he was too young to give him when Charlie was taken off to jail and left the boy in charge. The thing I regret, as I say, is that you didn't spend a good deal more time on it. I have a feeling that it could have been very much intensified and improved by being compressed into half the length. (The various darkies are excellent.)

What are you going to work on now? There must be lots to do with New Orleans today that its natives never seem to do. Have you read Faulkner's new book?* I haven't, but want to.

Have you read Elinor Wylie's idiot sister's book about her? I was quite touched by it in spite of her half-wittedness and the fact that she gets everything I know anything about wrong. You and I appear in it in cockeyed guise.

---

* *Pylon.*

I've got my Googleheim and am trying to get off to Russia, sailing May 4. I expect to come back in the fall. I'll be extremely glad to get away. I haven't been to Europe for fourteen years, and I'm fed up and disgusted with New York, have been full of the rancorous rankling of unproduced plays and uncompleted books. When I get back from my trip, if I still feel as I do now, I'm going to bury myself somewhere (outside of New York) and never be seen or heard from again except to emit an occasional work.

Do drop me a line, if you can, before I go, and tell me about your adventures in New Orleans.

Have you ever thought of rewriting *A. of D.* as a play? It might make a very good one.

Do you think this ballad justifies itself? Nobody likes it.

Love to Margaret.   As ever, EW

To JOHN DOS PASSOS   April 27, 1935
                                                                          Red Bank

Dear Dos: . . . If you can arrange for me to rescue your Russian rubles, I'll pay you back in dollars. I still haven't got my visa, though I'm planning to sail next Saturday. Have just read Faulkner's aviation story—the way it is written is a mess, he seems to have just been hit by Proust—but it made quite a powerful impression on me. I don't own it or would send it to you. Let me know what you think of Wilder. Also, I wish you'd send me a copy of your statement to the Writers' Congress, which seems to have started yesterday. They finally asked me, but I didn't go. I attended the party in celebration of Esther Murphy's wedding. There was a strange combination of high-class old relics of the Chester Arthur family and Administration with the usual Seldes cocktail crowd. There was also a large element of Utopianism abroad and I was buttonholed and given a sales talk by Mr. Reid, the high priest, which destroyed any faith I might previously have had in them. He is one of those hard Coloradoans who drill right through Californians, but I don't believe he can do much in the East. I must say I don't think much of Mr. Arthur, but then I haven't seen much of him and he may be all right. He's taking Esther West for the first time in her life . . .   As ever, EW

To JOHN DOS PASSOS   May 9, 1935
                                                                          Red Bank

Dear Dos: Thanks for your wire and letter. My tourist visa has come through all right and I am sailing tomorrow night. I had applied first for a six-month visa, and I understand that these are almost never granted and never without the most cogent reasons and credentials. I had made no special effort to build myself up but had simply gone around to the consulate and applied as a Guggenheim traveler who wanted to work in the Marx–Engels Institute. Since then I have put some machinery in motion.

I've read your statement with great interest. Something along these lines should certainly be said. But I'm not sure that you're not confusing two distinct sets of considerations.

In the first place, there is the literary question. The truth about this, it seems to me, is that there are a great many different kinds of writing varying between what may be called long-range writing, on the one hand, and close-range writing, on the other. Long-range writing (in fiction) gives a comprehensive picture of human life over an extended period of time, as Dante or Balzac does, or gives pictures of human beings generalized from wide areas and periods (Sophocles, Shakespeare, etc.). The type of short-range writing is the editorial, the public speech, the advertisement. Now for long-range writing to be possible, it is necessary to have a more or less established society in which the writer will be able to get leisure and have firm enough ground to stand on so that he will be able to look around. Some periods (more or less stabilized periods) make this easier than others; but it is no use pretending that it does not always mean a considerable amount of struggle to extricate oneself from the demands of the social complex to which one belongs or that it does not involve a good deal of spiritual solitude. It will be the same under socialism and will be so for more generations than we are able to imagine. And there is no use pretending that periods of genuinely anarchic social upheaval promote anything but the shortest-range writing; where everybody is trying to save his skin, there is no chance for the necessary *recueillement*. The literature of the French Revolution was the oratory of Danton, the journalism of Camille Desmoulins, the Marseillaise, and the few poems on current events that André Chénier got a chance to write before they cut off his head. And what is true of practically everybody when a revolution is on is true in ordinary times of all the people who are writing for the immediate interests of a party or a group or a class. Of course, a writer may work sometimes on the long-range plane and other times write for immediate interests. The Dante who wrote the *Divine Comedy* in exile is something quite different from the Dante who was so active in politics in Florence. There is a lot about politics in the *Divine Comedy*, but Dante has treated himself and his adventures just as objectively as he has treated some historical political figure like Hugh Capet, merely as an actor in a larger drama. His real subject is a thousand years of Christendom, and the Dante who wrote the drama is the Dante who had become convinced, as he says, that the "honorable" thing to do was to "make a party by himself" —the party we all have to belong to when we are aiming at the kind of thing that Dante was aiming at. And the Shakespeare who wrote patriotic propaganda in *Henry V* and celebrated Queen Elizabeth in *Henry VIII* is something quite different from the Shakespeare who wrote the magnificent long-range political plays, *Coriolanus* and *Antony and Cleopatra*. (Swift, whom you mention, is a queer case. The bulk of his work looks like close-range writing, but he is really a long-range writer. His will to power was stronger than his interest in any cause. When he missed his advancement in London, where he had hoped to get an important preferment, he went back to Dublin with the utmost reluctance but so furious with the English court that he was driven to identify himself with the Irish. The passion behind his Irish pamphleteering is in a sense irrelevant to the subject: he did the Irish a good turn when he roused them to rebel against Wood's halfpence; but he was afterwards just as savage on what was really the reactionary side as soon as the interests of the clergy were threatened. His great work of this period was *Gulliver's Travels*, which is one of the longest-range books ever written.) The important thing is to know what kind of writing one is doing and to take the necessary steps to do it properly. So that I am not sure your carburetor-cleaning and bead-taking analogy is a true one. The kind of writing that corresponds to our technological development in the mechanical field is the newspaper journalism and advertizing copy which, to be sure, has affected our whole literary field but which has itself been produced under the pressure of capitalist competition (as effective revolutionary writing of this kind is produced by revolutionary pressure). Some people work best under pressure; some people work only under pressure—and I am sure that their technical calculations are not always performed consciously. I don't believe, in short, that it is possible to formulate a set of conditions which will be right for all kinds of literary work. What it seems to me that you are really doing here is making out a case for the long-range writer. In spite of the charges of short-range propaganda which are sometimes raised against you, I never could see that you had much real taste for the kind of pamphleteering and polemics at which Upton Sinclair, for example, excels (or Lenin). Your characters arise and declare themselves and pass away to take their places in the bigger picture as Dante's characters do—it is simply that your system is different. And you have got to have your *recueillement*. Yet perhaps other kinds of writing perfect themselves under different conditions. Enough freedom for the attention required to clèan a carburetor or take a bead is surely involved in the conditions in any work where anything gets done at all.

The other set of considerations is political. It is the question of freedom of discussion on the left. The issue here, I am sure, is the issue between Russian traditions and habits and our own. They had never had any kind of working democracy and they are having a hard time getting it even under socialism. We have had; and I agree with you completely that whatever is to be accomplished in reorganizing American society will have to be accomplished in our way and not in the Russian way. This is not really a question of Marxism. You know that Marx and Engels said a number of times that the transfer from capitalism to socialism might be accomplished in England and the United States by ordinary parliamentary methods—adding, however, that a socialist government in England would be almost certain to have on its hands a serious Tory counterrevolution (as a socialist government here would have to meet those showdowns with U.S. Steel and the other large corporations that Roosevelt has invited but shirked). This is the source of the heresy of "exceptionalism." Lenin, however, said at the end of the war that whereas it had been possible to believe this at the time that Marx and Engels said it, it was impossible to believe it any longer. What the Communists mean by Marxism is Marx and Engels corrected and interpreted by Lenin and Lenin corrected and interpreted by Stalin. I don't think, however, that it is right for the politically non-active to do very much public railing at the political errors of the Communists—as soon as you begin discussing these matters in print, you find that you are being pushed into some political group. I've tried myself to keep outside the whole thing, but have gotten more involved in it than I wanted to and have recently resigned from everything that I was aware of being associated with. My policy at present is to keep away and in writing to try to ignore all parties and special doctrines. The situation seems to be peculiarly confused by the fact that the Kirov executions had been preceded in Russia by a period of unusual relaxation and tolerance. The last Writers' Congress in Moscow seems to have taken a new liberal line: We must learn from the bourgeois writers, etc. It is evident that the literary comrades over here don't understand their own damn line or at least are unable to carry it out. The new liberal dispensation was inaugurated by a characteristic act of terrorism: when the word came for tolerance, they cast about them for some signally intolerant comrade to sacrifice. That comrade was poor Granville Hicks, who had been working his head off to comply with what he understood to be the official attitude and who would unquestionably have done his best to follow the new line as soon as he found out what it was, but who was forthwith put out on his ear. I expect that the purge of the intolerant will be terrible: the whole outfit may ultimately be wiped out. I was invited at the last moment to the Writers' Congress, but didn't go. I've since written suggesting that they either ought to include the members of heretical groups or change the wording of the sentence in their program about inviting "all revolutionary writers." This is the only light on this subject, which has given me a good deal of perplexity lately, at which I have so far been able to arrive. My present intention, as I say, is to keep as far from the whole business as possible. In connection with your statement, I felt at first that you ought to be more specific: name the Communists and say what you think they have done that was wrong. (I believe that, due to the fact that you have been away, you don't realize that literary Communism is supposed to have passed into a new phase, the phase I have spoken of above: *The New Masses* is being edited by Bill Brown, Orrick Johns, and Joe North, and Earl Browder has been bringing pressure to bear.) But then if you are specific, you will find yourself involved in a political controversy. If you complain about anything done by Stalin, they think you're an adherent of Trotsky. They can't believe in the existence of people to whom Stalin and Trotsky don't matter in connection with the politics of the United States, and there is as yet no political party to which such people can belong.

You say a number of good things, in any case. One of the best of them is the remark you have crossed out about the people who are working out the new problems being in the exposed position, though I think you were right not to include it. Maybe the thing to do is to publish a strong statement on literature, ignoring Communist politics as much as possible. Why don't you send your article first to *The New Masses*?

I'm sending you some more odds and ends you might be interested in. If you haven't read Gerard Hopkins, the man that Spender, Auden and Co. have gotten so much of their stuff from, you ought to. I saw the Dietrich picture*—it is much better than anything else of Sternberg's I have seen, doesn't suffer so much from his awful taste. If you are responsible for this and for the detail, some of which is excellent, you got much further in Hollywood than most people do. It is really quite a good picture.

My address in Moscow will be care of The Open Road, Hotel National. Drop me a line over there. I'm going to take in Greece on the way back, if my money holds out.

. . . New Jersey looks particularly attractive to me this spring—because I'm going away, I suppose. I like these heavy, rich, and humid summers with the rank smell of the ocean coming in through the suburban greenery. I may spend my declining years here after I have had a look at Russia.

Best love to Katy—I hope she is better. Hope to see you both in the fall.

As ever, EW

One of the best things you say is about the abstractions and the human material. You can say this and ought to say it, because you have been doing this kind of work (though *The New Masses* tends to assume that you have been writing the novels of Gorky). And of course the same thing is true of politics; but who is going to make the criticism here? To make the criticism is to enter into politics oneself and to have to take political responsibilities. I myself became irked finally even by the kind of work I

---

* *The Devil Is a Woman.*

was doing writing up strikes and political meetings—from the moment when I had definitely the feeling that I was working without political direction (up to a certain point I had the satisfaction of feeling that I was bringing to the attention of the liberals things which they had been disregarding—that is, I was functioning as a kind of liberal). But now I don't see any political movement with which I'm prepared to ally myself and have myself been going in for *recueillement*.

U.S.S.R.

The first impression of Leningrad is absolutely dreamlike and dazing.
(Travels in Two Democracies)

To LOUISE BOGAN   May 13, 1935
                      On Board Cunard White Star *Berengaria*
Dear Louise: I'm sorry that the last night I saw you should have been
clouded by my sour humors. You've meant so much to me this last year—
in fact, your apartment was practically getting to be my home, and I was
beginning to develop in relation to you and Maidie a regular family
psychology. But I want you to know how appreciative of you and how
fond of you, my dear, I really am: I have never had this kind of com-

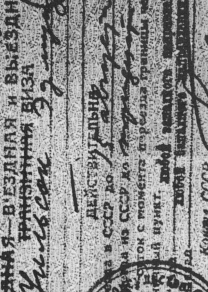

19

Passport visaed in Leningrad, May 23, 1935

panionship with a woman for any length of time ever before in my life, and I became so addicted to it this winter that maybe it's just as well that I'm going away: you and I really have too much fun together. I'm afraid that if I had a little more money, I'd decide to spend all the rest of my life drinking beer and stout with you.

I've enjoyed the voyage extremely so far—have felt the same sort of relief at getting away that I feel when I go up to Provincetown. There aren't many people, so that I'm able to have a room to myself—and the weather so far has been fine. I've read Mirsky's book on Pushkin, which I recommend to you. It makes him sound like the most interesting poet of that period and makes me eager to learn some Russian and read him. (Yours for a comprehensive culture, Morton Miltiads Label.)

Well, this is just a note to let you and Maidie know that Uncle Ed is thinking of you on the seas . . . Did I tell you that you ought to read John Brooks Wheelwright's poems? He published them himself in Boston —get him to send you one for review in *The New Yorker*. Malcolm knows his address. Am curious to know what you think of them. Did *Poetry* do anything about them? Give Maidie my love—I hope she has a good summer—and you, too, you old pretty pigeon.   As ever, Edmund

To Louise Bogan   [undated, 1935]
[Postcard]   Leningrad

Portrait of an old-time Persian lady doing a little quiet drinking. I just got your letter and was very glad to hear from you. Will write you some at length very soon, though there is so much to say that letters are inadequate. I've spent a good deal of time going to the theaters, because they are about to close for the summer, and I have never seen such wonderful productions anywhere. They are still packing them in with the Pushkin–Tchaikovsky operas and with Chekhov and Ostrovsky (a sort of Chekhov of an earlier period).   Love, Edmund

To Louise Bogan   1935
[Postcard]   Moscow

Great interest in your favorite Russian writer [Chekhov] now; they are celebrating the 75th anniversary of his birth—though some still can't quite forgive him for not having been more of a fighter. Of recent years the critical policy of dating the creation of culture and thought from the beginning of dialectical materialism has been abandoned, and you may now see pictures of Pushkin cheek by jowl with Marx and Engels.
                                                  Love, Edmund

To John Peale Bishop
[Postcard]

1935
1935
Moscow

This postcard is one of a series from Persian paintings which has just recently been brought out. The Soviets are beginning to be able for the first time to afford a little color, and these cards are one of their first attempts to satisfy the people's appetite. You can have no idea what the absence of color can mean till you see a Moscow amusement park—hardly a trace of color in clothes, posters, or buildings—like the ancients' idea of Hades. Where they lay themselves out on dyes, though, is in the theater, where the productions are the most gorgeous I have ever seen. Have had a great deal of caviar and vodka and have received a great deal of enlightenment.

Love, EW

To Maxwell Perkins

June 10, 1935
Moscow

Dear Max: Will you please have copies of *Axel's Castle* and *The American Jitters* sent to Sergei Alimov, Stoleshnikov 9, K. 12, Moscow—and a copy of *Axel's Castle* to Kashkin, Bolshoi Bozheninovsky Pereulok 21, K. 5, KV. 14, Moscow. I wish that you would also send Alimov Hemingway's *Death in the Afternoon* and *Men without Women*, if it isn't too much of a strain on your publicity supply. He wants to write something about Hemingway.

I'm very comfortably fixed here in Walter Duranty's* apartment while he's away but am moving on, I think, in a couple of weeks to take the boat trip down the Volga and see something of the south.

Best regards, Edmund Wilson

To Maxwell Perkins

June 11, 1935
Moscow

Dear Max: Won't you send some of your new American books to Sergei Alimov, one of the most interesting of the Russian writers, who reads English and is contemplating a book on American literature? I think he ought to see *Of Time and the River, Tender Is the Night,* and the books of Erskine Caldwell's which you publish. Some of this stuff ought to be translated, I think. They have just gotten out a volume of selections from Hemingway, and are mad about him. Alimov is very much excited over what I have told him about *The Green Hills of Africa*—do send him a copy of it when it is out . . . I've been more than ever impressed by our contemporary writing since I've seen how the Russians are influenced by it. They seem to read it more than any other.

---

* *New York Times* correspondent.

272

I can't do Moscow, etc., justice in a letter—but it's certainly more worth going a long way to see than anything else I have ever seen. Hope all is well with you.   As ever, Edmund Wilson

I suppose you know that Galsworthy was enormously popular over here, as at home—I don't know precisely what this signifies.

To Louise Bogan   July 7, 1935
                                                      Moscow

Dear Louise: It's impossible to make a really satisfactory letter, because there's so much to tell about—I understand why everybody wants to write books about Russia. I've got my student's visa and am living in relative magnificence in Walter Duranty's apartment while he's away. I've made some extremely interesting friends and spend my evenings drinking and talking with them very much as at home. Yesterday we went out to the Troitsk-Sergievsky Monastery, formerly one of the first strongholds of the Orthodox Church and a delirium of Byzantine ornament and barbaric magnificence—in some ways a little like Coney Island. I don't like the Greek Orthodox Church much and am not even very enthusiastic about the ikons of the first ikon painters. It all seems gaudy and barbaric, lacking in dignity and taste, after the Roman Catholic Church. It is all new to me, though, and fascinating. We ate a picnic lunch with much vodka in a little old queer hotel, the most primitive I have ever seen, traveled on crowded trains with hard seats, got off halfway to Moscow and went in swimming in a little river, and finally had dinner in the country with a prominent woman lawyer amid the combined families of a summer cottage which very much resembled Chekhov. It never really gets dark in the summertime here and you keep sitting on and drinking more tea under the impression that evening is just falling, when it is really getting on toward eleven. Some aspects of life here are quite idyllic. The collection of modern paintings of which these cards are examples is probably the best in the world. The Communists amalgamated two private collections made by rich men in Moscow before the Revolution and added to them anything else of the kind that turned up. I hope things are going O.K. with you. As my best audience, I shall entertain you on my return with many enthralling tales.   Love, Edmund

1936

AND

READING PUSHKIN

To John Peale Bishop   January 27, 1936
                                                        Red Bank

Dear John: I have been very much troubled to think that that nonsense
we sent you apropos of your firedrake poem could have discouraged you
about your work. It was simply that the poem contained both the firedrake and some other strange monster, and this set us off during some
convivial evening to compose a rigmarole in which Bill and Elinor and I
and somebody else, I think, each supplied a few lines in turn. As I remember, you had sent me at the same time the poem about Allegra and
the quince buds, which I have always considered one of your very best
lyrics. I had told you repeatedly around that time that I thought you were
developing your most successful and most original vein. However, *The
Waste Land* had just appeared during those first years when you were
abroad and it had a strange sterilizing effect on everybody—also the effect
of making them precious—it's apparent already in your firedrake poem.
I think it was all the worse for you, because you are certainly intended,
it seems to me, to be a poet of sensuous delight (which doesn't exclude
emotions, of course, connected with the soaring or passing or reflection of
sensuous delight), not self-torture and Puritan wistfulness like Eliot. I
don't think moods of pessimism really fit you. I don't mean that they're
not sincere, but that you haven't got the native vocation for them like
Eliot or A. E. Housman, and would really rather be enjoying yourself,
which is not the case with them. (Still, I suppose Eliot gave utterance to
emotions which ran pretty deep in everybody's life and revealed a central
social situation which was beginning to affect everybody.) I have just been
looking through *Green Fruit* again, and it is remarkable how well it holds

up—I don't know of anybody else's undergraduate verse which was in the same class with yours.

. . . I'm working at my book* and go to bed at six o'clock in the morning, so that I don't see much of anybody or anything.   As ever, Edmund W.

To Wolcott Gibbs   February 29, 1936
The New Yorker
. . . Here is the manuscript I spoke to you about. It is part of an account of a trip to Russia. I thought there might possibly be something in it you could use—for example, the part about the flophouse at Ulyanovsk or the part about the hospital at Odessa . . .

To John Peale Bishop   March 11, 1936
                                                              New York

Dear John: . . . I've just finished a book I have been working on and gotten it off to the printer, to my great relief. Now I'm going uptown to stay for a while with some Russian exiles who give Russian lessons. I find languages are a great relaxation: in the early stages, they introduce you into what seems to be a completely fresh new world, and there are no emotional connotations and no necessity for exercising the judgment. It is only at a later stage that you find people are saying the same things in the new language that they say in all the other languages . . .

As ever, EW

I also spent a week with the Gausses at Princeton. I thought that everybody was in a pretty sorry way, although they don't know it. I met the new president and he struck me as a master plumber. He is an extremely limited and conservative municipal politics professor from the more hardboiled milieux of Pennsylvania. I think that Gauss, who had rather hoped to be president himself, had his difficulties at first with Dodds's narrowness; and they seem to have passed into one of those ectoplasmic wrestling matches, such as Thurber so admirably depicts. But I discovered, when I went down there this time, that they had come out of it with Gauss all wrapped around Dodds. Dodds is stupid and Gauss is intelligent, and Gauss now feeds Dodds his speeches and seems to have become a personage of more importance in the administration of the university than he has ever been before. He is giving up his modern languages department, which, I think, is all to the bad, and has developed an official psychology which is incredible. He censors the *Lit.* and recently made one of the poets change the word "testicular" to "terrestrial." At the same time, he

---

* *Travels in Two Democracies.*

compensates by writing pseudonymous articles in which he says that leisure-class culture has no future—I think he's becoming schizophrenic.

To Phelps Putnam   March 24, 1936
                                                                Red Bank
Dear Phelps: I was glad to hear from you this morning. I was merely up at Washington [Connecticut] for a few days' visit (I didn't see Alfred [Bellinger], but have heard about him: it seems he has gone in for numismatics and tries to pay the bus drivers with obols, drachmae, and other ancient coins, which he carries around in his pockets)—and am now back here.

What the hell's the matter with you, you old fraud?—why don't you produce some literature? Haven't you heard about that one talent which is death to hide? Besides, during this ghastly period, when the world's in the doldrums, good work is all the more important: why leave the field to the phonies?

I'd like very much to see you; but shan't be able to go anywhere for a while, as I've got to attend to the proof of a book—not the *Finland Station*, but something else. The *Finland Station* is a lot of trouble but is coming along in a year or so, and in the meantime I'm getting out a couple of other things. I hope that this high productivity on my part will make you thoroughly ashamed of your own naysaying, malingering, Sicilian idling, false attitudes of ripe maturity, theosophy, easy living, narcissism and general hey-ho-lackaday!   As ever, EW

I learned Russian primarily, I think, in order to read Pushkin, inspired by D. S. Mirsky's book on the subject, as I had learned Italian in order to read Dante.   (To Leonard Kriegel, 1971)

To Malcolm Cowley   May 16, 1936
The New Republic   234 East Fifteenth Street, N.Y.

I understand that Avrahm Yarmolinsky is bringing out a translation of *Evgeni Onegin*, or a volume of translations from Pushkin containing it.* I'd be glad to write something about it, as I've been reading *Evgeni Onegin* in Russian and have some ideas on the subject . . .

To Louise Bogan   July 1, 1936
                                    234 East Fifteenth Street, N.Y.
Dear Louise: Why in God's name are you going to Quebec? I went there once as a kid, and though it is a little more interesting than the rest of Canada, it is still not very interesting.

---

* *The Works of Alexander Pushkin: Lyrics, Narrative Poems, Folk Tales, Plays, Prose*, translated by Avrahm Yarmolinsky and Babette Deutsch.

I have no interesting news—have done a lot of reading of Pushkin and have about decided he is the greatest nineteenth-century poet. When the translation of *Evgeni Onegin* comes out in the fall, you ought to read it. By the way, I was rather horrified at your handing Steve Benét so much in *The New Yorker*. When I was reading it, before I turned the page and saw your name, I thought, Good God! they've given poor Louise the gate and this is the kind of stuff they want. She never could have written this! What will Rolfe Humphries say! *Axel's Castle*, for some reason, is being translated into Japanese. I received a wonderful letter full of Japanese politeness and ending: "For the enlightenment of the literary circle at large, I hope your critical pen will prove facile and flourishing evermore." Maybe my destiny is to be a great writer in Japanese.

I am still having a good time in my eyrie, though I haven't been doing quite such furious entertaining lately as I did when I first moved in. I have my Russian ex-ballet girl to dinner occasionally to explain the hard parts of Pushkin to me.

. . . there was some talk—believe it or not—of selling *I Thought of Daisy* to the movies. I want to sell them *Axel's Castle* too, with Adolphe Menjou as Proust and the Marx Brothers as Joyce . . .   As ever, Uncle Ed

To MALCOLM COWLEY   September 2, 1936
                                                            Provincetown

. . . Can you find out precisely when Random House is bringing out that volume of Pushkin translations?—and could you get me advance sheets or, in any case, let me know what's going to be in it? . . .

To MALCOLM COWLEY   September 14, 1936
                                                            Provincetown

Dear Malcolm: That volume will evidently contain a large part of Pushkin and I only want to write about *Evgeni Onegin*, because I haven't got time now to read him all—so how would it be if I did merely a little piece about *E.O.* which could be used as a middle article? Then you could have somebody who knows Russian better do a review of the book. I suggest Max Eastman—about the only American literary man who knows Pushkin. I don't think you can give Pushkin too much space. I am about convinced now that he was the greatest poet of the nineteenth century and he is completely unknown in the English-speaking countries—though we have felt his influence at second-hand through Russian opera and fiction. He seems to have permeated their whole literature and the Soviet writers idolize him, so that to pay him a tribute is to contribute to the cultural entente cordiale. It is the second century [first century] of his death, and they are doing a lot of celebrating. *Evgeni Onegin* is a work of the order of *Le Rouge et le Noir* and *Madame Bovary* and, so far as I have been able to find, there is no decent account of it in English . . .

I'm not interested in doing anything about Chesterton—though somebody ought to.   As ever, Edmund

To Morton D. Zabel   February 19, 1937

. . . I've just read Pushkin's *Bronze Horseman* and am thinking of translating it—as Elton's translation is far from doing it justice. It is the best thing about Russia I have ever read—the Tsar wouldn't allow it to be printed, and I'm surprised that Stalin does . . .

To Malcolm Cowley   May 29, 1937

. . . Here is my piece on *The Bronze Horseman*, which is a companion piece to the one on *Evgeni Onegin*. I have cut down the introduction as much as I could; but if Bruce is filled with horror by its length, tell him that he can publish it in two installments, if he wants to; and that it will be a long, long time now before I send you anything else long . . .

To Malcolm Cowley   July 6, 1936
                                                                    Red Bank
Dear Malcolm: I've examined the English book on Engels and the German original and have decided that I'll have to read the German one anyhow and that it would be wasted effort to read the other one, which I am told misrepresents Meyer. Why don't you write about it yourself? I've got to cut down on book reviewing and don't want to do anything more except Pushkin in the fall. By the way, I've made several attempts to find out how my accounts with the *N.R.* stand at present and have never yet been able to get anybody to let me know. I wish you would send me a memorandum about it . . .   E.W.

To John Dos Passos   July 22, 1936
                                                                    Red Bank
Dear Dos: . . . I've just read *The Big Money*, and the whole thing is certainly a noble performance. The end of it suffers a little, I think, from comparison with the brilliance of the end of *1919*—it does sound as if you were getting tired of it. Aren't you a little bit perfunctory about the Sacco–Vanzetti case, for example? And I wished that when you brought your old characters on at the end, you had made them do more vividly characteristic things (though Dick Savage and Ben Compton are tellingly handled). When all the former mates are splitting up there, I don't think you always indicate sufficiently just what they think they are getting out

278

of it: it gets to seem a little automatic. But what happens itself is beautifully worked out, and the whole thing tied up at the end with unexpected inevitableness and point. I think that the best part is really Charley Anderson; but all the narrative parts have qualities which are very original and remarkable and seem to me rather different from what I remember in the other two volumes. As the Russians say of Pushkin, the writing has become "transparent"—they mean that the objects show through, but in your case it is experience which shows through and conveys its significance to the reader without any apparent effort on your part to underline it. One of the things which you have done most successfully—which I don't remember any other novelist's doing—is show people in those moments when they are at loose ends or drifting or up against a blank wall—such as a passage in the first volume which stands out in curious relief in my mind, when Moorehouse has washed up in Pittsburgh and simply lies on the bed for several days, not knowing what he is going to do next—moments when the social currents, taking advantage of the set of the character, will sweep the individual in. These moments and the purposive careers of your eminent men and women are the positive and negative poles of your book, between which you probably allow for more of life, cheat less on what real human experience is like (the principal exception to this is that I think you strip away too much the glamour and exhilaration of the good time which the Americans thought they were having during the Boom), than any other radical writer.

I'll be glad to get up to P'town. I've been down here most of the time lately. It's a great thing to get out into the great American summer again. I spent all last summer cooped up in Moscow and all winter writing at night—and have never appreciated our summer so much: we have more space and range, water, greenery, and sun than anybody.   As ever, EW

To ALLEN TATE   July 22, 1936
                                                        Red Bank

Dear Allen: Thanks very much for your book.* I've read it with much pleasure, which is something I can't say about any new poetry for a long time. In general, the ones I like best are the more lyrical ones—rather than the meditations. I wish there were more of your semi-dramatic subjects—things presented or described—in this volume: "The Robber Bridegroom," I think, is one of the very best. The one meditation which seems to me entirely successful is "The Ivory Tower"—which says something and is a good poem—though, as usual, when you get on the subject of Marxism, you seem to be combating the opinions, not of Marx, but of Marxist phonies. This is fair enough, I suppose, as there are plenty

---

* *The Mediterranean and Other Poems.*

around, and they have been making plenty of racket. But Marx and Engels would not have subscribed to any of the opinions—on *Oedipus, Lear*, etc. —nor even that beef and cheese washed down by Pilsen will necessarily solve all the problems—an opinion which I don't hold either, though you seem to attribute it to me—which you seem to think involved in dialectical materialism. Also, the ivory tower is not at all the same thing as what I meant by Axel's castle. They represent two entirely different attitudes toward life and art. I tried to make this clear in my book, but nobody ever seems to pay any attention to it. Alfred de Vigny's idea (after the Napoleonic Wars) was that human life was such a mess that you couldn't hope to do anything about it by intervening, but could only put the situation on record in art. He had a strong sense of tragic life and was worried by certain of the same aspects of the period as Marx and the other socialists. The *fin de siècle* attitude, on the other hand, which Villiers carried to such absurdity in Axel, was that you should get as far away from reality as possible—forget it, try to believe in a pure fantasy. This was the weakness of this kind of literature—that is, something which weakened its validity as art. For Vigny's ivory tower, on the other hand, I have always had a lot of respect.

Your poem about Landor haunts me, though I don't know quite what it means. As for my own muse, which you seem to invoke in your inscription, I've written a little verse of late years and may eventually bring out another book.

How are you? I'm not even certain where you are. I hope your family are thriving . . .   As ever, Edmund W.

To John Peale Bishop   August 27, 1936
                                                  Provincetown
Dear John: I believe that what I feel about your recent long poems is that some kind of intellectualizing activity has been tending to swamp the sensuous imagery which has always seemed to me your great forte. Somebody said to me something the other day about the "metaphysical" character of your poetry; and I was surprised at first, as I had never thought of your poetry as being particularly metaphysical. But then I realized that it had become so—that you were tending toward the same sort of thing as Tate. And I'm not sure that you ought to cultivate this kind of thing—which so many people have been doing and in doing which they have been making so little sense. In these long poems, for example, which you left me, what I like best are such passages of pure description as "Ducks flew in vain to the drained marshes," and the stanza in the other poem about the blue hills and the blackberry memories of meadow heat. The two great curses of contemporary verse, it seems to me, are metaphysical maundering and rhetoric; and your kind of exquisite sensuous impressionism (nonetheless, accurate description) is something which is very

rare. I believe that parts of your work nowadays are virtuosity rather than the real thing; and I've been thinking that I'd like to see you do a sequence of short poems which would compose into a whole. You could stick principally to the sensuous world and still convey all your emotion and thought (that Judas poem with its yellow marshes has always seemed to me in your best vein, for example). It's the point of view, the basic assumptions, not the "ideas," which matter.

I seem to have gotten around here to a criticism which sounds a good deal like your criticism of my Russian stuff. In regard to that, I think that you don't say quite what you mean. In writing, one cannot deal with "facts" at all without having some "opinion" about them. One's primary assumptions are opinions. I think that either your judgment *is* affected by the fact that you disagree with my point of view or that, simply, you have no taste for what seems to you my editorializing (though I thought I'd handled my thoughts fairly adroitly in relation to the other things). In any case, I'm returning the stricture by suggesting that you ought to write directly from the perceptions and feelings of the individual. (What about those birds of Monomoy, for instance?) I wish you would get rid, above all, of the ponderous Chirico machinery which has been weighing you down for so long (though in "Collapse of Time" you have translated the same theme into more modern terms). I'll say frankly that I *do* disagree with your point of view—which I take to be a Spenglerian vision of doom—and that I doubt whether any really sound writing can come out of a point of view essentially phony. What is authentic in the Chirico kind of thing— a sad and uneasy memory of what happened with the decline of Rome— is only one of the fleeting moods of our period: it can't be made to carry our realities. But the life of a man, if profoundly explored, is in itself a complete reality. Again, I seem to be passing your precepts back to you.

The important thing, however, is that you should come up here again. It was fine to see you and I was sorry not to have had more chance to talk to you, but thought that you would probably be glad to see Phelps. Let me know in advance, if you can, so that I won't make any other plans. Charley Kaselau tells me that the effect of your conversation on him was so stimulating that he attacked his painting the next morning with revived interest . . .   EW

To Louise Bogan   October 5, 1936
The New Yorker   Red Bank

Dear Louise: Here is a note about the Fenollosa book.* I suggest that as a recompense you allow me to keep the book, which has interested me very much and inspired me with a desire to learn Chinese . . .   Love, Edmund

---

* For *The New Yorker*.

The Chinese Written Character as a Medium for Poetry (52 pages, $1.50) is a reprint of the remarkable essay by Ernest Fenollosa first brought out in 1918 by Ezra Pound. Fenollosa succeeded in affording the foreigner a glimpse through the apparent opacities of the Chinese language, and he illuminated profoundly the whole subject of language and its relation to poetry in general. Of first-rate interest to all persons occupied with literature—especially the searching sidelight on Shakespeare.

I assume that this is for the Briefly Noted Department. If it's not what is needed, let me know.

To James T. Farrell   October 15, 1936
                                              Red Bank

Dear Jim: The trouble with [Serge] Dinamov is that in that passage he took exception to I had said that, from the point of view of proletarian literature, things in Russia seemed to have been working out the way Trotsky said they would. It is an indication of the state things are in over there. Just before that, he had been writing me letters of an almost maudlin comradely cordiality. I was glad to get the copy of your book, but, Jim, if you want me to read your complete works, you will have to write shorter and more to the point—I am an old concision-fetishist . . . Be sure to let me know when you're going to Russia.   Edmund Wilson

To Malcolm Cowley   November 2, 1936
                                              Red Bank

Dear Malcolm: Here is the Pushkin. It is long, but I think it is important that the whole thing should be run together. I know that, if you do this, there will only be room for about one other middle article, but there is no harm in that. People think they are getting a lot for their money. The N.R. did it with my Proust article and a couple of other things, with, as I remember, excellent results. This seems to me the best literary article I have given the N.R. since the *Axel's Castle* stuff and it is, so far as I know, the only essay on *Evgeni Onegin* in English—the only other treatments of the subject being the brief ones in Mirsky's book on Pushkin and in Maurice Baring's outline of Russian literature. I wish, also, for various reasons, that it could be published before the Yarmolinsky book comes out. (By the way, Max Eastman, to whom I have been talking on the telephone, seems to have misunderstood about the book of Pushkin translations: it has been done by various hands. He says that, if you will send it to him, he will let you know right away whether he can review it.)

I have some other ideas for articles in mind and want to make the

282

following proposal. Will the *N.R.* let me do for them for a while the equivalent of two articles a month? My idea would be to alternate discussions of contemporary literary events with more or less solid stuff about the past (of which the Pushkin could serve as the first specimen)—the whole thing to make more or less sense. What I should propose, specifically, would be as follows:

1. Pushkin.

2. Two articles which would go together, the first dealing with the general business of the literary (journalistic) scene both on the left and on the right; and the second dealing at length with Mr. De Voto—it is certainly time that somebody blew him out of the water. (If this is O.K., please send me the office files of *The Saturday Review* since his advent— and also his books, which I am sure you can get from the publishers—and, if you can get that, too, Pareto.)

3. The resumption of the *Finland Station* with two articles on pre-Marxist socialism.

4. A contemporary article or two—I have several possible subjects, and no doubt others will present themselves as the books come out.

5. Marx and Engels in the *Finland Station* series.

6. And after that, perhaps another breather till Lenin is ready.

This wouldn't necessarily mean a literary article every other week. The sets of two articles should be printed as successive works. Skipping a week between the two parts of John Reed's memoir did a good deal to weaken its effect—also, in the case of the Yeats pieces.

You could announce that I was going to be a regular contributor and that the *Finland Station* would be resumed . . .

If it is anywhere near where you live, why don't you come in to see me at Stamford? . . . I've got a house in the middle of the woods, where nothing is to be heard but the squirrels playing with acorns.

As ever, Edmund

To Babette Deutsch December 10, 1936
Trees, R.F.D. 1, Stamford, Conn.

Dear Miss Deutsch: Your letter was forwarded to me here and didn't reach me till after the Eastman review had appeared. I had, however, seen it in manuscript, and both Malcolm Cowley and I had done our best to induce him to tone down the personal aspect—as I see from the printed version, with imperfect success. I don't think you ought to be too much disturbed by it, though—because, unfortunately, he can't write about anything, even dialectical materialism, without appearing to make a personal issue of it, and people know and discount this. Aside from that, the positive parts, where he is simply dealing with Pushkin's poetry, seemed to me good; and in connection with what he says about the introduction,

I have had the same impression myself—not from the book, which I haven't seen, but from my conversations with you—that you and Mr. Yarmolinsky were somewhat unduly prejudiced against Pushkin. I'm sure, however, that Max Eastman has been unfair about your translation of *Evgeni Onegin*, which Louise Bogan, no indulgent critic, tells me seems to her remarkably good. It was a heroic feat to have carried it through in the original meter and rhyme scheme!

I have an article in the same number on *Evgeni Onegin*, which I'd be interested to have your opinion on. I'm anxious to see your book, which I'll get hold of when I go to New York. I'm sorry I hadn't seen it before I read Eastman's review.　　　　　　　Yours sincerely, Edmund Wilson*

> Old Zabel came out here for a night, and I enjoyed him very much.
> I think that his succeeding to the editorship of *Poetry* and his getting
> this gloomy-sounding anthology out has bucked him up quite a lot.
> （To Louise Bogan, 1937）

To MORTON D. ZABEL　　　　　　　　　　　　December 10, 1936
　　　　　　　　　　　　　　　　　　　　　　　　　　　　Stamford
Dear Morton: You misunderstood my letter. Of course I don't mind your reprinting from *Axel's Castle*. The point is that the chapters in the book were entirely rewritten and quite different from the *New Republic* articles, and that I was filled with horror at the prospect of having the old first drafts revived. And in regard to the other things, they were journalism written to last a week and oughtn't to be revived either. I hope that you put plenty of your own stuff into the anthology. Your reviews in *Poetry* have been exceptionally good lately.

I haven't seen the number with Louise's poems, but should like to.

Thank you for offering me the Coleridge and Leopardi books, but I have to concentrate now on articles I am doing for the *N.R.* By the way, there is somewhere in Coleridge's criticism a reference to Pushkin—where he is making a sort of survey of European literature. I have been through the volumes I have and can't find it. If you should happen to run across it, I'd be grateful if you'd let me know . . .

My retirement out here isn't a deliberate renunciation and as a matter of fact irks me a good deal and makes me cross. I'm fortunate in never having read *War and Peace* before, as I've been going through it in the evenings and go to bed feeling as if the house were all full of people.

　　　　　　　　　　　　　　　　　　　　　　　As ever, Edmund Wilson

---

* See pp. 459 and 460.

284

1937

To Evelyn Shrifte   January 23, 1937
Vanguard Press   Stamford

Dear Miss Shrifte: In view of the attempt which I understand is being
made to suppress James T. Farrell's new book, *A World I Never Made*,
I should like to say that I should consider such a step to be a very serious
blow to American literature. Mr. Farrell is one of the ablest and one of
the most serious American writers of his generation. His books are so far
from being pornographic that they are likely rather to alienate readers
through their earnestness and their bitter realism. Their effect on art and
morals alike should be wholesome.   Yours sincerely, Edmund Wilson

To James T. Farrell   January 23, 1937
                                                           Stamford
Dear Jim: Thanks for your letters and your convivial postcard. I wish I
had been with you. I've written to Vanguard about the suppression of
your book and have told Dos Passos about it. What's the matter?—are the
Catholics on your trail? I haven't answered before because I've been busy
struggling with a batch of stuff for *The New Republic* . . . What do you
think about the Radek trial? My theory is that it has been brought home
to them that the trials just before were an international flop, and that
they have decided to do the whole thing again and take more pains to
make it seem plausible. The idea that the accused were plotting with
Japan against the United States is a diplomatic gesture intended to cement
the entente cordiale with us . . .   As ever, Edmund Wilson

To John Dos Passos   February 12, 1937
                                                           Stamford
Dear Dos: I'm sorry I missed you when you were in New York. De Voto
has replied to my article this week and seems to have nothing to say. It is

all very disappointing. I don't agree with you about the Brooks book, which gave me a better idea of what Boston had meant to America in its day than anything else I ever read.*

What about the Russians? What the hell? It seems to me that one of the most important developments, to which no one seems to have paid any attention, was the speech by Troyanovsky, which came out the same day as the Radek verdicts and in which he said that the Soviets did not consider that the battle was one of socialism against capitalism. Did you see it? I've thought that the thing to do was to keep clear of the Stalin–Trotsky controversy, but find myself on this Trotsky committee and have been being agitated by Trotskyists and Stalinists in every mail and by telephone. Certainly Stalinism has been taking a pretty sinister turn and has triumphed over Trotsky to the extent that it has made it impossible at the present time for him to do anything except defend himself against these charges. In the meantime, I can't see that there's anything else left of international socialism. Do you think we're going to end up—see Troyanovsky's speech—with another one of these big wars to make the world safe for democracy?

I saw your Spanish film and thought it was awfully good—the best put-together picture I think I ever saw. It compared very well with the too-much-staged Soviet one.

I'm thriving on my present mode of life, which I think I probably ought to have adopted some years ago . . .   EW

To Malcolm Cowley   April 15, 1937
                                                       Stamford
Dear Malcolm: . . . In regard to your Russian article, I agree with the last part; but I believe you are mistaken about the trials. It would take too long to go into it in a letter, but you sound as if you had read nothing but the official report. You ought to read the Trotskyist and socialist stuff, too—and some of the most illuminating material has appeared in that little sheet called *The International Review*. Also, [W. H.] Chamberlin, who, in spite of his fundamental stupidities, is really about the best reporter on Russia. I guess that all the trials have been fakes since the time of the Ramzin sabotage trial. They have always been intended to provide scapegoats and divert attention from more fundamental troubles. In the case of these recent trials, I imagine that not a word of these confessions was true. The victims had, I suppose, been guilty of some kind of opposition to the regime; and the technique evidently is to tell them that they can only vindicate themselves by putting on acts which will be helpful to the U.S.S.R. We have to scare people about sabotage, Fascism, Trotskyism

---

* *The Flowering of New England, 1815–1865.*

286

(this is easy for men like Zinoviev and Radek, who hate Trotsky and whom he hates), terrorism, etc., and it is a patriotic service to sacrifice oneself in such a cause. This comes out clearly in the edifying speeches—like those of Radek—which the accused usually make before they are sentenced.

One extremely important factor which makes such things possible has not been emphasized enough: there is at the present time a complete double standard of truth in the Soviet Union, one for the official groups among themselves and another for manipulating the people. Nobody who hasn't seen the Russians at home will ever believe this, but the gap between the well informed and intelligent and the ignorant and dumb is still so great that the latter are always treated like children by the former. *Izvestia* and *Pravda* now—which are what the ordinary people read— haven't a word of news or sense in them. They are as bad as the Nazi papers. The real papers are those of the privileged groups, like the *Red Army Star* and the GPU bulletin—just as it is only the specially privileged people who are allowed to use the libraries. This makes it possible to pass the sponge every day over everything that has happened before. (Your article, it seemed to me, like a good deal else that is written about Russia nowadays, wasn't altogether free from the fault of having been influenced by this sponge-passing technique. One has to remember that everything that emanates from the government is pure propaganda intended to lead simple people and cooked up solely to meet immediate ends with hardly even the pretense of consistency or truth to the historical record. One has to check up on everything for oneself.) The higher-ups simply agree among themselves on what it is expedient to tell the boobs. The procedure is totally undemocratic. One of the things that surprised me most when I went to the Soviet Union was the scorn expressed by the—one scarcely knows what to call them: they don't correspond exactly to anything we have, but by the bright and self-advancing elements of the community toward the not-so-bright and backward elements. This produces a kind of snobbery which enables intelligent people to condone all this hornswoggling of the masses in the name of whom everything is being done. This psychology tends to affect everybody favorably disposed toward the Soviet Union. Louis Fischer has got to be an amazing example of it, and one has to watch it in oneself.

There would be a lot more to say, but I must pull up. They are evidently—as you intimate at the end of your article—up against fundamental problems now in connection with the relation of these masses to their governing groups. The authorities' real quarrel with Trotsky is that he is the only person who has kept these contradictions in view combined with bitter attacks on Stalin. Whatever you may think of Trotsky's deficiencies —which are real—in the way of political instinct and human relations, he errs on the side of being academic. His whole life is lived in a Marxist dream of history and to play the game according to the Marxist rules is his whole morality. The constant stream of books, pamphlets, speeches, and articles which he has been pouring out since his exile is consistent and obviously in earnest, and entirely incompatible with the charges against him. He undoubtedly has an underground influence in the Soviet Union —his books are bootlegged there. But these trials have not produced any Trotskyists—unless Muralov had been one. Trotsky in the publicity of the Soviet Union is simply what the Jew is to the Nazis.

I think my Paul Elmer More article ought to be run before the socialism articles begin, in order not to come out too late after More's death. I'm glad you're running something by T. K. Whipple, who really wrote the best book about the contemporary American writers.   As ever, Edmund

Don't send me the Bernard Shaw volume of musical criticism, but it might be interesting to see what Paul Rosenfeld would say about it.

It is all right about your allegedly pseudonymous letters—I thought they might have been one of the gaffes you occasionally pull when you are making the effort to be diplomatic.

To Phelps Putnam   March 3, 1937
                                                      Stamford
Dear Phelps: I was in bad shape seven years ago. My doctor sent me to a sanatorium, where my habits became regularized but where I wouldn't stay long. When I got out, I went back to my neurologist, who psyched me. Maybe a dose of psychoanalysis wouldn't be a bad thing for you. I have a high opinion of that doctor and will look up his name and address if you should want them. The younger neurologists nowadays have all the techniques at their fingertips and are thoroughly reliable with analysis.

Why don't you come out here to see me when you get out. Or come out for a holiday, if they will let you. If you're not supposed to drink, it will be easy, because I'm not drinking myself. I'd be delighted to see you and it's quite nice out here in the woods now. No sanatorium could be quieter. You could get yourself run over in a taxi.

I'm sending you the Pushkin article—also, a little vagary derived from my experience in the hospital in Odessa, when I had scarlet fever in four languages.   As ever, Bunny W.

Don't let them pull out your teeth—which is what they always try to do in those places.

To Phelps Putnam   April 7, 1937
                                                      Stamford
Dear Phelps: . . . The time that I drew a blank, my work didn't stop— in fact, I wrote the first chapter of my book *Axel's Castle* in the sanatorium, but it tended to confine itself to rather a narrow intellectual plane,

288

as can be seen in the book itself, which, as somebody said, gave out more light than heat. But everything else stopped. I was psyched over a considerable period—I forget exactly how long—and that was one of the only things that pulled me through. Your case is no doubt different, however. I wouldn't try to advise you. The only thing that has occurred to me to suggest—though without any positive assurance—is that it might be a good thing for a while to give up thinking about poetry at all and to start working at something else, maybe not literary at all. In the way of literary occupation, did you ever try any translation? I've been working lately on a translation of a long poem of Pushkin's (into a kind of iambic prose of my own invention) and I have thought again and again how I wished I had your gifts for poetry, as Pushkin's temperament and style are in some ways not unlike your own. There'd be no use in your versifying my prose, but I recommend the exercise for times when the original ideas are not running. It is quite interesting and agreeable and keeps the hand in . . . As ever, Bunny Wilson

To Louise Bogan

April 7, 1937
Stamford

Dear Louise: I was awfully sorry not to see you before you left. I didn't realize you were going so soon . . .

Your book finally arrived this morning and I read it with my coffee in bed.* I can only say, my dear, that I derived deep aesthetic satisfaction from it and that I was deeply proud—a feeling that I really don't often have—to be associated with it by your dedication. When I've read the poems more, I'll be able to talk about them more intelligently than I am now. I thought that you had finally succeeded in making "Putting to Sea" quite interesting—and the title is certainly a notable improvement. But I was sorry that you hadn't included the diabetes poem and the one about a bright crumb of forever, which is a special favorite of mine. It is really one of those accidental things that every once in a while turns out to be wonderful. The "Roman Fountain" I didn't remember, and it seemed to me one of your very best. I think that you are particularly good when you attach your attention to some object, as you tell me Rilke approves of doing, and I wish you would do it more. I believe you used to do it more than you do now. The one about Swift is wonderful. You ought to send it as credentials to Yeats.

Do write me and let me know about your adventures on the old sod.

It's really getting to be wonderful out here in the forest now. Crocuses of purple, yolk-yellow, white veined with purple, and white have suddenly sprung up in the front yard; and since the rain of the night before last

---

* The Sleeping Fury.

all the birds, plants, and animals of the woods seem to have burst out: frogs, turtles, tree toads, rabbits, peewees, wild ducks, orioles, pheasants. It is quite exhilarating to have lived among these trees all winter, with their monotony and the coating of the earth with dead leaves, and then walk out and find everything full of life and lively spots of color appearing. There are supposed to be trout in this river, and I am going to try to catch them when the season opens. I had a dream the other night in which I thought I was reading a poem by Pushkin about a trout: he addressed the trout as "little fox," which seemed to me very apt. And I must tell you about the poem I composed in another dream—the only dream poem I have ever been able to remember afterwards:

> The human heart is full of leaks;
> The human head is full of vapors.
> The crows disband; the mandrake shrieks.
> The scandal is in all the papers.

I'll spare you a description of the rest of the dream, but the words "the mandrake shrieks" were agreed upon beforehand and had to be worked into the poem, which was being written in a sort of *bout-rimé* game with very peculiar conditions. The crows were actually right outside my windows and make a terrible noise every morning. I suppose I thought that things had got so bad that they'd decided they might as well call it a day.

Well, it seems a long time now since I sat glowering at you over the whisky during the deep dark deathly days of late autumn. You really did much to save my life during that dolorous period. I have been missing you lately. You must let me know and come out here as soon as you get back. And write me in the meantime. I hope you have a marvelous time.

Love and gratitude as ever, Edmund

To MALCOLM COWLEY
The New Republic

March 9, 1937
Stamford

Dear Malcolm: On examining these articles of mine, I find that the longest of them is hardly four pages and a half, which is certainly not an exorbitant length. You are running Tom Wolfe's story to the tune of five pages an installment. Babeuf's defense is an important document, which has never, so far as I can discover, been summarized in this way before and which is particularly interesting at this time. The career of Enfantin is a queer and entertaining story, which, I think, relieves the rest of the record. And leaving it out would spoil the shape of the whole thing. The whole set of articles is packed with material. And you won't need to run any more *Finland Station* for as long as you like . . .   E.W.

To Malcolm Cowley   March 14, 1937
                                                          Stamford

. . . As for the socialism articles, it really doesn't seem to me worthwhile
for me to spoil my scheme, of which Enfantin is an integral part, in order
to take a thousand or so words out of an article which at longest can only
run four and a half pages. There is no hurry about printing these
articles. Hold them over till your glut of other material has been reduced.
I believe that your editorial psychology is sometimes getting the better
of your literary sense nowadays. It's a mistake to snip off arbitrarily little
bits of highly organized pieces . . .

To Malcolm Cowley   May 21, 1937
                                                          Stamford

Dear Malcolm: The book about the Commune is a good subject. I have
a lot of French stuff on the Commune here. Also, how about an attack on
Maxwell Anderson's poetic dramas? I've been wanting to do something
about them for some time. *Winterset* was one of the greatest impostures
ever put over on the American public. It oughtn't to be an encroachment
on Stark [Young]'s department because I should be considering them
primarily as literature—I haven't even seen the last two on the stage. And
I should want to quote Stark on *Winterset*. He was the only critic, so far
as I can remember, who said that the verse was lousy. You might get them
to send me his articles—I think there were two. Also, get the publishers
of *Winterset*, *High Tor*, and *The Masque of Kings* to send them to
me . . .   EW
     . . . Louise Bogan tells me that Oxford has already sent her the sheets of
the Swift. Are there any other editions of classics lately that haven't
been reviewed? Anything on Keats? The Fanny Brawne–Fanny Keats
letters have been reviewed, haven't they? Another possibility is H.D.'s
translation of *Ion*, which you sent me. *Ion* is a mysterious and much con-
troverted play. Verrall and Gilbert Murray have written about it no
end. I wish you'd send me Paul Elmer More's *Notes from an Oxford
Notebook* or whatever it's called (Princeton University Press). I imagine
it would be worth a short note at least.

To Bruce Bliven   June 9, 1937
The New Republic   Stamford

Dear Bruce: I've just had a letter from Malcolm, sending back my *Bronze
Horseman* article. I understand that he has sailed, so am writing you. If
The New Republic wants to do any further business with me, we will
have to have some kind of agreement that you will print what I write. In

other words, you will have to accept me as a regular writer on a basis like that of Stark or of Heywood Broun on *The Nation*. I don't, of course, want to write every week. In fact, I don't care how infrequently you run me. (You will have till the first of January to run the *Bronze Horseman*—when it is coming out in a book—and till autumn after next for the *Finland Station* stuff.) But it's essential, if I'm to do any more work for you, that you agree to let me write about what I please, say what I please, and write at any length I please, up to, let us say, five *New Republic* pages. If you will let me know how much stuff by me you think you want to run in a year, I will supply you with that amount. But I want your assurance that you will print what I write. It's too much of a nuisance to fight these absurd battles over every other article I send in. You will have to make up your minds whether you want my stuff enough and whether you have enough confidence in me to accept me on this basis. If you haven't, I'm ready to give you copy to cover my debt and call it a day right now. Sincerely, Edmund W.

To ALLEN TATE April 30, 1937
Stamford

Dear Allen: I was glad to get your letter. I had hoped I might see you up on the Cape last summer, as John Bishop seemed to expect you. I'm afraid it will be some time before I'll be going South, but if you and Caroline are ever North, I hope you'll come out and see me here. I've got quite a comfortable house, actually in the depths of a forest—have spent the whole winter here and expect to be here for another year at least. I hardly ever go to New York and am as rural as any agrarian. I do nothing but read and write—with a little fishing this spring in a river that runs past the house—and see nobody but people who interest me. Louise Bogan and Paul Rosenfeld have been out here to see me. Louise is now in Ireland. Phelps Putnam, as you know, is in a sanatorium in Hartford. I had a letter from him not long ago, and he seems to be getting along all right. I'm working on a book about the development of Marxism, which will be a sort of companion piece to *Axel's Castle*, but it is more trouble to do. The whole left literary movement got to be a pain in the neck, and now it has been completely demoralized—the political movement as well—by the Stalin–Trotsky controversy. I feel, however, that this is having the effect of considerably clearing the air. People will have to think for themselves, and those who can't think and can't write but have been hanging on to Stalin's mustaches—also the whiskers of Trotsky—will relapse into the obscurity where they belong—unless their poison pens turn up in the front ranks of a new war to save the world for democracy. Yours for a country life, Edmund

To Christian Gauss   June 2, 1937
                                                      Stamford

Dear Christian: I was afraid I was writing you down instead of up. I
have always felt that you were much too willing to say like Apollo in the
country of hunchbacks in Edna's Millay's poem: "Your roof is low for
me. The fault is mine." And there is something of this aspect of you in
my sketch, due to the fact that P.E.M. [Paul Elmer More] is the central
subject and necessarily holds the center of the stage.

I'm glad you have been reading my *New Republic* stuff. I'd be glad
to have your criticism of the *Finland Station* as it comes out. Will have
it sent to you up there if you don't get it. About the eighteenth-century
Utopians, it is a part of my scheme to leave out the eighteenth century—
which has been a good deal written about in this connection—except for
passing indications of what had been done between Vico and the beginning of the nineteenth. All that has come out so far is by way of leading
up to the main subject, which is the development of Marxism. In the
next installments the plot will begin to thicken. My great handicap, I
find, in dealing with all this is my lack of grounding in German philosophy. Dialectical materialism, which was in revolt against the German
idealistic tradition, really comes right out of it; and you would have to
know everybody from Kant down to give a really sound account of it. I
have never done anything with German philosophy, and can't bear it,
and am having a hard time now propping that part of my story up. It's
very important, though, to get at Marxism from that point of view. Its
shortcomings, I believe, are largely due to its genesis in the Germany of
that time . . .   As ever, EW

To Louise Bogan   July 8, 1937
                                                      Stamford

Dear Louise: . . . I'm very anxious to see you. What has been happening
to you? Drop me a line and let me know. I've been composing a long
satiric poem, which I want to show you. Have just read and written
about Edna's new book, which I didn't really think very much of.* I
have been predicting the demise of verse technique for years, but was
rather dismayed to see the old Grand Mistress of the mighty female line
turning into a sort of combination of Ogden Nash and Robinson Jeffers.
And there were moments when—due to the general tone—I was afraid
the grouse shooters had got her, after all. Maybe the burning of that
hotel was an Act of God. Not that there isn't a lot in it that's very witty,
and I thought during the first twenty-five pages or so that it was going to

---

* *Conversation at Midnight.*

be quite good; but I don't see that it comes to much. What did you think of it?

I have taken to collecting the big brightly colored night moths that come to the windows at night and have now a regular aviary in the back porch. I'm hoping there are some females which will lay eggs, so that I can see them go through their life cycles. I find that there are no companions like a lot of nice big moths. They sleep all day like me and give my life a touch of liveliness and color when I am working in my study here at night. Have never seen such beautiful ones as here.

As ever, Edmund

To Morton D. Zabel   July 12, 1937
                                                        Stamford

. . . I saw Louise after she came back from Ireland: she seemed rather disillusioned about the old sod.

Have just brought my daughter out here for the summer and am settling down to a lot of work—along with other things, I've got to give her some tutoring, as it turns out that the schools she has been sent to have failed to teach her even to distinguish the parts of speech. Her English teacher told me that they didn't cover nouns and verbs, etc., in her course but had been specializing that term in the gerundive, which I didn't know existed in English . . .

To Christian Gauss   August 25, 1937
                                                        Stamford

Dear Christian: When Carducci, in one of his sonnets on Dante, says,

> Odio il tuo santo impero; e la corona
> Divelto con la spada avrei di testa
> Al tuo buon Federico in val d'Olona.

—whom does he mean?—Frederick Barbarossa? I wanted to quote it but wasn't quite sure, as there's another Frederick who figures in Dante.

. . . have been getting together a book of ten literary essays: Flaubert, Pushkin, Henry James, Shaw, John Jay Chapman, and others.* I'd like to have you look at the one on Flaubert. Have been reading him again lately—biographical stuff and letters, which I hadn't read before—and have found in him a great source of inspiration just as I used to do. Some of his books resound a little bit like tombs; but, say what you please, he had in him the real principle of spiritual life. Certainly he was one of the great men of the last century . . .   As ever, Bunny Wilson

---

* The Triple Thinkers.

To Christian Gauss   September 6, 1937
                                      Stamford

. . . Thank you very much for your letter. What you tell me is precisely
what I was interested in knowing in connection with the Carducci poem.
I wanted to cite Dante as an example of a great writer whose political
ideas were completely mistaken—though I suppose his internationalism,
taken in the widest sense, was, or will be, the right idea in the long
run. I can't find that the val d'Olono is ever mentioned in *The Divine
Comedy*, and Farinata refers to *il secondo*, not *il buon Federigo*. I guess
that is all Carducci's

My idea about Flaubert, by the way, is that there is much more
politics in him than he is usually given credit for. The attitude may be
objective-nihilistic, but there are strong implications in the picture. Shall
send you what I write later. Have you ever read a book about him by a
man named René Dumesnil?—not especially inspired, but he explains and
justifies *Bouvard et Pécuchet* in a new way which seems to me very convincing. He believes that their characters were to have developed somewhat in the course of their researches and experiments; and that they
were to represent not the ineptitudes of the bourgeoisie but the limitations
of human accomplishment itself . . .

To Morton D. Zabel   [November 1937]
                                      Stamford

Dear Morton: It's Sunday, and we have the vapors.
We're even too jaded to look at the papers.
We've taken a walk in most wonderful weather;
But now we are sitting and moping together.
Louise says her heart has been giving her trouble:
Where it used to beat singly, it now vibrates double.
I tell her her poetry does not make sense—
Which arouses a fury of fraud and pretense.
Last evening we passed drinking three kinds of Scotch—
As a result of which folly I've broken my watch.
Louise would not stand for my pet Russian disks,
Wherein the most volatile melody frisks,
But *would* play the radio—things by Sibelius
Which I sharply declared to be Finland's worst failures.
We had rather a social afternoon otherwise,
Though she insists on assuming that my friends are all spies;
Then I read rather stutteringly extracts from Dante,
While the flaming old Fury drank like a Bacchante.
We attempted to talk about John Steinbeck's fiction,
Though, as neither has read him, our remarks lacked conviction.

Today we are thinking and talking of you,
To whom we are fastened by friendship's fine glue.
Ah, would you were here to clear up the confusions,
To foil the Frustrators and quell the delusions!
Ah, would you were here with your burning blue eyes
To sweeten our squabbles and banish the spies!
So take pen straight in paw and make us amends
With a shipment of prose* to your petulant friends!
          *Or verse, if you prefer.

A. J. Muste, whom I had known in my radicalizing and labor-reporting days . . . His shrewd and un-sanguine realism when you talk to him is a contrast to the intensity and eloquence of his speeches. (Notebooks of the sixties)

To A. J. MUSTE   December 31, 1937
                                                          Stamford
Dear Muste: I was very glad to hear from you. I had been much impressed by your article in *Common Sense* of about a year ago.

I think that the inefficiency and unreliability of the Russians is a good deal to blame for what happened in Russia; but certainly Marxism itself is also partly to blame. The trials of Zinoviev and the rest derive partly from the practice of "character assassination" inaugurated by Marx for the purpose of discrediting Bakunin and others; and the Marxists have been—and are still being—sadly misled through believing in the dialectic as a supernatural power which will bring them to salvation if they trust in it, without the necessity of thought or virtue on their part.

Best wishes for the New Year.   Yours sincerely, Edmund Wilson

To W. W. NORTON   November 25, 1937
                                                          Stamford
Dear Mr. Norton: My fee for reporting on a manuscript is $50. If you want to pay it, I will read the Rimbaud material.

                              Yours sincerely, Edmund Wilson

To W. W. NORTON   November 29, 1937
                                                          Stamford
Dear Mr. Norton: Of course I am not unsympathetic toward Rimbaud, Abel, or Norton. I get a good many requests to read and advise on manuscripts, and I answer them all in the same way. I am somewhat surprised that you should have been offended by my note. You made no mention of payment in your letter. I can only repeat that I'll be glad to report on the manuscript for a fee of fifty dollars.   Sincerely, Edmund Wilson

296

To W. W. Norton   December 6, 1937
                                                             Stamford

Dear Mr. Norton: I'm afraid I'll have to insist on a fee of fifty dollars, in
any case, for reading the Rimbaud manuscript—to be paid on receipt of
the report. That is my flat rate; and the length of the manuscript has
nothing to do with it. If you decide to have more translations of Rimbaud
made, I'll of course read them and give you my opinion about them—
and this will be covered by the original fee.

                                           Yours sincerely, Edmund Wilson

To W. W. Norton   December 17, 1937
                                                             Stamford

Dear Mr. Norton: I am sorry that I can't recommend as highly as I should
like this translation of Lionel Abel's. Rimbaud, in his regular verse, has
emphatic rhymes and a strong beat; but Mr. Abel has translated him
into irregular verse which is only half rhymed. Mr. Abel's near rhymes—
such as *bussed, phosphorus; dear, there; wanderer, vigor; bought, short;
arouse, mouth; flesh, breasts; darks, heart*; and many singulars rhymed with
plurals—seem to me altogether wrong for Rimbaud, who, in spite of his
unconventional imagery, was right in the resounding tradition of French
rhetoric. This kind of off-rhyming is fashionable now; and in some kinds
of poetry it has its justification; but not for Rimbaud. Mr. Abel carries it
through systematically in *"Bateau ivre"*; but in *"Tête de Faune,"* which is
an early and completely regular poem of Rimbaud, in which the rhymes
play a special role, he begins with regular rhymes and ends without any
rhymes. The rhymed *"Ô saisons, ô châteaux!"* he has translated without
rhyme; and there is very little left of it. It would be impossible in any
case to get anywhere with it by making it "O seasons, o castles!" He
would have to find an English equivalent for the sighing sound of the
French words. (In handling these off-rhymes, shouldn't a poem be
either all true rhymes or all off-rhymes—like the "Testament" in the
MacNeice–Auden book about Iceland—or alternate them according to a
definite schema?)

I don't say that these translations are bad, but in their present form they
are inadequate. Some of the translation of the prose sounds better—
though here, too, he ought to study more carefully Rimbaud's style, which
is both pithy and resonant—not elaborate into conventional grammatical
statement what is terse and telegraphic in Rimbaud—not miss the re-
echoing ring which Rimbaud has often managed to give to perfectly ordinary
words. *"L'Automne déjà!"*—I know that this last is very difficult from my
attempts to translate some passages from *Une Saison en enfer* for an essay
on Rimbaud once. There is a lot of dynamic energy in Rimbaud—that
the other Symbolists haven't got—which is difficult to get in translation.

                                                                    297

Mr. Abel has also made a number of actual mistakes in rendering the meaning of the text. For example: on page 15, "And I can live, ah. Life!" is really simply, "What a life!" If he wants to fill out the rhythm, a single adjective would be enough. "Anyone may beat me now!" should be "He can beat me now!" (the Infernal Bridegroom). At the bottom of page 8, it should be the white man, not Rimbaud, who is disembarking: Rimbaud is identifying himself with the savage, whom the white man will annihilate.

There is already a complete translation of the prose poems of *Les Illuminations* by Helen Rootham (published with a preface by Edith Sitwell). It is no better than these specimens by Mr. Abel, but neither seems to me quite what it ought to be. The partial translation of *Une Saison en enfer* by Edgell Rickword in *Rimbaud: The Boy and the Poet* (Heinemann, 1924) seems to me somewhat better than Mr. Abel's.

I have a suggestion of my own to make. Get out a really comprehensive volume of Rimbaud with all the important documents about him—like Yarmolinsky's *Pushkin*, published by Random House, and the one-volume *Poetry and Prose of William Blake*, and the other books in that series. Include the French text of Rimbaud (there is not very much of it) on one page, and an English translation on the other. Get the best translations already available and have the rest translated. There are two excellent translations of short poems by T. Sturge Moore in the Rickword book, and John Peale Bishop has done two quite good ones in his book of poems *Now with His Love* (Scribner's)—though one of them has the same fault I have objected to of making a rhymed poem partly unrhymed. And there must be others. I should think that W. H. Auden might be an ideal person to translate Rimbaud—if you can keep him from doing it all in off-rhymes, to which he is much addicted. Make Mr. Abel editor of the whole volume and let him put in some versions of his own—but make him work over them more! Then include the text and translations of Rimbaud's letters, of which, so far as I know, there are not many, but some of which are of prime literary importance; translations of Isabelle Rimbaud's *Reliques*, her memoirs of her brother's last days, and some selections from the memoirs of Ernest Delahaye and others; text and translations of Verlaine's poems about Rimbaud, and a translation of his essay on him; and finally get the rights to the English translation by Matthew and Hannah Josephson of Carré's *La Vie aventureuse de Jean-Arthur Rimbaud* (published by Macaulay, 1931) and put that in, too— it's very short, and I don't imagine it has much sale. There probably ought to be other material, too. I see that a book on Rimbaud in Abyssinia has just been published by the Oxford Press; and I believe that there is some new light on his later adventures. His reports on conditions in Africa ought also to be included. Such a volume would certainly be valuable; there would be nothing like it even in French; and it might have a steady sale. It would put the whole figure of Rimbaud before the English reader. His career was dramatic and has taken on a sort of symbolic significance; and one really has to know about it fully to appreciate his poetry. All these records by people who knew him are remarkable. The whole bulk of the material I have suggested would not be very big.

In my criticisms of Mr. Abel's translations I may sound a little pedantic. Of course, all I have said might be true, and yet the translations might be brilliant; but I don't think they are as yet. They might be if he worked over them longer and harder. Translating rhymed verse as rich and full of imagery as this is of course a most terrible job; but Mr. Abel (I take it) has asked for it. He oughtn't to be afraid to depart quite widely from the literal meaning of the original. Any translation like this, to be successful, must really be a new poem. The only real alternative is a prose translation that follows the original closely—such as Mary Colum has made of *"Bateau ivre"* in her new book of criticism, *From These Roots*. (In my suggested omnibus volume, you might print more than one translation of the same poem, if more than one good one exists.)

I should be much interested in seeing such a book published; and I believe it would have a much better sale than a mere translation of Rimbaud's poems. Let me know if I can help you further. I'll go over Mr. Abel's work with him, if you decide to print it.

Yours sincerely, Edmund Wilson

I don't find the first pages of *Une Saison en enfer*. I hope I haven't lost them.

To W. W. Norton   December 31, 1937
                                                            Stamford

Dear Mr. Norton: I'll be glad to advise you about the Rimbaud; but I don't want to write an introduction or to undertake the actual editorship. I suggest Haakon Chevalier of the University of California, who is bilingual, scholarly, and intelligent and writes well. He translated Malraux's *Man's Fate* and wrote an excellent book on Anatole France. I think he is likely to come East in the spring.

Thinking it over, I believe that the wisest thing might be to print the French text of the poems, a complete literal translation in prose, and only such verse translations as are really worth including. If you could get Auden to do some of it, it would of course be a great thing for the sale of the book, and his translations ought to turn out well.

Yours sincerely, Edmund Wilson

To Morton D. Zabel   April 1941
                                                            Stamford

This Rimbaud business is certainly an awful mess. I don't know why these boys who don't even know ordinary French should be so crazy to translate the *Saison en enfer*. Lionel Abel also attempted it. There were already, I think, two not so bad English translations. The André Breton howler about the woman's breasts which resembled flies drying on a reed is particularly amusing because it shows that young men who approach modern French poetry are prepared for anything.   EW

To ALLEN TATE   April 13, 1938
                                                        Stamford

Dear Allen: I laid your letter aside, thinking I should have plenty of
time to get in touch with you. I was occupied last week with finishing up
a piece of work; and then when I looked up your letter Sunday and called
you up, it turned out that you had already gone. To make things worse,
I didn't notice what time it was—I usually do my work at night—and
when I looked at my watch afterwards, it was half past one—so that I
owe your friend an apology. I'm extremely sorry not to have seen you—
had hoped you would come out here.

I'm married to a girl named Mary McCarthy, who has done some
writing for *Partisan Review* and *The Nation*. We'll be here until about
the second week in June, then probably go to Bermuda till fall.

I'm glad you liked my book. I'm struggling now with a book of which
the central theme is the rise of Marxism—which will fill the Marxists with
horror, I imagine—though I don't believe it will please the agrarians.
If God spares me, I may get it done by fall. Am anxious to see what you
say about the Triple T's.*

When you are coming up again, please be sure to write me and I won't
miss the train this time.

I have no special news except getting married. I have been living in
the country and hope to continue doing so, till Death takes me. I haven't
seen John Bishop for ages. Phelps Putnam and his wife were here for a
night last fall. Since then, I understand Phelps broke his kneecap on the
ice and was stimulated to do some work on his long-advertized poem. I
don't know whether he stopped when he got well. It was good to get
your collected poems.

Please give my love to Caroline. I hope the little girl is flourishing.
                                                As ever, Edmund W.

---
* *The Triple Thinkers.*

Yours till the Int. steeple topples!   —Hiram K. Antichrist

Marxism is the opium of the intellectuals.

All Hollywood corrupts; and absolute Hollywood corrupts absolutely.   —Old Antichrist's Sayings

      —To John and Katy Dos Passos, May 1938

Marx and Engels, Marx and Engels—
Left the boys in dreadful tengles.
Comes the trouble to a head:
Marx and Engels both are dead.

    —To Katy Dos Passos, April 1938

To Louise Bogan   April 13, 1938
                                                               Stamford
Dear Louise: How would you like to come out here the second weekend
in May, the 14th? We're very anxious to see you.

Did you see in *The Saturday Review of Literature* where some of the
critics voted you the best poet of the year? I thought I had it here to
send you, but can't find it.

I was delighted about Rolfe's getting the Guggleheim.

An Englishman named Tillyard who has written on Milton has been
down here to see me. He is from Cambridge—seems to be an older ally
of Empson, working along somewhat the same lines—which seem to be
largely fruitless. I've just been reading Empson's new book. Some of the
stuff about *Alice in Wonderland* is rather good, and a good deal of it
rather farfetched. He has one of those untrustworthy minds which in
their more uncontrollable forms prove that Bacon wrote Shakespeare.
Tillyard thought that Auden had made a great new lyric departure in
a poem from *The New Statesman* (I think) which he read me and
which really is pretty good.

I enjoyed Yeats's *Herne's Egg*—also the Housman book,* though it
seems to me that Laurence has done everything in his power to make it
lousy. I didn't like most of his humorous poems in the sadistic schoolboy
vein of "Ruthless Rhymes for Heartless Homes"—but the opera and the
poem on the Latin grammar are wonderful. I thought his excellent criticism of his brother's poetry the sort of thing I ought to have given you
the benefit of before *Sleeping Fury* was published—about remembering
that the reader knows only what you tell him, etc. Do look that passage
up and read it again!

We have got to get out of here in June and will probably go to Bermuda
till fall, as somebody has offered us a house there.

Do come to see us, Louisy, soon:

From the craving for your company I'm not immune.

In vain I imagine I'll look

For the notes you say you've prepared on my book!

                                                     Love to Madie, Edmund

What has happened to Morton?

To Louise Bogan   May 1, 1938
                                                               Stamford
Dear Louise: John Bishop is coming out here next weekend, and we are
planning a small fête champêtre or pique-nique en plein air for Sunday,
if the spring Graces smile on us and Jupiter Pluvius withholds his capri-

---

* *My Brother A. E. Housman.*

cious showers. Couldn't you come out Sunday morning and spend the night? If you can come, we'll arrange to meet you. Please let me know as soon as you can.   Love, Edmund W.

Your piece about *The Princess Casamassima* was fine and will probably remain the classical exposition of the subject.

To Christian Gauss   May 10, 1938
                                                               Stamford

Dear Christian: Thank you for your letter about my book. I'm well along with the Marxist book now and hope to get it done by fall or winter. I've just got hold of Marx's mathematical papers and am curious to know what they amount to. Marx thought he saw the dialectic in mathematics, and Engels believed that his work was important. You told me that there was a left mathematician at Princeton, who might be willing to look into them and tell me about them. Unfortunately, the text is in Russian; but I believe you said he had a Russian wife. In any case, however, it would probably be quite a chore to get through the stuff—there are 73 pages of mathematics and a long essay on the subject. What do you think? It may be that I can get Yarmolinsky to put me in touch with a Russian mathematician. I hope we can get down to Princeton to see you the end of this month or the beginning of next. I want to discuss the historicity question with you.   As ever, Bunny Wilson

To W. W. Norton   May 26, 1938
                                                               Stamford
. . . The book I propose to write is to be hung on the Philoctetes myth of the man with the incurable wound and the invincible bow.* It will have an essay on Sophocles, several on Russian authors, including Tolstoy, and essays on "The Malignity of Dickens," on Kipling, on Edith Wharton, on Casanova, and (if his book really comes out) on James Joyce's new work. There will be others, but I have not decided on the subjects. The essay on Edith Wharton is already written, and I'll do the rest beginning next winter.

If you can make me an advance of a thousand dollars, you can transfer a possible deficit to some other book of mine. Perhaps you could pay me two hundred dollars on the signing of the contract and the rest at intervals later . . .

To Robert Coates   August 20, 1938
The New Yorker   Stamford

Dear Bob Coates: I've always had a very high opinion of [Henry Allen] Moe. He is the only man connected with a foundation I've ever known

---

* *The Wound and the Bow.*

who didn't get fat and go to sleep on the job. I only served on the literary committee one year—1930–31—but, after doing so, I had the conviction that the whole thing would be better run if—in the literary department, at any rate—Moe were able to make all the decisions himself. He is intelligent, and he takes pains to inform himself about the candidates. I don't believe that he has ever allowed moral, political, or personal prejudices—from which he seems remarkably free—to obscure his judgment of a writer.

I was surprised to discover the year I served on the committee that the candidates he favored were the ones I should have picked myself: Hart Crane, Katherine Anne Porter, and [Edward] Dahlberg. What happened about Dahlberg was interesting. The higher committee, full of academic bullfrogs, got hold of some of his stuff and were horrified by it—particularly Louise Pound. H. S. Canby and I were summoned before this committee to defend our choice. We appeared separately, and I spent an hour arguing Dahlberg's case. Moe told me afterwards that if we stuck to our decision they would have to accept it. He had previously said that if any decision of our committee were overruled by the other committee, he himself would resign from the Foundation. But what we didn't count on was that that little s.o.b. Canby would let us down. As he was still half a professor himself, I suppose he was terrified by the academic bigwigs. He declared that he had never read the writings in question before, thought they were abominable, was so sorry that he had passed the author. So, as the decisions had to be unanimous, there was nothing that Moe and I could do. The point was that it was absolutely true that Canby had never read Dahlberg—neither, so far as I know, had Wilbur Cross, who was the other member of the committee. Neither of them had done a thing to inform himself about the candidates. They simply turned up for one committee meeting—though of course the Foundation had everybody's works on file and would send them to you. Moe and I were the only people who had any opinions, so Cross and Canby had to accept them. I don't know whether old man Cross would have approved of any of those three candidates if he had read them. I put over Em Jo Basshe, about whom neither of them knew anything either. Moe remonstrated with me about this, and I'm not sure he wasn't right. Now through all this the role of Moe was supposed to be simply that of an advisor. We sat at one end of a long table, and he sat at the other end. Actually, given the situation, his opinions were decisive; and I am sure that if it weren't for his presence on these occasions the Guggenheim would be as badly handled as the Pulitzer Prize.

I don't know who is on the committee now. I have heard that Edna Millay was; if this is so, I'm sure she's conscientious. I've been in to see Moe a number of times about various matters, and I've always been struck by his sympathy and understanding for different kinds of people and his tact in dealing with them. He always knows who can be trusted with the lump sum of the award and who will do better if he gets it in installments. He knows, I think, that projects don't mean a thing and that it doesn't matter whether or not they are carried out—and that different kinds of writers need to do different things with their money. He has worked to make as elastic as possible the conditions for enjoying the award and has arranged so that people don't have to go to Europe if they don't want to. The only thing that he has tried to prevent is their staying in New York.

In my opinion, however, the really bad feature of the Guggenheim is not incompetent committees, whose mistakes Moe can largely avert, but the fact that—so far as I can see—it is impossible for an unknown person to get the award. Is there any such case on record? I think you ought to go into this matter. You know that a preliminary sorting out of the candidates is made in order to save the committee trouble. I imagine that Moe does this himself. The dossiers on the better candidates are then submitted to the committee. I had the impression that nobody ever paid any attention to the other candidates, who have already in effect been discarded and thrust into the outer darkness. When I examined the list, I found the name of Kay Boyle among them. I seemed to be the only person who knew about her; her name and the work she had submitted evidently meant nothing even to Moe. And I reflected at the time that it was probably simply her lack of fame which had been the cause of her being relegated to the inferior list. I've never cared very much about her; but she was infinitely superior to some of the other women candidates who had been selected for more serious consideration. By this time, I imagine, she could get it—I'm not sure, in fact, that she hasn't. But I don't see how an obscure candidate could get it. Even if he were championed by Moe, Moe has no effective decision; and he would hesitate to try to put over an unknown person. And it may be the case that Moe is really unable himself to judge candidates on the merits of what they have written—that his good judgment is largely the result of watching the critical reviews and having a sense, as some publishers do, of what is important in writing without himself really knowing much about literature. I haven't seen enough of him to know. Though I suppose his interest in Dahlberg, who at that time had published only *Bottom Dogs*, might indicate that he did have some taste. In any case, I think it very regrettable that nobody can even be in line for a Guggenheim unless he has first made a reputation.

Moe himself, as I say, has won my esteem—and my experience of foundation functionaries had prejudiced me against them.

Please don't mention me in any use you make of this, and please don't use the Dahlberg incident. I'll be very much interested to see your story.

Sincerely, Edmund Wilson

To Louise Bogan   August 1, 1938
                                                  Stamford

Dear Louise: When I get *Das Kapital* liquidated in a day or two, I think I'll do a few parodies to go with yours. We will sell them to *The New Yorker* or, if they won't have them, we'll print them in *Partisan Review*. Why don't you do Auden and Muriel Rukeyser? I'll have these you did down here typed and send you copies. We will call them "Specimens of Contemporary Writing for Use in College Courses." Now post a bottle of gin at your elbow and let yourself go on Rukeyser! . . .

                                                Love, Edmund

To Babette Deutsch   September 13, 1938
                                                  Stamford

Dear Babette: I was sorry that we weren't able to get over—wish you were still out here.

    Thank you for sending me the poem, which I liked. Louise Bogan has written a poem about that little river, too—and I have tried it myself. Oddly, they are all something alike.

    The French woman is Louise Labé. There are some of her poems in the *Oxford Book of French Verse* and something about her in the preface. I see that I had her period wrong: she lived in the sixteenth century. Lanson says that she made *"le sonnet mignard aussi brûlant qu'une ode de Sapho."* There has been a big new edition of her recently.

    I have just written a parody of *Conquistador* called "The Omelet of A. MacLeish."

    Regards to the family.   As ever, Edmund W.

To F. Scott Fitzgerald   1928

. . . I have also read Archie MacLeish's *Hamlet*, which I consider a prime piece of bathos. Phelps Putnam, who had seen Archie and read the poem before it was published, had warned me that both he and I were pilloried in it. I figure that I am Rosencrantz and Guildenstern and Osric, the water fly, all rolled into one—and there were moments when I had suspicions that I was also Claudius, the adulterous uncle . . .

To Louise Bogan   September 22, 1938
                                                  Stamford

Dear Louise: More of your devil's work! All the better New Englanders think they know what New England girl's wickedness God had in mind when he hurled that hurricane upon them! . . . And now this letter from Clifton Fadiman, and MacLeish preparing to denigrate you in *The Nation!* . . . There has been no such retribution since the Atreidai!

    Thanks for your letter. I'll send you the Cowley verses when I've finished them. I learned from Peggy Marshall that MacL. was coming on *The Nation* just at the moment when I was about to propose their printing the "Omelet." But she told Mary to tell you that she would love to run some parodies by you. I might do critical notes to yours and print the "Omelet" somewhere else.

Love, Edmund

To WILLIAM MAXWELL October 6, 1938
The New Yorker Stamford

. . . I'm glad you like the MacLeish parody. Will you please send the manuscript back to me, as I want to make some changes in it before it is set up . . .

To GILBERT TROXELL 1939
Yale University
. . . I am glad you approved of my MacLeish poem; but my faith in the solidarity of Yale men has lately been terribly shaken at finding how many of them approve of it . . .

To GILBERT TROXELL 1942

Dear Gilbert: I never keep manuscripts of my things—I destroy them as soon as the stuff is published—so I haven't got the MS of the "Omelet." It is going to be published in a little book of mine called *Note-Books of Night* (Colt Press, San Francisco), out this month, I guess. . . . Do you know about a poem of Conrad Aiken's which I understand is addressed to MacLeish? I forget the title, and MacL. is not named, but it is something about a rooster exalting and flaunting himself . . .

As ever, Edmund Wilson

To JOHN PEALE BISHOP September 10, 1938
Chatham, Mass. Stamford

Dear John: We're planning to go up to Provincetown for the weekend Friday the 23rd. Couldn't we drop in on you people on the way and perhaps take you up there with us? We could pay our respects to the Walkers and the Dos Passoses.

Old Massa Tate has just been here with his wife, daughter, and dachshund. He seems to be on the crest of the wave this summer. We were sorry you weren't present last Saturday, though the party the next day didn't work out as we expected.

How about those poems you were going to send me? Myself, I've been concentrating on Marxism so long that any work of the imagination—

such as, for example, a fair foreign film like *Mayerling*—stirs me up like Shakespeare. I've just read the first fifty pages of Edith Wharton's posthumous novel,* and am intoxicated as by a rare bottle of absinthe.

As ever, Wilson

> Yet of the many kinds of intellectuals who were young enough to learn anything at all during the decade of 1910–20, it is probable that an enormous number owe a special debt to Max Eastman.
>
> (*The New Republic*, 1941)

To MAX EASTMAN   October 5, 1938
Stamford

Dear Max: I've been meaning to write you since I read your Marx and Lenin last spring in connection with my own work on Marx that it seems to me the best critical thing I've read on this philosophical aspect of Marxism and that it would be immensely useful if you would get out a new edition of it with new material—perhaps an omnibus of your writings on Marxism, including the preface to the Modern Library collection. I think the Marx and Lenin book itself suffers a little from the fact that it deals almost exclusively with negative aspects—that is, suffers from the point of view of readability; but it would have been a good thing if people had read it a few years ago when everybody was going crazy about Marxism. In any case, I've laid it heavily under contribution in what I've just been writing myself . . . I shouldn't think you'd have any trouble getting it reissued.

I'm enclosing a little playlet of my own which gives the main facts of Marx's career in an improved and simplified form† . . .

Sincerely, Bunny Wilson

To MALCOLM COWLEY   October 20, 1938
Stamford

Dear Malcolm: Here is the Bakunin. It is long, but I think the subject deserves it. Please don't send it to the printer till I have had a chance to correct the typed copy.

About your remarks on *Partisan Review*: those boys are still Marxists and so tend to gravitate toward Trotsky as the only outstanding Marxist still alive. They have still a residue of factional bitterness; but it seems to me that the last sentence of your article is a more serious distortion of the truth in the interests of factionalism than anything I have ever seen in *Partisan Review*. You apparently imply, for no better reason than that both

---

* *The Buccaneers.*
† *Karl Marx: A Prolet-Play.*

magazines have printed criticism of events in the Soviet Union, that *Partisan Review* is as bad as the *Mercury*—though you know perfectly well yourself that the *Mercury* is reactionary and even Fascist and that *Partisan Review* is edited by Marxists. In fact, you try to mislead the reader by one of those "bedfellow" tricks in which the *Daily Worker* indulges; and this seems to me almost as bad as the *Worker* at its worst.

What in God's name has happened to you? I was told some time ago that you were circulating a letter asking endorsements of the last batch of Moscow trials—though you had just published articles in which, so far as I could tell, you were trying to express a certain amount of skepticism. I don't suppose you're a member of the C.P.; and I can't imagine any other inducement short of bribery or blackmail—which sometimes appear in rather inobvious forms and to which I hope you haven't fallen a victim—to justify and imitate their practices at this time. You're a great guy to talk about the value of a non-partisan literary review after the way you've been plugging the damned old Stalinist line, which gets more and more cockeyed by the minute (did you see the interview with Stalin in *Liberty*, in which he invokes Peter the Great, Napoleon, and even Napoleon III, washes his hands of Spain and China, and returns a noncommittal answer to a question about an alliance with Hitler?)—at the expense of the interests of literature and to the detriment of critical standards in general!

I liked your poems in *Poetry* and your remarks about the revolutionary symbolists; and I wish you would purge your head of politics—revolutionary and literary alike—and do the kind of valuable work of which you're capable. I think politics is bad for you because it's not real to you: because what you're really practicing is not politics but literature; and it only messes up a job like yours to pretend it's something else and try to use it like something else. I was thinking a year ago that something must have gone very wrong with you when you could get yourself into a state of mind to praise Hemingway's Popeye-the-Sailor novel*—though I am sure that your natural instincts must have told you that it was mostly lousy and actually represented Hemingway in pieces!

Yours as ever, but with best wishes for a return to health.   Edmund

To MURIEL DRAPER   November 14, 1938
                                                                   Stamford
Dear Muriel: I don't think that the Comintern could have done any differently about the Czechs; but it seems to me that what happened definitely reduced to absurdity the nonsense about backing the supposed democratic nations against the Fascist ones—a policy which no Marxists at this time of day ever had any business advocating.

---

* *To Have and Have Not.*

About Russia: since I came back from there, I have read most of the books that have come out on the subject and to some extent the Russian press, and I can't see how it is possible to avoid the conclusion that the Stalin regime in its present phase is pretty hopelessly reactionary and corrupt. It is no more proper for people like you and me to approve it than it would have been for Marx and Engels to have approved the Second Empire in France on the ground that, after all, it represented the evolution of revolutionary France, that society was more democratic than it had been before the great revolution, and that Napoleon III was putting himself forward as the liberator of oppressed peoples. Now certainly the barbarism of Stalin and the administrative ineptitude of the Russians have produced an even worse state of things in the Soviet Union. They haven't even the beginnings of democratic institutions; but they are actually worse off in that respect than when they started. They have totalitarian domination by a political machine, which has been enacting class legislation for its own benefit; the morale of industry, according to this American engineer Littlepage, has been hopelessly broken down as the result of political espionage; and the GPU has turned up as the Department of Public Works executing "socialist construction" with forced labor. The Moscow trials seem to me clearly frame-ups designed to divert attention from the real causes of the system's working badly and the protests of the people against it—such as the terrorist activities of the young Komsomols. No doubt people like Zinoviev and Kamenev have opposed Stalin as much as they dared; but why shouldn't they? I can't imagine that you believe that the Stalin administration has been trying to achieve the aims of Lenin. I guess that the definite turn in the direction of reaction and repression was taking place just at the time we were there—when the current in the direction of brightening life up and letting up on the pressure of industrialization was met and overcome by the current of the policies of the group of officials who were somehow strengthened by the Kirov assassination. The hierarchy of social groups was already well established at that time, and I used to see signs of the resentment it was arousing; but I soft-pedaled it when I was writing my notes on Russia because I wanted to give them the benefit of every doubt. The tone of your letter, by the way, in regard to the men you designate as enemies, who were executed as a result of the trials, strikes me as very different from that in which you used to discuss in Moscow such incidents as the arrest of Yenukidze. Have you really become convinced since then that Yenukidze was a Fascist traitor?

I know that you have been working hard for the Spanish Loyalists; and up to now I should have left my opinion on this subject under the veil of what you call my mysterious reticences. But I can't see now that there is any possible reason for pretending that Russia is all right. The Russians certainly did little enough for Spain, and part of what they did was bad. They brought in the GPU terror and used it against the working-class left. I remember that you lived to forgive me for having been disrespectful years ago about Gurdjieff; and I hope that the moment is about to dawn when you will forgive me for being disrespectful about Stalinism.

Yours with love as ever, Bunny Wilson

To Maxwell Perkins   October 18, 1938
                                                              Stamford
Dear Max: Thank you for the Hemingway book and your letter. I have no complaint in this connection. I'm obliged to you for the advance and for helping me out the other day with your check.

But your apparent assumption that Scribner's has been remarkably generous with me in general moves me to expatiate on this subject. I remember that on one occasion some years ago I came to you with a request for what was certainly the very moderate sum of $75, and that at another time I tried to get Scribner's to be one of my sponsors when I was making a loan from a bank. You wouldn't do anything for me on either occasion at a time when you were handing out money to Scott Fitzgerald like a drunken sailor—which he was spending like a drunken sailor. Naturally you expected him to write you a novel which would make you a great deal more money than my books seemed likely to do. But, even so, the discrepancy seemed to me somewhat excessive. After *The American Jitters* came out, I never got the faintest sign of interest from Scribner's until Harcourt offered to publish my books. Harcourt has given me $1,700 on *To the Finland Station* and Norton has given me $800 for my next book of literary essays. *The New Republic* and *The Atlantic Monthly* pay me special rates (this is confidential). I don't know whether any of these people will make much money on me; but they seem to think it worthwhile to make me advances which enable me to do my work. Scribner's could of course have published *The Triple Thinkers* or the book which Norton will bring out, if they had thought it worthwhile to do anything about it. Let me add that your bookkeeping department has twice made miscalculations which gypped me out of part of what was due me for royalties—mistakes which you rectified when I wrote to you; and that you have never yet had corrected the inaccuracies in *Axel's Castle* which are continually getting me into trouble with readers—though I've spoken to you about it repeatedly and have given you lists of the corrections.

I attribute all this, of course, not to malice—you're the only person I ever see around there, and I've always felt I was on very good terms with you—but to the general apathy and moribundity into which Scribner's seems to have sunk. You people haven't shown any signs of life since old man Scribner died—except when you yourself have a paroxysm over some writer—usually very unreliable, like Scott or Tom Wolfe—upon whom you squander money and attention like a besotted French king with a new favorite. If you weren't stupefied by textbooks and general stuffiness, you couldn't have written me this letter in which you talk as if you had been backing me in a big way before I went to Harcourt.

Yours as ever, Edmund Wilson

To Maxwell Perkins

October 25, 1938
Stamford

Dear Max: I didn't think that you were criticizing me. I was criticizing Scribner's . . .

Thanks for the Hemingway book. I didn't think much of the play,* but the four new stories are wonderful. "The Short Happy Life of Francis Macomber" is as good as the *Green Hills of Africa* was bad. I've just written something about it for *The Nation*.

I've just had a telegram from Scott, who says he is going to arrive here this afternoon.

As ever, Edmund Wilson

To Christian Gauss

October 27, 1938
Stamford

Dear Christian: As my family gets larger, it gets to be more of a problem for me to make a living without a regular job; and I've been looking around for some kind of part-time work—which doesn't involve special writing, if possible. I was wondering whether there would be any chance of anything of the kind at Princeton. I know that teaching takes most of your time and doesn't pay very well; but what about that job that Archie MacLeish had a couple of years ago? I'm not clear precisely what it was. I know from experience that I'm no good as a lecturer in the regular way; but I'm scheduled to do a series of articles on literary subjects for *The Atlantic Monthly* next year, and I could always read them as lectures. I've done this at Harvard and Vassar and other places and seem to have gone over pretty well. I imagine that I could handle the preceptorial sort of thing.

I hope to get my Marx book done by January. The subject is a terrible one because it involves practically everything, and my book will be rather inadequate on the philosophical and economic sides.

We are still here in Stamford, though we've had to move from our forest retreat. We're expecting a baby in January or December. Scott Fitzgerald has just been here to see us. I have never seen so great and sudden a change in anybody I knew. He doesn't drink, works hard in Hollywood, and has a new girl, who, though less interesting, tends to keep

---

* *The Fifth Column.*

him in better order than Zelda (who seems to be fading out in the sanatorium). But the effect is very queer and disconcerting. As his personality was always a romantic drunken personality, it is something new for him to have to present to the world a sober and practical one; and he seems mild, rather unsure of himself, and at moments almost banal. There are times when you might almost mistake him for a well-meaning Middle Western businessman. It is melancholy to think of him in Hollywood, which has such a stultifying and oppressive effect on everybody who has anything to do with it. But I imagine he'll emerge from it eventually. He may work through to something new in the literary way. It's really a proof of his strength of character and physique that he's been able to survive at all. But it's very queer, as I say: it's as if he were looking at the world around him with grownup eyes for the first time, venturing tentative opinions about it and gradually acquiring a technique for dealing with it . . .   As ever, Bunny Wilson

1939

THE UNIVERSITY OF CHICAGO

To John Peale Bishop   February 1, 1939
                                                          Stamford

Dear John: I was glad to hear from you this morning—had been wondering about you. The baby arrived Christmas day, a boy—and he and Mary
have been in fine shape. We are down here surrounded by snow and deep
in domesticity.

My MacLeish piece came out in *The New Yorker*, and I understand
that he is sore. I'm doing another satire in verse on writers who go to
Hollywood. Aside from that and odd article-writing, I'm still occupied
with Marx.

Have I told you that Scott came to see us on a visit from Hollywood?
He is transformed in the most amazing way. Hollywood and strict non-
drinking have changed him—believe it or not—into something in the
nature of a well-meaning Middle Western businessman who takes a
diffident interest in the better kind of books. He had his girl with him—
a pretty little blond English girl who writes a syndicated movie column.
She is a steadying influence but not awfully interesting—I think that his
present normality and tameness are partly due to her. It occurred to me
for the first time that his madness had probably partly been due to Zelda.
I realized also that he had never before had a technique for meeting the
world sober. He is now evolving one in rather a groping way. It is as if he
were learning to walk for the first time among grownups. Maybe he will
emerge into a later period and accomplish something remarkable. I can't
imagine that he is doomed to perpetual Hollywood.   As ever, Bunny W.

The Walkers have written us about a wonderful house at Wellfleet,
which I'm going up to look at sometime soon, and which it might not be
out of the question that we might take.

To Max Eastman

February 1, 1939
Stamford

Dear Max: If I were compiling an anthology myself, I should certainly include "To Lisa in Summer," "Egrets," "Fire and Water," "A Dune Sonnet." If I had space for further selections, I should choose them from among "The City," "We Have Been Happy," "In My Room," "Morning," "Sea Shore," "Rainy Song," "To a Tawny Thrush," which seem to me nearly or quite as good. Among these new ones, the ones I like best are "The April Earth" and "Prayer"—though I think that the phrase "life-enhancing" in the last line of this latter somehow lets it down. I think that your best vein is when you are describing birds or the sea; all this glimmering mercurial stuff seems to me awfully good—sometimes the rhetoric of the emotions makes it turbid. And I should try to bring this out, because I don't think your lyrics have really had justice done them (poetry and poetry criticism have gotten to be such a racket, organized to a considerable extent by people who have nothing to show for themselves but their uninspired volumes of verse and who instinctively rule out of competition people who can do other things as well and can sometimes write lyrics a lot better) . . .

I was just going to write you to ask you whether you would lend me one of your volumes of the Marx–Engels *Nachlass*. It is the one that has in it Engels's articles on the '48 Revolution in the Palatinate—I think they came out in the *Neue Rheinische Zeitung*. I'd be grateful, because it's very hard to get these.

Another thing: would you or Eliena tell me what you make of the following passage in one of Marx's letters to Weydemeyer, which I've only been able to find in Russian.

"Несколько дней тому назад 'знаменитый' референдарит Шрамм встречает на улице знакомого и сейчас же начинает ему нашептывать: 'к чему бы ни привела революция, все согласны, что Маркс погиб. Родбертус, у которого больше всего шансов на успех, сейчас же велит его расстрелять.' "*

Are we to understand that Rodbertus was supposed to have ordered Marx to be shot? Did you ever notice that it makes you sick to read Marx in too prolonged doses? It's the negative criticism and the rasping which never let up for a moment (and, in their correspondence and in his polemics, Engels tries to imitate him). I'm just recovering from a slight bilious attack brought on in this way . . .   As ever, Edmund Wilson

---

* "Several days ago the 'well-known' junior barrister Schramm met an acquaintance on the street and immediately whispered to him: 'No matter how the Revolution may end, everybody agrees that Marx is perdu. Rodbertus, who has the best prospects, will immediately have him shot.' "

—Karl Marx to Joseph Weydemeyer, London, August, 1851

316

To H. L. MENCKEN   February 13, 1939
                                                    Stamford
Dear Mencken: Certainly, use whatever you want. The letter is to be
found in the Marx–Engels Gesamtausgabe, published by the Marx–Engels
Institute in Moscow—Dritte Abteilung, Band 1, page 148.

It was pleasant to hear from you. I hope that you are gestating a *Das
Kapital* or a *Madame Bovary* yourself.   Yours sincerely, Edmund Wilson

To CHRISTIAN GAUSS   February 23, 1939
                                                    Stamford
. . . I am grateful for your good offices with the creative arts committee.
The University of Chicago has offered me $1,200 to go out there for ten
weeks next summer, and I am going. I suppose this is pretty good academic
pay, isn't it?

I've had to drop the *Finland Station* lately in order to make a little
money, but I'll be back on it soon and hope to get it cleaned up before
I go out to Chicago . . .

To CHRISTIAN GAUSS   March 3, 1939
                                                    Stamford
. . . They have asked me to give two courses of four hours a week each
at Chicago: one to deal with a single author and the other with some
aspect of criticism. I think my author will be Dickens, about whom I'm
planning to write something—I thought that, since I'm new at teaching,
it would be well to choose something relatively easy. For the criticism
course, I think I'll give them social interpretation with Taine and some
of the Marxist stuff for texts . . .

To JOHN DOS PASSOS   May 3, 1939
                                                    Stamford
Dear Dos: . . . Have just read your book.* The theme is fine, and it's
an excellent thing to get it out at this time; but I don't think it's one of
your best things artistically. It seems to me that your systematic descriptions,
which you more or less succeeded in eliminating in *U.S.A.*, have all landed
back on you again. Shouldn't there be more about how the hero felt—
his hopes for society and for himself—and less landscapes, street scenes,
etc.? I think you really ought to take some exercises to correct your extra-
version. I wish the whole thing were shorter and sharper—I feel that the
kind of theme you have here doesn't lend itself to being presented through
the old rationalistic method. As soon as you begin putting things on a
moral basis, the delicatessen stores, Sixth Avenue El and other contemporary

---

* *The Adventures of a Young Man.*

junk oughtn't to matter so much. The Harlan episode is well handled and must have been rather difficult to do. The Kentucky girl is good, though I don't think the other girls are so good. I liked best of all the scenes where he looks at the animals in the zoo. I hope it will jolt people in some quarters . . .   As ever, Bunny W.

To Phelps Putnam   May 29, 1939
                                                          Stamford
Dear Phelps: I've delayed writing because I've been busy getting Marx liquidated and getting out of this house. We leave Thursday for Chicago, where I'm going to teach—God help me!—at the university summer school. I'm sending your poem on to Malcolm Cowley. They may not print it, because they've already had that page of verse by Auden about Yeats. I think you ought to try *Poetry, The Southern Review, The Kenyon Review,* and *The Virginia Quarterly.* I liked it, but didn't think it quite of your best. Shouldn't it mount up a little more to something at the end? I'm glad to see that your muse is definitely coming out of her stupor. You ought to read Joyce's new book,* parts of which are among the greatest poetry in the language—other parts a terrible pain in the neck. Allen Tate has a job teaching at Princeton next year . . .   As ever, Edmund W.

To John Dos Passos   July 16, 1939
                                                  The University of Chicago
Dear Dos: To begin with, I don't think your account of what you are doing in your books is accurate. You don't merely "generate the insides of your characters by external description." Actually, you do tell a good deal about what they think and feel. "Behavioristic" only applies properly to the behavior of rats in mazes, etc.—that is, to animals whose minds we can't enter into, so that we can only take account of their actions. Maupassant, in the preface to *Pierre et Jean,* announced his intention of abolishing "psychology" and using something like this method for human beings; but even he, as I remember, cheated; and in any case, how much or how little (in point of quantity) a writer chooses to tell you about his characters, or how directly or indirectly, is purely a technical matter. What has to be gotten over is what life was like for the characters (unless you're trying to give the effect of their being flies). You yourself in your books themselves make no pretense of not going inside your people whenever it suits you to do so. As for Defoe, he is so close to his people that you can't always tell whether he isn't merely ghostwriting them (since they tell their stories in the first person, he, too, gives you what they think and feel)—certainly,

---

* *Finnegans Wake.*

318

there isn't much criticism of them, in reference to moral standards, let alone social ideals, implied; whereas what you are doing is intensely critical and much closer to Stendhal–Flaubert–Tolstoy than to Defoe and the eighteenth-century novelists.

My idea about *Adventures of a Young Man* was that you hadn't conveyed—it doesn't matter by what means—the insides of Glen Spottwood. The sour picture of his experiences in New York is like *Manhattan Transfer* but off the track, it seemed to me, because the object of *M.T.* was to give a special kind of impression of New York, whereas in *Y.M.* you are concerned with the youthful years of an idealistic young man. You make all the ideas seem phony, all the women obvious bitches, etc.— you don't make the reader understand what people could ever have gotten out of those ideas and women—or even what they expected to get out of them. (In general, I've never understood why you give so grim a picture of life as it seems in the living—aside from the ultimate destinies of people. You yourself seem to enjoy life more than most people and are by way of being a brilliant talker; but you tend to make your characters talk clichés, and they always get a bad egg for breakfast. I sometimes think you consider this a duty of some kind.) And it seems to me that you have substituted for the hopes, loves, wounds, exhilarations, and depressions of Glen a great load of reporting of externals which have no organic connection with your subject. I never know what you are trying to do with such descriptions as those of the New Hampshire lake, of the New York streets, of Glen's arrival in Spain, etc. I feel that you ought to be showing these things in some particular way which would reveal his personality and state of mind or which would at least imply some criticism on your part of the whole situation. (You have sometimes done this admirably elsewhere—as when the Harvard boy in *U.S.A.* sees the façade of Notre-Dame in the twilight looking—I think—as if it were made of crumbly cigarette ashes.) Do you mean, for example, to suggest a contrast between the grandeur and beauty of the lake and the ignoble behavior of the man who runs the camp, to which the boys are subjected? I can't tell, because it seems to me that the descriptions are written exactly as you yourself might have written them in your notebook. And as for New York—though this may partly be due to my own rather moony tendencies—I believe that people get used to this kind of surroundings, so that they don't notice them but, as they are going from place to place, see their own thoughts instead. You don't spare Glen a single delicatessen store.

I must say, though, that the more I have thought about the book, the better it has seemed from the point of view of the idea itself, which, as one looks back on it, disengages itself and takes on life. But I don't think you quite wrote it. I take it, for example, that the critical moment is when

Glen declares in court that he doesn't believe in lying, because he believes in the dignity of man; but most readers, I find in talking to people, don't notice this at all, because you haven't built it up. You haven't told them enough about Glen's soul (or whatever it is). He seems too much on the plane of banality of the other characters—the reader tends to think that you mean to make him banal, too. (About the best review I have seen, by the way, is one in—I think—the English *New Statesman*, which regards the book as a sort of *Pilgrim's Progress*. Of course, the political issue has somewhat obscured it for people over here. They don't have the Trotsky–Stalin controversies in the same acute way in England.)

We've been having an awfully good time out here. The situation at the university is something fantastic—I can't do justice to it in a letter; but the faculty are much more lively and up-to-date and the students much more serious-minded than they've seemed to me in general in the East. The professors at least have the feeling that education has new possibilities and that they're really trying to do something in their work. At Princeton, they're resigned to stagnation, and make a point of being old fogies. It's ironical that at a time when at Princeton, which has always had so much to say about humanistic studies, the study of Greek is totally dead, they should be teaching the language here to quite a large number of students, who start in as beginners in college and are reading the *Symposium* at the end of the first year. I have students in my courses of all races, religions, nationalities, and colors—including a German Catholic nun. Some of them are very bright.

We've seen a great variety of people—including Gerry Allard and his colleagues, who have really made me feel a little that what the intellectuals write in New York has importance for the labor movement. Robert Morss Lovett got off to the Virgin Islands yesterday, looking very debonair and cheerful in a new Panama hat.*

I don't suppose there's any chance of your getting out here? I may stay on till the first of October, as I like it and am paying a rent for our apartment that covers the whole season. The Midway and the lake front up here beat anything in the way of a park in New York. The people are better-looking, too. It is a great sight to see them, over the weekends, in the water and on the grass . . . Mary sends love. She has written about your book for *Partisan Review*, so that if you don't know how to write the next one, it won't be our fault . . .

Love to Katy—and all the Provincetown incumbents.

As ever, Bunny W.

---

* Robert Morss Lovett was government secretary of the Virgin Islands from 1939 to 1943.

To MORTON D. ZABEL   July 18, 1939
                                    The University of Chicago
. . . That's all right, but Pater's father *was* born in New York—which, it
seems to me, makes Walter American enough to account for his excellence
as a critic . . .

To ALLEN TATE   July 24, 1939
                                    The University of Chicago
Dear Allen: . . . We've been having an awfully good time here—the
mixture of Aristotle and Aquinas with other things is fantastic, but it's a
very lively and interesting place. We've just seen Sherwood Anderson,
who is at Olivet, and reports that he and John Bishop and Padraic Colum
and Katherine Anne Porter are putting on a show together—they *all*
appeared and performed on one platform the other night—which is laying
them in the aisles in Indiana, and they think of taking it on tour in the
West. I find that I'm a little dismayed—though perhaps unnecessarily—at
seeing how many of the literati are taking to teaching as what *Partisan
Review* calls a "crutch."
     Love to Caroline and the little girl.   As ever, Edmund
     I was quite depressed to know that poor old [Ford Madox] Ford was
dead.

To W. W. NORTON   September 24, 1939
                                         Truro Center, Mass.
Dear Norton: I've been writing a piece on Dickens for that book I'm
doing for you. It's grown to something like 25,000 words, and it's occurred
to me that it might be brought out first separately as a small book for the
Christmas trade. The point of view on Dickens is more or less new, and
it is partly based on materials unknown to the general reader. It may even
come as more or less sensational to the ordinary admirer of Dickens. If
you think there's anything in the idea, I'll send it to you when I get it
typed. My idea is, of course, that it should be included in the larger book,
too.
     Thanks for the Rilke. How are you? Please give my regards to Mrs.
Norton.   Yours sincerely, Edmund Wilson

To H. L. MENCKEN   October 10, 1939
                                          Truro Center
Dear Mencken: I've been meaning for some time to write you how much
I've been enjoying your memoirs in *The New Yorker*—all the more as we
were still reading and eating in my time some of the things you read and
ate. I suppose it will come out in a book: it seems to me that it is some

of your best writing. That touch about the train going by while the little girl is playing a violin solo brings back a whole American landscape and period. Sincerely, Edmund Wilson

To Louise Bogan   October 22, 1939
                                                              Truro Center

Dear Louise: We both thought your piece on the Lawrence book the best review you have ever done. I think you ought to go in more for destructive criticism. Love, Edmund

To Louise Bogan   October 31, 1939
                                                              Truro Center

. . . I thought your piece about Max Eastman was awfully good, too. When you really say something, your reviews are excellent—and you seem to be getting over your inhibitions about saying things . . .

To Morton D. Zabel   November 26, 1939
                                                              Truro Center

Dear Morton: I'm terribly sorry that they should have tried to put that bill on you. I'd already paid it (November 17), so that they should have had it by the time you wrote your note. It had followed me around and reached me only a few weeks ago when I was down to my last dollar. On the other hand, I paid one of their bills twice by mistake last summer, so they oughtn't to hold it against me.

I've spent the better part of two weeks in New York on two separate trips, for the purpose of shaking down editors and publishers. I've never seen so many publishers before in my life, and found them a very melancholy crew. They have ceased to make any pretense of being interested in publishing books, but talk wistfully about religion and the fate of the human race. I saw Louise and learned with horror that she had sent you a letter of mine as a model of what correspondence ought to be or something. (I sent you that Christian Science literature when I was down there—I found it backstage in a Boston theater—in case you thought it was Louise.) . . . I'm hoping really to get the *Finland Station* cleaned up by Christmas. The early part of Lenin's life has turned out to have unexpected possibilities, as his family wrote wonderful memoirs about him that read like Russian novels. Harry Levin is awfully good about Joyce in *New Directions*. What did you think about Eliot's cats?—about the Newgate Garland on the cover of the anniversary number of *The New Republic*?—about MacLeish's great poem in it?—about the war in Europe? As ever, Edmund

To William Maxwell   December 22, 1939
The New Yorker   Truro Center

. . . Here is something which is fantastically out of your usual field. It is
an account of the early years of Lenin. But I think it has a certain special
interest, as it is quite unlike anything else on the subject in English,
being based partly on family memoirs that have never been translated.
I don't know whether it would be possible for you as an unconventional
kind of profile . . .

To Christian Gauss   November 29, 1939
                                               Truro Center

Dear Christian: . . . We're established up here on Cape Cod and probably
shan't get down to New York till the middle of January, when we may
stay a month. I'd be glad to go to Princeton, if they'll pay me something,
but I'm no good at making these little generalizing speeches, and I think
that the only thing I could do would be to read an essay on somebody that
I'd written. I don't know whether this would be what they'd want. I had a
very good time in Chicago and got on very well with my class (I liked
the Middle Western students). I got used to talking on my feet and
could hold them all right through my double classes of an hour and a half
at a stretch. I made it all more or less informal. They haven't said anything
to me about coming back, but offered to recommend me. Since then, I
have had an invitation to lecture at Columbia summer school. (The point
is about Princeton that I don't want to make one of these formal speeches
on tendencies or whatnot. Taking a class through a subject is something
different.) . . .   As ever, Bunny W.

To Allen Tate   December 3, 1939
                                               Truro Center

Dear Allen: I'd already heard from Gauss and written him. I'd be glad
to read an essay and talk to the boys afterwards. There are three subjects
I'll be writing on after the first of the year: Kipling, Kafka, and Sophocles'
play *Philoctetes*. How would one of these be? If this isn't what's wanted,
don't hesitate to say so. The point is that I'm no good at the ordinary
lecturer's spiel and can do better with a subject that I've devoted some
special thought to by reading a paper than by talking about it. Working
with a class, as I did last summer, is different from a solitary appearance.

We've seen quite a little of John, who is less demoralized than he was
last winter. I'm trying to get him to get out his collected or selected poems.
Max Perkins seems to be prepared to undertake it; but the difficulty is to
get John started. He is under the impression that he can't get his work

straightened out until he has the whole house to himself and can spread all his manuscripts out—something which he seems to think impossible— probably with good reason—as long as Margaret and the twins are around. It might be a good thing for him, I suppose, if he would stay at Princeton for a while when he goes down there. I wish you'd encourage him, in any case, to get his stuff together. He's also rather timid of publishers and needs to be steamed up to do business with them.

Love from us both to you both. We enjoyed "The Trout Map." I hope you'll get up here to see us. It's really beautiful where we are. I expect we'll live here more or less permanently.   As ever, Edmund

THE DEATH OF
F. SCOTT FITZGERALD
AND
JOHN PEALE BISHOP

Men who start out writing together write for one another more than they realize till somebody dies.

NOTE TO THE READER: The letters of the forties are preceded by this section on the deaths of two of Edmund's closest friends. These letters run from 1940 to 1944; they include the correspondence on editing F. Scott Fitzgerald's posthumous papers, and should be read as a separate episode.   —Elena Wilson

To F. Scott Fitzgerald   November 1, 1940
                                                              Stamford
Dear Scott: I was awfully glad to hear from you and to know that you
like the *Finland Station*—also that your own book is coming on.* I hope
it's about Hollywood—I've just read practically all the novels ever written
on the subject, and none of them really does much with it. They all either
deal with the fringes—the extras, etc.—or just treat Hollywood as an
episode in somebody's life; I suppose they are all really scared to go to the
mat with the industry itself.

We've been living up on the Cape, but have come back here for the
winter, because I'm back on *The New Republic* for a time. I'm also
writing a novel of a new and strange kind.

If you come East, do be sure to look us up.   As ever, Bunny W.

To Zelda Fitzgerald   December 27, 1940
                                                              Stamford
Dear Zelda: I have been so terribly shocked by Scott's death.† I had had
two letters from him lately, in which he had sounded as if he were getting
along well with his book. Though I hadn't seen much of him of recent
years, we had a sort of permanent relationship, due to our having known
one another at college and having started in writing at the same time. It
has brought so many things back—the days when you and he arrived in
New York together—and I have been thinking about you a lot these last
few days. I know how you must feel, because I feel myself as if I had
been suddenly robbed of some part of my own personality—since there
must have been some aspect of myself that had been developed in relation
to him. You must let me know if there is ever anything that I can do for

---
* *The Last Tycoon.*
† Scott Fitzgerald died on December 21, 1940.

you or for Frances. Max Perkins tells me that she is a very fine girl. All my love and sympathy, Zelda. I hope I shall see you sometime before too long. We have been hoping to take a trip South some winter, and shall look you up when we do.   As ever, Bunny Wilson

To John Peale Bishop   January 2, 1941
                    The New Republic

Dear John: I saw Sheilah Graham, Scott's girl friend, last week. She was with him when he died. You know that he'd been doing a lot of work on his book and had not been drinking for a year. He'd been writing all that morning, was feeling pleased at having got over some difficult scene. He had had a heart attack about three weeks before, and the doctor came to see him every week. That day he was feeling so well that he phoned the doctor not to come. That afternoon he had been talking to Sheilah about Scottie, with whom he carried on an elaborate correspondence, and had just finished a chocolate bar, after which he had licked his fingers. He suddenly started out of his chair as if he had been jerked by a wire, made a clutch at the mantelpiece, and fell dead. The man in the book he was writing was to have died of a heart attack. It was a novel about Hollywood, which he was keeping a secret, because he didn't want the people out there to know about it.

There is a lot more that I will tell you when I see you. In the meantime, I want to do something about him in a literary supplement to *The New Republic* which I'm going to get out in February.* (Aside from that, I've stopped working in the office and am now out here at Stamford all the time.) I wish you would write something about him—a poem or something in prose. Do please let me know right away whether you won't do something. I'm glad to have the Paris poem—I'll either send it on to the *N.R.*, or, failing anything on Scott, put it in the supplement. But do try to write something about him—preferably a poem. Perhaps you could come down here for a weekend and we could discuss the whole matter. I may ask John O'Hara to write something, too. He adored Scott and was one of the only people who had heard any of the new novel. There is also going to be a question of publishing a volume collected from his manuscripts and letters.

I had written him that he oughtn't to be offended by what you had written in *The Southern Review*, that you had no invidious feeling about him, etc.

Do try to get down to see us. I have felt Scott's death very much—men who start out writing together write for one another more than they realize till somebody dies.   As ever, Bunny W.

---
* "In Memory of Scott Fitzgerald," *The New Republic*, March 3, 1941.

328

To John Peale Bishop   January 7, 1941
                                                       The New Republic

Dear John: I am awfully glad you are writing something about Scott.
I am writing Glenway Wescott, Dos, Thornton Wilder, John O'Hara, and
a man named Budd Schulberg, Jr., in Hollywood, who I understand is a
great admirer of his. If you have any suggestions, let me know. I wish
you were in reach so that we could discuss it.

I was going to write you that, on rereading your Paris poem, I didn't
think it one of your best. There's too much of Eliot's "Triumphal March,"
and I have often deplored the day when you came under the influence
of Chirico. This is, of course, not to say that it isn't distinguished, but it
would be very much to the point in *Direction*, and I would much rather
have you on Scott. It was strange to look through *This Side of Paradise*,
and find a scene of a night walk at Princeton that paralleled one of your
poems and must have sprung from some old Princeton conversation.

How long is the Simenon? I think they could probably take a thousand
words.   As ever, Edmund Wilson

To John Peale Bishop   January 14, 1941
                                                              Stamford

Dear John: I don't remember saying anything about objecting to the
dream element in your poem—it was the Chirico element that I wasn't
enthusiastic about (also in the other poems of yours in which it occurs).
Please don't be hurt. My note was written in haste from the N.R. I only
drop in there for moments in order to transact necessary business. My
administration there (except for this supplement) is over—so you ought
to transact business with Nigel Dennis. I'm sending him your review,
which is first-rate. I liked your pieces about Edna and Pound—I think you
are good in this vein of reminiscence.

I do hope you do the poem on Scott. Glenway Wescott has written
something and a man named Budd Schulberg in Hollywood—whom Scott
thought a promising novelist—is writing an appreciation from the point of
view of the youngest generation. I'm also trying to get John O'Hara and
Dos. The supplement is not coming out till sometime in February, but
I think I ought to have all the material, if possible, by the end of this
month.

It's extremely depressing to me that Joyce should have died, too—even
though I suppose his work was finished. Yeats, Freud, Trotsky, and Joyce
have all gone in so short a time—it is almost like the death of one's father.
I think, though, that Scott at the present time needs commemoration more
than Joyce, because his contemporaries have done him less justice.

I'm sorry you're feeling exhausted—but come! Somebody's got to survive
and write.   As ever, Bunny

To John Peale Bishop   February 17, 1941
                                                                  Stamford
Dear John: Just received your letter—and this is a last appeal to do something about the "dives." It is the noun that particularly worries me. It is
a raffish and slightly antiquated word that somehow has comic connotations and is out of the key of your poem*—so that I am sure people will
think you mean "plunges." Not that I want to induce you to change it
against your own best judgment if you think it is all right. I will go over
the page proofs carefully.

   I have just read Scott's unfinished MS, and it has made me feel very
sad. It would certainly have been very good. But the sense of his approaching death hangs over the last pages he wrote in a strange and tragic way.
                                                                  As ever, EW

To John Peale Bishop   May 18, 1942
                                                                  Wellfleet
Dear John: My poem about Scott is in this week's *New Yorker*—improved,
I think, but far from perfect; I'm going to work over it some more before
it appears in the book.

   I'm expecting the proofs on my book of verse this week and should like
to consult you about them. Mary will probably have to go to New York
the end of the week—perhaps you could come up here for a night then.

   I've sent the Fitzgerald material off. Your producing those nonsensical
and gossiping letters made me get out some to me that I had excluded, and
I think the whole picture now is much more complete and typical. I
think that we ought to go over the proofs of this very carefully together.
There are several points still that will have to be cleared up.

   Drop me a line and let me know what days this week you will be free.
If my proofs come in the middle of the week, I might try to arrange to
get down to South Chatham and show them to you.   As ever, EW

To Allen Tate   September 28, 1943
                                                                  Wellfleet
. . . John Bishop has sunk into another of his dreadful declines. Margaret
is now a major general or something and always appears in uniform. She
came in here one day to fetch him back when he had been staying with
us, and we felt that we had had a brief visit of inspection from a very
busy and important official. One of her staff was waiting in the car, and
she couldn't stay a minute but whisked John right out of the house. She
has got him enslaved down at Chatham—he apparently has to make all
the beds and wash all the dishes while she is attending to her official

---

* "The Hours," published in "In Memory of Scott Fitzgerald."

330

duties, and he says that his life has become so sordid that he no longer has the heart to write anything. I have seen him only twice in the last year, as she will not let him get away any more at all. The Dos Passoses stopped off there the other day and report that both John and Robert appear to be faint and thin with starvation. John told me himself when I last saw him —last spring—that he did not want to let himself in for another winter there. Can't you get him a little job in Washington or at least write him a letter to buck him up? It is really no joke. There was a period when he first got back from working in New York that he did some remarkably good poetry; but the impulse ran into the sands as it always does under Margaret's pressure and with no encouragement from friends on the spot . . .

To ALLEN TATE   October 22, 1943
                                                      Wellfleet

. . . I have called up John Bishop, and he tells me that he has decided to take the Washington job. You evidently acted just in the nick of time. He told me that Margaret had to go out to Columbus to attend a stock-holders' meeting or something, so important that she had not been able to get anybody to take her vote, at which, I dare say, the question is to come up whether they shall sacrifice their incomes to patriotism. It would be an ironic but terrible thing if she really became dependent on John now . . .

To JOHN PEALE BISHOP   December 2, 1943
                                                      Wellfleet

Dear John: I have just had a postcard from Margaret. I had already heard that you were ill and had written you a letter; but it has haunted me since that it did not get mailed, though I have not yet been able to find it. I'm sorry you've been in bad shape, but you probably needed a rest, and there is nothing so satisfactory as a couple of weeks in the hospital if you have earned it. But I hope that, whatever you do, you won't give up your job and go back to Chatham. We up here are getting into the stuffy, moldering, freezing, too-much-whisky-drinking state that comes on toward the end of November, and shall be glad to get away Sunday, when we are driving down to New York. We'll be all winter at the Gramercy Park Hotel, and I hope you'll be getting to town so that we can see something of you.

I wish you would use your lying-up period to get together a new book of poems. I was reading your poem about Scott the other night and thought even more highly of it than before. And nobody except a few friends has seen the OBK poem. Don't bother to answer this letter—but do come to see us if you can on your way back to Washington.

As ever, Bunny W

To CHRISTIAN GAUSS   December 12, 1943
                                                      The New Yorker

Dear Christian: Thank you for your letter. I had heard about John. I don't think he is seriously ill. I think it will be a good thing for him to get away from the Cape and get really started at Washington. The situation in his household has been pretty grim, and that is partly, I think, what has been the matter with him . . .

Love to the family.   As ever, Bunny W.

To JOHN PEALE BISHOP   March 25, 1944
                                                      The New Yorker

Dear John: I've sent you some books that I thought you might like to see. Please don't let them get away from you. I'll pick them up when I come to see you sometime. How are you? The Dos Passoses have just told me about seeing you. Have also seen the Nabokovs (Nicolas)—Nicky is very amusing about Washington and rather somber about St. John's, between which he seems to alternate. I've been having a pretty good time with this job, which is child's play compared to either *Vanity Fair* or *The New Republic*. New York is not particularly exciting—I have felt a bleakness and emptiness about it that I have never felt before, and will be glad to be back to the country, where one can at least make a kind of world inside one's own house and not have so much the consciousness of the larger world's opening out into the naked interstellar spaces, in which bombing planes are doing their best to blast the work of humankind off the earth. Don't bother to answer this if your energies are limited. I hope we shall be seeing you soon. We expect to go back in May. Love to Margaret.   As ever, Bunny W

I wish you would send me some of those recent poems, which I think *The New Yorker* might use. Cap Pearce is now in the army, and the poetry selecting is done in the office.

To STANLEY DELL   April 13, 1944
                                                      The New Yorker

. . . I suppose you read about John Bishop's death. It is very sad. We had seen quite a lot of him, as he was living at South Chatham, not far from us . . .

To CHRISTIAN GAUSS   May 15, 1944
                                                            Wellfleet

Dear Christian: It was very kind of you to do that little memoir for the *Library Chronicle*, which has just reached me.* It is sad to think of those

---

* Edmund Wilson, the Campus and the Nassau 'Lit,'" in *The Princeton University Library Chronicle*.

John Peale Bishop

F. Scott Fitzgerald

When I'm with John [Bishop], I say: "Well, John, you and I are the only real artists," and when I'm with Alec [McKaig], I say: "You and I are the only ones who understand the common man," and when I'm with Townsend [Martin], I say: "Well, Townsend, you and I are the only ones who are really interested in ourselves," but when I'm alone, I say: "Well, Fitz, you're the only one!" —*The Twenties: From Notebooks and Diaries of the Period*

"frohe Tage" today when Teek Whipple, Scott, and John are all dead and Stan Dell seems to be a confirmed neurotic who does nothing but translate Jung. I miss John terribly, coming back up here this year, as he lived down the Cape at South Chatham, and I had seen a lot of him in recent years. His life was a tragedy, like Scott's, and it gives me the deep sense of a loss that can never be retrieved to read your description of him —so vivid to me—of the impression he made in his undergraduate days. He underwent a rapid and dreadful change in his late years and was really prematurely senile when he died—yet he saved his art through it all and, at the time he made his elegy for Scott's death, struck a fresh vein which flowed for some time. I believe that some of his best work was written then. I have been thinking about the whole group, and I believe that, in certain ways, Princeton did not serve them very well. I said this to Mary, who has had considerable opportunity to observe the men from the various colleges, and she said: "Yes, Princeton didn't give them quite moral principle enough to be writers." Instead, it gave you too much respect for money and country-house social prestige. Both Scott and John in their respective ways, I think, fell victims to this. I don't want to be pharisaical about them: I was more fortunate than either of them, not in gifts, but in the opportunity to survive, because I had enough money for study and travel in the years when those things are most valuable, but not so much that—like Stanley—I didn't have to think about earning some. One's only consolation is that Princeton did give us other things that were good—a sort of eighteenth-century humanism that probably itself was not unconnected with the rich-patron relationship of the university to somebody like M. T. Pyne. And then if we had gone to Yale, though we should probably all have survived in the flesh, we might never have survived in whatever it is that inspires people not to take too seriously the ideal of the successful man.

There are a few things that you say that are inaccurate. I never took economics at Princeton, only at Columbia summer school—and not really economics but a course in "Labor Problems." My bad grades were chemistry and coordinate geometry in my freshman and sophomore years. My tests in contemporary literature were rather different from the picture of them you give. Shaw and Wells had been my gods at boarding school, and I was still very much under their influence. Don't you remember those Shawesque articles that I used to write about campus problems? I considered myself a social reformer. *Fabian Essays*, which I read at college, made a great impression on me. And, whatever I may have said at some point, I very much admired some of Masefield: his sonnets and *The Everlasting Mercy*, parts of which I used to know by heart. Frost and Amy Lowell I never cared for at all, but I did like *Spoon River Anthology*. On that first occasion when we met (not at the Nass but somewhere else) we hadn't asked you to talk about Zola: Zola was merely one of the subjects that came up. In general, though, your description of that period and all of us seems to me absolutely correct. It is interesting to me to see how it looked to somebody who was older than I at the time.

Reading your article has made me want to talk to you about all this. I wish I could have got down to Princeton last winter, but I was working on a book as well as doing my *New Yorker* stuff, and my mother was very ill, so that I had to be at Red Bank a lot. I have heard good reports of you from several people. I saw Katherine in the Princeton Club just before I came away, and she told me you were still in doubt as to whether you ought to retire. I should hate to see you go—unless there is something you would rather do. What would the college do without you?

We have just come up to the country here. I am thoroughly glad to get away from New York, which I always find difficult to live in and which nowadays seems strangely empty.   . . . As ever, Bunny W

ON EDITING F. SCOTT FITZGERALD

1941–1944

*The struggle to be a good artist—which had also a tragic ending—
was one of the principal elements in Scott's career.*

"The Last Tycoon"
1941

To Maxwell Perkins   February 16, 1941
                                                        Stamford

Dear Max: I have just read Scott's MS, and it is heartbreaking, as you
say. I think the book would have been very good. It is much superior to
anything else about Hollywood. And it is the only one of Scott's books
that shows any knowledge of any field of human activity outside of
dissipation.

Here is what I would suggest for a book:

1. *The Great Gatsby*, if it is out of print. Otherwise, perhaps not. (It
   is out of print in the Modern Library.)

2. This MS just as it is, except for the few changes he has indicated.
   There should be a note explaining what he meant to do with the
   story—which I can't make out from his plan. But Sheilah Graham
   must know. I will edit the MS myself, if you want me to. There
   are spots where it ought to be compared with the written copy. The
   plan probably ought to be reproduced, too: it shows how carefully
   he was working it out, and it gives a good idea of the kind of effects
   he was aiming at.

3. *The Crack-Up*. I think you ought to consider this seriously. I hated
   it when it came out, just as you did; but I have found several
   intelligent people that think highly of it. There was more truth and
   sincerity in it, I suppose, than we realized at the time. He wanted

it published in a book himself, and after all I dare say it is a part of the real Fitzgerald record.

4. Possible other unpublished MSS. I have an idea that his notebooks were interesting, and selections from these might be included. And Sheilah told me that since Scottie had been at Vassar, he had written her a remarkable series of letters about how she ought to conduct herself and life in general, over which he took a lot of pains.

5. The memorial articles by other writers which I am running in *The New Republic*. The first installment was in last week, and the second will be in next. The Glenway Wescott piece and John Bishop's poem are really topnotch things—John's poem one of the best he ever wrote. Dos couldn't give much time to his piece, because he was finishing a book, but talked as if he intended to write something longer about Scott's work later on. John O'Hara wanted to write at more length and tell more anecdotes about Scott, and as he shows a good sense of Scott's personality, it might be worthwhile to have him do this. [Robert] Benchley, whom I hadn't thought of asking, volunteered to contribute something; but I wasn't able to take any more space in *The New Republic* for it.

I feel definitely that Scott will be read in the future and that people will think him significant, and such a book will make valuable materials accessible, even if it doesn't sell enormously.

I am going to New York the Wednesday after next and expect to have my book ready by then—so couldn't we have lunch that day? I will meet you at the Shelton at one if it is O.K.

Thank you for the Joyce article, which is interesting.

As ever, Bunny Wilson

To MAXWELL PERKINS   March 13, 1941
Stamford

. . . Here is a letter from Sheilah Graham explaining about Scott's book. Please send it back to me. Make a copy if you want to. John Biggs* has just written me, and I am going to see him next week.

I will get in touch with you again before we leave. Am going to work on the novel as soon as I have cleaned up a few odd jobs.

I saw [Edward] Weeks in Boston and told him about Scott's first chapter, in which he expressed a great interest. If you send it to him, don't you think you ought to send a copy—keeping the MS with Scott's penciled notes yourself? . . .

---

* "John Biggs is Scott's executor . . ."

To Maxwell Perkins   March 27, 1941
                                                      Stamford

Dear Max: Sheilah Graham has just written me asking me whether she
can't have a copy of Scott's MS, so that she can go over it carefully before
she comes on. Can you send her one?—or should I apply to John Biggs?
Another thing: couldn't Scribner's pay her fare to come up to see me on
the Cape? I will just have gotten settled by May 8, which is when she is
coming; and I don't want to have to come down again for the purpose. It
would be difficult to go over the MS in a New York hotel anyway. (Perhaps she can come straight from the West to Boston.)

About *Esquire:* I think you had better wait till we have produced a
cleaned-up text before sending them a MS. Otherwise, the names and
other things are going to cause confusion.

It was nice to see you and your daughter the other night. I hope our
combination of liquors didn't ruin you. We were a little the worse for it
ourselves.   As ever, Bunny W.

The Princeton class of 1917 . . . and John Biggs then a most promising writer of realistic fiction, now a learned and distinguished judge.
                                              (Christian Gauss,
              "Edmund Wilson, the Campus and the Nassau 'Lit' ")

To John Biggs   May 5, 1941
                                                      Wellfleet

Dear John: The above is now my permanent address—have just bought a
house up here. I'm working on Scott's MS and find that it's possible to
supplement the unfinished draft from these notes and sketches better
than I had supposed. I hope you can locate the original copy. There is
also among the notes a certain amount of personal stuff about his love
affairs, with names and dates, for example. When I am done with them,
I'll send them back to you, with a memorandum explaining how I used
them and what is in them. There are certain things that it may be of
interest to publish someday. I have an idea that an extremely interesting
book could someday be made up from his notebooks and letters. In regard
to his introducing the names of real people into his Hollywood novel, I
haven't come across anything that seems libelous. Real names have been
kept carefully out of the main action, and those that are used merely
serve to give the reader his bearing. They are used in just the same way
that real names would be used in any novel about a special field.
Hemingway in *For Whom the Bell Tolls* introduces real people by their
names to a far greater extent and treats them far more harshly. H. G.

Wells's novels are full of real political and literary figures introduced under their real names.

I haven't received the books you want me to autograph. I'll send you my new one when it's out, if you have the faintest interest in it.

As ever, Bunny Wilson

To Maxwell Perkins   May 24, 1941
                                                              Wellfleet

Dear Max: I am enclosing:

1. My foreword, which ought to stand at the beginning of the MS.

2. My synopsis of the unfinished part of the story. Please have them make three copies of this and send them to the following persons, whom I am writing to have them check up on it in various ways: Sheilah Graham, 1443 North Hayworth Avenue, Hollywood, California; Miss Frances Kroll, 7 West Eighth Street, New York; and E. E. Paramore, 2073 Coldwater Canyon, Beverly Hills, Hollywood, California.

3. Scott's outline, which ought to be copied for the MS.

4. The rest of the *Esquire* stuff (under separate cover). I have put on the top the three articles which recapitulate the adventures of the Fitzgeralds. They are well written and, in their relatively light way, have a certain autobiographical interest. If you publish a volume later with the *Crack-Up* articles and other things in it, I think that these might be included. I hope that you will keep all these *Esquire* articles on file.

If you will send me a copy of the whole typed MS, including the above parts, I will go through it and get it right back to you.   As ever, EW

To Maxwell Perkins   June 13, 1941
                                                              Wellfleet

. . . I shall have to put in a month or more of work on the *Tycoon*, and I think Scribner's ought to pay something for it. I don't want to make money out of Scott, but I think you ought to put, say, $500 to the credit of his account, so that the family will get the benefits of it. I'll send you the MS in a day or two . . .

To Maxwell Perkins   June 19, 1941
                                                              Wellfleet

Dear Max: Here is Scott's MS ready to go to the printer.

1. Sheilah Graham found another outline of Scott's and I have dug up some other data which make it possible to give a much better account of how the story was to have ended. I have therefore rewritten my synopsis, and it ought to be typed again. I do not need to see the typed copy, as I can check on it in the proofs; but I wish you would send carbons to the same three people to whom they were sent before. The other new pages

in pencil (mostly on this yellow paper, but also including the last page of the main text of the story on white paper) probably ought to be typed too.

2. I have included a suggestion for a title page. I don't want "Edited by EW" on it, as you proposed. My name at the end of the foreword will indicate my part in the matter.

3. The typographer ought to pay attention to the problem of setting my commentary in the notes in smaller type than the documents by Scott, so that it will be easy to distinguish the two without using quotation marks for the latter. This is the way it is always done.

4. It ought to be possible to get the big outline on two facing pages, so that it could be read by turning the book sideways.

5. I want to see proofs on the whole volume. And please send me back Scott's books when you have transferred the corrections from them.

6. I enclose a letter from Harold Clurman. I suppose you will want to send him proofs—unless it's a bad idea to let them see the book out there before it actually appears . . .   As ever, EW

Just got your letter. About the "Pat Hobby" stories: You know I didn't want to include them all, but only four or five, which I picked out. They aren't very good in themselves, but I think that they do add to the general picture of Hollywood. I felt that all this Hollywood material combined to give an impression of Scott's point of view on the movies that you don't get from *The Tycoon* alone. Sheilah Graham says that he thought some of them were rather good, and I was partly guided by her selection. At worst, it can't do any harm to stick them in at the back of the book. I have sort of apologized for them in my foreword . . .

To Maxwell Perkins   July 3, 1941
                                                       Wellfleet

. . . I don't think the "Pat Hobby" stories ought to be included in the volume with *The Crack-Up* . . . Unless [Samuel] Roth wants to bring out a volume containing all the "Pat Hobby" sketches (which I don't really think is worthwhile), the volume you are bringing out is the place for them. Leave them out if you feel so strongly. It isn't very important— but I thought that the ones I picked out would make some impression as a group and that parts of them were very amusing . . .

To John Biggs   August 11, 1941
                                                 Princeton Club

Dear John: You will remember that I agreed to donate my editorial work on Scott's book. It has occurred to me since that I ought to make sure that it isn't donated merely to Scribner's—which, so far as I can see, will be the case unless they make some payments to Scott's estate. Max

Perkins, whom I have just seen, points out that Scribner's is canceling Scott's debts to them; but I don't see that what Scribner's does in relation to Scott's estate has anything to do with my connection with the editing of the book—which is a transaction between Scribner's and me. I've put in on it at least six weeks' work, which is worth about $500, and I think that they ought to pay $500 to the estate. Otherwise, I simply give the work to Scribner's. If they had gotten someone else, who was not a friend of Scott's, they would have had to pay him something. I wish you would let me know what you think about this situation. If possible, please drop me a line here at the Princeton Club, so that I can get it before I leave Friday afternoon, as I want to take it up with Max before I go.

As ever, Bunny W.

To MAXWELL PERKINS   September 8, 1941
                                              Wellfleet
Dear Max: I am sending back the page proofs on Scott's book.

My foreword was not included with these proofs. This, I suppose, was because the early pages of a book are always printed separately; but I wish you would check up, so that I'll be sure to get it.

The printers have made something of a mess of the setting of the notes, etc., by beginning my summary of the conclusion on the same page on which the last chapter ends, and by running everything along after this, without starting the new sections on new pages. This is contrary to the indications of my copy; and I don't think it can be due to an attempt on the part of your office to keep the number of pages down, because you have taken an extra page for the title of each of the short stories. The first of these eyesores I have been able to straighten out; but to do anything about the rest would involve resetting a large part of the book.

The proofreaders at your printers' have lived up to the criticisms you have often heard me make by failing to straighten out the usages and spellings. One of the primary functions of a proofreader is to make these uniform; but this proof looks as if it had been read by a number of different people who had not agreed on a uniform practice. I have attended to the things I noticed; but I discovered when I was going through the latter part of the book that the word "good-by" was spelled differently there than it was in *The Last Tycoon*. Somebody ought to go through the proofs and make this uniform. The spelling I prefer is "good-by" rather than "good-bye."

Somebody has checked on Scott's references to the First Division on page 201. I'm not in a position to straighten that out up here. If you want to make this passage consistent with the facts, you might get the same person who discovered the errors to substitute references which would be correct. Of course, they would have to be regiments that men such as Scott is describing would have been likely to be in.

342

I have taken out the first reference to Metro; but the second one is all right, because Scott is merely indicating the different techniques of moviemaking peculiar to the different companies. There is no identification of Stahr with Metro.

The "Bald Hemingway characters" ought to be left. I can't imagine that Scribner's nervousness about Hemingway extends to barring any reference to his work. What conceivable objection can there be to referring to the characters of any novelist?

The references to Tommy Manville, etc., and to the _____ brothers (who were not the Warner brothers, as John Biggs seems to think, but the Fisher brothers), are completely innocuous. John seems to be under the impression that real people are never mentioned in books . . .

I assume that you will send copies to Zelda and Scottie, and I should like two or three for myself.

Could you send me the group of *Esquire* articles of Scott's that I picked out as worth printing? Not the Hollywood stuff, but *The Crack-Up* and associated pieces.

Will you please send me Scottie's address?   As ever, Edmund Wilson

To CHRISTIAN GAUSS   September 8, 1941
                                                          Wellfleet

Dear Christian: Your secretary at Princeton has just written me, and I am terribly sorry to hear about Alice's illness. I hope that she is well on her way to recovery.

This letter also brings the bad news of Duane Stuart's death—which is particularly a shock because I had just had a letter from him acknowledging a copy of my book which I had sent him. It had seemed to me, when I last saw him at your house, that he had managed to remain quite young and responsive to things. He was certainly one of the first-rate men at Princeton, one of the ones who really gave it distinction and kept up the standards when I was there.

I am just today getting off the last proofs of Scott Fitzgerald's unfinished novel, which I edited for Scribner's. It was very sad to do it. I think it would have been in some ways his best book—certainly his most mature. He had made some sort of new adjustment to life, and was working very hard at the time of his death. He had written the last pages the day before he died of a heart attack. In going through his MSS and notes, I was very much impressed to see what a conscientious artist he had become. I hope you will read the book. He always valued your opinion.

I have bought a house up here on the Cape, and am settled here permanently, I guess. *The New Republic*, which I was back on for a few months last winter, is now really an agent of British propaganda—since the Elmhirsts finance it and dictate the policy—and no place for me. I'm writing something in the nature of a novel, which I'm afraid is going to take years. Mary is well toward the end of a book that is something between a novel and a book of short stories—which I'm very much impressed by. I'm not sure she isn't the woman Stendhal.

Please give my love to Alice, and tell her that I hope soon to see her well. You people have had a lot of afflictions these last years.

As ever, Bunny Wilson

To James Thurber
February 9, 1942
Wellfleet

Dear Thurber: I was glad you were able to do that review of Scott's book —the only one which has had any critical value. I've been sorry to hear that you've been having such a bad time with your eyes. Everybody misses your stuff in *The New Yorker*. You know, Scott admired your work enormously and used to say that Thackeray had started in *Punch* in very much the same way. I hope that you will soon be able to write and draw again.

Yours sincerely, Edmund Wilson

"The Crack-Up"
1941–1944

To John Biggs
August 4, 1941
Wellfleet

Dear John: Thank you for your letter. The suggestions which you thought were Roth's originally came from me—I had asked him to send them to you. I have offered to edit the book (if this is agreeable to you), as he seems to want me to do. It is merely a question of assembling the material and writing a little foreword. I don't want my name to appear in connection with it, though, because I don't want to include all the memorial pieces that I published in *The New Republic* and I don't want Zelda— who was hurt when I didn't print one she sent me—to know that I am in any way responsible for the book. I think the Wescott piece ought to be included—though it is not devoid of pansy malice and vanity—because it makes out a good case for *The Crack-Up* and is well written and pretty interesting, I thought. Dos Passos is going to enlarge his piece, and this ought to counterbalance Glenway.

I have a number of letters Scott wrote me at the time that his various books came out, with some very acute self-criticism in them. Have you anything of the kind? Letters about personal matters wouldn't be in order at the present time, but some of his observations on writing, etc., would be worth printing, I think. I haven't seen the letters to Scottie. I thought that they might be interesting because he devoted a lot of care to writing them, I am told.

344

I saw his friend Katherine Fessenden . . . (nee Tighe, of St. Paul) up here yesterday. She told me to let you know that she would be very glad to help with money if Scottie needed to get through college or anything.

As ever, Bunny Wilson

How about your writing something about Scott yourself? None of the things in *The New Republic* gave any really solid personal picture of him and I think you could do this.

To JOHN BIGGS   September 14, 1941
                                                Wellfleet

. . . This contract is all right: but if I can get the memorial pieces for nothing, he ought to make it 15 percent. So don't sign it till I've talked to the various people . . .

To JOHN BIGGS   December 8, 1941
                                                Wellfleet

Dear John: Here are some points about the book of material by and about Scott which the Colt Press is going to publish:

1. It looks as if Dos Passos and the other people whose memorial notices I wanted to include would all contribute their pieces for nothing. When I have definite notification that they will, you can sign the contract. The Fitzgeralds can thus get 15 percent.

2. There are two other items I want to include: Scott's article on Ring Lardner at the time of his death, of which I have a copy; and the letter that T. S. Eliot wrote Scott when Scott had sent him *The Great Gatsby*. I have written to Eliot and have just gotten permission from him to print this letter. Scott was enormously proud of it, and I remember seeing it pasted up in one of those scrapbooks he used to keep. It ought to be possible to find it there. Won't you have one of the many minions and myrmidons of whom you undoubtedly dispose in your present exalted position look this up and send me a copy?

3. Won't you also try to find that last letter Scott wrote me, which I spoke to you about on the phone? Haven't you any letters from him yourself that are interesting from the literary point of view?

4. Have you got any copies of *Esquire* articles? I have copies of *The Crack-Up* proper; but there are some other pieces which are related to these which I also wanted to include. Scribner's had them, but they seem to be under the impression that they passed them on to you. If you have them, I wish you would send them to me. They are reminiscences of European travel and of getting back to America afterwards, and there is one about lying awake at night.

5. Did you get the MSS of *The Last Tycoon*, which I sent you some time ago?

How are you?   Bunny Wilson

To JOHN BIGGS   January 6, 1942
                                                              Wellfleet
Dear John: Thank you for the Fitzgerald material. I think that the Tom
Wolfe letter might be included—especially if you could find a copy of
the letter of Scott's which inspired it. I remember seeing the T. S. Eliot
letter pasted up in one of those albums of clippings and things Scott kept.
Have you looked in those? I think it's important to include this, if
possible.

Thanks for your letter about my book. Have you had notification of
the celebration planned for the centenary of the founding of the *Lit.*?
They began by planning something too ambitious, and it has now
dwindled, I believe, to a simple banquet. I hope you will go.

                                                   As ever, Bunny W.

To GERTRUDE STEIN   February 10, 1942
                                                              Wellfleet

Dear Miss Stein: I am getting together a sort of memorial volume for
Scott Fitzgerald and should like to include the enclosed letter, which you
wrote him about *The Great Gatsby*. I should be grateful if you would
give me permission to publish it. You never did a portrait of Scott or anything of the kind, did you?

I hope that things are going well with you over there. The last thing
of yours I read sounded reassuring.   Yours sincerely, Edmund Wilson

To GERTRUDE STEIN   April 17, 1942
                                                              Wellfleet
Dear Miss Stein: Thank you very much for your letter. I am having
Scribner's send you a copy of Scott's unfinished novel, *The Last Tycoon*,
which you may not have seen. Scottie is in her last year at Vassar. She
looks like Scott and Zelda in about equal proportions. Zelda lives with
her mother and sister in Montgomery. The tragedy is so complete. Scott,
you know, had stopped drinking and was working very hard at the time
of his death. He had a British girl friend who—though not brilliant—
appreciated him and took very good care of him. His serious literary ambitions had reasserted themselves, and he was working on a book about
Hollywood, which I believe would have been one of his best things. He
had had a heart attack a few weeks before his death. The doctor hadn't
taken it particularly seriously; but one afternoon, when he had been
sitting talking, he got up and suddenly fell dead. He had been feeling
rather happy about the progress he was making with his book. I think
you are right: that he had the constructive gift that Hemingway doesn't
have at all—and I feel sure that some of his work will last.

                                          Yours sincerely, Edmund Wilson

346

To JOHN BIGGS   July 16, 1942
                                                                   Wellfleet

. . . I think that these notebooks of Scott's are extremely good and ought
to be included in our book. Dos Passos, who has seen them, agrees with
me, and even seems to think that they ought to be published *in toto*. I
think, however, that they ought to be weeded out to some extent—particularly the verse, a lot of which is terrible.

In the meantime, my friend Roth, who was going to publish the book,
seems to have overexpanded and announces he can't go on. Jay Laughlin—
I don't know whether you know who he is: a rich young scion of Laughlin
steel, who does non-commercial publishing*—has written me asking
whether he can take over the book. Laughlin has a reputation of not
paying his royalties on time and of grinding down his authors generally;
and I have written him proposing that he pay the contributors and the
editors something exclusive of the 15 percent to the Fitzgerald estate. I
don't believe he will agree to this; but I think the book would perhaps be
better handled by a regular commercial publisher. I believe that the inclusion of the notebooks will make it a book that can really be sold. I
have also collected highly entertaining letters from John Bishop and
Gerald Murphy. I don't see why Scribner's shouldn't bring it out—on
the same terms as *The Last Tycoon*—and I'll speak to Max Perkins about
it, if you think it's a good idea, when I go to New York in August . . .

To JOHN BIGGS   September 12, 1942
                                                                   Wellfleet

. . . Scribner's seems far from enthusiastic about bringing out the book
about Scott, but Houghton Mifflin are interested, and I think that they or
Laughlin will do it . . .

To JOHN BIGGS   March 20, 1943
                                                                   Wellfleet

. . . I am trying to make a deal with Reynal and Hitchcock for a book of
mine, and am trying to put over Scott's book, too—should know this
coming week, and will write you, also send you what I owe you . . .

To JOHN BIGGS   May 27, 1943
                                                                   Wellfleet

. . . Here is Laughlin's contract, which seems to me O.K. I meant him
to send the checks on the advance himself; but he has arranged it differently, so that you will have to. The list is as follows:

---

* New Directions.

$25 to John Peale Bishop, Sea Change, South Chatham, Massachusetts

$25 to John Dos Passos, 571 Commercial Street, Provincetown, Massachusetts

$25 to Glenway Wescott, 48 East 89th Street, New York City

$25 to Paul Rosenfeld, 270 West 11th Street, New York City

I am supposed to get $100. Since I owe you fifty, only send me fifty, and that will take care of my debt. Laughlin, as you see, is sending you $200 . . .

When you send the contracts back to Laughlin, ask him to send you a set of proofs when they are ready, so that you can check on what is being printed. I gradually accumulated quite a lot of material from you and Harold Ober and other people, and I think it will be quite a book. I will ship back to you this mass of Fitzgerald material I have when the book has finally gone to press . . .

To John Biggs   June 3, 1943
                                                          Wellfleet

Dear John: I have tentatively called the Fitzgerald book *The Crack-Up*. I am not especially keen on this as a title, and it occurs to me that it might make people feel better to change it to something else.

Two points that might be made are: that Glenway Wescott's appreciation is largely based on *The Crack-Up*; and that if you read *The Crack-Up* through, you realize that it is not a discreditable confession but an account of a kind of crisis that many men of Scott's generation have gone through, and that in the end he sees a way to live by application to his work.

I thought at one time of writing a foreword and explaining all this, but I decided that the documents explained themselves. Nobody who read the whole book would get an impression of final demoralization. Scott's last phase, when he was working on *The Last Tycoon*, figures both in his notebooks and in the letters; and Dos Passos wrote especially for this volume a piece which praises *The Last Tycoon*.

I hope that you can counteract with your influence any influence that Ober and Max Perkins may have had on Scottie, and that you can allay her misgivings.   As ever, Bunny Wilson

To John Biggs   August 25, 1943
                                                          Wellfleet

Dear John: I have just examined the Fitzgerald MS as edited by Laughlin. The passages and notes I omitted and that he wants to have restored come under the following heads: 1. Notes that have already been printed in connection with *The Last Tycoon*. 2. Things that are libelous or that would hurt or embarrass people. I had already struck out the reference to Anne. 3. Stuff that I thought not worth printing. Of the notes in this last category, I have put back three or four; I think that in most cases I was well advised. I am sending the MS back to you today.

I suggest that the way to proceed is as follows. Have copies made of the pages where omissions occur. This will prevent Scottie's being needlessly worried by anything that is not to be in the book, and it will also keep Laughlin out of temptation. Take the matter up with Scottie, and then, if it is all right with her, insist that Laughlin sign a contract that includes the following stipulations: 1. The text of the book is in every particular to be controlled by you and me. 2. The choice, number, and placing of the photographs is to be controlled by you and me. 3. I am to see both galleys and page proofs. I believe that he will publish the book. He cannot put things in against our wishes, as you seemed to fear when we were talking on the phone, if we give him a copy that hasn't got them on.

There remains the question of the letter to Joseph Mankiewicz (page 292). I think it is a very interesting document, and I want, if possible, to publish it. I don't see that there is anything libelous in it, and I don't feel that movie people of this type deserve any courtesy. But if you want to show it to him, have a copy made and do so—or I will do it, if you prefer.

If everything works out with Scottie and Laughlin, you can send the MS direct to wherever Laughlin says send it. I don't have to see it again till it is in proofs; but the originals of the pages from which the copies have been made ought to be sent to me so that I can check up later.

About the letters which don't seem to you worthwhile: I think I am justified in including them. They are interesting in connection with Scott's books. Some people to whom I have shown them think them very good. The only thing that worries me about them is that so many of them are to me. I wish I could have got more letters to other people . . .

As ever, Bunny W

I see that Laughlin has put on his title page: "Published by the Colt Press. Distributed by New Directions." New Directions is Laughlin; but the Colt Press is the outfit out in California that published my *Boys in the Back Room* and *Note-Books of Night*. They were originally to have published the Fitzgerald book; but the man who ran it became insolvent and went to Alaska as a soldier. The business, I was given to understand, folded up. I have the greatest difficulty getting anybody out there to do anything about my own books. I think that you ought to find out about this before signing any contract. You ought to be sure who is responsible.

To John Biggs   November 5, 1943
                                                       Wellfleet
Dear John: I saw Scottie before I left New York and did not find her
difficult at all. She wants some passages in the letters and notes left out,
and I am going to omit them. She seemed to feel a little hurt that I had
not asked to see the letters that her father wrote her at college. I told her
that I *had* wanted to see them; but that you and Max Perkins had told me
that they were not possible to publish, and that the copies she had made
of them had never been shown me. She has offered to send them to me.
What was your impression about them?

I am going to go through the whole MS in a day or two. On second
thought, I think it will be better to wait till we definitely know about
Laughlin before I do anything further about the MS. The letters were
put together two years ago and I had not looked at them again till my
interview with Scottie the other day. It may be that I was a little callous
in leaving things that were calculated to make Scottie uncomfortable. My
original idea was merely to print passages which bore on his literary work;
the whole subject of his personal relations might better be left for the
eventual biographer.

Now, in the meantime, I think the thing to do—even before we have
a new copy of the MS made—is to find out whether Laughlin will consent to a contract which makes him powerless to intervene in any way.
I suggested every stipulation I could think of in an earlier letter to you.
The question of the photographs should be mentioned, too.

                                                As ever, Bunny W
I have just written Maurice Speiser, enclosing all the references to
Hemingway, and asked him to get a release from H. Will dig up the
Gertrude Stein letter.

To John Biggs   November 9, 1943
                                                       Wellfleet
. . . There is no point in sending Laughlin the MS again in the form
in which we want it printed, because he has already seen it in this form.
The only changes that will be made will be the omission of a few personal passages about Scottie and one or two other people. In fact, the
book should *not* be sent to him again. Send him the contract with a new
clause. He will have to sign it or give up publishing the book, and I don't
think he wants to do this. If you want to authorize me to do so, I will
take the matter up with him myself. I am used to these literary negotia-
tions. If he should refuse, I feel sure that I can get somebody else to do it
when I go to New York.

We are going to New York December 6, and will be all winter at the
Gramercy Park Hotel. Do come to see us. I gave the hotel your name

350

as a "social reference" for the apartment we are taking there, and hope you will tell them that I am solvent.

Another point about the MS: on looking through it more carefully, I find that Scottie wants something done about certain references to an aunt of hers and one or two other things that it will be easier to take up with her when I get to New York. I will have another interview with her then, and go over everything. A new copy can be made after this . . .

To JOHN BIGGS   November 22, 1943
                                                           Wellfleet

Dear John: What have you done about Laughlin? I have just had a letter from him saying that he has not heard from you. He also tries to butter me up, due to the fact that I am going to review books in *The New Yorker*. All that is necessary is to tell him that the MS is the same as before, with the exception of a few omissions necessitated by Scottie's desire not to have her aunt offended, etc. If he will not agree on these conditions, there is no use bothering with him. I can get somebody else to publish it, I'm sure. The publishers are now eating out of my hand, and I receive honeyed letters from them daily. If you want me to handle the correspondence with Laughlin, I will; but do let us get the thing cleared up.

Thank you for your recommendation. I am afraid, however, that the high opinion you express of my literary abilities will not impress the hotel management much.   As ever, Bunny W

To JOHN BIGGS   March 10, 1944
                                                           Wellfleet

. . . Thanks for your letters and all your trouble about the Fitzgerald book. I am sorry that Mankiewicz objects to having that letter printed. He is certainly wrong in saying that Scott was "happy with the final script." I have just called up Maurice Speiser about the references to Hemingway in Scott's notebooks. Hemingway is in town, and Speiser is going to see him tomorrow and ask him about this. I will let you know what he says . . .

To JOHN BIGGS   May 19, 1944
                                                           Wellfleet

. . . Thanks for sending me your letter to Laughlin. Did you make it clear that he would have to agree not to tamper with any of my editing? I will write him about this, if necessary . . .

THE FORTIES

When I call myself a journalist, I do not of course mean that I have always dealt with current events or that I have not put into my books something more than can be found in my articles; I mean that I have made my living mainly by writing in periodicals. There is a serious profession of journalism, and it involves its own special problems. To write what you are interested in writing, and to succeed in getting editors to pay for it, is a feat that may require pretty close calculation and a good deal of ingenuity.

CHRONOLOGY

1940	**TO THE FINLAND STATION**
JANUARY	Truro Center: I've got my hands full trying to deliver two books by May.
SEPTEMBER	I'm going back on *The New Republic* during October and November.
	We are going to Stamford for the winter.
DECEMBER	Death of F. Scott Fitzgerald.
1941	**THE BOYS IN THE BACK ROOM; THE WOUND AND THE BOW***
JANUARY	I want to do something about him [F. Scott Fitzgerald] in a literary supplement of *The New Republic*.
SPRING	I've stopped working in the office.
	My book has gone through with Houghton Mifflin.
SEPTEMBER	I have bought a house up here on the Cape, and am settled here permanently, I guess.
1942	**NOTE-BOOKS OF NIGHT**
SEPTEMBER	I've been overwhelmed by finishing my anthology [*The Shock of Recognition*] and commencing a series of lectures at Smith College.
1943	**THE SHOCK OF RECOGNITION**
JULY	A series of Russian articles for *The Atlantic*.
OCTOBER	They have offered me Clifton Fadiman's job reviewing books on *The New Yorker*.
NOVEMBER	We are going to New York and will be at the Gramercy Park Hotel.

---

* *The Wound and the Bow*: Dickens: The Two Scrooges / The Kipling That Nobody Read / Uncomfortable Casanova / Justice to Edith Wharton / Hemingway: Gauge of Morale / The Dream of H. C. Earwicker / Philoctetes: The Wound and the Bow.

1944	Weekly review in *The New Yorker*.
APRIL	Death of John Peale Bishop.
MAY	Back on the Cape for the summer.
SEPTEMBER	We are at Henderson Place, a little blind-alley street at the very end of East 86th Street.
1945	*The New Yorker* is sending me to Europe.
MARCH	Sailing for Europe next Wednesday.
SEPTEMBER	Wellfleet.
1946	MEMOIRS OF HECATE COUNTY
	Henderson Place (New York City) and Wellfleet.
NOVEMBER	Nevada.
DECEMBER	Married Elena Mumm Thornton.
1947	EUROPE WITHOUT BAEDEKER
DECEMBER	Zuñi, New Mexico, for *The New Yorker*.
1948	A little girl named Helen Miranda born last February.
MAY	No other news except that I have more or less laid off *The New Yorker*.
1949	
MAY	c/o Eitingon, Hillcrest Park, Stamford, Connecticut.
NOVEMBER	I have persuaded *The Reporter* to send me to Haiti.

To Malcolm Cowley   January 26, 1940
                                                     Truro Center, Mass.
Dear Malcolm: Here are two book notes, which cover, I think, everything
I have from *The New Republic*. I haven't waited for the other things I
was going to review with them, because I wanted to get them cleaned
up and not do any more reviews, as I've got my hands full trying to deliver
two books by May.* So don't send me Shaw's *Geneva* or the Dos Passos
Tom Paine, which I asked for. You don't need to send me the typed
copies of these: just send me the proof.
    About your review of Krivitsky: I get more and more puzzled and
disturbed by your political position as time goes on. The literary editor
of the N.R. ought to be in a situation to be independent of entanglements
with movements, parties, and groups if anybody is in New York, but
you seem to have given hostages to the Stalinists in some terrible incomprehensible way. Just at the time when it seems to me that the normal
thing would be frankly to discard your illusions, you have been carrying
on in a way that matches *The New Masses* at its worst. Last summer you
were vilifying [José] Robles, about whom you obviously didn't know a
thing except what the Stalinists had been pouring into your ear. I knew
Robles, who spent a summer up here in Provincetown, and I can't imagine
anybody less likely to have worked for the Fascists. His family, as you
probably know, played rather an important part in Spanish politics under
the Republic; and he had been offered the governorship of a province. He
told me that he wouldn't take a job under the Republic, because he knew
that it would eventually get to the point of the bourgeois government's
suppressing working-class revolts. When I knew him, his left position was
quite clear, and he was certainly a man of excellent character. When the
war started, he thought he ought to go back, and by the time Dos had

---

* *To the Finland Station* and *The Wound and the Bow*.

arrived, he had been shot. This fact, however, hadn't been made public, and Dos, when he found it out, had the job of breaking it to his wife. There were various things that might have got him into trouble. He had a brother fighting on the Fascist side, and he was one of the few Spaniards who knew Russian, so that he may have known too much. He was personally aristocratic and not at all the sort of person who would be likely to suppress his disapproval. What finished him was probably his enthusiasm for the social revolution, which the Russians were putting down. Now, what do you know about Robles? You promised further revelations when Dos wrote his letter to the N.R., but they've never been forthcoming. Last week, in the case of Krivitsky, you presented more of what you described as information from reliable sources whom you don't name; but why on earth, after your handling of Robles, should anybody take stock in it? You write better than the people on the regular Stalinist press, but what you are writing is simply Stalinist character assassination of the most reckless and libelous sort. You didn't hesitate to call Krivitsky a coward. You may not regard members of the Russian Secret Service as particularly sympathetic individuals, but why in God's name was Krivitsky a coward: because he refused to murder Reiss or because he refused to go back and get purged? In what way did he play a "discreditable" role?   Edmund W

To ALLEN TATE   February 6, 1940
                                                        Truro Center
Dear Allen: I'll only just be getting my Marxist book finished by the end of this month, so that I shan't have had a chance to write anything new by the time I go down to New York then. I was planning to stay a week and could go down to Princeton if you would be willing to have me read my chapter on the early years of Lenin. It is based partly on Russian memoirs that have never been translated and that read like Russian novels—is quite unlike anything else on the subject in English and might, I think, be quite interesting to the students. I realize, of course, however, that they are awfully skittish at Princeton of anything connected with Communism and that the subject has nothing to do with "English." If these objections arise, I could come down later when I'll have had a chance to do something else. We hope to get down to Stamford for several months in the middle of April. In any case, please let me know, so that I can plan my movements.
    Love to the family.   As ever, Edmund W.

To CHRISTIAN GAUSS   March 17, 1940
                                                        Truro Center
. . . I've just finished the interminable book that began with Michelet almost six years ago—it's a great load off my mind. In revising it, I went

358

again through the notes that you'd made on the proofs of the first part, and I see that I failed to appreciate at that time your remarks on the supposed inevitability of the proletarian revolution. In the course of time, I've come to agree with you. I'll send you a copy when it's out. It's inadequate in several ways; but it contains all the contribution to the subject that I'm capable of making, I guess . . .

To MALCOLM COWLEY   July 17, 1940
                                                      Wellfleet

. . . As for reviewing my book, I can't bear Lerner's stuff. Do it yourself, by all means, if you want to. I was hoping that it might be done by a historical expert (not a Marxist) who might be able to throw some light on the subject. I'm not sure that Irwin Edman mightn't be good—though he's a philosopher. Meyer Schapiro knows a hell of a lot about the whole subject . . .

> My friend Daniel Aaron . . . is a professor at Smith College and one
> of the very best people we have in the field of American literature.
>   (To Charlotte Kretzoi, 1964)

To DANIEL AARON   1961

Dear Dan: Thank you for having them send me your book—which I have of course read with interest.* The ins and outs of these old controversies and organizations are, as I told you, so stale and distasteful to me now that I return to them with reluctance, but there are also certain things that are new to me, and, in any case, in looking all this up so carefully and clearing up its complications, you have provided a valuable record, which isn't likely to be superseded. Unlike many such books—about Greenwich Village, the "twenties," the "thirties," etc.—it is both intelligent and accurate. I sometimes wish you had characterized people a little more clearly, but I realize that this was difficult so long as most of them were living, and that by quotations from them and quotations about them you have done a good deal by implication.

The one important omission I feel is your failure to give attention to the later work of Max Eastman and myself, who seriously studied Marxism, extricated ourselves from the various official versions, and eventually provided a critique of it. You say nothing about the *Finland Station* or Max's book on Marxism and Stalinism—or Bert Wolfe's *Three Who Made a Revolution*. I don't understand your barely mentioning Wolfe,

---
* *Writers on the Left.*

359

who seems to me the only American Marxist theorist who was capable of any original thinking at all and who showed any real courage in the earlier phase. I think that you ought to have gone to the mat with the basic philosophy and fallacies of Marxism—which I like to believe we in this country did our share in bringing out into the open. . . .

As ever, Edmund

To F. W. Dupee   May 16, 1940
Partisan Review   Wellfleet

Dear Fred: You people are getting as bad as *The New Republic*. Dwight Macdonald was after me for that Lenin piece for months, constantly writing me and calling me up. I fixed it up for you when I was in New York at a time when you knew my book was coming out and what the piece would be like. At the same time you asked Mary [McCarthy] to do a piece on *Pinocchio* and *The Grapes of Wrath*, which she went to some trouble to see in order to be able to do the article on time. The next time you saw her, you told her that the piece was all off for what seems to me the fantastic reason that you wouldn't be able to make space for it— as if Sidney Hook's interminable articles wouldn't always be the better for cutting. Now you send back my Lenin with the suggestion that I do you a little something on the younger novelists. You are developing all the symptoms of the occupational disease of editors—among them, thinking up idiotic ideas for articles that you want the writers to write instead of printing what they want to write. (Mary wants me to ask you whether you think you're *The Saturday Evening Post*.) I've thought there was something wrong in your shop ever since you passed up that short story of Mary's which seemed to me the best thing she had written. You people certainly owed her a chance to develop, since she was one of your original group. It reminded me ominously of the implacable opposition which the *New Republic* boys always put up when one of their number showed any signs of trying to write anything but *New Republic* editorials. Please pass this letter on to Dwight.

Aside from all this, I hope you're prospering and that we'll see you up here this summer.   As ever, Edmund W

To Morton D. Zabel   August 30, 1940

Good sir, you much misapprehend my notion,
These are the objects of my deep devotion.
The more they fight a destiny unkind,
Contending with the demons of the mind,

Making them serve the offices of art,
The more I love to take the case apart,
Examining the structure of the mainsprings,
Whose strength from panic fear and buried pain springs.
Dickens, the Christmas caroler of Hell,
Pleases my taste for light from darkness well,
Marx, whose Promethean vulture-eaten pride
Set the fierce vulture on the other side,
Brought fuel from a dark and freezing mine
To stoke the souls of man and make them shine,
Whereas my grievance against Rudyard Kipling
Is that he let Mrs. K. control his tippling,
And served the world adulterated brandy,
Creating an immense sympathy for Gandhi.
And as for that most malodorous offender,
Old Hank the Ripper, the London *Kinderschänder*,
I would rather have written his smallest novelette
Than be head of the English Department at Olivet.

And I can't forgive you for not having bought up for me some of the items of that collection.

Your monumental letter has brought us a fund of merriment and stimulation, and that widening of the mental horizon which is only to be obtained through cultured and thoughtful travel. Seriously: I was delighted by your eloquence on the subject of the U.S.A.—I've had the same sort of feeling. I shan't take up all the topics raised in it, as I hope you will actually come up here. We are all very anxious to see you. Wellfleet is very easy to get to. You go as far as Yarmouth and then take a bus which drops you at our door . . .   Love from us all, Edmund

. . . I'm going back on *The New Republic* during October and November while Malcolm writes a book. I want to get you to do something for them.

. . . it is quite extraordinary that a novelist so young should display, from the first page of his very first book [*The Cabala*], so accomplished a mastery of form and a point of view so much his own.
(*The New Republic*, 1928)

To THORNTON WILDER   August 25, 1940
                                                Wellfleet
Dear Wilder: [Nicolas] Nabokov, the Russian composer, has been living across the street from me here, and has asked me to help him with the

libretto of an opera made from Pushkin's "Negro of Peter the Great." I read the story, and I think it is a natural for an opera; but I don't think I'm the man for opera librettos. I thought of you, because it seemed to me that Pushkin was very much in your line. He told me that he had already had the same idea, and I believe had spoken to you about it. He has asked me to write you. I don't know whether there is much of anything for a writer in doing librettos (though it might be theatrically interesting) or what your opinion is of Nabokov's music. I haven't heard any of it except a sort of cantata made from Archie MacLeish's awful poem "America Was Promises," which he played me the other night. It seemed to me quite good and the kind of thing which might promise an opera. He is an extremely intelligent fellow. He says that Lawrence Tibbett sees himself as Peter the Great, and that he can certainly get the opera produced. The story, which Pushkin never finished, is awfully interesting and has great possibilities. There is a translation of it in the Everyman's Library collection of Pushkin's stories called *The Captain's Daughter*. I can imagine the whole business as a masterpiece, which would take its place with *Boris Godunov*, *Le Coq d'Or*, and *Pique Dame*. I'm sorry you couldn't get up here.   Sincerely, Edmund Wilson

He is going to write you about it.

To Thornton Wilder   September 6, 1940
                                                          Wellfleet
Dear Wilder: Masterpieces are written by people of remarkable ability. You are one, and I thought that Nabokov might be another (though my ideas about music are rather unreliable). After all, somebody has got to go on writing great Russian operas.

About Flaubert: the bourgeoisie, in Rabelais's and Voltaire's times, hadn't gotten to be so formidable a menace as they had in the nineteenth century.

About the Marquis de Sade and the English: there is a wonderful book on the Marquis by an Englishman named Geoffrey Gorer, in which the author proves that the Marquis was a great political thinker, who never meant any harm but occasionally indulged in schoolboy hoaxes.

                                                      Sincerely, EW

To Cap Pearce   December 20, 1940
The New Yorker   Stamford

... Why don't you run some of Jarrell's poetry in *The New Yorker*? His writing interests me more, I think, than that of any of the other younger people ...

The New
REPUBLIC
40 East 49ᵗʰ Street
New York, N.Y.

. . . a considerable amount of work brilliantly up to her best. (1927)

To Léonie Adams   October 1, 1940
                                              *The New Republic**

Dear Léonie: I am back at *The New Republic* for a couple of months. I understand that you have a new book of poems coming out. Couldn't *The New Republic* have some of it? I might be able to arrange for a page of them.

How are you? Do you and Bill ever come to New York?† I wish you would let me know if you do . . .   Love, Edmund W.

I do hope you can let us have some poems: we're getting out a special book number in October (material has to be in by the 15th) and I'd like to have them for it, as I'm trying to make it particularly brilliant.

To Léonie Adams   November 12, 1940

Dear Léonie: Do please send me as many of your poems as you can as soon as possible. I'm going to get out a *New Republic* supplement which will be something in the nature of a literary magazine, with articles, poems, stories, etc.—so that I should have plenty of room to print them . . .
                                              As ever, Edmund W.

To Léonie Adams   December 3, 1940

Dear Léonie: Do please send me those poems if you can possibly manage it. I'm getting up a special literary supplement—all poems and articles and things of that kind: no reviews—and I want to include them in it. I'm sending you a copy of the Christmas number, with a remarkable effort by Louise. I'm going to have a group of poems by Rolfe Humphries in the literary supplement. I saw him the other day for the first time in years, as his Stalinizing politics had estranged us. He seems to have completely recovered. How are you?   Love, Edmund

---

* The following letters were written from *The New Republic*.
† Léonie Adams was married to William Troy.

To Malcolm Cowley   October 24, 1940

Dear Malcolm: . . . Everything has been going well here and I have
been enjoying the office—though I have found it a pretty serious problem to fight off the Wednesday afternoon boys and girls. You may be
glad to know that I had Joe Gould put out of his misery in a dark room
behind Jimmy's restaurant by a painless whiff of chloroform. Norbert
Guterman has been caught in an eel pot and shipped to the Near East.
And I am trying to persuade the younger visitors that they won't be
qualified to do book reviewing till they have finished the second year of
high school. So you will find the Wednesday afternoons quieter . . .
                                                            EW

To Morton D. Zabel   October 17, 1940

Dear Morton: Finding this self-addressed card on my desk, I am unable
to resist the impulse to send you a line. I have been haunted during my
first week in the office here by a little book on glass flowers. I took it up
to show Louise, with the result that she, too, became obsessed by it and
is now composing a long poem on the subject. This probably has some
social significance. Let me know what you think of my book number.   EW
    A volume of letters by Conrad has just come in—am sending it for
review with the other book.

To Louise Bogan   November 12, 1940

Dear Louise: Could you be induced to do a short notice of Jean Starr
Untermeyer's new poems—if you haven't written about them at length
for *The New Yorker*? I have always had a certain respect for her poetry,
which seems to me to shine by comparison with Louis's.
    . . . I am also sorry that I can't pay you as much for your poem as I
said I would in a moment of exhilaration, but I am doing the best I can
on the *New Republic*'s rates.   Love, Edmund
    You have left a foot out of one of the lines of your poem: "Eager to
free its something sticky foot."

To Burton Rascoe   October 31, 1940

Dear Burton: I was just going to write you about your MacLeish article,
which I thought was one of the best you'd ever done, when I found your
piece on the publishers in the office here. (I am back in my old job for
a while.) I had just been brooding, myself, on the subject of the publishers, and had had some idea of getting the subject up, and doing some
articles about it. Your article is very valuable; but there would be even
more to be said about the subject—the whole situation of the publishers at

present, who really don't know where they're at. What would you think of doing another article for *The New Republic?* I am planning a super-colossal Christmas book number, and such an article might make a good feature for this. Could you have lunch with me Tuesday of week after election week, and talk about it?

About the MacLeish: I thought I had cleaned up on the subject pretty well myself, but you have really added something. I thought you handled that letter of Van Wyck Brooks's just right. I was going to write Brooks a reply, but decided to refrain. Il Luce is wonderful.

As ever, Bunny Wilson

To James Stern*   December 3, 1940

Dear Mr. Stern: I like this review of Frank O'Connor very much. There are only one or two things in it I question. In the first paragraph, couldn't you just tell about O'Connor's early book and leave out Vincent Sheean—who, after all, I suppose, was only trying to help sell an author not known in the United States. Also, do you really think the books you mention represent absolutely, as you say, "the highest achievements in the art of the English story"? How about Poe, Conrad, Kipling, Henry James, and Stephen Crane?

In the second paragraph, I don't quite understand the last sentence. Why should this technique require any greater concentration than that of the ordinary book of short stories?

As I say, I like the review very much and hope you will do some others for us. Please let me know if there are any Irish subjects you are interested in.   Yours sincerely, Edmund Wilson

To James Stern   December 10, 1940

Dear Mr. Stern: Thank you for fixing up your review. I have cut a sentence or two, which you will have a chance to check on in the proof. When you get proof, please try to think up a title. I still think your statement about the Irish short stories rather extravagant. For many readers, the word *modern* would not exclude Henry James and others.

Yours sincerely, Edmund Wilson

To Louise Bogan   December 27, 1940

Dear Louise: Why don't you do me an occasional poem on the magician we saw the other night. Conjuring is full of beauty and implications. Do take this suggestion seriously.   As ever, Edmund

---

* "They do show his most unusual editorship, the interest he took (above all in one he had never heard of, and who, incidentally, at that time, was new to book review-ing!)."   —James Stern, 1975

To Louise Bogan   January 7, 1941

Dear Louise: Do do the poem on magic. I have always thought that the
subject had great poetic possibilities. Could you get it done within the
next two weeks?   As ever, Edmund

To Louise Bogan   January 20, 1941

Dear Louise: I'm awfully sorry that you've been sick. We all have, too.
It's all right about the poem, which I'm counting on and much excited
about seeing. If I can get it by the end of this month, it will be all right.
  I have had various ideas about magic, which I have refrained from
suggesting to you. You know, the art had made relatively little progress and had fallen into desuetude during the period when the movies
were killing vaudeville, until the time when it came back with the
night clubs. In the meantime, however, like a number of other things,
it had fallen a victim to science. Houdini became scientifically interested
in showing up the impostures of mediums, and, conversely, some professor of physics at Columbia conceived the idea of applying modern
physical technique to magic. He rigged up a laboratory (no kidding)
where he performed such miracles as Hermann and Keller and Robert
Houdon never dreamed: wax hands tapped the answers inside glass globes,
the chosen ace of spades popped out of the pocket of somebody in the audience, and the pits of the mysterious lemon danced the Nutcracker Suite
in mid-air. He initiated a few cockeyed colleagues, who were sworn to
guard the secret. With the result that night-club entertainments get
nowhere, at the same time that the practice of magic is obstructing the
progress of physics. (Blame Hitler if you like; I say that the trouble lies
deeper.) And the old secrets of magic which used to be more or less
kept are now—see the catalogue I sent you—being hawked to the public
for something between a quarter and $7.50.   As ever, Edmund

                        Joseph Conrad
                         1938–1941

To Morton D. Zabel   October 31, 1938

Dear Morton: I haven't written you before about *Under Western Eyes*
because we have been reading it aloud in the evenings and have only
just finished it tonight. The first hundred pages, as you say, are good;
and I was interested in it all through on account of its dealing with Russians, about whom he says many things that seem to me true and penetrating and giving a Polish slant on them; but my opinion of it differs so

much from yours that I am curious to know why you rate it so high. It seems to me about the worst-told story I have ever read and confirms my doubts about Conrad at the time years ago when I gave up reading him. I have always thought there was a good deal of bunk about the technical apparatus of non-participant observers, etc., which James and Conrad went in for and which caused them to scoff at Tolstoy and Dostoevsky; I've always thought the non-participant observers were alibis for not showing the main characters from the inside, as Tolstoy and Dostoevsky were able to do. But Henry James does get something out of this method: given the form and the theme, the story is wonderfully told; it keeps you in suspense and it progresses. But Conrad cannot seem to do either. He shifts back and forth between Razumov and the professor in what seems to me the most perfectly meaningless way. The narrative goes round and round in circles. He keeps going back and telling you what is behind scenes from which you have drawn the correct inferences; and these returns on himself simply drive me crazy. What is the use of going back, for example, to Razumov's experiences in Russia after you have seen him in Geneva? And where, in Henry James, every character or setting is strictly what they call nowadays functional, Conrad introduces various interesting characters and vividly describes a whole series of settings without making them do anything at all. The whole book from the end of Part Two seems to me a masterpiece of mishandling. You know from the moment that Razumov shows up in Geneva that he is going to be moved by Miss Haldin to perform some act of contrition and that is precisely what he does, in a way that occasions little surprise.

Of course, there is a good deal by the way that is remarkable: the picture of Geneva; the psychology of the illegitimate and motherless Razumov (the use of this in the confession part is splendid); and the characterization of the Russians—though I feel that this, deeply intelligent as it is, has a little the second-hand quality of most sketching of national types by foreigners. Isn't it much more satisfactory to read *The Possessed* or *Crime and Punishment*? But do tell us why you like the book so much, why you should go back to it and reread it, as you say.

In any case, Conrad is an interesting bird, and I shall be very much interested to see what you say about him. It must be true as I think you were telling me that some bad conscience or feeling of defeat about Poland is behind these characters of his who are always selling out or letting themselves down or disastrously going to pieces. Certainly his interest in Razumov is not, as he seems to imply in his preface, simply an amazed curiosity at the eccentric ways of Russians, the national enemies of Poles. I should think that the whole Slavic end of Conrad ought to be gone into.

You must certainly write about him: why not a book of three longish studies, like Thomas Mann's Wagner, Goethe, and Freud? Couldn't one of them be E. M. Forster? It seemed to me, by the way, in reading your piece in *The Nation*, that your writing has very much improved: you seem to have got rid of your old fault of verbosity—or I guess what I mean is prolixity—which sometimes used to swamp the form of your long essays.

In any case, we have much enjoyed both the book and the brandy—blessing you whenever we drank the latter and cursing you whenever Razumov, for every action of whose we felt you for mysterious reasons had desired to assume entire responsibility, got hung up for some too interminable conversations. (I'm afraid this last sentence sounds like Conrad.) . . .   As ever, Edmund W.

To Morton D. Zabel   December 13, 1938

Dear Morton: I was glad you wrote me about Bakunin: I was just about to write you pointing out the difference between him and Bukharin. I don't think the character in *Western Eyes* has anything in common with Bakunin except escaping from Siberia and living with a rich lady. I've been reading Mrs. Conrad's book about Joseph, which seems to me wonderful in its way: I'm not sure she isn't a better storyteller than her husband . . .   As ever, Edmund

To Morton D. Zabel   November 12, 1940

Dear Morton: I am sending you the Conrad book. Now, here is the question: would there be any way of combining a review of this book with what you intend to say at Yale? I could use a fairly long article. If this wouldn't work out, and you would rather do the review and the article separately, I suppose they ought to be some distance apart (in point of time). I am getting out both a regular Christmas book supplement, made up of reviews, and a little later, a literary supplement made up of poems, articles, etc., which will be more or less in the nature of a literary magazine. I'll be glad to have your remarks on Conrad in either of these. Please let me know how you would like to handle it.

We were greatly delighted with the yogi literature, which far surpasses any of the inspirational matter I sent you.   As ever, EW.

To Morton D. Zabel   December 11, 1940

Dear Morton: I'm immensely pleased with this Conrad review—one of the most interesting of yours I have ever seen. I think that you are doing work of real importance on this subject. The title is O.K.

The review is too late for the Christmas number. I'd like to run it as a leading review this week: but I'm afraid I can't on account of a long omnibus affair about books on education that I've got to unload.

368

Call us up when you get to New York or stop off at Stamford. We're anxious to see you. As ever, EW.

Betty Huling, who has just read the review on its way to the printer, thinks it's wonderful.

To MORTON D. ZABEL   March 15, 1941

Dear Morton: 1. Conrad. Can't you get this to me right away? I've got to make up the supplement now and want to know precisely what length to figure on. Have also got to write an ad for it right away.

2. Beethoven. I've read the Sullivan book and am immensely indebted to you for sending it to me. Mary read it. It ought to be read by all literary critics. Beethoven has always been the only composer that I liked as well as the great poets . . .

3. Kipling. I was rather dismayed to learn that you had given my piece to your class, as I had just finished rewriting it from beginning to end. The version in *The Atlantic* was a dress rehearsal and—especially in the second part—not very well written.

4. MacLeish. We have just read your second *Partisan Review* article, and are both of us very enthusiastic about it—and you know that in this department Mary is not easily pleased. Your use of the *Yale Review* hoax is masterly, and in this second part you carry the whole subject to a ground where it raises bigger issues and where you express yourself with eloquence and spirit. It is one of the best things that *P.R.* has published and good enough to go into a book. Why in God's name don't you get out a book of essays?—of which Conrad could be one.

5. Bernard Shaw. Stimulated by what you said about Shaw's music criticism, I sent for the volume published in America, which turned out to consist of notices dating from 1888–89, earlier and inferior stuff, which I discovered I already had. There is an interesting preface, however, and a couple of good later articles on Verdi; and if you haven't it, I'll send you my extra copy.

6. Carson McCullers. This last book of hers is quite entertaining— consciously as well as unconsciously humorous. From what I hear about her from Bob Linscott, she sounds like a remarkable person—has memorized all the musical classics without being able to read a note. He says she is the best pianist he has ever heard on or off the concert stage. She is twenty-three and ill (tuberculosis, I think), and may burn out, I suppose.

7. Auden. What did you think of his long poem in *The Atlantic*? I thought it was much the best thing he had written.

8. Disney. I thought *Fantasia* was terrible, too. Two or three of them might have been all right if they had just been shown as amusing shorts, to which the music was incidental.

9. Fitzgerald. Yes: I have always greatly admired that passage at the

end of *The Great Gatsby*. In fact, I think the whole last ten or twelve pages are one of the best things in the American prose of this period. His unfinished novel about Hollywood is most remarkable—returns to the more concentrated and objective vein of Gatsby rather than to his romantic vein.

10. Glenway Wescott: I don't agree about his piece on Scott. I thought it well written and quite stimulating—though marred in spots by the silliness of the tone . . .

11. Malcolm Cowley. He performs prodigies of bumbling in the current *New Republic* on Jarrell and on the Fitzgerald articles.

Love from us both, Edmund W.

To MORTON D. ZABEL   March 21, 1941

. . . The Conrad seems to me masterly. I am going to do my best to publish it all. This will entail either (1) running it in two installments in ordinary numbers of the magazine or (2) displacing other things from the supplement and cutting down your piece a little to fit such space as can be made. There is a third possibility (3) that since I only contracted for 2,000 words from you, they may not let me buy it in this form at all (our relations are none too cordial at present)—it must be something like 6,000 words. I'll let you know as soon as I know what I can do . . .

To MORTON D. ZABEL   March 24, 1941

. . . I am happy to announce that I can run the whole of your piece. I have just reread it, and it seems to me one of the most *approfondi* literary studies that anybody has done—almost sets a new standard after the rather two-dimensional literary criticism we are used to . . .

To MORTON D. ZABEL   January 6, 1942

. . . Allen Tate tells me that your Conrad paper seemed absolutely dazzling amid the dullness of the M.L.A. . . .

Wyndham Lewis
1928–1960

To WYNDHAM LEWIS   December 3, 1941
                                                              Wellfleet

Dear Lewis: I no longer have anything to do with *The New Republic* and can't do anything for anybody in that quarter. They have sent me your letter and kept the article, which they'll let you know about. I have no connections now with any paper. I was asked to lecture once at the University of Toronto, but something happened about it. I'm sorry to hear you're marooned up there. I suppose you know the various magazines that might be a market for you—*The Atlantic Monthly, Harper's, The Nation, Partisan Review* might be worth trying, though they won't pay much. *Esquire* would pay you quite a lot—also, *The New Yorker*. It's hard to advise you, because I don't know what your article is about.

Yours sincerely, Edmund Wilson

To ALLEN TATE   July 17, 1928

. . . When you say that Wyndham Lewis's reasons are always "just because," you have hit the nail on the head. When I tried to argue with him about his notions, urging objections which he should have foreseen and already been prepared to meet, I was surprised to find that he was completely nonplused and would simply become silent, presently breaking out more peevishly in another place. He isn't really peevish, however, but a very agreeable person and quite interesting to talk to when his own personal egoism, though even this is not of a very poisonous kind, doesn't get into the discussion. My conversations with him about America, by the way, reduced me almost to a condition of 100 percent patriotism and imperialism. He was himself born in America and his father, he tells me, died as an American citizen, whatever that means, and he thinks he knows a lot about America, when he is really completely ignorant of everything outside of New York publishers' offices. He asked me where Cape Cod was, also St. Louis. I had already been coming to the conclusion that the United States was due about now to become the salvation of the Western world and, if anything had been needed to convince me, Lewis's attitude toward England, which he also extended to America, assuring me that America was just as bad as Europe since the war, and in exactly the same way, was all that was needed to clinch me . . .

To WILLIAM K. ROSE   April 4, 1960
                                                   Cambridge
Dear Mr. Rose: I don't believe I have any letter of Lewis's, certainly none of any interest. I first met him sometime in the twenties when Holliday of the Holliday bookshop in New York took me to lunch with him at the Algonquin. I saw him several times on that visit. The last time I saw him was after the war began, when he had felt obliged to leave England on account of his previous admiration for the Nazis. He came to see me at *The New Republic*, and seemed to want me to help him in some way but never appeared again, and I heard that he had gone to Canada. I don't remember any letter as late as 1951.

I have always been curious to know who and what he really was. In a conversation about him with Sibyl Colefax and T. S. Eliot, I discovered that he had told each of us a different story about where he had been born. He had told me in Philadelphia; one of the others, on a boat in mid-Atlantic; and I believe that during his days in Toronto he said that he had been born in Canada. In his memoirs, he has a photograph of his mother and father but tells you nothing at all about them. I came to the conclusion that he was somebody's illegitimate son. Can you throw any light on this?

I did not particularly like him, and did not like his writings, though I thought some of his pictures were very good when I saw the exhibition at the Tate Gallery. His delusions of persecution, which he would never seem to shake off, were a nuisance, and I always had an uncomfortable feeling that I was dealing with someone not completely sane. I used to wonder what it was that was wrong with him.

Yours sincerely, Edmund Wilson

To WILLIAM K. ROSE   April 15, 1960
                                                   Cambridge

Dear Mr. Rose: Thank you very much for your interesting letter. I thought that Lewis was afraid of being thought to be pro-Hitler because when he came to my office at *The New Republic* he brought a copy of his book on the Nazi movement. He said he was going to leave it with me in order that we could see what he had really said about Hitler. "Some people were fooled about Hitler," he said pointedly, "but then other people were fooled about Stalin." But he took the book away with him.

You know that when Lewis was in Toronto he saw something of Morley Callaghan, and he may have written him letters.

Yours sincerely, Edmund Wilson

RUSSIAN LITERATURE
1941–1944

I always enjoy talking to Russians, who, like Americans, have rather an outside point of view on Europe.

I wanted to remind you, too, about Vladimir Nabokov, of whom I spoke to you when I was in Princeton . . . His English is perfect (he went to Cambridge, England). I'm amazed at the excellence of the book reviews he's been doing for me [in *The New Republic*]. He is a brilliant fellow . . .   (To Christian Gauss, 1940)

To VLADIMIR NABOKOV   October 20, 1941
                                                          Wellfleet
Dear Vladimir: I've just read *Sebastian Knight*, of which Laughlin has sent me proofs, and it's absolutely enchanting. It's amazing that you should write such fine English prose and not sound like any other English writer. You and Conrad must be the only examples of foreigners succeeding in English in this field. The whole book is brilliant and beautifully done, but I liked particularly the part where he is looking up the various Russian women, the description of the book about death, and the final dreamlike train ride (as well as the narrator's long dream). It makes me eager to read your Russian books, and I am going to tackle them when my русский язык * is a little stronger.

I hope you will get somebody at Wellesley to read your proofs—because there are a few, though not many, mistakes in English. You tend to lean over backward using *as* instead of *like* and sometimes use it incorrectly. The critic's remark about Sebastian's being a dull man writing broken English, etc., is not a pun, but rather a *bon mot*. If the conjuror with the accent is supposed to be American, he would never say *I fancy*, but probably *I guess*. I am sure that your phonetic method of transliterating

---
* Russian (language).

Russian words is one of those things that you are particularly stubborn about: but I really think it's a mistake. It looks outlandish to people who don't know Russian and is confusing to people who do. I boggled for some time over your version of А у ней на шейку паук.* Combinations like *neigh* and *sheik* (and do these really represent the Russian vowels?), into which I fear you have been led by your lamentable weakness for punning, are not the logical phonetic way of representing these sounds; they introduce irrelevant ideas. You were right in thinking I should object to *smuggled smugness,* though in other cases your sensitivity to words provides you with some admirable observations and effects. I agree about the word *sex*—it is an awful word. But what about *Geschlecht—das Geschlecht!*

Now, can't you and your family come up here and spend Thanksgiving (the third Thursday in November) with us, staying on afterwards? We'd love to have you and have plenty of room for you all. If you're tied up for the holiday at Wellesley or otherwise, perhaps you could come up some weekend—almost any after the first of November? In the meantime, we may be in Boston some weekend before then, and we might have lunch or something . . .

I haven't really told you why I like your book so much. It is all on a high *poetic* level, and you have succeeded in being a first-rate poet in English. It has delighted and stimulated me more than any new book I have read since I don't know what.

Our best regards to you both.   As ever, Edmund Wilson

To VLADIMIR NABOKOV   April 20, 1942
                                        Wellfleet

Dear Vladimir: If I had the leisure, I'd be glad to translate your book. I'd like to see you translated, and I'd probably learn a lot of Russian. But I've got so many things to do that I couldn't possibly. I'm working on a couple of books, and I think I'll have to take on a part-time job that has been offered me at Smith. The truth is, besides, that my Russian is so uncertain that going over my work would probably be nearly as much trouble for you as translating the book yourself. How about Alexander Werth, who translated Ognyov's *Communist Schoolboy?* You don't have to have an American, do you?

I acquired in New York a volume of your poems called Горный Путь [*The Empyrean Way*]. I didn't know it existed. It looks like an *oeuvre de jeunesse.*

I'm glad you'll soon be back in this vicinity—will look you up when I get to Boston.

---

* Ah-oo-neigh na sheiku pah-ook: There is a spider on her neck.

By the way, I find that Henry Sweet in the article on Phonetics in the Encyclopaedia Britannica confirms my opinion that in Russian all the vowels tend to be long. What we do with longs and shorts you do with softs and hards. Since reading more Pushkin, I think I understand better the misunderstandings behind our argument at Stamford. Mirsky speaks of the versification of one of Pushkin's dramas—I forget which—as showing the flexibility of Shakespeare's later plays. When I read the play, I found that this was ridiculous. Beside the verse of Shakespeare's later plays, Pushkin seems pedantically regular. He almost never varies the iamb, whereas with Shakespeare any substitution is possible. I don't remember in Pushkin even any such verse as "Never, never, never, never, never!" in *King Lear*. It may be that neither you nor Mirsky, trained on classic Russian verse, quite realizes what English verse is like. I read French poetry for years without really understanding what they were up to—and probably don't fully understand yet.

There is a wonderful example of the handling of soft and long l's in the *Skazka o Tsare Saltane* [*The Tale of Tsar Saltan*]:

Ты, волна моя, волна! *
Ты гульлива и вольна —

This kind of thing, of course, we have in English; but my theory is that it is more important in Russian. Don't you think that Pushkin is particularly good when he is describing the way things *move*?—as he gives the movement of the wave with the alternating l's. Don't the л's *look* like waves, too? Also the ballet girl in *Evgeni Onegin* and the wonderful picture of the cat creeping after a mouse in *Graf Nulin*.

Best regards from us both to Vera—I hope she is better for her vacation. It will be nice to see you again.   As ever, Edmund W

To Vladimir Nabokov   June 12, 1942
                                                        Wellfleet
. . . By the way, don't you think that Pushkin in the Русалка [*The Mermaid*] intended to have the Prince come back insane after an interview with the mother русалка [the mermaid] herself? Isn't that what his speech about insanity at the end of the scene with the miller-raven portends? He would come back and be unable to make connections with the human family at home. The wife is developed on a scale which makes one think that she must be meant to figure later in an even more pathetic way.

---

* "O thou, my sea, my sea!/So indolent and free."   —E.'s translation

375

August 8, 1942
Wellfleet

Dear Vladimir: How are you? I've been reading more Pushkin, with great enthusiasm, and wish you were around to talk to—Nina Chavchavadze is rather inadequate on such subjects. I was disappointed in Каменный Гость [*The Stone Guest*] and don't quite see why Mirsky thinks it is a masterpiece. Цыганы [*The Gypsies*] is a masterpiece, though; and the humorous ones, Граф Нулин [*Count Nulin*] and Домик в Коломне [*The Little House in Kolumna*], seem to me absolutely wonderful, though they don't seem to be so much read. (I found at Cambridge, however, that the beginners in Russian at the summer school were being made to memorize Граф Нулин!) What are the theories about Домик в Коломне, of which Mirsky speaks? There *is* something a little queer about it? Do you know what the theory is about the countess whom he sees at church and who has no obvious connection with the story? Also, do you think he had any intention beyond what is obvious in the Гавриилиада [*The Gavriliada*]? Did he mean to imply that we can't be sure whether Christ was the son of Gabriel, the Devil, or God? The part about the Garden of Eden is quite beautiful—I prefer it to Milton on the same subject.

We are still pursuing our activities up here regardless of Clifton Fadiman and Pearl Harbor. I hope that Vera is better in the country. Do let us know when you are back. As ever, Edmund W

I met while I was lecturing at Smith an extremely intelligent Russian woman who speaks and writes English absolutely perfectly . . . She is Helen Muchnic. (To Vladimir Nabokov, 1943)

To Helen Muchnic November 15, 1942
Wellfleet

Dear Miss Muchnic: I've been reading your Dostoevsky thesis and think it is awfully interesting. I'd like to talk to you some more about the Russians. Couldn't we do something again this week after the seminar, with anybody you like? Let me supply the drinks this time. I'm afraid you will have had more than enough of me, but I have only three more visits to Northampton and want to arrange to see more of people before it is over. I'll bring you Proust and Дьявол.*

Yours sincerely, Edmund Wilson

To Helen Muchnic November 28, 1942
Wellfleet

Dear Miss Muchnic: Yes: I'd love to have another evening of the Russians. I want to hear you talk about Dostoevsky—I've done too much talking

---

* *The Devil* by Tolstoy.

myself when I've seen you before . . . The part about Dostoevsky and the other novelists in Proust, by the way, begins on page 236 of the second volume of *La Prisonnière*.   Yours sincerely, Edmund Wilson

To Helen Muchnic   February 9, 1943
                                   215 East Fifteenth Street, N.Y.
Dear Helen: I'm not very well posted about Russian plays. Have you looked into Ostrovsky? I saw a play of his in Moscow—Таланты и Поклонники [*Talents and Admirers*]—that seemed to me awfully good—and it is probably the kind of thing that amateurs could do. There is a volume of Soviet plays translated: Хлеб, Страх [*Bread, Fear*], etc. There is a revolutionary play called Дни Турбиных* which is supposed to be better than any of these. I gather that it is quite exciting, and a real revolutionary piece of the earliest vintage, i.e., of just after the Civil War.

You are very appreciative of Nabokov. I haven't read Подвиг [*The Exploit*], but it sounds like the other things of his I know. I have been saving up his books to read when I've been through more of the classics.

I'm glad you liked my poems. I doubt whether I'll write many more, though. I might do one or two more longish ones like the ones in the second section.† "The Good Neighbor" owes something to Pushkin's tales, by the way. I'm still reading Pushkin and find that I sometimes have entirely different ideas about the merits and interest of his respective works from the conventional Russian ones. Полтава [*Poltava*], which is a national classic, seems to me, for example, though very finely written, relatively dull; whereas Братья Разбойники ["The Robber Brothers"] and the unfinished Тазит ["Tazit"] much more characteristically Pushkinian and interesting.   Yours as ever, Edmund W

To Helen Muchnic   April 22, 1943
                                   Red Bank
. . . I was interested in Chernyshevsky on Tolstoy. I never know quite what you mean, though, when you say that Tolstoy only writes about himself—he seems to me more objective than Dostoevsky and to give even more the illusion of creating independent beings. I've just read Смерть Ивана Ильича [*The Death of Ivan Ilyich*] and was a little bit disappointed in it. Such a man as that could never exist: if he was capable of that last moment of grace, his life would have had something more to it than Tolstoy allows it in his description. It is a clever enough parable for Tolstoy's later moral purposes, but rather irritating after *War and Peace* and *Anna Karenina*, where the characters are so humanly convincing. I'm reading Исповедь [*Confession*] now—there is something about all this side of

---

* *The Days of the Turbins* by Mikhail Bulgakov.
† *Note-Books of Night.*

Tolstoy that interests me just the same—his feeling of having run through all the satisfactions that you can get out of the things men do, and asking, what then? I can understand this feeling—but where he loses me is where he turns to religion. I think we have got to learn how to get along without religion, though I don't know how it is going to be done . . .

To Helen Muchnic   June 8, 1943
                                                     Wellfleet
Dear Helen: Thank you very much for sending Mary the *Gallic Wars*—it is just what she wanted. It is very pleasant up here, and I am delighted to get back. You must come to see us . . .

About the Comintern: I don't think the announced dissolution of it really means a thing. I've just been reading a symposium on the subject in the socialist *New Leader*, by a variety of labor leaders, journalists, and radicals, and not one of them takes it seriously. Have you seen Earl Browder's letters to the *Times*? When he was interviewed by reporters on the subject, he said that it didn't affect him at all, as the American Communist Party had been disassociated from the Comintern since 1940. This is supposed to have been true, of course, but the American C.P. has continued to be, just as it was before, simply a tool of the policies of the Kremlin. The truth is that the Comintern has for years been merely a setup of dummies. The Communist Parties abroad have really been directed by the GPU and the Soviet Foreign Office.

I have been reading Griboedov's Горе от Ума [*Woe from Wit*], which I found appallingly difficult. The long speeches are almost as much trouble for me as the choruses in the *Agamemnon*. I called in the assistance of my neighbor Nina Chavchavadze (whose husband is a great-nephew, I think, of Griboedov's wife of the same name), and was rather relieved to discover that she didn't understand it all either. It is full of archaic words and locutions, and written very tersely and colloquially in extremely closely organized verse; but it moves with so much liveliness and rapidity that it has carried me over its many obstacles. I think you said you had never read it. You should sometime, because it is really brilliant—something halfway between Beaumarchais and *Hamlet*. I've also been reading Barbey d'Aurevilly, whom I'd never explored before. I had an instinct that his book *Les Diaboliques* had something in common with the stories I am doing.* I find that I was right, but Barbey's stories are not so absolutely wonderful—though not at all bad—that they discourage me.

It was so nice to see you, as it always is. Good luck to your book and your garden from us both.   As ever, Edmund Wilson

---
* *Memoirs of Hecate County.*

378

To Helen Muchnic   September 28, 1943
                                                              Wellfleet
Dear Helen: I am going down to New York the week of October 10.
Could you have dinner with me that Tuesday or Wednesday night? I
take back what I said about Gogol's probably losing less than other
Russians from being translated into English. I finally came to the conclusion that, on the contrary, *Mertvye Dushi* [*Dead Souls*] must be about
the most difficult book to translate, because the language is so important
and special. I began by thinking the Russians overrated it, but ended by
being very much impressed by it. He did well to call it a poem, however:
it doesn't have the solid reality and clear atmosphere that one expects in
Russian fiction. It is really all a monologue by Gogol in which the similes
are just as real as the incidents because the incidents, too, are images that
represent emotions and impressions of Gogol's and take form and dissolve
in his mind. The houses and the people that Chichikov visits are not
really known and created as the Rostovs and the Bolkonskys are. They
are goblins that, as Harry Levin says, have their Walt Disney side. Do let
us talk about Gogol when I see you. He is certainly a very strange man.
Mertvye Dushi has given me the creeps; but it is magnificent just the
same. Some passages—troika, Chichikov imagining his dead serfs, the
picture of Russian revelry against the dark background of the forest that
figures Russia in the scene at Pushkin's house—have a dense and sustained poetry that seems to me much more extraordinary than Chateau-
briand or De Quincey. I seem to be writing a literary essay . . .
                                                       As ever, Edmund W

To Vladimir Nabokov   November 1, 1943
                                                              Wellfleet
. . . I have just read Gogol's *Viy*, which is certainly one of the greatest
stories of the kind ever written. That little wooden church out on the
edge of the town with the dogs howling around it is wonderful . . .

To Helen Muchnic   August 7, 1944
                                                              Wellfleet
. . . The Nabokovs are here in Wellfleet and the Grynbergs* in Provincetown. We all had dinner together the other night. Vladimir and I have
been giving each other quizzes on our respective languages. Here is one
of his most interesting questions. How would you answer it? Put into
Russian the following sentence: At the harbor I saw many masts and had
many daydreams (using мечта† for daydreams.) . . .

---

* "Roman Grynberg . . . He is extremely well-informed about Russian literature."
† *Mechta:* daydreams; *machta:* sail.

379

To Helen Muchnic   October 25, 1944
                                                    The New Yorker

Dear Helen: . . . You can feel perfectly free to use Nabokov's translations.
The "Mozart and Salieri" came out in *The New Republic*, and most of
the others are about to appear in a little pamphlet published by New
Directions—which your students could get when it comes out . . . You
might drop a line to Nabokov (8 Craigie Circle, Cambridge), asking him
whether he minds your using his translations.   As ever, Edmund W.

   You ought to take in the movie Пиковая Дама [*Queen of Spades*] if
it is still on when you get to New York. It seems to have been made in the
Occupation, and, without departing very widely from Pushkin and
Tchaikovsky's opera, the producer (said to have been active in the underground) seems to have weighted it with anti-Nazi implications. The old
countess is France and Hermann the invading Germans. He tries by
violence and monomanic determination to wrest from her the secret of
her power and prestige and causes her to collapse, but, after her defeat,
she undoes him and mocks him. It set me to thinking about the meaning
of the fable again. It is certainly a very strange story.

To Helen Muchnic   November 1, 1944

   . . . Tchelichev tells me that I am all wrong about the *Pique Dame* film:
it was made ten years ago . . .

To Helen Muchnic   November 1, 1944
                                                    The New Yorker

Dear Helen: You should have asked Doubleday for $250 down and $250
on delivery of manuscript.* That is what Donald Elder intimated to me
they would give you. But what he wrote you leaves the way open for you
to ask for some more later on. It is better to collect what you can as an
advance because (a) it gives the publisher more stimulus to sell the book
and get his money back and (b) you will not be able to collect your
royalties till *ten months* after the book has come out. (You get the
report at the end of six months but, by one of the swindles of the publishers' trade, they don't send you the money till four months later; in the
meantime, they are using it for their own purposes and of course ought to
be paying you interest.) I am trying to get you started out as not quite so
much a babe in the woods as most beginning authors are. You must get
over the instinctive idea that the publishers are doing you a favor or have
anything in mind but their own gain.   As ever, Edmund W.

---

* *An Introduction to Russian Literature from Gorky to Pasternak.*

To Alyse Gregory   November 25, 1941
                                                         Wellfleet

. . . It was very pleasant to hear from you . . . and to hear that my book was making an impression in England (it has done rather badly over here) . . .*

To Alyse Gregory   April 9, 1942
                                                         Wellfleet

Dear Miss Gregory: The repetitions of words you speak of leap at me every time I open the *Finland Station*. Someday I may be able to correct them.

"Muzzy" is a perfectly good English word. It has a derivation, though I have forgotten what it is. I have always liked it ever since I saw it in Wells's *Tono-Bungay*.

We are very much isolated up here—almost at the end of Cape Cod. I never could work much in New York.

I agree with what Anatole France says about *Adolphe*. I was much relieved when I read it—just after I had read the novel.

I'm so glad you enjoy De Quincey. He's always been a favorite of mine, and I don't think people read him much nowadays. He is one of the few really *great* literary journalists. I never could read Hazlitt—can you?

I'm writing a kind of long novel,† whch I am afraid is going to take years, as the *Finland Station* did, as I keep having to interrupt it, as I did the *Finland Station*, in order to do other work . . .

My wife is dark—half Irish. She is twenty-nine—has just written a book of fiction which seems to me very remarkable (Mary McCarthy—her name; the book is called *The Company She Keeps*) . . .

---

* *To the Finland Station.*
† Unfinished novel.

I have adopted this itemizing method of answering letters, because writing without transitions makes me nervous, and this seems to me the logical way of dealing with the problem.

I enclose Marianne Moore's characteristically oblique memoirs of *The Dial*, which I thought you might find entertaining. They appeared in a magazine called *Partisan Review*, of which my wife used to be one of the editors and to which I have to some extent contributed. It is much the same sort of thing as *Horizon*—the best thing of the kind we have had during these last years, I think. I hope it may survive the war, though most of the subsidized magazines are going under. On second thought, I will mail you two copies under separate cover: the Van Wyck Brooks controversy might interest you, too. It was awfully pleasant to hear from you and to know that you liked my book.

Yours sincerely, Edmund Wilson

The critic I was telling you about. I think you ought to see his studies in contemp. Am. lit.   (To John Peale Bishop, 1941)

To MAXWELL GEISMAR   April 25, 1942
Wellfleet

Dear Max: You are much too grateful about the Guggenheim. Max Perkins did as much about it as I did: he told me that you were the first non-Scribner's author he had ever recommended. Also, Moe's judgment, as I told you, is extraordinarily clairvoyant. What you want to remember, most of all, is that what a writer like you gets (if he gets anything), he gets on his own merits. You are too grateful to people for recommending you just as you are too grateful to publishers for publishing you. On the other hand, of course, the other thing can be overdone. I got Jim Tully's first book published—*Beggars of Life*—back in '24 or '25. I had seen him in Hollywood and he was growling that the publishers in New York were all too respectable to bring out a raw hunk of life like what he had just written. I told him this was nonsense and took the MS back to N.Y. with me. The first publisher I showed it to—Boni—brought it out, and Jim Tully came on to the East—he never wrote me or looked me up, but I heard he was going around complaining to people that I had done him an ill turn, because I should have gotten him a better publisher. Years passed: a year or two ago I suddenly got a letter from Jim Tully, speaking of something I had written and thanking me for marketing his first MS. He went on to complain that the Eastern publishers were all so respectable that they would not print the kind of raw bleeding stuff he wrote. The fact that I belong to an older generation is rather painfully brought home to me by my tendency to tell you these old anecdotes. It is a real disease of encroaching age.

Love to Anne and the kids. Tell the latter that I have perfected an improved model of the mouse that has wings and flies. I hope the baby will soon have arrived happily.   As ever, Edmund W.

To Maxwell Geismar   May 6, 1942
                                                                    Wellfleet

. . . About Eliot: he has certainly not been done so completely that there's no point in writing about him. On the contrary, the trouble is that he's fallen into the hands of the most pedantic and limited school of poetry critics and that though they have written about him interminably so that people are tired of hearing about him, nobody has really done him from the social and human point of view. I didn't either, in any complete way. He certainly is one of the first-rate writers of his time—though I don't think he is exactly a great writer like Yeats, or even perhaps of the stature of A. E. Housman. I didn't care much for *The Rock*—or *The Family Reunion*, or those later long poems . . .

To Maxwell Geismar   May 27, 1942
[Postcard]   Wellfleet

Dear Max: I can give you my impressions of Eliot better in conversation when I see you. He is, as you say, full of contradictions, which are quite obvious when you meet him. His opinions when he writes them always seem judicious and specific, but his personality is really rather incoherent, and that is what his poetry comes out of. But I felt about him that he was probably the most highly refined and attuned and chiseled human being that I had ever met and couldn't help being rather awed by him. I gave him bootleg gin—he is so shy that you have to drink with him to talk to him—and we both got into bad condition. The next morning he had an awful hangover and said his joints creaked, and I felt as if I had wantonly broken some rare and exquisite vase. I have felt guilty about it ever since.
                                                                    EW

To Maxwell Geismar   June 10, 1942
                                                                    Wellfleet

Dear Max: I have just read the last chapter of your book* and have been trying to get an idea of the thing as a whole. Here are certain suggestions I want to make† . . .

There did, of course, develop out of a period of literary whoopee a kind of general social consciousness in fiction during the period you are writing about; but it seems to me that when you come to write about the

---

* *Writers in Crisis: The American Novel, 1925–40.*
† Three pages of suggestions, corrections, and errata omitted.

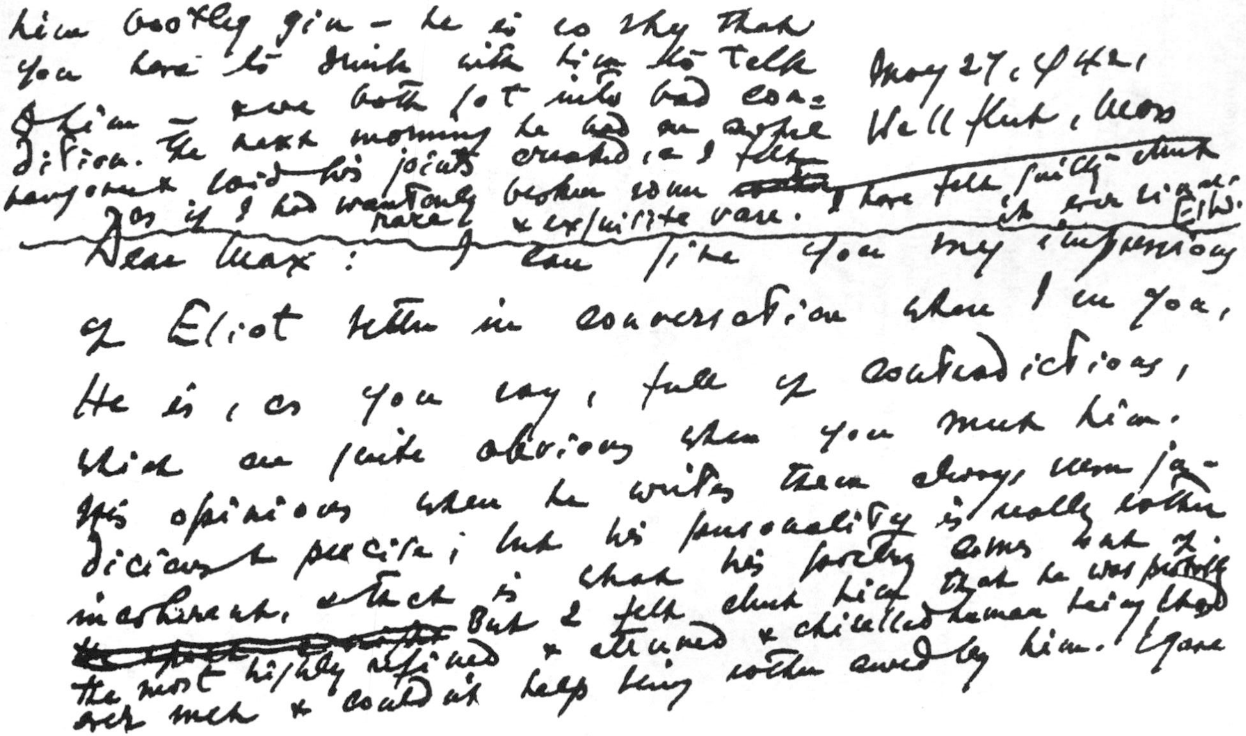

See letter to Maxwell Geismar, May 27, 1942

immediately preceding period, you ought to take into consideration that there had been a lot of social consciousness during the period between the Civil War and World War I. I've just read Howells's *A Hazard of New Fortunes*, which, though I think it's rather overrated as a novel, is certainly full of socialist social consciousness—as all the later work of Howells was. Edith Wharton's *The Fruit of the Tree* was quite Marxist. Upton Sinclair, Edward Bellamy, and Jack London were all socialists of one kind or another. Robert Herrick, Henry B. Fuller, Frank Norris, David Graham Phillips, and Harold Frederic were all, I gather, more or less acutely aware of social problems. So was George Cable, though in connection with a community which may not seem typical of the situation of the rest of the country after the Civil War. The truth is that the fireworks of the twenties were in the nature of a drunken fiesta in the general course of American thinking since the Civil War.

I think, too, that you tend perhaps to overestimate the artistic and intellectual importance of the social-consciousness enthusiasm that mounted so rapidly during the thirties. Aren't MacLeish and Sherwood, whom you cite, as well as most of the other people that you mention on page 288, as well as Steinbeck, perhaps, himself, really second- and third-rate writers? May it not possibly turn out to be true that they represent merely the beginning of some awful collectivist cant which will turn into official propaganda for a post-war state-socialist bureaucracy? With MacLeish and Sherwood at the White House as they are now, the whole thing makes me rather uneasy. It may be necessary for a subsequent set of writers to lead an attack on phony collectivism in the interests of the American individualistic tradition. One hopes not, but we don't know. You try to forestall this situation by what you say on page 289, and I approve of the ideals which you formulate in this chapter, but I shouldn't trust the Steinbecks to realize them, let alone that list of fellow travelers on page 288. One question which has still to be disentangled is the relation of the Russian Communist influence to the tradition of true American radicalism which you will encounter when you go back of the twenties. This influence has sometimes been seen in work that was distinguished and sincere, but it has sometimes nourished writers who might lend themselves to something like Fascism with a readiness in proportion to the closeness of the approximation of Stalin to Hitler—which is a good deal more readily than I can imagine that patriarchal old Southern landowner Faulkner doing.

All this doesn't mean that the story you tell doesn't have its validity as an account of what went on in fiction during the period with which you are dealing. It is only that I am not quite sure that the work got intellectually and artistically better as the writers got more socially minded. You already know how well I think you have told this story.

Best regards as ever, Edmund Wilson

"The Wound and the Bow"

> . . . he did not hesitate to assert himself as a single unique human being: he was not afraid to be Alexander Woollcott; and even when Alexander Woollcott was horrid, this somehow commanded respect.
>
> (*Classics and Commercials*, 1943)

To ALEXANDER WOOLLCOTT   February 16, 1941
                                                   Stamford

Dear Woollcott: The Kipling and the Dickens both are coming out along with other things in a book that is supposed to appear in July. The Dickens is rather a long affair which has a great deal more in it than came out in the magazine articles. The Kipling I am revising now, and I should be extremely glad of any further light on Kipling and the Balestiers. Do write me about it. I didn't know about the Waugh memoirs—I'll look them up.

I wish you would write something about Kipling's American adventures. My uncle was his doctor when he was at Lakewood, and he never paid the bill. I have heard a number of sour stories about him and no pleasant ones. And where is that memoir of the Phalanx you were going to write?

How are you? I was glad to hear from you—sorry to hear of your illness on the Coast.   Yours sincerely, Edmund Wilson

I heard you on "Information, Please," and was shocked at your indifference to *Bleak House*, which I've always thought perhaps Dickens's most successful book.

To ALEXANDER WOOLLCOTT   February 22, 1941
                                                   Stamford

Dear Woollcott: I'm afraid I can't get to Washington or Philadelphia—though I should like to see you. I have to stay here to work on my book.

I have read "Proofs of Holy Writ" since I wrote the version of the Kipling that is coming out in *The Atlantic*. I've just rewritten the whole essay, so that it is a lot better—and I'm rather sorry you read it in the magazine. I've just discovered the original ending of *Great Expectations*. Did you ever read it? If you haven't, you can find it in the Public Library. There's no question it's much better than the other one.

I've rewritten *The Crime in the Whistler Room*, too, and have no doubt that it will be triumphantly revived.

                                        Sincerely, Edmund Wilson

To Alexander Woollcott   March 4, 1941
Stamford

Dear Woollcott: I was very much interested in your account of Kipling, which has done a good deal to fill in my picture. It was kind of you to take the trouble to write me at such length. I hope that we can meet sometime and talk about it. Yes: I have seen the piece about *The Tempest* —though it hadn't occurred to me to connect it with *Captains Courageous*.

Reading your letter has made me feel that you could probably write a wonderful book about all that period—as well as before and after. Why don't you?   Yours sincerely, Edmund Wilson

To Florine Katz   March 1, 1941
Stamford

Dear Florine:* I asked Perkins about Max Geismar, and he told me that his reason for not taking the book was that he had already arranged to publish my essays and that he was afraid of publishing anything about Hemingway, no matter how appreciative, because he carries on like a madman about everything that is written about him. However, I have insisted on having a piece on him in my own book,† and I think this might have the effect of paving the way for Geismar's. Perkins is completely sold on him and spoke with the greatest enthusiasm of the essays he had seen. He said that he would like to see the others, and I think that Geismar, unless in the meantime he finds another publisher, ought to try him again later on. My book is supposed to come out in July. Please tell Geismar to keep it under his hat about Hemingway . . .   Edmund W.

To Florine Katz   March 7, 1941
Stamford

Dear Florine: My letter about Max Geismar needs a slight corrective in view of recent events. I gave my manuscript to Scribner's a few days ago, and when they laid eyes on my essay on Hemingway, they protested that they could not print it, and as I refused to withdraw it, broke their contract (though on terms pretty favorable to me)—this in spite of the fact that the essay had appeared in *The Atlantic Monthly*, that Max Perkins had read it and knew it was to be included, that what it said was mainly favorable, that they had made me a considerable advance, which they are forfeiting, and that they had been genuinely enthusiastic about publishing it. Hemingway has been getting worse (crazier) of late years, and they are scared to death that he may leave them. So you may conclude that Max Geismar's chances with them are not very good. Please tell him to

---

* Florine Katz was a friend of the Geismars and the Wilsons.
† "Hemingway: Gauge of Morale."

let me know if I can do anything to help him market his book. It must be good because Max Perkins thinks so highly of it. I am trying Houghton Mifflin with mine.   As ever, Edmund W

To Maxwell Perkins   June 9, 1941
                                                               Wellfleet
. . . Hemingway has heard about my book and is threatening to get an injunction against Houghton Mifflin to prevent their publishing it; but I don't think he is going to get anywhere with it. Houghton Mifflin have already printed 3,000 copies of the book . . .

To Maxwell Perkins   July 3, 1941
                                                               Wellfleet
. . . Hemingway has been raising holy hell about my Houghton Mifflin book—which is, however, coming out in August. I made only a couple of slight changes in what the lawyer was able to show were misstatements of fact . . .

To Morley Callaghan   1962
Toronto
. . . I have just read *That Summer** with, of course, intense interest. You have performed the feat—rare in the literary world—of writing about other writers truthfully and with understanding and yet without malice. You must be the first person—I haven't read the family memoirs—who has really told what Hemingway was like. You evidently got the benefit of the charming side of both him and Scott more than I ever did. I saw Hemingway —always on his visits to New York—probably not half a dozen times, and my relations with Scott were somewhat embarrassed by my position of seniority and mentorship at college, from which he never recovered. You speak, somewhere near the beginning, of "fierce passions" which, without your expecting it, were to be set off in Paris by your relationships with one another. If you meant this to be taken seriously, isn't it a little strong for Hemingway's childish sulks and a certain youthful touchiness from which all of you seem to have suffered? A good deal of the story is extremely funny. It will probably, in any case, survive as a classic memoir, like Trelawny on Shelley and Byron . . .

To Morton D. Zabel   July 5, 1941
                                                               Wellfleet
Dear Morton: We were awfully glad to hear from you. We've acquired a house up here, but had to do so much to it that we weren't able to move

---

* *That Summer in Paris: Memories of Tangled Friendship with Hemingway, Fitzgerald and Some Others.*

388

in till about a week ago. We're hoping to give a housewarming in September, so do try to come up and be here then.

About Russia: I'm still hoping they'll be too much for Hitler. It is significant that he's already complaining about the weather. It rains all the time in that part of the world in summer, and that may interfere with his advance. I'm reading *War and Peace*, which gives me a feeling of comfortable assurance that the story is coming out right.

Philoctetes* is coming out the middle of August—I'll have them send you one. I'm lecturing at Columbia for a week in August—am writing Louise to find out whether she and Maidie will be away then and whether I could stay in her apartment. Our literary activities have been rather impeded by constant moving and interruptions, but we are still forging ahead . . .   As ever, Edmund W.

"The Shock of Recognition"

To MAXWELL GEISMAR   September 11, 1942
                                                              Wellfleet

. . . I did finally get a title: *The Shock of Recognition*—from a sentence in Melville's Hawthorne essay: "For genius, all over the world, stands hand in hand, and one shock of recognition runs the whole circle round." What do you think of it? . . .

To H. L. MENCKEN   March 23, 1942
                                                    The Princeton Club

Dear Mencken: I am getting out an anthology of American criticism, and want to include your essay on Dreiser from *A Book of Prefaces* and a piece on the prose style of President Harding called "A Short View of Gamalielese," which you published years ago in *The Nation*. I am arranging with Knopf about the former of these. I hope you will have no objection to my reprinting it, and I hope very much that you will also let me use the Harding piece, which I believe is not included in any of your books. I admired it very much when it came out, and have just looked it up and reread it and it seems to me as good as it did then. I want to have some discussions of examples of the peculiar kinds of bad writing which have come to flourish in America—Poe on some of his contemporaries, Mark Twain on Cooper, etc.—and nobody in our own time has handled this kind of thing so well as you. The piece is certainly as good as the best things you reprinted in your *Prejudices* and oughtn't to be

---

* *The Wound and the Bow.*

left buried. If you are willing to let me include it, please let me know what anthology fee we should pay you.   Yours sincerely, Edmund Wilson

To H. L. Mencken   June 3, 1942
                                                                     Wellfleet
Dear Mencken: As I know that you are usually prompt in answering letters, I am afraid that something may have gone wrong about a letter I wrote you a couple of months ago asking whether you would allow me to include two pieces of yours in an anthology I am getting out. The anthology is a collection of American critical documents written by first-rate figures about other first-rate figures: Emerson on Thoreau, Henry James on Hawthorne, Santayana on William James, etc. I wanted to use your piece on Dreiser from *A Book of Prefaces*, and shall be able to get Knopf's permission for this. I also wanted to get an old piece of yours about the prose style of President Harding—"A Short View of Gamalielese" —which appeared in *The Nation*, April 27, 1921. It has remained in my mind ever since I read it, and when I looked it up lately, it seemed as good as it did then. I wanted to include some discussions of characteristically bad American writings: some of Poe's comments on his contemporaries, Mark Twain on Cooper, etc., and I do hope you will let me have this. I believe you have never reprinted it, and it ought to be preserved. I would pay you an anthology fee or royalty, whichever you would rather have.   Yours sincerely, Edmund Wilson

To H. L. Mencken   June 10, 1942
                                                                     Stamford
Dear Mencken: Thank you very much for your letter and generous permission to use your pieces. I called at the Princeton Club before writing you again, but your first letter has vanished without a trace. Nothing has been as it should be there since the Dartmouth Club moved in on us.
                                                  Yours sincerely, Edmund Wilson

To Van Wyck Brooks   September 11, 1942
                                                                     Wellfleet
Dear Brooks: I am getting out a sort of anthology of American literary documents—not literary criticism proper, but the American writers on each other: Lowell on Poe, Emerson on Thoreau, Henry James on Hawthorne, Howells on Mark Twain, etc., etc. I wanted to include also the series of letters written to you by Sherwood Anderson and published in the Anderson memorial number of *Story*. This seems to me a very interesting document because it indicates Anderson's idea of his relationship to Whitman, Mark Twain, and others. I have the permission of Mrs. Anderson and also of the editors of *Story*, and I should like to have your permission to

use your notes and introduction. I am paying Eleanor Anderson for the letters and will pay you whatever you like.

I hope your new book is flourishing. I liked part of *Oliver Allston*— the part that seemed to me to have been written years ago; but I hopelessly disagree with most of what you say about the moderns!

Yours sincerely, Edmund Wilson

I was interested in what you said about the size and shape of critics. I hadn't thought about it before, but believe there is something in it.

To MAXWELL GEISMAR   December 12, 1942
                                                            Wellfleet

. . . I'm correcting proofs on my anthology and reading up a lot of American classics that I hadn't read before. I'm surprised to find that I like Cooper very much . . .

To Max Eastman   August 27, 1942
                                                  Wellfleet

. . . I'd like to talk to you about your poem [*Lot's Wife*], which I've just read. I wish you would give it another month or so of work before you publish it. It ought to be wonderful, but you really haven't got it into shape. It is full of lines that are metrically impossible—I don't mean merely irregular, but impossible to read—and stop-gap phrases where you haven't yet found the right words. Where you *have* found the right words and written the lines, though, the style has a realism and vigor quite different from anything I remember in your other poetry. I think you learned something from Pushkin for it. The Americanisms mixed in go surprisingly well. I like particularly the opening about Caedmon and the description of Sodom (the city itself) and of Lot and of the daughters. When I started it, I thought it was going to be tops; but as I went on, it got to seem to me like an uncompleted draft of which only parts had been *menés à point* . . . Have you shown it to Edna Millay and Cummings? I think it might be a good idea to. The story is splendid: when I looked up Genesis, I saw that it was right there, but nobody else seems to have thought of it . . .

To Max Eastman   October 5, 1942
                                                  Wellfleet

Dear Max: I have been looking at *Lot's Wife* in book form, and it seems to me somewhat better—perhaps because I steer clear of the poor parts as I do in rereading Dickens. But do make the next one a masterpiece!

                                                  As ever, Bunny W

To Max Eastman   November 15, 1942

Dear Max: Our controversy about your poem seems to be rolling up with what Trotsky used to call geometrical progression, and I haven't answered your letter before because I haven't had a chance to digest the mass of materials which you have sent me . . .

In regard to my criticisms in general, they were stimulated, not by preconceived ideas about metrical rules, but by the fact that I stumbled over certain lines in reading the poem. Then, when I wrote you, I analyzed them to see what was the matter. I am often not aware of rhyme patterns or even meters when I read poetry; and if you had handled your off-rhymes and delayed rhymes more dextrously, I should probably never have noticed them. Your story held me as a reader, but I kept coming croppers over those things. Since you invoke a scientific basis of discussion, I recommend to you Oliver Wendell Holmes's essay on "The Physiological Basis of Versification" (in a volume called *Pages from an Old Volume of Life*—I wish I had a copy to send you), which seems to me absolutely sound. He says that our system of beats and pauses is based on the rhythms of the breath and the pulse, and that the metrical phenomena that jar us and seem to us impossible are violations of these rhythms and produce some sensation of physical constraint. Are you sure that your heart and your respiratory system were all right when you wrote parts of that poem?

I am, in any case, giving you an opportunity to retaliate by sending you a volume of verse of my own. But don't tell me you have found off-rhymes in it! My point is not, as you seem to suppose, that off-rhymes are not the thing to do, but that they have to be handled with some system.

I have enjoyed *Lot's Wife* . . . and our controversy. Most of the poetry and writing about poetry put me right to sleep. Ted Spencer, by the way, on a small scale, seems to me one of the better people. I'll send you his little book from Boston. I reread the other day your translation of Pushkin's "October." It is a beautiful poem and one of the only two really first-rate translations of P. I have ever seen—the other one of "Anchar" by Nabokov . . .   As ever, EW

To Allen Tate   January 31, 1943
                                                        230 East Fifteenth Street, N.Y.
Dear Allen: I think these poems are extremely good—though I feel about them, somewhat as I did about the other one, that while the general picture is clear, it is not clear stanza by stanza precisely what you are saying. What one reads is merely the images, not definite statements you are making; and though the images and language are wonderful, this always worries me a little. I think it would be worthwhile to send them to *The New Yorker*, and will do so if you approve. The *Pervigilium Veneris* I had already sent to Weeks [*The Atlantic Monthly*]. Why don't you give *Partisan Review* the one you sent me first—thereby improving their poetry department?   As ever, Edmund W.

To ALLEN TATE   March 20, 1943
                                                            Red Bank
. . . I'm eager to see your new poem. It may be that from one point of
view your spell at Princeton was a good thing for you: I think it is sometimes a good thing for a writer to stop writing altogether—as I did when
I went to Russia. When he starts in again, he is able to pick up from a
new point, and his abilities, instead of being atrophied, turn out to have
been refreshed . . .

To HELEN MUCHNIC   June 30, 1943
                                                            Wellfleet
Dear Helen: I have delayed so in answering your letter and thanking you
for the radishes because I had to go away for a week and got no chance
to write any letters. First of all: we were delighted with the radishes. I
am especially fond of radishes, and these are the best I have had for years.
When I was a child, I used to cut them in little slices and eat them on
bread and butter, and I ate a great many of these that way, made the
better part of a lunch and a supper on them. Many of the radishes you
buy or get in restaurants have been allowed to get too big and coarse, and
the taste is too sharp. You seem to have pulled these just at the right time.
   Let me take up the other topics seriatim:
   1. I like some of Hardy's poetry, but I don't think it is really first-rate.
I'm not sure that his prose is either, though his novels are better than his
poems. I haven't read him since I was in college, so that I don't have any
very fresh ideas on the subject. I used to object to the practical jokes that
he made God play on his characters, and regretted that he gave up novel
writing just when, in *Jude the Obscure*, he was beginning to make the
fate of his people depend on their own personalities.
   2. I don't care much for Allen Tate's essays, though there are a good
many good things in them. It is as a poet that he is really remarkable.
   3. The opening scene of the *Antigone* between the two sisters is
wonderful. The note of Antigone's character is struck perfectly in that
first speech, and the whole tragedy is anticipated in Ismene's failure to
understand her passionate feeling.
   . . . I've been asked to lecture on Russian literature at Yale. They're
going in for Russia in a big way. They offered me a full-time job, but I
am, of course, not qualified for it, and shouldn't take it now if I were,
because I want to do other things. I have agreed to lecture for a week in
the fall, and am trying to persuade them to ask you and Nabokov and
other people to come on and lecture about special subjects.
   We want very much to see you . . . we hope to have a Finnish girl
helping out here. She is writing a novel and wants a part-time job. I
hope it will not be too many writers in the household. Good luck with
your book!   As ever, Edmund W.

To Morton D. Zabel   July 15, 1943
                                                                 Wellfleet

. . . I was much interested to hear about your reconciliation with Louise.
You see that the course of conduct I recommended turned out to be
efficacious . . . I've got a series on Russian literature coming out in *The
Atlantic,* and have done a piece on Joseph Davies's prose style which
may be the first of a series in the *Mercury.* The proposition at Yale is at
present in rather a state of vagueness . . . My principal idea at present is
to make a little money writing articles and get my book of stories done.*

By the way, I reread Kipling's horror story, "At the End of the Passage,"
the other night. For some reason I didn't reread it at the time I was doing
that essay, and now, good God! I discover that it ought to have been my
prime document. Take a look at it from that point of view. The horror
that scares the man to death comes straight out of that experience of
Kipling's childhood, and the spur that he sleeps with to keep himself from
being overcome by it is an obvious symbol for Kipling's extroversion on
discipline, mechanical techniques, etc.

I played the *Figaro* album all over again the other night when I was
on the verge of writing something about Pushkin and Mozart. I must get
the rest . . .

To Morton D. Zabel   September 20, 1943
                                                                 Wellfleet

Dear Morton: I was awfully glad to get the Musorgsky songs (properly
so spelled). Most of these I had not heard. The one called "Ballade"
I had in the other album; but, as you say, this recording is much better.
It happens to be one of my favorites of Musorgsky's songs—the first one
that made an impression on me. A musical friend of mine with whom I
shared an apartment just after the last war in New York used to play
it on the piano.

I neglected, while you were here, to talk to you about your Graham
Greene article. I think it is one of the very best of your pieces of this kind;
and I wanted for that reason to mention the only passage that I felt
weakened it. At this point, I referred to the article and find the passage
less obscure than I had thought when I first read it. I think I do understand what you mean; but it is the kind of thing that tends to make your
writing seem rather opaque in spots:

> "The identity Greene's heroes pursue is the selfhood of a con-
> science implicated in the full mystery and terror of their natures;
> if the 'destructive element' engulfs them, it is their resisting pas-
> sion for a spiritual destiny that stains and brightens the flood.
> And it is because he sustains a dialectic between the oblivion of

---

* *Memoirs of Hecate County.*

naturalism and the absolute tests of moral selfhood that Greene has brought about one of the most promising collaborations between realism and spirituality that have recently appeared in fiction," etc.

It seems to me that this is an example of brilliant writing running aground in abstraction. An assemblage of abstractions is likely to become meaning-less—that is, to become unintelligible. In the first sentence here, you are trying—what is difficult—to state Greene's essential point of view, and by imagery and poetic vocabulary as well as by a kind of philosophical analysis, you admirably succeed. But then, when you have him sustaining a dialectic between the oblivion of naturalism and the absolute tests of moral self-hood, the reader is likely to draw a blank: he is first checked by being uncertain as to whether it is Greene who is being oblivious of naturalism or naturalism which is being oblivious of something, and what follows, with its further abstractions stretched along after this ambiguous one, is likely to give the reader the feeling that the whole thing has faded out. This is not at all a flagrant example; but in some of your articles you lead the reader into a regular briery bush of these abstractions, and it isn't always possible for him to jump into it a second time and get his eyes back again (as I think I have been able to do with this one). I know from my own experience that one of the great difficulties about literary criticism is finding ways of making general formulations of the qualities or points of view that appear in imaginative writers. If one is tired or stale, it becomes arduous to produce a concrete imagery of one's own or a pointed way of putting things, and one tends to fall back on piling up abstract phrases that to the reader are simply a wad of words. I think that this was really what that man was getting at who was trying to kid you about some article of yours in a letter in *The New Republic* of some time back, and I believe that to some degree he had a legitimate complaint. Even in the case of the present brilliant piece, he might have felt, as I say, that you had eluded him when you seemed just on the verge of making the final revelation. Of course, another thing that happens is that when one gets to the end of a short article like this, written for a paper like *The Nation*, one finds that one has only arrived at the fundamental problems of the subject, which one hasn't got the space to deal with, and the most that one is able to do is knock together a few unsatisfactory phrases. But do watch these festooned abstractions—and forgive this gra-tuitous advice! On second thought, I withdraw the excuse just suggested above. You have no business doing such little articles at all. You ought to be saying something definitive in books that would be absolutely sound in style and thought!

. . . I've been reading Stendhal's autobiography, the *Vie de Henri Brulard*. It seems to me very remarkable—in its method quite unlike any other book of the kind. But, curiously enough, in spite of the dryness and precision of the writing, it is something like James's memoirs: Stendhal is trying to tell only what he really remembers, regardless of inconsistencies and lacunae, and he is presenting the whole thing as a frankly subjective record. It progresses not like a chronicle but with a curious spiraling movement.

We look forward with lively expectation to your adventures in Brazil. Remember your peculiar responsibility to Anglo-American culture down there. Your only predecessors have been Kipling and Waldo Frank!

As ever, Edmund W

> Why is it that the novels of Miss Dawn Powell are so much less well known than they deserve to be? . . . Her real theme is the provincial in New York who has come on from the Middle West and acclimated himself (or herself) to the city and made himself a permanent place there, without ever, however, losing his fascinated sense of an alien and anarchic society. ("Dawn Powell: Greenwich Village in the Fifties," in *The Bit Between My Teeth*, 1962)

To Dawn Powell   October 4, 1943
                                                              Wellfleet

Dear Mrs. Ward: You will recall that for the last ten or fifteen years you have been in the habit of sending me your books, and that I have been filing them away as things I must someday read along with Newman's *Apologia pro Vita Sua* and works in foreign languages that require the use of a dictionary. You will be glad to know that I have finally read two of them, and that I am as much surprised as delighted to find in them a fund of wit, humor, and lively observation. I had definitely made up my mind years ago that you could not be any good as a writer; and, after telling you so frankly, I believe, on the occasion of our last supping at the Pickwick, I decided that I ought to check up on my intuitions—which have very seldom betrayed me. Imagine my amazement at discovering how good your novels are and that I had been taking you all these years for an incompetent! I was enchanted by *Angels on Toast* and am now devouring *A Time to Be Born* with voracity. Don't imagine, however, that I don't think there is plenty wrong with them. I do, and I am eager to tell you about it. Will you not spend next Thursday, the 12th, with me—beginning with rather a late breakfast. I shall call you up Sunday morning.

Yours always cordially, Ernest Wigmore

To Dawn Powell   November 13, 1944
                                                          The New Yorker

Dear Mrs. Humph: What I was groping for in our conversation at the Café Royal last Friday was the thought that the reader of your novels

397

WIGMORE BROODING ON "MARCIA'S CASE," ROMAN = FLEUVE IN 8 VOLUMES — STUDY SPECIALLY DRAWN FOR THE HERALD TRIBUNE BY JOHN SARGENT

For years Dawn Powell and I carried on a correspondence in which she was supposed to be Mrs. Humphrey Ward and I a seedy literary man named Ernest Wigmore. Later on, we were a sophisticated French pair: Raoul and Aurore.   —Note in E.'s handwriting attached to Dawn Powell's letters

who is just settling down for a treat of a high order is likely to find himself suddenly landed in something akin to George Kaufman—mere comic ideas, i.e., gags. One doesn't need to be an addict of Walter Pater to be disconcerted by the experience. If you don't like what I said about Katherine Anne Porter, substitute Gogol instead.

I am sorry, however, that I chose—without knowing it—such an unfavorable moment for unloading my criticisms. I am terribly sorry to hear that you have been laid low by so menacing (as Marianne Moore once wrote me years ago when I came down with the measles) and immature a disease; and I hope that I didn't contract it from you in the course of our close conversation when we were sputtering and snarling across the table. Please be sure to let me know if there is anything I can do for you in the way of supplying you with reading matter or whatnot.   Ever thine, Wig

I have stuck the delightful pictures in my mirror.

To ALLEN TATE   September 28, 1943
                                                            Wellfleet

. . . It is difficult for me to think of anything that I should be less likely to write than an essay on the influence of Symbolist poetry. I will go even further and say that it seems to me absurd in the extreme for *The Kenyon Review* at this time of day to devote a special number to the subject. And I will even go on to explain that I would not write anything whatever at the request of *The Kenyon Review*. The dullness and sterility and pretentiousness of the *Kenyon*, under the editorship of Ransom, has really been a literary crime in this period when the market for serious work has been so limited. Mary and I have both sent Ransom some of the best things we have written of recent years, and he has declined to print any of them—invariably keeping them for months and usually not sending them back till we wrote him or wired him. Of Mary's book he published a stupid and impudent review apparently composed by the office boy; my books he has not reviewed at all. I should be glad to have you send him this letter, as I should have written him in some such terms if the request had come directly from him . . .

To ALLEN TATE   October 22, 1943
                                                            Wellfleet

Dear Allen: I was very much pleased and honored to get the *Pervigilium Veneris*, which has just arrived. No kidding: it must be one of the best verse translations from Latin ever made. What really rejuvenates the poem and makes it your own is your getting away from the original meter, which makes it impossible to put any backbone into it in English. The introduction, too, is just right . . .

I brought the Henry James number of *The Kenyon Review* back from

New York and Mary has just read it all. I could only read it in patches, and she confirms my impression that it almost all sounds as if it had been written by the same person. It does seem to me to show an extraordinary lack of something or other on Ransom's part to get up these symposia on these very obvious subjects such as Henry James and Symbolism which have already been written to death, and induce a lot of writers, most of them mediocre, who have really nothing to say on the subject, to contribute articles about them—instead of finding out what people who are worth reading have written or want to write. Everybody we have seen has been complaining about this. The Yeats number of *The Southern Review* was a monstrosity. It didn't so much honor Yeats as make a fool of *The Southern Review* by the discrepancy suggested between Yeats and his commentators . . .

Mary, by the way, has been reading your Jefferson Davis poem in Horace Gregory's gruesome anthology, and wanting me to explain to her what it means. I finally had to confess to her that I couldn't. Why is Davis another Orestes? Is this some reference to history that I don't know?

I'm going to be in New York again next week . . . so do let me know if you are there. Our conversation the last time was troubled and curtailed.   . . . As ever, Edmund W.

To Christian Gauss   September 28, 1943
                                                                         Wellfleet

. . . I have been indulging my periodical dreams of starting a new literary magazine. I have very definite ideas about what could be done—I believe that I know at this moment of enough first-rate unpublished material to fill such a magazine for six months; and I am convinced that this would be the moment to launch such a project, because the old publications of the kind are mostly dead or decayed and there will probably be at the end of this war a new period of literary activity, as there was at the end of the last one, which a new magazine could help to promote and exploit . . .

THE
NEW YORKER

No. 25 WEST 43RD STREET

1942–1960

To HELEN MUCHNIC   April 22, 1943
                                                      Red Bank
. . . I am strongly reacting against academic communities after trying to
do something with teaching and rather enjoying it at first. Now I've
decided that the whole thing, for a writer, is unnatural, embarrassing,
disgusting, and that I might better do journalism, after all, when I have
to make money. (Please don't tell them this, though, at Smith!) . . .

To ALLEN TATE   May 12, 1943
                                              25 East 86th Street, N.Y.
. . . About the Louisiana job: I'm afraid that twelve hours a week is a
pretty heavy schedule, and I've decided to try to hang on with journalism
and publishers' advances . . .

To HELEN MUCHNIC   October 10, 1943
                                                      Wellfleet
. . . They have offered me Clifton Fadiman's job reviewing books on *The
New Yorker*, and I've decided to take it for a year, though I doubt
whether anything good but money will come of it . . . *

---

* E. wrote for *The New Yorker* from 1943 to 1972.

Dear Ross: Why don't you start a literary magazine and make me editor? The subsidized highbrow magazines are folding up because, on account of the war, their subsidies are being taken away from them: *The Southern Review* and *The Kenyon Review* have gone, and *Partisan Review* may go. On the other hand, *Harper's* and *The Atlantic* are so stuffy and second-rate that nobody interested in literature reads them. Except for *Partisan Review* in its small way, there is not at the present time a single magazine in the country that publishes serious writing.

I am convinced that such a magazine could be a success. There is no question that the material exists to make it brilliant. I believe that I could list offhand enough first-rate work—stories, poems, essays, etc.— by writers I know or know of to fill half a dozen numbers (the magazine I contemplate would be a monthly). It would also have regular critical departments, heavier than the ones in *The New Yorker* but, unlike most of that stuff in *The Nation* and *The New Republic*, done by readable and first-rate people.

I'll bet I could make such a magazine go, and it shouldn't cost such a terrible lot to get it out for a year. You may think that the present time is an unfavorable one for a literary magazine, but I don't believe this is true. On the contrary, the English magazine *Horizon*, which does on a much smaller scale what I should want to do, has been a considerable success and there has been, I understand, more demand for it than they are able to get paper to supply.

The New Yorker in my opinion is the only American magazine outside the Luce group which shows any imagination, and the only one that has any real distinction—so I thought I would suggest this idea to you. It seems obvious and perfectly sound: there is certainly a place for a magazine of this kind. But I know from having tried it some years ago that it is hard to get anybody to put up money. In other countries such magazines are published by book-publishing houses; but it seems to be impossible to get the New York publishers interested. There was *The American Mercury*, published by Knopf. I imagine it was a success when Mencken and Nathan were running it.   Yours sincerely, Edmund Wilson

I've had a good deal of editing experience—was managing editor of *Vanity Fair* and literary editor of *The New Republic* for years.

Dear Ross: Thank you for your letter. I forgot that you didn't publish *The New Yorker*. Yes: I'd be glad to have you talk to people about the idea.

I agree with what you say about business managers. Bad business managers have especially been the curse of literary and idealistic magazines. When I used to have visions of reorganizing *The New Republic*, I had a prospect picked out—a man who had been successful in a slightly different field; but he now has a job in Washington.

Do let me know if you hear of anyone who would back me for a couple of years.   Yours sincerely, Edmund Wilson

To Harold Ross   May 22, 1942
                                                           Wellfleet

Dear Ross: Thanks very much for all your trouble. Aside from the magazine question, I'm looking for some kind of regular—preferably part-time—job, and I'd be glad if you would let me know if you ever thought there was anything I could do in connection with *The New Yorker*. I don't know whether I would really fit in there; I could handle some kind of department, I suppose—though I imagine that most of your departments are run by people well over military age. There might be special articles of a kind I could do sometime. The point is that I am working on a book that is going to take me years and be completely unsalable to magazines, and I'll have to do something else in the meantime.   Yours sincerely, Edmund Wilson

To Harold Ross   October 17, 1943
                                                           Wellfleet

Dear Ross: Here are some points that we ought to discuss in connection with the book-review job:

1. *The New Yorker* has always had the practice of not mentioning the name of publishers. Couldn't this be changed? I have found it a nuisance. I never get used to it: I look up some book in *The New Yorker* to try to find out who publishes it and am always frustrated. I think it also does a certain amount of injustice to small or obscure publishers, as it sometimes makes it difficult to order their books.

2. I believe that Fadiman has been in the habit of doing all his work at home; but would it be possible for me to have an office there, to which the books could be sent and in which I could work? Also, could I have the services of some secretary in the office? The work for her would consist merely of typing my articles, doing letters in connection with the books, and making a comprehensive list at the beginning of every publishing season with their dates of publication.

3. What have you been in the habit of doing about books on the theater, music, art, and the movies? At *The New Republic*, we occasionally had problems come up about these, as the people who wrote regularly on these various things tended to claim all books on their subjects, and

to try to prevent other people from writing about them. If your writers in these special departments control the books that deal with their subjects, it is perfectly agreeable to me; but I should like to get it clear at the beginning. In the ordinary course of things, I should want to write something, for example, about such a book as Sir Thomas Beecham's autobiography. Louise Bogan, of course, does all the poetry, and is one of the best people writing on the subject. I believe that in her case there have been one or two conflicts of interest between Fadiman and her. That will not happen with me, because she is an old friend of mine, and I should be glad to have her write not only about poetry but about books of criticism of poetry and biographies of poets, if she wants to.

4. How would you feel about an occasional article on a reprint or somebody's collected works? I don't think Fadiman has done this.

5. Can't we have some signed agreement about my copy not being changed by other people? I don't anticipate trouble of this kind, but I should like to have it stipulated that *The New Yorker* will print what I write unless it chooses to suppress my articles or me altogether. (This does not, of course, apply to questions of the libel or obscenity laws, which of course I don't expect to get you into trouble with.) The only thing that worries me in this connection is the problem of dealing on occasion with books that raise religious problems. I have no intention of persecuting any religion; but I am myself a complete unbeliever, and I know from experience that both the Catholics and the Christian Scientists invariably make an awful squawk if anything critical is said about them. I remember that *The New Yorker* once printed a piece of mine in which I made fun of the Buchman group; but I have had the impression, perhaps wrongly, that you have been more careful about hurting the susceptibilities of the Catholics. Now I know that the Catholic Church as a pressure group is a formidable power at the present time; but I think it is important to stand up to it. For example, I have just read the Catholic biography of G. K. Chesterton, published by Sheed and Ward. If I had been reviewing books, I should certainly have had to review it; and if I had reviewed it, I should certainly have had to say that it suffered from the intellectual squalor of the Catholic Church in America. This would have brought you indignant letters and probably some people would have stopped their subscriptions. In the case of *The New Republic*, what the Catholics did didn't matter; but it may be more serious with you.

6. How would it be if I tried it for a year at $10,000, with $3,000 for expenses? I should move down to New York sometime in December and start my articles the first of the year. During the months when I should be in the country, I could make regular trips down to town.

7. I'll be in New York again the first days of next week and could

404

come in to see you Tuesday or Wednesday afternoon if you will let me know when you will be free.   Yours sincerely, Edmund Wilson

To James Thurber   May 15, 1959

Dear Jim: Thank you for having your book sent me.* I read it, of course, with delight. You have built him up more and made him more attractive than you did in the *Atlantic* installments. Both as a literary portrait and as a chapter in the history of journalism, it will certainly be a classic.

Here are a few comments on details:

p. 9. You have that scene in *The Gold Rush* turned around. It was Charlie, not his companion, who turned into the chicken.

p. 71. Waldo Frank tells me that it was he who invented *The New Yorker*'s use of profile. He wrote the first ones, you know.

On I don't know what page: "spinach." Frank Crowninshield used to use this word to mean unimportant space-filling matter. I always thought it was an old word of the trade.

Also—p. 85—the old lady in Dubuque. Crowninshield used to say, when confronted with something that he feared was too esoteric: "Remember, there's an old lady sitting in Dubuque, and she has to be able to understand everything we print." I do not think he invented this idea: he did not really take it seriously, treated it as more or less of a joke. I thought it was some old cliché of New York editorial offices. The slogan of *The New Yorker*—that it was *not* intended for the old lady in Dubuque—was, I think, simply a defiance of this cliché.

It seems to me rather queer that Ogden Nash should have valued Ross's praise so highly. I never thought he knew anything at all about anything *I* was writing; but maybe I underrate him.

That story about Harold Winney is amazing; but I am so careless about money myself that I am wondering whether, had I been in Ross's place, the same thing could have happened to me.

It occurs to me that Ross's conception of himself as continually perplexed and frustrated may have been somewhat reflected in the humorous pieces, rather typical in one period of the magazine, in which people were always helpless to cope with some commonplace situation. Or Ross perhaps, due to his own difficulties, found them specially sympathetic. People at one time in *The New Yorker* were always being "puzzled," and one of [Rogers] Whitaker's favorite words is still "puzzled." I was glad that you paid him a tribute, in spite of his early inimical treatment of

---

* *The Years with Ross.*

you. As Yeats said of Ernest Boyd's book on the Irish Renaissance, you "avoided many opportunities for malice."

Yours with much enthusiasm, Edmund Wilson

To James Thurber   July 15, 1959
                                                        Talcottville

Dear Jim: William Fenton has just been to see me. He is the great authority on the Iroquois Indians. He has been reading your book about Ross, and told me that, from the photographs of Ross and from your description of him, he definitely had the impression that he might be part Indian. It is possible that his suspiciousness, innocence, ignorance, deadpan humor, bursts of resentment and general feeling that everybody and everything was against him, and general inability to "integrate" in the social community were derived from an Indian strain. I remember his curious behavior in connection with my articles about Zuñi—in his Southwestern part of the world. He blocked them and made objections about them for weeks. He had never really wanted me to write them, and they had to be put over by Shawn.

We are going to be in West Cornwall next week, and I may give you a call.   As ever, Edmund W

Another Indian trait of Ross's: reckless and unscientific gambling.

                                                        EW

To Cap Pearce   1940
The New Yorker

... This is the only verse I have on hand.* Perhaps it may appeal to the nature lovers among your customers ...

To Cap Pearce   1940

... That poem is supposed to be dreamy and fluent, one thing pressing into another imperceptibly—hence the lack of punctuation. If you try to punctuate it any more, it will make less rather than more sense ...

To Cap Pearce   1940

Dear Cap: Though I approve in principle the rigorous editorial checking of *The New Yorker*, these seem among its less inspired suggestions. Summer, from my point of view and from the ordinary point of view, arrives any day toward the end of May or in the early part of June which is recognizable as a summer day. The days keep getting longer up to about

---
* "Birth and Death of Summer."

the twentieth of June. As for chlorophyl, it fades in the same sense that any coloring matter fades. I prefer the spelling with one final "l," which is the one recommended by Funk and Wagnall.

Best regards, Edmund W.

I've put in a little punctuation, which probably *is* needed.

To Louise Bogan   February 9, 1944
The New Yorker

Dear Louise: I thought this last set of poetry notes remarkably good. I agree about all three of those poets. I don't know why you sent me the Auslander book, by the way, unless you didn't want to have it in the house.

I have been getting the most abusive letters I have had since I came back from Russia and threw aspersions on Stalin. One lady who adored Kay Boyle's novel wrote me a letter which began: "I do not love thee, Dr. Fell."

We should like to see you but have despaired of ever luring you from the sibylline fastnesses of a Hundred and Something Street. Isn't Morton in South America going to be wonderful?

As ever, Elfton B. Wilsiman

To Louise Bogan   March 15, 1944
The New Yorker

Dear Louise: I made a few changes in the proofs of your notes—I thought the sentences were sometimes a little carelessly framed for your high standard. If you don't like what I've done, change it as you please. We'll call you up about dinner—I haven't got your card here. As far as I know, we'll be delighted to come. I've come down with gout, an affliction in my family which I'd so far escaped, and have been enacting the role of the irascible old man with one foot up on a chair. It seems to be passing off, though, today. I'm supposed to lay off liquor, and it really makes me feel I am aging. Watch for me on Louis Bromfield week after next!

As ever, Edmund W

To William Shawn   May 28, 1944
The New Yorker   Wellfleet

Dear Shawn: You now have three articles of mine for the issues of which the deadlines are May 29, June 5, and June 12. They ought to be run in this order: Rockets, Esmé of Paris, Jane Austen. I am coming to New York the 15th and will be in the office the following Friday and Monday. At that time I will give you another article—on Dali's novel. After that, I will take my vacation—though the weeks that I skip don't need to be

407

consecutive. There are a couple of books that I want to do coming out in the course of the summer—Woollcott's letters and Dos Passos's new book—and I will write about them at the time they appear. Besides these, I still have the anthropological books and Jaeger's work on Greek civilization, and I want to do something about *The Robe*. With my four weeks off, this accounts for nine weeks of the summer and should get me to the last week of August, of which the deadline is August 28. (I assume that you are not going to suspend publication every other week.)

There is one book coming out in the summer that ought to be seriously thought about: the final volume of Thomas Mann's *Joseph* series. I want to have this book done in one of the weeks that I skip, because I am really incompetent to write about it. I have never read Thomas Mann except for a few short stories and essays, and in order to review this book properly one ought at least to know the rest of the series of which it is the last installment. Ham Basso has probably read it. If he hasn't, I don't suppose you would think it a good idea to ask Fadiman to do an article for that one week? He is a great admirer of Mann and has followed the *Joseph* series.

Here is another problem. A man named Parker Tyler has written a book called *The Hollywood Hallucination*. It is a quite well-written attempt to study the Hollywood menace, and I should like to have something done about it in *The New Yorker*. Miss Farrell writes me that Lardner would like to see it, and the ideal thing would be for him to write something about it. If he doesn't want to do this, however, I want to run a note about it . . .   Yours sincerely, Edmund Wilson

To Hamilton Basso   May 28, 1944
                                                              Wellfleet
Dear Ham: . . . Shawn tells me that you are going to do the leading articles the weeks when I don't appear. One serious problem I am sidestepping: I don't know a thing about Thomas Mann, never having read anything by him except a few short stories. I haven't read the *Joseph* series at all, and the last installment of this is coming out this summer. It ought to be done, of course, by someone who knows the other volumes. I hope you will write about it if you do know them. Otherwise, I have suggested to Shawn getting Fadiman to do an article about it—as he is a great Mann and *Joseph* fan—though *The New Yorker* (and Fadiman) may not like this idea. Please let me know whether you are prepared to take *Joseph* on . . . A book that I had intended to write about, but which I have now decided to skip if it comes out this summer, as it is supposed to, is Henry Wallace's collected speeches and papers. I thought it might be worthwhile to characterize Wallace and discuss his ideas; but if this doesn't interest you, don't bother with it. Of course you can choose your-

self the books that you do articles about—though somebody will have to do something about Thomas Mann, the pride of German letters . . .

I hope you are getting along painlessly. I'm coming to New York the 15th and will hope to see you then.   As ever, Edmund W

To JANET TROXELL   October 18, 1944
                                                    The New Yorker

. . . Thank you for your note. Yes; I am indeed being overwhelmed by indignant letters from detective-story fans, all of whom tell me I have not read the right ones; but I am afraid that nothing could ever induce me to get through another detective novel . . .

To CHARLOTTE CHAPMAN   July 29, 1946
The New Yorker   Wellfleet

. . . Please try to get the Shaw birthday volume to me right away, as I want to send the article in next Monday. I think I will skip the Valtin. I'd like to have Matthew Josephson's *Stendhal* (September 19: Double-day) and Mary Colum's *Life and the Dream* (October 24: Doubleday). Keep the copy of *Animal Farm* for the checkers: I have a copy of the English edition—also keep the bound copy of Dos Passos. I wish, however, that you would get the checking department, when it is done with the books I review, to give them to you, so that they can be sent to me here. I have never seen bound copies of the Gertrude Stein book or the Cyril Connolly book. If the publishers did not send any, please get after them. Dodd, Mead really ought to be blown up for not sending the Shaw volume. I wish you would also order from Dodd, Mead, at my expense, if they've got them (in the "standard edition"), Shaw's *Love among the Artists* and the *first* volume (only) of *Our Theatres in the Nineties* . . .

To KATHARINE WHITE*   November 12, 1947
The New Yorker
Dear Katharine: I have read the Nabokov stories, and I think they are both perfect. Not a word should be changed. From the way you talked about "Signs and Symbols," I had imagined something like the work of the French naturalists at their most malodorous and ghoulish; but the details in Nabokov's story are of the most commonplace kind. The point is that the parents of the boy are getting "ideas of reference," too, and without these details the story would have no meaning. I don't see how anybody could misunderstand the story as you people seem to have done

---

* Katharine White was E.'s first editor at *The New Yorker*, long before he began to write regularly for the magazine.

or could object to the details in themselves, and the fact that any doubt should have been felt about them suggests a truly alarming condition of editor's daze. If *The New Yorker* had suggested to me that the story had been written as a parody, I should have been just as angry as you say he was (I'm surprised that he has not challenged somebody to a duel), and as I should be every time I get a *New Yorker* proof of one of my literary articles, if I thought I was obliged to take seriously the ridiculous criticisms made in the office and did not know, having once been an editor myself, that they were the result of having read so much copy that the editors could no longer pay attention to what was being said.

Besides this, there is, however, the whole question of *New Yorker* fiction—about which I hear more complaint than about anything else in the magazine. It is appalling that Nabokov's little story, so gentle and everyday, should take on the aspect for the *New Yorker* editors of an overdone psychiatric study. (How *can* you people say it is overwritten?) It could only appear so in contrast with the pointless and inane little anecdotes that are turned out by the *New Yorker*'s processing mill and that the reader forgets two minutes after he has read them—if, indeed, he has even paid attention, at the time his eye was slipping down the column, to what he was reading about. *The New Yorker* has got to the age when magazines get hardening of the arteries: it thinks it is obliged to supply something that it thinks its public likes and is continually afraid of jarring that public, though the only thing that any public wants is to be interested. It is also, as a humorous magazine specializing in comic newsbreaks, morbidly afraid of printing anything that could possibly seem unintentionally funny.

I am speaking mainly of the fiction; the nonfiction side, it seems to me, has been lately a little bolder. But I have a personal interest in the fiction side, too, because I have felt that there were stories in both my last two books that might perfectly well have appeared in *The New Yorker* and that the only thing that kept them out was that they were done from a sharp point of view, that they were not pale and empty and silly enough.

I have written this out at length so that you could show it to anybody who objected to the Nabokov story and use it perhaps in your anti-editing campaign.

I have just read "My English Education," and it, too, seems to me perfect for *The New Yorker*. I can't imagine what doubts you would have about it. It doesn't get anywhere, it is just a little reminiscence, but in this respect it doesn't differ from Mencken's childhood memories, of which *The New Yorker* printed any number. If it's a question of writing, as I thought you implied, I am not sure what is meant by the word *raiser* in the fourth line of page 5, but otherwise I don't see anything to which exception could possibly be taken. And since I have become aroused, I might go on, in this connection, to protest against the *New Yorker*'s idea of style. The editors are so afraid of anything that is unusual, that is not expected, that they put a premium on insipidity and banality. I find, in the case of my own articles, that if I ever coin a phrase or strike off a picturesque metaphor, somebody always objects. Every first-rate writer invents and renews the language; and many of the best writers have highly idiosyncratic styles; but almost no idiosyncratic writer ever gets into *The New Yorker*. Who can imagine Henry James or Bernard Shaw—or Dos Passos or Faulkner—in *The New Yorker*? The object here is as far as possible to iron all the writing out so that there will be nothing vivid or startling or original or personal in it. Sid Perelman is almost the sole exception, and I have never understood how he got by.   Edmund Wilson

To KATHARINE WHITE   November 5, 1948
                                                           Wellfleet

Dear Katharine: All the verses *do* deal with mistaken meanings. The point about "anotherguess" is that you think when you first see it, and never really get over the idea, that it has something to do with "guess"— whereas it is apparently one of the distortions of "another genus" (another sort of). I have never seen it hyphenated—it certainly isn't in the authors I mention. I can't have the "serifs" omitted, because it seems to me one of the best. What bothers you? Daniel Updike (I see that I spelled his name wrong) was one of the greatest, and I had supposed the most famous, of American typographers. I thus stand on my original text, and if you people don't want it the way it is, the priceless thing will go to Bill Benét.

I was glad to hear that Volodya was well. He had written me that he was a lot more comfortable in his job than he had been at Wellesley. By the way, when I showed him the first of those backward-rhyming poems of mine, he immediately produced a Russian quatrain he had written in which the whole of each line read the same backwards as forwards. This tendency to write poetry backwards may be one of the symptoms of the end of civilization.   As ever, Edmund W

To HELEN MUCHNIC   March 6, 1947
                                                           Wellfleet

Dear Helen: I was just going to write you to suggest that, since I want to review your book in *The New Yorker*, it might be a good idea for you not to dedicate it to me, as this might make it rather awkward for me to praise it as highly as I should like—and *The New Yorker* is particularly wary about anything that looks like logrolling. I should value very much the honor of your dedicating it to me, but I think that it is important, since this is your first book, to call people's attention to it.

I asked Doubleday to send me proofs, but they have probably forgotten it, and you might mention to them that I'd like to see page proofs. I'm delighted about your full professorship. Thanks for the valentine.

We've been leading an extremely quiet life up here—Elena working on the house, and I writing. It is a great relief after a year of rocky households, and I am really getting caught up on myself in a literary way.

I hope you will read the Malraux books. I have a very high opinion of him. He must be the most important French novelist since Proust.

I am disappointed in Volodya Nabokov's new novel and for that reason don't think I'll review it.* Am curious to see what you will think of it.

Love as ever, Edmund

To ALLEN TATE   September 27, 1945
The New Yorker

Dear Allen: Here are my suggestions for *The Sewanee Review*:

1. Poems and other things by Allen Tate. I think you have been influenced by Eliot in your policy of printing your poetry elsewhere. This, in my opinion, was a great mistake of Eliot's: he was trying to qualify as an Englishman by a conspicuous display of modesty. The result was that people bought *The Criterion* because it was Eliot's magazine and then found very little in it except tiresome articles by young men who were hanging around Eliot and whom he didn't have the energy to brush off. It would be absurd for you to follow his example.

2. If I were editing a magazine like yours, one of the first things I should do would be to get Paul Rosenfeld to write a musical chronicle like the one he used to do for *The Dial*. He is the best writer on music we have—the only one who is really a writer. *Modern Music*, the musical quarterly, seems likely to fold up, and there will be nothing but Virgil Thomson left. You will have to struggle with Rosenfeld sometimes about his style, but this is part of the editor's task.

3. Have you been reading any of the things that Anaïs Nin has been writing? I liked her little book of short stories, and I have just read a new book which she is getting out. This is the first section of a long novel based on her celebrated diary. I don't think she has quite got the hang yet of what she is trying to do, but the stuff has very brilliant passages, and is really extraordinarily interesting from the point of view of its exploration of the psychology of the destructive modern woman—the kind of thing we were talking about the other day. I think you ought to look into this book and ask her to send you some of the later chapters. Her address is 215 West Thirteenth Street.

4. John Jay Chapman, when he died, left complete manuscripts of

---

* *Bend Sinister.*

two small books: one on Goethe and one on Shakespeare's sonnets. I read the first of these and thought it was extremely good. It was rather along the lines of Gide's recent essay on Goethe: he tries to distinguish between the great genius and the stuffed shirt. The essay is extremely well written—he has taken a lot of trouble over it. The Shakespeare thing would probably be worth looking at, too. You can find out about them by writing to Chanler Chapman at Sylvania, Barrytown-on-Hudson, New York.

5. Paul Rosenfeld has just told me of the apparition of a young writer whose work he has not seen but who has impressed him as being rather remarkable. His name is David Moore—he is a nephew or something of George's—and he has been living in Richmond and went to college at Chapel Hill. Paul could tell you how to reach him.

6. I don't know whether you are interested in translated stuff, but somebody probably ought to do something about Moravia (Alberto), who is probably now the principal Italian novelist after Silone. *Horizon* has printed a very bad translation of one of his short stories; but it would be much more to the point to print the translation which is coming out in England of his short novel or long short story called *Agostino*. This translation ought to be good because it is by Arthur Waley's old girl friend, whose queer name escapes me. It is being published by Secker and Warburg, 7 John Street, Bloomsbury, London, W.C.1. If you write to Roger Senhouse, mentioning me, I'm sure he'll send you proofs. I read this book in Italian last summer, and, though I don't think Moravia is a master, he is a writer of some importance. He and Silone have really succeeded for the first time in rescuing Italian prose from D'Annunzio. Moravia writes a concise and sober style which is quite startling on the part of an Italian, and he is particularly interesting to a foreigner because he tells you about the things that are going on in Italy at the present time. There is a shorter story of his called "L'Ufficiale Inglese," about the British in Rome, which is an excellent picture of the relations between them and the Italians and would have a certain topical interest. I tried to get *Horizon* to run it, but don't know what they have done about it. I may have a copy of it in a box of books I sent from Italy.

7. How about Scott Fitzgerald's letters to you? Would they be worth publishing by themselves?

This is all I can think of at the moment, but I'll send you other suggestions as they occur to me. I think that, in general, as an editor you suffer from inhibitions in respect to anything which differs strongly in tone or technique from the work of your own group. I am much more of a journalist than you and like to astonish people with startling discoveries and novel juxtapositions.

. . . By the way, do you know whether anything was ever done about getting that fellow paid for compiling John Bishop's bibliography? Christian Gauss was going to speak to the library about it.

As ever, Edmund

To Allen Tate   December 4, 1945
                                                                   The New Yorker

. . . What's the situation about Pound? I've been feeling a little worried. I think that a lot of people haven't got the right attitude about him. I understand that Random House has excluded him from some anthology they're bringing out . . .

To T. S. Eliot   June 15, 1946
                                                                   Wellfleet

Dear Eliot: Yes: do come up here in July. Please let me know in advance, if you can, just when you will be able to come.

I am hoping to get some news from you about Pound. I've been worried by what I've heard, and I wish he could be quietly let out. I don't think that the writers and artists here have behaved terribly well about him. The case has never really been thrashed out in print, and nobody even knows what the evidence against him is. In any case, he is such a crackpot politically that his "treason" shouldn't be taken seriously. And he didn't admire Mussolini any more than Bernard Shaw and Winston Churchill did at one time!   Yours sincerely, Edmund Wilson

"EUROPE WITHOUT BAEDEKER"
1945

To Vladimir Nabokov   March 12, 1945
                                                       The New Yorker

Dear Volodya: . . . I get aboard my boat Wednesday—a little Norwegian
steamer that lands me in England. I'll be away from four to six months.*
Good luck in the meantime. By the way, if you really want an academic
job, you might write to Lewis Jones, president of Bennington, and say
that you are the person I mentioned to him a couple of years ago. I'm
sorry I haven't had a chance to see more of you this winter. Our conversations have been among the few consolations of my literary life
through these last years—when my old friends have been dying, petering
out, or getting more and more neurotic, and the general state of the
world has been so discouraging for what used to be called the humanities.
Love to Vera and Dmitri. I hope to see you all in the fall.

                                                       As ever, Bunny W

To Helen Muchnic   March 31, 1945
[Postcard]   London

Dear Helen: I'm writing this from the ship—have just arrived in England.
I didn't sail till about two weeks later than I thought at first, but had my
hands so full with all kinds of things that I couldn't have gone to Smith
anyway. I hope that things are going well with you. Do ask me up again
next year. I've brought some Russian books with me, but don't know how
much time I'll be able to work on Russian, as I'll probably have to go up
to Germany, and shall have to get up German, which I'm extremely bad
at. I wish life nowadays was a little more like the picture on the other
side of this card. Take care of yourself.   Edmund W

---

* A trip undertaken for *The New Yorker* magazine in the spring and summer of
1945.

WAR DEPARTMENT
BUREAU OF PUBLIC RELATIONS
WASHINGTON

This is to identify __Edmund Wilson__
(Name)

whose signature, photograph, and fingerprints appear hereon

as an accredited __news__ correspondent

representing __NEW YORKER MAGAZINE__
(Organization)

__25 West 43rd St., New York, New York__
(Location)

__Edmund Wilson__
(Signature of correspondent)

Loss of this card will be reported to the Director, Bureau of Public Relations, Washington, D. C., without delay, by the correspondent named hereon, together with a statement of the circumstances attending its loss.

Date of birth __8 May 1895__

Color of eyes __brown__ Color of hair __reddish__ Weight __200__ lb.

Height __5__ ft. __6__ in.

GPO 592244

Date issued __13 March 1945__

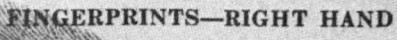

FINGERPRINTS—RIGHT HAND

THUMB

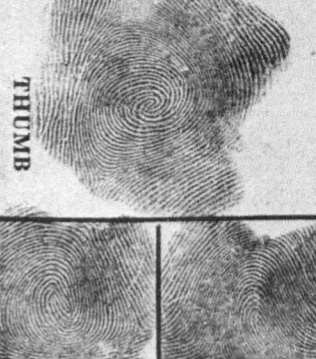

> A London girl whom I very much liked . . . She is an extremely
> bright and able girl, with the same sort of all-round competence that
> the young Englishmen from the universities have.
>
> *(Europe without Baedeker)*

To Mamaine Paget

April 28, 1945
AFHQ. PRO, Detachment A
A.P.O. 512, Naples

Dear Mamaine: I miss you and have been thinking about you almost all
the time since I left London this morning. I keep imagining your going
to places and seeing things with me and I must stop before I get addicted
to daydreams that can't correspond with any reality. The flight from
London to Naples today was one of the most fascinating trips I have ever
taken. We flew so low that you could see everything, and it was marvelous to have the map of England, France, and Italy unrolled underneath
you, all in a few hours. All the countries looked perfectly beautiful with
their various kinds of green and brown fields, sometimes with a few
clouds over them casting large shadows. I will skip descriptions—which
are a bore in a letter—but I wonder that the painters don't paint landscapes from the air: the effects are so different from anything else. At
the airport, I thought I wasn't going to get off again, as the British
officials, baffled in their first attempt, pounced upon the manuscript and
proofs of my book* and decided that it would have to be censored. The
man read quite a lot of it, and I think it was only Sylvester's [Gates]
name on the wrapping paper in which it had been sent that saved me
from having it held. The plane went only as far as Naples and I am going
to stay on here a day before going up to Rome. I took a long walk tonight
before it got dark. Naples is absolutely ghastly and makes the East End
of London look relatively cheerful. I saw nothing but either ruined streets
with fragments of walls rising like crumbled sand castles out of mounds
of pulverized plaster or battered buildings with garbage strewn on the
pavements, a few gruesome cuts in the butcher shops and thousands of
dirty children running about the streets. No police, no street lamps, no
traffic except an occasional donkey cart. Such lighting as there is seems
precarious and the lights in the hotel here have gone out several times
while I have been writing this letter. It is also very strange to go out of
the world of London—hotels and friends—into the world of the army,
and to find yourself, in Europe, being transported by American facilities,
with American food at every stop, and recent American magazines, and
even the New York papers handed you on the planes. There is also the
American conception of the various European cities—I will tell you the

---

* *Memoirs of Hecate County.*

legend of Naples when I see you. At the same time, it is all a little bad-dream-like going away from you now.

Please don't fall in love with anyone else before I see you again—and write me.

All my love, Edmund

A book (a new play) of Silone's has just appeared, the first thing of his that has been published in Italy. His magazine is advertized all over.

To Mamaine Paget   May 13, 1945
Albergo della Città, Via Sistina, Rome

. . . I have seen—and like very much—Silone and his Irish wife. He is very quiet and, I feel, a little *abattu*, but occasionally comes to life and makes a few trenchant remarks. I've read his new book, which I don't like much. It is a sort of Christian mystery play, all in terms of Fascists and anti-Fascists—partly based on *Bread and Wine*. He now seems to be engaged in trying to get the Christian value into socialism (so is Alberto Moravia), and he seems even to have had some sort of religious experience and to believe in God in some form. He read a long paper on this subject to a packed and impressed audience the other day. I sympathize with them for wanting to humanize socialism, but I always feel depressed and let down when religion raises its ugly head. Silone is one of the people on the central committee or whatever it is of the Socialist Party—he has just gone to Naples to see Blum. Of course it's hard for old radicals of his generation to get themselves started again. —I suppose that there's going to be an awful slump of almost everybody and everything all over Europe now. The fighting kept them up. I was in Milan just after the partisans had taken over and the Allied troops came in. They told me that there had been wild excitement during the first days of the expulsion of the Germans, the Mussolini execution, etc., but immediately afterwards everybody relapsed into a kind of state of tense exhaustion. The people looked awful: starved and stunned, and with deeply stamped expressions of anxiety and resentment such as I have never seen anywhere else. I'm very well fixed at the correspondents' hotel, with a room at the top of the house that has a balcony and looks out from the Pincian toward St. Peter's. Stendhal used to live in the next street and writes about having had a similar view. What I have been writing in this room has so far, however, been rather inferior to Stendhal . . .

To Mamaine Paget   May 22, 1945
Rome

. . . I went to the country last Sunday for lunch with an American woman married to an Italian Prince Caetani, who has a medieval place out on the edge of the Pontine Marshes. I was taken out by the British minister to the Vatican along with a young Englishwoman, the daughter of somebody named Cadogan in the Foreign Office. They had a wonderful very low-voiced and almost telepathic conversation on the way, which made me brood on the shortcomings of the British abroad. We passed through towns absolutely demolished by shellfire and bombing, where we could see families visiting around in half rooms, the other half having been completely destroyed. My companions through all this kept remarking with quiet disapproval on how well fed and well dressed the people on the streets looked in comparison with the people in England—which was not at all the case. And the only comment on the ruins made by your minister was when we passed some sort of church that had been blown up and he murmured: "Sad to see that shattered." When we arrived at Ninfa, however, we found the whole American delegation to the Vatican, the regular minister and his wife, and Roosevelt's "personal representative," a monumental product of the steel industry (one of the men who have made it what I told you it was), named Myron C. Taylor, and his terrific wife—they seemed to me so awful—so stupid, so uninteresting, and so unappetizing—that the English guests seemed charming by comparison. There was also a big-finance Italian, the Italian representative of J. P. Morgan, if you know what that is: the New York bankers; and I began to feel as if I were taking part in one of those now very old-fashioned Soviet melodramas in which types of the various Western nations are seen —caricatured by a few obvious national traits—preying on the people of China or somewhere, while an insurrection is brewing. The difference, however, was that, instead of being greedy and ferocious, all these people were rather subdued and fully expecting left developments in Italy. The only person I really liked was the old prince, who was pleasant and rather amusing, worried about the drought and mainly occupied with getting his place into shape after the various things that had happened to it in the war, and who disappeared soon after lunch. I decided that, after all, the Latin peoples did have something gracious and human that the Anglo-Saxons lacked. Later I found out that his mother was English and that one of his grandmothers had been Polish. I'm not sure what the moral of all this is.

Day after tomorrow I'm going out into the country for three days with the UNRRA people to see their efforts to distribute food and medicine. —I've just read *Pane e Vino* of Silone, which is certainly awfully good and so much better than the semi-religious play he has made out of one of the episodes in it. I've realized, however, in reading it, that Silone has himself a good deal of the priest about him. —I've met quantities of people here— some of them most attractive and interesting. You must come here and see them, too, and then we can talk about them . . .

To Mamaine Paget   May 28, 1945
                                                                     Rome

. . . I was interested in your account of V-E day (this "V-E" business is idiotic). It was just like that in 1914 during the bank holidays after the first war was declared: people rode around on the tops of taxis and gathered in front of Buckingham Palace and made the King and Queen come out on the balcony—they would yell, "Mary! Mary! We're wyting!" I think that the people are pathetic on occasions like this: they don't really know what they're cheering about, just that they're expected to make some demonstration. The ends of wars are never exciting: everybody has seen them coming and everybody is completely worn out. At the end of the last war I was in Chaumont, the American GHQ in France. A few French and American soldiers got drunk and walked through the streets brawling feebly. An American newspaperman in the army whom I'd been having dinner with kept saying, "Well, b' gosh, we beat Purdue!"—by which he meant to compare the celebration to the excitement over a football victory in a very small Middle Western college. Here in Rome it was also on the Purdue level. —I've just had dinner with Dorothy Thompson and her husband, whom I'd never met before. I began by thinking how awful they were, but ended by deciding they were not so bad—though she is so ignorant and so silly that one wonders why anybody has ever let her go on in print about politics and he is one of those all-too-heavy jolly Viennese lightweights . . .

To William Shawn   May 14, 1945
                                                                     Rome

FA21 XBX RMP30 SANSORIGINE 95 14 1632 PGE 1/50
PRESS WILLIAM SHAWN NEWYORKER MAGAZINE NEWYORK
SORRY SO LATE WITH THIS MOVING AROUND SO MUCH HARD TO WRITE
WANT TO DO TWO SUMMER LITERARY ARTICLES ONE ON NEW WORK
MALRAUX AND SILONE WHICH IS IMPORTANT ONE ON VISIT TO SANTAYANA
FASCINATING THOUGH CANNOT QUOTE MUCH OF WHAT HE SAID AM GOING
TO TRY SOMETHING ABOUT FOOD DISTRIBUTION AND PRESERVATION
WORKS OF ART IN ITALY IN FORM OF FICTION PLEASE SEND ME SOME
MONEY AS SOON AS YOU GET THIS CORRECT ADDRESS AFHQ COMMA
PRO COMMA DETACHMENT A COMMA APO 512 PLEASE NOTIFY FAMILY—
EDMUND WILSON

To Mamaine Paget   May 28, 1945
                                                                     Rome

. . . I have been out in the Abruzzi for three days—went all the way to the Adriatic in a jeep. The country is wonderful—like the Vosges or the New England states in America—the people sober and tough, with a pretty high standard of living; but the devastation is unimaginable, large towns with not a building left and the country still planted with mines, which the young men are getting killed digging up for 20 lire (20 cents) a day—miles and miles of this. These places affect me with more repugnance, I think, than anything else I've ever seen. I came back feeling more strongly than ever that it was just silly for anybody in Europe to work for anything but international socialism. I was glad I'd happened to read Silone just before going out there, as his books had supplied me with all the vocabulary for the region. I stayed in his province and passed quite close to the towns where his stories take place. I had a long reunion with the Silones last night. He talked very interestingly about the Comintern in Moscow in the early days. He knew Lenin and Trotsky and all the rest of them. He said that he believed that Pietro Spina in his books was the only modern revolutionary character who could not equally well have been a Fascist. I don't agree with him, though, about this—I think that he is rather unfair to Malraux, whom he regards as what he calls a "nihilist," that is, someone who wants to get results without caring about the moral purpose of what he does . . .

To Mamaine Paget   June 1, 1945
                                                              Rome
. . . I saw the Silones again the other afternoon. She told me before he arrived that she had been crazy about his books: she had read them all through and then started reading them again. I think that there is something about him that particularly appeals to women. I noticed that both you and Mary seemed to feel about his books the same way as Mrs. Silone, whereas, good though I think he is, his work doesn't excite me to quite that degree. I believe that it is the priest in him that women like. Personally he is a queer mixture of priest and Communist underground worker. —One of the most personally interesting people I have met here is the Surrealist painter Leonor Fini. She is much better as a painter than I had thought from the few things of hers I had seen in New York, and as a woman almost incredibly attractive and extremely intelligent about pictures and such things. She lives with a young diplomat marquese who under her influence is also becoming a Surrealist painter, at the top of an immense old palazzo, which has a single finger from one of those gigantic Roman statues standing up, like a "Surrealist object," on a pedestal on one of the stair landings. It is always a great relief and reassurance to me nowadays to find an artist who is really producing and interested in his work. I feel the same way at home, where there are so many people who have petered out. It's dismaying, in a time like this, to realize how few writers, etc., are capable of keeping on under their own steam because they can do something and enjoy doing it . . .

Dear Mamaine: After I wrote you yesterday, I went out to mail the letter
and, by a coincidence, found a shop with wonderful marionettes for
Reuel: kings, princesses, devils, brigands, etc., all beautifully dressed. Then
I had dinner alone at Fajiano's, which used to be one of the best restaurants in Rome and still has a certain glamour—it's been taken over by the
Allied forces; then I went to an Italian show called *Tentazione*—something
between a revue and what we call in America a burlesque show. It was
pretty terrible, but not so sordid as it would have been in New York.

Since you are interested in Silone, I'll tell you an anecdote about him.
The Princess di Bassiano, who is by way of being the local Lady Colefax,
invited the Silones to dinner. She said to me that Silone was a dear fellow
but never opened his mouth. The other day Mrs. Silone gave me her own
account of this occasion. It seems that, while they were there, somebody
came to tell the prince that the stationmaster from Ninfa, their town in
the country, had come all the way to Rome to ask him for a little corn—
he had a wife and ten children, and no work because the railroad out
there was wrecked. The prince, whom, as I wrote you, I found so agreeable, refused, saying that all his corn had been taken by government
pools. His American wife begged him to do something, as she knew the
family well, suggesting that he might find the man a job at a station where
the trains were running; but the old man said there was plenty of work
for people like that to do on his estate. They wouldn't work for him at the
present time because they wanted 300 lire a day and he refused to give
them that, but he knew that if he waited they would soon be in such
straits that they would have to work for 100 lire. Mrs. Silone (who is
Irish) was shocked by this and said it sounded like the things that used
to happen just before the French Revolution. The prince had sent the man
away without even speaking to him. But Silone, with his Marxist training,
merely smiled and said that all landowners were like that.

It is a beautiful day today—not hot. When I have finished this boring
but valuable article, I am going to spend a week merely seeing people and
places, trying to saturate myself with certain things, before I start in on
my grandiose project. I am absorbing quite a lot of Italian—reading modern
Italian literature, which I hardly knew before. I have an Italian lesson
almost every day with a nice young fellow who teaches literature and
writes poems in the magazines. I have cut down on eating and drinking,
as I had been getting fat sitting around Rome. This time of year at home
I do a lot of bicycling and swimming, and I miss it here.

The Italian countryside around here never seems to me quite real as
country—partly because, being so dry, there are no real country smells of
fields, flowers, trees, etc. The English UNRRA girl in the Abruzzi told

me she had the same feeling. Furthermore, the dry medieval towns do not seem to me the kind of thing that you ought to be finding in the country, and the hill towns that look as if they were part of the rock, built like wasp's nests in the corner of a barn, disconcert me by their resemblance to bunched-up Indian pueblos in New Mexico—I cannot help feeling that that isn't the way that white people ought to live. I hope these letters don't bore you. I'm hoping to find one from you this afternoon.

After I've been to the post office, I'll come back to the hotel for tea. The tea is an issue between the British and the Americans who share this correspondents' hotel. The Americans resent the fact—it made me furious myself when I first came here—that they cannot have dinner till 7:30 because the British have arranged tea from four to five. They then discovered that the shortage of sugar at meals was due to a lot of it having been used up to make little cakes for the British tea, which no American ever avails himself of. I am the only American here who has tea—because I have taken to skipping luncheon. Now the British correspondents and officers and soldiers are all turning up in socks and shorts—which for some reason drives the Americans crazy; they think they look like overgrown Boy Scouts. The mixture of all kinds of people here is really very entertaining—I also know some Russians. I seem to get along with Russians better, in general, than with any other people in Europe—perhaps because they are not really Europeans but have an outside point of view like Americans. I'm still under the illusion that you are my companion almost everywhere I go and that I am talking to you about things.

Best love as ever, Edmund

To Vladimir Nabokov   May 31, 1945
                                                                    Rome

Dear Volodya: I was walking the other day in this little street on the Pincian where my hotel is and eyeing with curiosity the row of *hôtels borgnes*, the blind doorways of which open up at night to let in the soldiers with their girls, when what was my astonishment to see on one of the façades, though it belongs, I guess, to a relatively respectable apartment house, a marble plaque with a bronze bas-relief of Gogol's head and an inscription which explained that he здес писал Мёртвые Души,* put up by the Russian colony in 1901. I had already discovered that I had D'Annunzio's house right across the street, Stendhal's house in the next street, and the house in which Keats died at the bottom of the Spanish Steps that go down at the end of the Via Sistina—nor is the house of the немецкий пошляк† Goethe very far away. I do not believe, however, that

---

* Here wrote *Dead Souls*.
† German vulgarian [Vladimir Nabokov's translation].

I have as yet written anything here that is as good as *Dead Souls* or the best of Keats—though (all at the expense and by the benevolent arrangement of the Allied occupying forces) I have a wonderful room on the next-to-top floor, with a bed on which I can spend part of the day and see a splendid view of Rome.

There would be so much to say about everybody and everything that I shouldn't be able to do it justice in a letter . . .

It will suffice for you perhaps as a bulletin from Rome to tell you, also, that Mario Praz, the erudite and slightly eccentric author of *La Carne, la Morte e il Diavolo nella Letteratura Romantica,* who is engaged in studying Russian and has just got through Шинель [*The Overcoat*], talked to me enthusiastically about your Gogol book, which he had somehow or other got hold of, and that I have even seen a copy of it in a bookstore. Aside from this, I'm afraid that Europe, as you must already have gathered, is at present in pretty bad shape. The ruined parts of Italy affect me with more repugnance than anything else, I think, that I have ever seen, and when I am in them, my principal feeling is that I want to get away from them as far as possible. The inhabitants constantly beg you to have them all taken to America (where a lot of their friends and relations have already gone), to arrange to have Italy somehow annexed as one of the United States. Rome is almost untouched and delightful—though I found a cousin of Nina's whom she told me to look up living in a section that had been bombed, with the house across the street destroyed and the poor old lady's panes all broken and replaced either by opaque glass or not at all. The mixture here of all nationalities over the grave of Italian Fascism is fascinating, and I am going to try to do something about it—perhaps in the form of fiction—in *The New Yorker.*

I hope that your affairs are prospering. Give my love to Vera and Dmitri. It really is awfully queer to think that Chichikov was выдуманный * by Gogol in the pleasant little street in the clear Italian light—all that world of *Dead Souls* seems so far away. How are your butterflies and how is your novel?   Regards as ever, EW

To John Dos Passos   June 3, 1945
                                                        Hotel de la Ville, Rome
Dear Dos: Your letter of May 18 has just reached me here in Rome. I was awfully glad to hear from you. I've been so far only in Italy and England—a month in England, six weeks in Italy, two weeks in England, now back here again. I'm going to Greece for two or three weeks—then home sometime in August. Europe is pulverized and the atmosphere is suffocating. The war seems to have made most people more provincial and more nationalistic, when the only thing that can save them is a

---

* Invented.

424

European federation (with England as the Massachusetts and Italy as the Louisiana), and the only thing that can bring this about is international socialism. Except for a few first-rate artists, the only people at all cheering I have seen have been old socialists like Silone and Harold Laski who have stuck to their guns through the war and are now becoming active again and working to wake up the socialist movement. I believe there's a chance that, if the socialists are let alone by England and America, they may be able to stand up to the Stalinists. (In England I went around electioneering with Laski and was much impressed by the seriousness and realism of the Labor audiences—also by Laski, whom I felt I'd underrated, or perhaps his present role gives him a dignity he didn't have before.) I don't understand what I have taken to be your loss of faith of late years in your old more or less socialist ideals. Everything else except reviving socialism seems to me, in Europe today, decadent, disgusting, and hopeless.

Rome has been fascinating this spring on account of all the variety of people and things here, but I am now getting horribly sick of it. When you begin to sink down below the surface—so much more modern and brilliant since Mussolini than it was when I was last here in 1909, at the age of fourteen—you find a corrupt and stagnant swamp. It is one of the most delightful of provincial cities, but no one can really do anything important among the debris of so many strata of the past that have become at once overpowering and rubbishy. I'm getting rather impatient to go home . . . but want to stay in this part of the world long enough to absorb enough of what is going on to do some fiction on the subject.

Love to Katy. I hope you'll both be there when I get up to the Cape, probably late in August. As ever, Bunny W

My [Wellfleet] neighbor Nina Chavchavadze . . .

To Nina Chavchavadze   June 7, 1945
                                                              Rome

Dear Nina: I went over to your cousin's again last night and had dinner with her and the friends with whom she lives. I think that I gave you perhaps too gloomy a picture in the letter I wrote you before. Since I had seen her then only in her own room, I didn't know that she was really part of a large household, with whom I think she is fairly happy. Downstairs there is a whole family of Troubetskoys and Fersens—I never got them quite straightened out; two sisters, a daughter, and a grandson, I think—and an elderly man whom I didn't identify. There was also the daughter of a Count Benckendorff whom I had met in London—a captain (the girl) in the British Mission which is on its way to Vienna, waiting for the Russians to let them in. I had an awfully pleasant dinner with them. They have been rather badly off—while we were fighting the

Germans here—and have not had all they needed to eat, but are decidedly better off now, and have made a little world of their own out there. Mrs. Daehn seems to be reconciled to Rome—though she says she hopes to see her family again. She thinks America would be too difficult because she could never afford to live there as relatively comfortably as she does over here. She is terribly thin, but it must partly be her illness, because the other old ladies are not so thin. She is very alert for an invalid and does not complain. They listen to the radio, read *Stars and Stripes* and the European edition of *Time*, and follow quite closely what is going on. I always enjoy talking to Russians, who, like Americans, have rather an outside point of view on Europe. It seems to me that the Russians and the Americans used to think themselves provincial in relation to the European countries, but that all these little fiercely nationalistic and yet pathetically helpless states seem provincial now in relation to us. They all asked about you and the Kutuzovs and I was sorry I was not able to tell them about the other members of Sofka's family.

The little Benckendorff girl—nineteen—seems British to the last degree. Like all the British girls in the army and UNRRA, she talks and behaves exactly like a young Englishman—I imagine this male manner for active women in England is more or less a product of the war. It is the ultimate triumph of the British male that even when women enter the same fields they should themselves become exactly like young men instead of feminizing—as they do with us—the hitherto masculine employments. —The Troubetskoys have a garden in back of the house, in which they have planted beets and carrots sent them (the seeds) by someone in California. They sit out there after dinner. We listened to Attlee's speech against Churchill on the radio, and I was struck by the fact that all the old ladies seemed to be convinced that public utilities ought to be nationalized and more or less expect socialism in Europe. The little Britishized Benckendorff, however, announced that she would leave England if Labor won the election!

Are you back on the Cape or still at Camp Edwards? I have sometimes missed Wellfleet this spring, but Rome is absolutely fascinating now with its mixture of nationalities and the struggle that is going on in Italy between the various political elements.   Best regards, Bunny W.

Gogol wrote **Мёртвые Души** [*Dead Souls*] only a few doors away in this street. There is a plaque to him put up by the Russians.

To WILLIAM SHAWN   June 9, 1945
                                                         Rome
Dear Shawn: . . . It is fascinating here, and I want to do a series of little stories on the various elements in Italy now: one on UNRRA in the ruined towns; one on the British officials; one on the American correspondents; one on the Russians; one on Santayana (disguised) and, com-

bined with, a member of the art-salvaging department, etc. I have been working on these and will send you a couple and you can see whether you think they are working out for you. I really think I have something here . . .

. . . I've been having a very good time with [Philip] Hamburger. My stuff will not conflict with his. Best regards, Edmund Wilson

To WILLIAM SHAWN   June 25, 1945
                                                    London

GMQ WBG8 JG 149 AM PW 37
LONDON 111 25 1850 VIA PREW
PRESS WILLIAM SHAWN NEW YORKER MAGAZINE NY
I CAME TO LONDON ON PERSONAL BUSINESS PLANNING RETURN ITALY
THIS WEEK BUT HAVE SEEN BENJAMIN BRITTENS OPERA WHICH IS
GREATEST MUSICAL DRAMATIC EVENT IN DECADES AND HAVE BEEN AROUND
ELECTIONEERING WITH HAROLD LASKI AND THOUGHT THESE TWO SUBJECTS
AND PECULIAR PSYCHOLOGICAL ATMOSPHERE OF END OF WAR MIGHT
MAKE INTERESTING SET OF NOTES IF YOU SHOULD CHANGE MIND
ABOUT LETTING ME TRY THIS WIRE ME HERE GUARANTY TRUST WILL
RETURN ROME AND FINISH WORK THERE PERHAPS LATER TAKING COUPLE
WEEKS IN GREECE COMING HOME EARLY AUGUST IS THIS SATISFACTORY
WAS MALRAUX SILONE ARTICLE IMPOSSIBLE YOU CAN CUT QUOTATIONS IF
YOU WANT TO   EDMUND WILSON

To MAMAINE PAGET   September 11, 1945
                                               Wellfleet

. . . It's been very queer getting back here. I came so fast from Europe that I didn't get a chance to prepare myself for the change to America, and I saw it as if it were another foreign country, noticing a lot of things that I hadn't been aware of when I left. The people all seem enormously large and, compared to the Europeans, rather lacking in focus and flavor (though the flavor is sometimes rather bad in Europe). A lot of the things that used more or less to interest me now seem to me unbearably boring. With the great role that we seem to be called upon to play, I don't see that we are doing much of anything to supply inspiration or ideas. Our only great contribution has been the atomic bomb. I feel a certain nostalgia for London—those nice little restaurants and Cyril Connolly and his champagne and his house in Regent's Park . . .

To MAMAINE PAGET   November 5, 1945
                                               Wellfleet

. . . The confidence in Truman is declining here. The U.S. is only just beginning to adjust itself to its international role and hasn't really got a policy yet. I am disgusted at the tendency of people over here to take their line either from the Russians or the British. The country seems to me to be going through a very strange phase, quite different from anything I remember. Our isolation has been definitely blown up, and one feels that a lot of things have gone with it. The fact that we have been having as never before a nationalistic propaganda in glorification of the American tradition is, in my opinion, an indication that that tradition may be dying— as Virgil and Horace celebrated the Roman ideals and virtues when Rome had just begun to decay . . .

To MARGARET MARSHALL   1947
The Nation
Dear Peggy: Thanks for the *Nation*s. I liked your article, but I think that one reason why people don't take British socialism seriously is that England without her empire is ruined and nothing that happens there now can be very important or interesting.

I don't want to answer Spender's review. I was surprised that his reaction should have been so conventionally British. It is the traditional howl of indignation that has always greeted American criticism since Hawthorne wrote *Our Old Home*, though they themselves have written countless denunciatory or supercilious books about America. You couldn't tell from Spender's review that there was anything but complaints about the English, though there is a lot of praise of British people and things, and a good deal about Russians, Italians, and Greeks that he almost entirely disregards. Nor did I think I was letting the Americans off so easily. The Americans that I describe are certainly not Henry James characters. Did you look into the book at all yourself?*

As ever, Edmund W.

Evelyn Waugh and W. H. Auden
1944–1947

To EDOUARD RODITI   March 10, 1944
The New Yorker
Dear Mr. Roditi: Thank you for your very interesting letter about Evelyn Waugh. I agree that he is a very complex person and that he dramatizes the various elements in his nature in a way that sometimes makes it difficult to say that he is in sympathy with one character rather than another. I didn't feel, however, that Ambrose Silk was the real hero of *Put Out More Flags*. Don't you think he is represented as rather a

---

* *Europe without Baedeker.*

weakling? I thought that the balance was weighted very much on the side of the Englishmen, whether flamboyant or stodgy, who were actually taking part in the war.

Apropos of what you say about Waugh's Catholicism: I have never really been able to see any Catholic point of view in his novels. He might equally well, it seems to me, be just a Church of England conservative. If I had not been told that he was a Catholic convert, I should certainly never have known it from reading his books.

Yours sincerely, Edmund Wilson

To Elizabeth Huling* July 4, 1945
The New Republic Rome

. . . Am going to wind up my work here in Italy and take two or three weeks in Greece, then go home. Europe, though interesting, is disgusting at present, and, as the swimming and bicycling season wears on, I think more and more longingly of God's country . . .

I saw Evelyn Waugh again. The great topic of conversation was his new novel,† which I guess hasn't come out yet in the United States. It is partly extremely trashy and unintentionally—which is sad for Waugh—comic, so that the malicious London literary world were having a field day about it. He wallows in his snobbery to an unbelievable degree (having married a wife from the Catholic nobility), and shows off his inside knowledge of how things are done in the great houses, and his aristocratic friends were making him miserable by telling him that he had everything all wrong.

Auden had just been through on his way to Germany, where he is to investigate the psychological effects of bomb damage—he is a captain in the American army. When I had been in London before, people were being very mean about him, and Stephen Spender, his old buddy, said to me that he thought it would be the hardest thing in the world for Auden ever to come back to England. A few weeks later, however, he turned up and, as Spender said, took the arrogant line when he might have taken the humble line. Without showing the least embarrassment, he complained about the coldness of English houses, and of other hardships of life in England, and told them that London hadn't really been bombed. They were speechless with indignation, having, they said, politely restrained themselves, when he explained to them the purpose of his mission, from remarking what a pity that he had had no personal experience of the

---

* Elizabeth Huling worked at *The New Republic* from the early days and remained a close friend of E.'s until her death in 1969.
† *Brideshead Revisited.*

psychological effects of bombing. He also assured them—being a homosexual chauvinist—that General Eisenhower was queer. I love this story, because the English are such experts at putting other people down that it is wonderful to see an expatriate Britisher coming back and working out on the boys at home . . .

To Mamaine Paget   February 4, 1946
The New Yorker

. . . I've been seeing quite a lot of Auden and having a very good time with him. I find him very easy to talk to now and great fun—I think, because he's been here now so long that he feels at home with Americans —he's just taking out his second citizen's papers. He's gotten away from teaching in little colleges and is living and writing in New York. It's very interesting about him: I understand better now his coming over here. He told me the other night that he supposed he'd come to America in order to become a good cosmopolitan. In fundamental ways, he doesn't belong in that London literary world—he's more vigorous and more advanced. With his Birmingham background and his early training as a mining engineer— in spite of having been to Winchester and Oxford—he is in some ways more like an American. He is really extremely tough—cares nothing about property or money, popularity or social prestige—does everything on his own and alone. At the same time, he is homosexual to an almost fanatical degree—tells people that Eisenhower is queer and assured me the other day that Wagner's Tristan and Isolde were really a couple of Lesbians, because a man making love to a woman couldn't really get into that rapturous state—he would be "thinking about something else." He has induced me to read *Eric, or Little by Little,* that old Victorian schoolboys' book, on the ground that it "contained the key to the English character." I have found it rather hard going, and suspect that it has for him a kind of erotic interest that it doesn't have for me.

Connolly sent me *The Condemned Playground*—I thought the burlesques were terribly funny. I also read and liked *Rock Pool*—though it is good, not precisely as a straight novel, but more or less in the same way as the burlesques . . .

To Mamaine Paget   February 23, 1946
The New Yorker

. . . I've been seeing something of Auden lately. I like him very much and he's awfully interesting about Europe and America—has just written an introduction to Henry James's *The American Scene,* in which he discusses the differences. I agree with him as far as he goes, but he has become so much preoccupied with theology that he has rather lost touch with the social-political factors, and it is as if he had never read Marx. He thinks that the United States is the only place where it is possible at present to be truly international, and I have felt this very strongly since I have been back. The intellectual and artistic vacuum that was created over here by the war is beginning to be filled now, and things are becoming more interesting . . .

To W. H. Auden*   October 9, 1947
                                                    The New Yorker

Dear Wystan: First of all—much as I usually approve of you—I have some very severe criticisms to make of certain of your recent activities. I hope that you will concentrate on the following sins any irrational feeling of guilt that may be haunting you.

1. Your mangling of the *Duchess of Malfi*, eliminating the last act so as to spoil the whole curve of the drama, and having the Duchess's voice reply from the tomb before she had even been killed.

2. Your title for Betjeman's book, which is not very good in itself and altogether out of keeping with a writer so English and local and entirely un-Americanized.

3. Your regurgitation in *The Age of Anxiety*, in the girl's speech over the sleeping boy, of the last pages of *Finnegans Wake*. This is the only misstep in this poem, in which the influence of Joyce, where it elsewhere appears, is pretty completely absorbed by your own style.

4. The blasphemous strictures on Yeats in which Stephen Spender tells me that you have been indulging. Bob Linscott at Random House, who is an authority on the subject, can explain to you the Byzantium poem. It seems that *the dolphin-ploughed, the gong-tormented seas* is an image for the human consciousness disturbed by the flesh (the dolphin) and religion (Buddhist gongs).

I have also some other more fundamental complaints, but am putting them into a *New Yorker* article on Baudelaire's journals.

Aside from the echo of Joyce, I thought *The Age of Anxiety* was wonderful—as an exploit in language and imagery, it really rivals *Finnegans Wake*. Don't let anybody tell you that your recent work isn't your best.

I have been inspired by your poem in *Horizon* to try writing in reversed rhymes:

> The man in the tavern was livid
> And told him to go to the devil:
> "You mumble, your costume is seedy,
> Your leering reveals your ideas.
> Your walk has the lurch of a felon
> Whose alphabet starts with an aleph.

---

* From a carbon copy found among some of E.'s papers at *The New Yorker*.

Be off with your threats and appeals!
In my feathers you never shall sleep!"
Said the stranger: "I flee from the tsar of
This blind and Siberian forest," etc.*

The rhyming is subtly connected with the subject, because the refugee turns out to be Stalin. I haven't yet been able to decide who the new tsar is going to be.

I'm sorry you didn't come up with Spender the other night. We're having some people for cocktails tomorrow (Hotel Carlyle, 35 East 76th) and would love to have you come if you can stand it.

As ever,

To WILLIAM McFEE   October 10, 1946

. . . As for Auden, he seems to me one of the top writers in English at the present time and one of the three first-rate poets writing English in our time, the other two being Eliot and Yeats (counting Housman as belonging to an earlier period). Auden did not try to evade the war. He came to the United States with the intention of becoming a citizen. He hoped to serve in the U.S. forces and was drafted, but rejected—and was very much sunk about it. He has a much bigger public than you realize. His collected poems, published last year, sold in an amazing way. The truth is that, unlike Eliot, he represents a reversion to the old-fashioned "family" poet—Longfellow, Wordsworth, Browning—who can be kept around and read in bulk and who provides a kind of moral pabulum. Do look into his *Collected Poems*, published by Random House, in which he is to be seen at his best . . .

---

* "Reversals, or *Plus ça change*," from *Wilson's Night Thoughts*.

432

"MEMOIRS OF HECATE COUNTY"
1941–1957

Hecate County was intended as a suburban inferno . . .
                                                  (To Mario Praz, 1952)

To Maxwell Perkins   December 5, 1941
                                                  Wellfleet

Dear Max: Being up against it lately again for money, I knocked off from my novel* and wrote the second of the enclosed short stories. The first was written on a trip last summer. I turned it out with the idea of selling it— and did sell it to *The Atlantic*. Then I had the idea of doing a whole series of them, all dealing with the same locality, Hecate County. Hecate County might be any community of the kind in Connecticut, Pennsylvania, or New Jersey—you are never told where it is. The stories are all about different kinds of people, but they all have an element of fantasy and a kind of odor of damnation. The last one will deal with the house mentioned at the end of the first section of "Ellen Terhune": it will turn out that the Devil lives there. He is in rather a bad way, too. I have planned seven—am going to do one more before Christmas.

Bob Linscott has seen these and has suggested that Houghton Mifflin give me $1,000 for them. I have just had a letter from him saying that he expects it to go through Tuesday—so far as they are concerned. I wanted to put it up to Scribner's, too, though. I have written a good deal of the first part of my novel—though much of it is still in first draft. I have had to drop it repeatedly to do other things: Scott's book, lecturing at Columbia last summer, writing these stories, etc. I have just had to have heating put in this house, which has been an awful expense, and I am confronted with no income again. *The Wound and the Bow* has done better than any other book I have ever published (in the same length of time), and

---

* Unfinished novel.

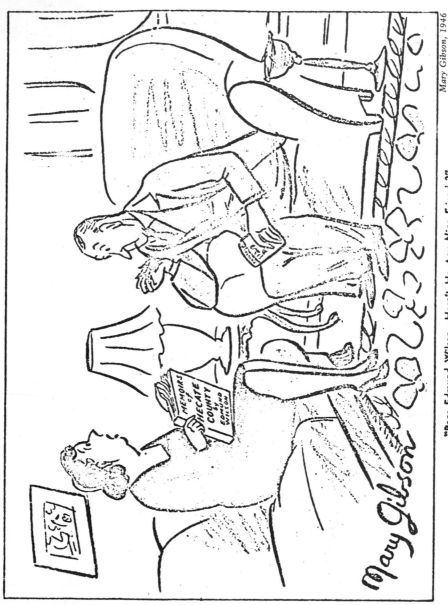

Mary Gibson, 1946

"Poor Edmund Wilson—Hasn't He Any Nice Friends?"

I shall probably be making something on it after the first of the year; but this won't meet my overhead.

I have just had an offer from Cornell to go to teach there for $6,000—which would solve my financial problem—though not till next fall; but I know from my experience at Chicago that it is absolutely impossible to teach two courses, as they want me to do, and do any writing at the same time. I am extremely anxious to stick to fiction writing now and get somewhere with it. I know that Scribner's have already given me quite a lot and have as yet had nothing in return; but isn't there some way that we could work it out so that I could get some more money from you? —on the basis of both the novel and the *Hecate County* book. Say $2,000 —$1,000 down and the rest in monthly installments. Perhaps I could agree to supply you with an anthology of American criticism—an idea which I have had for a long time and in which both Norton and Houghton Mifflin have taken an interest—if I don't present you with a substantial portion of the novel within the next year. The advantage, from my point of view, of having the novel and *Hecate County* both brought out by the same publisher is that I want to sandwich the short stories in-between the various drafts and sections of the novel, and if you are doing them both, you won't be clamoring to get the short stories out. If I can sell these stories to *The Atlantic*, who have asked for some of them and are announcing them, and other magazines, I'll have done a good deal to solve the financial problem. The house here, which I own, is now completely equipped, and I hope to live here till I've written these books.

Please let me know about this as soon as it's possible, because I am anxious to get some money before Christmas.

In reading the stories, please remember that the first one was first aimed at *The New Yorker* and that its sketchiness is due to my effort to keep down the length. *The Atlantic* has a better version, and it still requires some rewriting. I am also going to do some further work on the second one. The imaginary musical compositions which I have attributed to my heroine are too much the kind of thing that writers without musical training tend to concoct for their special purposes, and I am going to check up on it with a musician in order to make these parts more plausible. The next story is going to be about a very rich young man on the order of Felton Elkins and Hermann Oelrichs, who ends up as a magician in a night club. The one after that is a love story of a very peculiar kind. There is also one about refugees.

I forgot to say that the title is to be *Memoirs of Hecate County*. There will be a quotation from Ovid's *Metamorphoses* on the title page—they all deal more or less with transformations. I was going to give it for a subtitle, "Bedtime Stories for the Middle-Aged"; but decided it sounded dreary and might appear to limit the appeal too much. What do you think? . . .   As ever, Bunny W

To ALLEN TATE   December 9, 1942

. . . I'm glad you liked my story. It is one of a series I'm writing—it will
be a book called *Memoirs of Hecate County* . . .

To ALLEN TATE   March 20, 1943

. . . What you say about my writing is more or less true. I feel that I have
not really, in general, gotten myself out in my books, and am trying to
do so now . . .

To MORTON D. ZABEL   September 10, 1943

. . . I am nearly done with my long story, which is probably the best
damn thing I ever wrote—at least, it has given me more satisfaction, as
far as I can remember, than anything else . . .

To MAXWELL GEISMAR   September 21, 1943

. . . I've been working, not on the long novel, but on one of those Hecate
County stories, which has turned into much more of a project than I
contemplated when I wrote the first stories . . .

To MORTON D. ZABEL   November 9, 1943

. . . Both Houghton Mifflin and Scribner's are scared to death of the story
I have been writing, and neither one will bring out the book. If all else
fails, I am going to take some of my *New Yorker* money and publish it
myself . . .

To MORTON D. ZABEL   January 24, 1944
                                                The New Yorker
. . . My book of stories is all right: Doubleday is going to bring it out—
they are not at all worried by its impropriety . . .

To JOHN BIGGS   March 22, 1946

. . . I'm sending you a copy of my new book. Do not let it fall into the
hands of the children . . .

To JOHN BIGGS   March 26, 1946

Dear John: I was really very glad to get your letter, as I have been getting
some pretty sour reactions to my book from friends whom I shouldn't have
expected to be shocked . . .   As ever, EW

436

To Louise Bogan   March 22, 1946
                                                       The New Yorker

Dear Louise: I was very much pleased by your letter—because I've been
getting some pretty sour reactions, not only from my colleagues on the
newspapers, but also from friends like Peggy Bacon, who has been so
much shocked by the book that she can't bear to speak to me about it.
Most people—including V. Nabokov—sound as if they thought that I had
made an unsuccessful attempt to write something like *Fanny Hill*. From
Betty Huling, that old romantic, I have not heard a word . . .

                                                              Love, EW

   Robert Van Gelder on the *Times* called me up to ask for a picture and
tell me that he was enthusiastic about *H.C.* and running a long article
about it by Alfred Kazin on the front page of the Literary Supplement.
I thought this was a little queer, but looked forward eagerly to finding
myself on the front page of the *Times*. Of course, it never appeared—and
I've heard from Doubleday that Van Gelder's boss got wind of the book
and told him that he could not run so favorable a review. Kazin has taken
his article to *Partisan Review*, and the *Times* has run nothing at all. I
must say that Hal Smith, on *The Saturday Review*, has been very sporting, if not particularly lucid, about the book, in view of the fact that he
must know that it was his career in relation to the Van Dorens and Canby
that inspired the Milholland story.

To Louise Bogan   April 5, 1946
                                                       The New Yorker

Dear Louise: I'm sorry that I'll miss you. I'm going away for about a
week next Thursday—to Charlottesville, Virginia, with my sole surviving
Virginian cousin. —I have a high opinion of Ken McCormick, who is
trying—not without success—to get some quality into the Doubleday lists.
I have done business with him and have got on better with Doubleday
than any other publisher I have ever had. Be sure not to be afraid to ask
them to pay you a lot of money, they have quantities and are not niggardly
about it.

   I'm charmed by the idea of the Trumans with my book. I have been
getting some very strange responses—one poison-pen letter. Betty Huling
hates it—she said to me, "You haven't convinced the reader that that man
was in love with those women!" One man wrote me that he hoped I
would do an extended study of Devil worship and the Black Mass, in
which he was sure I must be very interested, and wanted to know whether
I didn't agree with him that "the idea of good is a hoax and that the
Devil has been right all along." Somebody has suggested that it's a feeler
from the Old Man himself. Let me know when you get to town again.

                                                              Love, EW

To Mamaine Paget   March 26, 1946
                                                         Wellfleet
. . . I'm sending you a copy of *Hecate County*, though you've already
read it. It's been having a curious reception—selling, for me, pretty well,
but I've been getting extremely sour reviews from most of my fellow
critics and some horrified reactions from friends that I shouldn't have
expected to be shocked. Most people don't seem to understand that story
about the two women—which I should have thought couldn't have been
plainer. It registered so successfully with you, when you read it, that I
wasn't prepared to have people puzzled . . .

To Mamaine Paget   May 1, 1946
                                                         Wellfleet
. . . My book has become a best-seller—mainly, I'm afraid, because people
think it's scandalous—and I'm making no end of money. I'm also getting
some very queer letters. One man wrote that he hoped I would write at
length on Satanism and the Black Mass, a subject in which he was sure I
must be much interested, as he was, and asked me whether I didn't agree
with him that "the whole idea of good is a hoax and the Devil has been
right all along." The White House, it seems, has bought a copy, and I've
been feeling rather uneasy at the idea of Harry and Bess perhaps attempting to read it aloud in the evening . . .

To John Biggs   July 24, 1946
                                                         Wellfleet
Dear John: Did you know that Sumner of the Anti-Vice Society was
trying to suppress *Hecate County*? He has been raiding the Doubleday
bookstores. The case is supposed to come up at General Sessions, in
September or October, when we shall need people to testify that it is a
serious book. Does your position as a federal judge make it impossible for
you to appear in this connection? I imagine that it does, but thought I
would ask. Doubleday's lawyer is a man named Dwyer or O'Dwyer, who
says he knows you. —Is there any chance of you and Anna getting up
here? I'd love to see you.   As ever, Bunny Wilson

To H. L. Mencken   July 23, 1946
                                                    The New Yorker
Dear Mencken: Thanks very much for your letter—though I don't care
for George Moore. I've never read *Memoirs of My Dead Life,* but may
unconsciously have plagiarized the title. Sumner is out after *Hecate
County* and has been raiding bookstores in New York.
    I sometimes think, in connection with my *New Yorker* job, of your
campaign of the 1910's and '20's, and wonder whether the literary situation
is worse or better now than then. It was harder to get an honest book

438

published in the early years of the century than it is at the present time; but, on the other hand, Hollywood, Henry Luce, *The Reader's Digest*, and the government propaganda service are today eating up all the talent. During 1910–30, the writers had to have the courage to swim against the current and had to have something of their own to offer. The younger generations of the post-Depression period have been much less sure of themselves and much more susceptible to being swallowed by the big businesses mentioned above and by such groups as the Communists and the Catholics. I am afraid it is the American form of the same state of mind that Goering and the Kremlin have exploited. I'm trying to hope we'll survive it. Best regards, Edmund Wilson

To MAMAINE PAGET September 9, 1946
Wellfleet

. . . The case of my book in New York is to come to court October 14. If they suppress it, it will be an awful nuisance, as it will be difficult ever to get it reprinted. In the meantime, it has been selling madly. Hearst— if you know who he is: the American Beaverbrook, but a great deal worse —has been conducting a campaign, evidently aimed at Catholic readers, against indecent books, with special virulence against *Hecate County*, on the ground that they debauch the young and ruin family life, and I have been getting a lot of abusive letters and literature like the enclosed (be sure to read the story about the man who tried to dodge the Devil). The situation in England seems to be even worse: Warburg writes me piteous letters, saying that he cannot get a printer to set *Hecate County* and is begging me to change the text . . .

To ROBERT WARSHOW August 17, 1946
Wellfleet

Dear Mr. Warshow: Thank you for your letter. You seem to have the right idea about *Hecate County*, which has sometimes been mistakenly criticized on the ground that it is an unsuccessful attempt to write something attractively erotic. Yours sincerely, Edmund Wilson

To ROBERT WARSHOW December 9, 1947
Wellfleet

Dear Mr. Warshow: Thank you for your letter and the copy of *Commentary*. It was reassuring to read something by somebody who did not think *Hecate County* was an unsuccessful atempt to rival *Fanny Hill*. Apart from that, I was much interested in your essay. I am sure that some such condition as you describe exists, and I can see that it is a much more serious matter for the writers who have grown up in the Depression and after than it was for my generation . . .

Yours sincerely, Edmund Wilson

To Norman Kemp Smith*　　　　　　　　　　　　January 9, 1947
　　　　　　　　　　　　　　　　　　　　　　　　Wellfleet
Dear Kemp Smith: Thank you for your letter and the clipping. I was
afraid that you mightn't like *Hecate County*—though I don't think it is
any more unpleasant or somber than some of those gloomy Scottish
novels that you and Edwin Muir were recommending to me in Edinburgh . . . With allowance made for fantasy and satire, I think I can
claim that *Hecate County* is not at all an untrue picture of that kind of
life in America. Your memories of the country all date from before the
Depression, and it has really changed very much from the period when
you were living at Princeton. The community, for example, that I live
in on Cape Cod has lately reached a stage of deterioration that would
have seemed absolutely incredible even fifteen years ago. I may not have
made my characters real, but—aside from the supernatural element—
what they do and are is not too eccentric for the contemporary reality. A
good deal that may seem to you bizarre in the book is based on things that
have really happened.

I've just got married again and am going up to the country to spend
the rest of the winter. I've had a very rocky year and a half since I got
back from Europe, what with domestic difficulties and the various prose-
cutions of my book, which the Hearst papers and the Anti-Vice Society
have been trying to get suppressed; and am delighted to be settling down
again.

I look back with much pleasure on my week in Edinburgh. It has been
a great stimulation and a source of pride to have maintained contact with
you through the years.　　　　　　　　　　. . . Yours as ever,

To Mamaine Koestler†　　　　　　　　　　　　June 19, 1951
　　　　　　　　　　　　　　　　　　　　　　　　Wellfleet
. . . *Hecate County* is out in England, and Cyril Connolly has given me
a hideously bad review. I try to think he is jealous of the sales—the first
printing seems to have sold out in a week—but am afraid this is not true
and he honestly doesn't like the book . . .

To John E. Austin　　　　　　　　　　　　　　1957

Dear Mr. Austin: Thank you for sending me this thesis, which I have
read with interest. I think that you have handled my books intelligently
—especially *I Thought of Daisy*—though you don't seem to understand the
underlying idea of *Hecate County*. All the women except Anna are

---

* From a carbon copy found among some of E.'s papers at *The New Yorker*.
† Mamaine Paget had married Arthur Koestler.

witches, and even Jo is turning into one in the narrator's dream at the end—hence the title of the book. Hecate herself appears in the final story. I am afraid that as a writer you are not yet mature enough for this to be published anywhere. It is essentially a student production, and I am sure that you will in time do much better.

Here are a few inaccuracies:

p. 9. Our house was at the bottom of a hill, not *on* one.

Except that there are blond daughters, the Grosbeakes are not based on the Gausses. Grosbeake is based on Whitehead: both his physical appearance and his conversation. I have given him Frieda Lawrence for a wife.

"Bunny" was a family nickname, which carried over to school and college. I don't stutter and never have. (Also p. 156.)

p. 17. I had hardly read Yeats in college. It was only after college, when I read *Responsibilities*, that I began to find him interesting.

p. 20. I have met Floyd Dell only once in my life, so have never been in the least "close friends" with him. George Cram Cook, I knew only casually.

p. 28. Max Eastman was not my guide in my radical days. At the time I was most Marxist and pro-Soviet, he was showing the fallacies of Marxism, attacking the Soviet regime, and even undermining the assumptions of Trotsky, whom he had at one time greatly admired. Eventually, when I had gone more deeply into Marxism, I came to see what he was driving at, and his writings influenced me the other way.

p. 29. I never had any intention of applying for C.P. membership. The Communists had usually been indignant about what I wrote about them and, after I came back from Russia, they put me on their blacklist of people who were never to be allowed to go there.

p. 34. I was never a "week-to-week" reporter for *The New Yorker*. I went to Europe for them in '45, to Zuñi in '47, and to Israel in '54.

p. 47. Hugo Bamman has no connection whatever with John Peale Bishop.

p. 117. *Hecate County* sold something under 60,000.

p. 121. I spent only one summer in Europe during the early twenties.

p. 139. Anna was Ukrainian, not Polish.

p. 146. The girl mentioned here was also Ukrainian.

p. 152. You mean *credibility*, not *credulity*, here.

These errors are of two kinds: the kind of slip everyone makes—I make them myself, but when I am writing for *The New Yorker*, their admirable checking department corrects them—and the kind of mistake which is based on guess or rumor: you ought to train yourself never to make an assertion which is not based on positive evidence.

Good luck to you!   Sincerely, Edmund Wilson

. . . among the writers who have really devoted their lives to the study of our literature—I hope that I am not doing anyone an injustice—I can think of only two who can themselves be called first-rate writers: Van Wyck Brooks and Newton Arvin.

(The Bit Between My Teeth)

To Newton Arvin   May 24, 1946
Wellfleet

Dear Arvin: Thank you very much for your letter and the book. I have been having a very good time reading it. I won't discuss it further now, as I've written about it in *The New Yorker*. I'm pleased that you liked *Hecate County*. It turned out, though I hadn't planned it so, to be rather in the Hawthorne tradition. I had never had much real taste for Hawthorne, but he has certainly proved, in American fiction, a strangely powerful and lasting influence. Last summer, when I was in Rome, I read *The Marble Faun* for the first time and thought it a remarkable book —all that he says about the effects on an American living a long time in Rome is equally true today. I found passages that were classical expressions of precisely the same feelings that I had been trying to put into my notebook under the illusion that they were something new. I happened also to read Douglas's *South Wind* and discovered, to my surprise, that his theme was very much the same as Hawthorne's and that he had borrowed Hawthorne's plot. What is most curious is that Douglas, with his façade of sophistication, is so much more simple-minded and obvious in dealing with the moral situation. Like the moralistic Scotchman that he is, he has arranged to have the killing by the wife of the considerate husband an act to which no blame can possibly attach, so that he really lets himself out of the consequences of the point of view he pretends to present. Hawthorne does not do this: Miriam is a really mixed character, and it is not so easy to judge her.

My opinion, in general, of Hawthorne's novels is just the reverse of the usual one: taking them in chronological order, I like each one better than the one before—so that I admire *The Scarlet Letter* least and *The Marble Faun* most, and *The Blithedale Romance* more than *The House of the S.G.* It seems to me that in his later books the backgrounds become less shadowy and the characters live with an intense life. I should like to talk to you about *The M.F.* If the denouement has a deeper meaning in respect to the poetic fate, I don't think I understand what it is. Henry James throws no light on the subject, and I don't think he gives the book enough credit—especially since, in something like *Roderick Hudson*, he obviously owed it so much.   Best regards, Edmund Wilson

To MAXWELL GEISMAR   August 17, 1946
                                                      Wellfleet
Dear Max: I was glad to hear from you. Thanks for the Tom Wolfe *Portable*. If anything can induce me to read him, it will be your volume of selections. I've already been dipping into it—I find that I just can't believe in those scenes with his friends in Paris, where they are ribbing him about his French, etc.

I'm up here struggling with the household and what Mencken used to call beautiful letters . . .   As ever, Edmund W

To R. P. BLACKMUR   November 6, 1946
                                              The Minden Inn, Nevada
Dear Blackmur: In reply to your mysterious letter: you may quote me to the effect that magazines of the type of *The Dial, The Little Review,* and *Partisan Review* have done an immensely valuable service in printing the work of important writers who were rejected or had not yet been discovered by the commercial publications, and in keeping the discussion of literature and art on a level of high seriousness. In my opinion, however, the existing magazine that most needs and deserves support is *Modern Music*, rather than any of the literary magazines. (I understand that P.R. is fixed up with a subsidy now.) *The Kenyon Review* is indescribably awful. Allen Tate, before he left *Sewanee*, never succeeded in lifting the shadow of the influence of J. C. Ransom or being able to refuse filling its space with the writings of his cousins and aunts. *Accent* is perfectly piffling; and *Poetry*, except when, with obvious and ignominious timidity, it recently tried to do something for Pound, has been as dead as Hull-House for years. It would, of course, be a great thing to have a new literary magazine, but it would have to be a lot different from most of these that you name. You may quote me, too, if you like, to the effect that it would be a great thing to have a new first-rate magazine that

would serve both as a critical review and as a reliable vehicle for new creative writing. A monthly of this kind has been needed for years.

Best regards, Edmund Wilson

To Vladimir Nabokov

December 1, 1946
Nevada

Dear Volodya: I knew that I would get a rise—but I am perfectly sincere about Malraux. Some of your points against *La Condition humaine* seem to me badly taken, the others of little importance. As for enchantment, he has always enchanted me since I read *Les Conquérants* (though I don't care for *Le Temps du mépris*). *La Condition humaine* seems to me the novel I have read which has best expressed the crises and emotions of its period—and the first installment of *La Lutte avec l'ange*, written during the war, in some ways even more remarkable. (I admit that he has no sense of humor: *La Voie royale*, though an exciting book, has its unintentionally humorous aspects.) He is surely the only first-rate imaginative genius that the French have produced since Proust. Inaccuracies, clichés, and clumsiness do not in themselves invalidate a writer. You and I, besides, differ completely, not only about Malraux, but also about Dostoevsky, Greek drama, Lenin, Freud, and a lot of other things—about which, I'm sure, we will never be reconciled; so that we'd better, I suppose, stick to the more profitable discussion of Pushkin, Flaubert, Proust, Joyce, etc. (Your enthusiasm for *South Wind*, by the way, seems to me an extravagant example of the betrayal of a man of taste by his enjoyment of a special kind of thing—in this case, malicious humor—which hasn't necessarily anything to do with first-rate literature.)

Do you know Silone at all? I've also been reading out here the books of his I hadn't read. He and Malraux now emerge, I think, as the masters of this political-social-moral semi-Marxist school of fiction that is the great development in its field since the analytical psychological novel; but their points of view are entirely different. You might like Silone better—though he's not really so great a man as Malraux.

I'm very eager to see your own book. Do have them send me the proofs. *Hecate County* was convicted in New York by a vote of two to one. Doubleday is going to appeal. The dissenting judge wrote a very intelligent opinion; the other two—what is rather unusual—voted *Guilty* without explanation. It is all an awful nuisance and is putting a crimp in my income.

I have been having a very quiet and not unpleasant, rather purgatorial, time out here. It is a queer and desolate country—less romantic than prehistoric and spooky. I made some money one night at roulette, and then threw it all away. Gambling, however, is a weakness of the great Russian writers that is incomprehensible to me. As an amateur magician, I can more or less see how the roulette wheels, the dice, and the *vingt-et-un* (blackjack) deals are being manipulated. The pretty girls they get out here to do the dealing in the card games are simply wonderful with their fingers and most have had months of preliminary practice. I like to go in to watch them.

I'm looking forward to getting back to Wellfleet and hope you people can get up to see us . . . As ever, EW

The death of Paul Rosenfeld has left me, not only shocked at the unexpected loss of a friend, but with a feeling of dismay and disgust at the waste of talent in the United States. ("Paul Rosenfeld: Three Phases," in *Classics and Commercials,* 1947)

To JOHN PEALE BISHOP
March 21, 1941
Stamford

. . . Rosenfeld . . . needs work badly. He did some excellent pieces for me—especially one taking down the Sibelius cult, which hasn't been published yet. His work improves when he is encouraged and given a little scope . . .

To JEROME MELLQUIST
March 4, 1947
Wellfleet

Dear Jerry: I shan't be able to finish the book I'm working on till some-time in the early part of September, and as soon as I have, I'll have to apply myself to catching up with my *New Yorker* articles and getting out a volume of John Bishop's writings, which is long overdue. I'll be glad to write something about Paul but I couldn't possibly get to it before the end of May. Your suggestion of my writing about Paul as "An Amer-ican Voice in Literature" is, however, I am sorry to say, a perfectly mean-ingless and inappropriate one—so far as one can tell from this title. He was more like a European voice in America. In any case, I am sure that you will simply discourage people from contributing to your volume if you make such suggestions to them—or, in fact, any suggestions at all. The way to make such memorial volumes successful is simply to invite the old friends and admirers of the subject to write anything they are moved to write. (The volume in celebration of G. B. Shaw's ninetieth birthday is a good example of how not to do it.) In the meantime, you ought to get a publisher lined up and have some understanding about dividing royalties among the contributors (not, of course, that the book will make money). You ought to be sure that the book will be published before you get the people actually to write the pieces. I forget what you told me about this. Best regards, Edmund Wilson

445

PAUL ROSENFELD

Since the death of Huneker, the chief musical critic in America capable of interpreting music in terms of life.

—*Vanity Fair*, 1921

To Jerome Mellquist   October 3, 1947
                                                       The New Yorker
Dear Jerry: I am very glad to hear that you have got a publisher for the
book about Paul. I'll try to do something for you by November 1, but that
doesn't given me much time, and it won't be long.

I have been getting together a volume of John Bishop's prose, and it has
occurred to me that you might like to include a long review of one of
Paul's books that he once wrote for *The Dial* (though I understand, of
course, that it might not go with the other things). If you should want
it, I'll arrange to have you have it and not include it in the other volume.
If John were alive, he would certainly want to contribute.

                                              Best regards, Edmund Wilson

To Alyse Gregory   January 11, 1948
                                                       Wellfleet
. . . I look forward to seeing the memoir that I understand you have
written for the memorial volume for Paul Rosenfeld. I miss him very much;
his death was all the more depressing because his later years were full of
illness and discouragement. He no longer had a market for his work. I
often regret the *beaux jours* of *The Dial* . . .

To F. O. Matthiessen   June 2, 1947
                                                       Wellfleet
Dear Mattie: Thank you very much for the Cheney book. I have only
looked through it and read in it as yet, but it *does* carry me back to the
twenties, when people mixed art and literature with their liquor, and it
makes me sad to think of what has happened to Phelps Putnam and
Farwell Knapp and a lot of other people that it seems to me I used to get
so much more out of seeing than I do of the representatives of the later
vintages.

I tried to get hold of you when I was in Boston last weekend, but you
had evidently gone out of town.   As ever, Edmund Wilson

To Mary Colum   June 28, 1947
                                                       Wellfleet
Dear Molly: It seems that Max [Perkins] simply came down with a cold
one day, rapidly developed pneumonia, and died. I had talked to him on
the phone not long before. Dawn Powell tells me that the last time she
saw him he seemed to her horribly weary of the publishing business and
talked to her mainly about incidents of his youth when he had worked
for a time on a newspaper. I think that the great tragedy was that he was
never able to do much at Scribner's after the old man died.

Dawn also told me that Gladys has opened the doors for Van Wyck to a larger and livelier social life than Eleanor had ever encouraged. I have never cared much for Gladys, but maybe she is just the right thing for Brooks.

I am sorry that you have been ill again. I got your message when I was in town and tried to call you up but couldn't get you, and then had to leave. But do be sure to make connections with us this summer. Come up here and we will have a more satisfactory conversation. Best regards to Padraic.   As ever, Edmund W

To MALCOLM COWLEY   July 8, 1947
                                                                Wellfleet
Dear Malcolm: Thanks for your trouble over the Bishop essay. About the transfer: I don't see what *The New Republic* has to do with it—it is a problem for the publishers of the book.

About Whitman: I've always thought that the part of Whitman's work included in the Everyman's edition of *L. of G.*—everything through "Blue Ontario's Shores"—gives a better impression of him than the complete edition with the later installments, which, though there are some good pieces among them, get more and more diluted. I read this volume through during the first war, in France, and felt a unity and completeness about the work as a whole that most people don't seem to see. I thought that even the long passages of cataloguing that seem silly if looked at by themselves had their value when read with the rest. By the way, when you wrote about Whitman in the *N.R.* some years ago, I thought you gave rather a false impression by comparing him with Charlus: he was an entirely different kind of homo. It never seems to have made him in the least uncomfortable or given him a bad conscience—because, I suppose, he felt himself in the position of being admired by weaker and less masculine people. I suppose you've seen, in the various editions of *L. of G.*, how he kept working on it and improving it. But the first edition is particularly astounding, appearing as it did with no warning or explanation. As you say, it is much more like Rimbaud than like a Currier and Ives print of a frontiersman. (Do you really think Lautréamont is wonderful? He seems to me juvenile and second-rate.)

I should be working on an article on Sartre—hence this long interesting letter.   As ever, Edmund Wilson

To JOHN DOS PASSOS   November 24, 1947
                                                                Wellfleet
Dear Dos: I have never expressed to you my sympathy over Katy's death, though I have had it much in my mind. I know what you must have been going through from my own experience after Margaret was killed; and I

448

can't say anything conventionally consoling, because I know how demoralizing it is. But I can tell you that you will get over it and get over the morbid feelings of guilt connected with it—though I never did quite till I remarried, when, in spite of my difficulties with Mary, I began to function normally again.

One curious effect in September was that I kept hearing Katy commenting on the behavior of our various friends, as I had heard her do so many times—especially on Eben's rather too pressing desire to get all his favorite still-living neighbors buried in the family plot. But they were not being characteristic on the day when the funeral took place—I have never seen the people up here so stunned, and it was a relief to get to the cemetery, which looked so light, clean, and dry and yet human up there among the old four-square churches and from which the view was incredibly lovely. The horrible weather we had been having, which seemed to have some connection with what had happened, cleared up and showed the bay all silver in the four o'clock light and the bright waterway winding in-between the sands and the marshes. I thought about what the water had meant to us all, and afterwards it took me back as nothing had ever done to all my life on the Cape, and, though I have always, by a reflex action, tried to disassociate myself in my own mind from the rest of the community up here, I had to see that I was part of a local group a good deal more than I had realized or had wanted to be—since it was already a whole life that I had lived here, now going back through many phases for all of twenty-five years—and that Katy had been from a phase now far past somehow at the center of it as a principle of imagination and intelligence and beauty and charm—so that her death and the little hilltop cemetery seemed to give the whole thing a kind of dignity such as I did not ordinarily grant it. Everybody seemed much older, both from strain and from losing Katy, who had always remained so young. We had all been getting old together, and it was already, I say, a whole life behind us, with many things that we could never have again.

The worst thing is that really clever and sensitive women are very hard to replace, and that, once you are over forty, you find that you can't bear the idea of living in the country or traveling with even attractive and amiable ones of the kind that you can't really talk to. Katy must have been a wonderful companion—I had the impression that you were never bored with her, and that—rather shy with most other people—she must have been inexhaustibly entertaining with you and inexhaustible in her gift of investing life with something that the statistics don't add up to but that is one of the only reasons why one would like to see life continue on this planet.

Do let us see you in New York. We'll both be there for a few days after the 7th, before I go out to Zuñi.   As ever, Bunny W

November 15, 1948
                                                        Wellfleet

Dear Stark: Thanks very much for your book, which I have been reading
with pleasure, but with the melancholy realization that the kind of criticism we practiced on the N.R. is now completely out of fashion. What
do you think of the awful stuff that comes out in *Sewanee* and *The
Kenyon Review*? I don't believe that the extreme distaste it inspires in me
is due to old-fogyism on my part. They represent, on the contrary, dreadful young or middle-aged fogyism of half-baked academic types who don't
know anything, are devoid of taste, and have no real interest in literature.
On the other hand, you have Luce and the drivel in the daily papers. The
old *New Republic* looks to me from here like the court of Lorenzo de'
Medici.

I have been so much disgusted with *The New Republic* in its latest
phase, in which it looks like toilet paper and reads like the Soviet magazine
Bolshevik, that I had missed your reviews of recent productions, and was
very glad to read you on the Old Vic, *The Iceman*, and *The Duchess of
Malfi*. I must say that the latter, though, was terrific when I saw it in
London, unadapted and much better acted. The New York production
was about as bad as it could be, but the play *can* have dramatic power. I
think that you could have afforded to include even more of your reviews
than you did. The few first-rate collections of dramatic articles are always
of great interest when their period in the theater is over—witness Max
Beerbohm and Shaw. You are always so good on comedy—Molière, Shaw,
Chekhov, etc.—that I'm sorry you didn't include that preface you wrote
for Goldoni.   Best regards as ever, Bunny Wilson

January 10, 1948
                                                        Wellfleet

Dear Orwell: I have sent you Brooks's Mark Twain book and another
book of his, *The World of Washington Irving*, which is, I think, the best
volume of his literary history of the United States. It deals with an
exciting period over here and might interest you. If you have any extra
copies of books of yours I haven't read, I'd be very glad to have them, as
they are hard to get over here. The ones I have read are *Burmese Days,
Animal Farm, In the Belly of the Whale,** the Dali, the Dickens book, and
The English People. I've been particularly wanting to read a book called
Keep the Aspidistra Flying.

In *The English People*, by the way, I see that you persist in the error
that I tried to dispel when I saw you in London: that the various kinds of

---

* *Inside the Whale.*

insects in America are indiscriminately known as "bugs." Of the list you give, it is true that a cockchafer is known over here as a June bug and that a ladybird is sometimes called a ladybug, but a cricket and a daddy longlegs are known by the same names as in England, and even when we call insects by different names or have different insects to name, we do not often call them bugs. Bugs with us mean only beetles or beetlelike insects, and a cricket or a daddy longlegs couldn't conceivably be referred to as a bug. As for wild flowers, they all have separate names, just as they do with you. The ones that are not found in England sometimes have Indian or translated Indian names. The truth is that we are rather rich in the nomenclature of flora and fauna, and that the difficulty sometimes is that there is a confusion between the different names for the same thing in different parts of the country.

As for the verbs in *-ize*, it seems to me that the British have produced the most remarkable one—to womanize—which I have been seeing in highbrow English journalism. It is apparently a derogatory word used in connection with men who have a sexual interest in women.

Yours sincerely, Edmund Wilson

To Helen Muchnic   May 11, 1948
                                                    Wellfleet

. . . No other news except that I have more or less laid off *The New Yorker*. I have just done a very Freudian study of Ben Jonson, which I have a feeling they are not going to print. Last December I went out to the Indian pueblo of Zuñi to see the big annual festival, which is extraordinary and well worth the trouble involved. My pieces about it for *The New Yorker* won't be out till fall, because Harold Ross thinks that articles about things that take place in cold weather can only be published when the weather is cold . . .

. . . Did you know that Vladimir Nabokov was going to teach Russian at Cornell? They are immensely pleased about it, as it means a good salary, and it happens to be one of the only colleges where serious work with butterflies is done . . .

To Louise Bogan   November 5, 1948
                                                    Wellfleet

Dear Louise: The enclosed will enable you to gauge the degree and quality of Boston's awareness of T. S. Eliot. By the way, has it ever occurred to you lately that the dear old master is being a teeny-weeny bit overrated? I still don't like *Four Quartets*. I bought the recording of it, but it irritated me so that I never played it through but once. I was glad to see you do something for poor old Pound. I myself have been writing

451

some remarkable poetry in an unconventional form which I invented. I will send it to you if you take cognizance of this letter; otherwise, not.

We went over to call on Edna when we were at Lenox last summer. She has changed very much—so much that I don't think I would have recognized her—was evidently pulling herself out of some very dark neurotic period. She has been writing poetry again at a great rate, and it is mostly perfectly good stuff in her old vein. She has her war poetry terribly on her mind as a delinquency that she has to atone for. Going over there brought back our days at Hillsdale.

We have been living up here all the time, with our complicated family coming and going: Rosalind, Reuel, Elena's son, and a little girl named Helen Miranda, born last February . . .

Have just read Ellmann's book on Yeats, which all takes place in a void: an abstract psychological analysis with no conception of the Dublin background or of the passionate dramatized personalities of the people he is writing about. Every time he quotes from Yeats, you are startled and ask yourself what the poetry is doing there: you have to readjust your mind in order to take it in. —Don't you think the highbrow magazines are horrible? —How is Rolfe Humphries? —Who are the people nowadays that you don't see? (You always say that you don't see anybody, and then it turns out, on close examination, that you have regular familiars and admirers who visit you on regular days.) What are the works that you say you are writing but aren't? Please write me, answering all these questions, and let us effect a meeting before we have been put in prison by John Crowe Ransom and his academic commissars. Love to Maidie and all the Frustrators. Edmund W

To Louise Bogan   December 22, 1948
                                                              Wellfleet

Dear Louise: Thanks for your card. My poem is coming out in *Furioso*,* and I'll send you a copy—I suppose care of Morton in Chicago will reach you. I have just read you on Edith Sitwell, and I am so glad you have not been taken in by the ballyhoo about her recent poetry—which, as you say, is much inferior to her early stuff. Osbert, too, is being overrated. His autobiography (I've read only the last volume), though extremely literary, is not really well written, and he manages to be most uninteresting about the writers and people he's known. The Sitwells seized the moment, in England, when letters were ebbing low on account of the war to put themselves over as important figures—though none of them, except Edith in her *Gold Coast* days, ever had any real talent.

---

* "The Pickerel Pond."

452

But why on earth did you say, in writing about John Bishop's poems, that that volume represented a selection? It is his complete collected verse, assembled with great care by Allen and myself, and full of interesting unpublished material. I don't believe you even opened it.

Merry Christmas to you and Maidie. We hope to see you when you are back from Chicago. You will have an amusing time. Give our love to Morton.   As ever, Edmund W

To John Dos Passos   January 27, 1949
                                                              Wellfleet

Dear Dos: Just got your card. The other night when I saw you I had had almost no sleep for forty-eight hours, had taken a couple of stiff drinks before setting out in the hope that they would buck me up, but they extinguished me completely. Elena says you were wonderful on South America, but I wasn't quite sure you were back from there.

I enjoyed *The Grand Design*—I think it is much the best of the three. It is enormously skillful in the writing (much less burdened by the naturalistic detail of which I used to complain), and in the swift and subtle presentation of social-political processes. But I do think it is true that your characters (in your words) are becoming less and less convincing as human beings. I feel that as you get older it costs you more and more of an effort to imagine the mediocrities that you insist on writing about. Everybody connected with the New Deal was not as mediocre as that, and even in the case of the ones who were, I don't think you are the person to write about them, as you haven't enough mediocrity in you to get into the spirit of the thing. I wish there were some Jeffersons, Joel Barlows, and Tom Paines in your fiction nowadays. Above all, as a brilliant conversationalist, why do you persist so in making everybody talk in clichés? Almost nobody talks like that. Sometimes you give the impression of those writers who like to show off their mastery of the idiom of some African tribe by retailing conversations with the natives. I think, though, that part of the hostility that *The Grand Design* has aroused has been due to the fact that it has shocked people as blasphemy against the Great White Father. He was never any great hero of mine, and I am glad that you have shown up his inadequacies, but there was certainly more to those administrations than anybody could learn from your book—you hardly touch on the labor side of them, for example. The "field" expeditions are admirable —and so are the meeting at which the old man is high-pressured into following the Communist line, and the death of Miss Washburn (though I couldn't really believe in her sleeping with that guy), and a lot of other things. I shan't reproach you with your personal tendency to represent everything in America as always deteriorating, as I am working on a play,

453

supposed to take place in the immediate future, beside which your recent series looks like a smile by Truman.

We are going down to Stamford February 12. We will be staying in a cottage belonging to Mottie Eitingon. The number is in the telephone book, but it has been interchanged by mistake with the number of the same people's other house, so you have to remember that when you want the "cottage," you give them the number of the "residence." Do call us up when you are going to be in New York—perhaps you could come out for a night or so.

I am enclosing a poem of mine dealing with life in Wellfleet—one of a series, I hope. Note the reversed rhymes—so far as I know, an invention of mine.   As ever, EW

To Mamaine Koestler   [undated]*
                                                              Wellfleet

. . . The second floor of the main house has three bedrooms, two bathrooms, and an attic which I am about to have expanded with dormers in the narrow eaves and made into two bedrooms. On the top floor are two bedrooms. These old-fashioned American frame houses are, however, not in the least like any English houses, and I don't think you can imagine it correctly. It is the kind of thing that is painted white and has a green roof and green shutters. Around it are horse-chestnut trees, lindens, holly trees, black walnuts, etc., and white and purple and Persian lilacs and a variety of other shrubs, and privet and box hedges. There is a wonderful rose garden, now in very bad shape—I'm going to try to get it attended to this fall; and the side of the house which you see here on the right is covered with several kinds of ramblers . . .

To Mamaine Koestler   June 6, 1949
                                                              Wellfleet

. . . Isaiah Berlin . . . has just spent a weekend with us. He is an extraordinary Oxford don, who left Russia at the age of eight and has a sort of double Russian-and-British personality. The combination is uncanny but fascinating. We spent the whole time talking brilliantly, covering rapidly, but with astonishing knowledge, sure intelligence, and breathtaking wit, an incredible variety of subjects. Since he has left, it has occurred to me, however, that, having hardly known him before, I unloaded on him all the best stories, bon mots, and stimulating ideas of virtually my whole life as if they were new and spontaneous, and that he may have been doing the same thing with me. He is about to go back to England, and I think you ought to know him . . .

---

* Written on the back of E.'s plan of the Wellfleet house. See facing page.

MAIN ROAD

DRIVE

PORCH WITH COLUMNS

FRONT DOOR

STAIRS

LIVING ROOM

← LITTLE VESTIBULE

LARGE KITCHEN

DINING ROOM

BIG GARDEN NOW MOSTLY A JUNGLE

DOOR?

HALLWAY

EXTREMELY PLEASANT MIDDLE ROOM

DOOR INTO GARDEN

STAIRS

MY STUDY

WOOD=SHED

BATH=ROOM

This is all an independent unit, really a separate building connected with the rest of the house only by the corridor on the ground floor. Above the study are a bedroom & an attic.

OLD WINDMILL USED AS TOOLHOUSE

FURTHER BACK AN OLD BARN

... Isaiah Berlin paid us a fleeting but animated visit the other night at an hour of almost Proustian lateness. His idea was that he was passing through incognito, but had announced this to innumerable people and asked them to keep it a secret ...

To Gilbert Highet

November 7, 1949
Wellfleet

Dear Highet: I have just read your book,* which is a splendid piece of work. I am paying my respects to it in *The New Yorker*, for which I am doing a brief return engagement, so I won't express my appreciation further here. But I could not discuss it in *The New Yorker* in so detailed a way as I could have done in a more literary magazine, so I am writing you on some points that interested me.

1. In the Middle Ages, you fail to mention Hrotswitha, the German tenth-century nun, who wrote Latin plays in imitation of Terence. Whether she was a real person or, as some think, an invention of Conrad Celtis and other German humanists, who wanted to provide Germany with a medieval literature, I should think she would have been very much to your purpose. There is an admirable paper on her by Zoltan Haraszti, unraveling the whole controversy, in the *Bulletin of the Boston Public Library* for March 1945.

2. I think that there is something more to the influence of Virgil on Dante than your account of it indicates. Dante seems to have taken his cue for all his dramatic meetings from the Sixth Book of the *Aeneid*. Of course you mention his debt to this; but it is curious to see how he has picked up and exploited in his own poem all the notes struck there by Virgil: Deiphobus, as I remember, is echoed by several angry characters in the *Inferno*, and it seems to me that the pathetic effectiveness of the Palinurus incidents may have suggested Buonconte in the *Purgatorio*. Also, in pointing out that Dante treats certain incidents in a style very different from Virgil's, you don't take account of the fact that he deliberately imitates Virgil's style, just as he does with Arnaut Daniel's when he wants to evoke Virgil's personality. The meeting of Virgil with Statius involves an impersonation of Virgil's style and characteristic mood. Compare

Frate,
Non far: ché tu se' ombra, ed ombra vedi, etc.

---

* *The Classical Tradition.*

456

with something like

> *Dixit et ex oculis subito, ceu fumus in auras*
> *Commixtus tenuis, fugit diversa, neque illum*
> *Prensantem nequiquam umbras . . .*

And when Virgil finally disappears, you have not only *Manibus o date lilia plenis*, but also a sort of Virgilian plaint, with the pathetic iteration of his name. I believe, too, though this is harder to pin down, that Dante's alliterative system owed a good deal to Virgil's. I have a theory that the sounds in Virgil's name sometimes influenced those in his lines (as Dickens's name haunts the titles of his novels), as in

> *Qualis populea maerens philomela sub umbra*

or

> *Et iam summa procul villarum culmina fumant,*
> *Maioresque cadunt altis de montibus umbra.*

The *p v f* combination is, of course, a natural one; but there seems to me something Virgilian in the conclusion of the Brunetto Latini canto, and a *p v m* harmony that is certainly intentional and significant is made to sound in the farewell to Virgil, as you have *p v f m b* in the meeting of Virgil and Statius.

3. You say, on page 79, that Dante makes Statius a Christian "doubtless because of the medieval tradition of his conversion, and also because of his boundless admiration for Virgil." But apparently no such tradition is known. In the posthumous volume of Verrall's *Collected Literary Essays*, there are two fascinating papers on Dante's reasons for believing that Statius was a Christian. You ought to look them up, if you don't know them. They are a wonderful piece of [omission] work.*

4. On page 801, you speak of the notion of Dante's having prefigured the Renaissance. Had you thought of his Ulysses in connection with this? Ulysses wanted to know the world from the point of view both *de li vizi umani e del valore*, and was incited to venture out beyond the Pillars of Hercules to satisfy his curiosity. Dante evidently has him founder because, like Rimbaud, he "lacked the moral sense." There is, in classical antiquity, so far as I know, no such interpretation of Ulysses. Where did Dante get it? Some such spirit must already have been in the air.

5. You say, on page 284, that Housman was Bentley's disciple, but

---

* The original of this letter was lost and this carbon copy was found in Gilbert Highet's book *The Classical Tradition*. E.'s handwritten corrections have been inserted, but it is possible that on the actual letter Mr. Highet received, others had been added, as was the Greek text missing here.

quote only a derogatory phrase. The *lucida tela diei* passage in the preface to Manilius shows an enthusiasm for Bentley which is positively passionate, whatever he may have said elsewhere about his myopic and pedantic side. (By the way, do you know the very funny parody in the Martinus Scriblerus papers, in which Bentley is made to emend and flatten out a passage from Virgil?)

6. By what process did the French alexandrine grow out of the iambic hexameter in which Greek tragedies are written? I take it that alexandrines are simply a rhymed and less flexible version of this. I have wondered about it but never looked it up.

7. I was amused by the couplet on page 320. Did you concoct this yourself?

8. Elegiacs. I was very much interested in your discussion of this meter. I think it is a little misleading for you to say, as you do on page 381, that the difficulty of reproducing it in a modern language is partly due to the difficulty of finding spondees.

All dactylic verse in Latin and Greek involves spondees; but we don't need to look for spondees in English—in fact, a spondee at the end of an English dactylic hexameter would not produce a happy effect. All you need is trochees. But I don't understand why elegiacs have been so little attempted in English. The only good examples I can think of are Swinburne's "Hesperia" and E. A. Robinson's "Pasa Thalassa Thalassa." (D'Annunzio, though, wrote some beautiful ones in his own *Elegie Romane.*) I have been thinking about this lately, because I am very fond of this meter, and have been trying to write it with a turned-around rhyme at the end of each half line, my idea being that this might produce the effect of point that the ancients got without using rhyme. This wouldn't suit many subjects, though! I am enclosing a specimen, which might amuse you.

9. p. 683. I thought it was Sainte-Beuve who first mentioned the ivory tower. I have read a learned discussion of this, but can't remember where.

10. Mrs. Belloc Lowndes's story about Renan and France, p. 687, does not sound to me very reliable. Renan, in his *Saint Paul*, describes Paul appearing before Gallio and remarks that such a Roman gentleman could not have conceived that the future was standing before him in the person of *ce laid petit juif* (as he calls Paul in another connection). France, disputing this, undertook to show in *Sur la pierre blanche* that it was Gallio and not Paul who represented the real future, the forces of civilization that must triumph over fanaticism and superstition.

11. p. 461. I am glad to know where it is that Flaubert speaks of Virgil. I remembered it, but could not find the reference when I was writing years ago on the subject. I think that Virgil deeply influenced Flaubert, I have something about it in *The Triple Thinkers*—in the essay called "Is Verse a Dying Technique?"

458

12. p. 696. Joyce made a diagram of Ulysses, in which everything is perfectly clear. He gave a copy to Herbert Gorman, who gave a copy to me. Joyce would not let it be published (though it ought now to be printed in every copy), but he allowed Stuart Gilbert to make use of it for the purposes of the latter's book. The way Gilbert made use of it was a mess. He mixed it up with his own vaporings, so that you cannot tell what comes from Joyce and what is imagined by Gilbert. He prints some of Joyce's indications, but leaves out others that are very important. He tells you, for example, that the scene in which Dedalus walks on the beach represents the combat with Proteus, but he does not tell you that Joyce meant Proteus to be "primal matter."

13. p. 506. The relations of Bloom, Mrs. Bloom, and Dedalus have more meaning than you seem to realize—and a closer moral connection with Homer. It is, for example, as a result of his meeting Bloom that Dedalus will find the subject for his masterpiece—*Ulysses* is dated at the end as having been completed at just the time that Dedalus has told Buck Mulligan he would produce one. I have stated my view of all this in my chapter on Joyce in *Axel's Castle.**

14. p. 512. It was not *Ulysses* but Dos Passos's *Manhattan Transfer* that Paul Elmer More called "an explosion in a cesspool." I don't seem to have, so can't give you the reference—but I think it was in an essay in the volume called *The Demon of the Absolute*.

15. It is true that the Russians were but little affected by the Western revival of learning, but, in the case of Pushkin, the classics played a very important role. He had studied Latin at school, and though he later complained he had lost it, he tried to get it up again. He made some translations of Latin poems, which are said to owe more to the versions in French in his set of Latin classics than they do to the Latin itself. But a foreigner reading his poetry is struck by a Latin turn which sometimes reminds him of Horace (whose *Exegi monumentum* he puts at the head of one of his poems). Russian resembles Latin in not having any articles, and a good deal of the work of our prepositions is done, as in Latin, by endings, so you can separate modifiers from substantives and achieve effects of balance and concision not possible in modern Western languages. In the later years of Pushkin's short life, he set out, as Tolstoy did, to learn Greek, and there appears in his notebooks a crude attempt, supposed to date from 1833, to put the opening lines of the *Odyssey* into Russian, as well as copies in another hand of Sappho's ode to Aphrodite and [omission] with Russian versions that he was evidently making with the help of someone else's Russian prose. (All the information about his Latin and Greek is in the Soviet edition of these notebooks, called *Rukoyu*

* See p. 179ff.

Pushkina.) But he also did a bogus Sapphic fragment and some bogus translations from invented Greek writers, in hexameters and elegiacs (which, however, are quite successful and plausible: in some ways Russian is rather good at giving the effect of Greek), an elegiac distich on Homer and a strange unfinished poem in terza rima called *For a Translation of the Iliad*, in which he describes the effect on him of the statues in the garden of the lycée where he went to school. Besides this, all his verse, realistic though it became, is full of mythological allusions and the conventional classical masks, the Aglaias and Laises and Adonises, that he had evidently picked up partly from the French eighteenth-century poets that he began by imitating. And, in a more fundamental way, his method and temper are "classical" in the sense that he is well balanced and well proportioned and likes to put the right word in the right place. Russian literature looks different from the Russian end than it does from the point of view of the English-speaking reader of translations of the Russian novels, who thinks the Russians disorderly writers and the people they write about madmen. The life of the Russians itself was more feudal and barbaric than that of the West, but their literature was extraordinarily sophisticated, and the influence of Pushkin was lasting and almost all-pervasive—it can be seen in even Dostoevsky. But to talk about this would take too long.*

16. I am sorry that you left out D'Annunzio—especially since you gave considerable space to both Swinburne and Carducci. His novels, his poems, and his plays are all heavily plastered with the classics, and his version of them is something peculiar to the Italy of the day before yesterday. He is, besides, it seems to me, rather underrated nowadays—he is completely out of fashion in Italy. You could have done something interesting with him.

But you have covered an immense amount of ground and have been interesting as well as intelligent about such a variety of subjects! All these points are of no great importance—they have merely supplied a pretext for me to talk to you about literature . . . I have been much cheered and stimulated by your book.   Yours sincerely,

---

* See p. 276ff.

HAITI AND THE MARCELINS
1948–1957

To VLADIMIR NABOKOV   September 9, 1948
                                                              Wellfleet
. . . I'm very much interested in a Haitian novelist, Thoby-Marcelin. I
think you might like his books: *Canapé Vert* and *La Bête de Musseau*.
I don't know anything like them. The first one seemed to me anthropo-
logically fascinating, but, when I read the second one just now, I saw
that he was a decidedly distinguished, perhaps even important writer.
There is a third one coming out which is said to be terrific. It is all a
critique of morals from a point of view which enters into both the voodoo
and the Christian religions, and by no means of such special local interest
as you may think when you first encounter it. Haiti seems to be producing
quite a remarkable culture. I'm thinking of trying to get *The New
Yorker* to send me there for a visit . . .

To PHILIPPE THOBY-MARCELIN   August 30, 1948
                                                              Wellfleet
Dear Monsieur Thoby-Marcelin: Dawn Powell tells me that you are in
Washington and that you will be in this country for some time. Is there
any chance of your being in New York in September after the 21st? I
should like very much to see you, and if you should be there, I wish you
would let me know. You can reach me at the *New Yorker* office. I am
very much interested in your work—have just read *La Bête de Musseau*,
which, though not on so large a scale, seems to me in some ways even
more successful than *Canapé Vert*. Mrs. Jakobson has written me about
a new book of yours, which she is sending me in manuscript and which
I look forward to reading . . .   Yours sincerely, Edmund Wilson

To PHILIPPE THOBY-MARCELIN   September 8, 1948
                                                     Wellfleet
. . . In the meantime, do send me the MS of your poems. As for a preface,
I had been thinking of writing something about your work as a whole.
Wouldn't this be a better idea? . . .

To PHILIPPE THOBY-MARCELIN   December 6, 1948
                                                     Wellfleet
Dear Marcelin: Thank you very much for the manuscripts. I was greatly
interested in the memoir of Hippolyte. I wish you had made it complete
and written about his death—I think you said you were there at the time
he died. A good deal of the poetry is very successful, exquisite—it seems
to me very original and not much like anything I know in French—a
genuine literature of Haiti. You ought to have all your poems brought
out in a volume . . . I haven't yet received *Le Crayon de Dieu*.
    We immensely enjoyed seeing you in New York . . . There is so much
that I still want to talk to you about.   Best regards, Edmund Wilson

To PHILIPPE THOBY-MARCELIN   July 16, 1949
                                                     Wellfleet
. . . I am sorry that neither Farrar, Straus nor Rinehart would bring out
Le Crayon de Dieu . . . have you got or could you get any extra copies of
Canapé Vert and *La Bête*? I should like to send them to people in France
in the hope of interesting somebody in bringing them out over there.
Sartre has recently published an article on an anthology which included
work by Jacques Roumain, and I was sorry not to see you mentioned . . .

To PHILIPPE THOBY-MARCELIN   September 28, 1949

. . . About going to Haiti. I had hoped that I could get *The New Yorker*
to send me there at the end of November, but they have just definitely
decided not to do so . . .

To PHILIPPE THOBY-MARCELIN   November 5, 1949
                                                     Wellfleet
. . . I have persuaded a new magazine, *The Reporter*, to send me to
Haiti to do them some articles on Haitian literature and politics. Would
there be any chance of your being able to go, too, at some time? . . .

To ELENA WILSON   November 26, 1949
                                              Miami Beach, Florida
. . . I rather enjoyed the trip yesterday—sitting in a comfortable little com-
partment in all those well-fitting new clothes. The train was so clean and

modern that even you wouldn't have minded it. It was stimulating after Wellfleet to see the industrial efficiency of Philadelphia and Wilmington for the first time in years. I went through quite a lot of my Haitian literature. The report on the UNESCO mission there—which *The Reporter* wants me to check on and write about—shows that the "capitalist" countries are being driven to at least make some gestures in the direction of meeting socialism halfway. It is curious to read about these attempts to encourage rural cooperatives and popular education in Haiti, and then read Bellegarde's book about the American occupation, in which it appears that we did everything possible to prevent them from having schools.

I . . . woke up early to see the dazzling golden light on the green palms and little pine trees strung with Florida moss. I have never been in Florida before and was fascinated by the pageant of bird life that goes past the window: snowy egrets, several kinds of beige and bluish heron, and other darker long-winged birds that I take to be buzzards—all looking as if they had flown right out of Audubon—he must have gone crazy when he came here. There are also smaller birds that fly in flocks with quick wingbeats, and it gives an almost musical pleasure to see the contrasts of tempo between these and the slower rhythms of the longer-winged birds. They all fly close to the train and not far above the endless pale swamps and plains. It is wonderful to see an egret alighting and folding its wings from the flying position with deliberate dignity and grace.

Miami is not so attractive—it is, in fact, of an unimaginable awfulness—much like other American seaside resorts but on an unprecedented scale: acres of cheap white shops, mountain ranges of white hotels. After lunch, I had a taxi drive me over to Miami Beach. It goes on for miles—thousands of hotels and houses and monotonous lines of palms. I can't imagine how people live here or why so many of them come: it all seems a great insipid vacuum—less amusing than Southern California, because there is no touch of fantasy about anything . . .

To Elena Wilson   November 28, 1949
                              Hotel Oloffson, Port-au-Prince, Haiti
. . . I had a very pleasant plane trip here yesterday—only about an hour and a half from Miami to Cuba and two hours from there to Haiti.

I am very much impressed with the Haitians. You have only to see them to realize what a wretched life we have made for the Negroes in the States. The Haitians with whom I traveled on the plane and the officials who handled the passengers at the airport were entirely different from our Negroes. It is not merely that they are quick and polite but that they have no consciousness of inferiority—so that their faces and bearing are different. I went out for a walk yesterday afternoon and got the same impression from the ordinary people on the streets. They are extremely good-looking, and to see the children playing and the older people taking their Sunday afternoon walks made me realize that our Negroes are never at home. There is no squalor (in this part of town, but, driving in from the airport, I went through a more African-looking quarter), though most of the houses seem rickety or flimsy—many of them are decorated with this wooden lace. They were all wearing their best Sunday clothes—not stylish, but very clean. What is fascinating is to see people of a different race really (as they don't seem to be in the U.S.) at their physical best. They seemed quick, sober, and gentle . . .

I came on the plane with an amiable Belgian ex-consul, who said that the people were "a little slow." They liked to write here but were perhaps a little too "lyrique." He seemed to feel that the production of poetry was one of the main industries of Haiti. He told me that the climate was "delicious"—which seems to be true—quite warm, but in the morning and at night there is a cool little breeze. There is an agreeable fragrance of cooking and coffee in the air. The only thing it reminds me of is a little of New Orleans.

I had dinner on the verandah, which corresponds to the balcony on the second floor and has a good view of the town and the harbor. The food here is not fancy but it is all right. I went to bed after dinner and read Aimé Césaire's long Surrealist poem and the book that Waldo lent me on Toussaint L'Ouverture. They are both extremely painful. Césaire's poem —*Cahier d'un retour au pays natal*—seems to me about the best thing I have read in the school of Rimbaud and Lautréamont. It is infinitely superior to the Surrealist stuff because it is about something important: Césaire's situation as a Negro from Martinique who has been civilizing himself in Paris. The account of the slave trade in the other book almost made me sick. You are closer to all that out here. Our idea of it is blurred in the States, where, bad though the situation was, the slaves must have been treated somewhat better.

In Miami, I went to a movie after dinner. I didn't remain long, but it made an appalling impression on me, and Miami, in fact, in its way, has been as much of a revelation as Haiti. The theater was not a very big one, but represented the last degree of luxury: seats, with some kind of specially soft cushions, that swing back to let people pass; soft indirect lighting from the ceiling on a gray and pink interior decorated with big metallic mythological figures, like the Paul Manship bas-reliefs on Rockefeller Center, framed in cameolike white seashells, and great white plaster exfoliations that looked like the legs and defensive antennae of the sea crawfish in the Miami aquarium. The picture (*Oh, You Beautiful Doll*) was a Technicolor that covered the whole surface of a large screen with some trumped-up sentimental romance intended to create glamour about the writer of mediocre popular songs that were current no longer ago than my college years. They were commonplace and vulgar enough then, and, revived, they are simply sickly. All these attempts to exploit the immediate past show the rapidity of the bankruptcy of the movies as purveyors of popular entertainment, but the Miami audience showed that there is a public that enjoys their product. They were the characterless devitalized drove that seems to populate Miami, and they sat in a muffled atmosphere that smelled like scented face powder—I couldn't tell whether the theater was perfumed or whether it was due to the fact that the women all used the same kind of cosmetics. The characters in the picture represented the same kind of insipid people, brightly colored and gigantically magnified. The three shorts all dealt with animals: a hunting number, an animated cartoon, and a picture about racing whippets. I felt that the human beings were no good as animal organisms any more, and that we had had to fall back on the lower animals, who were at least good examples of their various species.

I don't think it had been brought home to me before how all this side of America had been developing, and how it looks today to foreigners who come here. It is only when you go to the airfield and see them handling these big planes that you are made to feel better as you become aware that the personal deterioration has been offset by these mechanical creations—which somewhat restores your pride. I find that I am putting into these letters the kind of thing I usually write in my notebook—so please be sure to save them! . . .

To Elena Wilson   December 7, 1949
                                                                Haiti

. . . I abstained, after the theater, from going to a party for the actors, because I had to leave at four the next morning for Cap Haitien . . . The Bogats drove me. The road, which is the best in Haiti, is in perfectly awful condition, almost as bad as the bomb-blasted ones in Europe: great holes and an overflowing river through which the car has to be driven. It took us about eight hours, but it was tremendously interesting for me. You go between cane fields and banana orchards and a countryside that must be like Africa, with the people all living in thatched mud huts. Cap Haitien is quite different from Port-au-Prince and gives you an idea of the past. There is a big and fine Spanish church, built in the fifteenth century,* and the old gates of the planters' great places, sometimes opening on wild fields. In the town, there are planters' mansions which have been kept up and used for various purposes. There is an absolutely first-rate hotel in one of them, with beautiful garden and grounds. We slept in the

---

* E.'s note in margin: "!! 17th century, more likely. Columbus didn't get there till 1492."

465

afternoon, and I got up early the next morning and went to see the palace of King Christophe, Sans Souci, built in imitation of Versailles, but looted after his death and gradually dismantled by the peasants, so that there is not much left of it now—and afterwards made the trip up the mountain to see the citadel he built. You go up on horseback, and it takes about two hours. It is the thing I have most enjoyed since I have been here. The hills, which look like peaks plucked up in a starched tablecloth, lifted themselves into a fresh dazzling morning light, where little round clouds poised above their summits. You climb right up into this light through a forest of mahogany, coconut, cocoa bean, coffee bean, breadfruit, pomegranate, mango, banana, orange, avocado, calabash, bamboo, and all kinds of other things, with citronella and anise underfoot, smelling and tasting just as they do in the preparations of them we use. This will bring to mind an image of fruit salad, but actually everything is green and not junglelike, but wonderfully fresh. At the top, you find the formidable citadel, futile as it turned out and never completed, where Christophe, beaten and ill, shot himself with his golden bullet*—but a source of pride to every Haitian, because it somehow represents for Negroes an affirmation of will and a defiance of the world.

We came back Sunday night. Bogat himself drove instead of the one-eyed driver who had brought us, and made it in five hours. I liked him: he is completely black but aquiline, so that he looks like an American, a Negro type I have rarely seen. He is a businessman, not intellectual, but very well informed and intelligent—kindly and equipped with the Haitian charm. He is the only Haitian I have seen who seemed to me to have anything of the Roman national heroes of the revolutionary period . . .

I was roused out of bed this morning by the arrival at eleven of the Marcelin brothers. They had breakfast with me and then came up here and talked till after two. I was very much interested in them. Pierre, who writes the novels with Phito, was different from what I had expected . . . He is in some ways much more attractive than Phito, has an almost feminine good looks, sensitiveness, and charm (without giving a pansy impression). I think that he is probably the more important of the two in their literary collaboration. My guess is that their collaboration is very close . . . and I imagine that what will happen is that Pierre will join Phito in Washington and that they will write another novel together. Pierre speaks even more indistinctly than Phito, and when he is talking about anything at all delicate, absolutely whispers, so that the things I most want to hear are completely unintelligible to me. The other brother [Milo] attends the voodoo ceremonies and commits them all to memory without writing them down. He is publishing texts of all their rites. They

---

* E.'s note in margin: "No: he shot himself in the palace, was carried up to the citadel afterwards."

466

talked about voodoo mythology. I think that they are rather *fin de race* and at the same time rather *déséquilibrés* between their French tradition and their African heritage. They have all three made a cult of *"le peuple"* —these two told me, as Phito had, that the peasants represented *"le meilleur de l'Haiti,"* and that their life is really richer than that of the bourgeoisie because they think they are surrounded by the spirits of the voodoo mythology and in constant communication with and possession by them. The Marcelin family is very distinguished here—there are a *rue* Marcelin and a *pont* Marcelin—but I am told that, with their considerable Negro admixture, they don't belong to the very top layer, which, it seems, consists entirely of people who are almost entirely white, who marry only whites or each other and who only engage in business, never politics.

The only example of this I have seen is the woman who runs the wonderful hotel at Cap Haitien and whom I took for a white French-woman. She gave my black guide a horrible tongue-lashing, which made me feel sorry for him. He had expounded the citadel with much elo-quence. This guide, though a little of a fraud, I found rather sympathetic. He was full of misinformation. In the forest, I asked him what the bird was which was giving a harsh cachinating cry. *"C'est le rossignol, mon-sieur,"* he said. Was it really, I asked, the nightingale that was celebrated for its song? *"C'est le même oiseau, monsieur,"* he answered. They told me afterwards that it was some kind of woodpecker.

The big layer of political and professional people, to which the Marcelins belong, has a sort of social equality with these, but does not intermarry with them. Below is a third stratum of government employees, which continually takes in black blood . . .

In-between writing this letter, I have been to an embassy party . . . I became involved in a conversation with the younger embassy and State Department people, who finally rather disgusted me by their plugging of the beneficent purposes of the U.S. in respect to the rest of the world. I suppose that what we are doing in the West Indies and South America is all right, but I react unfavorably against attempts to represent it as dis-interested. The First Secretary's house is in a section of large and hand-some residences that I hadn't yet seen. Life must be rather agreeable here. I found a former cultural attaché who had been superseded but was just staying on. No Negroes except a Negro agricultural expert, an American, attached to the embassy, with his wife . . .

To Elena Wilson   December 12, 1949
                                                                                Haiti

. . . I was right in my idea that Haiti has a unique importance and interest. It is the only place where you can see independent Negroes, with a tradi-tion of victory behind them, trained in a highly developed culture. One curious thing I had noticed, that Yvonne Sylvain talked about explicitly:

the Haitians make a point of not visiting and not knowing much about the other West Indian islands, where the Negroes are still kept in an inferior position. They have lately taken a little to amusing themselves in Havana, but otherwise, except for sending young ladies to learn English in Jamaica, they simply ignore the rest of the Antilles. When they make trips, they go to France or the United States. She says that the slums of Port-au-Prince are as bad as any anywhere, but that I am right in my impression that all except the poorest people in P.-au-P. are clean. Soap, she says, is one of their chief articles of consumption . . .

To Philippe Thoby-Marcelin   January 26, 1950
                                                          Wellfleet

Dear Phito (Do let us stop calling each other Mister): How are you? We were sorry that you had to go so soon when you were here at New Year's . . . I never got around to talking to you about a lot of things I had hoped to discuss.

I should like to ask you a few questions, if it isn't too much of a nuisance, in connection with my Haitian articles, on which I have been working . . .

I admired the cathedral at Cap Haitien and was told that it dated from the fifteenth century, but this can hardly be true. I can't find any description of it in anything I have except a little travel book, which simply mentions it as the "Centenary Cathedral." Do you know when it was built—it looks more like the seventeenth century—and why it is called the Centenary Cathedral?

Can you tell me Cassagnol's first name and the proper way to spell his last name? Is *Parti populaire chrétien* the right name of his party? Was it in his paper (what was it called?) that Foisset's exposé appeared? I should be grateful if you could lend me Foisset's articles. You said that you thought you had them.

Could you write me briefly the career of Colonel Roland as you told it to me when we were driving to Wellfleet?

What do you hear about recent political developments in Haiti?

Do you know the first name of the Bourdelle who has painted the execrable murals for the Exposition buildings? Am I right in thinking that he is the son of the French sculptor Paul Bourdelle?

Am I right in thinking that Estimé's term of office normally expires in 1952? Have you heard anything about the results of the January elections? Do you now have both a Senate and a Chamber of Deputies, and are these the bodies that would have to vote on changing the Constitution so that the President could be reelected?

I understand that Arthur Bonhomme served about two years in jail in connection with an attempt on the life of President Vincent. When was this?—in 1940?

468

Do you think that it would be embarrassing for Lespès if I said that in conversation I found him more open-minded than one nowadays expects a Communist to be?—that he expressed himself as well disposed toward the United States, in spite of the fact that, as I understand, he had been printing in his paper the most fantastic stories about us.

I should be grateful if you would read my stuff when I have finished it and had it typed . . .

I have been reading Seabrook's book,* and I agree with you that it has some value, in spite of the fact that he is more interested in telling a story than in reaching scientific conclusions. What is bad about it and what must have contributed to making the Haitians dislike it are the illustrations of Alexander King—one of the world's worst artists, who had at one time an unaccountable vogue among American editors and publishers.

How are you? I have sent *Le Crayon de Dieu* to Houghton Mifflin, but they haven't yet made up their minds about it.

Yours as ever, Edmund Wilson

To PHILIPPE THOBY-MARCELIN   April 29, 1950
                                                   Wellfleet

. . . In rewriting my own section on Haitian literature, the thing that I most need is a copy of the volume of Roumer's poems. The only one I could find in Haiti was in the Bibliothèque Nationale, and I had to write about him from memory without the book before me. Can you think of any way that I could buy or borrow a copy? It doesn't seem to be any use applying to the libraries in Port-au-Prince. Do you think Roumer would send me a copy himself? Other books I want to get are Frédéric Marcelin's novels, Lhérisson's *Zoune chez sa ninnaine* (I was very much amused by *La Famille des Pitite-Caille*), and any or all of the books of Roumain, except *Gouverneurs de la rosée* and *Bois-d'ébène*, which I have. I should be extremely grateful if you could think of any way I could get them. (What do you make of Duraciné Vaval's *Histoire de la littérature Haïtienne*? I have found it very useful, but have the impression that he has given himself a prominence that he does not quite deserve!)

Please give your brother my best regards . . .   As ever, Edmund W

I hear very good reports about *Le Crayon de Dieu* from Houghton Mifflin . . .

To JOHN DOS PASSOS   September 5, 1950
                                                   Wellfleet

. . . Phito Marcelin has expressed a desire to see you. He is lonely in Washington and gets dreadfully deprived on account of segregation on the one hand and lack of Negro friends on the other—spends as much time

---

* *The Magic Island.*

as possible in New York. He has been up here a couple of times and I have got to know him pretty well. He is a very first-rate fellow and most interesting to talk to when you get past his conventional politeness. He knows Haiti inside out and—when he is really speaking with candor—is very realistic and intelligent about it. The best of these educated Haitians —though rather shy and sly with foreigners—always surprise me by being so little provincial, but, of course, between the two Americas and America and Europe and the black and white worlds, their position for observing and comparing must be unique . . . Marcelin's address in Washington is 1712 16th Street, N.W. He works during the day at the Pan-American Union. He and his brother were at Yaddo this summer but the brother couldn't stand it and went back to Haiti . . .

To Eva Thoby-Marcelin   March 7, 1953
                                              Princeton
. . . We were very much pleased with the little book of Phito's poems. They seem to me better than ever—have been brought out by the selection and, I suppose, some revision. His personal accent is now unmistakable. I like *"une flamme hirondelle dans l'ombre absolue,"* and so many other things. They are among the very best Haitian poems and as good as anything recent I have seen from France . . .

To Phito and Eva Thoby-Marcelin   August 10, 1957
                                            Talcottville
Dear Phito and Eva: I was very glad to hear from you—had been wondering what had happened to you . . . I was glad to hear that Milo [Marcelin] got a Guggenheim . . . I've been here almost all summer working on my book about the literature of the Civil War . . .

This year I read Dujardin's book *Les Lauriers sont coupés* that Phito gave me a couple of years ago—I thought it was awfully good, a masterpiece in a small way. I have received the first six volumes of the complete and unexpurgated Goncourt Journal—published in Monaco—which is so hair-raisingly scandalous that I could hardly tear myself away from it to return to the more humdrum literature of the Civil War period.

I passed through Cazenovia once this summer—isn't that where Eva comes from?—and was much struck by how pretty and well kept it was . . .
                                        As ever, Edmund

THE FIFTIES

I am much more of a journalist than you and like to astonish
people with startling discoveries and novel juxtapositions.
                                                    —To Allen Tate

I seem nowadays to be obsessed with minorities.

CHRONOLOGY

1950	CLASSICS AND COMMERCIALS
APRIL	We have been in New York for most of two months [17 East 84th Street].
AUGUST	Talcottville: We are spending a few days up here in a house belonging to my mother . . . *The Little Blue Light* is now definitely to be done in Cambridge August 14 . . . with Jessica Tandy and Hume Cronyn.
OCTOBER	My old friend Edna Millay died.
1951	
JANUARY	We are going to New York to spend the rest of the winter [11 East 87th Street].
MARCH	[Edmund's mother died in Red Bank.]
APRIL	*The Little Blue Light:* It's finally going to be done April 15 by ANTA.
AUGUST	Talcottville.
NOVEMBER	We spent two weeks in Red Bank going through my mother's house.
	Christian Gauss died at Princeton.
1952	THE SHORES OF LIGHT
FEBRUARY	We moved everything out of Red Bank the week before last . . . We are going to spend the rest of the winter at 17 East 97th Street.
AUGUST	I shall be up in New York State till after Labor Day . . . I'll be in Princeton to perform for the Christian Gauss Foundation from the beginning of October.
1953	
SPRING	I was in Virginia.
SUMMER	Wellfleet, Talcottville.

1954	**FIVE PLAYS***
JANUARY–MAY	When we were in Europe—London, the Basil Street Hotel; Paris, Hôtel du Quai Voltaire; the Salzburg Seminar of American Studies; Munich, Frankfurt, Rapallo.
MARCH	*The New Yorker* is sending me to Israel.
MAY–JUNE	Wellfleet.
JULY–AUGUST	Talcottville: I'm up here doing prodigies of work.
1955	**THE SCROLLS FROM THE DEAD SEA**
FEBRUARY	26 East 81st Street, New York.
JULY–AUGUST	Talcottville.
1956	**RED, BLACK, BLOND AND OLIVE; A PIECE OF MY MIND:** *Reflections at Sixty*
JUNE	Honorary degree from Princeton. First attempt to settle income tax.
JULY–SEPTEMBER	London, Paris, Munich, Paris: I am almost ready to yield to the charms of the older and more gracious civilization of Europe.
NOVEMBER	Wellfleet: Let down by the election.
1957	
JANUARY–MAY	16 Farrar Street, Cambridge.
SUMMER	Wellfleet, Talcottville.
DECEMBER	I am writing about the Iroquois Indians for *The New Yorker*.
1958	**THE AMERICAN EARTHQUAKE**
FEBRUARY	My trip to the Indians was immensely successful.
NOVEMBER	I spent most of the summer on the Iroquois.
1959	*Apologies to the Iroquois* in *The New Yorker*.
SUMMER	Wellfleet, Talcottville.
SEPTEMBER	I've accepted for 1959–1960 the new Lowell lectureship at Harvard—shall give them my Civil War.† 12 Hilliard Street, Cambridge.

---

* *Five Plays:* Cyprian's Prayer / The Crime in the Whistler Room / This Room and This Gin and These Sandwiches / Beppo and Beth / The Little Blue Light.
† Chapters of *Patriotic Gore: Studies in the Literature of the Civil War* ran intermittently in *The New Yorker* from 1948 to 1961.

1950

February 24, 1950
                                                17 East 84th Street, N.Y.

Dear Christian: I have just sent you a copy of André Gide's anthology
of French poetry, which I think will interest you, if you haven't seen it—
simply, I think, because it is a little unconventional. Some people object
to Péguy's being left out—for which I, however, am grateful. The introduction seems to me admirable. He has produced some amusing modern
poets—such as Franc-Nohain and Henry J. M. Levet, of whom I had
never heard. Do read these, if you don't know them.

I am glad to hear from Katherine that you are doing well. I have been
trying to imagine you in Florida. I had never been there till just before
Christmas, when I went through and spent a night in Miami on my way
to Haiti. I thought the bird life was fascinating but the vacationers insipid
to the point of horror. Miami is truly appalling—it is on such a gigantic
scale! But the country and the water, when you get away from all that,
must be very pleasant.

I have just read the whole of the manuscript of Arthur Mizener's book
on Scott and am very much worried about it.* He has assembled in a
spirit absolutely ghoulish everything discreditable or humiliating that ever
happened to Scott. He has distorted the anecdotes that people have told
him in such a way as to put Scott and Zelda in the worst possible light,
and he has sometimes taken literally the jokes and nonsense that Scott
was always giving off in letters and conversation and representing them
as sinister realities. On the other hand, he gives no sense at all of the
Fitzgeralds in the days when they were soaring—when Scott was successful
and Zelda enchanting. Of course, Mizener is under a disadvantage in not
having known them or their period, but his book is a disconcerting revelation of his own rather sour personality. I am disturbed about it because I

---

* *The Far Side of Paradise*, a biography of F. Scott Fitzgerald by Arthur Mizener.

am, I suppose, partly responsible for his having undertaken it, and his brief biography of Scott in that book about eminent Princetonians and one or two other things had led me to think that he would be a good person. (The worst of it is that I have also an uncomfortable feeling that he is exploiting to some extent my own technique of emphasizing the miseries of a writer's life in order to bring out the glories of his work—because he does praise Scott as a writer, though in rather a woolly and boring way.) I am going to remonstrate with him about it. Please don't say anything about all this.

We are down here in New York for a few weeks. Cape Cod is bleak and deserted at this time of the year. —The T. S. Eliot play is really very good—you ought to see it when you get back.* It has even, apparently, been a success and ought to be still going. I had just been getting rather discouraged with him—I thought his *Notes toward a Definition of Culture* was twaddle, and was getting ready to contribute my obol to condemning him to the fate of Aristides, which Allen Tate says he is ripe for. I have just written a play myself, which I am publishing in the spring.†

I have been reading up Haitian literature at a great rate. It is relatively enormous: they have published more books in Haiti in proportion to the population than any other American country with the exception of the United States. The standard is very high. They have written an enormous amount of poetry, much of it very accomplished. Some of this is a pale imitation of French, reflecting everything from Romanticism to Surrealism; but the remarkable thing is that they have produced some very original—and often very curious—work, especially the novels of the Marcelin brothers and the poetry of Emile Roumer. Do you know the work of Aimé Césaire, the Martinique Negro poet?—now the deputy to the French Chamber from Martinique, since the island has been given the status of a department. I think that his *Cahier d'un retour au pays natal*, discovered and reprinted by André Breton, is probably (though I don't necessarily take Breton's opinions seriously) the best thing that has been done in its genre of the declamatory full-length prose poem since *Une Saison en enfer*. I have found a copy of this at Brentano's and am going to send it to you. The emergence of these West Indian Negro writers represents a new flowering of French that may have some even more interesting future.

To go back to Arthur Mizener: reading his books has given me new insight into how literary biographies are written—makes me understand the biographer's misunderstanding of what happened and his ignorance of important things that people close to his subject knew but that nobody

---

* *The Cocktail Party.*
† *The Little Blue Light.*

would have been willing to tell him. It is queer to find one's own day before yesterday turning up as literary history. I thought that Arthur, having been to Princeton, would be good on the Princeton part; but he is actually rather misleading. He once told me of his permanently gnawing chagrin at not having made the right kind of club, and he seems to suppose that in our time there was a social life and a literary life that was something quite different. I am apparently represented as having written the Triangle play in my senior year in order to acquire prestige.

I suppose that you are depressed, as I am, by the deadlock that Russia and the U.S. have reached. Of course, these enormous wars promote all kinds of technical progress, and this is one of the elements of civilization; but I wish we could work round to a phase that would bring into prominence again the elements that I have more personal interest in. The kind of thing that is going on makes a writer feel so helpless—especially if he has spent years on *The New Republic* and celebrated the makers of the Russian Revolution.

Don't bother to acknowledge this letter, as I'm sure you oughtn't to bother with correspondence. I hope to see you when you get back to Princeton. I often think of you and continue to count on you even when I don't see you often.   . . . As ever, Edmund Wilson

To Arthur Mizener   February 22, 1950

. . . You have done a remarkable job of research, of assembling and sorting out scattered materials, and have understood admirably a good many things that the ordinary biographer would have been likely to miss . . .

To Arthur Mizener   March 3, 1950
                                                17 East 84th Street, N.Y.
. . . I ought to tell you that I saw Inez Haynes Irwin a year ago (she used to be a well-known writer, is quite an old lady now), and she told me that she had met Scott only once, but that he had made on her a tremendous impression—looking distinguished and talking brilliantly. "He was like a Renaissance prince," she said. Undoubtedly this was not the light in which he appeared when he went to see Edith Wharton, but if he had had a chance to know her better, I imagine that they would have gotten along, as Gertrude Stein and he did, and the bordello in which he and Zelda were supposed to have spent a week would have fallen into perspective as a joke. (I don't believe, by the way, as you seem to, that Gertrude Stein's interest in him was prompted solely by her pique against Hemingway. She was a very good judge of writing, and the only time I ever met her she talked about Scott with intelligence. She said—what is perfectly true—that he had much more sense of form than Hemingway.)

In Zelda's case, though you describe her as she later was, you don't give any idea of her appearance at the time she first came to New York, except for her provincial clothes—of which, when I spoke to her later once of the first time John Bishop and I had seen her, I discovered she was still ashamed, but which none of Scott's friends at that time had thought anything but romantically Southern. Yet her astonishing prettiness then, with what John called her "honey-colored" hair, is a very important "value" in the picture. Nor do you, I think, make clear that even when her mind was going, the writing and painting she did had her curious personal quality of imaginative iridescence and showed something of real talent. In the earlier days of her married life this talent came out mainly in her conversation, which was so full of felicitous phrases and unexpected fancies that, in spite of the fact that it was difficult to talk to her consecutively about anything, you were not led, especially if you yourself had absorbed a few Fitzgerald highballs, to suspect any mental unsoundness from her free "flight of ideas" . . .

. . . It is true that you have the advantage of not having known the Fitzgeralds or seen anything of the gaiety of the twenties, whereas you must have had a first-hand impression of the desperate hangover of the thirties. But you can't really tell the story without somehow doing justice to the exhilaration of the days when Scott was successful and Zelda at her most enchanting . . . The remarkable thing about the Fitzgeralds was their capacity for carrying things off and carrying people away by their spontaneity, charm, and good looks. They had a genius for imaginative improvisations of which they were never quite deprived even in their later misfortunes . . .

. . . Since I wrote you, I have got hold of a copy of Zelda's *Save Me the Waltz*, which I hadn't seen since it came out . . . I have the impression that you have quoted or depended on the novel in such a way sometimes as to make it appear that you have some kind of direct authority for attributing behavior or thoughts to Zelda which are actually out of the story. Of course, you would give your source in the notes; but wouldn't it be a mistake to take incidents in the story as literally true, since so much of it is obviously fictitious? I am thinking of the episode of the aviator and his departure and the heroine's tearing up his letter and photograph, etc. Have you independent confirmation that all this really happened as she tells it . . .

To Arthur Mizener   April 4, 1950
                                                                                    Wellfleet

Dear Arthur: I have badgered you enough about the Fitzgerald book but I had been thinking of sending you some general tips and your last letter encourages me to do so.

It is important, in writing a biography, to remember that you are telling a story and that the problems of presenting the material are in many ways just the same as those of presenting a subject of fiction. You cannot take for granted, on the part of the reader, any knowledge whatever of your particular subject. You have to introduce it to him so that he will understand it every step of the way, and you have to create your characters and background and situations just as you would those of fiction. You must put yourself in the reader's place. *The Kenyon Review* and the rest of them are not a particularly good school for this, because they are always making allusions to writers and movements and books without explaining what these things mean to them (very often they don't quite know). They assume that the reader will have read the same books and made the same assumptions as themselves.

And the biographer has not only to choose and place every detail of his picture, but to calculate the tone of every sentence. It is quite obvious that, in dealing with Scott, you have produced, by not hitting the tone, an effect you didn't intend. This has sometimes happened to me when some completely irrelevant feeling has got into something I was writing. To correct it, you have to approach the thing in a perfectly objective way and readjust it step by step, systematically, so as to put it in a different light. In spite of the fact that the biographer is given his materials in the shape of letters, memoirs, etc., he is just as much responsible for the portrait that emerges as Scott was for the Great Gatsby.

But, in dealing with the given data, you do have a different problem from the writer of sheer fiction, because you have to have some principles for deciding what constitutes evidence. Biographers, of course, have dealt with this problem in a variety of different ways. It is always a lot of trouble to check on facts, and in the case of an amusing or romantic character, anecdotes grow rapidly into legends. I recommend, in this connection, that book about Henry James called *The Legend of the Master*,* in which the author tries to run down the truth about some of the most famous James anecdotes. When I was writing about Lenin in the *Finland Station*, I tended to accept the memoirs published in the Soviet Union. I hadn't realized how early the deliberate mythmaking had been begun. Now I am not at all sure that some of my details of his return to Russia were not made up out of the whole cloth for the purposes of a volume of eulogies, of the authenticity of which I was convinced by the proletarian status of the supposed witnesses, but by which I may well have been taken in. Trotsky, whose first volume of a life of Lenin is one of the best things on the subject, does not even believe in the memoir published by Lenin's sister, which I decided to accept. You don't have any such baffling

---

* A collection of memoirs of Henry James compiled by Simon Nowell-Smith.

problem in finding out about Scott, but it is always an awful nuisance to try to get at the truth behind conflicting accounts, and though you are scrupulous and scholarly with texts, you have not had any occasion before to train yourself in examining evidence. In regard to the nut-kicking incident, for example (if it was nuts: I thought it was something else, which shows how legends vary), I suggest that you write to John Dos Passos . . . explaining that you have heard several versions and asking him exactly what happened. He was there and he is an accurate observer and is likely to tell you the truth.

Well, I seem to be having a field day as an Elder Biographer giving advice. Don't feel, by the way, that you are bound to accept all my or anybody else's suggestions about the MS.   As ever, Edmund W.

To Christian Gauss   April 27, 1950
                                                        Wellfleet
Dear Christian: I have just been thinking of you in connection with the early text of *Madame Bovary* that I have been examining (edited by Pommier et Leleu: Librairies José Corti). The Princeton library ought to have it; you ought to look it up if you haven't seen it. It is tremendously interesting and shows that Flaubert's methods of writing were somewhat different from what I had imagined. If you look up one of his most marvelous passages—young Charles Bovary looking out of the window at Rouen, or the old farm servant at the Comices—you find that the earlier version is likely to be quite flat (in the former passage you don't find at all the sentence that gives the scene all its poignancy: "*et il ouvrait les narines pour aspirer les bonnes odeurs de la campagne, qui ne venaient pas jusqu'à lui*") and full of realistic details that he hasn't yet reduced to essentials. He seems first to have assembled materials, and the really transforming touch didn't come till a comparatively late stage. That this touch could be so magic is what surprises me. What a distance, in the scene at the window, between (early version) "*Sous lui, en bas, la rivière, qui fait de ce quartier de Rouen comme une Venise de bas étape, coulait safran, ou indigo, sous les petits ponts qui la couvrent,*" and "*La rivière, qui fait de ce quartier de Rouen comme une ignoble petite Venise, coulait en bas, sous lui, jaune, violette ou bleue entres ses ponts et ses grilles.*" It somehow gives me an even higher opinion of Flaubert to see him bringing these paragraphs to life, turning on the music and color only after the data have been lined up.

How are you, and are you back from Florida? If you are, I shall be in Red Bank next week, and I should like to come over to see you . . .

Arthur Mizener has behaved very well about the criticisms I made of his biography of Scott and has been revising the manuscript, but I have my misgivings about the results of his trying to put Scott in a more genial light . . .   As ever, Bunny Wilson

To Morton D. Zabel   April 28, 1950
                                                                     Wellfleet
Dear Morton: I have had and enjoyed both your letters—have not answered them before because I have been overcome by a series of disasters. I was ill most of the time I was in New York and am not well yet. There is something wrong with my vocal chords—God's punishment for talking too much and too loud—and I am not supposed to speak. In the meantime, my mother—who is eighty-five—had a rather alarming collapse and had to spend two weeks in the hospital. I only came back from Red Bank last Monday—she is back at home now—but am going down again next week.

We saw *The Cocktail Party* and the Henry James play. I think you ought to take them both in when you come on. The former is in many ways preposterous but a very effective play, and the best thing, I think, that Eliot has done in years. It may not look like much in the printed text —partly because there is no stage business indicated. I thought that some of the most moving touches were entirely in the silent business, and I have been wondering whether Eliot invented them himself. The scene between the girl and the psychiatrist, following on the scene with the married couple, is the pivot of the whole thing and somehow very impressive, even if you don't, as I don't, take any stock in Eliot's religious point of view. What gets over and what he really feels deeply is the sensation of spiritual emptiness which the girl in the play identifies as a conviction of sin. This is something, it seems to me, very New England and Protestant: she has to fill her life with good works. I can follow him up to the point where he makes connections with Christianity, but, except in the crucifixion idea and the rather corny scene at the end of the second act, where they are holding holy communion or toasting the Trinity or something, he does not plug this much here. Of course, from my point of view, she might just as well have become a Communist of the crop who were converted in the twenties.

The *Turn of the Screw* play demonstrates how much dramatic interest exists in a latent state in Henry James; it isn't impossible that the movies may do (but probably won't) something exciting with *The Wings of the Dove*. The best scenes—and they are very effective—come right out of the story itself. Poor Miss Straight* is exceedingly weak; but the children are absolutely remarkable. The adapter has contributed a passage in which

---

* Beatrice Straight played the governess.

the little girl tells about eating beetles, of which the Master would not have approved. We also saw *The Consul*, which I think is not really good. Menotti is a very peculiar case: he is a composer who is a master of theatrical tricks, and he is better at these tricks than at music. *The Consul* is simply a succession of them, and the score is more or less on the order of Eliza crossing the ice. (I think *The Medium*, which you've probably seen, was better.)

We went to the *New Yorker* party celebrating their twenty-fifth anniversary. It was enormous—a thousand people invited—and far less attractive than the one fifteen years ago, when there was a smaller staff and fewer contributors. The evening, in fact, was one of catastrophes, and it has been suggested that *The New Yorker* ought to write it up in the vein of Hersey's *Hiroshima*. Prominent persons whom I will not name were guilty of wholesale malignant rudeness; other people were extinguished by blackouts and woke up the next morning in suites at the Ritz, which were generously paid for by the magazine; old bores that one thought one had left behind sometime back in the thirties turned up, aged and sallow and very drunk, and bored on a shattering scale that even their earlier efforts could not have prepared one for. Instead of the expected champagne, agreeably remembered from the earlier party, nothing was served but ready-made highballs passed around by waiters. I was ill, had already lost my voice, and had a relapse the next day. Vladimir Nabokov, who had come down from Cornell for the occasion, hearing that Stanley Edgar Hyman was there, went up to him and asked him what he meant by calling his father "a tsarist liberal." Hyman, who was evidently afraid that Nabokov was going to attack him physically, replied, "Oh, I think you're a great writer!—I admire your writing very much!" Nabokov went back with acute neuralgia and has spent a long spell in the hospital. And as somebody pointed out, the Ritz itself is just about to be pulled down. Harold Ross, who had conducted a successful campaign against the commercial broadcasts at Christmastime in the Grand Central Station, had invited the man who manages the Grand Central—in order, I suppose, to have somebody he could talk to—and devoted most of his time to him. Fifteen years ago, Ross and Katharine White stood at one end of the room as a sort of ill-at-ease receiving line. This year Katharine took to her bed several days before the party and did not show up at all. We were with Auden and Louise for part of the evening. They got away early, and I hope no misfortune befell them. (Louise also came to dinner with us one night when Padraic Colum was there. She and Padraic had a long conversation about Irish and Welsh history and got along madly. I was struck by the fact that Louise had lost a good deal of her shyness—I never heard her talk so readily in company. I think that Chicago and Washington have in this way done a good deal for her.)

I have finally, after abstaining through all the early stages, struck a blow in the *Saturday Review* controversy. I hope to get *The Nation* to print my correspondence with Hal Smith apropos of his editorial on the Bollingen award to Wallace Stevens. The Lord has delivered him into my hands. Aren't you glad to know they have mastered Stevens after having so much difficulty with Pound?

I am sorry about your sister's illness. Such things—with their uncertainty and sadness, as I know from my recent experience with my mother—make it difficult, not only to move, but even to pay attention to other things. Let us know if you manage to come East . . .   As ever, Edmund W

To ALLEN TATE   April 14, 1950
                                                                        Wellfleet

Dear Allen: I have just sent this wire to *The Saturday Review*: "Glad to know you have mastered Stevens, whom I personally find more difficult than Pound. What is your interpretation of what he communicates? If, however, art for art's sake has been or ought to be destroyed, then the poetry of Wallace Stevens has been or ought to be destroyed, and I do not understand how it is possible for you to applaud him. Please elucidate these matters in an early issue."

I'll call you up at the end of the week, if I'm still here.

                                                             As ever, Edmund

Dear Allen: I wanted to keep you *au courant* with this controversy . . .*

To HARRISON SMITH   April 27, 1950
The Saturday Review of Literature   Wellfleet

Dear Mr. Smith: Thank you for your letter—which I must say does not do much to vindicate the literary competence of *The Saturday Review*. In attempting to demonstrate that Stevens is less obscure than Pound, you say: "Since I have sent you a quotation from the *Pisan Cantos*, it is reasonable to confine my quotations from Stevens to his latest book, though I believe that his poetry has become less obscure with the years." You then transcribe several passages from what you describe as "his 1947 volume," *Harmonium*. Now, *Harmonium* was Stevens's first, most famous, and for many years his only book: it was published in 1923. If it is a question of comparing epochs in the work of Stevens and Pound, I do not remember anything in the work of Pound at that period so difficult as many of the poems in this book. There is, for example, a piece called

---

* A note scribbled on a copy of the following letter to Harrison Smith, which was among Allen Tate's letters from E.

"The Emperor of Ice-Cream," which I have never been able to understand. I have been told that the Emperor of Ice-Cream is Death, but I do not see how the first three lines are to be explained on this assumption. And what do you make of "Le Monocle de Mon Oncle" and the last lines of "A Nice Shady House"? Are they likely to be understood by anyone who can make nothing of Pound?

As for your quotation from the *Pisan Cantos*, which is intended to prove Pound's unintelligibility: you have yourself made the first lines meaningless by omitting the five lines that precede them—about Lorenzo de' Medici —from which the next lines follow. The whole passage evidently deals with Pound's adventures in Italy, when he was arrested at the end of the war. The usual echoes of things he has read are running through his mind. No one, of course, can recognize all his references, historical, literary, and personal, but most of them can be looked up, and it is usually clear what value he means you to attach to any given item in his scrambled chronology and topography. Ezra Pound is a naïve man, with a few very simple (and sometimes crank) ideas. He has emphatically explained in his prose the themes that he has used in his poetry. Wallace Stevens, on the other hand, has written out of something like what Matthew Arnold meant by "the buried life," and only partly emerges. His imagery is much trickier than Pound's and his puzzles cannot be solved by consulting encyclopedias and dictionaries.

I think that you ought to familiarize yourself with the works of these two admirable writers before sounding off about them in a journal supposed to be devoted to literature. And it seems to me that accusations of irresponsibility of the kind your editorial brings do not nowadays come very appropriately from the editors of *The Saturday Review*. You assert in your letter that you "have never felt or said that 'art for art's sake ought to be destroyed'"; yet the title of your editorial was "The Destruction of Art for Art's Sake." You seem to suggest in the article that the judges for the Bollingen award* have proved either the absurdity of this doctrine or their insincerity in professing it, and the implication of the title seems plain that the doctrine has somehow been discredited and ought to be discredited.

Sincerely, Edmund Wilson

To ALLEN TATE

February 15, 1955
The New Yorker

. . . I don't see much in this correspondence. It seems to me that Robert Fitzgerald plays almost as unpleasant a role as Ezra. Why on earth should

---

* The first annual Bollingen Prize, awarded to Ezra Pound in 1949, had stirred up a large controversy because of Pound's Fascist broadcasts from Italy. *The Saturday Review* devoted an entire issue to attacking the Bollingen committee for its award.

he make such a point of rubbing the nose of Ezra Pound's daughter in the vomitings of her father. I have seen the worst of Pound's broadcasts, and it seems to me that they are simply the ravings of a crank, which are unlikely to have done any harm and have to be disregarded. There is no question that, in certain ways, he is a very unsympathetic character. But I am all in favor of letting him out. I do not understand what effect you expect these letters to have on Eliot. He will unquestionably deplore Pound's language, but Eliot is anti-Semitic himself and was at one time inclined toward Fascism. As for Hemingway and MacLeish, I don't see that they needed to intervene, since Ezra's problem was quietly solved . . .

To Mamaine Koestler   April 3, 1950
                                                            Wellfleet
Dear Mamaine: I have had both your letters and was glad to know that you were better. I haven't sent you my book because the publication has been delayed.*

We have been in New York for most of two months, but have been back here a week. It is the first time since we have been married that we have been away that long. We enjoyed it—though I found it was an error to suppose it would be much fun to look up all your old friends. We took them on night after night in relays and talking with them and drinking with them exhausted one so much that I finally collapsed and spent a week in bed. The whole project was based on a fallacy, as I had forgotten that people in New York never see one another when they are living there. As Dorothy Parker said, If you go away and stay, they don't worry: they just think you're dead. I believe it is unlike London in this respect, where the writers, etc., seem to huddle together . . . I have just been reading the most extraordinarily grisly lot of books, most of them about prisons, which probably seemed even worse on account of my depleted condition: the complete edition, just published, of Oscar Wilde's *De Profundis;* a book on Wilde and Douglas by the present Marquess of Queensberry; Jean Genet's *Notre-Dame-des-Fleurs* (have you read Genet at all? you have to be feeling strong, but it does have some interest and merit—though it seems like the ultimate low in French morale and culture); two books about their prison experiences by American conscientious objectors; and a book about American confidence games by a curious professor of linguistics who is probably the greatest noncriminal authority on the American underworld and whose attitude toward confidence men is almost as perversely admiring as that toward his own favorite kinds of criminal. Have also been reading Chekhov—for the first time in bulk and in Russian. Taken after these other books, he seemed relatively cheerful

---

* *Classics and Commercials.*

and normal. Have you read him? I think you would like him. I think that English and American readers often somehow have a wrong idea of him. He has much more solidity and point than I had expected from the things that are said of him, and he is particularly interesting just now, because the petty "technicians" and officials, and the rising ex-serfs that he writes about, whom he presents as most cowardly and incompetent, are the people who came to the top with the Revolution, and the later phases of whom may be studied in the Soviet Union. Though Chekhov came from this class himself, he did not seem to see very much hope for them except in a remote and problematical future . . .

Give my regards to Koestler. His and Silone's pieces are the most valuable ones in *The God That Failed*. (I wish he could have persuaded Crossman not to give the book that title.)   As ever, Edmund W.

I was awfully sorry about George Orwell—I had a feeling that he wouldn't last, as if the thing he represented were doomed to fade away, and it is disconcerting to have it gone.

To ALFRED KAZIN   May 12, 1950
                                                               Wellfleet

Dear Kazin: Thanks very much for the Blake. The introduction is much the best thing of yours I have seen—and reassuring after so much of the dreary stuff that people have been putting out lately. The first part is brilliant—especially the Blake–Beethoven comparison. I think that your most serious fault is imprecision of language—this sometimes gets you into trouble in explaining Blake's ideas, which are so difficult to get hold of anyway. Writing for *The New Yorker* may be useful for you in this connection, if you don't take them seriously beyond a point. I also liked the *Commentary* piece. (I suppose you know what *solovey* means in Russian.) Beethoven, Blake, and Brownsville all seem to be better subjects for you than any in that American book.

I am sending you in return my own latest opus. Is there any chance of your coming up here? I have spoken to Elizabeth Freeman about you, and she says there is a house with a view of the sea where you could get a room and board.   Sincerely, Edmund Wilson

To ALFRED KAZIN   June 10, 1950
                                                               Wellfleet

Dear Kazin: Thanks for your letter. *The Little Blue Light* was intended as a satire and warning, as *Hecate County* was. In the long view, I am not pessimistic (though disgusted with a good deal that is going on), and don't know why you should have been depressed by the last part of *Europe without Baedeker*, where I was talking in my own person and quite hopeful in a number of ways. In any case, I can promise you that my

486

next production will tell a more cheerful story than those of my *Hecate County* period.

I think that Mizener's book on Fitzgerald, which is supposed to be out in the fall, will be more helpful to you than I can. He knows all the literature on the subject. The best thing I ever wrote about him, I guess, is the poem at the beginning of *The Crack-Up*.

Solovey means *nightingale*, so the name was well chosen.

As ever, Edmund Wilson

To John Dos Passos

July 21, 1950
Wellfleet

Dear Dos: I'm glad that you were impressed by my play—which really isn't one of my own favorite works. I don't think that stories and plays that are supposed to take place in the future are ever quite satisfactory. I'm doing another one now that takes place in a fairy-tale fifteenth century—on a theme like *The Sorcerer's Apprentice*: a young magician who has to take over from the old magician before he has learned the business.*

Have you been keeping up with the Sartre novel? I think that the most recent episode—the last part of *La Mort dans l'âme*, with its sequel in *Temps Modernes*—is one of the best things he has done: the reflection of the crisis of Communism in the relations between French Communists who are organizing concentration camps. Sartre, who is not a great artist, is certainly a first-rate journalist. He and Steinbeck and the Italian Moravia and the Soviet writer Leonov all seem to me to represent more or less the same sort of thing. They mostly depend on ideas and devices provided by other people, and they do not produce great literature, but they are able reporters on their period and worth reading for this reason. I've also been reading the installments of Malraux's *Psychologie de l'art*, an original and remarkable work. The supplemental volume on Goya which has just come out is wonderful. The French are certainly the only people in Europe who are still doing anything serious in literature. I'm not sure that Genet isn't a top-notch writer—better in some ways than Sartre. (At his best he is a master of language.) Have you read *Journal du voleur* and *Notre-Dames-des-Fleurs*? The latter of these is terrific. It is sensational in an obvious way, but beyond that he manages to get out of his apparently highly special personal experience something that has a certain ghastly truth for the whole Western world at present. The English, so far as I know, have nobody comparable to these three writers—not even George Orwell was.

Next week I begin going down to Boston to assist at the production of the *Blue Light*. After it opens, we hope to get off to Talcottville for a

* *Cyprian's Prayer.*

487

while and miss as much as possible of the local August. The summer so far has been pleasanter than usual. The weather has been almost like early fall. Both the village and our place are quieter now that they are bypassed by the new road. Reuel and Helen have been growing rapidly and filling out like fresh ripe peaches. The woods where the Matsons and Phillipses used to be are now full of émigré Hungarians, Dwight Macdonald, and the remnants of a nudist colony. I never venture that way at nightfall, it's like the Tonta Wald in one of Andrew Lang's folk stories. (I'm exploiting this vein at present.) We are constantly shaken by target practice up the Cape.

Everybody sends love. Eventually I hope we'll get to Virginia. Let me know if you come up in the meantime.   EW

To MORTON D. ZABEL   July 20, 1950
                                                                Wellfleet
Dear Morton: You couldn't have sent us anything that would have pleased us more than the Schumann–Heine records. Elena knows the songs well, but I had only occasionally heard them sung and did not really know them—so I have been enchanted by them, listening to them with the text. Schumann was certainly one of the greatest of the romantic poets. All the lyrics are not of Heine's best, and he has sometimes really made them better. It is true that I have been weak in the department of lieder, and I am now going to cultivate it. I left Wellfleet with my head full of these songs, which we had been playing the night before . . .

The *Blue Light* is now definitely to be done in Cambridge on August 14, with Jessica Tandy and her husband, Hume Cronyn. He wants to bring it to New York (if it seems viable in this tryout), though without Miss Tandy, who is signed up for the fall for something else.

We enjoyed your visit immensely. That is the best time for a visit up here—before the season gets started. Now old and dear friends are arriving in droves, and one has to protect oneself against them in the interests of one's professional and family life.

. . . The [Henry B.] Fuller book I haven't seen is *The New Flag*, a satire in verse. If the University Library has it, I'd be grateful if you'd send me a photostat and let me know how much it is. *Lines Long and Short* I have . . . I have read Angus Wilson's article on Dickens. It is a little disappointing, sounds like a fragment from a preface, but I think it is worth reading . . .

In New York I saw the English picture with Alec Guinness in it—*Kind Hearts and Coronets*. You ought to take it in if it comes out there. I went with Louise. She is in splendid shape—was evidently feeling set up by her adventures in the West, where she says the young people all know and swear by her work . . .   As ever, Edmund

Have you people read Angus Wilson's stories? I think they are
terrific.*   (To Celia Paget, 1950)

To ANGUS WILSON   July 21, 1950
                                                   Wellfleet

Dear Mr. Wilson: Thank you for your letter and the Dickens article—
which, as a matter of fact, I had just read. I was much interested in it but
rather sorry that you hadn't dealt with the subject on a larger scale.

As you know, I have very much admired your stories and have been
hoping you would do a novel. You are the first writer I have read who
has done for England in its present phase something of what Sartre has
been doing for France. (Sartre, of course, is more or less of a journalist,
doing a different kind of thing from yours.)

Have you read Gathorne-Hardy's memoir of Logan Pearsall Smith? It
sounds like an overelaboration of a story invented by you.

Is there any chance of your coming to this country? You must be sure
to look me up if you do.   Yours sincerely, Edmund Wilson

To MAXWELL GEISMAR   August 8, 1950
                                                   Wellfleet

. . . I'm going down to Cambridge tonight to watch rehearsals of the
Light—it opens next week. The man who is doing the Wandering Jew
is wonderful on the different accents and has acted in the Jewish theater,
but doesn't like the comic lines and wants to leave out the passage about
Palestine—partly, I am afraid, because he thinks it may offend somebody . . .

To JOHN DOS PASSOS   September 5, 1950
                                                   Wellfleet

Dear Dos: I haven't answered your letter, because I have been involved
with the play, a trip to Talcottville, and the final paroxysms up here at the
end of the summer season. The Brattle Square people did pretty well with
the Blue Light, considering that they had only ten days to rehearse. The
last days, a lot of theatrical people came up from New York to see it, and
it looks as if it would be done either by the Theatre Guild or by Whitehead and Harold Clurman—but you know how uncertain those things are.
The success of The Cocktail Party has given Broadway the idea that there
is money in the intellectual drama—so that my Wandering Jew may ride
into town in the wake of Eliot's religious psychiatrist. The Cocktail Party,
by the way, acts much better than it reads. Preposterous as a good deal
of it is, it is really very effective on the stage. Eliot's uncritical Anglicanism
is, in my opinion, all poppycock, but the play does have a certain intensity

---

* Such Darling Dodos.

of old-fashioned puritanical New England moral passion that begins by making you uncomfortable and then grips you in the second act.

The best French bookstores in New York are La Maison Française in Rockefeller Center and the Librairie Lipton, 791 Lexington Avenue. The former seems to have driven the French department at Brentano's almost out of business. But, if you are ordering by mail, I should think that the best and probably cheapest way would be to write to Mr. Muller at Schoenhof's, 1280 Massachusetts Avenue, Cambridge. They have *La Monnaie de l'absolu* (*Psychologie de l'art III*) and *Saturne* (about Goya) of Malraux, and Genet's *Journal du voleur*. *Notre-Dame-des-Fleurs* is somewhat harder to get . . . (Waldo Frank has borrowed mine or I'd lend it to you.) Sartre has been writing an enormous and very *approfondi* introduction to a new complete edition of Genet. Why don't you write him, as I have done, and say that you want to subscribe to it or something? . . .

I was very much impressed by *Intruder in the Dust*—wasn't I telling you about it when it first came out? It is better if read in conjunction with the book *Go Down, Moses*, to which it is a sequel, and was written before Faulkner had gotten himself into a state of mind about the Civil Rights program and has less boy's adventure story in it.

I have been reading Chekhov in bulk in the Soviet edition. It is most remarkable and somewhat different from what I had expected. The stories are presented here in the order in which they were written, and you see that, in his later years, he was doing a series of what are really short novels, each of which studies intensively a different social milieu and which together provide a sort of anatomy of Russian middle-class and peasant society on the eve of the revolutionary period. (The volumes of the English translation mix up these elaborate pieces with the shorter and lighter ones written many years before, so that you do not get any sense of the direction and intention of his work.) It is immensely interesting at the present time because these half-baked incomplete bourgeois and liberated bewildered serfs are the people who came to the top under the leadership of the Bolsheviks and who had to run Soviet Russia. Chekhov, though he came from these strata himself, is with them but has very little hope of them. There is only an occasional gleam of belief that they may accomplish something in the very long run. He was as far as possible from Tolstoy's faith in the wisdom and virtue of the present. Some of these stories are masterpieces—or rather, the whole little *comédie humaine* is a masterpiece. It's strange to think that, with all contemporary cultural expression completely shifted in the Soviet Union, they should continue to get out, volume by volume, this admirably edited and printed edition . . . By the way, I learn from Roi Ottley's book *Black Odyssey* that Jefferson's colored servant and bodyguard actually did sleep, as the guide told me, in that curious bunk above his bed at Monticello—that I was asking you about once. Is there something rather interesting that has been kept out of sight about Jefferson's relations with Negroes? Did he have close and unpublicized relations with them that made up to some extent for his lack of close relations with white people? I learn from the same source —and for the first time—that he had several mulatto children.

I expect to go to New York sometime the middle of next week . . . Do let us know if there is any chance of your being there.

As ever, EW

To MAMAINE KOESTLER   September 7, 1950
Wellfleet

. . . I have gone back lately to reading Gibbon—there is nothing like it during periods of political strain—having read only about half of it years ago. I think it is really one of the greatest English books. In its intellectual grasp and enormous scope in time and space, it has something in common with *Das Kapital*, which it also resembles in having an advantage of detachment through not dealing, except incidentally, with the historian's own country. It always has a peculiar effect on me—both calming and stimulating. Have you read it? I am sure you would like it. If you haven't, do begin at once. It throws such an immense amount of light on so many obscure things, and has a dramatic and narrative fascination that few of the big historical people can exercise. Very curious reflections on the future of Europe, when he is summing up the breakdown of Rome, just before the reign of Theodoric. He says that Russia won't be a menace because she is becoming civilized and that any progress in military technique that could make her a dangerous enemy would proceed with an enlightenment that would prevent her from behaving aggressively. But *if* Europe should be overrun by anything like another Mongol invasion, all the enlightened people could simply take ship for America, which has already been conveniently settled by six million Europeans. But you may know already about all this . . .

To MAMAINE KOESTLER   October 24, 1950
Wellfleet

. . . My old friend Edna Millay—whom you told me you had read—died suddenly last Thursday. Her husband had died last year. We went to see them two summers ago. After what seems to have been a very neurotic period, she had begun writing poetry again—was repenting bitterly of the patriotic stuff she had written during the war. She went on living alone in the house—very lonely in the country, a large farm—and apparently had a stroke when she came down to get breakfast in the morning. Though I hadn't seen much of her of recent years, we occasionally corresponded, and I am very much depressed by her death. You are not really old, so you still have old friends, but some of the ones I counted on most are dead. The people of the twenties over here were quite different from the crops that have come since—the Depression made the difference, because it cut down money and freedom and inhibited people in various ways. I find that I can only talk comfortably with the writers of my own era—am always shocking others or seeming frivolous to them . . .

To Morton D. Zabel   November 19, 1950
                                                                  Wellfleet
. . . I have opened this to ask you to give me an opinion on George Dillon as a possible biographer of Edna Millay. Houghton Mifflin wants to get a book on her, and I can't seem to think of anyone else—though I really know nothing about him, except that he translated Baudelaire with her and published some not bad poetry of his own. I've heard nothing about him since, but I see from *Who's Who* that he's still alive and lives in Richmond, Virginia. I think they ought to get somebody who knew her. Her poetry is so much out of fashion that I should hesitate to send them to somebody like John Berryman, who has just done an excellent book on Stephen Crane. Do let me know who and what Dillon is. Wasn't he the fellow who edited *Poetry* after the big crisis? You might have some other suggestion . . .

. . . also John Berryman has sent me some extraordinary stuff.
                                                    (To Allen Tate, 1959)

To John Berryman   November 19, 1950
                                                                  Wellfleet
Dear John: Thanks very much for sending me the book,* on which I congratulate you. I had already read it in galleys and written about it for *The New Yorker*, so I shan't discuss it at length here. It is an important book and likely to last as long as there is any interest in Crane, which I agree with you in thinking will be a long time. There's just a chance I may get over to Princeton if I go down to New Jersey before Christmas, in which case I'll look you up.   Best regards, Edmund W.

To Morton D. Zabel   July 20, 1950
                                                                  Wellfleet
. . . By the way, how much would Chicago pay me for performing in the winter for a quarter?

---

* *Stephen Crane.*

October 16, 1950
Wellfleet

Dear Christian: What was that fellowship that was given Eliot, so that he could live and work at Princeton? I was wondering whether it was something one could apply for. As happens to me periodically, I'm hampered in my literary undertaking by the necessity of doing journalism and other odd jobs, and have been casting about for some solution.

I've been wanting to go over to Princeton when I've been down at my mother's in Red Bank, but have never had time enough. Later I expect we'll be in New York for a few weeks, and I hope to make it then. A play of mine is going to be done in New York this winter. It was tried out in Cambridge last summer, with a certain amount of success—got a good notice in *Variety*, at any rate!

Have you read Malraux's *Psychologie de l'art?* The last volume is now out. I am tremendously impressed with it. I'm not sure it isn't one of the really great modern books. I'm sure it would interest you, if you haven't read it. There's nothing else like it . . .   As ever, Bunny W.

To Christian Gauss   October 27, 1950
Wellfleet

Dear Christian: I am sorry to hear that you have had to go to the hospital and hope you are out by now.

I have just read Sartre's little book on Baudelaire. He hardly pretends to deal with Baudelaire as a poet, and his Existentialist ideas about free will and *engagement* seem to me naïve, but I think it has a certain validity. It explains to me why I have always found Baudelaire personally unsympathetic and rather uninteresting. He is a rebel who has to have Authority constantly present on the stage in order to make his act effective, a rebel who is not going anywhere, is not rebelling in the interests of anything, has no countermorality to propose. His political and social ideas, and even his religious one—since he has to have God in His heaven in order to give his blasphemies force—are completely reactionary.

As for my literary projects, I am working on another play, and that is the immediate thing that I want to get time to do. But if they would prefer to hear of something more "scholarly," I am also working on a book of American literature between 1870 and 1910, which is going to take me years and on which I am also held up by the continual necessity I am under of writing articles and doing other jobs.

I have sent you a copy of my new book—though it is just a collection of my old articles.*   As ever, Bunny W.

---

* *Classics and Commercials.*

To Christian Gauss   November 19, 1950
                                                            Wellfleet
Dear Christian: Thank you for your letter and your *démarches* on my
behalf. There's just a bare chance that I may get down to New Jersey
before you leave, in which case I'll come over to see you. Did you know
Edith Wharton? I wish you would tell me about her. As for my ideas
about the effects of American life on literature, I got most of them out of
Brooks in the first place, the early Brooks of *The Ordeal of Mark Twain*.
                                                      As ever, Bunny W
     You might be interested to read Budd Schulberg's novel based on
Scott. Having known him, as well as being more intelligent and intuitive
than Mizener, he really comes closer to the truth of both the Fitzgeralds
and the period. Not a very good novel, though.

To Morton D. Zabel   November 19, 1950
                                                            Wellfleet
Dear Morton: Thank you for your letter. I should like to come to Chicago
again, but I am a little appalled by the idea of *two* courses—also, by the
probability that the $2,000 offered would be largely eaten up by the
expenses of having the family out there. What I am fishing around for
is a job which would make it possible for me to occupy myself with the
first stage of my proposed study: the literature of the Civil War and the
careers of distinguished writers who were in it and affected by it—Holmes,
John De Forest, Weir Mitchell, Ambrose Bierce, Sidney Lanier, and
Cable—probably ending up with Henry Adams. So I'll say no for the
present. Thanks for all your trouble in going into the matter . . .
                                                      As ever, Edmund W

To Philippe Thoby-Marcelin   December 19, 1950
                                                            Wellfleet
. . . Dawn Powell, who is in Paris, has been writing gloomy letters saying
that she hates the French—but many Americans feel that way when they
first go to Europe late in life; later they find that they love it . . .

1951

To Allen Tate   January 4, 1951
                                                     Wellfleet

Dear Allen: I had already heard with regret from Malcolm [Cowley] about your conversion—particularly because I was afraid that it would prevent your appreciating my New Year's card. My animus against the Catholics lately has been due to their efforts to interfere with free speech and free press. They had a good deal to do with the suppression of *Hecate County* and they actually almost succeeded in persuading the Oxford Press to break their contract with me for a new edition of *The Triple Thinkers*, on account of a single footnote in the essay on John Jay Chapman. Everybody in the publishing world knows what an impudent nuisance they have lately become. You probably think that the Catholics who do these things are misguided, that there is room in the Church for all kinds, etc., but this is as much a mistake as it was for the sympathizers with Communism in the thirties to imagine that they could influence the policy of the Stalinist Comintern or that this policy could be anything but intolerant, unscrupulous, and tyrannical. Cardinal Spellman and the Holy Name Society are what the Catholic Church *is*: by their fruits ye shall know them.

I hope that becoming a Catholic will give you peace of mind; though swallowing the New Testament as factual and moral truth seems to me an awful price to pay for it. You are wrong, and have always been wrong, in thinking that I am in any sense a Christian. Christianity seems to me the worst imposture of any of the religions I know of. Even aside from the question of faith, the morality of the Gospel seems to me absurd. If one combs out the contradictory passages in which Jesus appears as an arrogant and militant Jewish moralist, as Trotsky tried to do, you get a doctrine of weakness and non-resistance which, if followed by the inhabitants of the supposedly Christian countries, would not allow them to survive ten years. It does not imply Christian tendencies that one tries to cultivate kindness and respect for the rights of others—qualities, as a matter of fact, for which I am not always remarkable and which I do not regard as always important; qualities which, besides, Christianity did not invent and for which the Catholic has, especially, not been remarkable.

We are going to New York the 15th to spend the rest of the winter. Do let us know when you are in town—you can always reach me through *The New Yorker*. Love to Caroline. As ever, Edmund

To Malcolm Cowley   January 5, 1951
Wellfleet

Dear Malcolm: I have only two or three copies of the *Reliques** left, and I want to keep them. I sent one to [Van Wyck] Brooks—am sorry I forgot about Kenneth Burke, whom I haven't seen for years (was much amused by the passage you quoted from his letter) . . .

My backward-rhyming in "Reversals" is strictly based on sound, disregarding spelling—like any other kind of rhyme. I've done a long and more ambitious poem in this form.

I yesterday had a letter from Allen announcing his conversion and acknowledging my New Year's card. It is a very odd letter, because, though couched in a facetious vein, it shows a determined-effort-to-adapt-himself attitude. He makes against me, however, a malicious, libelous, and baseless charge of crypto-Christianity. It is strange to see habitually waspish people like Allen and Evelyn Waugh trying to cultivate the Christian spirit. Waugh—in *Helena*—makes a pathetic attempt to show his heroine making the attempt to sympathize with the Roman plebs, but then immediately turns his inveterate snobbery into other channels—so that all heretics, dissidents, and Byzantines become automatically dreadful people with whom one wouldn't care to mix. I remember that even Cummings, in the winter of '45–'46, had a phase of Christian piety and turning the other cheek which made him so disagreeable that I have never looked him up since. I hope, though, that conviction will soften Allen, who has lately been excessively venomous about his literary contemporaries. He never could forgive any kind of success: when *The Cocktail Party* was a box-office smash, he even threw over Eliot—so I suppose that after that there was nothing for it but Christ. For myself, I have been finishing Gibbon (begun fifteen years ago), and am speaking on him tonight before the Wellfleet Friday Night Literary Club. It is one of the greatest English books and particularly instructive and, in a way, reassuring to read at the present time.

---

* New Year's card: *Wilson's Reliques:* The Mass in the Parking Lot / Reversals, or *Plus ça change* / Cardinal Merry Del Val.

We are going to New York the 15th to spend the rest of the winter . . .
Call up someday when you are coming to town—I want very much to
see you.   As ever, Edmund

To ALLEN TATE   January 18, 1951
                                                        The New Yorker

Dear Allen: I thought I knew you well enough to be frank about my
reaction to your conversion. I shan't apologize for being unfeeling, because
I don't pretend to be, and don't want to be, a Christian. But how on
earth can you say that I've been indifferent to your work? I've often said
both in print and in conversation how highly I thought of your poetry.
In spite of our unusual loathing of one another's views, I'd very much
like to see you . . . I promise not to make myself unpleasant about the
Assumption of the Virgin. (I understand that she wrote Graham Greene
a charming little letter about his article in *Life*.) Do come to see us and,
if I turn up at Princeton, please don't forbid me the house (as a Christian,
I don't think you ought to).   Yours as ever and God bless you, Edmund

To ALLEN TATE   January 30, 1951
                                              11 East 87th Street, N.Y.

Dear Allen: Your two letters have just reached me. I don't understand
your position in your letter about *The Miracle*. At one point, you say
that [Cardinal] Spellman has the authority to condemn a film and "command the obedience of the faithful," but elsewhere you seem recalcitrant
to this authority, and since you have gone to the picture yourself, he has
obviously not commanded your obedience. What *is* the force of Spellman's
condemnation and who is obliged to accept it? I am not kidding—I really
want to know what the position of an intelligent Catholic is. It was fine
to see you the other day.   As ever, Edmund

To LOUISE BOGAN   May 26, 1951
                                                        The New Yorker

. . . Was glad to read this morning of the honor bestowed on you by the
Institute.* Why don't they elect you, so that you can wear the purple
ribbon diagonally on your shirt with your evening clothes? Did you know
that this was one of the privileges? . . .

To HELEN MUCHNIC   September 3, 1951
                                                            Wellfleet

Dear Helen: Thank you for your paper on Gorky and O'Neill, which is
very interesting and able. It is better on *The Iceman Cometh* than any-

---

* National Institute of Arts and Letters.

thing else I have seen: but I don't think you bring out sufficiently the fundamental irony that Hickey has just murdered his wife, and that the influence of moral regeneration which he is able to bring to bear on the people in the bar is due to the special euphoria—a psychiatric phenomenon —which has followed and offset his crime. When the play was done, the dramatic critics all said that they couldn't understand it. The idea seemed so shockingly cynical that they couldn't accept it or even grasp it. I thought that the *Iceman* was O'Neill's best play, but hate is the only emotion which he is really good at conveying, and there is nothing in the play but hatred. This is a serious limitation. Did you notice that O'Neill's own son committed suicide last year?

We are rather the worse, as usual, for the summer season with its many children and their guests. I have been quite productive, though—have finished another play, done two long articles of a new and better series that I have undertaken for *The New Yorker*, and have gotten together the materials for a book of selections from my articles of the twenties and thirties.* Newton Arvin and [Truman] Capote have been here, and we have had a couple of very pleasant evenings with them. Also saw Dan Aaron earlier.

. . . It was wonderful to see you last spring, and I do wish you would come to see us when we get to New York again. Will you be there all winter, or do you go back to Smith in the fall?   As ever, Edmund W.

Signor Praz is chiefly known as perhaps the leading authority in Italy on English literature . . . He loves the grotesque, the incongruous, and his books, among other things, are cabinets of curios . . . But this will give no idea of either the beauty or the range of his work.   (*The Bit Between My Teeth*, 1965)

To Mario Praz   September 11, 1951
                                                    The New Yorker
Dear Praz: Random House is sending you Capote's books. He was in Wellfleet when your letter came—I know him but haven't read him. *The New Yorker* will send you the other books. Steinberg's *Art of Living* is wonderful. He is really one of the great comic draftsmen. Thanks for the *English Miscellany*, which I thought was more interesting than the first number. I hope eventually to do short essays on Edward Lear and R. H. Barham of the *Ingoldsby Legends* and might send them to you if you thought you could use them. I have received the new edition of *The Romantic Agony* and hope to do a *New Yorker* article on it and on the vogue of the Marquis de Sade. It is easy to see the reasons for this

---

* *The Shores of Light.*

vogue, but what puzzles me is how people manage to see in him all the things they do—so that [Geoffrey] Gorer can call him a great political thinker and someone else can write a book to prove he was a great Christian. There is a good deal of unintentional humor in some of these recent writings on the subject. Have you seen the introduction to the collected papers of Maurice Heine by the man who is at present carrying on the torch? They have even looked up and photographed the sordid-looking place where the marquis and his valet had the episode with the prostitutes.

The biography of Scott Fitzgerald I mentioned in my last letter was the one I had already sent you—I had forgotten about it. I'd be glad to have *Gesù fate luce*, though I'm way behind on the other books you've sent me. I hope to get to Italy eventually. When is the Venice festival—or is it going on now? Did you hear the Stravinsky–Auden opera?*

As ever, Edmund Wilson

To the Editors   April 14, 1966
The New York Review of Books   Wellfleet

The full-page advertizement for a translation of the Marquis de Sade's *120 Journées de Sodome* which appeared in your issue of March 17 is as mendacious and misleading as possible. It begins by stating that *The New Yorker* had "devoted" to its "subject matter" "the reading space of 38 pages of its issue of September 18."† I wrote the article in question, which is a biographical and critical study of Sade and devotes only one paragraph to the *120 Journées*. The ad then goes on to a statement which will make anyone who knows the book laugh: "He [Sade] sets up his story like a magic mirror. Standing before it, you can see yourself at your best and at your worst, where you began and where you'll wind up." The characters in Sade's novel never show humanity at its best. They are wholly fantastic monsters, and it is hard to imagine that anyone will "wind up" like them. Even the account of the manuscript is false: "There was no book until Dr. Bloch hunted up the most important of the lost parts, connected them with what was authentically de Sade, discarded the unscrupulous rubbish added by others, and so brought to light one of the true gems of mankind." Actually, the only known manuscript was acquired by Iwan Bloch all in one long scroll of Sade's handwriting. Nothing was added to it by anyone else. Bloch published a defective version of this, and later Maurice Heine made a better one.   Edmund Wilson

---

* *The Rake's Progress.*
† "The Documents on the Marquis de Sade," reprinted in *The Bit Between My Teeth.*

September 24, 1951
                                    Wellfleet

Dear Waldo: I have had to make a couple of trips, so that I haven't been able to settle down to reading anything and only finished your book yesterday.* Here are some notes I have made on it:†

I have gone into these matters so minutely, because my impression is—especially from the days of *The New Republic* when we used to struggle with you over *The Rediscovery of America*—that you don't know what people mean when they complain about your writing. It has seemed to me since I have been seeing you up here that you have a real (I suppose partly unconscious) antagonism to Anglo-Saxon culture, in general. For example, you tend to tax me with overestimating the English writers, though the ordinary specialist in English, who has never read any other literature, usually thinks I underestimate them. I believe that you are disrespectful toward the English language itself. I can't imagine that, in using French, you wouldn't try to get the prepositions right—you would make a point of knowing that it was *essayer de* and not *essayer à*; yet you allow yourself mistakes in English of exactly the same kind. You complain that your books go over better in Spanish than they do in the United States, and I am sure that this is partly due to the fact that the kinks of which I speak would naturally be ironed out and turned into idiomatic Spanish, whereas the English-speaking reader is exposed to having his teeth set on edge or even to being brought up short—as sometimes happens to me—by something that he can't understand, where it is a question, not of some conception of yours that is difficult to express, but merely of the statement of some simple fact.

Now let me get on to the positive side, which, though it will take up less space than my list of errata, outweighs the technical blemishes. The first chapter seems to me, as I told you, the best writing of yours I have ever read. The last sentence is very fine, and shows how you *can* find the right words for a feeling deeply poetic (though I'd write *by* instead of *in* the blood). And, of course, there are other successful things from the point of view of pure writing, when poetic imagination makes the prose incandescent—for example, the description, I can't remember where, of some style of architecture, in which you speak of its impalpable perfume and its fernlike archaic texture.

You have, in any case, compensated for your faults of style by the broad range of vision and the long perspective you have been able to bring to the subject—which make you, I suppose, unique in this field. I feel that I have not only learned a lot from the historical point of view—

---

* *Birth of a World: Bolivar in Terms of His Peoples.*
† Seven pages of criticism, corrections, and errata omitted.

the book has created for me a whole living picture to fill a complete blank
—but that the book enables me to estimate Bolivar's career in relation to
the rest of the world in a way that an ordinary biography would not.
You are in general, I think, at your best when you are lighting up the
cultural and moral role of some figure or nation or race. The last chapters
are especially brilliant—though are you living up to your promise in your
preface that "when thoughts or motives are given as Bolivar's, they derive
from the letters," etc., when you report the dying Bolivar's reflections as
he is looking out the window at the Pico Plateado? If this is merely what
you imagine he thought, you ought to indicate that fact, in order not to
fall into fictionalized biography; but the passage is splendid in itself—the
seizing on the peak as a symbol for Bolivar's far-reaching ideas, incom-
mensurable with the world in which he worked.

I hope the book goes well. You have been getting very good (that is,
favorable) reviews, and they're giving you quite a lot of advertizing.

Having given your prose such a combing, I suppose that the least I can
do is to offer you a chance to retaliate by criticism of my play,* which
I'll be glad to have you read if you want to. Albert Marre doesn't like it,
and Elena is dissatisfied with it, but Mr. Breen, the former head of ANTA,
claims he is going to produce it. He is an escaped Dominican monk, who
once put on the ur-Faust in Chicago and seems to know a lot about the
Faust legend, so I suppose he has a special interest in the subject.

We are going down Thursday to stay at the Algonquin a week—shall
see you when we get back. I hope you will read that James Hogg story—
a very curious and powerful thing that has a particular point just now.

As ever, Edmund W.

To Waldo Frank   September 28, 1951
                                              The New Yorker

Dear Waldo: I am certain that a good deal of your trouble in *The Bolivian*
is due to working with your Spanish sources. I have had this experience
myself where I have been reading or translating from some other language
and have hit upon foreign locutions which I found it difficult to change,
because I couldn't think of the idiomatic English. But I wish I could make
you see the point about the other things I object to, most of which, though
you try to defend them, are really indefensible (the dictionary is no guide
to taste). As you say, I am not pedantic; and it does not dispose of such
objections to say that all the great writers have broken rules or been guilty
of solecisms or to declare that the critic complains of your style simply
because he is resisting your revelation. You present an unusual case somewhat similar to that of a composer who should have a great love of music

---

* *Cyprian's Prayer.*

but be partly tone-deaf, yet for whom imagination and will should sometimes allow him to triumph over deficiencies of technical skill. For these moments in *The Bolivian*, I am grateful. I got quite a lift out of the beginning and a lot of illumination from the end. (My only objection to the passage where Bolivar looks at the mountain is that, in view of your assurance in the foreword that you have evidence for everything you tell, the reader might be misled into supposing that the reflections attributed to Bolivar were based on a journal or a letter.) And the whole book is a valuable contribution to the breaking-through of cultural partition, the unified vision of history, that is one of the great tasks of our period. It has something of what I admire in Malraux's *Psychologie de l'art*.

We are enjoying ourselves down here . . . The theatrical season, however, has started off most depressingly, and there is nothing we want to see. The most interesting thing I have found is Sam Behrman's profile of the art dealer Duveen, which is to run in six installments in *The New Yorker*. It is not only incredibly entertaining but also fills in a whole chapter of American cultural life. I hadn't realized how important Duveen was, that the whole rather chilling artistic side of the big-millionaire period was mainly Duveen's creation. I think you ought to read it . . .

As ever, EW

To Waldo Frank   October 5, 1951
                                                                The New Yorker

Dear Waldo: Here is this play.* I'm rather dissatisfied with it and should be glad to have your opinion. Let us meet soon. This correspondence is getting to be like those two Russians of divergent (not disparate or dissident) philosophical and political views who wrote each other long letters from opposite corners of a room in Moscow.   As ever, EW

         S. N. Behrman, the New York dramatist . . .

To S. N. Behrman   September 30, 1951
                                                                The New Yorker

Dear Sam: I was so fascinated by the first installment of your *Duveen* that I got the proofs of the rest of it and have just read the whole thing. So far as my memory goes, it is the best Profile *The New Yorker* has ever printed—incredibly entertaining and at the same time a filling in of a chapter of American cultural history that hadn't been written before. Particularly good is the discussion, at the end, of the reasons why the millionaires of that period went in for buying works of art—and the story

---

* *Cyprian's Prayer.*

is all pervaded with your unobtrusive humor, wisdom, and sense of ultimate values. I like the light but firm touch with which you keep the people in their places, yet refrain from scoring off them in the meaningless, mechanical way that *The New Yorker* sometimes falls into, and allow Duveen at last to emerge as capable of a certain disinterestedness.

They tell me here you are now in Boston, but coming back this week. We are at the Algonquin for a few days and should love to see you if you're here. Sincerely, Edmund Wilson

To John Dos Passos   November 27, 1951
                                                                Wellfleet

Dear Dos: Our holidays—with the four children—are already so complicated that the idea of going to Virginia, though attractive, is unthinkable. Eventually, I hope, we'll get there on another trip to the South. I don't believe we'll get to New York till after Christmas . . .

We've just read *Chosen Country* and were fascinated. I find it rather hard—which happens rarely with me—to judge it as a book, because, knowing the originals or components of so many of your characters, I keep seeing the real people and get partly thrown off the track of what you are trying to do. What comes through to me is the Peter Pan fantasy of the Smoolies or the horrors of life with Griffin Barry, which seem to me wonderfully caught, but I can't gauge the effect of all this on a reader who hasn't known them. I will hazard, though, a few specific criticisms. Negative: colorless title—you seem to be getting addicted to them—which doesn't convey the idea you intend (till I read the book, I thought it meant *Choice Country*—i.e., country appropriate for farming or something) and isn't likely to lure the reader; dependence in conversation on clichés— you are here at last dealing with people who are supposed to be clever and charming and sometimes profound and brilliant, yet you still make them carry on even among themselves an exchange of catch phrases and platitudes. You do get away from this to some extent, and at moments very successfully, in the case of Jay and Lulie* and the elder Pignatelli—but I think you still a little give the impression that the guy who is writing the book is the only master of language in the United States, a country where the language of everybody else is a tissue of the ready-made phrases that go with his profession or milieu. And this brings us to the positive remarks: you have never written more beautifully or fluently—having dropped your naturalistic impediments—in evoking sensations and places. That is, I think, the real development of your latest books. You seem to be able now to turn off easily and with breathtaking rapidity—the last setting in Maine, for example—descriptions that depend for their effectiveness on

_____

* Lulie, in *Chosen Country*, was based on Katy Dos Passos.

an extremely subtle use of language. This makes the travels in Italy go admirably—a kind of thing that can be very boring and hold the story up. I think, though, that from the point of view of the characters, the last chapters go a little too quickly. Jay seems to be functioning in court in that Sacco–Vanzetti trial without any previous experience—and haven't you got the Communist movement getting into its overtly cynical phase a good deal too early, as well as Jay reading *Ulysses* before it came out (in 1921)?

We spent two weeks in Red Bank at the end of October going through my mother's house—quantities of papers and photographs, old books and old clothes, and all kinds of other things. I am going to ship part of it up here and part of it to Talcottville, so that, as soon as the house down there is sold, the whole New Jersey exploit of my grandparents and parents will be closed—I haven't a single relation left there. I went back through their whole lives and my own partly forgotten early life, and though interesting, it got to be too much for me, at moments rather suffocating and sickening —all the more as I was working at the time on a book of my old articles of the twenties and thirties, which also made me relive the past. Then Christian Gauss died at Princeton, and I had to go over there and relive my college days. When I got back here I read your book and relived your early years; the result is that I'm feeling as I never have before that I belong to a past era from which I'm not sure I'm capable of emerging, and I see myself in relation to the rest of the world as a probably rather moldering and mellow old codger from the frivolous twenties who looks back on a world they can never know as the older generation I saw in my youth could look back on the years after the Civil War, which seemed so far away to me. This is annoying and seems hampering, but I suppose it will partly pass. Love to Betty from both of us.   As ever, EW

To GILBERT HIGHET   January 15, 1952
                                                   Wellfleet

Dear Gilbert: I will consent to your doing a broadcast about me only on
the following conditions:

   1. 20 percent of the fee, with an extra 1½ percent for every minute
over fifteen.

   2. A guarantee that there shall be nothing in the broadcast not calculated to promote the sales of my book—the text to be checked by my
lawyer and public-relations man.

   3. An announcement at the end that I am returning to my original
occupation as a magician and Punch-and-Judy showman, with a concession
in Macy's basement. (This is due to embarrassment at America's failure
to provide the leadership required of her and my discouragement at not
being able to do anything about it. You will begin to feel this way, too,
after the first exhilaration of citizenship wears off.)

   4. The recording on a silver spool, with an apparatus for playing it.

   5. A Baskerville edition of Juvenal, with a complimentary inscription
from the author.

   6. A case of Old Forester whisky.

   If all this seems too much trouble, just forget about it and make the
broadcast anyway.   As ever, [unsigned]

To JOHN BIGGS   January 17, 1952
                                                   Wellfleet

Dear John: . . . From a non-legal point of view, though, the whole discussion of mental responsibility seems rather idle. In my opinion, the
great reform needed is a law to authorize the chloroforming of imbeciles
and hopeless psychiatric cases. Of course, mistakes would be made, and
the people would have to be very carefully checked, but we already put

a lot of other matters into the hands of Boards of Health, etc., and it would be better than shutting up such cases in miserable asylums.

I was a good deal impressed by Justice Douglas's statement that appeared in the magazine section of the *Times* last Sunday. I agree with him completely, but I have an awful feeling nowadays that nothing anybody says along those lines any more is going to make any difference and that we are headed for a war with Russia—that's all we seem to be planning for—which will result in a fiasco for us, even though Stalin may be upset in the course of it. The Soviet Union in the backward East is, of course, getting its ascendency through false pretensions, but our pretensions are beginning to be bogus, too.   As ever, Bunny W.

To Elizabeth Huling   February 3, 1952
The New Republic   Wellfleet

Darling Betty: You and Dawn [Powell] both sent me that gout clipping, and it has set me up no end.

Would you do me the following favor? In *The New Republic* of April 24, 1929, there is (in the correspondence department) a controversy between Virginia Woolf, myself, and somebody else. This issue I have, but later on Virginia Woolf answered my letter. Would you mind looking this up and getting Polly Murset to type it, as well as any other correspondence on the subject (giving the date of the issue or issues)? Also, what was the date of the appearance of V. Woolf's article "On Not Knowing French," which started the controversy off?

We moved everything out of Red Bank the week before last and came back up here to take it in. The house is like an anaconda that is trying to digest an enormous meal; but Elena has been getting it in and stowing it away at a great rate, and the rooms are getting to look more distinguished —our old furniture was sometimes on the junky side.

We're going down to New York the 13th to spend the rest of the winter . . . and hope to see you soon thereafter.   Love, EW

To Chauncey Hackett   February 8, 1952
                                                             Wellfleet

Dear Chauncey: At the moment I got your letter, I had just been moving up here from New Jersey innumerable bound volumes of *Littell, St. Nicholas, Century,* and *Harper's* (the latter going back to the fifties, to the very beginning, I guess). The house is now full of books and furniture, which we're having some trouble absorbing. I have around me here a large stuffed owl, a most elaborate jigsaw clock, in the shape of an old-fashioned steamboat, made by one of my uncles in his boyhood, and a broken plaster gargoyle from Notre-Dame, acquired by me in my boyhood. There are also many diplomas carefully preserved in tin cylinders. These are harder to know what to do with than used razor blades. They can never be thrown away but have to be moved around from one attic to another. There is also a whole library on Arctic and Antarctic exploration, a subject which fascinated my father but has always profoundly depressed me.

. . . As ever, Bunny W.

To Ada Nisbet January 15, 1952
Wellfleet

Dear Miss Nisbet: I was very much interested to hear about your Dickens discoveries, and should be delighted to read your paper—though I don't know that I can do much to help to get it published . . .

I am glad that something is being done for a real edition of Dickens's letters. The Nonesuch edition as a whole was a scandal, and the whole situation about Dickens is a disgrace to English scholarship.

Yours sincerely, Edmund Wilson

To Ada Nisbet February 12, 1952
Wellfleet

Dear Miss Nisbet: I have been fascinated by your Dickens paper. You have certainly settled this business. I have been trying to think what you ought to do with it. The presentation is just right, but the length is an awkward one from either the book or the magazine point of view . . .

Yours sincerely, Edmund Wilson

To Morton D. Zabel February 12, 1952
Wellfleet

. . . Miss Nisbet has definitely got the goods on the Dickens business. I am asking her to send you a copy of her paper. You will be fascinated. She has discovered passages in his correspondence relating to Ellen Ternan by having the parts inked out treated with infrared photography.

To Ada Nisbet April 21, 1952
New York

Dear Miss Nisbet: I showed your Dickens MS to Farrar, Straus, my own publishers. They told me that they thought it was the kind of thing that ought to be brought out by a university press, and suggested that you try California. I am glad that the press out there is interested, and shall be glad to do a little introduction. I was already going to suggest it, if you thought it would help—but of course you would have to take out the complimentary reference to my essay. Let me know when you want me to send it. The press ought to pay me, say, $100 . . .

Yours sincerely, Edmund Wilson

To ADA NISBET   May 6, 1952
                                                        New York

Dear Miss Nisbet: I'll try to give you the Dickens preface by the end of
May. I don't see my way at the present time to doing much more than
a foreword—since you have made most of the points yourself. Be sure to
remove the reference to me from your text . . . I think that it would be a
very good idea to print as many documents as possible. Are you going to
add chapters about his married life, as you suggested doing in one of your
letters? If you do, please be sure to let me see them, I ought to know the
exact contents of the book.*   Sincerely, Edmund Wilson

To JOHN BERRYMAN   August 2, 1952
                                                        Talcottville

Dear John: We have left the Cape and shall be up here in New York
State till after Labor Day. The Dos Passoses are in our house. Sorry to
miss you, but I'll be in Princeton—to perform for the Christian Gauss
Foundation—from the beginning of October to the middle of February,
and we hope to see you then.

   I'm glad you liked the Millay book. I'm afraid that the rest of the book
isn't all equally interesting.   As ever, Edmund W.

To ALLEN TATE   November 23, 1952
                                                        Princeton

Dear Allen: I have never said anything whatever about refuting your
ideas about my criticism in my seminars or anywhere else—in fact, didn't
even know that you had expressed any ideas about my criticism.

   We look forward to seeing you in December. We went to dinner the
other night with some young people who are living in your old house in
Linden Lane. The place was rather bare, and it made me sad at first—
I missed Caroline's romping dachshund and your old Confederate flag
that used to hang on the wall in the back room. They are using for a
nursery the room that you used as a dining room and in which I remember
some wonderful dinners. It all seems longer ago than it ought to.

                                                   As ever, Edmund

To CHAUNCEY HACKETT   December 9, 1952
                                                        Princeton

Dear Chauncey: . . . I was interested in your theory about Falstaff, but
I doubt whether Shakespeare's mind worked in the way that would be
implied by the allegory you suggest. I read your letter to John Berryman,
here, who is an expert on Shakespeare and has been going into his life

---

* *Dickens and Ellen Ternan,* by Ada Nisbet, with a foreword by Edmund Wilson.

very deeply, and he says that he has been unable to find any positive evidence that he ever became a Catholic.

Thank you for the Adams book, which I am soon going to read—when I get back to Grant again. My lectures don't begin till next week, and at present I am struggling with Harriet Beecher Stowe, whose writings are voluminous and about fifty percent terrible.

We are very comfortably settled here and have really been enjoying it very much. What is your delightful quotation about "the diversion of a lonely man," etc.?

Dos spent a night with us a few days ago. We always begin with a super-animated conversation, then I become exasperated with him and begin to tax him with his absurdities, then I become depressed about the whole thing and wonder whether we are not both getting into our crotchety fifties.

Love to Bubs, and from all of us to all of you.   As ever, EW

To FLOYD DELL   December 23, 1952
                                                    Princeton

. . . I, too, grew up on the school of Wells and Shaw, but though I still regard Shaw as a great man, I don't really think much now of the rest of them—except, in a smaller way, Max Beerbohm. At least, I certainly don't feel that our American crop that came a little later compare with them at all unfavorably. I can't imagine that anybody in the future will take Galsworthy very seriously—or Chesterton. That period seems to me now to have consisted mainly of three great Irishmen: Shaw, Yeats, and Joyce . . .

To MAMAINE KOESTLER   April 27, 1953
                                                    Wellfleet

Dear Mamaine: . . . When I was reducing the bulk of my books before I left Princeton, I sent you a copy of a book on Dickens and his curious love affair, of which I had several copies and which may or may not interest you. I have just come back from a week in New York and a trip to Talcottville. The family have been here, and though the weather is horrible this time of year, we are glad to get back *dans nos meubles*. I really don't fit very well into academic communities—always find it more of a strain than I expected—I'm about to start in on a new book and have entered a period of fasting and prayer. I've been going in for the Jews and all that and am reading Renan's *Histoire du peuple d'Israël*, which is wonderful and which you should read when you finish Gibbon. It was interesting to begin it just after reading Malraux's introduction to his *Musée imaginaire de la sculpture*, which is a very exciting book and much the same sort of thing as Renan—in the great French philosophical and

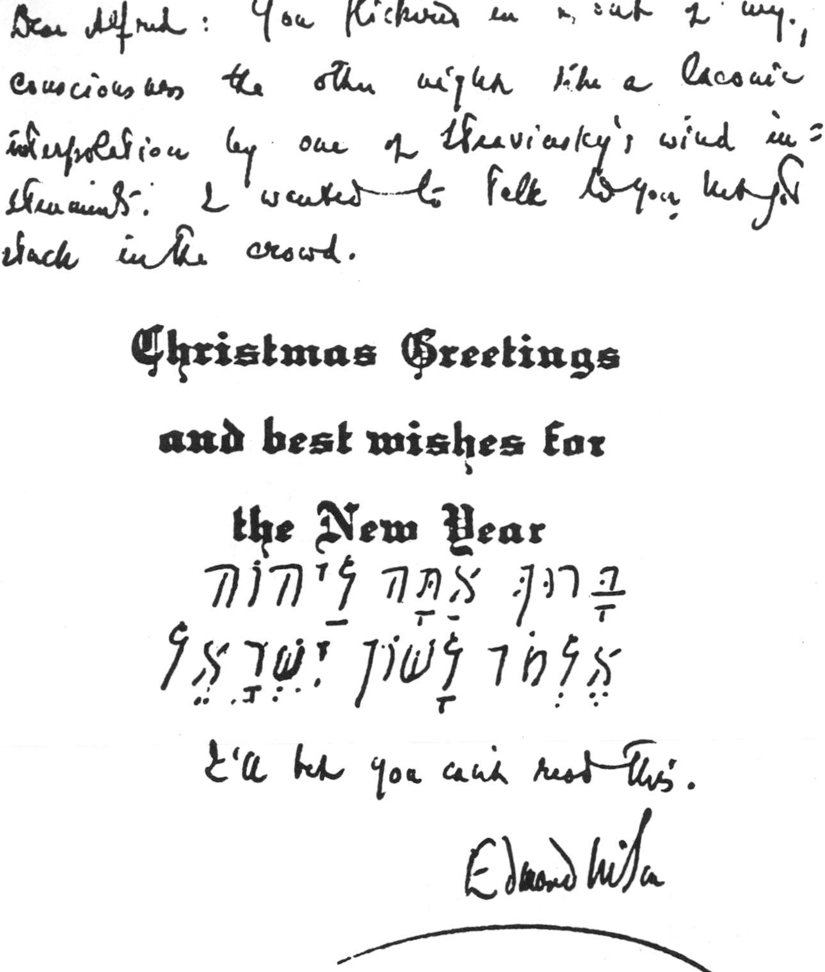

Dear Alfred: You flickered in and out of my consciousness the other night like a laconic interpolation by one of Stravinsky's wind instruments. I wanted to talk to you but got stuck in the crowd.

Christmas Greetings

and best wishes for

the New Year

ברוך אתה ליהוה

אלמד לשון ישראל

I'll bet you can't read this.

Edmund Wilson

To Alfred Kazin

December 1952
Wellfleet

Dear Alfred: You flickered in and out of my consciousness the other night like a laconic interpolation by one of Stravinsky's wind instruments. I wanted to talk to you but got stuck in the crowd . . .*

I'll bet you can't read this. Edmund Wilson

* In Hebrew: "May you be blessed by the Lord. I will learn the language of Israel."

international tradition, but written in such a labored and poetic and often obscure way that Malraux, as Elena says, sounds more like a German than a Frenchman. I think, though, that this art series of his is really one of the most important modern works. If you have taken up Greek on your own, ἐγὼ ὑμᾶς ἐπαινῶ *—my Greek master used to say this in order to make sure that we had to make an effort to understand his infrequent praise. I have just been stung by a wasp and will bring this letter to a close. Elena sends love. I don't know when we'll ever get to England. I wish somebody would produce one of my plays over there.

As ever, Edmund W

To JOHN BERRYMAN   April 27, 1953
Wellfleet

Dear John: I have been reading and rereading your poem "Homage to Mistress Bradstreet" on my travels (I only got back to Wellfleet the day before yesterday) and am very much impressed by it. It is certainly far and away the best thing of yours I have ever seen and quite unlike anything that anybody else has written. The intensity of expression and the language are startling both in contrast to your other poetry and in contrast to most current verse. The only thing that sometimes worries me is that I'm not always quite sure what is going on. Would it be a good idea to have a gloss, like *The Ancient Mariner?*: Here she lands in New England; here she has a change of life, etc. Maybe not—since what you're trying to do is stick close to an inner experience. There were one or two details I was going to mention, but I haven't got the MS by me. The only one I can remember is "Jack's pulpit," which sounds perhaps a little too Meredith–Browning and gives the impression of overdoing the staccato rhythm.

I hope you get off on your trip. Elena sends love to you both. We are glad to get back to our place up here, though the weather is a good deal less pleasant than Princeton. I am about to begin a new book and have gone into a period of prayer and fasting.   As ever, Edmund W

To JOHN BERRYMAN   May 25, 1953

Dear John: In Rome, look up Mario Praz (who wrote *The Romantic Agony*), 147 Via Giulia; and Margaret Caetani—Principessa di Bassiano—Palazzo Caetani, 32 Via Botteghe Oscure. You probably know who she is: an American woman, who gets out a trilingual quarterly called *Botteghe Oscure*. I am writing them both by this same mail.

Hope you are enjoying yourselves. Elena sends love.

As ever, Edmund W

---

* I praise you.

July 12, 1953
                                                        Wellfleet

Dear Mario: Dr. Melchiori's book is very able. I think he has got hold
of something in his ideas about tightrope walking and the baroque style,
though I'm not always sure that his points are relevant to his thesis—
not, on the other hand, that I necessarily think that books ought to be
dominated by theses. A few of these points seem farfetched or unimportant; but he has brought out many interesting and curious things. (I
don't agree, by the way, that Bloom in *Ulysses* "fails": like Odysseus, he
triumphs, or at least survives, through a combination of cunning and
integrity.)

There are one or two faults of writing that I wish you would bring to
his attention. He sometimes misuses *instead*. It shouldn't appear at the
beginning of a sentence as it does on page 147 . . . On page ii, it isn't clear
whether the sentence about progress represents Eliot's opinion or the
author's . . .

But these errors are very rare; and the whole book is better in every
way than most of this kind of criticism over here. I continue to be
astonished at the competence of the Italians in Anglo-American literature.
I will try to get the book published . . .

I've been asked to do a month at the American Seminar in Salzburg,
so we are going over for February. I'm afraid we shan't get to Italy, but
hope to take in Paris and London on our way. If you are anywhere near
us, do let us know.

I am leaving for New York State next week . . . for the rest of the
summer. On my way, I am going to pick up Paolo Milano, who has been
staying at a place called Yaddo near Saratoga Springs. I don't know
whether you know what this is. You really ought to have seen it for your
collection of curiosities. It is the estate of a millionaire which was left as
a home for deserving writers and other practitioners of the arts, and one
of the most extraordinary examples I know of the taste of the turn of the
century. You must certainly see it if you come again. Paolo is coming to
visit me, and we are going to read Belli, on whom he has been working—so
I shall at last be getting some use out of the many editions you have sent
me.

As for the Rosenbergs, it was not another Sacco–Vanzetti case. The
fuss made about it in Europe sounds like a combination of anti-
Americanism and Communist agitation. I suppose they were guilty and
that they had a fair trial, but I don't think they ought to have been
executed. I think that there is something in the theory that the judge
leaned over backwards because his own wife's name had been Rosenberg.

. . . I don't want any more Italian fiction now, thanks: I am not caught
up on the books I have.   Best regards, Edmund W

. . . Mrs. Ames of the Yaddo community wrote me recently asking whether there was anyone I wanted to recommend for invitations there. I wrote her suggesting you and your brother. She has sent me their applications for you. I don't know whether you know what Yaddo is. It is a foundation left by a millionaire for the purpose of helping artists and writers by giving them a place to work . . . The whole thing is free (including food); so far as I know, you don't have to pay a cent. You could spend two months or the whole summer there. It might be worth your thinking about. You would see a lot of writers and artists—most of them, I imagine, second-rate. One of the dubious features of going there used to be that about one evening a week you had to listen to Mrs. Ames read aloud from the very bad poetry of the wife of the founder, but I'm not sure that this has been continued. If you don't want to go, you don't need to do anything about the applications.   As ever, Edmund W

> Leon Edel's biography of Henry James, which presents the results of exhaustive research and acute psychological insight with so much lucidity and elegance, will undoubtedly stand as a literary classic.
> (1963)

To Leon Edel   May 25, 1953
                                                               Wellfleet

Dear Leon: Thank you for the Lincoln article. About the English: this anti-Americanism annoyed me at the time of the war; and I think that, in general, they have been becoming most disagreeable, not only with foreigners, but also with each other. It seems to me that the kind of thing I found in 1945—on the part of the kind of people I mostly saw—has been admirably described in Angus Wilson's hideous stories and Stephen Potter's amusing books. But, of course, you grew up in Canada, where the people consider themselves more or less English, whereas I have had a certain anti-English tradition behind me.

An error that I made at Princeton in taking you around the town was in telling you that that big yellow house on the corner was called Morton and was a replica of Pope's villa at Twickenham. The original Stockton house, of which this was true, was just beyond that monument to the Battle of Princeton. The house on the corner, however, was also a Stockton house, because a Stockton married the daughter of the family that lived there.

I was amused by your account of the reviewers who identified themselves with the various members of the James family. Shows that you made it real to them . . .   As ever, Edmund Wilson

To LEON EDEL   December 21, 1953
                                                          Wellfleet
Dear Leon: Thank you for your Sturges paper, which has interested me
very much. I don't remember hearing about him in connection with the
class of '85. It was a rather unfortunate class, one of those that came at
the time when there was almost always a serious conflict for men who had
set out to fit themselves for one of the old-fashioned "learned professions"
and then found they had to compete in the Big Money post-war world.
Many came to tragic ends—died young, went insane, committed suicide.
Sturges, you see, took refuge in England. By the time my father was
thirty-five, I don't think he had a single college friend living, and his
brother, who had been contemporary with him at Princeton, had died of
practicing law in Pittsburgh.
    I bought this little Henry James Grolier Club booklet in Boston the
other day, then found I already had it, so am sending the extra one to
you, though you probably have it, too. By the way, there is an amusing
page about James in the *Life and Letters* of G. W. Cable by his daughter
Mrs. Bikle.
    We are sailing for Europe the 30th . . . I am going to Israel to do
some articles for *The New Yorker* . . . Best wishes for the holidays from
both of us.   As ever, Edmund W

To ELIZABETH HULING   November 8, 1953
                                                          Wellfleet
. . . I am making money out of my paperback editions (have sold four
books to the Anchor–Ballantine series), and feel a little, for the first time
in my life, as if I were a real success . . .

To MARIO PRAZ   February 16, 1954
                         The Salzburg Seminar of American Studies
Dear Mario: I'm afraid now that I shan't get to Rome. When I leave
here the middle of March, I'm going to Rapallo to see Max Beerbohm,
but shall then probably sail from Marseilles for Israel. I'll be leaving my
family in Germany and shall come back to Paris and sail from France.
If, however, I should go by way of Italy, I'll certainly hope to see you
in Rome.
    . . . If I knew your Paris address, I'd recommend your going to see
Genet's *Les Bonnes*, a hair-raising little play that seems to me to go
somehow embarrassingly deep into the psychology of contemporary
France.
    I was interested in your broadcast. It really isn't true, though, that I
think all my articles important. The articles in *The Shores of Light* were
only a few out of many that will never be reprinted, and among those
that I did reprint there are a number that were included, not because I

514

thought them particularly good, but because, in my panorama of the twenties, I thought they might interest American readers in recalling the kind of thing that was going on.

There are a lot of Italian students here—from Milano, Torino, Bologna, Sicily, Como, Florence, Rome—and a number of Yugoslavs. I seem to get mostly the Britishers: one Irishman, one Scotchman, one Welshman, one Cornishman, one true-blue Englishman. The whole thing is rather interesting—though the weather is monotonously gloomy, and the castle, once inhabited by Max Reinhardt, is cold and somewhat battered by the war, and full of plaster cupids and bogus Austrian portraits. You might find some of the incongruities piquant. As ever, Edmund W

To Mamaine Koestler*   February 20, 1954
                                                        Salzburg
Dear Mamaine: Thanks ever so much for sending the letters from the hotel. We all got ill in Paris, and haven't quite recovered even now. What finished us was going to see Genet's play *Les Bonnes* in the freezing little Huchette theater. But be sure to see this bothering, hair-raising piece if you go back to Paris. It is very well acted and embarrassingly close to the kind of thing that is now going on in Europe. We saw Malraux and had a very good time with him. He had just spent three weeks in New York and Washington and had come back with a lot of his characteristic formulations about the U.S. that didn't always seem to me to make sense. I think that he is much happier and much better off with his attractive current wife than with the one he was married to when I saw him last. I think that it is also a relief to him not to feel any more that he has to worry about politics and to be able to devote himself to writing . . .
                                                        Love, Edmund

To Elizabeth Huling   May 24, 1954
                                                        Wellfleet
. . . We spent a couple of afternoons with Malraux, who does a good deal to redeem the otherwise rather sorry state of France . . . I was beginning to have some of my old feeling for Paris and was rather reluctant to leave and come back to the McCarthy atmosphere . . .

To Vladimir Nabokov   1950

. . . About Genet: the tough boy who kills and betrays and remains impenitent to the end—of the type of *Notre-Dame-des-Fleurs*—represents his

---

* "I had a letter from Celia dated the 3rd, telling me that Mamaine had died three days before. A part of the attraction of London is gone."—Notebooks of the fifties, June 7, 1954. Celia Paget Goodman was Mamaine's sister.

ideal and appears in everything I have read of his. I agree about his pornographic passages, but they are the kind of erotic fantasies, more or less detached from reality, that people seem to cultivate in prison (like the Marquis de Sade in the Bastille). They are only carried off by the fact that the story is not really that of the author's invented characters, but that of Genet in prison trying to project himself into a novel. The men are all dream men, and even Divine—who, I grant you, is somewhat more convincing than the others—is to some extent a dream tapete. Genet's life, as he tells about it in his memoirs, *Journal du voleur*, has certainly been miserable. I believe that he was in with a life sentence when Sartre and Cocteau got him out of jail. I'm very much amused by the remark that he's reported to have made about Gide: "*Il est d'une immoralité douteuse*" . . .

To John Dos Passos   August 11, 1952
                                                          Talcottville
. . . I hope you read Genet to the end. The entire element has the weakness of being made up of prison fantasies. Where the book is remarkable, I think, is in showing the active and passive-loving elements of the period combined in one being of ambiguous sex. It takes the lid completely off this mess. He is anti-social to the last degree . . .

> Edward Dahlberg, the author of *Bottom Dogs*, is writing a new book, and I have suggested his showing it to you. I thought *Bottom Dogs* very remarkable.   (To Maxwell Perkins, 1931)

To Edward Dahlberg   March 11, 1954
                                                     Frankfurt, Germany
Dear Edward: I found your first three letters when I arrived at Salzburg a month ago, and the fourth later reached me here. I wasn't able to answer them at the time, because I was kept busy with my work at the American Seminar. Do you know about this institution? It is a very curious affair—I don't know that there has ever been anything like it. The American universities have raised money to rent Max Reinhardt's old Salzburg Schloss and bring over American lecturers to give courses in American culture to students from all over Europe. I found it quite interesting: some of the students—especially the Yugoslavs—are ravenous to read American books and find out about the United States.

I am leaving for Israel at the end of this week. I have lately been studying Hebrew and getting interested in Jewish history, and I have persuaded *The New Yorker* to send me to do some articles for them. You know, I have always felt that you had a strain of the specifically Hebrew literary genius—imagery, rhythms, hardness, and fierceness—but I am afraid that you also authentically belong to the type of Hebrew prophet who inevitably—like Jeremiah, wasn't it?—gets put down a well. Yet maybe you are really happier there, and your squawks (jeremiads) that people won't pay attention to you are simply a part of the act. What you give the world is so atrabiliar that you can't honestly be surprised that it puts people off. I am sorry, though, that you are having difficulty in getting your work published. One trouble is, I think, that you produced so little—only *These Bones* and the *Flea*—over a long period of years that your earlier reputation lapsed, and you are up against the problem now of getting yourself known again. Why don't you try the new magazine *Encounter*, published in London by Stephen Spender and Irving Kristol? Mention my name, if you like, or perhaps it would make more impression to get Herbert Read to forward something to them. There's also another new English literary publication, *The London Magazine*, edited by John Lehmann.　　　　　　　　　　　　　　　　All good wishes, Edmund W

To Edward Dahlberg　　　　　　　　　　　　　　June 22, 1954
　　　　　　　　　　　　　　　　　　　　　　　Wellfleet

Dear Edward: Thank you for the *New Directions* and the copies of *Poetry*. I'm glad to see that you're getting printed. I haven't acknowledged them before because I've been heavily enmeshed in three thousand years of Jewish literature and history—a subject almost entirely new to me, on which I've been trying to write. I enclose my first article, which might interest you. Israel—modern Israel—is not like what you think or what I expected. I'm going to write about it, more or less from the Biblical and rabbinical point of view. Tel Aviv is quite a pleasant little Mediterranean city, with a sort of Viennese atmosphere: theaters, coffeehouses, bookshops. I have been reading up Philo, Josephus, and Pliny in connection with the discovery of the Dead Sea scrolls—a wonderful story that I am going to write.　　　　　　　　　　Best regards, Edmund W

To Edward Dahlberg　　　　　　　　　　　　August 10, 1954
　　　　　　　　　　　　　　　　　　　　　Talcottville

Dear Edward: I wrote Henry Moe to sound him out about your chances [Guggenheim Fellowship]. He was away on vacation, and I got this reply from his secretary. If I were you, I'd apply, and get Herbert Read to write to them, and somebody else who will impress them, if possible. I'll do my best for you. Thanks for your interesting letter. I'm now in the midst of the third of my Hebraic articles. There is an awful lot of work in them. It is a field of which I knew almost nothing—3,000 years of Jewish history!　　　　　　　　　　　　　　　　As ever, Edmund W

To LOUISE BOGAN   May 23, 1954
                                                      Wellfleet
Dear Louise: I am moved to write you again by the arrival of Marianne
Moore's *La Fontaine*. My affection for her and my liking for her other
work are not able to blind me to the fact that it was not at all a good
idea to have her translate La Fontaine. It is perfectly plain in the verse
here—what I have always maintained—that her sense of both rhythm and
rhyme is defective and underdeveloped. The oddity of her own poems is
partly due to this—it is not, as people think, deliberate—and here both the
pulse and the point of La Fontaine disappear. In my opinion, this translation and Auden's attempt to do a libretto for the Stravinsky opera are
the two major literary mistakes of our time. I'm interested to know
whether you agree with me about Marianne. I do hope to see you in
the course of the summer. I want to show you sometime the strange
sequence of poems by Edna inspired by T. S. Eliot. Most of the stuff in
this new book I thought weak. There are more interesting unpublished
poems than these.   As ever, Edmund

To LOUISE BOGAN   July 18, 1954
                                                    Talcottville
Dear Louise: Iris Origo has just written me asking me to do something
about her Leopardi book. I'm not in a position to now, but thought you
might have some interest in it. I am sure *The New Yorker* would send
it to you if you want it and haven't got it . . . I get the impression that
it's a pretty good book.
    I'm up here in New York doing prodigies of work, living alone in this
house, with a woman from the village getting meals for me. I have two
Persian kittens that I bought for Helen. The family are coming the
first of August.
    I have just read the Day Lewis *Italian Visit*, and your note about it.
There *is* something unsatisfactory, in spite of his inventiveness with
images and his metrical virtuosity—some inescapable banality of the
regular patterns of thought of the London literary world. Nevertheless,
it is better, I think, than the other things of his I have read.
                                              Love as ever, Edmund

To LOUISE BOGAN   August 9, 1954
                                                    Talcottville
. . . John Betjeman's new book is wonderful—it has some of the funniest
poems ever written. I also think rather highly of Edward Gorey's *Listing
Attic*, which really ought to be taken cognizance of by *The New Yorker*'s
poetry department . . .

To HARRY LEVIN   August 4, 1954
                                                   Talcottville

Dear Harry: I've just sent the following to Isaiah Berlin:

> Said David Cecil to Cecil Roth,
>   "You don't think I'm only a bit of froth?"
>   "A problem with which I'd prefer not to wrestle!"
> Said Cecil Roth to David Cecil.

I've developed a new literary genre: reporting my own table talk. Living here alone for weeks, I've found it pleasant to do this. After all, William Beckford forged his own correspondence. I've also invented a man who reports it—a Boswell who rather dislikes me. Hope you are enjoying Wellfleet more than I should.   As ever, EW

THE DEAD SEA SCROLLS

AND

STUDYING HEBREW

1952–1956

The Dead Sea Scrolls were not discovered by archaeologists but by the Bedouin, and their importance was brought to the knowledge of the world at large, again not by an archaeologist, but by a very scholarly amateur, Edmund Wilson. Were it not for the Bedouin, on the one hand, and Wilson, on the other, I'm not so sure that the subject of the Dead Sea Scrolls would have been known at all. Wilson sensed very early in the research on the scrolls that one of the most important aspects is the relationship between the writings of the Essenes and the birth and beginning of Christianity. Quite a lot of scholars were very shy to jump to conclusions, or to make these conclusions better known at the time. The problem of how Christianity was born out of Judaism intrigued him and appealed to him. He always comes back to that particular problem. He not only contributed to the fact that the Dead Sea Scrolls were known in the lay world but he also influenced some of the scholars in the way they dealt with the scrolls, because he was very provocative in his writing. He was trying to put questions. He was trying to define the views of some scholars perhaps more boldly than they dared.
                    (Yigael Yadin, *The Listener*, September 20, 1973)

To Mario Praz   July 13, 1960

... About my interest in the Dead Sea scrolls: it was studying Hebrew that led me to this, not the other way around. I took a course at the Princeton Seminary, and apropos of this, Paolo Milano told me that he

---

Note to the Reader: In the winter of 1952–1953 Edmund gave the second series of the Christian Gauss Seminars at Princeton. He had been preceded by Paul Tillich and followed by Leon Edel. Edmund's six lectures were first drafts of what were to become six chapters of *Patriotic Gore*. That same winter he took a course

had heard from a friend who had just been in Jerusalem that there seemed to be something fishy going on in connection with the scrolls . . .

To Daniel Aaron
October 20, 1952
Princeton

. . . I am taking a course in Hebrew in the Theological Seminary here so that I can lecture to Waldo Frank about the Jewish Genesis . . .

To Waldo Frank
November 18, 1952
Princeton

Dear Waldo: Thanks for your letter about my *Shores*. I am sorry about your book and have written both Roger Straus and Jack Wheelock about it.

I have been enjoying Tillich's seminars. He is an attractive man and a rather noble character—also intelligent and widely read—and has been influenced both by Marxism and by Existentialism. In spite of the fact that the interpretation of Christian theology in terms of German philosophy is not exactly my cup of tea, he is interesting from the points of view both of what has happened to the Christian religion and of what has happened to Germany. What he is really doing is expounding a system of morality of his own which almost anybody might approve of, but my reaction to the whole thing is that it is a pity he had to start from the Scriptures and feels under the obligation to interpret the New Testament in such a way as to accommodate his own conceptions. By the time he gets done with the words of Christ, they are made to have meanings

---

in Hebrew at the Princeton Seminary, where he was, I believe, the only lay student among the seminarians. It was also then that he became extremely curious about the scrolls of the Essene sect which had been recently excavated in the area around the Dead Sea.

Reading the Old Testament in Hebrew turned his mind to the "cramping theology" of Calvinism in his family history. In "the larger historical sense," to use his own words, his approach to Israel was that of "an Anglo-Saxon of Old Testament Puritan background." A "similar revelation" came to him, as his studies progressed, of how "the imagery of the Hebrew Scriptures have been an element of literature in English from the King James translation on." These ideas recur in the chapters of *Patriotic Gore* (1962) and in the earlier chapter, "The Jews," in *A Piece of My Mind* (1956).

On the other hand, Edmund's "acquiring a little Hebrew" furthered his exploration of the Dead Sea scrolls controversies, which resulted in *The Scrolls from the Dead Sea* (1955), and the sections on Israel and "On First Reading Genesis" in *Red, Black, Blond and Olive* (1956). Nearly all the chapters of these books came out alternately in *The New Yorker* in the fifties and sixties. In this volume the letters relating to the Dead Sea scrolls are in "The Fifties," while letters pertaining to *Patriotic Gore* will be found early in the sixties section. The revised and expanded version of *The Scrolls from the Dead Sea* was published in 1969 and retitled *The Dead Sea Scrolls*.

To the very end of Edmund's life, he would be found at his desk surrounded by Bibles and dictionaries, "keeping up with new developments," deciphering the Old Testament and facsimiles of fragments of the scrolls. —Elena Wilson

which would have amazed the Apostles. At the same time, though he prefers, as he says, to dispense with the word *God* and to talk about the Power of Being, his fundamental philosophic ideas seem to me to depend on a pre-assumption of God that, at a fairly late stage of his exposition, is smuggled in under the name of Being; and as for me, *je n'ai pas besoin de cette hypothèse.*

Realizing that I had the chance down here to study Hebrew with experts, I have been taking a course at the Seminary, and I find that it would hardly be possible to begin it without some help from a teacher. It is important to read it aloud. The difficulty at the beginning is that the accents, many of the vowels, and the values to be given to the consonants are written in and under and above the consonants in a complicated system of dots and dashes, and that the consonants are sometimes vowels. The verbs are also rather complicated, but they tell me that, after you have mastered these matters, the rest is not very difficult, and the boys who take this course seem to read quite well at the end of the year. I've found the subject fascinating. The opening of Genesis is very impressive and gives the effect of an epic poem. The verbs are a revelation: of the seven conjugations you learn, three are intensive aspects (to kill *brutally*, to search *diligently*, to break *to bits*, etc.), and two are causatives (God *made* the grass to spring forth). Besides these, there are a jussive form (Let there be light) and a cohortative form (I will eat flesh), and—what seems most extraordinary—a prophetic use of one of the aspects that is distinguished from the simple future and expresses the conviction of the speaker that something will *certainly* come to pass. The Hebrew verbs are thus more dynamic, more full of conviction and determination, than those of any other language we study. The sense of time, time by the clock, is vaguer than even in Russian—there are no real tenses of the Western sort.

We study a simplified grammar—Yates's *Essentials of Biblical Hebrew*—which I recommend. The Jews who know the language here tell me that in certain respects the pronunciation of the Seminary is better than that of the Sephardic rabbis, who, from living in countries where there is no *th* sound, have changed all the *th*'s to *s*'s; but then I can see that the Jews have the hang of certain other sounds which the students of the Seminary will probably never learn. If you get any chance this winter, you ought to get somebody to read with you. I don't know whether I'll be good enough when I get back in the spring to go through the early stages with you myself. But I hope we can attack it together. There is sure to be somebody in the course of the summer—Sam Wolman, for example—who could give us a little assistance.

We are comfortably fixed here . . . I don't begin performing till December 11. Elena sends love to you both, as do I.   As ever, Edmund W

The Charlie Chaplin film is wonderful (sentimental, but it doesn't matter)—and his greatest piece of acting.* He has been getting the good reviews he deserves in London—stimulated, no doubt, by the idea that he is a victim of American intolerance—but intolerably stupid ones over here.

Do you remember where that precept of Newman's is that you were telling me about?—his saying that once the Catholic had accepted the faith, he ought to tell himself afterwards that the matter had been settled once for all. I want to use it in connection with Holmes.

To ALFRED KAZIN   May 25, 1953
                               Wellfleet

Dear Alfred: I was very much pleased by your letter. I had it on my mind, when I was writing about Laski, that I ought to say something about his Sovietism—which was one of the outstanding examples of his capacity for being unrealistic; but I had to deal with so many other matters in connection with him and Holmes that I decided to leave it out. I might have known that Sidney Hook would repair this omission.

I am going through a sort of Judaizing period now and read with rapt attention the articles on the origin of Chanukkah and the interpretation of the Zohar in *Commentary*, which I formerly used to skip. I want to have some essays on Jewish subjects in my next miscellaneous book—have arranged to do *The New Yorker* an article on the Pentateuch! Have been reading Renan's *Histoire du peuple d'Israël*, which seems to me one of his best things. It must be unique as a study of the Bible by a non-Jewish and non-clerical Hebrew scholar who was also a first-rate writer and attacked the subject simply as a critic and historian. There is a remarkable chapter, for example, on the Jehovist author of Genesis, which is just the kind of thing I should like to do but shall never be qualified for . . .

Miss Freeman tells me that you found a house. I hope to see you at some point. Won't you be staying into September?

Please remember me to your wife—who, I think, is extremely good for you.   As ever, Edmund Wilson

To ELIZABETH HULING   November 8, 1953

The New Yorker will send me to Israel . . .

To ELENA WILSON   [undated, March 1954]
                       King David Hotel, Jerusalem

. . . The difference between people here and the "intellectuals" that we have seen in Europe is that these people have something to live for, to passionately care about . . .

---

* *Limelight.*

523

. . . a rabbi who now runs the publicity of the Weizmann Institute at Rehovoth discovered I was interested in Hebrew and Jewish history—a novelty for them, I gather, on the part of a visiting Gentile . . . he invited me to lunch and we had a long conversation. They seem to be on the point of liquidating the old religion, which, in its more rigorous form, is difficult to reconcile with a modern community. This man had visions of a more rationalized cult, based, however, on the Bible, that would permeate the whole life of the country.

. . . I called by appointment on a terrific old scholar, the head of the Hebrew language department at the university. He received me, with one of his colleagues, in a room so devoted to study that there was nowhere for people to sit and talk: it was almost completely filled by books and an enormous desk. His hair was tousled like Auden's, and one of his eyes was half closed from peering at manuscripts. He was charming but got rid of me rapidly, having selected one of his staff to read Hebrew with me. We cannot begin till Sunday, because Friday afternoon (today) and Saturday are Sabbath . . .

To Elena Wilson   April 10, 1954
                                                        Jerusalem
. . . The day that I wrote you from Tel Aviv, I walked around the town by myself and found it rather pleasant, though everybody from Jerusalem runs it down: little alleys with lime trees, esplanade along the sea, bookshops, pastry shops, theaters, cafés, coffeehouses, and a livelier pace, though it is hardly the beehive that the people here had led me to expect—there is something like a touch of Austria. I was invited in the afternoon to tea at the house of Schocken, one of the principal publishers here and the editor and publisher of what is said to be the best paper. The contributors to his literary section were there—the usual conversation: American novels, translations from the Russian, etc. In the evening I went to *Fledermaus*. Everybody at Schocken's had warned me against it, and I found out how right they were.

The next day I had lunch with the man from New York, Grodzensky, who had the *Finland Station* translated. I enjoyed him very much—most of his life has been spent in New York. We walked around the city in the afternoon. One end was built by people from Germany and the other by people from the Slavic countries: the Germans don't quite trust the Slavs, and a little bit, I felt, look down on them. We ended by calling on a woman poet named Leah Goldberg, very sensitive and sweet and cultivated. She reminded me of Helen Muchnic—though her position in Tel Aviv is something like that of Marianne Moore. She lives with her Russian-speaking mother and is approached with a certain reverence. She had just translated *War and Peace* and Petrarch's sonnets.

. . . The next morning, a little after nine, I started off on a motor trip under the guidance of a very well informed young man from the Press Office. There were also a young woman, originally from Poland, who had spent the last seven years in Cleveland, and a gloomy and grim young man from Switzerland, a specialist in the psychiatric aspects of law. The latter always insisted on eating in kosher restaurants and put on his little round cap while he ate, but was horrified and revolted when he had to face a typically Jewish breakfast, much relished by other members of the party but quite unlike what he was used to in Switzerland—sour cream, chopped carrots, radishes, olives, and pickled herring. He rose and moved as far as possible to the other end of the table. We had lunch at, and explored a little, the Arab town of Acre, visited the mosque and bazaar. The Arabs live in squalor—from the Western point of view, it is all a great slum. The country in what used, in Biblical times, to be Israel, the Northern Kingdom, full of the scenes of Biblical events, is the same land of stony little mountains as, lower, around Jerusalem. The landscape of Palestine is mild, rather pleasant, but rather monotonous. To see where the great battles and religious crises of the Bible took place is to find them reduced in scale. We visited the old town of Safed, "picturesque" and looking out from a very high hill, which now has an artists' colony and is by way of becoming a Santa Fe or Provincetown. From there we went to the Lake of Tiberias, the New Testament Galilee. I had never quite believed in Renan's idyllic description of it in the *Vie de Jésus*, imagining that he had somewhat subdued it to the suavity of pretty French prose; but it is actually as idyllic as he says—all dim blues and greens, with a background of low wrinkled yellowish hills— quite a large lake, sparsely inhabited (it is supposed to have been more of a center of civilization in Jesus' day). We spent the night at the town of Tiberias, now a popular resort, with t.b. sanatoriums, hot baths for rheumatics, and many small summer hotels. The little rise—with a little church—where the Sermon on the Mount is supposed to have been preached is at one end of the lake.

The next day we came back to Jerusalem through Cana, where what my British-trained guide called "the old wedding feast" is supposed to have taken place, and Nazareth, now a mainly Arab town, where we were besieged by Arab souvenir sellers and taken by an Arab guide to see two churches built over ancient caves, in one of which the Annunciation is supposed to have taken place and in the other of which the family of Jesus is supposed to have lived.

. . . Just out of Tiberias, we stopped in the morning at a cooperative settlement where I called on a woman to whom Joseph Brand, the man who runs Schoenhof's, had given me a letter. She was an old friend of his from Prague and one of the pioneers of the settlement—having come there in the first years of the century—which was itself the pioneer cooperative of Palestine. They had been intellectuals, inspired by Tolstoy to return to the land and work with their hands. "We started the whole movement," she said, "were called revolutionaries. Achtung!" she added humorously. They are immensely proud of themselves—had a battle with the Syrians right on the premises and have preserved a captured tank and some of their trucks as memorials. Several children of the community were killed. Now they have a special building and school for children made orphans by the Nazis and suffering from severe neuroses as a result of having seen their parents massacred or something of the kind, and other "problem" children. She was a splendid old type. Her room was full of books and she had done a good deal of teaching; but we found her in the mending department working a sewing machine. I was glad to have seen this and got a very good impression of the place, as I had of similar settlements—very different from the Russian collective farms; on a higher level of education and without the undercurrent of resentment. They are supposed to work pretty hard, but the atmosphere is quite a relaxed one, and one has the feeling that the people are getting along well together. They stroll in a leisurely way along the paths from place to place among their trees that they have planted themselves and their now brightly blooming gardens. The children, who live here with their parents (as is not always the case in these settlements), seem to get a good deal of considerate attention.

We arrived back in Jerusalem late yesterday afternoon. I called up the consul and found that they think they can be sure of arranging for me to go over to Jordan long enough to see the Old City and visit the Dead Sea excavations. Fritsch from Princeton is there, and the American School of Oriental Studies has offered to put me up. I am very much pleased about this. I'll come back here in time for Passover, and then be leaving the following Tuesday . . .

To FELIX FRANKFURTER   May 10, 1954
                                                           Wellfleet

Dear Felix: We just got back from four months abroad, and I have found your letter and the copy of your speech. I was grateful for them both, and very much interested in the latter—don't see how you managed to extemporize so invariably to the point. I know, from my attempts at the Salzburg Seminar (where I gave them the Civil War), that I can't do this at all and have to fall back on reading something I have written. I went also, having persuaded *The New Yorker* to send me, for a month to Israel and Jordan, leaving the family in Europe. The subject of Israel (in its larger sense) has somewhat been seducing me from the Civil War, though I can't pretend to do anything with it except in a journalistic and more or less superficial way. But on this level there is something to contribute, I think, and I am going to do a few articles—one in *The New Yorker* this week. The implications, for example, of the Dead Sea scrolls have never been brought out in a popular way, and the most recent astonishing discoveries have hardly even been reported. Israel now, in spite of their troubles with the Arabs, seems relatively cheerful compared to Europe—they at least feel that they have something to work for; and the tension there is nothing compared to here.

Our love to you both, Edmund W

To Alfred Kazin
May 17, 1954
Wellfleet

Dear Alfred: We got back a couple of weeks ago. I spent a month in Israel and had a very good time. It is unlike any place else on earth, and quite bracing and cheerful after Europe—in spite of their troubles with the Arabs—since they feel, as the Europeans don't, that they have something definite to work for. Yet the tension is much less than you might expect—nothing to what we have here. But, of course, I had no responsibility there, and here I tend to worry about America's mission.

I found here an old January *New Yorker* with a review of Cummings by you which is one of the best things of the kind you have written. That autobiographical book did your writing a lot of good, I think.

. . . Best regards to your wife.
As ever, Edmund W

To Lee Grove
Oxford University Press
June 28, 1954
Wellfleet

Dear Mr. Grove: I am wrestling with my Biblical and Hebraic subjects and don't now expect to be done with them much before the first of September. That part of the book alone will run to some 50,000 words . . . How soon I can get the book to you depends on when I finish with this Hebrew material. After that, I can tell you more definitely. The first of these essays, by the way, has proved to be more successful—from the point of view of letters and requests for reprints—than anything else I ever wrote.* *The New Yorker* is printing several thousand copies for use by theological seminaries, the Chicago Linguistics Institute, and other institutions which have asked for them. This won't hurt the sale of the book, but, on the contrary, ought to promote it.

Sincerely, Edmund Wilson

---

* "On First Reading Genesis."

527

To Lee Grove   October 5, 1954
                                                                  Wellfleet
Dear Grove: . . . The New Testament Apocrypha finally came, but it
turns out that it does not contain the things I want. These are:
Didache (Teaching of the Twelve Apostles)
The Pastor of Hermas
The Dialogue of Justyn Martyr. These or some of them are probably to
be found in the Oxford Library of the Fathers and the Ante-Nicean Library. Do you publish these titles? If you have them in stock, please see
if they include the above works, and if they do, send them to me . . .
                                                Sincerely, Edmund Wilson

To Alfred Kazin   October 29, 1954
                                                            The New Yorker
. . . I've been involved in a long job (Dead Sea scrolls) that I've only
just finished . . . I am still struggling in the toils of the three thousand
years of Jewish history. Once you really get into it, you find there is no
easy way of getting out again. Have you ever tried reading the Talmud?
It is a very strange work—difficult at first to get the hang of—but it
exercises a certain fascination. I think that I may settle down to reading
it through. There seems to be no other way of really finding out what is in
it . . .

To John Dos Passos   November 1, 1954
                                                            The New Yorker
. . . I was sorry not to see you when I went to Baltimore yesterday. I
arrived in the black clothes that I wear to reassure Biblical scholars and
that sometimes cause me, in bars, to be mistaken for a clergyman on a
trip, to see Albright, the Biblical archaeologist at Johns Hopkins, about
a piece I am doing on the Dead Sea scrolls. I have discovered, however,
that the top scholars in this field are no longer at all clerical, but cultivated men of the world, sometimes nattily dressed and delirious with
excitement over the scrolls—which are subversive of Christian beliefs—
who seem only to be discreet about the divinity of Jesus in order not to
upset those of their students who come from pious homes . . .

To Waldo Frank   December 14, 1954
                                                                  Wellfleet
Dear Waldo: Thanks very much for your letter—which is good Waldo
Frank, if my article is good Wilson. I have just had a letter from an ex-
Israeli criticizing me, perhaps rightly, from the opposite point of view,
on the grounds that I have written only about the lunatic fringe and

have disregarded the great mass of steady and moderate people. I think that you much overrate the danger and fear of the Israelis. I got the impression that the Arabs were a good deal more afraid of them than they were of the Arabs. After all, they have succeeded, in a very few years, in doing with that barren country what the Arabs were unable to do in more than a thousand, and the real unconfessed preoccupation in Israel which I did not touch upon is a kind of imperialistic drive to expand in a territorial way and become a power in the Middle East.

In general, the approach to Israel (in the large historical sense) of an Anglo-Saxon of Old Testament Puritan background is something entirely distinct from that of either the rabbinical or the Europeanized Jew. It is based on a reversion to the Bible without the intermediate Talmudic and medieval experience. I have never seen this situation brought out: most Jews do not recognize it, and most ex-Puritans do not realize how strongly it, the Hebraic factor, is there. I have not yet written about this directly, but I shall get to it later on, and the pieces I have already done are merely attempts to take account of this rather peculiar relation to Hebraic religion and history. They are thus primarily addressed to people in my own situation, so you are so far right in saying that I am writing of myself in relation to the Bible, Israel, etc. Your position is quite different: you have *lived* the Jewish experience in terms of European culture and the actualities of American life. For me, it is merely one element involved in an American training, to which I am trying rather belatedly to do justice. By the way, I owe you some debt in all this: it was partly your book, I think, that started me off.

We're going to New York tomorrow—back by the middle of next week. I'll lend you Agnon then. I borrowed my copy of *The Bridal Canopy* and had to give it back, but am going to get another.

In the meantime, בברכת ידידות, "with shining blessings," as one of my Jewish correspondents always signs himself. EW

Also, חג שמח, though I may see you before then.

To Waldo Frank   December 27, 1954
                                                          Wellfleet

Dear Waldo: The only person I saw in Israel who talked the way you do was the former wife of John Gunther. She is Jewish and has been trying to rejoin her Judaistic background by living in Jerusalem; but she told me she was sometimes afraid that the Israelis were dooming themselves to repeat the pattern of Babylon, Spain, and Hitler. I hope not, and do not believe so, but it is true that in such matters I am likely to be over-optimistic. What is happening, it seems to me, at the present time is that they are actually becoming strong at the expense of developing a psychology not unlike that of the Soviet Union in the early years of the Revolution. The Arabs have no such drive, no such unity, no such technique of modern warfare and organization. It would take a lot of backing by Russia to enable them to wipe out Israel.

Am hoping to see you soon.   Edmund

To WILLIAM SHAWN   January 4, 1955
The New Yorker   Wellfleet

Dear Shawn: I don't know whether you will still feel that parts of this are too technical. I have got to the point with it where I should have to have suggestions from somebody else, if anything is not clear. The part at the end about the Metropolitan* is still unsatisfactory, because it has not been checked. Albright tells me that it is not true that somebody crept into the Chicago Museum and photographed his scrolls by infrared rays. It seems he imagines things. I have to check everything he tells me by other people's evidence.

Thanks for the Christmas card—and Happy New Year.   EW

To CELIA PAGET GOODMAN   April 15, 1955
                                                     The New Yorker
. . . I am staying on through the first week of May to see my scrolls article through the press. I have devoted the better part of a year to it: a terribly complicated subject, but the story has never yet been properly told and seems to me fascinating. I understand that the Vatican is getting a little worried and is about to make a statement telling people what they ought to think, but I hope to beat them to the rap. I'll send you the piece when it's out. It is only an abridgment of a longer thing, which is later coming out in a book; but it will probably be quite enough for you . . .

To UPTON SINCLAIR   June 8, 1955
                                                     The New Yorker
Dear Sinclair: Thank you very much for your book, with its inscription. I was particularly interested in discovering, in your postscript, the present position of the Episcopal Church. Like you, though younger than you, I still grew up at a time when a good deal more dogma was demanded. The professor under whom at college (Princeton: notoriously Fundamentalist, of course) I took a Bible course was immediately afterwards dismissed

---

* "The Syrian Metropolitan, at the Monastery of St. Mark in Old Jerusalem, Mar Athanasius Yeshue Samuel."   —*The Scrolls from the Dead Sea*

when he published a book in which he treated Jesus from the "historical" point of view. So, in publishing my article about the scrolls, I thought that I would be bringing down a lot of complaint and denunciation. On the contrary, to my surprise, I have had complimentary letters from rabbis, Jesuit priests, and ministers of several denominations. Dean Pike at St. John the Divine's, it seems, preached a sermon expressing agreement as to the Essene background of Jesus. I was somewhat disappointed at not having shocked people more!

Long life to you and please give my regards to your wife, if she still remembers me. Sincerely, Edmund Wilson

My most interesting professors at Princeton were Norman Kemp Smith and Christian Gauss . . . He [Kemp Smith] was a Scot from Dundee and . . . held the chair of Moral Philosophy at Edinburgh . . . He was much liked in both Princeton and Edinburgh and I felt I had a friend in him all my life. (*A Prelude*)

To NORMAN KEMP SMITH July 6, 1955
Talcottville

Dear Kemp Smith: The Dead Sea scrolls article—in expanded form—is coming out as a book; and the other two Hebraic pieces are part of another book. I'll have copies of both of them sent you. Several people have written me complaining about the interspersed advertizements. I had an urbane letter from a Jesuit at the Jesuit seminary in Massachusetts. He said that they were recommending my article to the students and regretted that the bathing-suit ads made it impossible to give it to the Sisters of Notre Dame. He also amused me by saying that he thought I had handled with moderation the "rather neuralgic subject" of the relation of Jesus to the Dead Sea sect. I understand, by the way, that the Vatican is about to make a pronouncement telling Catholics what they are to think on the subject.

The enormous advertizing that *The New Yorker* carries just before Christmas and in the spring is all to my advantage because it makes it possible for them to run my long articles.

I am up here in my old family place in upstate New York. I spend a certain amount of time here alone every summer, concentrating on some piece of work: two summers ago, the Hebrew Bible; last summer, the Dead Sea scrolls; this summer, Calvinism and early New England—the stiffest assignment, I fear, of all. I have always rather avoided it but must now attack it, in connection with a book I am doing about the literature of the Civil War. It is absolutely quiet here—a little village of eighty people, in rolling dairy country on the edge of the Adirondacks, fine old stone house, built at the end of the eighteenth century when the first settlers arrived. The place has changed remarkably little—much less than most of America—since I came here as a child.

I shall be glad, however, to see my family, who are arriving this afternoon. As ever, Edmund Wilson

To Norman Kemp Smith September 25, 1956
Wellfleet

Dear Kemp Smith: . . . I was in England at the end of July and wanted to come to Edinburgh, but had only a short time and a good deal to do in London. Was also in Paris and Munich. It seemed to me that, even since two years ago, a new phase had become perceptible. The young post-war people in Europe seem more like Americans and Russians. They are not much interested in politics, are thoroughly disillusioned with great leaders, and are interested mainly in television, refrigerators, and fast cars. This may be a hopeful sign. It may be easier for the various countries to get together on this materialistic basis.

It has become for me a pleasant occupation to make connections with the secular scholars who have been working on the Dead Sea scrolls, and give them moral support. They are under heavy attack from the Catholics, and are even becoming alarmed for fear the Catholic priests, who now predominate in the team that is working on the scrolls in Jerusalem, may be capable of suppressing embarrassing documents. (I have an article on the general situation in the *New Statesman*'s autumn book number.) A number of interesting things have turned up since my book was written. The next number of the *Journal of Biblical Literature* will contain a most important text. The New Testament, as you know, is full of citations from the Old Testament intended to show that the coming of Christ had frequently been predicted; but many of these quotations are not to be found in the Old Testament in the quoted form. The passages have been sometimes rewritten, and, in other cases, passages from different parts have been taken out of their contexts and fitted together to produce the desired sense; and there has long been a theory that the early Christians had collections of Testimonia to be memorized and made use of in argument. Such a collection has now turned up, and it includes some of the New Testament quotations as well as other Messianic predictions arrived at by similar methods. This collection must be pre-Christian like the other documents from the caves.

About Santayana: I haven't read much of his philosophy, but greatly admire his other work. He says of himself that he only became free when he ceased to teach philosophy at Harvard, and it seems to me that his writing enormously improves after that. For he *was* primarily a writer. He once said to Irwin Edman, who had published something about him:

"You don't say the obvious thing—that I'm a poet manqué." But he was brilliant as a critic of ideas, of points of view, of civilizations. I read his novel *The Last Puritan* last winter and thought it was very remarkable. The friends of my college days had a good deal in common with the hero, and it is astonishing how well Santayana, the Spaniard, was able to understand such people.

. . . I am glad to hear that your health is good. We feel better for our trip this summer. It suddenly came over me when I was back here what a struggle—whatever you are doing—it is to live in America. The country is still so new that there is always, at the bottom of everything, the anxiety about making it work as well as of maintaining one's own position.

Elena sends love. I hope we shall see you on our next trip.

As ever, Edmund Wilson

During the summer I spent in Moscow, she was working for the Open Road Travel Agency, through which I had to make my arrangements. She was married to a young American, the son of one of the engineers who had been brought over as advisors on the planning of Soviet industry.   (*Red, Black, Blond and Olive*)

To Lily Herzog   June 5, 1955
Wellfleet

Dear Lily: I am completely non-religious, and it is only by an effort of the imagination that I can even understand how people come to believe in gods and creeds. In saying that discouragement with social improvement tends to make people fall back on religions, I was merely stating an historical fact. I do not approve of this, and my interest in Marxism was partly due to my accepting it as what it pretends to be: a secular philosophy and practical program. There has always been, however, concealed in it, a strong element of religion—which is what makes it go so to people's heads. I have written about this in *To the Finland Station* . . .

Love, Edmund

To Mario Praz   January 2, 1955
                                                              Wellfleet
Dear Mario: Here I am in Technicolor—in return for the photograph of
yourself you gave me. I have been meaning to write to you for ages, but
have been struggling with a rather complicated book—to be called *Red,
Black, Blond and Olive; Studies in Four Civilizations: Zuñi, Haiti, Soviet
Russia and Israel*—which is now nearly done. I am sorry that we did
not get to Rome when we were in Europe last year. I only passed through
Rapallo at the suggestion of a friend [S. N. Behrman] who was staying
there and knew Max Beerbohm and offered to take me to see him. Though
over eighty, he is perfectly clear in his mind and talks extremely well.
Did you ever meet him? As the years have gone on, I have come to realize
that he and Bernard Shaw are the only British prose writers likely to
survive out of the group of contemporaries I read in my youth. I got the
impression, by the way, that Max really disliked Shaw.

. . . Have you seen the new Pléiade Proust, which I have found fascinating. It is the only sound text that has been published, and it is full
of *inédit* material, including a whole episode that he never got around to
working in. I have not read much that is new, because I have been occupied alternately with the American Civil War and the 3,000 years of
Jewish writing and history—the latter of which it is difficult to extricate
oneself from, once one has got into its coils. Do you happen to know
anything about a new MS of Petronius that is supposed to have turned
up recently in Egypt, I think? I ran across a mention of it in reading up
excavations in the Middle East, but can't find anybody who knows anything about it.

Best regards for the New Year, which may see us all vaporized.
                                                     As ever, Edmund

To Harry Levin   January 25, 1955
                                                      Wellfleet

. . . Do you ever get at all bored with Albert Schweitzer? I really know
nothing about him but can't help feeling that there is something phony
somewhere. It may be merely the publicity, but where does all that publicity emanate from? Have you ever read any of his books? I can't bear
the way he looks . . .

To Louise Bogan   February 7, 1955
                                                  The New Yorker

Dear Louise: We are in town . . . We want to see you when we are a
little better settled; but in the meantime, I suppose you are going to
Auden's birthday party on the 21st, and I suggest that you and I compose
for him a joint sonnet—like the one that Max Beerbohm and Gosse did
about Henry James—contributing alternate lines. Here is my beginning:
                Auden, that thou art living at this hour . . .
Write or phone me your 2nd line.   Love, Edmund

To Mario Praz   March 31, 1955
                                                  The New Yorker

Dear Mario: Your articles just came this morning, and I have only had
a chance to read the passage you marked. I was touched by your missing
my Christmas card. I send them out only every other year—am planning
a brilliant one for next Christmas—unless I get vaporized: I had supposed
that my place in upstate New York, in dairy country and a long way from
any factory, would be quite out of the way of bombing, but I have
lately found out that it is right next door to the radar station for all that
region and that there is a mysterious "government project" not far away,
enclosed in an iron fence. In my opinion, the inhabitants of the United
States ought to strike against paying the income tax till the government
ceases to spend the money on this insanity.
    Apropos of taxes, it sounds ridiculous that your American editions
should be taxed. I have never had taxes deducted from any of my Italian
advances, or from my English ones—though for those latter I had to make
out applications in form.
    I am enclosing some of the fruits of my Hebraic studies—which may
not much interest you. There is a third one on the Dead Sea scrolls coming
out in three or four weeks. This is really a sensational story, which has
never yet been told in any complete and easily comprehensible way—
something of a theological scandal . . .
    I can't keep you posted on new American writers, because I never read

them any more—have entered the old-fogy stage when one reads a lot of history and doesn't care what the young people are doing . . .

As ever, Edmund

To Stanley Dell
March 18, 1956
Wellfleet

Dear Stanley: I doubt whether I'll get to the reunion. I make a point of not paying my class dues and disapprove on principle of the whole idea of class get-togethers. But I do have to be in Princeton the 12th of June—reunion is, I think, the Thursday of the week before—and if you are going to be there then, should love to see you. If there is a real prospect of seeing you, we could come on Monday the 11th. I miss my old friends nowadays—so many are insane, dead, or turned Roman Catholics. Dave Hamilton, Morris Belknap, and Larry Noyes have all died in the last few years. Dave was the only one, however, that I still continued to see. Remember me to your wife . . . As ever, Edmund W.

To Morton D. Zabel
September 1, 1956
Hotel Vier Jahreszeiten, Munich*

. . . I live pleasantly at this hotel. Have been finishing the *Young Werther*, which I began twenty-three years ago when I was learning German for Marxist purposes. It seems appalling that young men all over Europe should have been committing suicide on account of this book. My principal amusement is the opera. The Richard Strauss numbers—which are given in progression—in themselves rather annoy me, but they are beautifully staged and directed, and, what is incredible, well acted. But I expect you know all about Munich . . .

To Morton D. Zabel
September 22, 1956
Wellfleet

Dear Morton: I got back last Tuesday and found your letter at the club. Sorry to miss you. I was interested in your description of what Munich was like before the war. But, even bombed, I prefer it to New York and Boston. After a lifetime of back-breaking patriotism, I have been having an unexpected reaction in favor of that gracious Old World civilization and may end as a Henry James character living in Paris and working on a marvelous book about America. As ever, Edmund

To John Dos Passos
September 26, 1956
Wellfleet

Dear Dos: Your postcard reached me in Germany—was glad to hear you had visited Frijoles. I got back last week and find—with a certain surprise—

---

*E.'s itinerary included London, Paris, and Munich.

that I am rather out of tune with the U.S. It has suddenly come over me that, whatever you are doing, functioning in America is a terrible struggle —in the long run, it wears you out. In spite of a lifetime of patriotism, I am almost ready to yield to the charms of the older and more gracious civilization of Europe. Not that I have any illusions about what is going on there now, but for a mellow old American of literary tastes and well enough off for a comfortable hotel, Paris offers strong attractions, and even Munich, while partly in ruins, is a more attractive city than such horrors as New York and Boston. So don't be surprised if you hear of me filling in for Henry Miller—while he is busy with his yogi role in Carmel—sitting in a good café and watching the Seine flow by while I sip an apéritif and leisurely slice the pages of the latest pornographic novel.

One of the things that I most enjoyed was giving moral support to the secular scholars who have been working on the scrolls. They are now under constant attack from the Catholic Church, and the conflict has become exciting. I am the only outsider who knows anything about the subject, and am coming to play, in connection with the scrolls, a role not unlike that of Hemingway with bullfighting. As Hemingway used to go around with Sidney Franklin and coach him, so I try to coach young John Allegro, who has stirred up a hornet's nest by drawing upsetting conclusions from the documents that had been given him to decipher.

Love to the family. We may move to Boston after Christmas. Reuel has just entered Harvard, and Helen needs a better school.   As ever, EW

To Leon Edel   October 19, 1956
                                                            Wellfleet

Dear Leon: I congratulate you on your discovery, which is full of interest. What a story for James at twenty-one!* And it does bear out your idea about the psychological importance of the father's accident.

                                          Sincerely, Edmund Wilson

To Leon Edel   November 9, 1956
                                                            Wellfleet

Dear Leon: I have been reading your two James paperbacks with the greatest interest.† The American one especially is fascinating. You have really done a service in collecting this stuff. What is particularly valuable to me—with my interest in the American writing of the latter part of the century—is the series of letters written in 1895 and giving a kind of cross section of current publications. It is wonderful to have James on Grant, John Jay Chapman, Whitman, and all the rest. And Robert W. Chambers!

---

* "A Tragedy of Error."
† *The American Essays of Henry James* and *The Future of the Novel.*

There is one key passage in the discussion of Roosevelt which I am going to use when I get around to doing a full-length study of T.R.—in which he quotes and takes exception to Roosevelt's statement that "an educated man must not go into politics as such . . . or he will be upset by some other American with no education at all." Actually, from the point of view of the political career, Roosevelt was perfectly right. His great strength as a young man was that he didn't adopt the attitude of what was then called the silk-stocking reformer, but plunged into the political bear pit and dealt with them on their own terms. James objects that "a better way than to barbarize the upset . . . would be to civilize the upsetter." The result of James's following his line was that he got quite out of touch with his American public; the result of Roosevelt's following his line was that he ended up almost as unscrupulous and blatant as the New York politicians he began by fighting.

The more one reads of James's journalism, the more impressed one is. I wish, though, that someone would compile a volume—or more likely two or three—containing *all* his essays. It annoys me that Sweeney, in his recent collection, shouldn't have given us the whole of James's writing on the plastic arts.

In speaking, in your introduction, of James's casual treatment of Thoreau, were you forgetting the passage about Thoreau and Emerson in the Concord chapter of *The American Scene?* By the way, in introducing that early story, you speak of Leland's "Hans Breitmann sketches." They were ballads, not sketches. You may be thinking of another series by Leland: *Meister Karl's Sketch-Book.*

The cover of the American book enchants me. I assume that you did not design it. I can't make out whether James has been bandaged or turned into a barber pole, or whether there is supposed to be some reference to the Stars and Stripes.

We are dull up here and let down by the election. We expect to go to Cambridge or Boston to live about the first of the year. If you come on, do let us know. You can always find out from the Levins where we are.

As ever, Edmund W

I was also very much interested in the little description of Harriet Beecher Stowe. Though I have read a good deal about her, I have always had difficulty in imagining what sort of appearance she made. James had undoubtedly hit her off in these few words—which confirm my impression of her: vague but very observant.

To Leon Edel   November 21, 1956
                                                         Wellfleet

Dear Leon: You seem to see everything, so I suppose you have seen Oscar Cargill's paper on *The Turn of the Screw* in the summer *Chicago Review.*

But do you know about a man named Harold C. Goddard of Swarthmore —now dead—who, before Edna Kenton had published her note, assumed on first reading the story that the governess was supposed to be insane, and was surprised to find that other people took it as a conventional ghost story? His daughter has sent me an essay on the subject by him. I think it ought to be printed but couldn't get *Encounter*. You and Cargill and he all, I think, have quite distinct ideas about how the governess was able to give, or appear to give, an accurate description of Quint. Cargill's seems to me the most plausible. She had found out from the little girl. I don't think you had thought of this—or had you?

Don't bother to answer this—we can talk about these matters when we meet.   As ever—and love from Elena to you both, Edmund

You know the Turgenev letters, don't you? in the University of Oregon's *Comparative Literature*.

To Leon Edel   November 30, 1956
                                                    Wellfleet

Dear Leon: Here is the Goddard paper. If it is published, it ought to be explained that it was a pioneering work—written even before Edna Kenton. It is long, but might perhaps be cut.

I am glad to hear that my book* gave you something to do on Thanksgiving Day, which has always seemed to me an utterly empty holiday. The point was that the Puritans did not celebrate Christmas, so that this was their Saturnalia: they had all sorts of rituals and jollifications—now we have nothing to do. I don't seem to have got over to you in my last chapter precisely what I intended. For one thing, I have given quite a wrong impression if I led anybody to think that there was anything "mercurial" about my father.   As ever, Edmund

William Faulkner
1948–1958

To Vladimir Nabokov   1948

. . . I am curious to know whether or not you ever read *Light in August*. Of course, he has no message . . . is merely interested in dramatizing life. In spite of his carelessness, I should think he would be rather congenial to you. I have been reading him spellbound lately. I think he is the most remarkable American novelist . . .

---

* *A Piece of My Mind.*

. . . Does Faulkner ever get to New York nowadays? I should like to meet him if he doesn't hate meeting people. I've just been reading his collected short stories. He spoke in very warm terms of you in a letter he wrote me several years ago about my review of *Intruder in the Dust* . . .

To William Faulkner*   September 25, 1956
                                                        Wellfleet

Dear Mr. Faulkner: I don't believe in these national propaganda schemes and have always refused to take part in them. I was surprised to hear that you were involved in this. I have just come back from Europe and found your books being sold in London, Paris, and Munich. How can you, or any other writer, make any better propaganda than by books that get themselves translated because they have something to say to people in other countries? There is a lot of anti-American feeling in Germany, England, and France, and propaganda can do nothing to improve relations. In fact, my impression is that our own—which is often puerile—has, if anything, contributed to making them worse. But the Kammerspiele in Munich, for example, the serious theater there, now does practically nothing but American plays: Wilder, Miller, Wolfe, Faulkner, and others. No committee with a "program" sent them these. The Germans made an effort to get them. These authors do not, as a rule, glorify "the American way of life," but they make people respect America.

The President is well intended, but his talk about "our American ideology" and "the great struggle being waged between the two opposing ways of life" is, in my opinion, nonsense. The American ideology is not to have any ideology, and the Soviets and the States, for good or ill, have all along had a good deal in common, more perhaps than either now has with Europe, and have in various ways been imitating one another. The Russians have been learning and will learn from us, not what we want to tell them, but what they find is valuable to them.

Make any use of this you please.   Sincerely,

To The New Statesman   1958

Sir: I have never made the statement—which seems to me silly—attributed to me by Mr. Walter Allen in his review in your issue of February 1, that William Faulkner has "genius without talent."   Edmund Wilson

---

* Carbon copy, the original of which has been lost.

James Branch Cabell
1953–1956

To ROGER W. STRAUS, JR.   1953

. . . Did you publish the Cabell *Smire*, etc., trilogy? If so, I'd like to have it—have never read it. Please send it to Wellfleet, if you have copies, next week. We saw him when we were in Richmond—much the worse for a case of flu and an Aureomycin cure. He had had a heart attack and wasn't allowed to climb stairs, so his bedroom had been moved to the bottom floor . . .

To MAXWELL GEISMAR   1953

. . . Apropos of Ellen Glasgow: I have been working up a belated interest in Cabell. He is more interesting than you may think, and you probably ought to have done him. I take the apparently paradoxical position that he is rather a bad writer from the point of view of style, but at moments a powerful moralist. There is a conception of damnation in his work as well as an ideal of uncompromising rectitude that derive from Scotch Presbyterianism and go deeper than the preciosity and the romantic Southern trappings. I saw Cabell last spring when I was in Virginia. He is under the impression that nobody now is taking any interest in Ellen Glasgow. I told him that you were writing about her. I'm sure that he would like to see your book. Why don't you get Houghton Mifflin to send him a copy "with the compliments of the author," or, if you send it to him yourself, you will get a queer but interested response . . .

To JAMES BRANCH CABELL   November 21, 1955
The New Yorker

Dear Cabell: Thank you for the letter and the books . . .

I have been making up for my long neglect of your books by becoming something of an addict to them, and have read you almost completely through. I have done an article on your work as a whole—hung on your latest book—which ought to be out in *The New Yorker* soon. I'll send you an advance copy. You may not like what I say—which, like everything of mine, is rather heavily social-historical—but I can assure you that it has been written with much admiration and that I have had a great deal of pleasure in reading you. I have, at least, I think, got away from the old clichés of Cabell criticism.

I have recommended to Roger Straus that he bring out the *Smirt*—

Smith—Smire series in one volume. It seems to me one of your very good things—it is a pity that so few people know it. I have also suggested his bringing out a volume containing *Figures of Earth, The Silver Stallion, Jurgen, The High Place,* and *Something about Eve.* Do you think this is a good idea? I am not sure that he will do either, though the idea of publishing an omnibus originally came from him.

The [John] Macy anthology is the kind of thing that I never read myself, and that I wonder whether anybody reads. I don't enjoy fragments of books, and fragments of novels seem to me impossible. For example, your episode of the "Troubling Window" is more or less unintelligible out of its context, and a good deal that is important is left out.

Writing about you made me think of Burton Rascoe, whom I hadn't seen in years. I went to see him yesterday, and my call was more cheerful than I had expected. I told you in Richmond that I had heard that Burton was off his head, but I thought he made more rather than less sense than he used to. I have always been rather puzzled as to why—with his abilities as a literary journalist—he has failed to make more of a career.   Sincerely, Edmund Wilson

To James Branch Cabell   January 30, 1956
                                                          Wellfleet
Dear Cabell: My article is so long that it can't be published till early spring, when the Easter advertizing will give them enough pages to carry it. In the meantime, I keep rewriting it—as my habit is—in proof. It is now in the teletype stage—rough and ragged columns. When I get better proofs, later on, I am going to send you a copy. I don't know about Straus's plans but shall ask him when I talk to him again. It may be that, for some reason, he is waiting for my article.
                                               Sincerely, Edmund Wilson

To James Branch Cabell   April 10, 1956
                                                          Wellfleet
Dear Cabell: I am sorry about the delay with the article. It is simply a question of waiting till the spate of spring advertizing can float it. My article on the Dead Sea scrolls last year didn't come out till the middle of May, when it was larded with bathing-suit and lipstick ads.
                                               Sincerely, Edmund Wilson

To James Branch Cabell   April 12, 1956
                                                          Wellfleet
Dear Cabell: "The Cabell Case" will definitely be out next week, and I have asked them to send you an advance copy. They sometimes keep my articles for six months or more, but I don't complain because, if it were

542

not for *The New Yorker*, they could never be written at all. No other magazine in the country now would allow me to write at such length on such neglected subjects of interest as yourself and the Dead Sea scrolls. I am enclosing a review of Tolkien. Do you know his work? I think it is awful.   Sincerely, Edmund Wilson

To James Branch Cabell   May 16, 1956
                                                  Wellfleet

My dear Cabell: Thank you for your letter, and especially for your telegram, which reached me, in the morning, as a delightful surprise.

I am still getting letters about my article. They fall, in general, into three classes: a) people who have always admired you and know your work well; b) people who explain *Mispec Moor*—I answer them by saying that the form the anagram took is significant; c) people in or from Georgia, who write me rather ill-bred letters to say that my version of the Southern point of view is all wrong, that almost nobody has that point of view in Georgia. Never having been in Georgia except to pass through, I am rather interested in this. I thought they were all sub-Virginian down there—instead of, as they claim, more up to date . . .
                                                  Sincerely, Edmund Wilson

To Roger W. Straus, Jr.   May 10, 1956
                                                  Wellfleet

Dear Roger: I wish you could persuade yourself to take a chance on the Cabell book in spite of its length. If you don't, he will be disappointed, and it would be, I believe, in any case, something of a service to American letters. You say that you don't aim to be entirely commercial. I will practically make you a present of my *New Yorker* article, which ought to provoke some reviews, and the whole thing—with a new title—will come as virtually a new book . . .   As, ever, Edmund W

EDITH WHARTON

To Van Wyck Brooks   February 7, 1957
The New Yorker

Dear Brooks: I have just been reading your book on the twenties with great interest and pleasure.* I was so much enchanted and moved to be brought back to that period again that I sat up most of the night reading it. I am sorry I sounded so disagreeable about the Yeats review. I shouldn't have supposed I could produce an impression equivalent to a pack of wolves. I have lately been taking that new drug from India, Rauwolfia serpentina (I may not have the spelling quite right); it reduces my blood pressure so that I never get angry any more.

The narrator of *Hecate County* was not derived from Paul Rosenfeld. I had other models in mind, and the place where he lives is a house in which I lived several years outside Stamford.

I was very much touched by your speech at the Institute.† So few people who write about me seem to know more than two or three of my books.

I am sorry never to see you. We are living in Cambridge now—16 Farrar Street—and if you should ever be coming on there, I wish you would let us know. Please remember me to Gladys.

Sincerely, Edmund Wilson

To John Dos Passos   May 10, 1957
Wellfleet

Dear Dos: Mario Praz, who came over here several years ago under the auspices of the State Department, told me that an official greeter in Wash-

---

* *Days of the Phoenix: The Nineteen-Twenties I Remember.*
† E. was awarded the gold medal of the National Institute of Arts and Letters. The citation was read by Van Wyck Brooks.

ington remarked to him that the Potomac had once been called the Tiber, evidently giving him a cue to say that Washington was now a second Rome. I want to use this incident, but am not sure that Praz got it right. I seem to remember from my Civil War reading that it is one of the small streams that run into the Potomac that is or was once called the Tiber. Can you throw any light on this? I can't find anything about it here . . .

. . . I found Harvard extremely stimulating. Should like to discuss it with you. In spite of Pusey and some recent developments, they are intellectually much more serious and more on their toes than Princeton.

Have you been reading Salinger's stories about the Irish–Jewish Glass family in *The New Yorker*? I think they are very remarkable, quite unlike anything else. Don't bother to look them up if you haven't. They are coming out in a book.　　　　　　　　　　　　Love to the family, EW

Edith Wharton
1947–1957

To Blake Nevius　　　　　　　　　　　　　　　　July 31, 1953
　　　　　　　　　　　　　　　　　　　　　　　　　　Talcottville
Dear Mr. Nevius: Thank you very much for your book . . . I have read it with much interest. You are at your best, I think, in the chapter called "The Trapped Sensibility," which is a real contribution to the criticism of Mrs. Wharton. I hadn't realized before how constantly this theme recurs. There are many other good things, too—your discussion of her attitude toward artists, for example . . . I think it is a pity, in treating Mrs. Wharton on such a large scale, to omit all references to her poetry, which is important biographically and sometimes very good.

I believe that it is misleading to present Mrs. W., as you and everyone else has done, as an out-and-out *grande dame*, a true representative of old New York society. When R. M. Lovett was writing his little book on her, he was told by one of her friends that she was probably an illegitimate child and that her brothers, on this account, are supposed to have treated her rather badly. I asked the late Theodore Spencer to check on this with Mrs. Winthrop Chanler, and she told him that the well-known scandal was that Edith was the daughter of an English tutor who was staying with the family at Newport, tutoring the boys; and that Edith herself believed this and had made an expedition to England with the purpose of looking him up, only to find that he was dead. Now, it is plain that she tends to identify herself with women (like Lily Bart) whose social position is precarious; and it is striking that the public, the official Edith

545

Wharton, who was a stickler for formality and demanded deference, does not, so far as I remember, really appear in her novels, is certainly, at any rate, not glorified. And if one knows the story of the tutor and the anomaly of the brilliant girl appearing in—and disconcerting—the entirely non-intellectual family (as the Joneses are said to have been), one can see them turning up in the fiction—at the end of *The Age of Innocence*, for example, where somebody (I think) runs away with a tutor, and in the governess of *The Buccaneers*, the tutor's feminine counterpart. The conflict between passion and convention must have occupied Edith's mind from before the Walter Berry affair.

Why do you omit from your bibliography the prefaces to the later editions of *Ethan Frome* and *The House of Mirth*? Since the latter appears only in the English World's Classics edition, not many people here know about it . . .

You speak of Cabell as neglected today. Have you looked into him lately? I have been reading him this summer and doing him belated justice . . .   Yours sincerely, Edmund Wilson

To Blake Nevius   August 10, 1953
                                                                        Talcottville

Dear Mr. Nevius: Good luck with your further work on Edith Wharton. I am glad you are going to look up her old friends . . . Don't hesitate to ask them about the illegitimacy business. Have you seen Mrs. W.'s place at Lenox? You should visit it if you haven't: it is very characteristic. It's now a girls' school.

  I was sorry that you didn't include the poetry in your bibliography, because I came across a very curious poem—personal and, I suppose, revelatory—in an old copy of *Scribner's* . . . that I found in this house last summer. I was wondering whether there was much other uncollected stuff.
                                                          Sincerely, Edmund Wilson

To Blake Nevius   November 19, 1954
                                                                          Wellfleet

. . . About Walter Berry: a neighbor of mine here who knew him had a very high opinion of him, and remonstrated with me for basing a description of him on Percy Lubbock's account. I met him once in his late years but did not have an opportunity to get any very clear impression. Frank Crowninshield had brought him to the Coffee House Club, and his own characterization of Berry has, however, remained very clear in my mind, and fits in with the accounts that disparage him: a man of fashion in Paris, who knew all about French literature and a lot of other things, but was somehow a little hollow. But then Crowninshield was no heavyweight

546

himself, and represented another variety of the same species. If you ever do anything with this subject again, you should consult Caresse Crosby's dreadful memoirs. Harry Crosby was a relative of Berry, who left him all his library . . .

To CHAUNCEY HACKETT   October 15, 1947
                                                      Wellfleet
Dear Chauncey: I was very much interested in your account of Walter Berry. I met him once, when he was pretty old, and didn't get much impression of him. But I used to hear about him from Frank Crowninshield, whose picture of him seemed to fit in with Lubbock's—that is, he talked about him as if he were a little too perfect and rather empty. But this may have been partly Crowninshield, who didn't particularly like people who made him feel inconsequential; and it is clear that Percy Lubbock holds it against Berry that he was a hard-boiled rationalist who, as he thinks, prevented Edith Wharton, at the end of her life, from becoming a Catholic. I am going to keep your letter, which may eventually be useful to something I am planning: a new excavation of the American literature of about 1870–1910.

I wish we saw you more often. There are many things I should like to discuss with you . . . When I see you, I want to tell you an amusing story about Horace and Elinor Wylie and Berry.   As ever, Bunny W

To VAN WYCK BROOKS   October 6, 1957
                                                      Wellfleet
. . . I was very glad to have the Everyman edition of your history. I am going to install it at Talcottville so that I'll have a set in both places. Like the other edition, it is an excellent piece of bookmaking.

I have been rereading in *The Confident Years*. About Edith Wharton: did you know that she was said to be, and apparently believed herself to be, an illegitimate child—by a young Englishman, who was tutoring her brothers? She was born a good many years later than they and is said to have been the only member of the family who had any intellectual interests. Mrs. Winthrop Chanler told Ted Spencer that Mrs. Wharton tried to look up her supposed father in England and found that he was dead. I have heard from another source that her brothers would not really accept her and did not treat her very well. This would explain her typical heroine, who is never a great lady in the sense of the role that, in private life, Edith Wharton herself liked to act, but an impoverished hanger-on like Lily Bart in *The House of Mirth*, a soiled and outlawed character like the girl in *The Reef*, or a governess like the woman in *The Buccaneers* —in every case, a half outsider (even Madame Olenska in *The Age of*

547

Innocence belongs in this category). There seems also to be an echo of the affair of the tutor at the end of *The Age of Innocence*. The recurrent theme of the intellect and natural instincts at war with conventional habit is probably involved with this, too. There is a short story—I forget the title —about parents who find themselves embarrassed at having produced a too clever daughter. There is another old legend that Edith's parents destroyed all the copies they were able to get hold of of her early book of poems, which she had had printed without their knowledge. You are right, of course, in saying that among the old-fashioned there was a certain tendency in America to be frigid and stiff with the populace, to keep them at arm's length; but Mrs. Wharton—whether or not it was true that she was an accidental daughter—would have had special reasons for standing on her dignity. Her unfortunate marriage to Wharton—with whom she seems to have had nothing in common—may have been due to a need to feel that she was solidly established in society. But you may know all this already.

Conrad Aiken tells me that he has now learned definitely from England that *The Sweeniad* was written by a man named Victor Purcell, whom neither of us has ever heard of but who he says is in the English *Who's Who*. I have been brooding on Eliot since our conversations. He has lately been involved in a curious controversy in the London *Times Literary Supplement*, which it might interest you to see (I think it was all during August). The writer of an anonymous leader called *Classic Inhumanism* charged him with anti-Semitism and Fascist sympathies, and Eliot replied, denying these as well as a number of statements about his relations with Pound and [T. E.] Hulme. The author of the article demonstrated that Eliot was in error about the facts of his own life and cited his favorable references to Fascism. He did not return to the anti-Semitic charge but would have had no trouble in producing evidence. Aiken tells me that Eliot has now made an ineffective rebuttal (by the way, it is only lately that it has dawned on me that Myra Buttle = My Rebuttal). What is curious here is that Eliot be so vague about himself. My explanation is this. As I was saying to you, I think, there is a scoundrel and actor in Eliot. It was the young scoundrel who wrote the good poetry and it is now the old scoundrel who is putting on the public performance. In private, he is humorous and disarming about his reputation, but the performance still goes on; and just as his poems are all dramatic monologues, so all of his public utterances, except when he is writing about literature—and sometimes even then—are in the main merely speeches for one or other of his dramatic "personae." When he is writing for clerical papers or addressing a Conservative dinner, he allows himself reactionary audacities which he rarely hazards with his larger audience. (He did let some of these loose in the lectures collected in *After Strange Gods*—delivered at the University of Virginia, where I suppose he thought it was safe to let his snobberies and antiquated loyalties rip—but when hostile repercussions reached his sensitive ear, he did his best to suppress the volume.) But these dramatically slanted opinions are so dim and make so little sense that I don't see how they can do much damage. I was talking about this just now with Arthur Schlesinger, usually an up-in-arms liberal, and—rather to my surprise—he anticipated my opinion by saying that all this side of Eliot didn't matter. In his poetry and in his personal relations, he is sensitive, gentle, and rather touching. In spite of his assertion to the contrary when I talked to him years ago, he is ready to converse with unbelievers, and he is not disagreeable to Jews; and he makes fun of all the old gentilities that he otherwise pretends to represent. The shrewd Yankee operator who always remains discreet but gets away with murder is balanced by the Yankee idealist who—in literature, the only thing about which he feels intensely—is able to stand by his convictions and, on occasion, without sticking his neck out (as Lewis and Pound habitually did), to show a firm courage. In his tiresome performances as the humble great man, he is more and more betraying his vanity: he talks about his own work in far too many of this last collection of essays. He is absurd in his pretensions to pontificate—did you know that he has recently announced that it is proper not entirely to despise Longfellow? But the literary and academic worlds are apparently full of people who want nothing better than to follow his directives. He enjoys his conspicuous position, and I imagine that this has been one of the few compensations in a life of which the sufferings and conflicts have been finely and frankly expressed in his poetry.

But I know that you regard him as a more sinister figure. This long letter is due to my not having had a chance to talk with you, when you were here, as much as I should have liked. I hope that you will come to see us in Talcottville. Love from us both to Gladys.

Sincerely, Edmund Wilson

To Van Wyck Brooks   December 18, 1957
Wellfleet
. . . I am somewhat puzzled, though (as *The New Yorker* likes to say), by your habit of carrying through your *pensées* along from one book to another. This is the third time that I have read that note about the Indian path and the Roman road. It is in both *Oliver Allston* and *Chilmark*. I am interested in your theory about what you call the avant-garde—though I can't imagine what they are ahead of. I hadn't thought of that explanation—had assumed that the whole thing was merely the latest form that academic mediocrity had taken . . .   As ever, Edmund W

Edmund Wilson Interviews John Wain

In 1957 I visited Talcottville with the purpose of interviewing
Edmund for The Observer . . .*Very characteristically, he typed out*
a number of questions he wanted to ask me.

(John Wain to Elena Wilson, 1974)

1. Do you ever have a feeling that English literature is rapidly shriveling up and that there will soon be nothing turned out that anybody is likely to remember except an occasional poem by John Betjeman and an occasional story by Angus Wilson?

2. Whom would you prefer as a successor to John Masefield as poet laureate? Do you think that Betjeman would have a chance? It would be interesting to see whether he would have the effect of making the Royal Family look suburban.

3. How do you explain the overpowering prestige of "Mr. Eliot," which seems to have become so great that no one ever criticizes a word he writes! Of course he has written some very fine things—in his cautious New England way—has stood for the highest standards, but a good deal of his writing of recent years has been sounding more and more like self-parody: his address at a Conservative banquet, his poem about Christmas trees. He is sometimes still good on literature, which he understands and about which he feels intensely; but his utterances on political, social, and theological questions seem to me utter twaddle. Some of his plays are good and have deserved the success they have had; but *The Confidential Clerk* was dreadful. Yet when I went to see it in London nothing had prepared me for its feebleness and dullness. I was therefore afterwards surprised when the editor of one of the leading English literary reviews told me that he considered it one of the six worst plays that he had ever seen in his life. Why did no one say this kind of thing in print? Since Eliot turned up for the Nobel Prize with the Order of Merit around his neck, people have been afraid to say boo to him. Maybe the old boy needs a jolt. One does not like to see him fade out so dismally.

4. On the other hand, why are so many people down on Cyril Connolly? It is true that he produces very little, and one wishes that he would not spend his energies on those articles in *The Sunday Times;* but the little he has published I find I reread as I rarely do contemporary writers. What is striking, however, is that the feeling against him seems always to take the form of moral indignation. During the war, it seemed to be felt that he was not taking the war effort seriously, though in bringing out *Horizon* he was undoubtedly making to English culture a contribution of special importance. But what is the pretext now for this indignation still manifesting itself? *The New Statesman* went out of its way to give

a slating to "Shade Those Laurels," a mere episode—published in a magazine—from an uncompleted novel. Indignation again. No one seemed to be aware of what I should have thought was obvious in every line: that it was a high-class burlesque like *Zuleika Dobson*. My own theory is that it is the Irishman in Connolly that makes the English indignant. They are troubled by the suspicion, precisely, that he may be making fun of them, that there is something in him which does not give a damn about their principles. They behaved in very much the same way about Sterne and about Wilde—and even at times about Swift and Shaw. What is your explanation of this phenomenon?

5. Would you agree that in England at the present time there is a tendency, in the writing about literature, to neglect the greater figures in favor of the minor ones? One rarely finds a study of Joyce, about whom there is surely a great deal to be said. The review of the volume of his letters in *The Times Literary Supplement* was one of the worst pieces of snidery I have ever read, and even the relatively far-ranging Pritchett struck me as falling below his level when he tried lately to discuss *Ulysses*. Among recent English authors themselves, A. N. Whitehead and W. H. Auden seem to me the most considerable, and nobody could be more English; but one rarely hears about them in England. Both came to live in the United States, and there seems to be a certain policy of dropping a man when this happens. Yet this cannot be the whole explanation, for the great English writers of the past and the great writers of other countries are also rather generally ignored. The only two serious studies that I remember to have seen lately of top-flight writers are Angus Wilson's little book on Zola and Isaiah Berlin's essay on Tolstoy. It has been one of the encouraging things about the juvenile Colin Wilson that he has rediscovered a lot of great writers. One would think from the way he treats them that he never heard anybody speak of them. Would this have been true, and if so, why?

6. English culture is, it seems to me, at the present time at its best when it is closest in touch with what is going on in the larger world: in *The New Statesman* and *Encounter*, for example—we have in the States at present nothing of the kind that is half so good. So I am glad you are visiting us. I should like to have your opinions on (a) American women, (b) American cooking, (c) American literature, (d) the comparative merits of the British Foreign Office and the American State Department.

"APOLOGIES TO THE IROQUOIS"
1957–1965

To WILLIAM SHAWN December 3, 1957
The New Yorker Wellfleet

. . . Please send me a letter explaining that I am writing about the Iroquois Indians for *The New Yorker*, and whatever assistance, etc. Nobody asked me for my credentials except Standing Arrow, who has none himself, having been repudiated by his clan; but I think it might be as well for me to have some—especially since I shall next time be traveling with [William N.] Fenton and want to be able to make it clear that I am not a New York State official . . .

To JOHN DOS PASSOS November 19, 1958

. . . There is lots that I'd like to talk to you about but it can't be handled in a letter. I'm still entangled in the Civil War, which, as Liebling at *The New Yorker* says, is like the Tar Baby in *Uncle Remus*. I've also taken on the Iroquois Indians, who are having themselves a nationalist movement against the United States. Mad Bear, the Tuscarora leader, is the first person in history who has succeeded in stopping Robert Moses, as you must have been seeing in the papers. Investigating these Indian situations has taken me into the big power projects, the St. Lawrence Seaway, the proposed Kinzua Dam, and other developments in New York State, and it is appalling to see how much this country is getting to be run by engineers, bureaucrats, and the Armed Forces . . .

To VAN WYCK BROOKS December 18, 1957
  Wellfleet
. . . By the way, I have been rereading your chapter on Parkman and find —page 178 of the old edition—that you speak of the Mohawks and the

Iroquois as if they were different tribes. *Iroquois* is the collective name for the Confederacy of the Six Nations, of which the Mohawks were one. I am particularly up on this because I have discovered, to my great surprise, that I am surrounded at Talcottville by an Iroquois national movement—not unlike Scottish nationalism and Zionism—with a revival of the old religion and claims for territory of their own. They have some legitimate grievances because they are losing their property in their reservations on account of the St. Lawrence Seaway. I went over there in October and found some very strange things going on and am going again at the end of January, when the Iroquois celebrate their New Year, and will eventually write something about it . . .

I had wanted to talk to you about Fenton before you saw him. He is the country's greatest authority on the Iroquois Indians—brilliant and quite free from anthropological jargon. He grew up among the Indians in the southwestern [part of] New York and knows them intimately in a personal way. (To Roger W. Straus, Jr., 1958)

To WILLIAM N. FENTON   October 29, 1957
                                                              Wellfleet
Dear Dr. Fenton: Thank you very much for your helpful information and the Iroquois literature. I was able to catch a plane immediately, so went on to Boston.

It would be immensely useful to me to go, as you suggested, on a tour of the reservations at the Iroquois New Year. If you can go, I hope you will take me along. I'll be better informed by that time.

By the way, I did not catch the name of the epic you said you had translated. I cannot find it in your bibliography.
                                        Sincerely, Edmund Wilson

To ELENA WILSON   January 24, 1958
                                                           Salamanca, N.Y.
. . . toward evening it began to snow, we stopped off and spent the night at Geneva. Fenton talked a blue streak all the way . . . and gave me quantities of information, all very much to the point . . .

We stopped off in the late morning at the Tonawanda Seneca reservation, where Fenton had spent two years, and called on a most extraordinary old Seneca. He had been to the old Indian college Carlisle, now discontinued, was a power in politics, played the piccolo and flute (had once played in Sousa's band), and was something of an Indian scholar. Though you never would have thought English was his native language, he spoke it with an unexpected felicity and exactitude, and seemed more like a cultivated old Russian or Oriental than like anything in upstate New York, though he had some of the old-fashioned New York turns of phrase and ways of speaking. Fenton himself comes from this part of the state and knows everybody and all about the local affairs, as well as knowing more about the Iroquois than anybody else alive. The Indians receive him as a local boy whose family have been here for generations and an authority on their own history and religions . . .

We then moved on to the Cattaraugus and Allegany reservations. These two are inhabited by the children of the 1848 revolution . . . These Senecas had revolted against the sachems and chiefs who had been selling their lands to the whites, had deposed them and set up a council, with an elected president at its head. They are organized—incorporated, I think— as the Seneca Nation . . . missed the beginning of the ceremonies, which included one of the things I most wanted to take in. This is a kind of opera or cantata, which is entirely done in the dark and lasts all night till dawn. Fenton and the old man at Tonawanda were telling me about it, singing parts of it, and making it sound wonderful—a legend of the good hunter, who was scalped by the Cherokees but then rescued by the animals, to whom he had been considerate; they brought him back his scalp and raised him from the dead . . . we might spend the last night near Tonawanda, to look in on the ceremonies there . . . Tomorrow begins a round of ceremonies. The woman who gave us the dinner told me I should have to dance in spite of my gouty foot, and that once you started dancing, it was impossible to stop. Due to the protests of the Buffalo humane society and the dying out of the special breed which used to be raised for the purpose, they no longer, I was rather relieved to find, sacrifice the white dog . . .

This country is monotonous and grim in the wintertime—gray sky and gray snow, bristling with small black woodland . . .

To Roger W. Straus, Jr.   February 5, 1958
                                                                        Wellfleet
. . . My trip to the Indians was immensely successful—I saw most of the New Year's festival and got a pretty good understanding of the most important of the Iroquois' grievances: that one of their reservations will be completely destroyed if a flood-control dam on the Allegheny River is put through as proposed by the government. The Indians in that part of the world are fortunately rich enough to have hired a smart Washington lawyer, and there is a chance that they may succeed in saving their reservation. I'll be doing an article or articles on the overall situation of the Iroquois in the United States, and there may possibly be a small book in it . . .

To Elena Wilson   June 9, 1958
                                                         Talcottville
. . . Philip Cook, the Mormon Mohawk, has asked us to supper at St.
Regis on Thursday. This will probably be a two-day trip. The Strawberry
Festival takes place, apparently, the 22nd and the Little Water Ceremony
(of the resurrected hunter) is sung the night before. Bill Fenton has told
me what to do to get admitted, and I hope I may succeed. We shall
probably, however, start on our trip next Sunday and give it a whole
week: Syracuse, Niagara Falls, then the southwestern corner of the state,
where I went with Fenton last winter . . .

To Elena Wilson   June 14, 1958
                                                         Talcottville
. . . We got back last night . . . We had a very successful two-day trip.
Cook is full of affection and good will and has a kind of natural authority.
All through the evening, people kept dropping in or coming to see him
about something—an aluminum worker to get him to find him a new
house, a young man who had just graduated from Hamilton and wanted
a job. The next day we went to a place near Saranac Lake to see another
Indian expert, who has an Indian museum there but earns his living as a
schoolteacher. He is a curious character: his father was Irish, and he looks
and behaves like an Irishman—has red hair and blue eyes and a terrific
gift of gab. But, having grown up in the Mohawk reservation with his
Mohawk mother, he has canalized all the eloquence, wit, and fighting
spirit which used to be devoted to Irish patriotism into the cause of the
Six Nations. The boys in the St. Regis reservation have gone in for
having their heads shaved, in the traditional way, leaving only a strip of
hair down the middle for a scalp lock . . .

To Elena Wilson   June 19, 1958
                                                          Salamanca
The situation at the Tuscarora reservation has been very tense lately.
I went to the house of a family in which the father had been the head of
an Indian Defense organization and one of the sons had taken part in the
recent riot. The father was rather suspicious at first—a sheriff's car was
patrolling the reservation—but then the son came and recognized me from
having seen me at the Onondaga reservation when I was put out of the
Longhouse by that old man. Everybody in the Indian world seems to
know about this incident—it is just like the Russian grapevine. They
ended by asking us to supper, having talked for about three hours. I
then looked up the Tuscaroras' lawyer [Stanley Grossman], who came
to see me at the hotel. He turned out to be a very bright young Jew, full

of enthusiasm for the Indian cause, who believes that he, too, can get his case before the Supreme Court and, in any event, hold up the power project at least a year . . .

To Elena Wilson   June 21, 1958
                                                        Salamanca

. . . The evening after I wrote you last, we went to call on the Crouses. Reuel thinks that he is like a German burgomaster. He is also like all the husbands of clever and sought-after wives—quiet and polite. Myrtie is the Sibyl Colefax of the Allegany reservation, who entertains visiting palefaces just as Lady Colefax entertains visiting Americans . . . The next day we went to see Cornelius Seneca, the president of the Seneca Nation—very satisfactory interview . . . He said that he sometimes wondered whether he wouldn't have been happier in the Indians' primitive state. Since he wouldn't have "known any better," he wouldn't have missed the things they didn't have; and life would have been so much quieter. They only killed such animals as they needed to eat, and otherwise lived on good terms with them. It is curious that the loss of good relations with the animals seemed to be one of the things he most regretted.

   . . . Then I went to call on the man who is the custodian of the sacred medicine of the Little Water Ceremony, to which I was hoping to get admitted. The Indians I had talked to about it were dubious about my succeeding. No Indian can be admitted unless he has taken the medicine and become, by having done so, a member of the fraternity, and very few people are willing to take the medicine—compounded of all those parts of animals—even in the extreme emergencies in which it supposed to be efficacious. The keeper of the Little Water told me that the ceremony had already taken place, but did not discourage me from applying in September. He said that he would have to consult his fraternity mates . . .

To Elena Wilson   June 23, 1958
                                                        Talcottville

. . . The Strawberry Festival was animated but brief. The confessions and the reciting of the Handsome Lake code had taken place before, as, to my disappointment, had the Little Water Ceremony. There is only one dance—the Feather Dance, which is done in costume, with such terrific stampings by the men that you think it will bring down the Longhouse. Myrtie Crouse asked us afterwards to lunch . . . Excellent lunch of ham, potato salad, some kind of beans, cole slaw, and a tremendous strawberry shortcake. At the festival, the strawberries are served in pails floating in strawberry syrup and offered to everyone in turn in a dipper. Then people—especially the children—go and take as much as they like in glasses or cups . . .

To Arthur Schlesinger, Jr.   June 24, 1958
                                                        Talcottville

Dear Arthur: . . . I am sorry to be missing you at Wellfleet. I should like
to hold an old-fashioned school debate on "Resolved that the United
States is an international menace and nuisance"—you, I assume, taking
the negative. I have just come back from a tour of the Iroquois reservations, which has confirmed my worst suspicions as to what Washington
and New York State are doing to the Indians. What has surprised me,
however, is that there are quite a few white people who hope that they
will win their cases. I think that many people nowadays are nervous about
their rights.   As ever, Edmund

To Daniel Aaron   [undated, 1958]
                                                        Talcottville

Dear Dan: I have had the following idea. There is going to be a pageant
at the Six Nations reservation in Canada—near Brantford, just west of
Niagara Falls—which I want to go to: August 15–16. Would you like
to come here, say, the 14th, and drive me?—all expenses paid by *The
New Yorker*. I have business in the Tuscarora and Tonawanda reservations, which would be right on our way, and this would enable you to
see quite a little of the Iroquois . . .   As ever, Edmund

To Daniel Aaron   [undated, 1958]

Dear Dan: Here is a souvenir of our trip.* Mad Bear and Stanley Grossman were summoned to St. Regis by the Mohawks in connection with
the income-tax crisis—which, I guess, developed after you left (the
Mohawks refuse to pay the state tax)—and had dinner with me on their
way back. I got Mad Bear to tell me the prophecy again and took it
down word for word. Hope you are enjoying yourself.   Edmund W.

To Elizabeth Huling   November 4, 1958
                                                        Wellfleet

. . . I spent most of my summer on the Iroquois Indians, who for various
reasons are having their reservations taken away from them or ruined.
They have worked up a nationalist movement, are bringing suits against
the U.S. and the State of New York, and are threatening to appeal to
the U.N. They have taken some beatings in the courts but have also had
some rather remarkable successes and have the glory of having been the
first people in history to stop the operations of Robert Moses. All too long

---

* "Deganawida's prophecy as told me by Mad Bear (Wallace Anderson), August
31, 1958."

to tell about in a letter, but it will be coming out soon in *The New Yorker* . . .

To William N. Fenton   February 28, 1959
                                                          Wellfleet

Dear Bill: . . . We would be delighted to have you March 23rd. By that time I hope to have the whole Indian thing done and typed. I am only just getting to the Seneca, which I keep till last for the *pièce de résistance*. You, of course, know about the remarkable victory over Moses of Mad Bear and Stanley Grossman. Mad Bear, I gather, is becoming, as I thought he would, something of a big Iroquois leader. The last news I heard from Niagara was that he was first going to have a conference with Mrs. Roosevelt and then advance on Washington with four hundred Indians.

                                                          Best regards, Edmund

To Mary Meigs and Barbara Deming   April 2, 1959
                                                          Wellfleet

. . . My friend Bill Fenton, the Indian authority from Albany, spent two highly animated days with us. He brought unpublished records of Indian music that I wish you could have heard. The Six Nations Reserve in Ontario has declared its independence of Canada and upset their puppet government. The Mounties were sent in to put it back. I don't know what will happen . . .

To Mary Meigs   April 11, 1959
                                                          Wellfleet

. . . I am just starting off on another Indian trip—to attend the hearing, in Canada, on the Iroquois chiefs who have proclaimed their independence and been arrested . . .

To Elena Wilson   May 1959
Talcottville

. . . It is a marvelous day and I feel full of energy. Mad Bear called me up before seven. Stanley Grossman is taking the defense of the Indian who is supposed to have shot that trooper. He is a first cousin of my friend Papineau at Onondaga. They claim that he did not do the shooting but was framed by the police. He himself was shot and is in the hospital at Watertown. Grossman and Mad Bear are presumably coming to see me the last of the week. Fenton tells me that the state authorities have "got their backs up" against the Indians . . .

To Robert Lowell   June 8, 1959
                                                          Wellfleet

Dear Robert: Thanks for the poem. When you come up here again, you must engrave it below the other one. I've just come back from two weeks at Talcottville, interspersed with trips to the Indians. I finally succeeded in hearing (it is all in the dark) the Little Water Ceremony—wasn't I telling you about it?—which is terrific and makes you realize how much life there is left in the Indians. I hope you are back home or in Europe. Love to Elizabeth. Edmund

To Mary Meigs   July 3, 1959
                                                                 Talcottville

. . . I am here all alone, but productive and enjoying myself. Besides doing the Indians, I have completely revised the text of *Hecate County*, which I do think is my best book. I like sitting here in this house, which seems to be practically part of the prehistoric limestone formation, and receiving Indians, lawyers for Indians, state officials, and local relatives. It makes me feel like Sir William Johnson—if you know who he was . . .

I finally succeeded in hearing the Little Water Ceremony—the thing that I missed before. Fenton got me in, and we were the only people there. It is really terrific, quite unlike anything else I have ever heard, except the other song cycle which they also sing in the dark, and not even much like that. I won't describe it here because I am writing about it at length in my book. The Iroquois nationalist movement is now going ahead so fast that what I am writing about it can hardly keep up with it . . .

I have been reading mostly local history—Mormonism, Indians, etc.— all very queer and violent . . .

To Mary Meigs   August 4, 1959
                                                                 Talcottville

. . . Last week two Canadians came to visit us in connection with Indian matters. Canada is itself nowadays developing a passionate nationalism. They feel that they have got away from England, but that they now have to contend with the United States. It was amusing to find that my guests and I were presently competing as to which group of Iroquois—ours or the Canadian ones—was the more authentic and important. Since the Iroquois sided mostly with the British at the time of the Revolution, the Canadians regard them as their loyal vassals, who defended them against the nasty Yanks. Mad Bear, the Iroquois leader, has just sent me a card from a big hotel in Cuba, where he says he is the honored guest of Castro. I don't know what this means . . .

To William Shawn   September 1959
The New Yorker   Wellfleet

Here is the whole thing. I held over Part III, hoping to get the latest news about the Kinzua Dam. It still hasn't come, so I'll have to attend to

559

this in proof . . . The point I have omitted on pp. 284–5 is really, I think, important, but the article will read more smoothly without it.

Anyone who edits the MS or reads the proofs ought to know that the Allegany reservation, the Allegheny River, and the Alleghany Mountains are all spelled in different ways. My writing of the Indian names does not keep to a consistent usage, but I'll straighten that out in the proofs. EW

> She is a very pretty Seneca woman . . . who comes from the Allegany reservation and went to the Indian school—married an Italian psychiatrist who went to Princeton and now practices there.
>
> (Notebooks of the sixties)

To BETTE CROUSE MELE   August 10, 1960
                                                               Talcottville

Dear Mrs. Mele: Thank you very much for your letter. It happened to arrive when Bill Fenton was here visiting me, and he told me that he remembered your mother well, that she was a beauty, and that he was once allowed to be present when she was ill and they were performing ceremonies to cure her—he and I and a lot of other people are doing what we can to avert the Kinzua Dam. I suppose you must be related to Clifford Crouse of Quaker Bridge (I described his family in my book) and Elon Crouse of Tuscarora.

I should like very much to meet you, but I almost never get to New York—I live in Massachusetts in the winter. Do you ever get to this part of the world? . . . The little village I live in is Talcottville, Lewis County. It is about an hour's drive north of Utica. I should be very glad to see you. Or if you should come to Boston, I'll be at 12 Hilliard Street, Cambridge, this winter.

I was interested in what you say about Seneca family life. I hadn't been aware of this, but I suppose a somewhat uncomfortable situation is created by each new generation's being drawn more and more strongly toward the non-Indian world about them.

I am very much pleased that you wrote me.

                                                   Sincerely, Edmund Wilson

To BETTE CROUSE MELE   December 16, 1961
                                                               Cambridge

Dear Mrs. Mele: I understand that Kennedy spent part of a day looking up the Kinzua Dam situation and decided that it was something that had been settled during the Eisenhower Administration and that there was nothing he could do about it. William Fenton, when I last saw him, told me that the reservation was now doomed. It is outrageous—like a lot of other things that our government has been doing.

Christmas greetings, Edmund Wilson

To BETTE CROUSE MELE   January 2, 1963
                                                        Cambridge

. . . I was glad to have news of Quaker Bridge and the Senecas. I get their bulletin about the Kinzua situation, and it always makes me angry to think what has happened to them . . .

To BETTE CROUSE MELE   April 3, 1964
                                                        Rome, Italy

. . . About taxes: The Mohawks in St. Regis not long ago forced a show-down with the tax authorities. They put up a battle but lost. They should certainly not have to pay taxes, when they refuse to be U.S. citizens. Of course, I should be very much honored to belong to the Hawk clan, but I don't think it is a good idea to bring pressure to bear for this purpose . . .

To BETTE CROUSE MELE   June 13, 1965

Dear Mrs. Mele: I am glad to hear that the baby has arrived, and I am honored that you have wanted to name him after me. But I do think it is something of a mistake to give a child so many names. I have only one myself and have always been glad not to be loaded with initials. Every-body, I imagine, will call your boy Tony and forget about the rest. After all, he may never read my books and may not like them if he does . . . My regards to your husband . . . Best wishes to you and Tony. Edmund W

In 1963 I met Edmund Wilson in Talcottville. I had written him fol-lowing the New Yorker *articles which became the book that is the best contemporary work on the Iroquois. Mr. Wilson took the Iroquois out of the libraries of archaeological and anthropological texts into the modern world. He presented us in a most sensitive fashion, as people capable of handling our own destiny in spite of the overwhelming odds against us, due to the multiple water projects in New York State at a time when the general U.S. population was not aware of Native Americans east of the Mississippi . . .*
. . . I had the child named Antonio Edmund Wilson Mele so that Mr. Wilson's name would be on the Seneca rolls . . .
The Memorial ceremony for Edmund Wilson was in Wellfleet. But part of the memorial tribute to Mr. Wilson belongs to us, for the legacy of Apologies to the Iroquois, *which made an impact on both the Indian and the non-Indian world at a critical time in Iroquois history . . .* —Bette Crouse Mele, "Edmund Wilson, 1895–1972," in The Indian Historian (Fall 1972)

Compton Mackenzie

To Sir Compton Mackenzie   August 18, 1958
Edinburgh, Scotland

Dear Sir Compton: I have lately been interested in the nationalist movement of the Iroquois Indians in New York State. They occupy reservations their title to which and jurisdiction in which were supposed to be
guaranteed to them by treaties with the federal government made after
the Revolution, when they were recognized as a sovereign nation. They
have recently been deprived of certain rights, and are fighting not to be
put out of several of their reservations, which the New York or U.S.
authorities are threatening to take for various public projects. I am going
to write something about this situation, which, with your interest in small
nationalities, you will recognize as typical of a kind of thing that has
been going on all over the world.

But in the meantime, in connection with this, I want to ask you about
what seems to be the somewhat similar situation in the Scottish Outer
Isles that you dramatize in *Rockets Galore*. Curiously enough, I was reading this book at the time of a visit to a reservation in which a tribe of the
Iroquois (the Tuscaroras) were successfully resisting the efforts of the
engineers backed by the police to take a part of their land for the Niagara
Power Project. The quiet obstruction and sabotage were so like the behavior
of your islanders that I actually sometimes confused the incidents that I
was hearing about and reading about. What I should like to know is
whether anything of the kind did occur—in South Mist, for example,
which you mention in your foreword. We have had, so far as I know, no
news of the local reaction to proposed rocket sites in Britain, as you, I
imagine, have had no news of the recalcitrant Iroquois, and I should be
grateful if you would send me any clippings or information on the subject.

By the way, since I saw you in Edinburgh, I have read with great
interest and pleasure your *Winds* series and Scottish series as well as
some of your other books. It seems to me that the failure of British
criticism to give serious attention to your work as a whole is one of the
most striking signs of its increasing London provincialism and general
shrinking of scope. I realize that I'll have to write something myself! but
I haven't quite got through you yet.   Sincerely, Edmund Wilson

To Arthur Mizener   1949

. . . When he [F. Scott Fitzgerald] was in Capri, he went to see Compton
Mackenzie. I asked about their conversation. "I asked him," he said, "why

he had petered out and never written anything that was any good since *Sinister Street* and those early novels." "What did he say to that?" "He said it wasn't true." Scott then went on to tell me his theory that the trouble with Mackenzie was that he had missed the great experience of the war. I have thought about this recently since I have been reading up Mackenzie's books from the point where we all dropped him. It is not true at all that he missed the war. He was physically in such bad shape that nobody would accept him for service till Sir Ian Hamilton, who liked his novels, heard that he wanted to get in the service and gave him a job in the Gallipoli campaign, which enabled him, without actually fighting, to see a certain amount of fighting. When Mackenzie's health broke down, Hamilton sent him to Athens, where he had a very lively and rather dangerous career as head of the British Secret Service. He has written four volumes of memoirs and several novels about it, though I don't believe any of them had yet come out at the time that Scott himself felt that he had missed the war . . .

I suppose you have looked into the early Mackenzie, whose influence on Scott can't be overestimated. (The curious thing is that Zelda wrote like Mackenzie, too. I don't know whether she got it at first hand or through Scott or what.) But what strikes me, in reading Mackenzie today, is that, much better educated though he was than Scott, Scott's best is far better than Mackenzie's. Mackenzie is a very odd literary case. I may write something about him someday. He gets less attention now than he deserves. He has been—except perhaps in *Carnival* and *Guy and Pauline* —completely lacking in intensity and almost completely extroverted. I have a theory—his mother, I believe, was an American woman from the South and his father a Scottish actor—that he represents a peculiar breed —romantic but extroverted, intelligent but superficial, quixotic but rather mild—that is due to this mingling of strains and that doesn't find any appropriate role in the English public-school system in which he was brought up. His reminiscences of the war—so full of the enjoyment of adventure and moving quickly through foreign lands and so critically detached from the British cause, which he is supposed to be there to serve—might almost have been written by an American. In his later years, he went to live in Scotland and interested himself in Scotch affairs—is now doing a series of Scotch novels. He is, as I say, an anomalous case. His career has been disappointing, but I would rather read him than Somerset Maugham, for he seems to me a real and rather remarkably gifted writer. I met him in London four years ago at a rather dreary literary gathering and, unexpectedly, enjoyed him more than anybody else that evening. I was astonished, among all the limp and the dim, to find him so cheerful and brisk, small and wiry, and full of energy and delighted with himself.

I hadn't meant to go on at this length—it seems to be turning into notes for my Mackenzie essay . . . *

---

* E. had planned to include an essay on Compton Mackenzie in *The Devils and Canon Barham*, which was published after his death. He had gotten "through reading" the many volumes, but the essay was never written.

See p. 14.

1958–1959

March 18, 1958
                                                                      Wellfleet

Dear Arthur and Marion: I don't know whether you have seen this
passage in one of Laski's letters to Holmes:*

"I dined the other night at the house of Arthur Schlesinger *fils*. It was
a delightful assemblage of historians, literary as well as political. Van Wyck
Brooks explained that he had been trying to provide America with a usable
past, and Edmund Wilson said that he was grateful for this usable American past, and that he had often had occasion to use it. Young Schlesinger,
whose mind works with lightning speed, from time to time tossed in a
quip that had the older men laughing like schoolboys. He had just come
back from Washington, where he had had an interview with Eisenhower.
He had been told that the President was being kept in ignorance of everything going on in the world and that he must not say anything to upset
him. As a result, they talked about nothing but the differences between
the administrative systems of Columbia and Harvard and compared the
cuisines of their faculty clubs. It appears that Ike's recent *défaillance* has
been due to his learning, through some fluke, of such matters as the bombing in Tunisia and Nasser's alliance with Syria. Charles Beard sat blinking
like a chilly old eagle when Arthur praised Franklin Roosevelt. James
Ford Rhodes confessed his deficiency in Greek when John Finley talked
about Thucydides. I told him to read the Latin translation by Henry
Dodwell, whose edition of Thucydides (Oxonii, e Theatro Sheldoniano,

---

* E. is here writing a parody of Harold Laski's letters to Justice Holmes. "He
[Harold Laski] would freely invent stories that had often no basis whatever in fact
about people he did not know but whom he claimed to have met and talked with,
exploits he had not performed, scenes that had never occurred and books that he
had never read."
　　　—"The Holmes-Laski Correspondence," in *The Bit Between My Teeth*

1695, ligatured Greek with the Latin at the bottom of the page) I have just picked up at Goodspeed's for $7.50, an amazing find and bargain. It takes an accomplished Irishman to manage the eloquence of the Greek. Rhodes, I thought, leaned over backwards in discussing the *Trent* affair. The British case was not so strong as he thinks. When I got home, I reread Grotius, *De jure belli* and *Mare liberum*. I doubt whether any of those distinguished men is well grounded in international law. I topped off with *The Book of the Limerick*, the best half-dozen pieces from which I shall recite when we meet again."

So glad it wasn't like this. We enjoyed ourselves very much.   Edmund

To Arthur Schlesinger, Jr.   April 13, 1958
                                                                    Wellfleet
Dear Arthur: Just got your note from Barbados. I am returning your books with thanks.

The McClellan is interesting, with its alternations of querulousness and smugness, and such remarks as that Halleck is "a *bien mauvais sujet*, not a gentleman." It gives me a clearer idea of McClellan's personality than I had ever had in reading about him.

As for Plan B. presented by the Japanese, it doesn't seem to me that Langer and Gleason make out a very good case for our summary rejection of it.* Nor can I see that the intercepted telegram from Tokyo ought seriously to have affected the situation. (Of course, I start with the assumption that we had no business worrying about China.) I have just received, by the way, two pamphlets containing blasts by Harry Elmer Barnes. I am not well posted enough to argue all the points he raises, but I am in general sympathy with his point of view. (I haven't read the book of yours —*The Vital Center*—that he scolds you about.) It seems to me that there is a myth of the war and our position vis-à-vis the rest of the world which has been swallowing us up in an alarming way. Actually, we are disliked and feared by the rest of the world just as Napoleon and England and Germany have been. At the same time, we have worked up a self-justificatory fantasy about the nobility of our actions and aims. I agree with Barnes that the self-righteousness, the bogus moral principles of Dulles —exhibited in his *New Statesman* reply to [Bertrand] Russell—are a kind

---

* "The attack on our fleet at Pearl Harbor has become, in our popular history, an act of moral turpitude more heinous than the firing of the Confederates on Fort Sumter; but it has been argued, to me quite convincingly, by Charles A. Beard, Harry Elmer Barnes, and others, that this act was foreseen by our government and— in order to make our antagonist strike the first blow—deliberately not forestalled at a time when a Japanese delegation was attempting to negotiate peace."
                                                   —Introduction to *Patriotic Gore*

of thing that was begun under Roosevelt, and I am afraid it is true that McCarthy is an outgrowth of the Roosevelt Administration, too. (If you haven't seen and want to see these pamphlets of Barnes's, I'll have copies sent you, but I imagine you know all about his point of view.)

The point is that, whether one approves or not of the present activities of the United States, one ought, I think, to recognize that we are really an expanding power unit, and that all our idealism is eyewash. Of course there are many who actually believe that we stand for "the free world" and that American institutions are preferable to those of other countries; but, whether or not these beliefs can be defended, they have not been the cause of our far-flung adventures, and I think that what they have been based on has been rather going by the board as we have been getting more bureaucratic and monolithic.

I have just looked up, in this general connection, your old article in *Partisan Review* on the causes of the Civil War. I agree, of course, that the historian must have a moral point of view, but it ought to be his own, not that of the participants in the events he is describing. The contentions of the "revisionists" you criticize seem to me aside from the point—which is that the Civil War was simply, like the Mexican War, a consolidation within this continent of the big North American power unit. The Abolitionists were fanatical about slavery, but this moral issue, again, was merely something, like Hitler's atrocities, that was useful for propaganda. Neither Sherman nor McClellan regarded the freeing of the slaves as one of the aims of the war, and Garrison, on the other hand, was all for having the North secede from the wicked South. Allan Nevins in his history of the war takes a view somewhat similar to this, but the difference between him and me is that Nevins enthusiastically approves of everything the U.S. has done since in the way of intervention and expansion.

Let's talk more about this when I see you again.   As ever, Edmund

To Hamilton Basso   July 14, 1958
                                                    Talcottville

Dear Ham: Your letter arrived at a low moment and made me feel even lower—aside from the fact that I was glad to hear from you. The ideas you express are very much the same as those that, since I wrote *A Piece of My Mind*, have been going through my own mind, and you confirmed me in my gloomy conclusions. I am thoroughly depressed with the U.S. and its present role in the world. I shan't go on about this at length; but here are comments on some of your points.

1. I tried to make it clear in my book that I did not equate the values I was talking about with New England–Anglo-Saxon Protestantism . . .

2. In connection with not making our republican sense the "touchstone

567

of American merit," I say specifically that I am thinking of certain artists and engineers . . .

3. Marxism never had the effect of destroying my belief in literature. All through the thirties I was defending literature.

4. Did you know that I am a relative of Cotton Mather? One of my great-great-grandfathers, who was a preacher up here, married a first cousin of Cotton's, and my mother's middle name was Mather. He was a rather dreadful man, I think. Did you read Barrett Wendell's excellent book about him? Good luck to you. We all need it nowadays.

As ever, Edmund W

To Van Wyck Brooks

June 8, 1958
Talcottville

. . . If you attempted to read *Cadmus*, you would not think it was meant to be a joke. They tell me that Eliot, since his marriage, has become a new man—almost embarrassingly affectionate and cheerful. He touched Conrad Aiken almost to tears—having always hitherto treated him with a certain lack of cordiality—by publicly embracing him at Cambridge, and in Texas wanted to know why the young men were all so gloomy when there was so much to be happy about . . .

To Van Wyck Brooks

September 23, 1958
Wellfleet

Dear Van Wyck: I am sorry to have been slow in acknowledging your *Arcadia*. I have been enmeshed in the Civil War, the Indians, and the Pasternak novel all more or less at once. I have enjoyed the book very much—you have woven a kind of prose poem out of all those old wanderings in Italy. But I kept hoping you would get more interested in the people and their personal problems. You do, of course, make the reader feel the personality and pathos of Margaret Fuller; but how about Constance Woolson's suicide and the strange destiny of the homosexual [Henry] Fuller, forced to shuttle back and forth between Italy and Chicago? Don't you think that Charles Godfrey Leland must have been rather an insufferable man? I lately read his autobiographical book in the Civil War connection but I became so disgusted with him that I dropped it in the middle and had to make myself go back to it and finish it. There is a boast on every page. He took no real interest in the war—his exploits in it are on the same level for him as his expedition looking for oil—and, in spite of his many talents, he seems never to have done work of any importance on any of the subjects with which he amused himself. He only wants to "blow" about himself and repeat the compliments that people have paid him.

I am saying this because I wish you would give more play nowadays to your insight into personality, which you exercised so acutely in your early books. It seems to me that—for your different purposes—you shut it off in *Makers and Finders*, and that it has been reappearing since in your autobiographical volumes.

By the way, Leon Edel, who has just been here, says that he and somebody else are bringing out the James–Howells letters. I gathered from what you told me that you have seen some that are not in the Harvard Library.

It is a pity you are not here this September. This is much of the best time of year to be here. Do by all means come to Talcottville on your way to Canada next summer. I thought you were really interested and want to show you some more sights. Love to Gladys.   As ever, Edmund

To HARRY LEVIN   September 29, 1958
                                                                Wellfleet

Dear Harry: I don't object to *contrived* in the sense that a Maupassant story is contrived. What I was interested in was the disparaging use of *contrive* in England. "Well-established usages" mean nothing to me. There are many well-established usages that I would like to see disestablished.
                                                        As ever, Edmund

To HARRY LEVIN   October 3, 1958
                                                                Wellfleet

Dear Harry: No usage is established for long. It is inevitable that the meaning of language should change. What I was interested in, in my articles,* was the significance of some recent changes. It is the states of mind they represent, not the fact that the changes have occurred, that I view with disapproval or uneasiness. In the case of the current meaning assigned to a word like *demean*, which is based on a false derivation, this usage is better "established" than the one which associates it with *demeanor*. The word was used in this way all through the nineteenth century by some of the best English writers. I am enough of a scholar to be somewhat annoyed by this—but I recognize that this is the way language is made, and that a language which was prevented from changing would soon be completely dead.   Edmund

To NEWTON ARVIN   January 8, 1959
                                                                Wellfleet

Dear Newton: Thank you for your paper, with which I agree. What you say about Dante, however, is, I think, a little misleading. "The strong

---

* "Words of Ill Omen" and "More Notes on Current Clichés," in *The New States-man*, September 6 and 13, 1958. Reprinted in *The Bit Between My Teeth*.

severe personal image" is not the product of biography, but mainly his own creation, in the *Commedia*, the *Vita Nuova*, and the *Letters*. It is he who tells about his exile, in the *Paradiso*, and invents himself as a character. Of the early biographies of him (brief "lives"), the nearest to being contemporary is Boccaccio's—as a child, he had once seen Dante. He is, so far as I know, aside from Dante himself, the only real witness for Dante's personality (he is very amusing on the subject, since his own personality is so different from Dante's, and he tells us that he feels as he writes that Dante, in heaven, is disapproving). I was sorry that we could not manage anything last summer, and hope it will be possible next.

Best regards, Edmund W.

To James Thurber   February 16, 1959
                                          Wellfleet
Dear Jim: I was glad to see [Arthur] Miller's letter. [Henry] Brandon's interview with me I thought much the weakest of his series. As Miller guesses, it is much chopped up and doesn't really hang together. Brandon's idea in his little introduction that he disrupted my serenity is absurd. He expected to find me something different from what I am like: that is, he expected to find me a cloistered and mellow old man of letters—and kept asking me questions about books—a kind of thing that bores me, especially when I haven't read the books. You probably surprised him, too. Don't worry about the reaction of the Whites to your *Ross*.   As ever, Edmund

To Alfred Kazin   January 26, 1959
                                          Wellfleet
Dear Alfred: Your O'Hara and Schlesinger pieces were excellent. I have been confirmed, reading you lately, in the conviction that I have been gradually brought to that writers are much better off outside colleges. I am glad you have a regular place to review in *The Reporter*—to have space at one's disposal and no pressure to qualify as a professor is really the great thing.   As ever, Edmund

To Alfred Kazin   March 13, 1959
                                          Wellfleet
Dear Alfred: I don't think that Tolstoy really, in the long run, believed that Trollope was better than he was. At the time when he was writing *War and Peace*, he was impressed by *The Bertrams*, which he was reading, but later notes in his diary that it is "too conventional." Even when he is being enthusiastic about Trollope, he doesn't imply that he can't compete with him. All that I can find on the subject is in Aylmer Maude's *Life*. Otherwise, an admirable essay.

Having just advised you to steer clear of the academic life, I've accepted for 1959–1960 the new Lowell lectureship at Harvard—but shall give them my Civil War; it will help me get through it.   As ever, Edmund

To JACOB LANDAU   December 15, 1956
Tavern-Bar Wines and Liquors
131-133 Queen Anne Road, Bogota, N.J.
Dear Mr. Landau: Thank you for your letter. I shall make a point of stopping in at your tavern if I ever go through Bogota.
                                                        Sincerely, Edmund Wilson

To JACOB LANDAU   May 16, 1958
                                                        Wellfleet
Dear Mr. Landau: *Levi* for *Zevi* was a misprint, which I had corrected in later printings. Didn't know that, while running a tavern, you were also a Hebrew scholar. By the way, I'm not a professor. חז חז חז לך *
                                                        Edmund Wilson

To JACOB LANDAU   July 22, 1958
                                                        Talcottville
Dear Mr. Landau: Thank you very much for your letters, etc., especially for פרקי אבות. † (I hope you didn't deprive yourself of a valued book.) I had only read it in the translation included in Charles's *Pseudepigrapha*, and it didn't make much impression on me. I had never seen the Hebrew text. I am astonished at how much more interesting it seems in Birnbaum's translation—full of wisdom, in fact.

The passages you have written in your beautiful Hebrew script will be useful to me, as I have difficulty getting the hang of this script. When I get letters written in it, I sometimes have to get them printed out. Your writing is so clear that I can use it as a standard. I also have difficulty in making out Yiddish, not having accustomed myself to it. I always forget which Hebrew characters represent which German vowels . . .

I think it was a good idea to read the [*American*] *Earthquake* at a high altitude, since the book describes the country at such a low level of morale.

I should of course be delighted to have the whisky if you can find any way of sending it . . . I am glad you like *Beppo and Beth*, which I have always thought one of my best pieces of writing. Few people have paid any attention to it . . . I enclose a book of poems that you may not have seen . . . (The English printers dropped out a word or two somewhere, so that one of the lines comes out wrong.) חז חז לך   Edmund Wilson

---

* Thank you very much.
† *Sayings of the Fathers,* a section of the Mishnah.

To Jacob Landau   August 13, 1958
                                                                   Talcottville
Dear Mr. Landau: Thank you so much for *The Book of Books* and the
whisky. Unfortunately, the Old Taylor got broken on the way, but I am
putting in a claim and hope to replace it. The delicious Scotch was drunk
yesterday, and very much appreciated, at a family gathering here. *The Book
of Books* is most interesting in its collection of such varied tributes.
                                                                   Edmund Wilson

To Jacob Landau   September 5, 1958
                                                                   Talcottville
Dear Mr. Landau: Your terrific Harper whisky hit me like a thunderbolt—
I hadn't noticed that it was 100 percent proof. I also much enjoyed Rabbi
Herzog's sauterne. When I was in Jerusalem, somebody wanted to take me
to his Seder, but he said that he already had too many guests. When I
get back to Wellfleet next week, I'll try to find you a copy of a Christmas
booklet of mine which contains my only Hebrew—or partly Hebrew—poem.
                         Once again, תודה רבה,* Edmund Wilson

To Jacob Landau   February 16, 1959
                                                                   Wellfleet
Dear Mr. Landau: I have been so busy since Christmas that I haven't been
able to acknowledge your letters and gifts sooner. The liquor, I am sorry
to say, has never arrived. The book about the Bible I was very glad to
have, and I have spent a good deal of time trying to figure out דער טאג , †
in which it was wrapped—sometimes it completely baffles me. What, for
example, is the character I have marked on this clipping (the other word,
Strahlen, I understand)? It looks like a Hebrew *tav*, but I thought that
Yiddish didn't have this character. Your New Year's greeting I was able to
read, except for the word מאמין .‡ If I were anywhere near where you
live, I would ask you to tutor me in these languages. (Where is Bogota?
Near Hackensack?)

You speak of not being able to get some of my books. If I have extra
copies, I'll be glad to send them to you—though some old books of mine
I'd be just as glad to have scrapped. Of recent years I've been revising and
republishing everything I think is worth saving.

I hope that you have by this time entirely recovered from your operation.
                                                        Yours sincerely, Edmund Wilson

---

* Thank you.
† *The Day*, a daily Yiddish newspaper.
‡ Believe.

To Jacob Landau   February 26, 1959
                                                   Wellfleet
Dear Mr. Landau: Thank you for your reading suggestions, but I have
any quantity of Hebrew grammars, ancient and modern, and H. E. Goldin's
Yiddish grammar. The letter *tav* does not occur anywhere in Goldin's book.
I suppose it is used in Yiddish only in proper names. I was stupid not to
recognize "Nathan." I thought of it but assumed that the next two words
were part of the same word. I cannot get used to having Hebrew characters
spell out German. I still cannot find your word מאמין* in any of my
Hebrew dictionaries. It must be a participle of אמן.†
    Thank you for the article about *Zhivago*. I already knew that the Jewish
patriots were angry about Pasternak. But in regard to this matter he
(Pasternak) has—I suppose deliberately—completely disregarded the historical approach, as he has in dealing with the Russian Revolution. I am
going to write something about all this presently—shall send you a copy.
    I don't have a copy of *The American Jitters*. With the exception of two
pieces—one of them not by me—the whole thing is reprinted in *The
American Earthquake*. I had to beg a copy from a friend in order to paste
up the *Jitters* for this purpose . . .   Sincerely, Edmund Wilson

To Jacob Landau   March 15, 1959
[Postcard]   Wellfleet

Dear Jacob (let us drop the Mister; we seem to have become quite good
friends without ever having met): I already have the Chomsky book, so
ought to return the copy you are sending me. Am immersed in *Zhivago*,
the Iroquois, and the Civil War all at once—hope I don't have a stroke till
I get out of it all.   Sincerely, Edmund W

To Jacob Landau   December 14, 1959
                                                  Cambridge
 . . . What is the meaning of the last three characters עמש‡ in the salutation of one of your letters? A young Israeli who was here the other night
wasn't able to tell me but thought it was an abbreviation for a prayer.
                                             As ever, Edmund Wilson

---

* Believe (ma-amin).
† The root letters of "ma-amin."
‡ Until 120 years (an abbreviation of a common Hebrew expression wishing a life
fully lived).

December 27, 1959
                                                            Cambridge
Dear Jack: Your present arrived before Christmas and exactly took care of
our needs. We are immensely grateful for it. I gave the children a magic
and puppet show, and your stimulants helped to get me through. I'll be
sending you a copy of my Indian book presently . . .

                                        Greetings of the season, Edmund Wilson

"A WINDOW ON RUSSIA"
1954–1960

To GLEB STRUVE   June 7, 1954
Department of Slavic Languages   Wellfleet
and Literatures, Berkeley

Dear Struve: Thank you for sending me your paper, which I have read
with much interest. It has helped me to understand those gerunds, which
have always puzzled me somewhat. I wish you had explained your dis-
agreements with my ideas about the Russian tenses. It seems to me that
your quotation from Dostoevsky and your note about eighteenth-century
correspondence confirm my impression of the vagueness of the Russian
way of dealing with the past. What worries the foreign reader is that the
Russian writers don't seem to know, in the case of a main verb in the past,
whether a gerund dependent on it that represents a simultaneous action
or state should be put in the past or the present. I find in Nevill Forbes's
grammar Будучи в городе, мы зашли к вам;* but быв† would be equally acceptable, wouldn't it?

Elena sends love. We recently saw a lot of your relatives in Paris. I
wanted to see your brother, but didn't have a chance. I was interested in
your father's [Peter Struve] memoirs of Lenin.

                                           Sincerely, Edmund Wilson

To GLEB STRUVE   July 8, 1954
                                                      The New Yorker

Dear Struve: Of course, I don't dispute the subtlety and interest of the
Russian verbs. I have written about it in an article on Russian that came
out some years ago and that I am going to include in the same book with
the other essay. I didn't mean to give the impression that Russian was not

---
* Being in the city, we dropped in on you.
† Having been.

an expressive language. But it does lack the precision of tenses that the Western languages have.

As for Old Slavonic, isn't it true that its more elaborate machinery of tenses was imitated, like its sentence structure, from Greek? It was a literary language, not a spoken language, and involved from the beginning with the Greek Church. When the spoken Slav dialects emerged, the various Slav languages—except for one or two survivals of the Old Slavonic tenses—all exhibited the same verb system, with its much simplified tenses and its fundamental aspects of perfective and imperfective.

Do you know W. K. Matthews's book *The Structure and Development of Russian*? I have been reading it for light on this subject. Page 82 has a number of instances of the vagueness of the time sense in Russian.

I'll certainly get *Novy Zhurnal* and read your Chekhov article.

Sincerely, Edmund Wilson

To GLEB STRUVE   December 27, 1954

Dear Struve: Thanks very much for your papers, which I have just read with great interest. When I reprint an article of mine on Chekhov, in which I praised the Soviet edition, I'll take account of your discoveries. You are good on Aldanov and Nabokov, but I am rather surprised to find a Russian saying that the latter is quite outside the Russian frame of reference, even outside the social world. Surely his great distinction is to have described the situation of the exiled Russian . . .   Edmund Wilson

To GLEB STRUVE   September 5, 1955
                                              Wellfleet

Dear Struve: Thank you for your letter. The D.P.'s letter was written to Mrs. Barbara Wolkov Mourontzov, who is now living in England. It was given me by Seta Schouvalov, about whom you probably know—she is teaching Russian at Syracuse.

A Russian woman named Vera Traill, whom we met in London, has written me to say that she knew [D. S.] Mirsky in Moscow, and that he was arrested "in the very first days of June 1937 (I think it was on the 3rd). He had never been arrested before—though he might have been through some kind of interrogation." I do not know whether it is possible, as I think you say in your book, that he had already been given the "minus six" (or however many minus it is). I certainly take the word of E. H. Carr that he saw him after I did—and it must have been in Leningrad or Moscow.

I am glad that you are doing a bibliography of Mirsky. It would be useful to have a collected multilingual edition of his writings . . .

Sincerely, Edmund Wilson

To Elizabeth Schouvalov   March 25, 1955
                                                 The New Yorker
Dear Miss Schouvalov: I am returning the Mirsky letter. Mrs. Mourontzov
has given me permission to publish it, asking me to take out the reference
to the writer's feet having been half amputated. She says he has returned
to Russia and is afraid he might be identified by this detail . . .

    I am asking Oxford Press to send you a copy of Forbes's *Russian
Grammar*. I have found it very useful, but Russians usually exclaim in
horror over it. The attempt to reduce the Russian language to something
that can be neatly explained in English has rather a curious effect . . .
                                       Sincerely, Edmund Wilson

To Gleb Struve   June 2, 1957
                                                  Talcottville
Dear Struve: Thank you for your letter about Mirsky. He had a prodigious memory, and it wouldn't surprise me to know that he had been
able to supply all the quotations without texts. I looked up your brother
in Paris last summer and had a very pleasant conversation with him. I
have your book on the Russian writers in exile, but haven't had a chance
as yet to do any more than look into it. I have just been to visit the
the Nabokovs at Ithaca and was somewhat surprised to find that Vladimir
regarded *Lolita* as his most important effort in either Russian or English.
I think, though, that for the first time he is beginning to make contact
with a larger public—curiously enough, through *Lolita* as well as *Pnin*. A
women's college in California has offered him a good job on the strength
of the latter! . . .   Sincerely, Edmund Wilson

To Helen Muchnic   August 18, 1955
                                                 Talcottville
Dear Helen: . . . I spent Monday and Tuesday with the Nabokovs at
Ithaca. He is an associate professor with life tenure, but is a little appre-
hensive about what will happen when the new book* about which I have
been telling you comes out—since it seems they can dismiss you for moral
turpitude. Don't mention this, lest it get back to academic circles. I have
never seen them, however, so cheerful, and I had a very good time with
them. I brought them that magnum of champagne, which I thought I
couldn't drink alone. He has made a translation of *Evgeni Onegin*, with
an enormous commentary that emphasizes, needless to say, the stupidities
of other translators and editors. The translation is good, I think. He has
more or less accepted my method, in the passages I translated, of following

---

* *Lolita*.

577

the text exactly and writing lines of irregular length, with a metrical base of iambic pentameter . . .

I loved your visit—have just had a nice note from Miss [Dorothy] Walsh, whom I hope to see again. She is sending me some Multiple Purpose Food and addresses me as "Dear Magician." I have been meditating on that remarkable card trick, of which I want to increase my mastery, and I realize that, although it is possible to make the blacks and the reds come out in any proportion, it is not possible to make them alternate, card by card: a red, a black, a red, a black, etc. This I shall never achieve. I have been greatly enjoying the record, shall play it again tonight. As ever, Edmund

Nabokov has just discovered that Stendhal is a complete fraud, and is about to break the news to his class. He has also read *Don Quixote* for the first time, and declares it is completely worthless. I wasn't able to agree with him, since I have never read it myself. He has come to the conclusion that **Смерть Ивана Ильича** [*The Death of Ivan Ilyich*] is the best thing Tolstoy ever wrote. What I don't like about it—its not being true to human life—is precisely what enchants him. The way that he tells you about it, savoring its cruel little ironies, makes it sound like a Nabokov story. When I said that it was too much of a moral fall, he was astonished and indignant. He had forgotten all about Tolstoy's view of life, and thought it was the kind of thing he writes himself.

Ivan Turgenev

TO HELEN MUCHNIC   September 2, 1955
                                                      Wellfleet

. . . I have been having a very pleasant time here, with all the children back, concentrating on home life and reading Turgenev through, which I find enchanting and soothing. Am now on **Отцы и Дети** [*Fathers and Sons*]. I read it in English in my youth, and it made almost no impression on me, so that I had never quite believed in it, but now it seems to me wonderful, a masterpiece . . . I find that I have two copies of Zhitova's memoirs of the Turgenev family. I think that you ought to read it. I hadn't realized what a monster Turgenev's mother was. What seems to me interesting is that, so far as I have read, there are no such households in his fiction—though *Mumu*, it appears, is based on one of Varvara Petrovna's barbarities. He likes to represent his country families as comfortable and well equilibrated. The wonder is that his mother's violence was not reflected in himself, but I suppose that it was a case of reacting in the opposite direction . . .

578

To Lily Herzog   March 26, 1956
                  Wellfleet

. . . Have been reading Turgenev through. He has a soothing and beneficent effect. Do you remember Дым [*Smoke*] and Новь [*Virgin Soil*]? They are brilliantly satirical. He gives, it seems to me, a more objective picture of Russia than Tolstoy or Dostoevsky—a picture that explains the failure of the Russians since the Revolution to build themselves a modern state.

Were you surprised at their repudiating Stalin? I don't see how it can be anything but a good sign . . .

To Vladimir Nabokov   September 18, 1956
           Cunard Line, *Queen Mary*

Dear Volodya: I have been reading the correspondence of Mérimée and Turgenev—*Une Amitié littéraire*. It turns out that you were mistaken in assuming that Mérimée knew no Russian, had his translations fed him by some lady. He was coached by Turgenev for over ten years. He translated a number of Turgenev's stories and checked on the translations of most of them. The dictionaries he used were inadequate, and he was always having to call on Turgenev. His deficiencies appear in these letters, but he does deserve a good deal of credit for pioneering in this field in France. I found the book very interesting and think that you ought to look into it. Mérimée on Pushkin is curious. He appreciates him in certain ways, but admits that he is no judge of poetry. What he really admires in Pushkin is the *côté Mérimée*. I had forgotten how prudish and Victorian the Second Empire was. Turgenev is always being expurgated by the editor of *La Revue des Deux Mondes*; and Mérimée himself protests about the cruelty of Turgenev's stories.

I was able to get an earlier sailing, so am coming back earlier than I expected—landing today and shall be in Wellfleet by the end of the week.   As ever, EW

To Helen Muchnic   November 30, 1956
                  Wellfleet

Dear Helen: Jason Epstein of Anchor Books so much admired your Talcottville photograph that he somehow had prints made of it and has sent me one. I think I must give him one in color. Of course, I was grateful for Newton Arvin's review—why on earth should I have been offended by it? But I wish he had had more space to develop his dissent from my opinions. I should like to know, for example, what he can find to say in defense of Christianity. The thing that annoys me about most of the reviews is that the stock thing seems to be to say that I'm "mellow."

Here is something I'd like to ask you. I've been translating passages from Turgenev and then looking them up in Constance Garnett and Isabel Hapgood. (Both are full of errors that even I can detect—which shows that they must have worked very fast, never checked on their work, and never read their translations to Russians.) Now, at this point will you refer to the fifth chapter of Дым [*Smoke*] and look at a speech of Potugin's which begins "И этого нет-с, а у него много воли-с."* Later on, he makes a statement which begins, "Мы толкуем об отрицании как об отличительном нашем свойстве…"† I assume he meant some negative attitude of a distinctly active kind without understanding exactly what, but I found that Hapgood made it *renunciation* and Garnett *skepticism*—both of which are perfectly nonsensical in view of what follows: you can't be either skeptical or renunciating with your fists or a sword. Hapgood must have confused отрицание with отречение.‡ What do you think Turgenev meant?

I am planning to spend a long season at Talcottville next summer, and I hope you will come to see me. We will read Pasternak together. I also hope to stop at Northampton on my way before college closes.

I eat, sleep, and spend the whole day in Turgenev—there is nothing here this time of year to distract my attention. You really didn't do him justice. Have you read the terrific story Конец ["The End"] that he dictated on his deathbed? It is not in the old editions—was not published till after his death. You can find it in Volume 8 of the new Soviet edition.

As ever, Edmund

To Helen Muchnic   January 8, 1957
                                                           Wellfleet

Dear Helen: I wish you would read Turgenev's story Часы ["The Watch"] and tell me what you make of it—also Собака ["The Dog"], which seems to be associated with it. What is the meaning of the watch? The symbol-exploiting critics would have a field day with these stories if they got around to Turgenev. The idea of mysterious destinies—irresistible devils and guardian angels—evidently grew on him in his later years, with the devils usually getting the better of it; but these two stories stand out in seeming to show the working of a *beneficent* destiny. Часы, however, somewhat baffles me. Isabel Hapgood says that she can find nothing about it in Russian criticism.

Love, Edmund

---

* There is none of that either, but he has a lot of will power.
† We talk of negation as of our distinguishing quality.
‡ Negation, renunciation.

To Helen Muchnic   February 7, 1957
                                                   The New Yorker

Dear Helen: Thank you for your letter and the passage from Shchedrin.
The latter seems to me typical of contemporary Russian comment on
Turgenev—which is always involved with politics, tendencies, groups, and
so forth . . . I think that the watch in *Chasy* is something of a social
symbol, which stands for the corruption of the old regime. With the
exception of the exiled uncle, the older men are all crooks, and the
watch itself seems to have been stolen. Dating the story in 1850 is simply,
I think, one of Turgenev's devices for getting it out of range of the
suspicions of the censorship.

They are doing my play *Cyprian's Prayer* at the uptown students'
theater of New York University the week of Washington's birthday, and
I have come on to see about it. I think it will be great fun . . .

                                                   As ever, Edmund

To Lily Herzog   May 30, 1957
                                                   Talcottville

. . . I have just sold to *The New Yorker* 17,000 words on Turgenev—
quite a feat, I think. I read him all through in Russian and got so fond
of Ivan Sergeyevich that I felt as if he were a personal friend . . .

To Lily Herzog   October 11, 1957
                                                   Wellfleet

. . . I am mailing you a copy of Turgenev's plays . . . The later ones are
quite good. I recommend Провинциалка [*A Provincial Lady*] (who I
suppose derives partly from his terrible mother) and Месяц в Деревне
[*A Month in the Country*]. I also liked the little sketch—written not for
the stage but for a well-known reciter—Разговор на Большой Дороги
[*Conversation on the Highway*]. One trouble with Turgenev's plays is
that, not being accustomed to the stage, he thinks he has to make the
people do everything they would do in real life—say: How do you do.
Won't you sit down? Talk about the weather, etc. That is one reason why
they are usually too long. In a story you can simply say that somebody
came in a room, greeted the ladies, and sat down. He didn't realize that
this has also to be abbreviated on the stage . . .

Целую ваша хорошенькая ручка,* as Turgenev used to write to the
actress Savina . . .   Edmund

---

* I kiss your pretty hand.

Boris Pasternak

To WILLIAM SHAWN   December 3, 1957
The New Yorker   Wellfleet

. . . Do you know about the novel by Pasternak, which the Soviets are
suppressing in its original form but which an Italian publisher is bringing
out?* I sent for their Italian translation but now learn that it will later be
published in English. I thought I might write about this, since Pasternak
is a first-rate figure—about the only one they now have—and the novel
sounds interesting. Please let me know about it, and whether, if you want
a piece on it, you think it would be a good idea to write about the Italian
or wait for the English. There was a story in the *Times* about this book, but
there is a more informative article in *The New Statesman* of November
16 . . .

To HELEN MUCHNIC   September 12, 1958
                                                             Wellfleet

. . . I have the Russian text of the Pasternak novel, which, so far as I
have got with it, I think is wonderful. It is brilliantly written, so don't
read the English . . .

To AVRAHM YARMOLINSKY   November 1, 1958
                                                             Wellfleet

Dear Avrahm: I have just finished my article on the Pasternak book and
am sending the Russian text to Helen Muchnic, asking her to send it on
to you. I should eventually like to have it back. I think that it is one of
the great books of our time, but shan't discuss it here, since my review
will soon be coming out.† You will find a lot of important details in the
Russian which have been stupidly omitted by the English translators. But
those Russian writers of fiction seem to be able to survive anything! Love
to Babette.   Edmund W

---

* *Doctor Zhivago.*
† "Doctor Life and His Guardian Angel," in *The New Yorker*, November 15, 1958.

Janet Flanner
Has a crusty manner
She sits in a bar
Like the St.-Lazare Gare

And from there she pounds out her wonderful letters
Which makes us all her eternal debtors.

(Notebooks of the sixties)

To JANET FLANNER   November 21, 1958
                                                  The New Yorker

Dear Janet: Thanks very much for your letter.

Didn't you notice how dreadful my article was, style-wise? I am used
to taking any amount of time and having any number of proofs on my
New Yorker articles; but on account of Pasternak's being so much in the
news, I had to hurry this one through and had to do all my revising on
the phone in a two-hour session with Whitaker. The result is a lot of
wrong grammar, sentences that don't quite make sense, and other casualties.
I was quite depressed about it, so your letter was reassuring.

Of the translations I have seen, the French one is much the best. You
are quite safe with it. If you will compare it for length with the English
one, you will see how much has been omitted in the latter. The French
translation has even made an effort to reproduce Pasternak's Audenesque
off-rhyming—so when you find *heures* rhymed with *feutre* and *perles* with
déverse, don't conclude that the translator is incompetent. I am wondering
who did this conscientious job. No translator's name is given. (Have
learned that six people were involved.*)

There was not, so far as I know, anything clandestine about Feltrinelli's
edition of the Russian text. It seems that the Vatican people at the Brussels
Fair bought up a lot of copies and were handing them out free to Russians
outside the Soviet Pavilion. (Have learned that a version of the text, with
forged interpolations, *was* printed in Holland and distributed by the émigré
organization called N.T.S. The Vatican, so far as I know, had nothing to
do with it.†) Pantheon has announced that it is importing this edition
over here, but in the meantime the University of Michigan has got hold
of nobody seems to know what manuscript and is also going to bring out
an edition. I had the page proofs of the Michigan edition as well as
photostats of the original typescript, which Pantheon lent me.

By the way, I have just heard from a Russian friend that, according to
the Greek Orthodox calendar, the name Larissa means *seabird*.

Elena sends greetings.   As ever, Edmund

---

* Handwritten inserts.
† Handwritten inserts.

To GLEB STRUVE   December 1, 1958
                                                           Wellfleet

. . . I have just had a conversation with Max Hayward in Boston. He is
embarrassed about the translation. I was right in thinking that they had
not had time to do it properly. The version published in England had
had the advantage of revisions which were not included in the American
one, which, besides, was somewhat mauled in the New York office.
Hayward is now making further corrections . . .

To HELEN MUCHNIC   January 28, 1959
                                                           Wellfleet

. . . I am going to do another article eventually on Pasternak—have been
collecting his works. I have several things which you probably haven't seen
. . . On the other hand, you may have in the Smith library some things
which I can't find in Widener—there is, in fact, not a single volume of
Pasternak to be found on the shelves there now! . . . I'm going to publish
some further notes on *Zhivago* in *The Nation** . . .

To HELEN MUCHNIC   February 6, 1959
                                                           Wellfleet

. . . About *Zhivago*, it has a whole *Finnegans Wake* element that people
are now getting to work on . . .

> I think that you and Evgenia Lehovich ought to be brought together
> . . . She is a very remarkable person—runs the New York City Ballet
> school and has so much energy left over that she has written a short
> book on *Zhivago* and at one time made herself an authority on the life
> cycle of the eel. She is the granddaughter of the Princess Ourousov,
> who lived in Paris and was a friend of Turgenev, as well as of Henry
> James. She has letters from Turgenev to her grandmother and copies
> of his books that he sent her.   (To Helen Muchnic, 1962)

To EUGENIE LEHOVICH   February 1, 1959

Dear Evgenia: I am not sure that I agree with you about Larissa's representing the Revolution. Wouldn't it be rather that she represents the more
civilized (than Pasha) European element, deriving originally from France
but with a Germanic strain (Belgium) that sympathizes with the "oppressed
classes"? . . . Max Hayward pointed out to me that the death and resurrection idea is contained in the first lines of the book: "Кто хоронят?"

---

* "Legend and Symbol in *Doctor Zhivago*," in *The Bit Between My Teeth*.

584

"Живаго (живого),"* etc. In the article in *Time* on Pasternak, it was said that this is connected with an old ballad about somebody's being buried alive. What is this ballad? Do you know it?

I do hope that you can come up here, so that we can talk about this fascinating subject . . .   As ever, Edmund

> Gleb Struve recalls that it had already been thought that "Pasternak had inspired Stalin with some mysterious fear."
> *(The Bit Between My Teeth)*

To Eugenie Lehovich   February 14, 1959
                                                                                   Wellfleet

. . . I was much interested in the thing about Pasternak and Stalin, and think it might be worthwhile to translate the last pages. I am wondering whether there can be any connection between the Christianizing tendencies of Dacian's wife in the St. George legend—for which her husband, according to Voragine, "took her by the hair and did do beat her cruelly"—and the incident of Pasternak's message to Stalin at the time of the death of his wife. I think, in any case, that the author of this article may be right about Stalin's reason for protecting Pasternak . . .

To Eugenie Lehovich   February 26, 1959
                                                                                   Wellfleet

Dear Evgenia: Thank you for all the *Zhivago* material . . . The article by Koryakov† somewhat shook my confidence in him. I think that what he says about *Zhivago* as an oculist and the "concealed polemic" against Mayakovsky is all nonsense. But I do think there may be something in his theory about Pasternak's relations with Stalin.

Thank you for all the trouble you have taken about this.

                                                                         As ever, Edmund

To Eugenie Lehovich   March 23, 1959
                                                                                   Wellfleet

. . . We have just come back from Boston, where we saw Max Hayward. He has had a graduate student working on *Zhivago* and the Мения Чета [*Lives of the Saints*]. He has discovered that the original Larissa was burned —hence, apparently, the smell of burning with which she is so often accompanied: the smell of the frying blini, the burning of the clothes she is ironing, etc. She died with many other victims—hence the concentration

---

* "Whom are they burying?" "Zhivago" (one who is alive).
† "Novoe Russkoe Slovo."

camp. I don't think I told you that Hayward had discovered that in some old directory of Soviet writers in which the names are not listed alphabetically, Pasternak turns up beside a Dr. Zhivago. He tells me that Pasternak left or was removed from Peredelkino just before the Macmillan visit, and that he has never been heard from since. At the time of the Nobel Prize uproar, the government posted a doctor and a nurse at Peredelkino, who accompanied him everywhere he went, even to the bathroom, to prevent his committing suicide—which he had no intention of doing—and the resultant большой скандал.* This was why, in one of his public statements, he said he was "surrounded by doctors."

We hope to get to New York by April 17. The Zhivago Research Center can then hold a meeting. By that time the article should be in proof.

As ever, Edmund

To Eugenie Lehovich   December 27, 1959
                                                                    Cambridge
Dear Evgenia: I have been kept so busy that I have had no chance to answer your letter. Now the first semester is over, my Indian book is done with, and Christmas is happily liquidated. About the collection of Russian articles on *Zhivago:* I usually find this kind of book rather indigestible . . . Kurt Wolff, Pasternak's American publisher, had the idea of doing something similar . . . and I rather discouraged him. When he wrote to Pasternak about it, Pasternak discouraged him flatly. I have just read the Автобиографический Очерк ["An Essay in Autobiography"], intended as an introduction to Pasternak's collected poems (called in English *I Remember*), which is most interesting and, like *Zhivago*, stimulating. Then I tried Охранная Грамота [*Safe Conduct*], which floored me. I resorted to a translation and found that certain passages still remained obscure. Have you read this? I wanted to do another article about his earlier prose which is now coming out in English, but I don't think that I can really get at it.

Your boy came to a party that I gave for my seminar, and he told Elena that he saw that I had there "вся красота Радклифа."† We are looking forward to your visit. In the meantime, holiday greetings to all the family.

As ever, Edmund

To Eugenie Lehovich   June 19, 1959
                                                                    Wellfleet
Dear Evgenia: Here is a letter from Pasternak, in which he seems to scoff at our ideas about Moreau and Vetchinkin, etc. But he emphasizes, as you

---

* Great scandal.
† All the beauty of Radcliffe.

This is a valentine note for Evgenia
With whom I now share a common mania
Since we both have developed a marvelous knack
For finding false meanings in Pasternak.

see, his fluidity. Please send it back to me . . . Thank you for the clipping, and especially the St. George, which I am going to have framed. I suppose you know that Surkov and the head of the Komsomol have been fired, and that Pasternak is presumably to be reinstated. *Encounter* made a mess of our article. Love to you both.   Edmund

To GLEB STRUVE   August 3, 1959

. . . You are right, of course, in saying that the attempt to compare Pasternak with Tolstoy carries people completely off the track.

Pasternak has written Kurt Wolff that Evgenia Lehovich and I were quite wrong in our Joycean reading of Moreau and Vetchinkin, but he doesn't deny the saints' legends . . .

To EUGENIE LEHOVICH   January 6, 1960

. . . Isaiah Berlin tells me that Pasternak's sister showed him some kind of silver trophy that had been given Pasternak père, and that the silversmith's name was Zhivago . . .

To GEORGE L. KLINE   August 12, 1959
Assistant Professor of Philosophy   Cambridge
Columbia University
Dear Mr. Kline: I am sorry to have delayed so long in acknowledging your letter and enclosures. I wanted to wait until I had read the Pasternak memoir—which I have only just been able to do. I was interested to hear about the Tsvetaeva poems. I notice that in Pasternak's denials—in an interview in *The Nation* and in an unpublished letter in German—that he intended the riddles I found in *Zhivago*, he never discusses the question of the saints' legends.

The text that Magarshack used in translating the "autobiographical sketch" was evidently different from the one I have. The part about *Zhivago* at the end must have been added later. The second paragraph of the twelfth section of the pre-war chapter is curiously different. Pasternak says that he did not understand Mayakovsky's propagandist activities, his "подчинения голосу злободневности."* Magarshack seems to be translating something quite different. But in my Russian text Nikolai Trubetskoy is said to be, not a philologist, but an "известным философем."†

---

* Subordination to the voice of burning issues of the day.
                                                   —George L. Kline's translation
† Well-known philosopher.

I think your translations are excellent—it is a good idea to imitate, as you have done, Pasternak's off-rhymes. Thank you for sending them to me.

Yours sincerely, Edmund Wilson

To Eugenie Lehovich

June 4, 1960
Cambridge

. . . I have been very much depressed by Pasternak's death. I suppose they really killed him by putting him through such an ordeal—if not literally, as they evidently did Gorky: I thought it a little suspicious that he should have been reported to be suffering from so many serious ailments . . .

THE SIXTIES

It takes me some time nowadays to get through the literature sent me in connection with the subjects that I've written about. I am inundated with books and papers on psychoanalysis, the Bible, the Dead Sea scrolls, socialism, the American Indians, the Civil War, Canada, Jewish history, the Symbolist movement in literature, the Soviet Union, and Hungary. I wish sometimes that I hadn't been so various.

CHRONOLOGY

The winter of 1960–1961 was overshadowed by worry about the income tax. I borrowed the money from Roman Grynberg and Barbara Deming, then paid it back by selling my papers to Yale.   (Notebooks of the sixties)

1960	APOLOGIES TO THE IROQUOIS
APRIL	Cambridge: Next week I have my last two lectures.
SUMMER	Talcottville: I have taken up the study of Hungarian.
NOVEMBER	We are spending the winter in Cambridge, coming up here [Wellfleet] sometimes for weekends and holidays.
1961	NIGHT THOUGHTS
JANUARY	I hope to get done with the Civil War by Easter. We have been more or less enjoying our winters in Cambridge . . . we quite often get away to the Cape.
SUMMER	Wellfleet, Talcottville.
SEPTEMBER	Cambridge.
1962	PATRIOTIC GORE
MARCH	Copies of the book will be ready on Friday. The Internal Revenue people have cut off my sources of income.
SUMMER	Wellfleet, Talcottville.
SEPTEMBER	I am leaving for Canada . . . to investigate Canadian literature.
OCTOBER	I spent a month in Canada—Toronto, Montreal, Quebec —and had a delightful time.
1963	THE COLD WAR AND THE INCOME TAX
JANUARY	We have had some hideous winters in Cambridge . . . tax troubles and various ailments.
SUMMER	Wellfleet, Talcottville.

SEPTEMBER	We are going to Europe in a few days.
OCTOBER	London, Basil Street Hotel.
WINTER	Paris, Hôtel de Castille.
DECEMBER	We had quite an exciting . . . trip to the Vosges, where I spent the first war.

1964

MARCH	We have come down from Paris to Rome [Hotel Victoria].
APRIL	A month at the Hotel Gellert in Budapest.
SUMMER	Wellfleet, Talcottville.
AUGUST	The Edward MacDowell Medal.
SEPTEMBER	Our address from the end of this month will be 131 Mt. Vernon Street, Middletown, Connecticut [The Center for Advanced Studies, Wesleyan].

1965 O CANADA

MAY	Middletown: We're coming up to Wellfleet for the weekend, May 7–9, when I'll be seventy years old.
OCTOBER	I spent most of my summer at Wellfleet this year.

1966 THE BIT BETWEEN MY TEETH

SPRING	I am working on my academic comedy [*The Duke of Palermo*].
JUNE	Talcottville.

1967 A PRELUDE; GALAHAD and I THOUGHT OF DAISY, revised edition

APRIL	I am going to Israel and Jordan at the end of April to bring my Dead Sea scrolls book up to date [April 27– May 29].
JULY	Talcottville: It seems marvelously quiet up here and the telephone rarely rings.
NOVEMBER	Wellfleet: My age is beginning to tell on me.

1968 THE FRUITS OF THE MLA in *The New York Review of Books*

JANUARY	My recent grandchild—Jay Hilary Wilson.
SUMMER	Wellfleet, Talcottville.
OCTOBER	Session on the Iroquois at Utica College.

1960–1961

To Helen Muchnic   April 30, 1960
                                                                 Cambridge
Dear Helen: I have asked [Renato] Poggioli about the Last Judgment,
also another expert, and they both tell me the same thing. The souls will
rise now *equipped with their bodies*. Those who are in Heaven and Hell
will be sent back to their old rewards and punishments, but they will now
be experiencing them in the flesh. Purgatory will by that time be cleaned
out: all the souls there will have graduated. And the world will now have
come to an end.

   Next week I have my last two lectures—after that, nothing but papers.
Love to you both. I may possibly turn up again.   Edmund

To T. S. Matthews   April 4, 1960
                                                                 Cambridge
Dear Tom: I have been reading your book with great interest.* You have
turned out to be a writer, after all. I think that you did well to decide to
do a straight autobiography rather than the usual autobiographical novel.
I am sorry that our last meeting was disagreeable, and when I heard that
you were leaving *Time*, I had the impulse to wire you congratulations. I
hope to see you again in a more cheerful way. It was dreadful to read
about Julie's death.

   Here are some observations: First of all, I was surprised to discover that
I was only six years older than you. I had thought of you as so much
younger. The point is that the younger people are, the more difference a
few years make. At first, it did not seem to me plausible that you should
have been in England in 1911—I was there in 1908 and 1914—and that

------
* *Name and Address.*

you should remember the old-fashioned Fourth of July. (You don't mention that those paper balloons were sometimes in the form of animals.) I also read Ralston's *Russian Fairy Tales*, which was in my grandfather's library, and also thought they were among the most frightening. You know Gogol developed his story *Viy*—which I think is the most hair-raising modern tale of horror—from one of those vampire stories.

p. 105. It was not Simon Legree—in the novel, or even, I think, in the play—who was chasing Eliza across the ice; and the bloodhounds are not in the novel. They were first introduced in one of the versions for the stage only in 1879; but, of course, they have become since then an inalienable element of the legend.

p. 190. You omit the important point that Pauline's [Hemingway] cotton éclair was produced on the first of April.

p. 192. My eyes, far from being "pale," are of the dark brown kind that is sometimes called black.

p. 194. I don't believe this baseball story, and I doubt that it is true. It could not have been my "parents," in any case, who presented me with the equipment: my father was as unathletic as I was.

p. 195. You misunderstood the Fitzgerald story. It was in my radicalizing days, and Scott thought that when the revolution came, I should inevitably be made Secretary of State.

p. 196. I perfectly well know—having learned about printing at *Vanity Fair*—how much trouble I was giving the printers and you [at *The New Republic*]; but I have always been keenly aware that literature demands not only all one can give it but also all one can get other people to give it. In this respect, working for *The New Yorker* has been an ideal arrangement for me, since they allow and even encourage any amount of correction in the page proofs as well as the galleys, and I need never have twinges of conscience. On my Dead Sea scrolls article I corrected eleven proofs.

p. 197. I did not "learn Russian and later go to Russia"; I went to Russia and there began studying Russian. And I was there not six months but five.

p. 202. I had supposed that Schuyler Jackson's peculiar behavior the night we went to dinner there was an exercise—rather ill timed—of the Orage–Gurdjieff technique of making rude personal remarks in order to jolt the patient into grappling with his real personality. Somebody afterwards told me this.

p. 205. Tony Luhan was not a Zuñi but from Taos. The self-contained Zuñis only rarely intermarry even with their neighbors the Hopis, let alone with fancy whites.

p. 297. I share your personal reactions to what is going on in this country: Russia and the U.S. are getting to be more and more alike; and sometimes I feel that I have reached the point when, as the old adage says, good Americans can die and go to Paris.

Please remember me to Martha. We must eventually have a *New Republic* reunion—possibly without Bruce Bliven.

As ever, Edmund Wilson

To Dawn Powell   March 17, 1960
                                                        Cambridge

Dear Dawn: We were delighted by your "Inside Yaddo" letter. How long are you going to be there? I may be going to Talcottville in April, and if you were still there, should make a point of stopping to see you.

We have lately had two fatiguing but highly interesting sessions with a delegation of Russian writers that included [Leonid] Leonov but nobody else I had ever heard of. They were accompanied by a Soviet interpreter, an old-fashioned Russian witch, who, Arthur Schlesinger tells me, was fastened on to him on his recent trip to Russia and even slept above him on the train; and by a blank-faced blond young man, who, at the time people were being introduced, said simply, "State Department." Later on, I asked one of the writers whether it wasn't possible for them to meet people here "without interpreters and without State Department *chinovniki*" (*chinovniki* being the old tsarist officials that Gogol and the rest of them wrote about). The *Baba Yaga** interpreter herself was present at the conversation, trying to make me speak English instead of the bad Russian in which I could more directly express my thought, and this remark, in some magic way, was immediately communicated to the man from Washington, who a few minutes afterwards confronted me and said: "I am the State Department *chinovnik*."   Love, Wigmore

To Lily Herzog   June 24, 1960
                                                        Wellfleet

. . . In Boston we saw something of four Soviet writers who were visiting. The only one I know anything about was Leonid Leonov. He had known the Alimovs and told me that Sergei was dead, which I had already heard, and that Maria Fyodorovna had married a critic. He [Leonov] was very clever at parrying the leading questions that people asked him, but he seems to have spoken quite freely to Elena, to whom he expressed a certain interest in religion and in her relative Pyotr Struve, an old socialist who fell out with Lenin and who has always been denounced by the Communists. He spoke of having lived through all those terrible years and added, "Я очень хитрый "† . . .

---

* Russian fairy-tale witch.
† I am very hypocritical.

Mary Meigs and Barbara Deming—they bought Mary McCarthy's old house on Pamet Point Road [Wellfleet] . . . We invited them more and more.   (Notebooks of the fifties)

To Mary Meigs   August 22, 1960
                                                  Talcottville

Dear Mary: . . . I wonder whether your ideas about the landscape up here have anything to do with the tax situation that was preying on my mind. But I think there is something in what you say about the wilderness being held at bay. I enjoy that feeling myself. I like to see that the wild flowers are getting into the garden and growing along the front porch and that the limestone of the steps and pavements surges with the riverbanks. I spent a day on Tug Hill with the small-mammals man. It was interesting and in some way disturbing. It was the first time I had had revealed to me the whole world of invisible life that goes on in such isolated places without contact with the human one: by flying squirrels, jumping mice, moles, shrews, meadow mice, and wood mice, all with more or less different habits but adjusted to one another. It was most satisfactory to go through these woods with someone who knew what everything was: birds, animals, trees, flowers, ferns, mosses, and how they all lived. He was not doing any live trapping, but catching them in mousetraps and rattraps in order to examine their stomachs and other organs, and this made a rather painful impression, though at the same time inspired respect for scientific procedure. Some of the little animals turned out to be nursing mothers, and I suppose the babies simply die or are eaten up by owls. The young zoologist . . . told me on the way home that he sometimes felt badly about it. He took me also to a sphagnum swamp. I had never seen sphagnum before—it is a great thick blanket of moss that floats on the surface of the water. You can walk on it where it is most solid, but it gives and it is as if you were walking on a hammock. There are insect-eating sundews and pitcher plants, the latter in great clumps that seem almost as animal as the big frogs in the central pond . . .

I have taken up the study of Hungarian. Two of my plays have been translated in Hungary. They have been published and, I believe, are to be produced. In the volume, the translator explains that they know nothing of my other work in Hungary, but that I am obviously a first-rate dramatist. I was so pleased with this that I think of starting soon for Budapest. There are a good many Hungarians in this part of the world, and I have found somebody to give me lessons. The only thing that worries me a little is that they have only translated two plays that were written in the early thirties,* and the translator explains in a note that I am depicting the decay of the capitalist world and indicating the correct

---

* *This Room and This Gin and These Sandwiches* and *Beppo and Beth.*

598

line of escape through following the party line. But I am sure that those Hungarians are capable of playing certain scenes ironically.

I am writing all this to you because I assume that Barbara is absent. Here is one of these Cuba bulletins for her. In answer to her inquiry about the nose rosettes of the star-nosed mole, they are little feelers of flesh that naturally dry up when they die.

About Constable, when I get back to Wellfleet, I'll show you how he derived from Rowlandson's landscapes. I have acquired a vast volume of the caricatures of Rowlandson's contemporary Gillray, who turns out to be quite different from Rowlandson, even when Rowlandson is grotesque and outrageous. It is really a political history—extremely dramatic and exciting if you follow it from beginning to end—over 500 engravings: thirty years of the reign of George III. What is astonishing nowadays is the hair-raising satire on the royal family both in their public and their private lives.

I ought to explain to Barbara—if she hasn't found it out already—that I was all wrong about Nigeria and Ghana: they are two different countries. —I have just had a letter from Stephen Spender, who says he is writing her about her article. He came to see me here before he left. We sat on stones in the middle of Independence River and talked London gossip. He composed a poem for one of my panes.   Love, Edmund

To Newton Arvin   November 26, 1960
                                                         Wellfleet
Dear Newton: I had the impulse to write to you when I heard about your recent difficulties; but I wanted first to find out from the people at Northampton exactly what had happened, then to know how my own embarrassments were coming out, so that I might more appropriately condole with you. In my case, I was actually guilty of income-tax "delinquency"; but in your case it seems to me that the way you were treated was gratuitously insulting and outrageous. What happened with me, however, was equally revealing of what is now going on in the "Free World." All my books seem to have been examined in Washington with the idea of showing that I was a subversive character, and it was even brought up against me that I had been married four times. Fortunately, the matter was handled in upstate New York, where I am known and which still manages to preserve a certain relative tranquillity and independence, and they honorably refused to say anything at all about my political opinions or *Hecate County*, or the fact that I had, in my Indian book, exhibited in a not entirely favorable light the judge who had to decide my case. In your case, I am told that the judge was reluctant to pass any sentence at all.

I hope that this episode will not discourage you but perhaps in the long run prove stimulating. It will not detract in the least from your literary reputation. If it is impossible now for you to teach at Smith, you ought not to have any difficulty in publishing reviews and articles. Would you like me to speak to *The New Yorker* and *The Nation*? I have always thought you didn't write half enough. Then there are *The New Statesman* and *Encounter*, which I'd also be glad to write to.

We are spending the winter in Cambridge—coming up here sometimes for weekends and holidays—and if you should ever get to Boston, I hope you will let us know . . .

Goddam all this interference with people's personal affairs! I had to submit to an interrogatory covering my whole life.

Yours as ever, Edmund Wilson

I don't think I have spoken to you about Barbara Deming's book *Prison Notes* . . . She spent twenty-seven days in jail in Albany, Georgia, for taking part in one of those marches, and her book is not a mere piece of agitation but a notably well-written document that throws more light than anything else I have read on the meaning of their non-violent protests for the more serious of these demonstrators. (To William Shawn, 1966)

To Barbara Deming   January 23, 1961
                                                                        Cambridge

Dear Barbara: We were much interested in your letter . . . When I went to the heart specialist in Hyannis, it turned out that I had a touch of angina (not at all serious), for which he has given me pills and put me on a regime of sobriety and diet. The results have been excellent: I am now able to get around comfortably, which I wasn't before. But our life has been rather monotonous and dreary. Elena reads Arthur Schlesinger's Roosevelt biography, and I read endless Civil War lit. Arthur is going to Washington as White House assistant to Kennedy, though he doesn't seem to know exactly what he is going to do. We were invited by the Kennedys to the inauguration by a telegram announcing that the new Administration "hoped to seek a productive relationship with our writers, artists," etc. Elena would have liked to go but wasn't able to, and I had no great desire to, having attended two inaugurations in my time and knowing how dreadful they are. I'm glad I missed hearing Robert Frost read that terrible poem . . . We have been feeling very cheerful about the advent of Kennedy, but as John Strachey, who has been here, says, new Administrations are always disappointing.   Love to both, Edmund

To Robert Lowell   January 5, 1961
                                                                        Wellfleet

Dear Robert: We were glad to hear from you. It seems incredible that you should want to live in New York, but you have had more of Boston than we have. I wish I could perform for Harriet's birthday, but it will probably be weeks or months before we get to New York. We came up here for the holidays but shall probably be back in Cambridge in a few days . . . We have missed you very much this year. Since I haven't had a job it hasn't been as arduous for me as last year. We have had very little social life and have come up here as much as possible.

I hope to get done with the Civil War* by Easter. I keep adding more and more people and things and am now having difficulty to prevent the book's bursting at the seams. As soon as I have finished it, I am going to write a hilarious farce-melodrama of academic life,† which I should like to have produced at the Loeb Theatre. Projecting it has cheered me up as a kind of "breakthrough" of high spirits from the Civil War and other depressing matters. We enjoyed Elizabeth's [Hardwick] article in *Harper's*. I hear enthusiastic reports of your *Phèdre*. The Loeb Theatre, by the way, is really adding a lot to life in Cambridge. They have put on excellent performances of *Troilus and Cressida* and Brecht's *Caucasian Chalk Circle*, which take on the whole text and last from eight to eleven, while you are sitting in comfortable seats, all of which have a comfortable view of the stage.

Happy New Year from both of us—it couldn't be worse than the last.

Edmund

To Morton D. Zabel   March 18, 1961
                                                          Cambridge

Dear Morton: We were awfully glad to hear from you. We had hoped to be coming to New York about now, but I'm afraid we shan't make it till after Easter. Be sure to see Nichols and May—you may already have seen them in Chicago, but I am sure that what they are doing now is much more remarkable. *She* is the greatest thing of the kind since Ruth Draper. He is terribly funny, but she really creates her characters. The brokers will charge you $12.75 a seat, but I simply went to the box office and found that I could buy tickets, though not very good ones.

My Civil War book has become a Penelope's web—longest and most complicated thing I've ever attempted—but I am now really getting toward the end of it. It won't be out, however, till spring of 1962—by which time the market will be glutted. All the fuss that is now being made about the war bores the life out of me. Why do the Southerners feel that they have to reenact the whole fiasco? It is apparently going on for four years! And those special features in *Life!*

The Joycean texts in my Christmas card are precisely attempts to write down when awake the prose that I compose in my dreams—though from

---

* *Patriotic Gore.*
† *The Duke of Palermo.*

the moment I am able to remember these things it is probable that some intentional element enters in. I then draw pictures to fit them.

We have been more or less enjoying our winters in Cambridge. The best of the faculty are brilliant, and a real exchange of ideas goes on; but it is a cramped claustrophobic place. This year, however, since I don't have a job, we quite often get away to the Cape . . .   As ever, Edmund

To Jacob Landau   June 29, 1961
                                                       Talcottville
Dear Jack: I arrived up here two days ago and found your whisky awaiting me. I have been drinking Bob's with much enjoyment, and am keeping the Grand Macnish for guests. Have finished my Civil War book, all except the Introduction—which I am dreading because I want to try to put the war in perspective of our foreign policy before and after. I come up here alone at this time every year and have a period of work and tranquillity. I'm sure you'll enjoy your retirement. I'm sorry that I forgot to send you the Hebrew books from Wellfleet but shall do so when I get back. By the way, I was delighted to find in a little dictionary שכה, which was defined as "wander around lasciviously." When I looked it up in Gesenius, however, I found that the sole occurrence (Jeremiah 5:8) was in a very special context and that the root was rather dubious. תודה רבה הויסכי *
                                                      Edmund W

To Alfred Kazin   July 8, 1961
                                                       Talcottville
. . . I wish I could have seen more of you; but the Wellfleet summer festivities are too much for me. Tonight I am dining out for the first time since I have been back here, and have seen almost nobody except a handsome Hungarian girl [Mary Pcolar] who types for me, drives me, and teaches me Hungarian. I am going to read their great poet Ady, but have never heard of any other Hungarian writer that I thought I particularly wanted to read.

I was somewhat upset by Hemingway's death. Of course he often made a fool of himself, but it is as if a whole corner of my generation had suddenly and horribly collapsed. I knew that the desperation in his stories was real, and his suicide—as it evidently was—makes his drinking and posing seem pathetic, because it must have been an effort to counteract and cover up the other thing.

In my own case, besides the onset of senility, the U.S.A. is getting me down. Have you seen the special number of *The Nation* devoted to the C.I.A.? I don't see how you still manage to believe in American ideals and all that.   Yours in low spirits, Edmund

---

* Thank you very much [for] the whisky.

To Mary Meigs   August 19, 1961
                                                     Talcottville
. . . Helen and I are preparing our annual Punch and Judy show, with
which to conclude the Talcottville season. We have written down the
script for the first time, and I feel that, like Nichols and May, we have
perfected it through the improvisations of years. Some of the features
date from when Helen was a little girl. My Hungarian assistant is now
typing it.

My great revelation this summer has been making connections with the
Hungarians here. It seems to me that even in Europe they are always at
a tangent to everybody else. They are rather, as a people, self-contained
and proud and likely to be fiery if provoked. As in the case of the Indians,
their Mongolian origins come out in unmistakable ways. I have read some
Hungarian poetry, and it is true that, as they claim, it is full of color. I
think that Bartók's music really tells you a good deal about Hungary. I
have always very much admired it, but it will interest me more now—
the alternations between brooding depression and rousing peasant dances,
with flashes of spirited self-assertion . . .

To Helen Muchnic   September 22, 1961
                                                      Cambridge
Dear Helen: I have delayed writing you because I wanted to have a
chance to read your book.* I've now read the part that I hadn't read
before and am very much impressed by it. I see now that it develops a
general theme which I hadn't been aware of before. The opening is
dramatically excellent; the discussion of Gorky masterly. I had never read
enough on him to know what he was really like, and your chapter has for
the first time given me a clear idea. About *The Lower Depths*: I was
fully aware that Luka was a benevolent fraud, but I thought that Satin,
too, was a fraud. Certainly Kachalov seems to make him one in that
record I once played for you—but then, Russians when they are delivering
orations always seem to me fraudulent. As you say, he only cares about
humanity when he is drunk. Don't he and the Baron, in their drinking
conversation, represent two opposite kinds of bankruptcy? But I haven't the
play here and may be mistaken. I don't approve of your saying, in connection with O'Neill's *Iceman*, that it is amazing how different the results
can be when different authors treat similar themes, and then not telling
how O'Neill and Gorky differ. This is not good critical practice. How
does the reader know what you mean? There is no question that O'Neill
was imitating Gorky, and it seems to me that the plays are much the same.
In both cases, the saviour is a fake and has nothing but illusions to give.
I was surprised that you didn't mention the reminiscences of Lenin as

* *Russian Writers: Notes and Essays.*

603

well as those of Tolstoy and Chekhov, and discuss Gorky's relations with Lenin. I hadn't understood till I read your chapter why they got along so well together, and how well equipped Gorky already was to be a spokesman for Lenin's revolution. You say that Trotsky was accused of killing Gorky but not that this is incredible and that, on the contrary, there is a strong suspicion that Stalin had him killed because Gorky was a thorn in his side. George Kennan believes this to be probable.

In any case, this must be the very best book that exists on the subject in any language. You are not hampered by political partisanship and you see the whole thing in a "context" of creative literature in general in a way that I don't think anybody else has done—at least, on such a scale. I am glad to see that the publishers have given you bold type and a distinguished format, which was not the case with the other book—since you yourself as a critic have improved with what Trotsky and other Marxists used to call "giant strides."

I was delighted with the Punch and Judy puppets. I have never seen a set like them and wish I could get the rest. It is the only Punch I have ever seen who really looks cruel and malignant. The traditional Punch is jolly in his way and bursts into song after committing his crimes. In England, the male spectators, after seeing him dispose of his family, the landlord, the police, the hangman, the devil—all enemies or impediments to the ordinary man—used to want to shake his hand and offer him a drink. But this Punch looks so disagreeable that I thought at first he must be the hangman—though the cap would seem to show that he is really Punch. The urbanely sneering barrister or judge is also something I have never seen before. This set seems to represent an original interpretation in which the characters are made more hateful . . . Love to you both . . .

As ever, Edmund

To Daniel Aaron   October 11, 1961
                                                           Cambridge
Dear Dan: Thanks for telling me about the Matthews article, which I have read with interest. I don't believe he is right in thinking that Punch and Judy weren't real to the spectators. The men in the audience, in England, used sometimes to want to shake Punch's hand and offer to buy him a drink, and this must have been due to the fact—as John Wain suggested to me—that he represented the victory of the ordinary man over everything that hampered and oppressed him: domestic life, the landlord, the law, and the fear of hell (why the doctor, I don't quite know). I am much interested in the introduction of the Crocodile, which appeared at a fairly early date. It is not true, as Matthews says, that Punch also vanquished the Crocodile. In every show I ever saw, the Crocodile got Punch in the end, and I think that the immorality of the original ending

was too much for the Victorian age, which couldn't let him go unpunished. The Punch and Judy show, you know, came in from the Continent with the Restoration, and the play originally ended with Punch's saying, "Hurrah, the Devil's dead!" Brander Matthews does, however, throw some light on where the Crocodile may have come from. I must read George Sand's essay.

I finally got Kate Chopin's *At Fault* on a microfilm from the Library of Congress, so if you ever want to read it, I have it. Though she arranges a happy ending, it is—like *The Awakening* and some of her short stories— extremely unconventional for its period. She is a curious and interesting writer, and I have never seen anything good written about her. I have hardly done her justice in my book.

It is taking me about a week to rewrite my Civil War Introduction. I think that you and Stuart [Hughes] were right in saying that it ought to be longer or shorter, and I am making it considerably longer.

Let us know when you get to Cambridge. As ever, Edmund

To Helen Muchnic   November 6, 1961
                                                Cambridge

Dear Helen: I have delayed so long in acknowledging the puppets because I have been correcting the proofs of my book. This set is very much like one that I have had for years and with which I used to do soap operas for the children, but these things were always made by hand, and there are always interesting differences—the Devil is quite different. The policeman is, however, the same, except that the German manufacture is shown by the double eagle on his helmet. Elena says that the Punch figure is probably not Punch but Kasperl, the German equivalent of Punch. In the other set that you sent me, I am inclined to think—after studying Cruikshank's drawings of the old Punch and Judy characters—that the figure you thought was Punch is the Hangman. I am preparing to make use of him in our coming production as an apparition that represents the irreducibly evil side of Punch's nature. I am delighted to have all these figures. One of the ones in the second set is completely unrecognizable to me and must represent something in the German play that I do not know about—perhaps a lawyer.

I see a great stack of your book at the Harvard Coop and hope it is going well. I haven't seen any reviews. Love to Dorothy. Edmund

To John Dos Passos   November 7, 1961
                                                Cambridge

Dear Dos: I regret the demolition of the Princeton Club. We are now in the Columbia Club—a rather queer and to me rather uncomfortable place. Yes, I admire Salinger—haven't read the Hapgood book.

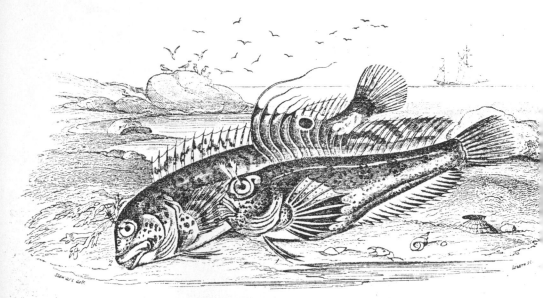

1 Butterfly Fish. 2 Gattoruginous Blenny.

To Morton D. Zabel   Christmas 1961

[Postcard]

Dear Morton: On the other side you will find, not a message of Christmas cheer, but a symbolical representation of the plight of the literati—you and me—in the present state of the world. I didn't testify for [Henry] Miller; wasn't asked to. My book will be out in March or April.

Everybody sends love. Edmund

I've just finished the page proofs of my Civil War book—have written a long Introduction which nobody is going to approve of. I think that the U.S. is now even more of a mess than I did at the time of the Depression and wish I could spend my declining years somewhere else.

I've been studying Hungarian in more or less the same spirit that other people do crossword puzzles. (It does have the relevance, however, that in Talcottville I am surrounded by hundreds of Hungarians who came over in 1914, and I have gone on to them from the Iroquois.) I am full of discomfitures produced not only by the state of the world but also by unpaid back taxes and gout, which is constantly aggravated by the horrible climate of Cambridge. I was upset by Hemingway's death, but it makes it more understandable to know that he had been taking shock treatments and was part of the time quite out of his mind.

There is an important and fascinating new book in its field—*Cavalier and Yankee* by William Taylor—about the reciprocal myths created about the North and the South in the first half of the nineteenth century.

Love from us both to the family, and, as Benchley used to say, be sure to drop in when you come to Fall River.   EW

To Robert Lowell   December 11, 1961
                                                                Cambridge
Dear Robert: Sorry to hear about your chicken pox. I had both measles and scarlatina when I was grown up and have never been sicker. Mrs. [Esther] Brooks invited us to dinner for this Saturday, but Helen and I are giving our Punch and Judy show at five in the afternoon, and we shouldn't be able to get there in time. Couldn't you come to the show? I have made Punch and Judy into a great ritual drama—which I suppose it always more or less was. That was a very good poem of yours in the *Observer*.   Love to Elizabeth, Edmund

"PATRIOTIC GORE"*
1947–1962

To Philip Vaudrin   April 21, 1947
Oxford University Press   Wellfleet

Dear Mr. Vaudrin: Thank you for your letter. The book I contemplate
is a fairly elaborate affair, which will begin with the literature of the
Civil War and go up through Edith Wharton. I have been working on it
off and on for some time, but shall not have it written for years.

The idea is to excavate a period which, though it is just behind us, has
been really very little explored. We have set our values straight about the
Hawthorne–Emerson–Melville generation but are still quite in the dark as
to what is first-rate and what is second-rate after that. When you go into
it, you find many surprises. I shall write about G. W. Cable, De Forest,
Harriet Beecher Stowe, Miss Woolson, Grierson, and Fuller, Crane, Norris,
Clyde Fitch, J. J. Chapman, Harold Frederic, Kirkland, Owen Wister,
Santayana, etc.

If you are interested in anything so remote as that, we might talk about
it. I'd have to have $2,000 down and a straight fifteen percent.

Sincerely yours, Edmund Wilson

To Philip Vaudrin   May 17, 1947
                                                    The New Yorker
Dear Vaudrin: . . . I enclose a memorandum for the English office. By the
way, do you think it would be any use to try to interest them in *The
Shock of Recognition*, that collection of documents on American literature
that Doubleday published? I thought, when it first came out, that Secker
and Warburg would be interested in it as a guide to our literary history.
But they didn't show the slightest enthusiasm. I didn't realize till I went

---

* From 1948 to 1961, *The New Yorker* published chapters of *Patriotic Gore*.

to London two years ago how earnestly anxious the English were *not* to learn about the United States.   . Sincerely, Edmund Wilson

The book I am working on is to deal with some of the more important figures in American literature between the Civil War and about 1910. The pre-Civil War period has, during the last quarter century, been pretty well studied and cleared up. We are able to see now who was first-rate in that period better than the people of the time could. But the later half of the century, though it lies just behind us, has never really been excavated yet. Everybody knows Mark Twain and Henry James; but one finds, when one begins to read in it, that there are writers of the first importance whose work is today scarcely known. I propose to throw these into relief and to let lesser people, even though more famous, sink more or less into the background.

I shall begin with a general discussion of the literature of the Civil War, which is more abundant and more interesting than is usually realized, and go on to discuss the effect of the war on the writers who had fought in it and survived it—a Southerner like Sidney Lanier and a Northerner like Ambrose Bierce* . . . The book will differ from those of Van Wyck Brooks in being more critical and less historical.

To Peter Davison   June 26, 1958
Atlantic Monthly Press   *The New Yorker*

. . . My original idea was to write a book about the American literature of the period after the Civil War, but I became so interested in the period of the war that I decided to do a book about it. I hope eventually to get on to the later period, but it will have to be for some years hence . . .

> Have only just finished my seminars [the Christian Gauss Seminars, Princeton, 1952–1953], for which I had to write some 10,000 words a week about the American literature of the Civil War . . .
>
> . . . suggested giving them [the American Seminar in Salzburg, February 1954] the Civil War . . .
>
> . . . the new Lowell lectureship at Harvard 1959–1960 . . . shall give them my Civil War . . .

To John Dos Passos   September 8, 1952
                                                              Princeton

. . . I've been reading up the literature on the Civil War—some of which is wonderful. There are a number of books that ought to be classics but

---

* Deletion of list of names which appear in letter of April 21, 1947.

are not because the Civil War has to some extent been a taboo subject. The South wouldn't read the Northern books about it, and the North wanted to forget the whole thing. There are some books that every American ought to read, but that haven't been assigned in schools and colleges, because they wouldn't go down with the Southerners: *Herndon's Lincoln; Grant's Personal Memoirs;* Thomas Wentworth Higginson's *Army Life in a Black Regiment; Uncle Tom's Cabin;* Francis Grierson's *The Valley of Shadows . . .*

To John Dos Passos   April 30, 1953
                                                            Wellfleet
. . . Have changed some of my ideas about the Civil War since I was talking to you last winter. It is a period that has always been hard to grasp because it is hard to face—though so much is being written about it nowadays. But in my opinion Carl Sandburg is the worst thing that has happened to Lincoln since Booth shot him, and I can't imagine either Grant or Lee getting through *John Brown's Body . . .*

To Mamaine Koestler   December 5, 1953
                                                            Wellfleet
. . . My English publishers—W. H. Allen—are showing some recalcitrance about the book I am doing now. It is a book about the American literature of the Civil War period and the writers who were affected by the war, and Allen's point of view seems to be that the British have no interest in this. I know that it is true that the English did used to be rather ignorant about it. An aunt of mine whose sister married an Englishman discovered, when she went to visit her, that her brother-in-law and his friends had never heard of our Civil War or of anybody connected with it. But I get the impression nowadays, from *The New Statesman* and *The Times Literary Supplement*, that people over there are paying more attention to American literature and history. Do you suppose that your publishers would have any interest in bringing out an English edition? It will certainly be one of my best books—in some ways, more like the *Finland Station* than like, say, *Axel's Castle*. The chapters, as I now plan them, are: Harriet Beecher Stowe; Francis Grierson; Lincoln; Grant; Frederick Olmsted; the Women Diarists; Sidney Lanier; George W. Cable; John De Forest; Ambrose Bierce; Justice Holmes. You have probably never heard of most of them. It was not a period when belles-lettres particularly flourished, and the novelists and poets who had been in it before they began to write never quite got over it or adjusted themselves to post-war America, where commercialism ran riot. But I don't know of any other historical crisis in which everybody was so articulate. They wrote their whole drama so thoroughly that their

speeches and articles and diaries and letters and memoirs make most fiction about it seem pale; and a study of the literature of the period becomes more or less a history of what happened. (This is a little blurb.) . . .

To ALFRED KAZIN   February 5, 1954
                                               American Seminar, Salzburg
. . . I found, by the way, in Paris and London, that some educated people didn't know the difference between the Civil War and the Revolution, and that in England they were likely to think that I was going to lecture about Cromwell . . .

To HAMILTON BASSO   June 5, 1955
                                                        The New Yorker
. . . We were interested in what you say about the revival in the South of the spirit of 1861—I had been getting that impression from reading the papers . . . I am back on the Civil War, reading more Southern diaries. Did you happen to see my article on that hair-raising book, Sut Lovingood? I am going to put Sut into the middle of a chapter on Sidney Lanier . . .

To LEON EDEL   December 4, 1952
                                                           Princeton
Dear Mr. Edel: Somewhere Henry James writes—in a letter, I think— about Justice Holmes's little volume of speeches, saying that he finds it somehow unsatisfactory. I thought it was in a letter to William, but cannot find it, and I can't find among my James documents the correspondence with Holmes that I know was published somewhere. I am applying to you, because I know that you have James at your fingertips.
     . . . I'll be grateful if you can tell me about the James reference, but don't bother about it if you don't know it right off.
                                               Yours sincerely, Edmund Wilson

To FELIX FRANKFURTER   April 20, 1953
                                                        The New Yorker
Dear Felix: Thank you for your letters and the opinions, which I read with interest. If it is not too much trouble, I wish you would send me— as Holmes did with Laski—any others, as they come up, that you think I ought to read. I am glad that Marion approved of the Grant article. I hope you will read the one on Holmes and Laski, which ought to be out in a couple of weeks. Our conversation helped me in writing it. I'll look up the article on Holmes's early writings when I go into the subject more thoroughly, as I'll have to do later on.
     Thank you, also, for the tickets to the Senate and House and for your

other kindnesses in Washington. The new Supreme Court Building, which I had not seen, is certainly a splendid and impressive affair.

We immensely enjoyed our evening with you. My family have gone back to Wellfleet, and I am going back there next week. I am about to start on a new book, on some aspects of which I should sometime like to talk to you. Where is it you go in the summer, and how far is it from Pittsfield? I'll probably be going through there sometime, and might stop off to see you, if it's not too far.   As ever, Edmund W

To Felix Frankfurter   May 28, 1953
                                        Wellfleet

Dear Felix: Thank you for the letter about my Laski–Holmes review, and for the corrections, which I'll attend to when I revise it. I was especially glad to know exactly when Holmes reread Marx, because I couldn't find out from the correspondence and was wondering whether I had put it too late.

I have become very much interested in the Old Testament tradition in America. I ran into it in connection with the Civil War and realized how important it had always been in this country for everybody connected with the early New Englanders or strongly influenced by them. I believe that it was at one time proposed to make Hebrew the language of the country. Later on, when Calvinism went to pieces like the Wonderful One Hoss in the fable of the elder Holmes, people wanted to get away from the rigors of the old discipline and from the apocalyptic notions of the Civil War. But these were something fundamental in our civilization and have 'been among the elements that have differentiated us from England, where they never had the same scope. I took a course in Hebrew last winter at the Princeton Theological Seminary and got a better idea than I had had before of the power of the Jewish moral vision and what its effects had been. I have arranged to do for *The New Yorker*—no kidding—an article on reading the Pentateuch for the first time, and I shall have to deal with the whole subject in connection with the Civil War, when I come to do my book.

Love from us both to Marion. Perhaps I may see you this summer.
                                        As ever, Edmund W

To Felix Frankfurter   May 1, 1956
                                        Wellfleet

Dear Felix: It was curious to get your letter the other morning, for I had just got around to reading—with much interest—your Marshall address the night before. I shall have to try to deal with these matters when I get to my chapter on Holmes—and shall reread it then.

612

Thank you for the review, which I hadn't seen.

In looking up something this morning in Theodore Roosevelt's correspondence, I was amused to read his ferocious letter to you, of 1917, apropos of the Mooney case.

I am sorry to hear that Marion has still not wholly recovered. Please give her our love. As ever, Edmund W

To Felix Frankfurter December 14, 1957
Wellfleet

Dear Felix: I was glad to hear from you—have often thought about you lately struggling with all those damned problems.

I sent you *A Piece of My Mind* mainly on account of the memoir of my father. Now I am trying to get finished by some time next year a book about the literature of the Civil War. Tell Marion that I am more and more impressed by Grant, in spite of his weakness as a President. I wonder whether she has ever read a curious, amusing, and valuable book called *Around the World with General Grant.*

Eventually I hope we may get to Washington and have a chance to see you. In the meantime, love and Christmas greetings. Edmund W

To Felix Frankfurter July 28, 1961
Talcottville

Dear Felix: Thank you for your letter about Holmes. The man who wrote to *Commentary* said that the story about the Wendells being Jewish came directly from you; but I am not going to say that in my book. About Barrett Wendell: he was inclined to believe in a theory that most of the original New Englanders were Jewish because they had come from a part of England that was mostly inhabited by Jews. There was actually a Jewish self-identification, by way of the Old Testament, on the part of the early New Englanders. You find it in some of Harriet Beecher Stowe's novels and elsewhere.* This was undoubtedly what was at work in Barrett Wendell's mind. The older Oliver Wendell Holmes, by the way, was strongly pro-Jewish. Please remember me to Marion.

As ever, Bunny W

---

* "Hebrew," he writes, "is the principal tongue in the hierarchy of languages, the mother of profound and exalted emotions, the most primitive and authoritative medium for the expression of transcendent praise and ineffable sorrow."
—Francis Grierson, as quoted in *Patriotic Gore*
". . . no doubt, the traditional prestige which the Jews have had in New England is due to the self-identification of the Puritans with the Old Testament Israelites."
—"Justice Holmes," in *Patriotic Gore*
"Julia Ward Howe, when she composed 'The Battle Hymn of the Republic,' went directly back to Isaiah." —"The Jews," in *A Piece of My Mind*

To ARLIN TURNER   August 18, 1957
Duke University   Talcottville

Dear Mr. Turner: I am wondering whether the next step might not be
to try to get Anchor Books to bring out, in one volume, *The Silent South*
and *The Negro Question*, with *My Politics* as an introduction—as [G. W.]
Cable originally intended it to be—to the second edition of *The Silent
South*, and a preface by you which would summarize the whole interesting story of the reaction to these writings of Cable's. Do you think it would
be possible to get permission to bring out *My Politics* in this way? It is
so important and interesting that it seems to me it ought to be published.
Have you seen Richard Chase's discussion of *The Grandissimes* in his new
book . . . I think it is extremely good. I have just been through your book
again in the course of doing my essay on it and Cable—every student of
American literature must be grateful to you for having done it so well . . .
I am sorry that, on page 158, you do not tell what the incident was that
led Cable to speak out about the Negro question. The reader expects to
be told and I did not find out till I read *My Politics*.
                                        Yours sincerely, Edmund Wilson

To ARLIN TURNER   August 31, 1957
                                                           Talcottville
. . . About the proposed Anchor Book: I don't think Cable's short stories
would combine very well with his essays. I am afraid that it would
bewilder and put off the book buyer. The two books on Southern problems, with *My Politics* and an introduction by you, would be quite
enough material for an Anchor Book—some of them are not that long. It
could be called *The Negro Question* . . .
    I have just been talking to [Jason] Epstein, and he seems to think that
it might also be a good idea to bring out a volume of stories. I would
suggest a selection from *Old Creole Days* and *Strange True Stories*—
actually the latter book seems to me at least as interesting as the former
. . . One other small point in your book . . . you seem to say that by 1888
Cable was definitely discouraged by the enactment of state laws restricting
Negro rights. Isn't it true that the first disfranchising enactment was the
poll tax of 1890 in Mississippi and that the other similar laws were spread
through the following decade? . . .

To CHAUNCEY HACKETT   March 3, 1958
                                                             Wellfleet
. . . I am still struggling with the Civil War, have been reading military
memoirs. My greatest surprise has been Sherman's book—I had had no
idea that he was such an interesting character—rather complex, even a

little unbalanced. My chapter on the subject ought to be out in *The New Yorker* sometime before Easter . . .

To ALLEN TATE — July 3, 1959
Talcottville

. . . I am going to be at Harvard next year unloading my book on the Civil War, which I hope to finish then. My view of it, I can see from talking to various people, is going to be very unpopular . . . Your article on Southern literature was one of your best. But have you read [John Pendleton] Kennedy's *Swallow Barn* (1832)? It is just as realistically observant as Longstreet and a good deal more distinguished. By the way, in rereading the other day your essay on Emily Dickinson—which, otherwise, I like, though I think that you overrate her a little—I found a certain vagueness in regard to New England. Thomas Wentworth Higginson was never editor of *The Atlantic Monthly*, nor did he try to correct Emily's poems. On the contrary, he was defending her incorrectitudes against the Boston editors. See the volume of correspondence that deals with it.

What has happened to Tate the poet? John Berryman has sent me some extraordinary stuff . . .

To SHELDON MEYER — April 17, 1961
Oxford University Press — Cambridge

Dear Meyer: Thank you very much for your letter. You have caught some inaccuracies, and I was interested in your comments. It is true that the chapters are sometimes rather lumpy—but, as in the case of John Brown and Stonewall Jackson, I had the peculiar problem of being obliged to introduce important characters not through their own writings but through what other people wrote about them. There are also some *longueurs* of quotation. You, however, I think, partly misunderstand what I am aiming to do. I want to show the *whole career* of all my major subjects, how they lived, what they thought about, and what their personalities were. *Uncle Tom's Cabin* is not, as you assume, the "focus" of the chapter on Mrs. Stowe. The crisis in Calvinism is a very important element in the history of that time. I return to it in the later chapters when I deal with the New Englanders of the next generation. Certain of your questions are evidently due to your not getting the clue to some of my themes—the corruption of the post-war period (Grant's later career), the psychology of men committed to war (the Shermans)—both of which themes are to be among the principal subjects of the soldier De Forest's novels. It is one purpose of my introduction to give the reader these clues, so that he will understand the direction of my emphasis. I am also trying to cover all the literature of any distinction inspired by first-hand experience of the war:

hence Melville's poem has to be dealt with, and it gives me a chance to start another theme, very important in the later chapters: the intimacy between North and South in their fratricidal relations.

But when I go down again, I'll bring your letter, and we can go over your points one by one. I hope to have the whole text by the beginning of May, with the exception of the Introduction.

Sincerely, Edmund Wilson

Max Nomad, whose first book, *Rebels and Renegades*, appeared in 1932, has occupied a unique position in the intellectual world of New York . . . What has made him a connoisseur of radicals?
(*The Bit Between My Teeth*, 1960)

To Max Nomad   June 20, 1961
                                                                              Wellfleet

Dear Max: First of all, thank you for the books. I was especially pleased with the alphabet book, which is fascinating. It is particularly useful to me because it has the alphabet of Hebrew script, which I have never been able to get anywhere else, and I have usually found it impossible to decipher letters that were written me in this script. I am also glad to have the argot dictionaries. I already had several, but not these.

I was delighted to hear that *Apostles of Revolution* is going into paperback, too. I have been reading *Non-believers* with interest. I don't know about the title, though. It isn't the non-believers who need it: they have already come to your conclusions . . .

I have finished my Civil War book—all but the Introduction, which I am dreading, as I shall have to try to put the Civil War in the perspective of our whole foreign policy before and after. I am going to compare Lenin, Lincoln, and Bismarck and show that they all had a good deal in common—which may well so offend some readers that they will not go on with the book.   Please remember me to your wife. Edmund W

To Daniel Aaron   February 5, 1962
                                                                              Cambridge

Dear Dan: Thanks for your letter, which reassured me. I had the book around so long that I finally got bored and depressed by it. I am sorry you read the galleys (please don't show them to anyone else): I made considerable corrections even in the page proofs. Did you get the revised Introduction? Please be sure to check any quotations with the text of the finished book. Let us know when you come to Cambridge.

As ever, Edmund

Yes: do send me your review.

To DANIEL AARON   March 5, 1962
                                                       Cambridge
Dear Dan: Of course, I was pleased by your article. Copies of the book
will be ready on Friday, and I'll have one sent you. Note the title page:
I also have a quotation from John Brown to balance the Southern one.
A few notes:
    p. 17. Did I really write "Nobody North nor South"? If I did, I
shouldn't have.
    p. 13. I don't understand the first sentence of the second paragraph:
what do you mean by "America could not escape history"?
    p. 9. I don't think you should use "insular" here—which properly ap-
plies to an island.
    p. 14. I hope that you and Mark Twain are not misusing "jejune" here.
It means arid, sterile, not juvenile.   As ever, Edmund

To HELEN MUCHNIC   February 9, 1962
                                                       Cambridge
Dear Helen: I have been reassured by Dan's enthusiasm, because I got
rather bored with the Civil War book . . . But I have now pulled myself
together and am writing about Swinburne—a pleasant relief. Don't let
your eagerness to read the Civil War book lead you to get the galleys
from Dan—it has been heavily revised since then, and I am sorry he read
it in this form. Elena is as enthusiastic about your book as you say Dan
is about mine—also tells everybody about it—so maybe literature flourishes
in spite of everything. Love to Dorothy. Eventually I'll be coming your
way.   Edmund

To HELEN MUCHNIC   April 4, 1962
                                                       Cambridge
. . . Thanks very much for your letter. I was afraid people were going to
be bored, but so far I have had mostly favorable reactions. I don't understand what you mean about there being a contradiction between the
Introduction and the rest of the book. The book is supposed to develop
the theme that I stated in the Introduction . . .

To NEWTON ARVIN   March 31, 1962
                                                       Cambridge
Dear Newton: Thanks very much for your letter. I deplore Henry James's
idea that the South "deserved" to lose, because it implies a moral judgment
of the kind that I am trying to eliminate. I remember how Woodrow
Wilson said, in connection with the war of 1870, that the French deserved
to lose on account of their frivolity and immorality.
    I look forward to your book on Longfellow, about whom I have never

read anything interesting, even in Van Wyck Brooks, but who could, I am sure, be made interesting.

We hope at some point to get to Northampton, though we don't know exactly when.   As ever, Edmund

To Barbara Deming   April 11, 1962
                                                      Cambridge

Dear Barbara: . . . In regard to the points you raise: I think that Lincoln, Wilson, and F.D.R. were all carried into war by the power drive behind them—though they all, as you say, must have had moments, Woodrow Wilson especially, when they hoped that it might be avoided. I don't believe that it is possible to be President and not be willing to lead the country into war. Nobody can get to be President who has not himself a strong drive to power.

I am not myself a pacifist. I think it was quite right for the American colonists to take up arms against the British, who were using force to keep them in subjection. In the case of resistance movements, I approve of the use of force if I sympathize with the people resisting—that is, I approved of the French when they were resisting the German occupation, but I don't approve of the resistance of the O.A.S. I am concerned in my Introduction only with national expansionism . . .   Love, Edmund

To Celia Goodman   October 5, 1962
                                                      Talcottville

. . . I'm glad you got something out of *Patriotic Gore*. The Introduction got me denounced in editorials in *Time* and in *American Heritage*, an illustrated magazine that glorifies American history. They rejected an appreciative review on the ground, I was told, that if they printed it they would be taking the bread out of their own mouths . . .

To Helen Muchnic   April 17, 1962
                                                      Cambridge

Dear Helen: I don't agree at all that, in the event of war, the "individuals have made certain choices, more or less consciously, and know that they must hold on to them for the duration." I have learned, from my experience of the army, that most non-professional soldiers don't know what it's all supposed to be about. They have simply been grabbed by the government and herded into service. Most of them don't want to be there, but know that if they deserted, they would be shot. Not that most of the professional soldiers know what wars are about, either. They may have chosen the profession, and in this case, they are not in a position to criticize the cause; but they have not always even chosen that: remember the case of Grant, who did not want to go to West Point and did not approve of the war with Mexico. I was much interested in that chapter of *War and Peace*. So

618

far from being unnecessary and better omitted, as some stupid people think, it is one of the few things that make the book great. I should have added above that the group psychology doesn't begin merely after a war has been declared. It is going on all the time, and we are all more or less victims of it. It takes self-discipline and usually education even partially to detach ourselves from it. Of course, there are also men in service who have responded to the group drive themselves or been persuaded by the official propaganda.

We do hope to see you soon—perhaps at the end of May.

Love as ever, Edmund

To Alfred Kazin   May 20, 1962
                                                                   Talcottville

. . . I found a copy of *The Reporter*, in which I reread your review. I don't think you quite understand my point of view. I didn't mean to imply that the Jews were responsible for the U.S. getting into the last war; but I don't think that we would have gone into the war at all in order to defend the Jews. Nor do I think that we fought the Civil War in order to liberate the Negroes. What I was trying to do in my book was to show that these conflicts are not moral battles but battles for power . . .

To Alfred Kazin   May 30, 1962
                                                                   Talcottville

. . . No clear line can be drawn between man and the other animals. You can't say that animals don't have "ideals." Their ideals, like those of men, are shown in what they have made of themselves. My Introduction is not unconsciously but deliberately non-political. I am trying to get behind politics. I believe, as I say there, that many intellectuals think in political and economic terms too much. They ought to pay more attention to zoology and anthropology.

Are the Germany, the Russia, and the United States established by the leaders I mention really so very different? We vastly admired modern Germany and they admired us. We and Russia are now competing and becoming more and more alike. The more we expand as a power unit, the more centralized we have to become, and Washington in many ways already exerts a tyrannical power . . .

To Alfred Kazin   June 2, 1962
                                                                   Talcottville

. . . To continue our conversation. You asked whether the Manchester mill workers and the foreign volunteers in the Civil War were deluded because they supported the North. They were, in the same sense as those American workers and others who supported the Soviet Union. They did not know what was going to result, and that this would not be to the advantage of the cause they were hoping to serve. Of course, this seemed at the time to be the right thing to do, but it is foolish, in the long run, to support either the Kremlin or the Washington government when they are doing something completely different from what they had promised to do and what such people expected of them. It is dangerous to continue to defend a war or to continue to be loyal to a revolution because it seems to have accomplished some aim one desired. We were all delighted when Hitler was smashed—so much so that we did not notice that our indiscriminate bombing of German cities only discredited our moral case, or at the time feel very much regret at annihilating those Japanese cities. We were all out to get Hitler, but in order to do so, we made an ally of another modern tyrant who had been doing the same things, on the same monstrous scale, and allowed him to carry out his own predatory conquests, than which Hitler's could hardly have been more oppressive. I think we ought to train ourselves to disassociate our views of war from these moral attitudes, which are mostly romantic literature such as a government that is bent on making war can always manufacture and exploit in an improved and streamlined form. In the case of the Civil War, I believe that the most embarrassing policy the North could have adopted with the South would have been to allow them to secede. They would have been stuck with their unworkable economy and would have had to come to terms with the modern world (their aggressiveness, of which you speak, could never have been effective), just as at present the most embarrassing thing we could do with Russia would be to abandon nuclear testing . . .

To Robert Penn Warren   August 12, 1962
                                                      Talcottville
Dear Red: Thank you very much for your article, which pleased me more than anything else that has been written about *Patriotic Gore*, because it got deeper into the book.

Of course the Introduction is full of moral indignation, and I thought, after it was printed, that I should have said, not that I was trying to remove the subject from the plane of morality altogether, but that I wanted to remove it from the old melodramatic plane and consider it from the point of view of an anti-war morality.

Best regards to you and Eleanor. Let us know if you get to Cambridge.
                                                      Edmund W

To T. S. Matthews   August 25, 1962
                                                      Talcottville
. . . I know that my Introduction is inadequate to the questions it raises, but I thought that they had to be raised in connection with the Civil War. What you are supposed to "applaud" is my anti-war "message."

Several people have complained that I talk about removing the subject from the moral plane, and then show moral indignation . . .

To Max Eastman   [undated, ? 1962]

. . . I'm sorry you found *Patriotic Gore* hard to keep open. That format which I use for all my books was designed to make them convenient to handle. I have suffered from these huge heavy American books that collapse on me when I am reading them in bed . . . I know my Introduction is inadequate, but I am supplementing it with a kind of pamphlet,* which I'll be sending you in due course. The chief reason that we're being soaked for taxes is that we're supposed to need billions for national defense against this Russian bugaboo, in which (the bugaboo) I do not believe. Surely the Soviet Union is also pulling in its claws. I suspect in you the survival of old-fashioned attitudes appropriate to the Stalin era. I can't conceive that there is or has ever been any danger of the Russians invading and dominating the U.S. . . .

* *The Cold War and the Income Tax.*

1962

AND

"O CANADA"

To Van Wyck Brooks

January 2, 1962
Wellfleet

Dear Van Wyck: This is to say Happy New Year to you and Gladys—though I don't have much hope for anything very cheerful for 1962.

I've finished my book on the Civil War literature and shall be sending you a copy in a couple of months. It owes so much of a debt to you that I really am unable to tell—in regard to my ideas about cultural phenomena —how much they were originally derived from you and how much I have contributed myself. In any case, if your books had not been written, this book would probably never have been written.

I read your *Shadow of the Mountain* with my usual enjoyment. You were clever to connect that passage in *Daisy* with our picnic at Independence River. There are three small errors, which I'll indicate since you aim at perfection. On p. 130, it should be Via Giulia—unless there is a *Villa* Giulia. At the bottom of p. 169, it should evidently be *scripsisti*. The Zuñis —p. 188—are in New Mexico, not Arizona. What makes it perhaps confusing is that they have a sacred lake in Arizona. I don't object to *all* of Howells's New England novels. I like one that you don't like: *The Minister's Charge*.

Waldo Frank has been here for Christmas. He has written—rather to my surprise, since I expected something pontifical and perfunctory like his books on Russia and Israel—a very fine full-length book about Cuba. It is the one of his books I have read that seems to me most successful. I am astonished at his continued vitality. I had been so much depressed myself by my negative feelings nowadays—I think that this country is a mess and I don't approve of anything that the government is doing—and the mainly negative character of my Civil War book, that it quite bucked me up to read anything so affirmative and so imaginatively colorful as Waldo on Cuba.

Have you seen William Taylor's *Cavalier and Yankee*—which seems to me a brilliant and rather important book.

Love from us both to you both. The Givens say they see you in summer and that you are active to a degree of which I am now incapable.

As ever, Edmund Wilson

To Mary Meigs   January 19, 1962
                                                          Cambridge

Dear Mary: I told you last night over the phone that my translation of *The Bronze Horseman* is in my book *The Triple Thinkers*.

We have seen the Chinese show, which is wonderful, though Elena says that most of the stuff is not of the very first rank. I could see that you must have been delighted with all those trees and twigs. How did you like the bamboo grove after the snowstorm and the green-eyed twelfth-century kitten? I was so enchanted by the calligraphic exhibits that I couldn't bear that I was too old to learn Chinese, which I've always wanted to do. Arthur Waley told me that I could more or less master it in nine months, but he attacked it just after he got out of Oxford. I have found that there is a man in the library here who repairs the bindings of books— a difficult job, it seems, unless you have them completely rebound—and I am going to take the Maurice Sand there tomorrow . . .

I don't think that *Our Mutual Friend* is really so good as *Bleak House* and *Little Dorrit*, but it belongs to the same group. Be sure to go on and read *Edwin Drood*, in which he is embarking on something different. I look back with much feeling to my last days in Wellfleet. I came to realize afterwards that I had never seen so much of you by ourselves before.

We are doing our Punch and Judy show Sunday. Helen is becoming quite proud of it. Tonight a Norwegian is coming to dinner who has been writing a thesis on Kate Chopin, that remarkable Franco-Irish Southern American novelist. You and Barbara ought to read her, but her books are quite impossible to find except in libraries. I am trying to get her reprinted. Do you know about her at all? She shocked and shook the nineties with a Lawrencesque novel (in subject, not style) called *The Awakening*. I am working on my journals, which I am turning into a kind of memoirs— though I don't know how or when they can ever be published. Am reading Swinburne's letters, which are delightful—they take my mind off other things, including my own past life. He almost never thought about anything but literature. Love to you both.   Edmund

To Mary Meigs   February 17, 1962
                                                          Cambridge
. . . I was very much interested in your ideas about *Edwin Drood*. Since
I wrote, there has been a long paper written on the probability that
Datchery is Bazzard. I'll lend it to you if you want to read it. You may
be right about Helena. The figure in the lantern light on the cover certainly looks like a woman. I didn't mean that Scrooge was clinically a
manic depressive—simply that his sudden change of disposition reflected
the alternations of Dickens. If you wanted to go seriously into *Edwin
Drood*, you would have to get Robertson Nicoll's book, which I don't think
I have. The corrections Dickens made in the MS throw some light on the
impressions that he wanted to give the reader—or rather, on the things that
he didn't want the reader to find out at that part of the story . . .

        . . . the other great Swinburne specialist, Mr. Cecil Y. Lang . . . who
        has edited for the first time the whole of Swinburne's extant corre-
        spondence.   (*The Bit Between My Teeth*, 1962)

To Cecil Lang   February 6, 1962
                                                          Cambridge
Dear Lang: I have been reading right through your Swinburne letters—
am now in Volume IV. I have really been enjoying them immensely: it is
pleasant, after years with the Civil War, to read again about somebody
who is occupied entirely with literature (one can't take his politics seriously). I see that the last two volumes are announced for April 1. I hope
that Yale will send me copies of the books as soon as they are ready . . .
since they will be easier to handle than these page proofs. I am planning
a long article for the spring. Thanks for having the index sent me.
    I congratulate you on this feat—your spotting of the many quotations
seems to me almost supernatural. You must have had a devil of a time
with the printers. I see that you have corrected a good many of the errors
—am including a list of other passages that caught my eye and that may or
may not be wrong.
    Where did you find the amusing self-parody (not from the *Heptalogia*)
which you quote in your Introduction? Is the text of the Bonchurch edition
as unreliable as Hughes says? Though I assume that nothing is as bad as
he says.
    I wanted to look you up on two trips that I made to Utica but was so
overwhelmed by income-tax difficulties that I didn't have the heart for
Swinburne. I expect to be coming over in the early summer. How long
will you be at Syracuse? I am anxious to have a long talk with you.
                                            Sincerely, Edmund Wilson

To Cecil Lang   February 24, 1962
                                                        Cambridge
. . . I find that the *Whippingham Papers* are here in Houghton, but I
think I can do without them. I should, however, be extremely grateful if
you could send me *La Fille du policeman* and *La Soeur de la Reine*, the
incidents of which I've partly forgotten. If you could send them registered,
I'll return them in the same way. By the way, isn't there something wrong
in the second line from the bottom of the last note on p. 142? Should
en nomme be *un nommé* perhaps? Here are some other possible blemishes:* . . .

I'm not sure I understand how your index works; but have been
struggling with one of my own and am only just coming to understand
the kind of problems involved. My own index may well be annoying and
eccentric . . .

To Cecil Lang   March 1, 1962
                                                        Cambridge
. . . I agree with you that "[sic]" is a nuisance. I have almost entirely eliminated it from my Civil War book. I warn the reader at the beginning and
then let Lincoln write *apparantly* for *apparently*, etc. . . .

To Allen Tate   February 9, 1962
                                                        Cambridge
Dear Allen: My copy of Mattie's [Josephson] book is at my lawyer's. At
first I had the idea of writing him a letter which should begin as follows:
"*Cher faux dadaiste démodé,* [illegible word] *immonde, farçi de merde,
dans les entrailles de Rousseau et de Stendhal.*" I also conceived the
project of writing a letter to the literary papers which should commence:
"When I first met Matthew Josephson in the early twenties, he persuaded
me to read the manuscript of a novel unusually lacking in promise. He
has now written another inferior work of fiction which he has attempted
to make more interesting by giving the characters the names of real
people." The course I decided on will appear from the enclosed letters
(which please return). The publisher's lawyer has written me that they
will omit the false statement about me in the next printing. I don't know
what could be done further except our all getting together for a mass
exposé of his slanders and misstatements, and that is hardly worthwhile.
As you say, he has evidently been suffering for years from resentments
against his betters, and he oughtn't to be allowed to think he has scored.

If you see or write to Katherine Anne [Porter], give her my love. It

---

* List of errata deleted.

was her beauty, not her storytelling, that "mesmerized" me the first time I met her, and I remember to have used this word in telling about it. But I don't remember ever to have printed it, and I don't know how Mattie came to know about this. In any case, he has of course got it wrong. I love her remark about him . . . As ever, Edmund

To Alfred Kazin   March 31, 1962
                                                                   Cambridge

Dear Alfred: I am proud of your dedication, and have been much enjoying the book.* The stuff seems even better collected—everything gets more weight. There is a lot that I have not read. You throw light for me on many matters. I disliked Karl Shapiro's book so much that I did not know what to do with it: I didn't want to send it to the dump and I didn't want to give it to a library, for fear it would mislead the young. Your review has persuaded me that the thing to do is to sell it to a second-hand book-store. I suppose you are right that the trouble with him is that he teaches and is reacting against the academic canon. As for Snow: I have hardly read his novels and don't want to try to read any more, and your discussion of them makes me feel that I know what they are.

I don't quite agree with you about Rexroth, whom I usually read with delight—and this does not date from his tribute to my poetry in his last collection of "Assays"—which I hope to have engraved on my tombstone. He has an absurd judgment or inaccurate statement on every other page, and I get tired of hearing him say that something or other is the greatest something or other "in any language." But he amuses me, and I approve of his reading so widely and think it is a good idea to disturb the accepted opinions by throwing the books around.

Your own book is a great bedside resource—I shall be reading it for days to come.

Love to Ann, and Elena sends love to you both and thanks for the inscription in the book.

This was written yesterday afternoon. Last night I read the very able political pieces in the latter part of the book. About Kennedy: I think you somewhat overrate his literacy. His historical allusions are likely to be inaccurate in a way which suggests that he cannot really have read much history. I suspect that his pretensions to "culture" are largely worked up by Arthur Schlesinger. (On Arthur himself you are perfect.) You speak of Kennedy's "immense power"; but what I am beginning to fear is that the President of the United States does not any longer have very much power—hence the blunders and frustrations of which you speak.

In the final essay on criticism, you say that I often declare myself to be

---

* *Contemporaries.*

"the mediator between artist and public." This is one of the clichés about me, but I don't remember to have said it. It is not my idea of what I do.

As ever, Edmund

To Alfred Kazin
April 13, 1962
Cambridge

Dear Alfred: I am still reading your book. The Dylan Thomas piece is particularly good—I hadn't given much thought to the subject. All the pieces gain weight from being massed together in this way. It makes it possible to take account of how far you have progressed since *On Native Grounds*. You are able to express yourself much better. I felt in your first book that you were better on contemporary writers than on the people further back; but now you have extended back your understanding of our literature and history. I was impressed by the political pieces, which I hadn't read before . . . Love to Ann.
As ever, Edmund

To Alfred Kazin
May 6, 1962
Cambridge

Dear Alfred: I am still reading your book, and I don't think my continued enthusiasm for it is due to the dedication, since I have usually in the past been suspicious of things that were dedicated to me. The generalizing pieces are very good, and this is a kind of thing that is not often done well. On top of this book the piece in *The Atlantic*—which may be the best thing you have so far written—makes me feel that you have really arrived in a way that you had not done before.
Best regards, Edmund W

In one of your Faulkner pieces, Major de Spain twice appears as *Mayor* de Spain.

To Jacob Landau
June 19, 1962
Wellfleet

Dear Jack: Do you know about Isaac [Bashevis] Singer, the Yiddish novelist? If not, I recommend strongly his novel *The Magician of Lublin*. (His new one, *The Slave*, I haven't read yet.) I met him at Cambridge and heard him read, and he has sent me this account of his visit. I want to write him about it, but though I can recognize Harvard and Rabbi Gold and Rabbi Zigmond and my own name, I am not geared for reading Yiddish. I should be extremely grateful if you would write me the substance of what he says. Note that I am now in Wellfleet. Thanks for your note about *Patriotic Gore*.
Sincerely, Edmund W

To Jacob Landau
June 25, 1962
Wellfleet

Dear Jack: Thanks so much for translating the Singer article. That evening was, as he intimates, a great personal success for himself as well as for

627

Rabbi Gold, who got it up. Gold is a fine man, much liked. He has a special knowledge of and a great enthusiasm for all the departments of Jewish literature; has been encouraging the translation of Agnon.

I was interested to hear about the Princeton commencement. I wish they hadn't named that library after John Foster Dulles!

Best regards, Edmund W

To Jacob Landau   October 5, 1962

. . . Did I tell you I saw Singer in Cambridge? He seemed to think himself that Yiddish would have to struggle to survive. I was very much impressed by him: he reads and talks so well that you don't notice his very heavy accent . . .

To Barbara Deming   August 4, 1962
                                                            Talcottville
Dear Barbara: Thanks for the books, which I haven't yet read, but I am about to attack that subject.* I had a long talk with Muste in New York, and he is getting for me information that I should otherwise have had trouble finding. He is interested in Stuart Hughes's campaign, which is getting much further than anybody expected—they now have 125,000 names. He will probably make inroads on Kennedy's vote, and somebody writing in *Newsweek* thinks he may have a bare chance of winning.†

I was interested to hear about the wildcat. There are many around here —they kill a good many deer, I am told, in the wilder part of the country west of Boonville, and it is something of a mystery why they should kill so many, since sometimes they leave them uneaten. Just the predatory impulse, I suppose. I have never, however, seen one alive except in a cage at the County Fair. He looked so frustrated and furious that I felt very sorry for him.

It was a relief to get away from Wellfleet—Reuel drove me up here the day before yesterday—I stayed perhaps a little too long. The pace seems to accelerate in the course of the summer. The Schlesingers, the Hofstadters, the Kazins, the Aarons, Ed O'Connor, the Wallings, sometimes the Jenckses, together with their summer guests, assemble in the afternoon on what Stuart calls *la plage des intellectuels*. Then they have drinks or dinner in various combinations. I enjoyed it up to a point, but there is more gossip and jokes than exchange of ideas, and I am glad to be settled down up here . . .

Love, Edmund

---

* *The Cold War and the Income Tax.*
† Stuart Hughes ran as a peace candidate against Edward Kennedy.

August 7, 1962
Talcottville

Dear Newton: I think it is obvious that—whether consciously or unconsciously on Holmes's part—*A Mortal Antipathy* is based on a straight homosexual case. Did you notice that he says in the foreword that women had said to him that he would be "afraid of" such a subject?—and then the hero's relationship with his servant may have been observed from life without Holmes's understanding it. But, then, it seems clear that he does not understand the importance of the masculine qualities of the heroine. All these three novels of Holmes's are psychologically interesting. The case of *Elsie Venner* is entirely implausible, but in the heroine of *The Guardian Angel* he has got hold of something real: a highly sexed girl in an undersexed community. There is a wonderful portrait in it of a certain kind of successful cold-blooded Bostonian—one of the men who wants to marry her.

We had a delightful time the other night—I wish I saw you all more often. As ever, Edmund

To Newton Arvin August 21, 1962
Talcottville

Dear Newton: Since you have read Holmes's other two novels, perhaps you ought to read *Elsie Venner*, too. Elsie herself is incredible, but the description of her New England life is excellent. It is supposed to take place in Northampton, you know, and I think that the sinister mountain where Elsie goes to meet her snake friends must be that abrupt and rather beetling cliff that you see when you are going from Mount Holyoke to Northampton.

I am very much interested in what you say about those Middle Western writers. I wrote about George Ade once, and was rather puzzled by him. What were they protecting themselves, as you say, against?—the dreary life around them? You must certainly write about this . . .

As ever, Edmund

To Newton Arvin September 4, 1962
Talcottville

Dear Newton: I do know Oberndorf's book, was going to tell you about it.

My objection to Elsie is that you really don't get inside her. She is a split personality all right, but a character in a fairy tale, not really accounted for clinically. Dan Aaron wants to know what would have happened if Roderick Hudson had fallen in love with her instead of with Christina Light.

My piece on George Ade was written some years ago when I thought

I was going to do the book on American literature in the post-Civil War period and the early 1900's that turned into *Patriotic Gore*. There are a handful of these essays, and I am going to write a few more and bring them out together later on . . .

I'm leaving for Canada on Wednesday to investigate Canadian literature. The Internal Revenue people have cut off my sources of income, but I'll be traveling at the *New Yorker's* expense, and I'll look forward to sitting around in comfortable hotels and buying dinners and drinks for writers. I expect to be gone several weeks, and I may perhaps become a Canadian citizen.

Best regards, Edmund

To Leon Edel

October 24, 1962
Cambridge

Dear Leon: When lately prostrated by a bad attack of gout, I read your two volumes straight through*—thank you for having them sent me—and they considerably alleviated my misery. I don't know of any other American literary biography which is comparable to it or, in fact, anything like it. It is an altogether original work, which, inspired by Henry James, is not subordinate to him—I only await the last volume (are you sure you won't need two?) to call it a masterpiece. It makes one realize that one never really knew before what sort of man James was or what his life was like. One sees that the equanimity of the years of his early maturity, which seems so well organized, so soundly based, and, from our present point of view, so enviable, is to give way, with Constance Woolson's suicide, and the fiasco of his theatrical efforts, to a phase of relative uncertainty and demoralization which, however, was to produce his most interesting work.

Here are a few misprints and queries on Volume II . . .

My *Patriotic Gore* was such a mess typographically that I am wondering whether your so much better results are due to your being so much better a proofreader than I or whether they proofread at Lippincott's in the office. They don't at Oxford!

I have just spent a month in Canada—Toronto, Montreal, and Quebec —and had a delightful time. I got *The New Yorker* to send me there to write about Canadian lit, which for the first time in history seems to me to be becoming interesting. I am eager to discuss it with you. As you undoubtedly know, at the present time they are going through a complicated kind of crisis, and the French Canadian world especially is in a great state of ferment, which is stimulating to literary activity.

Love from us both to Roberta.

As ever, Edmund W

---

* *The Conquest of London* and *The Middle Years.*

To CELIA GOODMAN   October 5, 1962
                                                        Talcottville

. . . I have just come back from a month in Canada, where I had persuaded *The New Yorker* to send me to investigate Canadian literature,
which seems to be getting more interesting than it used to be. Elena was
with me for a week, and we had a very good time. They are going
through a complicated crisis up there. The entry of Britain into the
Common Market will make them even more dependent on us, and they
combine being strongly anti-American with talking about joining our
Union. At the same time the French Canadians are revolting against the
domination of English-speaking Canada and talk about setting up as an
independent country (though I don't think they'll go that far) . . .

To PHILIPPE THOBY-MARCELIN   November 24, 1962
                                                         Wellfleet

Dear Phito: I meant to write you long before about the MS of folk
stories you left with me; but I went to spend a month in Canada not
long after you were in Talcottville, was then occupied with other things,
and am only now getting around to it. I think that the stories are delightful
and that you have told them in a charming style. Some of them are
familiar from the folklore of other countries, but some are entirely different
from anything I have seen before. You seem to have stuck close to the
originals—I suppose, from scholarly fidelity. Where did you get them from?
I am not sure that you couldn't have improved them from the literary
point of view by adding a few details of your own, and even an incident
here and there. Do you want me to send back the MS? I think that it
ought to be brought out as a book.
   My Canadian trip did me good . . . Montreal is now a delightful city—
French restaurants, French theater, French press—which is far from what
it used to be; and it is a relief to visit Canada, because the Canadians are
not under the horrible pressure that we are in the United States. There
is a nationalist movement in French Canada to get out from the domination of the English-speaking element, and there is a great fermentation
going on. The literature of French Canada is a good deal more interesting
than I had expected, and with the current political and intellectual excitement, there are now, I was told, in the whole of Canada, more books
published in French than in English. I remember your telling me once
that the Haitians felt a certain kinship with French Canada; but the
Catholic Church up there seems to have been more reactionary and rigid
than anywhere else in the world (in Haiti, I take it, the Church is not
taken anything like so seriously): it has been Jansenist and very puritanical,
and it has complete control of their education and exercises a certain

censorship on their reading. Now the general liberalizing tendency which seems to be sponsored by Rome has set off in French Canada an explosive revolt against the old constricting culture. I'm going to write about all this for *The New Yorker*.

We've come up for Thanksgiving to Wellfleet for the last time this winter—after that, 12 Hilliard Street, Cambridge.

How are you? By the way, did you carry off from Talcottville that great French novel *Histoire d'O*? If you did, please return it eventually. I make a point every Christmas of reading it aloud to the family. Love to Eva. Elena sends love to you both.   As ever, Edmund

To Cecil Lang   November 17, 1962
                                                 The New Yorker
Dear Cecil: I do seem to be popular with the Kennedys. Bobby reads me, and Jack read me and insisted on my being given one of those freedom medals, though they tried to fob Archie MacLeish off on him. I saw Arthur Schlesinger yesterday and told him that you expected me to be Secretary of State in the next Kennedy cabinet. He said he had been thinking of me rather for Secretary of the Treasury . . .

                                               As ever, Edmund

"O Canada"
1955–1967

In Toronto, for the first time, I met Morley Callaghan . . .
                                      (Notebooks of the fifties)

To Morley Callaghan   August 19, 1955
                                                    Talcottville
Dear Callaghan: I became so engrossed in your book *The Loved and the Lost* the other night that I read it through in about three hours. Elena had a similar experience. The smoothness and speed with which the story is told are not unusual nowadays, but there are few contemporary novels that have their foundations laid so deep and carry so much weight of meaning. I admire, also, the way that the background of Montreal is unobtrusively but solidly established . . . We very much enjoyed seeing you—hope to repeat the visit.   Sincerely, Edmund Wilson

To Morley Callaghan   May 9, 1961
                                                     Cambridge
Dear Morley: I was delighted to hear that your books were coming out in England. Yes: you can't overestimate the stupidity of publishers' offices.

In your case, I think that one of the troubles has been that they didn't realize how original your work was, because it did not seem eccentric. I am hoping in the course of the summer to make a trip to Montreal and Quebec . . . I haven't seen that part of Canada since my early teens. Am looking forward to your new book.   As ever, Edmund W.

To MORLEY CALLAGHAN   January 2, 1963
                                                    Cambridge
Dear Morley: . . . *The New Yorker* asked me to review *That Summer*, but I decided that I couldn't write about it without getting into it my own impressions of Scott and Hemingway, and I didn't want to do that, because it would lead me to expand in a way that would be out of place. It will be better done by somebody who didn't know them.

I have just finished *More Joy* and have started *They Shall Inherit. More Joy* is very fine. It has your characteristic subtlety of presentation and complexity of moral vision that the reader is not led to expect when confronted with what, at the start, seems a more straightforward situation. I think, though, that you have very much improved since then. It is as if with *The Loved and the Lost* you had entered on a new phase of your work . . . I believe you and Hemingway and Anderson evolved a kind of flat poetic vein which does nowadays sound rather self-conscious . . . I think that a vague use of the word *thing* and *things* is one of the keys to this . . . By the way, I don't understand where Kip at that point got the money to buy those expensive dress clothes. I have just been reading Balzac, who always tells you—and, to be sure, tells you more than anybody but a Frenchman wants to know—how much money everybody makes and how much everything costs.

Thanks for your letter about *Patriotic Gore*, which crossed with mine from New York. It pleased me very much. I hope to go to Canada again, but I can't go during the winter. Even this climate is supposed to be bad for me. I am not used to being hampered with ailments, and it makes me very impatient—with at the same time a certain complacency that comes from being an invalid. I hope that Lorrette has found some relief. New Year's greetings to all of you, as well as a few harsh gratings.   Edmund

    . . . another writer strongly to be recommended to anyone who wants
    to understand Canada.   (*O Canada*)

To HUGH MacLENNAN   November 18, 1964
                                                    Wesleyan
Dear Hugh: Thank you very much for your letter. I should be grateful if you would send me any clippings. I am sure that there will be com-

633

plaints that I have given too much space to French at the expense of English Canada, but the lopsidedness will be corrected in the book, where I shall have a long piece on Morley and some notes on other writers.

It may amuse you to know that one of the editors of *The New Yorker* remonstrated with me for sounding "too Presbyterian" when, in writing about your heroines, I said, in the original version, that I found it "a relief . . . to read, for a change, about some decent women who are capable of lasting affection." He had just seen Iris Murdoch's *A Severed Head* and thought it was wonderful—said that "life was like that." I refused to modify the passage, but when the magazine came out, I found that the word "decent" had been omitted. I can understand expunging obscenities—though this never seems to happen any more—but I didn't know that things had got to the point where you can't mention a decent woman.

Your letter has made me realize how much you people up there are still groping for an audience. I suppose that that is the reason that so many French Canadian novels are laid in an unspecified locality. They hope to be read in France, but what they write is alien to the French, and their stories can't be imagined as taking place anywhere except in French Canada.

Best regards, Edmund W

To HUGH MacLENNAN

April 29, 1965
Wesleyan

Dear Hugh: The enclosed may amuse you. It confirms my impression that the attitude of Canada toward its writers is one of either complete indifference or nervous unsureness.

I was interested in your story about Diem. I think the C.I.A. is capable of anything. Yes: there is a lot of feeling against Johnson's policy in Vietnam—Morgenthau and Walter Lippmann—but there are people such as Joseph Alsop who think it is just the thing.

Marie-Claire Blais, who has had two Guggenheim fellowships and now lives in the United States, is in fact our neighbor, has written a new novel which is certainly her best book* and one of the very best French-Canadian novels. When she first came here and told us about her early life in the lowest stratum of Quebec, we all told her that she ought to write about it instead of spinning her queer kind of fairy tales that were becoming more and more dreamlike. This she has now done—she might not have had the courage to at home—with hair-raising and desolating results. The picture of convent life and the clergy is so awful that she doubted, when one publisher rejected it, that it could ever be published

---

* *Une Saison dans la vie d'Emmanuel.*

in Quebec; but Jacques Hébert has now taken it on. It is also coming out in English.   Best regards, Edmund W

To Hugh MacLennan   July 23, 1967
                                                       Talcottville

Dear Hugh: I've just read the *Sphinx*, and shall give you my impressions of it, which are perhaps so subjective as to be unfair. I read the first two-thirds at Wellfleet before I came over here, with avidity and, as they say, unable to put it down. I thought that your dramatization of the Canadian situation was masterly. It seemed to me a much better book than *Two Solitudes*, that you were hitting all the nails on the head, with no *longueurs* or boring episodes, and the descriptions, so much briefer than in your other books, touched in with a very sure skill. The last hundred pages I read up here, and they held my interest to the end; but I had been so delighted, the night before, to get up in the country here, where it is perfectly quiet and the telephone rarely rings, away from the zooming traffic and the tumultuous summer visitors of Cape Cod (a good many of them now French Canadians and not the most attractive kind), that I rather overelaborated my arrival and finished your book the next day in a somewhat letdown condition. At the end, I was a little disappointed, but this may have been due to my own exhaustion. I had expected something more climactic and some more definite upshot—though I suppose you were making the point that the issues don't come clear in Canada and that the forces put in motion were reduced to a kind of stalemate. And I don't think I understand about the Sphinx. What is the Sphinx's return? Do you mean simply that the situation is puzzling? If you do, I agree—and I agree that it is not confined to Canada. (Still, anyone who wants to know about Canada ought to read your book.) . . . Don't you ever come to the States? We wish that you and your wife would come to see us in Wellfleet— sometime in October, say. The vacationers are gone by then, and there is a long Indian summer.   Best regards, Edmund W

To William Shawn   February 27, 1964
The New Yorker   Paris

Dear Shawn: Here is the copy of the first part of the Canadian piece. I'll be sending another installment as soon as I get the typed text from the office. There is to be another section dealing with Canadian politics and the literature it has produced, but I have decided that I'd better not write it till I get back . . . I think I ought to spend a few days in Canada in order to work up a strong and lively finale after the perhaps rather depressing sections on French Canadian fiction—general significance and importance of what is going on in Canada, etc.   Best regards, Edmund Wilson

To Celia Goodman   September 16, 1964
                                                         Wellfleet
. . . My Canadian articles have turned into a book, of which I'll eventually send you a copy. It is not one of my best, but informative—though I know that the English don't really have much interest in hearing about Canada. Neither have we had, but for the first time in history since the early French and English wars it is beginning to become interesting, and people ought to be instructed about what is going on up there . . .

To William Shawn   October 3, 1964
The New Yorker   Wellfleet

. . . I found the subject of Canada extremely difficult to handle, because the country itself is so uncoordinated, and it is so hard to present the French and the English sides in any unified way . . .

To Mary Meigs   June 3, 1965
                                                       Talcottville
. . . You might tell Marie-Claire Blais that I hear from Morley Callaghan that my book has set all the English Canadians against me—I don't know whether he means by this to include the Scotch and the Irish. A young Englishman who has only been in Canada three years has attacked me in one of the Toronto papers, on the ground of "ignorance," though he doesn't say what it is I am ignorant of . . .

To Sir Rupert Hart-Davis   January 20, 1967
Rupert Hart-Davis Limited, London   Wellfleet

. . . The book [O Canada] was not always well received in English Canada. There is too much about the French in it. The accepted idea up there—quite wrong—is that the poetry of English Canada is excellent and better than their fiction, and it irritated them to be told that the best Canadian poet was French. Most of them had never heard of him [Emile Nelligan]. I suppose you know that the French Canadian novelists have been having a mad success in France. Marie-Claire Blais won one of their prizes and has just come back from Paris almost groggy from having been made the toast of the publishing season. It is as if they had discovered French Canada for the first time since the battle of the Plains of Abraham . . .

636

1963

AND

EUROPE

To Helen Muchnic and Dorothy Walsh   January 7, 1963
                                                              Cambridge

Dear Helen and Dorothy: I am delighted with the little treasury of
impostures, which I find valuable on the subjects of vampires, early reports
of conjuring, and other matters. I particularly like those mid-century
English books that always have such an atmosphere of old libraries and
curious happenings—have also been reading a somewhat similar volume
(in appearance and atmosphere) of Dickens's *Life of Grimaldi*, a wonderful
book of his which no one seems to pay any attention to.

   Due to dieting and refraining from effort, my condition has been much
better lately, and we have almost painlessly survived the holidays.

                                                              Love, Edmund

To Dorothy Walsh   January 19, 1963
                                                              Cambridge

Dear Dorothy:* I was much relieved to get your letter, with the elucidation of the problem of the incubi and succubae. Ignorant as I am of
theology, I had been thinking of them as highly skilled labor who would
be prevented by conversion from following their trade, and who, even if
unconverted, might be put out of their jobs by automation.

   I am in much better shape than I was, though exercising the caution
I have to is, as you say, uncongenial to my temperament.

                                                  Love to you both, Edmund

---

* Dorothy Walsh, Professor of Philosophy at Smith College, and Helen Muchnic
own a house at Cummington, Massachusetts. E. stopped there nearly every year on
his way to and from Talcottville.

To JOHN R. B. BRETT-SMITH   March 2, 1963
Oxford University Press
Dear Brett-Smith: Thanks very much for getting that check through so
promptly. It makes it possible to get it to the tax people by Monday,
which is supposed to be the deadline. If you should get a notification that
the lien has been lifted before I come to New York, I'd be grateful if you
would let me know.   Sincerely, Edmund Wilson

To LOUISE BOGAN   March 18, 1963
                                             The New Yorker
Dear Louise: That is a good solid piece on Frost, but after I read it and
went on to the poems, I had my usual disappointing experience of finding
them flat and uninteresting, entirely devoid of the qualities you praise.
And how can you say that "The Pasture" is "a love song—surely one of
the loveliest in the language"? It isn't addressed to a woman—I always
thought it was addressed to the reader . . . Léonie and I enjoyed our visit
the other evening.   Love, Edmund

To LOUISE BOGAN   March 22, 1963
                                             The New Yorker
Dear Louise: I forgot to point out in my letter—in case you should reprint
your piece—that "The Widow in the Bye-Street" is in stanzas, not in
couplets. I was interested in your account of Frost's life, but it seems to
me that, on your own showing, he did not have a particularly hard time—
he had plenty of education.   Love, Edmund
    Have just been reading the posthumous volume of Robinson Jeffers's
poems, and it interests me much more than Frost.

To DANIEL AARON   March 26, 1963
                                             The New Yorker
. . . You will have heard about Newton's [Arvin] death. He came to stay
with us a night in Cambridge and I've never seen him seem to be happier
and more self-assured—pleased with his *Longfellow* and looking forward
to his new projects. It is ironic and dreadful, as Helen Muchnic has said,
that just as at last he was liberated, or as liberated as he ever could be,
and was free to give his time to writing, he should suddenly have been
cut off by cancer. Here is a piece that I began about his book before I
knew he was ill . . .

To JOHN DOS PASSOS   May 2, 1963

Dear Dos: We always mean to come South every spring but never get
further than New York. I have had a belated *rapprochement* with the
[Gerald] Murphys, and on our last trip went out to see them at Sneden's

Landing. They lived up to their tradition of gracious living by providing an incredible lunch—for which a special chef had been procured—with the menu, à la française, on little porcelain tablets. We always speak of you with a toast and a tear—but I suppose since your citation from Goldwater, you are insensible to such humble tributes.

We have had some hideous winters in Cambridge—aside from Cambridge itself, tax troubles and various ailments. I have pretty well got rid of the latter and the former are pretty well settled, but they have inspired me to write a tract which I hope will be the hottest thing since Tom Paine. The Americans at the present time are being tyrannized over by the federal government in a way that ought to give them more cause for complaint than the colonists had against the Crown, but they seem to take it lying down.

This is our last winter in Cambridge. We have been hoping to spend next winter in Europe . . . but I don't know whether we'll have been left enough money by that son of a bitch—Uncle Sam.

Love to the family, EW

To Jacob Landau   July 18, 1963
                                                    Cambridge
Dear Jack: Thank you for your letters. I'd be delighted to have the Hertz Pentateuch, if you really have a copy to spare . . .

I've just acquired a copy of a Christian seventeenth-century Hebrew Bible, which I find extraordinarily interesting. They have reproduced the Masoretic text to the point of printing the big *waw* and *lamed* which mark the middle of the Torah and the other special textual signs.

I've just finished a pamphlet called *The Cold War and the Income Tax: A Protest*—a copy of which I'll send you later on.*

I'm enclosing a copy of an article on language which I'm not sure that you have read.   Best regards as always, Edmund W

To Jacob Landau   August 21, 1963
                                                    Talcottville
. . . I am sailing for Europe September 6 . . . I'll be doing some work for *The New Yorker*—including bringing my *Dead Sea Scrolls* book up to date—a good deal has happened since I wrote it . . .

To Padraic Colum   September 3, 1963
                                                    Wellfleet
Dear Padraic: Thank you for sending me the poem, which touched me very much. I thought your volume of selected poems was wonderful. I

---

* "Arranged with A. J. Muste and Roger Straus to have the proceeds from my pamphlet [*The Cold War and the Income Tax*] go to Muste's peace movement."
                                                    —*Upstate*

wept while reading Elena some of them—not for sentiment, which doesn't often make me weep, but for the beauty of the lines. If everybody in Ireland hadn't been so much overshadowed by Yeats, you would certainly have stood out as one of the best poets in English of your time, and for me, that is what you are.

I wish we could make connections here, but we are going to Europe in a few days. We are putting Helen in school in Switzerland and spending the winter there.   Best regards as ever, Edmund Wilson

Europe
1963–1964

To Mary Meigs   October 22, 1963
                                            Basil Street Hotel, London

Dear Mary: . . . We have given ourselves up here to a life of pleasure and have been having a very good time: friends, shops, theaters, galleries, and short trips to the country. This Saturday we are going to Paris . . . Hôtel de Castille, rue Cambon . . .

I thought [Marie-Clair Blais's] *La Belle Bête* painful but quite powerful. I imagine that the English translation made it seem worse than it is.

We went to Rochester the other day. Though it isn't far from Canterbury, it is a place that no one visits. Dickens's house, Gad's Hill Place, has not been made a national shrine. I couldn't make out what was going on there. It didn't even look as if anybody lived in it. The cathedral is blackened on the outside and very cold and somber inside, and not very well kept up. I couldn't disassociate it from *Edwin Drood*. I could easily imagine the choirmaster smoking opium and something spooky taking place in the belfry. You know that Dr. Ward's father was Dean of the Cathedral—did I point out to you the curious parallels between his career and Jasper's? I didn't blame him, after seeing Rochester, for embracing something rather lurid. I also went to Gravesend, a few miles away, to see an old man who makes Punch and Judy puppets—apparently an expiring craft. He carves them, paints them, and costumes them, and the costumes are extremely elaborate. I am getting him to make me some. He is also an operator. He doesn't do the Devil and the Hangman, and only puts Punch in the stocks, but a show I saw in London had them, and had Punch get away from even the Crocodile. "Punch always has to score!" he told me. We have also seen a mediocre magic show, and not bad production of Musorgsky's *Khovanshchina*, the latest Ian Fleming film, a very bad ballet of *Le Sacre du Printemps*, the film of *Tom Jones*, which is perhaps worth your seeing, and a very queer and funny psychoanalytical

640

farce made by J. B. Priestley from Iris Murdoch's novel *The Severed Head*. Also, a show at the Tate Gallery of Soutine and Modigliani, which did not interest me much.

In spite of all our activities, it has been a great relief to be in England, which seems so quiet after America. Instead of being all keyed up, they seem to be slowly subsiding from their position as a great power . . .

Love from us both to both of you, Edmund

To Mary Meigs   December 2, 1963
Paris

. . . Yes: Elena was much upset by Kennedy's death. The whole thing made me feel sick. We were both suffering from bronchial and sinus ailments and sat dismally around the hotel rooms here reading the ghastly newspapers. I think that the United States is getting very bad and cracking under all these strains. Most people over here don't know this and believe that we are prosperous and comfortable. I was surprised to see, by the reaction to the Kennedy assassination, how much they had been counting on him. I worried about Barbara in jail in Atlanta. I didn't know whether this murder would give the South pause or make them feel they were getting away with it . . . I'm afraid that old Lyndon Johnson can't keep up this Kennedy tradition . . .

To Mary Meigs   December 18, 1963
Paris

Dear Mary: I am sending you rather a mixed Christmas package. The militant Louise Labé is for Barbara. She has always interested me, and I like her sonnets, which sound rather like Shakespeare's. Divide the rest however you like. I am sending the articles from the Paris papers because they reveal certain things which may not have appeared in the American press.

We have had quite an exciting five-day trip—Elena driving a hired car—to the Vosges, where I spent the first war, and to Rheims, where Elena was born. I hadn't been back for forty-six years, and Elena had been back to Rheims only once since she was seven years old. There are two things in Rheims, the cathedral and champagne, and they seem to have something in common. The cathedral is the most attractive I have ever seen and has a certain geniality and effervescence: the smiling figures beside the doors, the gargoyles that are animals instead of demons, the angels with spread wings, and the row of kings high up the towers. Nancy, which I used to love, has beautiful ornamental eighteenth-century squares and a museum full of Callot and Georges de La Tour, both of whom came from Nancy, and of the strange drawings of another Nancéien called Bellange. I had been told about him by one of Elena's Russian cousins, who specializes in enthusiasms for little-known artists. I'd never heard of him before—have you? It was terribly cold and as foggy as the Cape.

. . . We think of you often and miss you. We hope that Barbara is out of that hellish South and will not have to go back. [A. J.] Muste's latest letter said that the people, since the cattle-prod exploit, have been behaving better.   Love as ever, Edmund

To Mary Meigs   January 29, 1964
                                                                      Paris

. . . You and Barbara probably ought to read that German play called *Der Stellvertreter.** I sent an English translation, *The Representative*, which you can have if you want it. I have been sent another. Elena is much excited about it. It has been a sensation in Germany and provoked riots in Switzerland. We saw the Paris production the other night—which is better than the English one. All the productions are different, according to which scenes they choose to include. The English version was rather inferior because, as the German publishers told us, the English can't allow themselves to appear so ungentlemanly as the Nazi characters are supposed to be, so they left out most of the Gestapo stuff—as well as, unfortunately, for some reason, all the Jewish characters. Both productions left out all the women, except, in the English one, the waitress on her first appearance. The French, however, have much less trouble in acting nasty parts. When the Catholics were making trouble at the performances here, someone had the strange idea of releasing a lot of mice. A lady who was sympathetic to mice collected them and put them in her handbag . . .

To John Dos Passos   January 18, 1964
                                                                      Paris

Dear Dos: I haven't seen your offensive article. Why don't you send it to me? It's so long now since I've seen you that I don't know what line you're taking. The last I heard, you were receiving a citation from Goldwater, who is surely one of the biggest asses in our asinine country. How can he be all out for cleaning up on Russia and at the same time want to get rid of the income tax? What do you mean, by the way, by the "mass mis-informers" about the Kennedy assassination?

Paris is extremely dreary—the French themselves complain of it. Elena, who knows it better than I do, gets the same impression as I—that de Gaulle is way up in the empyrean with *la gloire*, la France, and Louis XIV, with Malraux performing prodigies of cleaning up the old buildings, which turn out to be yellow Palladian affairs, and reforming the opera, which believe it or not, now puts on brilliant productions—while the ordinary

---

* By Rolf Hochhuth.

people, on Montmartre on a Sunday, seem as drab, though not as driven, merely glum, as in Moscow, and really have no connection with de Gaulle's "image" of France.

Have just been reading Scott's letters—which are desolating, but I am perhaps easily desolated nowadays.   As ever, Bunny W

To John Dos Passos   February 1, 1964
                                                     Paris
Dear Dos: Here are some remarks on your article, which Farrar, Straus has just sent me:

1. My references to Hiss and the Rosenbergs were not liberal clichés. In the case of Hiss, I imagine that he was covering up for his wife, and perhaps himself; but that the typewriter business was a fake. Chambers was evidently a neurotic case of an imaginative writer manqué, and it was impossible to know how much of what he said was fantasy. In the case of the Rosenbergs, at first I took everything at face value—though I thought they ought not to have been executed. But the husband of a cousin of mine, Malcolm Sharp of the University of Chicago, who at the last moment brought in an *amicus curiae* brief for the Rosenbergs, went through the whole record of the trial—which very few people did—and wrote an able book about it. He is in general a supporter of the *status quo*, something of a special pleader for American business, but a strong civil-rights man, and he became convinced that the Rosenbergs were taking the rap for someone else, and that there was no evidence at all to justify sending Sobell to Alcatraz. He studied a number of these trials and came out believing that in that period the F.B.I. was systematically framing suspects.

I have never regarded myself as a liberal, because the word does not mean anything definite. If you don't have any fundamental political philosophy, there are a number of practical ways of dealing with the various problems. If you do have a political philosophy, you have principles that you try to stick to. But the "liberal" takes up neither position.

You've been railing against "the liberals" all your life, and my impression is that your conception of them is a projection of some suppressed alter ego that you perpetually feel you have to discredit. You used to assail this myth from the radical side, and now you assail it from the conservative.

2. What danger do you imagine the Soviet Union is threatening us with? Invasion and occupation of the United States? I don't understand how at your age you can continue to believe in these bugaboos and see everything in terms of melodrama. It seems to me that you are just as gullible as you ever were in the twenties. I get more and more skeptical myself.

3. "Army and Navy and Air Force men who are conscientiously trying to do their duty by experiments with new methods of warfare" is surely

a prize euphemism. It reminds me of "the final solution of the Jewish question." Your sympathy with the anti-militarists reminds me of Oscar Wilde on "these Christs that die upon barricades: God knows that I am with them in some things."

4. Shelters. Nothing I have read on this subject has convinced me that shelters will help. And even if they did keep a few people alive, it seems to me that if we have to resort to such expedients, we might as well call it a day.

5. Your talk about "dissecting the generalized commonplaces that obscure realities, sorting out truth from falsehood, extolling the good and decrying the evil" sounds like the meaningless banalities of an old-fashioned pastoral exhortation. You ought to dissect your own generalized commonplaces, which seem to me from here identical with the shibboleths of the Goldwater camp.

Thanks for the Brazilian book, which I have been reading with interest. I am half buried in Canadian literature *tant français qu'anglais*, which I have to get through for an article on Canada (very interesting now for the first time in history). What with the tax situation, I am "overextended" in my *New Yorker* engagements. When I get done with Canada, which I had hoped to do before I left, I'll have to go after the Dead Sea scrolls in order to bring my book up to date. Then I'm going for a long stay in Hungary, on which I've also engaged to report. I've become interested in the Hungarians since I discovered that Hungary was the only country where I was chiefly known as a dramatist. Also, I seem nowadays to be obsessed with minorities—French Canadians, Iroquois—feeling that I belong to one myself. From what I hear about Hungary and what Reuel tells me about Poland, I gather that, in spite of their Communists, the getting rid of the antiquated feudal regimes has had a stimulating effect on the young people in those countries such as there is nothing to give the French young people under de Gaulle except incantatory rock 'n' roll and allied activities. The Hungarians will get rid of the Russians, too. A Hungarian who had been there recently told me that there really was no such thing as a Hungarian Communist. The Communist leaders themselves, another Hungarian told me, are disguised old-fashioned nationalists.

As ever, EW

To John Dos Passos   March 18, 1964
                                         Hotel Victoria, Rome
Dear Dos: Your letter addressed to Wellfleet only reached me after our last exchange. Your lucubration in Rome seems to me an appalling production. I never expected to see you develop into such a hot-air artist. After the usual denunciation of the American writers for not being in contact

644

with the real world, you proceed to a lot of vague pronouncements and liberal pious hopes that make Dr. Frank Crane look like Socrates: management and labor harmonized by the realistic intervention of a "social engineer" and Negro rights won without "racial warfare." And what do you mean by saying that "the plain men and women who do the work of the world and cope with the realities of life"—these phrases are hollow clichés in a class with the Communist "toiling masses"—"respond almost automatically to these values"? What values? Different societies have different values. (The plain men and women in America are suffering from the monstrous taxation and the other impositions of the government without having the intelligence or the gumption to do anything effective about it.) Then, later on, you talk about the "firm belief that good is good and evil is evil" and the indispensable "conviction of right and wrong." Well, what is your conception of these moral abstractions? There is no general agreement about them even on the part of people from the same society. I believe, for example, that nuclear and biological weapons are entirely evil. You evidently approve of them as the noble achievements' of "Army, Navy and Air Force officers who are conscientiously trying to do their duty by experiments with new methods of warfare"—which impractical literary ninnies have no right to complain about. I note that you are having nowadays some difficulty in reconciling your early resentment against our government for vilifying Germany with your later complete acceptance of its behaving in the same way about Russia.

As for the piece about gas warfare: when in an article recommending these weapons I find the author talking about the free world, I immediately stop reading.

I really don't think you are well equipped for this moral political editorializing (I don't think I am at my best in it either). There is all the difference in the world between what you gave them in Rome and the descriptions and "constatations" of your book about Brazil. And what are you doing at those literary congresses, anyway? Nothing could drag me to one.

About the Kennedy assassination: my first thought and that of many people was that the lunatic rightists had done it. What interest would Khrushchev or Castro have had in killing Kennedy? Stevenson and the Texan Johnson had already been attacked in Dallas, and Kennedy, I am told by Schlesinger, had been advised by Stevenson not to go. When he arrived, he was confronted by a sign that said, "Let Goldwater barry King John." There has been running in the Paris *Express* a series of articles by a man named Thomas Buchanan, which it is said the American editors have been afraid to publish, but which I suppose will come out in a book. His theory is too long to try to outline in a letter, but he believes that

Kennedy was shot from in front from the wall of a railroad bridge. Oswald, on his record in the Marines, was a terribly bad marksman, and according to Buchanan, had another man with him who fired the later shots. (There was a cigarette package found in the room, and Oswald didn't smoke.) Oswald, well known to the Dallas police, had been chosen to take the rap but was deceived into believing that he would be allowed to get away. The whole thing, according to this theory, must have been a police conspiracy inspired presumably by the oil and John Birch interests. I feel sure that, if this is true, we shall never get an honest report from the official investigation.

We have come down to Rome from Paris—very glad to get away. There is sunlight and good air here, which is not the case in *la ville lumière*. But the city is very much changed since I last saw it at the end of the war. For the first time, the impression I get is not of being in a very old city that incorporates the whole history of civilization. The Forum and the Colosseum and all the rest are still here, but the past doesn't dominate the present. Rome and Paris both are getting more and more like everywhere else—that is, more like the U.S. One very striking thing is that the characteristic *smell* of these places is gone. I first came to Italy in 1908 and still remember how everything smelled: horses and spaghetti and I don't know what else—poverty, I suppose. Now one hardly smells anything at all.

Helen is coming from her school and Rosalind from Boston this week. We are here on Helen's account, having still the old-fashioned idea that it is a part of the young person's education to have seen a little something of Italy . . .   Best regards, Bunny W.

On Hungary
1964–1966

To CHARLOTTE KRETZOI   January 17, 1964
Budapest   Paris

Dear Mrs. Kretzoi: . . . I am arranging to come to Budapest on April 19 and to stay at least a month. I want to find somebody with a knowledge of literature who can regularly read Hungarian with me. Would this be possible for you, or, if not, is there someone you could recommend? I look forward, in any case, to seeing you.

Osziute tiztellettel,* Edmund Wilson

---
* Regards.

646

To CHARLOTTE KRETZOI   February 12, 1964
                                                                  Paris
Dear Mrs. Kretzoi: Thank you for your letter. I am delighted that you
can do some Hungarian with me, and I shall be glad to tell you anything
I know about American literature. I have applied for a visa, and since they
ask for the names of friends in Hungary, I have taken the liberty of
giving them yours and that of Professor Országh. I hope that you will have
no objection. I am greatly looking forward to my visit.
                                       Yours sincerely, Edmund Wilson

To CELIA GOODMAN   April 19, 1964
                                              Hotel Gellert, Budapest
. . . I am going this afternoon to meet a Hungarian translator of Homer.
The Hungarians have the only language in Europe in which accent and
quantity are of equal importance, and they boast that they are the only
people who can reproduce Greek meter. I am curious about this . . .

To MARY MEIGS   April 26, 1964
                                                  Hotel Bristol, Vienna
. . . Hungary has really interested me more than any other country I have
been in over here. The Russians are detested, and you cannot even mention anything Russian without its being coldly received. If they could get
the Russians off their necks, they would undoubtedly arrive at a compro-
mise society, part socialist and part free enterprise, the kind of thing that
all the Western countries seem to be tending toward. The Hungarians
themselves are most agreeable, and except for a Hungarian professor born
in the United States and only there for research, I have seen none of the
flamboyant and voluble kind that I have sometimes found fatiguing at
home. They seem stunned and subdued by their many misfortunes. The
old breed of Hungarian, I think, is only to be found abroad . . .
    . . . I look forward to getting back and seeing you. Am thoroughly tired
of waiters and hotel meals, foreign currencies and visas and taxis. Sometimes I wake up in the morning and am not sure what country I am in
and what language to use to say "Thank you" when the waiter brings
the inevitable *café complet* . . .
    I thought *Les Stances à Sophie* terribly funny—but it is also quite true,
I am sure, to the life of that generation—the young married and the professional beatniks—in Paris. She speaks of a number of unpleasant features
—bad air, boring dinners, etc.—which we had already noticed. When I
get back, I'll try to explain the argot. Some of the words were unfamiliar
to several people I asked, but I persisted, and I think I found out about
them all. The title is the name of an indecent song—*une chanson de corps
de garde.*

To William Shawn   June 26, 1965
The New Yorker   Talcottville

. . . the remarkable novelist Christiane Rochefort. I read her *Les Stances
à Sophie* when I was over there, and afterwards read her two other books.
I see that *Sophie* is coming out in English as *Cats Don't Care for Money*
. . . and I wish you would send me this translation. What I wrote will
save your reviewing it. I think she is an important writer . . .

To Charlotte Kretzoi   October 26, 1965
                                         Wellfleet
. . . I have been reading "Az Alföld,"* and I may not have understood it,
because I can find no passage comparing one of those wells to a mosquito.
The only reference to a well I find is:

> Deleléskor hosszu gémü kútnál
> Széles valya kettös ája várja.

What is *gémü?*† Is it a form of *gém?*

To Charlotte Kretzoi   December 31, 1965
                                         Wellfleet
Kedves Sarolta [Dear Charlotte]: . . . One subject we failed to discuss. It
seems to me that your insistence on calling the Slavic words in Hungarian
"loan words" derives from the old narrow Hungarian nationalism that made
people change their German or Slavic names into something *echt* Hungarian. Do you also call loan words the Turkish vocabulary that I understand is embedded in Hungarian? The Russians surely don't take this view
of the Tartar words that are part of their language—nor do we of the
Norman French which composes so large a part of ours. Of course, there
is more French in English than there is Slavic in Hungarian: but I am
not sure that you take account of how much that is Slavic there is—and
in some very fundamental words. For example, Russian возить, водить,
вести ‡ must have some close kinship with Hungarian *viszni* and
vezatui.

You and Miklós were a great success with everybody and added much
to our celebration. You must come up to see us again.

                         As ever, OB (Odön Bácsi) [Uncle Edmund]

---

* A poem by Sándor Petöfi.
† Heron.
‡ To bring.

To Charlotte Kretzoi   January 10, 1966
                                                              Wellfleet

. . . I said Slavic, not Russian; but I recognized the Slavic words from
Russian. The word *jövevényszo* [newcomer] itself must be a product of
the nationalistic eighteen-thirties, isn't it? . . .

To Charlotte Kretzoi   September 15, 1966

. . . Yes: I am writing about Hungary, and there are a number of things
I want to check with you . . .

To Charlotte Kretzoi   August 6, 1964
                                                            Talcottville

Very honored dear: Thank you for picture postcards. I am happy that
you are enjoying your vacation. I have no vacation. During the summer
I only work. For the last eight weeks I lived alone here, but my eldest
daughter has arrived to stay with me. My wife will come soon.

This is a very small village—eighty people—where my family house was
built at the end of the eighteenth century. The picturesque country sur-
rounds it. Friendly greeting to your husband.

                                        Sincere regards, Edmund Wilson
    Do you think I'm improving? I had very little help with this.*

To John Dos Passos   May 18, 1964
                                                              Wellfleet

Dear Dos: Your letter reached me in Hungary, but since mail is likely to
be read there, I am only answering it now that I'm back in Wellfleet.

You seem to mistake my point of view. I am not "between for and
against Marxism." The Marxism of the so-called Communist countries is
today mostly mere cant to cover their exploitation by the Russians. But the
problem in these countries as well as here at home is to prevent the
apparently inevitable tendency toward centralization and nationalization
from crushing individual initiative and any leeway for minority groups.
(The old vocabulary of "socialism" and "capitalism" seems to me completely out of date.) The Soviet imposition on Hungary and their alien
and mechanical system is detestable and frankly detested by all Hungarians
except those—not many—who have to pretend to go along with it. If they
could get the Russians off their necks, they would undoubtedly make their
own adjustment without all the repression and regimentation which even
after the explosion of 1956 they are still obliged to endure; but economically

_____
* Letter translated from the Hungarian.

Bossville R + D 1,
Oneida County, New York
1964. 6 augusztus

Kedves Méltóságos Drágám: Köszönöm a képes
levelezőlapokat. Örülök hogy élvezi a nyara-
lást. Nékem nincs nyaralásom. Nyáron csak dol-
gozok. Én már itt lakok nyolc hete egyedül, de most
az idősebb leányom megérkezett és tartózkodik
velem. Feleségem jön nemsokára. Ez van nagyon
kis falu — nyolcvan ember — hol van nékem családom
házai amely épült tizennyolcadik század végén.
Körülkerít képe. — Barátságos üdvözlet a
férjének.

            Szeretettel,
                Wilson Edmund

Do you think I'm
improving? I had very
little help with this.

See letter to Charlotte Kretzoi, August 6, 1964

they are tied to the Russians, having accepted from them loans and supplies, and with 40 percent of their trade with Russia. They yearn constantly toward the West and especially toward the United States, which they—disturbingly, to me—idealize; but we have stupidly refused to recognize the Kádár government, and our legation in Budapest, with Mindszenty on the top floor, is always guarded and subject to restrictions as representing a semi-hostile power. It is a spooky and uncomfortable place. But Hungary was the most interesting country I visited—not, except in certain imported features, like Russia, but like a partly and queerly metamorphosed Central Europe. Yet everywhere in the West is getting more and more alike. The people in the Budapest streets do not really seem so very different from the people in Paris and Boston.

I hope that we can soon get together and talk about all this . . .

As ever, Bunny W

1964–1965

To Barbara Epstein   June 11, 1964
The New York Review of Books   Wellfleet

Dear Barbara: Thank you for the copies of the *Review*. I think that it is
now really excellent. I enjoyed Gore Vidal on O'Hara—I hope it doesn't
lose O'Hara to Random House. On the other hand, I thought Roth on
the Baldwin play [*Blues for Mr. Charlie*] was dreary and very stupid. I
have just read this play, and though I can see that the last act might be
theatrically irritating, I think that it is very good. Roth's article seems to me
one of those supercilious pieces of destructive analysis that the New York
literati like to write in order to make themselves feel better when some
other writer both has become popular and is producing work of obvious
value. (Midge Decter on *Dr. Strangelove* in *Commentary* is another
example of this. Not content with an all-out successful satire, she objects
that the other side—the side that the satire is written from—ought to be
satirized too.)
   The Nabokov Pushkin has come. I shall take it to Talcottville and go
through it very carefully—hope to get you the article by the end of
summer. Just looking through it, I can see that Volodya's translation, sometimes in the same way, is almost as much open to objection as Arndt's.
It is full of flat writing, outlandish words, and awkward phrases. And
some of the things he says about the Russian language are inaccurate.
                                          . . . Love to everybody, Edmund

To Louise Bogan   August 6, 1964
                                                       Talcottville
. . . Morton Zabel's death made me sad. I wonder what the "thing" was
that he had been working on off and on for years and that he was rather
mysterious about . . .

To John Dos Passos   September 15, 1964
                                                      Wellfleet
Dear Dos: I was glad to get the stimulating postcard. But I feel obliged
to tell you that your article about the San Francisco convention sounded
like a teenager squealing over the Beatles. What on earth has happened
to you? How can you take Goldwater seriously? His utterances make no
sense and never have made any. But you seem to have arrived at a state
of pure faith where such questions no longer mean anything.

   We have seen something of Dawn [Powell] in Talcottville and New
York. She has been in and out of the hospital and seems far from well—
is suffering, she says, from anemia and is, for her, terribly thin.

   Our address from the end of this month will be 131 Mt. Vernon Street,
Middletown, Connecticut.   Bunny

To Jacob Landau   October 13, 1964
               Center for Advanced Studies, Wesleyan University
                                            Middletown, Conn.
Dear Jack: Thanks for your note. I am not teaching here. They give
fellowships to writers, artists, and scholars. It is delightful: they supply
you with everything from a house to postage stamps and pay you for
being here. If you should ever be in this neighborhood, I'd be very glad
to see you.   As ever, Edmund W

To Paul Horgan*   1967
Center for Advanced Studies
Dear Paul: I was just about to write you when your letter came. Barbara
Sutton has come to see us at Wellfleet and told us about you. She said you
had finished the [Maurice] Baring book and had enlarged your house,
which I hope someday to see. It must have been rather a relief to be able
to retire from that job. I kept thinking that it must be a trying, a very
exacting one, and you handled it very well. Juggling such diverse people
working in such different departments, and a different lot every year. But
it was profitable for the Fellows themselves to be thrown with a variety
of people of diverse faiths, nationalities, and interests. I should never, for
example, otherwise have had an opportunity of getting to know Father
D'Arcy—against whom I had had something of a prejudice—if it hadn't
been for the Center. We had dinner with him, by the way, not long ago
in Boston.

   I don't understand exactly what your Maurice Baring book is. You speak

---

* Paul Horgan, the novelist, was the director of the Center for Advanced Studies at
Wesleyan.

of it as a "compilation." It would give me, in any case, a pretext for an article about him . . . Could you send me a carbon or galleys? Who is publishing it? Roger? One point I'd like to make is that the only reproach to which Baring seemed vulnerable was that of wasting too much time on social life. There is a little flare-up of this kind in one of his letters in one of those memoirs you lent me. Do you remember where it is? If you do, I'd be very grateful if you would have the passage typed and send it to me. He behaves in a similar way in connection with the same accusation made against Pushkin—in one of his [Baring's] Russian books, which I have. Thank you for the Baring enclosures, which are interesting and useful. Thank you, too, for your own book, which hasn't yet arrived.

Best regards, as always, Edmund W.

To Mary Meigs   May 3, 1965
                                                                        Wesleyan
. . . I have become addicted to the novels of Maurice Baring, in which everybody is cultivated, well bred, well off, and extremely international. I recommend them in moderation . . .

To John Dos Passos   October 28, 1964
                                                                        Wesleyan
Dear Dos: Phoenician is supposed to have been very close to ancient— that is, pre-Bible—Hebrew. The Semitic alphabet is supposed to have been brought to Europe by the Phoenician traders, and all our Western alphabets have come out of it. There is a popular book which might be helpful called *The Story of Aleph Beth*, but I can't remember who wrote it. I happen to have two copies of Renan's *Histoire générale des langues sémitiques*, and would send you one, but they are in Wellfleet. But there is no difficulty about finding out about this. Don't you have an encyclopedia?   As ever, EW

To John Dos Passos   April 19, 1965
                                                                        Wesleyan
. . . I have seen the Gordon article—which is interesting. I knew that he believed he had identified Hebrew words in the Minoan script, but hadn't read him on the subject. Some scholars doubt his conclusions, but then some scholars always doubt genuine discoveries. Since you seem to be interested in the subject of Semitic languages, I am sending you an extra copy that I happen to have of Renan's history of their development. It is, of course, somewhat out of date, but Dupont-Sommer, Renan's successor at the Collège de France, tells me that he considers it excellent. I read it with much interest, but I am not sure that anybody who hadn't previously some knowledge of the subject would want to read it through. Look up

654

the parts about the Phoenicians and Carthaginians. Did you know that one of the most important items in the very scrappy remains of Carthaginian is a Carthaginian character in Plautus's *Poenulus* who talks in his own language? Nobody understood this scene till relatively modern times, when the speeches were put into the Hebrew alphabet and were found to be perfectly intelligible . . .

To MARY MEIGS   December 26, 1964
                                                              Wesleyan

Dear Mary: I missed you after you left New York and was going to write you, but as a result of walking back from Durlacher without a coat I came down with some kind of bronchitis and had to spend the next day in bed. My condition was aggravated by a strange evening I had spent the night before and in which I would have involved you if you had stayed. Arthur Schlesinger called me up rather mysteriously and invited me to a party "to meet," as they say, Jackie Kennedy and Tennessee Williams. It turned out to be one of the rites connected with the emergence of Mrs. Kennedy from mourning—in the house of a woman named vanden Heuvel, who is a big shot in the entertainment business. Lots of well-dressed ladies, very rich, and among them Saul Steinberg, John Galbraith, Truman Capote, and Arthur. I had some conversation with Steinberg, who is very much the solid, dogmatic, and serious-minded kind of Jew. He almost never allows himself to smile. On my other side was Galbraith, a very tall and equally dogmatic Canadian Scot, who smiles even more rarely than Steinberg. Mrs. Kennedy spent the whole evening talking to Tennessee W., then they left together, and for some reason I never grasped, we all went on to another party in the same building, where everybody was even richer; they seemed to be a mixture of old society (Vanderbilts and Whitneys) with café society—now to some extent, I suppose, the same thing. It was evidently a kind of housewarming for a tiny little white-mouse-like couple who had just furnished a huge apartment in what Augustus John, speaking of Wilde, called "impeccable bad taste." When you entered, you were confronted with one of Francis Bacon's yelling Popes side by side with a Vertes drawing, and beside the piano stood two products of pop art: a girl and a boy made of wooden boxes. On the walls of a big living room were absurd abstractions. People would say, "That's a _____, isn't it?" The host and hostess were referred to benevolently as "these children." I never knew why I was there or what it was all about. But you see what you missed by not staying over.

I got back to Middletown only half alive and took to my bed for two days—during which I read the Françoise Gilot book on Picasso, which is fascinating, and very illuminating when he talks about his painting. It confirmed me in my doubts about him. (You said you had read it, didn't you?) Doesn't he think too much about his public? He is so consciously preoccupied with shocking and at the same time always makes a point of putting in human or animal features in order that the ordinary person can find something he recognizes. There is something rather vulgar about him —in his art as well as his behavior.

. . . Am also enclosing an article on pop art. The author sounds very portentous and says that other people don't have the right attitude, but then doesn't seem to provide the expected illumination or to know where he stands himself. The man who teaches drawing here tells me that pop is already a thing of the past and that "op"—optical illusions—has taken its place.

We hope you will come on again soon and succeed in seeing the Hartford gallery. Love from all of us to everybody.   Edmund

To Mary Meigs   April 26, 1965
                                                         Wesleyan
. . . We're coming up to Wellfleet for the weekend, May 7–9, when I'll be seventy years old: it depresses me. I alternately think that I've had it and might as well call it a day, and that I must go into training and make an effort to accomplish a good deal more . . .

To Louise Bogan   October 7, 1965
                                                      Talcottville
Dear Louise: I'm sorry to hear from Betty Huling that you are back in Bloomingdale's, but maybe it is what you need after your year at Brandeis. (The young woman from there who wrote the life of Keats, Aileen Ward, spent the summer at Wellfleet, and we saw something of her and liked her.)

I spent most of my summer at Wellfleet this year, because all the family were converging there, but I have now come up here for a couple of weeks and am enjoying complete peace. I saw the [Glyn] Morrises the other night, who always inquire about you. He now has a projector in his basement and I brought up an avant-garde French film, which turned out to be pretty phony. The schools here are equipped with a whole library of documentaries, and we followed the story of neurotic impotence, in which Max Ernst, Fernand Léger, Cocteau, and a lot of other people had a hand, with the *Life of the Honey Bee*, which was fascinating. You see the honey scouts doing their dance, which indicates where and what the honey is, and the potential queens struggling to death for supremacy. My young Hungarian friend also remembers you and asks about you.

I have taken to reading Maurice Baring's novels, sometimes delightful, sometimes rather thin. Did you ever do anything with them? I wonder that more attention has not been paid to him. He knew more about Russia than any other Englishman had ever known. His books on Russian history, society, and literature, as well as his burlesques such as *Sherlock Holmes in Russia*—the only case in which he [Sherlock Holmes] was completely baffled: he couldn't tell who were the aristocrats and who were the revolutionaries, or what any of them was up to—were unique and are still, in some cases, the best things on their subjects in English.

This is not a brilliant letter, but what do you expect at seventy? I hope you will be out before long. Elena would send love, but I am up here alone.   Love from me, Edmund

To John Dos Passos   November 20, 1965
                                                              Wellfleet

Dear Dos: I was just about to write you. I have been rather upset by Dawn's death. I had always continued to see a good deal of her, and we were used to having her there. I went to see her in the hospital not long before she died, and she was more cheerful and animated than I was. Though she must have been full of sedatives, she was still making perfect sense . . .

We are spending the winter here for the first time after six years of Cambridge, Europe, and Wesleyan, and find it a great relief. We have settled down to an old-fashioned sort of domestic life—have had a fireplace built in the middle room and read Goethe aloud in the evenings. I am writing a farce-melodrama of American academic life, based on my recent experience. Elena sends love.   As ever, Edmund

חזק חזק ונתחזק

September 19, 1966
Wellfleet

To GLYN MORRIS
Lyons Falls, N.Y.

. . . I was delighted to get the Hebrew slogan and have put it up on the wall of my study . . . .

1966

AND

AWARDS

To Jacob Landau   March 14, 1966
                                                          Wellfleet
. . . By the way, what is the exact meaning of this at the end of the
Hebrew Bible? חזק ונתחזק המחוקק לא יוזק. I understand that it is an
exhortation to "be strong" and start reading the Torah again, but I can't
seem to identify what I take to be the other forms of חזק.* And how
should they be pointed?

                                          Sincerely, Edmund Wilson

To Jacob Landau   March 23, 1966
                                                          Wellfleet
Dear Jack: Thanks for your elucidation. I did know what the first part,
חזק, חזק ונתחזק,† meant and have often found it necessary to say it to
myself of recent years.   As ever, Edmund W

To Elizabeth Huling   April 26, 1966
                                                          Wellfleet
. . . I am feeling rather old myself, and even a pint of Scotch is likely to
enfeeble me the next day. But as the Hebrew Bible keeps saying at
intervals: *Hazayk, Hazayk, Venit-hazayk*—Be strong, be strong, let us
make ourselves strong . . .

---

* The root form of the word meaning strong.
† Be strong, and may we become strong.

I've always thought about you that you were like a girl of my own generation who had somehow turned up in the later one, and I found that your parents were much like the parents of my friends of my own generation. Your father seems to have the old-fashioned idea that the unemployed could always find work if they wanted to.

(To Clelia Carroll, 1966)

To CLELIA CARROLL   January 14, 1966
                                                            Wellfleet

Dear Clelia: I have already acquired *Tosca* and have played it twice. I think you must have seen it when you were very young and been carried away by the melodrama—of rather an old-fashioned kind: "Ha, ha, my proud beauty—your lover shall pay for this!" But there is a good theatrical movement at the end of the second act, when Tosca has just killed Scarpia and says,

> "E morto! Or gli perdono!
> E avanti a lui tremava tutta Roma!"

I have a recording in which Callas sings Tosca, and she seems to lower her register most effectively for this.

How are you getting along with the *Ring*? It is really much more interesting, I find, to listen attentively to an act or two at a time on the phonograph than to hear it in the opera house. I never thought seriously before about the meaning of *Götterdämmerung*. The false Siegfried is a strange conception. (Siegfried tells his life story too many times. As Bernard Shaw says, he is telling it again when they kill him.)

I have never read *The Hobbit*,* but Helen, when she was younger, read it or had it read to her innumerable times, so it must be a good children's story. I can't imagine it in an English course, though.

We have been madly reading Balzac—another valuable resource for spending winter in the country. I don't suppose you have enough time on your hands for this, but if you should ever want to, let me make you some recommendations. You have undoubtedly, at some point in your education, had to read *Père Goriot* or *Eugénie Grandet*. I read these early, and they rather put me off him, and I have only lately been getting interested in him. Some of them are immensely amusing . . .

My line about Truman Capote is that he wants to be the feminine Elsa Maxwell.

We expect to be in New York for a week or two at the beginning of February. Do let me know if you will be there.   As ever, Edmund

---

* By J. R. R. Tolkien.

To CECIL LANG   March 16, 1966
University of Chicago   Wellfleet

Dear Cecil: . . . This winter, for the purposes of something I am writing,
I have been reading the Elizabethan dramatists, together with Lamb,
Swinburne, Saintsbury, and Eliot on the subject. They used to amuse me
more than they do now. A good deal of it is awful rubbish, turned out at
top speed to make a fast pound. In the cases of collaboration, the parts
written by different hands are sometimes not even consistent. As for the
pretentious Chapman, so seriously taken by some, he seems to me the
most unreadable writer I have ever tried to read. The high praises of the
critics mentioned above often seem to me quite inexplicable. In my farce-
melodrama of academic life I have to have an Elizabethan forgery perpe-
trated by one of the professors, and I am in process of writing parts of
three acts of it. I find that I am having difficulty in making it extravagant
enough, and am discouraged at finding in a play of Shirley's—*Love Tricks,
or the School of Complement*—a set of parodies of Elizabethan drama and
prose that I can never hope to equal. Shirley came late enough [1596–
1666]—he already anticipates Congreve—to look back on his predecessors
and see how absurd they sounded.
   Please remember me to your wife. I hope that she is getting used to
Chicago.   Best regards, Edmund Wilson

To CELIA GOODMAN   March 30, 1966
                                                         Wellfleet
. . . I am working on my academic comedy,* which seems to me hilariously
funny, but although I can judge the effect of things that I publish in
The New Yorker, I never know about my plays . . .

To ELIZABETH HULING   August 23, 1966
                                                         Wellfleet
. . . Watch for my academic comedy in *The New York Review of Books*.
. . . *The New Yorker* was going to run my play but wanted me to change
the Elizabethan word *firk*, which doesn't mean what it sounds like but
which I exploit a little for comic effects . . .

To CECIL LANG   April 4, 1966
                                                         Wellfleet
Dear Cecil: . . . In regard to the question you raise in connection with
Sons and Lovers, I can't contribute an opinion because I've never read
the book. I've always been meaning to read Lawrence's novels—other than

―――――――――
* *The Duke of Palermo.*

Lady C.—but have never got around to it. I met him once and thought him ill-bred and hysterical, and his writing mostly affects me in the same way. Best regards, Edmund W

Have been reading through Swinburne's Elizabethan criticism, and in spite of his overstating everything, have been quite impressed by it.

To Alfred Kazin April 3, 1966
Wellfleet

. . . About your proposed march on Washington: I don't believe that a lot of writers will make any impression on Johnson except to influence him the other way. He already believes that the writers belong to the category who are not with him, so against him. But send me your statement, by all means . . .

To Alfred Kazin April 12, 1966
Wellfleet

Dear Alfred: All right: add my name to your statement.

Edmund

To Alison Lurie February 16, 1966
The New Yorker

Dear Alison: I have just got around to reading your book, and I am rather astonished by it.* I think it is a brilliant performance, without a trace of amateurishness. The dialogue, the descriptions, and the invention of incident are all first-class. How did you get to know so much about the beats and the Hollywood actors? The book amused me immensely. Not having read your first novel, I didn't know you had that much talent. The only thing that seemed to me forced was the wife's staying behind in California. It is a good comic idea, but didn't seem to me convincing.

My best regards to Jonathan [Bishop].† Perhaps you can both come over to see me when I am in upstate New York again.

Sincerely, Edmund Wilson

To Alison Lurie July 19, 1966
Wellfleet

. . . Thank you for sending me *Love and Friendship*. I enjoyed it, though not quite so much as the Los Angeles book . . .

I deplore your misuse of "disinterest" for "lack of interest." You have it on 214 and again on 219. The curious thing is that on the latter page you use "disinterestedly" a few lines below correctly. But then you misuse

---

* *The Nowhere City.*
† Jonathan Bishop, John Peale Bishop's son, married to Alison Lurie.

"disinterest" again on 230. "Semivierges" on 231 should be "demivierges," and it does not have an accent . . .

To Mary Meigs   May 23, 1966
                                                            Talcottville

. . . I have been reading Anaïs Nin's *Diary*, which reached me here. Elena says that another copy has been sent to Wellfleet. If you people would like to read it, ask her for it. It is undoubtedly Anaïs's most interesting book, but there is a little too much about Henry Miller's wife, who fascinated both Anaïs and Miller and about whom they endlessly talked, but who doesn't sound all that fascinating . . . The *Diary*, after the beginning, opens up and becomes quite absorbing. I think you really ought to read it . . .

To Mary Meigs   August 11, 1966

. . . About Anaïs Nin: she is much more attractive than the pictures in that book, which are mostly very bad. The only photograph that is any good is the one by Carl Van Vechten, and that doesn't look much like her. She doesn't really pose: that is what she is actually like—like nobody else I have known. She is a practical little Franco-Spanish housewife on one side of her personality, and yet I always felt about her that I was dealing with a lovely little nymph who was not quite a human being. What you might not gather from this book is that she can be extremely amusing. I like to talk to her—especially about people and books, which is all she is really interested in. When she gave me her last piece of fiction, she told me that it was frankly "a funny book," but it sounded very much like all her others, and if you didn't know her, you would think that it was only unconsciously funny.

When I saw her last, she had just come back from California and had been somewhat disconcerted to find Henry Miller living a thoroughly bourgeois life in Los Angeles, with a swimming pool and all the other status symbols . . .

> The novel about Hollywood with most teeth in it is still that intrepid satire by Miss Anita Loos called *The Better Things of Life*, which came out serially in *Cosmopolitan* . . .
>   (*The Boys in the Back Room*, 1941)

To Anita Loos   October 8, 1966
                                                            Wellfleet

Dear Miss Loos: I have just read your book with delight and fascination.*
The first part is a wonderful description of California the way it used to

---
* *A Girl Like I.*

be. The New York part plunged me back into the twenties and was quite exhilarating. It has a lot about people I used to know, with a good deal about them that I didn't know—including that poor old Alec Woollcott had always wanted to become a mother. Reading you makes me regret that, in those days, I only met you once or twice. Would it be possible, if you are in New York, to get you to come to dinner or something? Perhaps you feel, as I sometimes do nowadays, that you have already seen enough people.

I thought, by the way, that your last two novels didn't get the attention they deserved. Perhaps they came out too long after the first two. Can't you get Viking to bring out an omnibus of all four together?

Yours sincerely, Edmund Wilson

To ANITA Loos   November 23, 1966
                                                                        Wellfleet

Dear Anita (If I'm going to call you Anita, you must stop calling me Mr. Wilson): We hope to be in New York sometime after the first of the year and shall certainly see you . . . I don't know whether Arthur Schlesinger's research has gone so far as the *Princess* [*with the Golden Hair*]. He asked me to explain the difference between the behavior of the young people in *This Side of Paradise* and the ones in *I Thought of Daisy*, an earlier novel of mine. He didn't seem to have understood that even the cocktail-drinking debutantes of Scott Fitzgerald were a good deal more conventional than the inhabitants of Greenwich Village in the twenties, who had already been working at Free Love a decade. I am curious to see what he produces.   Best regards, Edmund W

To FRANCIS STEEGMULLER   October 28, 1966
                                                                        Wellfleet

Dear Steegmuller: I don't know how printable this anecdote is, I got it from an Oxford friend, who had been told it by the French professor who, on the occasion when Cocteau was given an honorary degree at Oxford, had taken him to see Bowra. Bowra, in his French of Stratford atte Bowe, was boasting of a decoration that he had been given in France: "*Et à la fin j'ai été baisé par le Président de la République.*" (Bowra's sexual proclivities are well known.) The professor, in telling the story, said, "*Et devant ces dames françaises! Cocteau ne broncha pas.*"

Best regards, Edmund Wilson

To FRANCIS STEEGMULLER   March 20, 1967
                                                                        Wellfleet

Dear Mr. Steegmuller: Yes: certainly tell Gallup that you may use any of Cocteau's letters that may be found among my correspondence. I saw him in Paris in the summer of 1921. I was struck—though I did not agree

664

with him—by his saying that Flaubert was always getting ready to shoot but did not hit the target, whereas Stendhal aimed and hit the mark again and again. I later found this idea developed at the beginning of "Le Secret professionel." I was interested then in Octave Mirbeau: he agreed that *Sébastien Roch* was good, but said, *"C'est toute une génération que notre génération a sauté."* He said of Anatole France that he was *fou de la politique,* but also too much preoccupied with such matters as imagining what Mme de Noailles and her lover were like in bed—she with her disproportionately large head.

I translated, for *Vanity Fair, Les Mariés de la Tour Eiffel,* and for some years he sent me his books.　　　　　Yours sincerely, Edmund Wilson

To JOHN DOS PASSOS　　　　　　　　　　November 26, 1966
　　　　　　　　　　　　　　　　　　Wellfleet

Dear Dos: I have just read *The Best Times* and very much enjoyed it. I wish we could talk about it. The part about your father is fascinating, and the account of your travels in Persia, etc., for some reason seems to me to come out better than when you wrote about it before. Why didn't you tell about your experiences during the Spanish War and the reasons—execution of Robles, etc.—for the coolness between you and Hemingway? —all this, so far as I knew about it, seemed so characteristic both of him and of you.

In my case, you are somewhat inaccurate. I was never "an honorary member of The Society of American Magicians," nor did I travel back and forth between New York and Red Bank on a motorcycle. I once bought a second-hand motorcycle in Red Bank, but I never tried to ride it more than once. It broke down, and since I had no idea what to do about it, I had to push it as far as I could, then get it picked up. I don't think that you and I could have been talking about Henry James at Sea Bright— I never knew you to be interested in him; but I remember that when we were jumping the waves, I was trying to expound Whitehead and modern physics. I think that you have also got one of your stories about Scott Fitzgerald wrong. On the occasion when he threw the vegetables—they were things like half grapefruit from the garbage pail, weren't they?—he had purposefully not been asked by the Murphys to meet their nobilities, and, in order to show his defiance, heaved the vegetables into the party from behind a wall. (Archie MacLeish is said to have gone out and socked him.) I know that he wrote on Margaret Bishop's dress with a lipstick. But did he do this more than once?

There are several mistakes in the foreign words, which I list in case you want to correct them for a paperback edition* . . . Writing so much for

---

* List of corrections deleted.

The New Yorker, with its checking department, has made me a stickler for accuracy. But my own books, to my disgust, always come out with mistakes.

Your pronouncements on current events continue to give me the creeps. I recognize you in *The Best Times*, but your latest article and previous ones in *The National Review* sound to me like some of the messages from Mark Twain or Oscar Wilde that are supposed to be transmitted through mediums. In regard to the most recent one that I have seen: I have talked with a number of people who take part in those demonstrations, and I have never yet found anyone who talked Marxist. Of course, the Communists try to infiltrate them as they always do such movements, but they don't seem to have much success, and there are few of them left now. As for Daniel and Sinyavsky: all the regulation protests and petitions have been made. I declined to sign one because (a) it was going to be drafted by Dwight Macdonald and (b) I was afraid that, coming before the trials, it would further antagonize the authorities. It seems to me that it is more to the point to protest against the mendacity of the President and of the Administration generally, and of the suppressions that are now beginning of opposition to the Vietnam War.

I hope that all these corrections and objections will in no way obscure the sincerity *de mes sentiments les plus distingués et les plus amicaux*. We may get to New York for a few weeks after New Year's. If you should be coming on, do let us know. You can always find out whether I'm there from *The New Yorker*. But I want also to go to Jordan and Israel to bring the Dead Sea scrolls up to date, and I'm not sure, at my age and with my ailments, how much I'll be able to move around. Travel tires me out, and I'm always only too glad to get back here. Please remember us to Betty.

As ever, Bunny W

Medals and Awards
1957–1968

Roger Straus was telling me about a seventy-year-old sculptor who began getting medals. When Roger congratulated him, he said: "The thing is to outlive the sons of bitches."

American Academy of Arts and Letters, New York
Gold Medal of the National Institute, May 25, 1955

Academy of Liberal Judaism, New York
Certificate of Tribute for *The Scrolls from the Dead Sea*,
    February 28, 1956

Princeton University
Doctor of Letters *honoris causa*, June 12, 1956

United States Presidential Medal of Freedom, 1963

The Edward MacDowell Medal (for outstanding contribution
to literature), August 16, 1964

The National Medal for Literature, 1966

Aspen Award, June 12, 1968

Festival International du Livre, Nice, France
Grand Aigle d'Or International, 1971

To Van Wyck Brooks   March 1, 1957
                                                 Cambridge

. . . About the Institute [of Arts and Letters]: I can't see that it serves any
good purpose, except for its handouts to writers and artists—and I don't
want to have to lobby and vote about them. Still less do I want to have
to worry about who is or is not admitted . . .

To John F. Kennedy   July 14, 1963
                                                Talcottville

Dear President Kennedy: I am of course extremely appreciative of the
award of the Freedom Medal. I am sorry that I shall be in Europe in
September, so that I shall not be able to be present at the ceremony.
                        Yours sincerely, Edmund Wilson

To Alfred Kazin   March 8, 1966
                                                 Wellfleet

. . . The [American Academy of] Arts and Science people couldn't be
vaguer, and have told me that if I want to know anything more, I ought
to apply to you. Don't bother about it, though. I suppose that in time
they'll let me know exactly what I'm supposed to do. This "Academy"
seems to me a phantom. I hope the thousand dollars is not . . .

To Mary Meigs   May 23, 1966
                                                Talcottville

. . . I am going to stay up here till I get my award* on June 3. The awarders
are coming to Utica. In the little speech of acknowledgment I have just
written, I end with a plug against Vietnam by way of the money's being
tax free . . .

---

* The National Medal for Literature.

To Loren and Mary Crosten   June 16, 1966
Boonville, Oneida County, N.Y.   Wellfleet

Dear Loren and Mary: The bestowal of the award went off painlessly
enough. It was a good idea to make them come to Utica and to give the
lunch myself, because I was able to curb the publicity and the number of
people involved. You are mistaken in thinking that I have stripped the
country of awards. I was told that I was in line for a $30,000 handout
from Aspen, Colorado, and we had it all spent in imagination. But I
missed out on that one . . . Perhaps it is just as well: I was beginning to
feel like a stuffed shirt.

     The lady-slipper that you found was, I take it, the *Cypripedium acaulis*.
There are a great many of them here—we gathered some yesterday. The
yellow ones are rarer, and the showy orchid—pink and white—rarest of all.
But I found a place last summer [in Talcottville] that had all three.
Walter Edmonds's son found a showy orchid on the Black River and
successfully transplanted it to their garden.

     I have been trying to come under the spell of Anton Webern, but have
not been—and I know never shall be—entirely successful.

                                              Best regards, Edmund W.

To Ada Nisbet   August 24, 1967
                                                            Wellfleet
. . . Thank you for the suggestion of an honorary degree from California;
but I have had one from my own university, Princeton, and have refused
all such offers since . . .

To Helen Muchnic   June 12, 1968
                                                        The New Yorker
. . . I am going to get the dough at a dinner tonight—unless some literary
enemy shoots me first . . .

To Mary Meigs   June 22, 1968
                                                            Talcottville
. . . The dinner to celebrate the Aspen Award turned out to be somewhat
unexpected: all big executives and oil millionaires. The wife of the president of the Institute said to me, "You wrote *Finlandia*, didn't you?" I
said, "No, that was written by a Finn" . . .

To Ada Nisbet   July 12, 1968
                                                            Talcottville
. . . I didn't go out to Aspen to get my award because I learned that it was
8,000 feet high and I couldn't on account of angina. They gave it to me in
New York . . .

1967–1968

AND

ISRAEL

To Morton D. Zabel   1942

. . . No, I've never read Balzac on a large scale, but once bought his complete works, like you—in the Conrad edition—and someday am going to attack them . . .

To Celia Goodman   January 31, 1967
Wellfleet

. . . We have been madly reading Balzac this winter. I never got "hooked" on him before. He is either quite wonderful or completely implausible and unintentionally funny. I don't think that anybody has ever treated on such a huge scale all the bad sides of the French character . . .

To Roger W. Straus, Jr.   January 20, 1967
Wellfleet

Dear Roger: . . . I thought that I wouldn't revise the text of *Daisy* and didn't reread it before I gave it to you. But when I began to go through the proofs I realized that I could not let it be reprinted in the often inept form in which I wrote it in the twenties, so have had to revise it drastically, at the rate of only about ten galleys a day (but I'm sending it back today). I'll have to have a costly revise on this, too. I ought, of course, to have foreseen this, but I thought I could get by. Redoing it is a nuisance for everybody, but I am having a certain satisfaction in seeing my books republished in a better format and text.

I also cut the *Prelude* all to hell and should be getting a revise on it in a week or so. As I get older, I revise more and more and have been somewhat spoiled in this respect by the fact that *The New Yorker* allows any number of proofs—eleven on the Dead Sea scrolls—and any amount of resetting. I suppose I'd hear the howl of the banshee if I suggested that, in the case of *Prelude*, Farrar, Straus and I should go halves on the cost of corrections.

Best regards. Shall be seeing you in early February.   Edmund

To Richard Ellmann   January 31, 1967
                                                          Wellfleet

Dear Mr. Ellmann: Thank you for your letter. I forgot to say when I wrote you that I was interested to learn that Joyce had read Mirbeau's *Sébastien Roch* before writing *A Portrait of the Artist*. I happened to read the Mirbeau book not long after the *Portrait* and was struck by the resemblances between them.* I mentioned it in an essay on Mirbeau in my *Classics and Commercials*. I think that Joyce must have been influenced by Mirbeau.   Yours sincerely, Edmund Wilson

To Helen Muchnic   March 31, 1967
                                                          Wellfleet

Dear Helen: I read your paper and Dorothy's paper with interest. I can't discuss Dorothy's in a letter but should like to talk with her about it. I also want to tell her about a brilliant Jesuit dropout whom I met in New York, an Irishman named Malachi Martin, a former associate of Cardinal Bea, who knows all about the Dead Sea scrolls and who, since he has left the order, is translating the Encyclopaedia Britannica into Arabic. He and I had the dinner table in roars of laughter telling about the adventures of the scrolls and the personalities connected with them. It was unpredictable that on such a subject we should sound almost like vaudeville comedians in what used to be called a "sidewalk conversation" . . . I expect to go to Jordan and Israel in the latter part of April in order to bring my Dead Sea scrolls book up to date . . .

I recommend Thornton Wilder's new novel, which seems to me the best thing he ever wrote.† It stirred me up more than anything I had read since *Zhivago*—though it is not really so remarkable—and I wonder whether it may not have been partly inspired by Pasternak. Have you read Chukovskaya's book? I have sent for it.

No other news in this *morte saison*.   Love, Edmund

To John Dos Passos   April 6, 1967
                                                          Wellfleet

Dear Dos: Mario Praz writes me that you have been awarded the Feltrinelli Prize, 20 million lire, "for narrative art," and intimates that I might let you know, but says to tell you not to talk about it, because it isn't to be announced till the end of May. He was on the committee that decided

---

* See "The Early Years," p. 40.
† *The Eighth Day*.

it, and since he knows a great deal about American writing, I imagine that he put it over. He is at Dumbarton Oaks at this moment and would probably like to see you—I congratulate you. It is delightful to be given non-taxable money . . .

I am going to Israel and Jordan at the end of April for the purpose of bringing my scrolls book up to date.

Have you read Thornton Wilder's novel? I think it is the best thing he has done. You might not like it so well—though it has certain things in common with *U.S.A.*   Love to the family, EW

To GLYN MORRIS   April 20, 1967
                                                   Wellfleet

Dear Glyn: Yes: the oil has been a nuisance. People rescue the poor birds and take them to the Audubon Society to be cleaned off . . .

I am taking off for Jordan and Israel on the 27th in order to bring my Dead Sea scrolls book up to date. (Am back plodding through the Hebrew Bible again.) I'll be gone a month, and when I get back shall have to stay here till after the Fourth of July in order to finish my manuscript. I have all my books and other things on the subject here. But shall then go over to Talcottville, where I look forward to seeing you. The weather here has been horrible. We had snow a couple of days ago . . .

                                                   Love to you both, Edmund
    If you have any time for such things, do read Thornton Wilder's new book . . . I should be interested to know how you react to the religious element.

To SHELDON MEYER   May 13, 1965
Oxford University Press   Wesleyan University

. . . The Dead Sea scrolls that are in Jerusalem have been housed in a new museum, the opening of which I was invited to attend but couldn't. They have, however, invited me to come any time at their expense and have offered to take me up on Masada—you probably know about the recent discoveries there. I have been thinking of making the trip, but shouldn't be able to do so till next spring. I should also, of course, go to Jordan, where the scrolls are kept that Oxford is publishing. This would delay the new edition of my book but undoubtedly make it more interesting . . .

ISRAEL, 1967—ITINERARY

Thursday   April 27   Leave Kennedy, Pan American   6.30 p.m.
                           Arrive Rome, Hotel Victoria   8.30 a.m.

Sunday	April 30	Leave Rome	12.10 p.m.
		Arrive Jerusalem,	4.45 p.m.
		American School of Oriental	
		Research, Jerusalem, via Amman,	
		Hashemite Kingdom of Jordan	
May 24		Leave Tel Aviv, Air France #139	8.45 a.m.
		Arrive Paris, Hôtel de Castille	1.15 p.m.
May 29		Leave Paris, TWA	4.15 p.m.
		Arrive Boston	6.50 p.m.

To ELENA WILSON   May 1, 1967
                                                        Jerusalem

. . . The next day I hired a car and went out to Bomarzo with Darina
[Silone] . . . Bomarzo, with its wild park and monsters, is more interesting
than I had expected. I think that I am going to write about it. The legend
about it is that one of the Orsini dukes was "a hunchback and deformed"
and that his wife went to bed with a handsome young brother. The Duke
killed the brother and then, to "express his anguish," began in 1560 on
the park of the monsters. What is striking about this is that the whole
thing, taken together, represents the emotions and imagination of a curious
kind of poet. The inscriptions that go with the figures and other objects
make an impression almost of Surrealism. Paolo Milano says that it is
"baroque before the baroque"; Silone says that it is a kind of thing that is
German rather than Italian: the Italians don't like works of art to be
grotesque and outlandish to that extent. I found that Mario Praz, who
had been excited by the monsters, was strangely disappointing when he
wrote about them, and I attribute this to two causes: that he did not want
to dwell on the Duke's deformity, and that, with his bad foot, he found
it difficult to get around the park. It is all on a steep hill, dominated by
the old castle high above, and—it was one of my tottery days—I had trouble
getting around myself. I didn't go down to the lowest level, because I
thought that I couldn't get up again. Darina went down and reported—
she copied out the inscriptions there . . .

To ELENA WILSON   May 11, 1967
                                                        Jerusalem

. . . I enjoyed my stay on the other side [Jordan], but I rather dislike the
Arabs. They are always waylaying you or leaping out at you and trying
to sell you something for which they overcharge you. As they told me at
the school, "There's no question of right or wrong. They just want to take
all they can get." (I went rather *octorogno** when I wrote you from Jordan

---

* Careful, cautious.

because correspondence is censored and sometimes suppressed.) Nor do I much like old Jerusalem. When you first go there, it stimulates the imagination, but on this visit I did almost no sightseeing. I did, however, on my last day, make a trip to Bethlehem, where I had never been. The road there is the most frightening I have ever been driven on: mostly on the edge of abysmal drops, with no guards to keep cars from falling off, and full of abrupt loopings—in going around one of these, you may suddenly be confronted with a huge bus . . . now you have to go eleven miles out of the way so as not to trespass on Israeli territory. The Church of the Holy Nativity at Bethlehem is much more attractive than the Holy Sepulcher: built by Constantine, rebuilt by Justinian. You enter by a small low door, intended for the double purpose of preventing the Crusaders from riding their horses and camels into the church and of promoting humility on the part of those entering in approaching the birthplace of Christ. I did not go down to the stable in which Jesus is supposed to have been born nor to the cell in which St. Jerome is supposed to have made his Latin version of the Bible, on account of the steep steps. Also visited Shepherds' Field, where the shepherds are supposed to have heard angels singing: a large cave, a little church. It was guarded by a single Franciscan, a chinless young man from Cleveland, who complained about the scorpions.

. . . I was driven over here yesterday morning in a car from the consulate. The city has been much cleaned up and built up since I was here before, and is now a well-developed town, which gives an impression of solidity. This hotel is crammed with very bourgeois and not particularly attractive visitors from all over, who have come for the festivities of Independence Day. They have given me splendid rooms, with a basket of fruit from the manager.

I had dinner last night with Moshe Pearlman. Do you remember that he came to dinner with me once in New York? He is likable and a very lively talker: politics, literature, language. The great question they now discuss is whether the original idealism is fading—since many are leaving Israel—and how they can carry on . . .

To Elena Wilson   May 14, 1967
                                                            Jerusalem
. . . The next day I went to see [Yigael] Yadin . . . He is tall, good-looking, and cosmopolitan. He speaks English incredibly well and has a great deal of charm. He held me spellbound for two hours and a half, talking about the scrolls. He and Père de Vaux think, as I do, that John Allegro is dotty in his theories about the New Testament. He tells me that the BBC had a recent symposium in London in which he and Allegro and two other scrolls scholars performed, and that it has never been published

as it was supposed to be—he believes because Allegro got rather the worst of it and has prevented its publication. He says it was the occasion for more plain speaking than has ever occurred before, and that I ought to try to get a transcript.

On Friday, Kollek the Mayor took me and an American photographer around the city, ending with a visit to Agnon. The old man has a very firm face—unlike the photographs, which make him look ugly. He speaks only German and Hebrew, so Pearlman interpreted between us, and we exchanged well-turned compliments. We drank "L-Hayïm," "to life," in cognac. He gave me a bunch of flowers, then another bunch of flowers from a vase in the living room, and then, as I was going, another flower, which he picked in the front lawn. He gave me one of his books with an inscription in Hebrew: "To the honored Edmund Wilson who has been graced by God with an eye to see and a heart to understand." (I am enjoying all these compliments.) Kollek had warned us that we mustn't stay long, since Sabbath begins Friday afternoon, and Agnon would soon have to be taking his ritual bath. His street has been named after him, but he lives in the utmost austerity. When asked what he would do with the Nobel money, he said that he did not intend to use any more margarine. (Butter is not kosher—at the hotel, you cannot get butter, or in the restaurants that are kosher.) He says that he is rather frightened at the prospect of his reception by the Jews in New York. He tells about getting the prize in a way that makes it sound like one of the stories he writes. He had spent the whole day attempting to get the plumber and always being frustrated. The man was never there or never seemed to get his message. Then late in the afternoon somebody knocked at the door, and he thought, "At last, the plumber!" It was a man from the Foreign Office announcing the Nobel Prize.

On Saturday, I went to the school of archaeology, the counterpart of the American School on the other side, where I met much the same kind of people: American archaeologists and Biblical scholars. They had a "cook-in" at one on the terrace. I met there a jolly and learned rabbi who teaches in the Cincinnati seminary, and we had a good round of American highballs . . . there is very little drinking here . . . they have no alcoholic problem, no one is ever drunk on the streets.

To Elena Wilson   May 20, 1967
                                                            Jerusalem
. . . I hope you are not worrying about the news. Nobody that I have seen takes this "crisis" seriously . . .

I went to the terrific "tattoo" and parade that the Arabs protested against and in which, for that reason, the armament display was limited.

Under pressure, apparently, by the British, with their interest in Saudi Arabia, the U.S. and French ambassadors did not attend, and the Israelis, I think, were rather miffed that almost nobody but the representatives of the African republics were there. The celebration was evidently regarded by the Arabs as a militant gesture, and Nasser has responded with a countergesture.

After witnessing the start of the parade from the stadium, I was taken to the house of the Mayor, Teddy Kollek: splendid library dealing with this part of the world, cupboards full of antiquities, two Chagalls. All kinds of people came in: the Liberian ambassador and his wife; a Chaliapin who is Dassia's brother; . . . a Jewish English lady, who contributed to the financing of the Masada excavation; an American advertizing man. After that, we went on to the house of one of the few resident millionaires, an American Jew named Shuover, who arranged our first loan to Russia, was suspected of being a Soviet agent and pursued or investigated, then enriched himself in Venezuela, and finally married an Israeli wife and built himself a very fancy and luxurious house, with specially made walls of mosaic and lots of pictures, mostly in very bad taste, but including a portrait by Repin which he bought when he was in Russia and of which he is very proud. We lunched in a modern-style pergola, with a roof like a kind of pinched-in bonnet. Everybody chic was there. The lady who sat next to me told me that her Sephardic family had come straight from Spain to Palestine in the sixteenth century and had been here ever since. I thought she was rather snooty about my friend Grodzensky, who used to work in New York on a Yiddish paper. She implied that she did not associate with the Yiddish-speaking element.

To Elena Wilson   May 23, 1967
                                                              Jerusalem
. . . The intellectuals I have talked to here have tended to shrug off the possibility of war; Teddy Kollek, the Mayor, and Yadin, who was Commander-in-Chief during the other war, seem, however, to take it more seriously. Yadin says that both the Egyptians and the Israelis have massed troops along the border, with 700 tanks on each side, and that the test of Nasser's intentions will be whether he goes so far as to block Israel's shipping. If he does, there will be war. The politics of the six Arab states—which I have never paid much attention to before—are extremely complicated: monarchists and republicans, who call themselves socialists, and England and Soviet Russia intent on acquiring or safeguarding oil.

. . . I have made another trip to the new museum, under the escort of the custodian of the scrolls building. It has a wonderful collection of copper and silver synagogue ornaments with a whole transported Venetian synagogue, and archaeological and paleontological remains that they have been collecting for fifty years. They bring you close to the various periods of the life described in the Bible . . . The architecture, the atmosphere, and the presentation of the exhibits made it seem the most satisfactory museum I've visited. It is situated on a hill, and the construction of the segmented building has been made to follow the contours of the slopes. Everything new in Jerusalem is controlled by a planning board. All the houses and other buildings have to be made of blocks of the same kind of pale stone. The highways have been planned with a view to connecting eventually with the rest of the city . . . I have seen the Chagall windows, which are gorgeous . . .

The weather is getting hot, and I shall be glad to get to Paris tomorrow . . .

To ANITA LOOS   June 9, 1967
                                                                  Wellfleet

Dear Anita: I am sending you a copy of my memoirs.* There is really not very much that was not in the *New Yorker* installments.

The timing of my departure from the Middle East turned out to be perfect. I had a flight from Tel Aviv to Paris the morning of the day before the consul called me up to say that he had had word from Washington to tell all the Americans to leave. Aside from the mess things were in when I left, my trip was highly satisfactory. (Note that the scrolls were found by the *Dead*, not the *Red*, Sea. The Red Sea is what the Egyptians are trying to keep the Israelis out of.)

Janet Flanner and Natalia Murray and I talked about you in the somber and palatial old bar of the Continental. I came back singing, "I loathe Paris in the springtime," etc.

Have a good trip yourself. Best regards to your household.   Edmund

To ALISON LURIE   June 24, 1967
                                                                  Wellfleet

Dear Alison: It's a great pleasure to have a friend whose wife writes novels that you really want to read. I think that *Imaginary Friends* is so far perhaps your most satisfactory book. It was especially interesting to me because I had just come back from the Middle East and had been brooding on the origins of religions. Have you read Fawn Brodie's book on Joseph Smith? It is really quite upsetting. Here you see the whole thing

---

* *A Prelude.*

676

being manufactured by a scoundrel out of nothing at all but his egoism. By the way, please don't let your narrator—p. 111—use "disinterested" in that false meaning that sets my teeth on edge.

. . . Best regards to Jonathan. Edmund W.

To ANITA LOOS   July 29, 1967
                                                                Talcottville
Dear Anita: Thanks for your letter. I got it the morning after I had finished reading the biography of Cole Porter—interesting, though rather illiterate—in which you sometimes figure. It seems strange to me now, at my age, that I lived through all that period, saw a good many of those shows, and knew some of those people. Hope to talk to you someday about the Porters. He was certainly a very special case: to have had that much talent and worked so hard with all that money . . . Love, Edmund

To MARY MEIGS   August 14, 1967
                                                                Talcottville
. . . Otherwise, nothing much of interest—I'll be seeing you soon, I expect. I read all Ibsen in college except the very earliest plays. I saw Kachalov and the Moscow Art Theatre do *An Enemy of the People*. He was wonderful in the scene where the Doctor makes his speech which takes him through the different phases of the reformer who at first is sorry for the common people and wants to help them and then realizes how stupid and crooked a bourgeois community is bound to be. This scene is very dramatic but it takes a very good actor, and in other inferior productions I have seen, it has always been speeded up and cut. In the Moscow Art Theatre production, the speech was addressed to the actual audience, and the Norwegian characters who heckle and interrupt were planted among them. You probably ought to read Bernard Shaw's *Quintessence of Ibsenism*— though he exaggerates Ibsen's interest in social reforms. What he was interested in was really the individual *versus* society—a conflict which he makes come out sometimes one way, sometimes another. Shaw doesn't understand or appreciate *Rosmersholm*, because the past is too much for the reformers. Don't you think *Hedda Gabler* represents a type still with us? . . .

To ANITA LOOS   November 11, 1967
                                                                Wellfleet
Dear Anita: Thank you for sending the Keynes book, but I thought you said *auto*biography. I have read Harrod. The [Lytton] Strachey book goes on and on and gets to be not so much a book as a way of life. The sexual

complications get to be more and more fantastic. Do read it when the second and more interesting volume appears.

. . . Love from us both, Edmund

To Celia Goodman   November 12, 1967
                                                              Wellfleet

Dear Celia: We were glad to hear from you. We have no exciting news. My age is beginning to tell on me, and I tend to go to sleep when I ought to be working. We have just come back, much fatigued, from a trip to upstate New York and New York City and found my new study and upstairs room at my end of the house finished (it is really a separate house; connected only by a corridor with the rest)—something that I had been looking forward to for years, but now am appalled at facing, because it means sorting out all my books, hundreds of which I am giving away or selling. Also, papers and phonograph records.

Do you know Penelope Gilliatt, who was married to John Osborne and did theater and movies for the *Observer*? She has taken up with Mike Nichols—do you know about Nichols and May?—and is working for *The New Yorker* now. We like her very much and she is coming up here for Thanksgiving. She is wonderful for me, because she laughs so heartily at everything I say that is meant to be funny.

. . . I went to the Middle East in April and May to bring my book on the Dead Sea scrolls up to date—left just before the shooting commenced. I am very much pro-Israel—don't see how those dopey Arabs can ever accomplish anything.

Have you read the first volume of the Strachey biography? . . . It is of enormous size and reading it becomes a kind of "way of life"—more like a long old-fashioned novel. All those people wrote so many letters that it is possible to follow them day by day, and the ins and outs of their love affairs, as they call them, are very queer, in every sense, and can be made to sound hilarious—though Strachey, with his ailments and frustrations, is really quite pathetic. By the way, what does Mrs. Waley mean when she says in the *T.L.S.* that Arthur Waley's papers have been stolen and nothing has been done about it?

You sounded cheerful and well. I was worried when you were ill.

As ever, Edmund

To Clelia Carroll   May 1, 1968
                                                              Wellfleet

Dear Clelia: We were going to stop over to see you on our way from Charlottesville to Baltimore, but, not having heard from you, I imagined you were away . . . We didn't run into any riots, though they seemed to have been expecting trouble in Charlottesville, and the atmosphere at

The Wellfleet Library

Gloria Watts

the hotel seemed rather tense. One change I particularly noticed was that the colored waiters and porters, who used to say "Yessah," now say "Yes, *sir!*" Those Virginians rather bore me nowadays that I'm not able to drink to keep up with them. One lady, whom I saw in the morning, said, "What do you like to drink after breakfast?" I said I didn't drink during the day. "Whisky sours are very nice on a hot day like this." They run on in their pleasant way about genealogy and local events, never seem to have any real curiosity about what is going on in the North or anywhere else. It seems to be inevitable at some point that you talk about dogs and cats.

After that, my evening with old [W. F.] Albright was absolutely exhilarating. He is now seventy-seven—told me that I was a mere child. I don't think I have ever seen a scholar who reveled so continuously in his work. He is the great demiurge, in this country, of Semitic archaeology, paleography, and scrolls interpretation, as well as an Assyriologist and, I think, Egyptologist. His ex-students are everywhere in more or less key positions. He laughed and giggled like a demon as he talked about the aberrations of other scholars, and gave me delighted gossiping digressions: one rather out-of-bounds Biblical scholar had "tried to date" the attractive wife of another extremely square one, and a veteran Bible man at Oxford, whom everybody in this field makes fun of, had succeeded in getting himself knighted by campaigning for Harold Macmillan. Albright has both glaucoma and cataracts and this makes it difficult for him to travel but he says that he has "nothing to complain about because it gives him more time at his desk."   . . . Love, Edmund

To Thomas F. O'Donnell   April 29, 1968
Utica College   Wellfleet

Dear Tom: . . . Ed [Edwin] O'Connor's death was totally unexpected and a dreadful shock. He suddenly had a cerebral hemorrhage. He had been telling his wife every other day how happy he was in his new apartment; had made arrangements for his play to be done; and was working on a novel about an old cardinal who couldn't understand what was happening in the Church.   As ever, Edmund W.

To Thomas F. O'Donnell   August 16, 1968
                                                          Wellfleet
. . . I thought you might like to see this [John V.] Kelleher article. I think it is the most intelligent thing that has been written about Ed. You see that he says the same thing that you did: that the Irish generation Ed describes now hardly any longer exists. Little, Brown is going to publish a volume with the fragments of his unfinished novels, this article, I hope, and the unfinished magician novel that he and I were writing together . . .

680

To Francis Steegmuller   April 17, 1968
[Postcard]   Wellfleet

Dear Mr. Steegmuller: The verse you inquired about is by George Du
Maurier and is to be found in Carolyn Wells's *Nonsense Anthology*
(Scribner's, 1903), along with some very amusing others of his "Vers
Nonsensiques." I see that somebody in the *T.L.S.* has explained that the
one you inquire about first appeared in *Punch*. I suppose they all did.
                                                    Edmund Wilson

To Francis Steegmuller   July 27, 1968
                                                    Wellfleet

Dear Mr. Steegmuller: Thank you for your card of congratulation.
  Here is another Du Maurier limerick:

              Il était un gendarme à Nanteuil,
              Qui n'avait qu'une dent et qu'un oeil;
                Mais cet oeil solitaire
                Etait plein de mystère;
              Cette dent, d'importance et d'orgueil

                                                    Sincerely, EW

To Francis Steegmuller   1969

Dear Steegmuller: I was delighted to get the Du Maurier limericks. I
have just been going through the two volumes of his *Society Pictures
from "Punch."* It is amusing but rather monotonous.
  I am sorry not to have had more chance to talk to you the other night.
I get so exhausted by these gatherings nowadays that I can't do them
justice.   Sincerely, Edmund Wilson

To Celia Goodman   October 30, 1968
                                                    Wellfleet

. . . I was interested to hear the new theory about the games with the
bulls in Crete. Have been reading Maurice Bowra's memoirs and am
surprised at what a good impression he makes. I did not like him particularly when I met him, nor have I in general been very much impressed
by his work. Have also, in the course of my program of getting through,
before I die, all the celebrated books that I haven't read, been reading
Macaulay's history. It is really a wonderful book—not so prejudiced on the
side of the Whigs as the Tories have liked to pretend, and really the best
eulogium of the greatness of England as it appeared in the middle of the
last century. Apropos of Bowra, I read any number of English books of

                                                    681

memoirs of the Edwardian age and the twenties: the Waughs, Kingsley Martin, Bertrand Russell, Lady Ottoline Morrell, A. C. Benson, etc. I read them at night before I go to sleep, and find them very restful. I really grew up on that period when the "American Renascence" was only just beginning, and it is comfortable to lapse back into it. Everything over here is hell now.

I've just discovered a young writer named Wilfrid Sheed—one of that Ward–Sheed Catholic connection—who seems to me awfully good. He has done an entertaining novel about his growing up partly in England and partly over here. He seems to know both sides about equally well. I am going to have a copy sent you . . .

To WILFRID SHEED   April 25, 1969
                                                            Wellfleet
Dear Wilfrid: I am sending back the *Middle-Class Education* because you say it is your only copy. It is perhaps more ambitious than *Blacking Factory*, but not, I think, so successful. It is maybe a little too long, and doesn't the time sequence get confused at one point, where you have your hero apparently finished at Oxford and go back to London, and then turn up for more adventures at Oxford? I have just read *Square's Progress*, which is something of a tour de force, because you manage to carry the reader without complaint through 300 pages of deliberate banality. I enjoyed it, though I don't really believe that such people exist—I don't believe in Tolstoy's Ivan Ilyich either. I doubt whether life seems like that to such people. What you and Tolstoy are doing is describing the way they seem to writers much cleverer than they are. I can't imagine either Fred or Alison settling down to such purposeless lives without even dreaming of some purpose—any more than I can Ivan looking back at his life without some satisfaction.   . . . Best regards to both of you, Edmund W

To MORLEY CALLAGHAN   December 26, 1969
                                                            Wellfleet
. . . I am going to send you a novel—*What I'm Going to Do, I Think*— by a young Finnish-American [L. Woiwode] which is a little in your line, it seems to me. The ending is unsatisfactory, and I don't think the author ever makes plain precisely what is wrong with his hero, but it does seem to show remarkable abilities . . .

THE AMERICAN PLÉIADE
1960–1969

To Mary Meigs   February 1, 1960
                                                      Cambridge

. . . I am overwhelmed by the gigantic unattractive books that were published just after the Civil War. They are almost impossible to hold—running sometimes to a thousand pages—and they come apart while you are reading them. These are the memoirs and historical works. The words are printed in very small type on paper that is now yellow and crumbly, and are sometimes in double columns. I look forward to a nice volume of the Pléiade again, with limp leather cover, thin paper, and two silk ribbons for markers . . .

To Sheldon Meyer   September 16, 1960
Oxford University Press   Wellfleet

. . . I have been working on the Civil War book all summer . . . I calculate that it will be about a thousand pages in my regular format—which you used for the *Scrolls* book and *Red, Black, Blond and Olive:* but I don't want any other format. If you will look at the Doubleday edition of my book *The Shock of Recognition*, which has 1,290 pages, you will see that, with moderately thin paper, this will make a volume that is easy to handle . . . I want to insist on this because it seems to me that American books are the worst produced in the world: too heavy, pages too wide, and too much type on a page . . .

To Roger W. Straus, Jr.   May 17, 1956
                                                      Wellfleet

. . . Oxford got out the *Scrolls* in that format—though I hadn't necessarily meant them to—and I think it worked out remarkably well: it made a small clear compact volume that seemed easy to read and handle . . .

Young Epstein of Doubleday came up here to see me . . . He is the only publisher I have ever met whom I have felt I have had to caution not to over-interest in my books.

(To Roger W. Straus, Jr., 1953)

To Jason Epstein*
April 18, 1961
Wellfleet

Dear Jason: I am glad to hear that you are going to take up with the Bollingen Foundation the possibility of bringing out in a complete and compact form the principal American classics. I have, as you know, been trying for years to interest some publisher in this project. It is absurd that our most read and studied writers should not be available in their entirety in any convenient form. For example, the only collected edition of Melville was published in England in the twenties and has long been out of print; and there is not, and has never been, of Henry James and Henry Adams any complete collected edition at all. The only serious attempt, on any large scale, to do reliable editions of our classics was the publication by Houghton Mifflin of such New England writers as Emerson, Thoreau, and Hawthorne, and these, too, are now out of print. For years there was no scholarly edition of Poe which even aimed at accuracy and completeness except that by James A. Harrison of the University of Virginia, also long out of print—though I understand that Mabbott of Columbia is now bringing out a new one through the Harvard University Press. The collected Stephen Crane was published by Knopf in a limited edition which can only be found in large libraries.

The kind of thing I should like to see would follow the example of the Editions de la Pléiade, which have included almost the whole of the French classics in beautifully produced and admirably printed, thin-paper volumes, ranging from 800 to 1,500 pages. These volumes, published by Gallimard, have evidently been commercially successful, for they are to be seen in every bookstore in Paris. Mondadori of Milan has been publishing the Italian classics in a similar format, though not on the same scale. The state-subsidized series of classics edited by Benedetto Croce—Scrittori d'Italia—has supplemented this series of the more popular authors. In England the Oxford Press has brought out the English poets and a certain amount of prose in cheap and well-edited volumes. Only the United States, at a time when the interest in our literature has never been so keen, has nothing at all similar. In the case of many writers of not necessarily the first importance, but such as are often included in the Pléiade series, there exist—except for random reprints by university presses, and occasionally by paperback publishers—no modern editions at all. Such writers need not be

---

* This letter appeared in *The Devils and Canon Barham*, 1973.

reprinted *in toto*, but there are several which should have a volume of selections: De Forest, George Cable, Henry Fuller, Harold Frederic, John Jay Chapman, Kate Chopin, and others.

Almost everything should be edited anew, as in the case of the Pléiade editions. It would be possible, thus, to establish, as has been done in the case of Proust, the only sound and full text that exists.

Of course, there would be questions of copyright, as in the case of Emily Dickinson's newly published poems or Mark Twain's posthumous writings, but these are the kinds of things that, after first being published in expensive editions, are likely afterwards to be sold to the paperbacks, and they might just as well be sold to a series of classics.

I hope that you will be able to interest the Bollingen people.

Sincerely, Edmund Wilson

To The New York Review of Books   March 14, 1968
Wellfleet

To the Editors: I congratulate Lewis Mumford and *The New York Review* on his article in your issue of January 18 on the new edition of the Emerson papers. The editing of the classical American writers has got to be an academic racket that is coming between these writers and the public to which they ought to be accessible. I have for a long time had the project of getting out the American classics in a series similar to the Pléiade editions published by Gallimard in France: complete works of the important authors, selections from the less important, well but not pretentiously edited, well printed on thin paper, and not impossibly priced. The Pléiade series has got the whole of the *Comédie humaine* into ten volumes—the whole of Henry James could probably be contained in less—Saint-Simon in seven volumes, and the whole of Montaigne in one. The three-volume Pléiade edition of Proust is the only complete and accurate one of *A la Recherche* that has ever been published. We have in print no such editions of Poe or Melville or James. What we get are, on the one hand, odd reprints of various works of these writers and, on the other, pedantic and expensive editions—such as the Ohio State edition of Hawthorne—published at long intervals, a volume or two at a time, by the university presses. I was given not long ago to understand that a sum of money had been allotted for my project by the National Endowment for the Humanities. My supporters and I were ready to go into action. But then I was told that the project had been "tabled" for reasons that were not explained, and that the Modern Language Association had somehow succeeded in having this money assigned to themselves. The next news of this that I had was that more of these stupid academic editions were being got under way. I was asked to do an introduction for one volume of George W. Cable, of whose work, good as he is at his best, there are only half a dozen titles that deserve to be widely read, and these books, since they are mostly short, could be included in one Pléiade volume. There is also the grisly news that some M.L.A. beneficiary is going to undertake a complete edition of the works of William Gilmore Simms, who seems to me one of the most unreadable and most unrewarding American writers —his work is both sloppy and voluminous—who has never had any reputation. He ought to be left on the library shelves, where special students can always find him. This shows that these exploits are being conducted with the same lack of taste and discrimination that has come largely to dominate the academic field of American literature. The professor who edits these unnecessary works may earn academic credit and promotion in the academic hierarchy by his industry in becoming an authority on some writer who he discovers has never been edited but that few people want to read.

I am of course indignant about this; but I cannot be bothered to do anything about it. I should be very glad, however, to hear from the Modern Language Association as to how and why they accomplished this operation of waylaying the funds we were supposed to get.

Edmund Wilson

To The New York Review of Books   June 5, 1969

To the Editors: I have been sent a copy of a pamphlet published by the Modern Language Association of America, called *Professional Standards and American Editions: A Response to Edmund Wilson*. I have already replied, in my own pamphlet, *The Fruits of the MLA*, to most of the complaints it contains. I find, however, that Mr. Oscar Cargill declares that I maintain, in *Axel's Castle*, that T. S. Eliot borrowed from Blake his phrase in "Gerontion": "Christ the tiger." Actually, neither in *Axel's Castle* nor elsewhere have I discussed this phrase, and I have never supposed it was borrowed from Blake. "After all," Mr. Cargill continues, "Eliot revolted against the Romantics, of whom Blake was one." But how can Blake be called a Romantic? Certainly Eliot did not think he was. See his essay on Blake in *The Sacred Wood*, where he calls him "a poet of genius."

This pamphlet leads off with a menacing statement by Mr. Gordon N. Ray:

"The recent attack in *The New York Review of Books* on the Center for Editions of American Authors of the Modern Language Association of America raises complex questions of taste and emphasis. It must be obvious at the same time, however, that this attack derives in part from the alarm of amateurs at seeing rigorous professional standards applied to a subject in which they have a vested interest. Here, at least, the issue is not in doubt. As the American learned world has come to full maturity since the second World War, a similar animus has shown itself and been discredited in field after field from botany to folklore. In the long run professional standards always prevail."

I have had some respect for Mr. Ray on account of his edition of Thackeray's letters—though I was slightly annoyed by his following Thackeray's epistolary shorthand so pedantically as to print all his *and's* as ampersands and his contractions of such common words as *should* and *which*, when a note of explanation or the facsimile of the page of a letter would have been enough to indicate this practice and leave the editor free to present a more readable text. But the statement above is absurd. In regard to scholarship of this kind, what is meant by "professional standards" which "in the long run . . . always prevail"? It is necessary to have a Bar Association to keep the legal profession in order and a Medical Association to prevent malpractice. But there is not and there is not needed any similar organization to protect the kind of literary scholarship to which I have been objecting. People like Mr. Ray try to behave as if there were, but I have been gratified to discover, from the approving letters I have received, that a great many academics, including a number of scholars who have proved their own competence, do not accept these policies and procedures. And, in this field, who are "the professionals"? the writers who produce the books or the non-writers who make it harder to read them? "A similar animus [to mine],"* says Mr. Ray, "has shown itself and been discredited in field after field from botany to folklore." What does he mean by this? Percy's *Reliques*, in which Bishop Percy allowed himself a pretty free hand in revising the text of his old English ballads, is a more valuable and more important book than F. J. Child's enormous repository, for which he took down and published so many inept and illiterate versions, so many tiresome repetitions of the same ballad. As for botany, I find it difficult to see what the analogy can be. Have the flowers been rebelling against classification? Or do they object to being picked and mounted, as our writers might well object to being trussed up and made inaccessible for CEAA† editions?   Edmund Wilson

To LEON EDEL   November 7, 1968
                                                                       Wellfleet

Dear Leon: . . . Thanks very much for your letter. We have had a good many supporting letters from academic people and publishers—as well as

---

* E.'s brackets.
† Center for Editions of American Authors.

some venomous and vulgar ones from the people involved in these projects. This morning, an abusive anonymous letter. There will be a selection of these in the next *New York Review,* and we are getting the articles out as a pamphlet, with my commentary on these letters, in time for the holiday conference of the M.L.A., where I understand it will be sold at a booth . . .

I am eager to see your fourth volume, but would rather read it in book form than proof. Best regards as ever to both of you.   Edmund W

To Fredson Bowers   January 4, 1969
University of Virginia   Wellfleet

Dear Mr. Bowers: Thank you for your letter and enclosure. The latter I started reading in the living room which was full of Christmas litter, and now am unable to find. I am hoping it will turn up. I am having a copy of the pamphlet sent you.* My remark about your lack of literary discrimination was not based on hearsay but partly on your attitude toward editing and partly on my conversations with you, in the course of which you twice referred with some surprise to the fact that Amy Lowell and John Gould Fletcher, who were, you said, regarded as important in the pre-First War period, seemed to have been completely forgotten. I thought this showed a lack of discrimination because I never knew anyone of any taste who ever took these writers seriously.† They were forgotten because they were not good poets. Please remember me to your wife.

                                        Very sincerely, Edmund Wilson

To Fredson Bowers   April 25, 1969
                                                                 Wellfleet
Dear Mr. Bowers: Thank you for your papers and the criticism book. I'm afraid that the Shakespeare studies do not lead me to change my opinion of your interest in literature as such. They are very much less impressive than the papers in the criticism book, which explain many points of curious interest. But what you say about Walt Whitman is not literary criticism except as it shows how he improved passages. It has long been known—though many people do not seem to know it—that Whitman worked hard over *Leaves of Grass* and that his successive editions show

---

* *The Fruits of the MLA.*
† "Mr. Wilson's imperfect recollection of a quite casual conversation led him, in *The Fruits of the MLA,* to attribute to me as a CEAA editor at the age of sixty-two the literary tastes of my reading at the age of sixteen."
                                        —Fredson Bowers to Elena Wilson, 1976

his many changes. What you report from exploring these manuscripts would be interesting to a biographer; but the finished product is the thing of importance. When I read something like your scrutiny of Whitman's early drafts, it confirms me in my resolution to destroy all early drafts of my own. As for the printer's errors, it is far more important that the masterpieces should be circulated in even a faulty text than not be available at all—which is the case now with so many of them.

About the *Hamlet* passage: "solid" seems to me much more probable than "sullied." I am not persuaded by the argument to the contrary. After all, his mother's betrayal cannot affect Hamlet's *flesh*. I was glad to know about Eliot's "Whispers."* In connection with Melville's "coiled fish": Auden tells me that someone who wrote a book about him made some point on the basis of a misprint in one of his poems, and that he was unable to set the author right because he had died before Auden discovered it.   Sincerely, Edmund Wilson

Edmund Wilson Regrets

TO ARTHUR MIZENER   1943

Dear Arthur: I almost never read variants, and I believe that the publication and comparison of the various drafts of a writer's work is mostly perfectly futile. I have a horror of having my own production circulate in a state of undress, and for this reason have always avoided reading other people's works in the same condition. It is mildly interesting to a writer to see how another writer goes about it to improve his stuff. I was quite impressed by and learned something from the successive versions of the same passages as they appeared in the various drafts of an unfinished dialogue of Anatole France's. But a little of this goes a long way. I don't mind leaving on record a few MSS of mine in their successive phases; but the chips and shavings of writing mostly belong in the dump heap. If you leave them around, they are likely to be edited or written about in theses by scholars in the universities who ought to be occupied with something better. The parts of a writer's papers that represent things not realized or not finished yet, or things that for personal or political or other reasons he hasn't been able to publish, are of course another matter; but they are the affair of a literary executor.   Yours as ever, Edmund W

---

* E. corrected "Whiskers" to "Whispers" and inserted in the margin: "I hope that this, though a typist's error, will be recorded in the eventual definitive edition of my collected letters."

EDMUND WILSON REGRETS THAT IT IS IMPOSSIBLE FOR HIM TO:

READ MANUSCRIPTS,

WRITE ARTICLES OR BOOKS TO ORDER,

WRITE FOREWORDS OR INTRODUCTIONS,

MAKE STATEMENTS FOR PUBLICITY PURPOSES,

DO ANY KIND OF EDITORIAL WORK,

JUDGE LITERARY CONTESTS,

GIVE INTERVIEWS,

CONDUCT EDUCATIONAL COURSES,

DELIVER LECTURES,

GIVE TALKS OR MAKE SPEECHES,

BROADCAST OR APPEAR ON TELEVISION,

TAKE PART IN WRITERS' CONGRESSES,

ANSWER QUESTIONNAIRES,

CONTRIBUTE TO OR TAKE PART IN SYMPOSIUMS OR "PANELS" OF ANY KIND,

CONTRIBUTE MANUSCRIPTS FOR SALES,

DONATE COPIES OF HIS BOOKS TO LIBRARIES,

AUTOGRAPH BOOKS FOR STRANGERS,

ALLOW HIS NAME TO BE USED ON LETTERHEADS,

SUPPLY PERSONAL INFORMATION ABOUT HIMSELF,

SUPPLY PHOTOGRAPHS OF HIMSELF,

SUPPLY OPINIONS ON LITERARY OR OTHER SUBJECTS.

Dear Cairns: I am sorry that I have had to make a rule not to give anybody, under any circumstances, a statement to be used on a book jacket.
I am sorry to refuse a favor—especially in view of your kindness on several
occasions—but I can't make an exception about this, as I have just refused
to write a blurb for a book by a cousin of mine, as well as a number of
other people. I shall look forward, however, to seeing your book.

Sincerely, Edmund Wilson

To Whit Burnett   1947
Story Magazine
Dear Mr. Burnett: You will remember that when I chose something for
your anthology *This Is My Best* you cut it, without my permission, in such
a way as to make it practically pointless—so that I am not disposed to
contribute anything to your new anthology. Now, don't write and tell me
that anything I suggest for it will be printed intact. I don't approve of
these anthologies anyhow and don't want to be associated with your
project.   Yours sincerely, Edmund Wilson

To Alfred Kazin   1951

Dear Alfred: I have had to make a rule not to give publishers plugs for
books. One reason for this is that I have several relatives who write and
I have to have something to tell them when they come to me with their
books. Aside from this, however, I think it is a bad plan for a professional
critic. He cannot really express himself about the book in the few lines
he gives the publisher, so he finds himself writing what is virtually
advertizing and undermining the authority of his criticism. The only
exception I have made in recent years was to allow Scribner's to print
part of a letter to Isabel Bolton, who is herself an exceptional case in
being an old lady just beginning to be known and trying to beat the
Grim Reaper, instead of a young writer with his forces undepleted and
all the rest of his life before him.

Best regards and best of luck, Edmund Wilson

To Roger W. Straus, Jr.   1950

. . . For some reason I have never understood, the writing of blurbs in this
country has usually been assigned by the publishers to more or less
illiterate people who do not understand books . . . Though far from an
Anglophile, I must say that the British publishers handle their publicity

better—with simple and sober announcements clearly telling what is in the books. Our book advertizing overdoes everything, and at the same time the raving is likely to be so sloppy and tired that it does not carry conviction . . .

To CHARLES NORMAN   1957

Dear Mr. Norman: I am sorry that I have felt I had to make a rule not to talk to people who are doing books about writers I have known. Someday I may write about them myself, and I would rather have my impressions come at first-hand. You will find what I have published about Cummings in my book *The Shores of Light*.   Sincerely, Edmund Wilson

To MALCOLM COWLEY AND DAWN POWELL   1958

Dear Messrs. Cowley and Powell: Of course I am delighted by your letter announcing that I have been deemed worthy of the long-coveted honor of election to the Club des Bibliophages. I suggest that a special meeting should be held in the near future to decide what is to be done with the coarser and less well-flavored books of which I constantly have large quantities sent me. One cannot ask one's friends to eat them, and I have been wondering whether it would be possible to sell them to Canada or South Africa. They get moldy if kept too long, and one does not like to send them to the dump when so many semi-literate people must be hungry.

   Acceptez, chers messieurs, les remerciements sincères et le respect inébranlable de   Edmund Wilson

To ALFRED KAZIN   October 4 1961
                                                              Cambridge
Dear Alfred: I meant you to get *page proofs* from the publisher. There is nothing I dislike so much as to have my books read before publication—but I didn't know you were adviser to that book club. No great harm done if you'll take account of my revisions.   Best regards, Edmund

To JOHN DOS PASSOS   April 19, 1965

. . . By the way, I have had two requests to make your letters to me available to people who are writing about you (they are with the rest of my papers in the Yale Library). I have refused, on the principle that it is only when people are dead that it is time to publish their correspondence . . .

Maybe the Patriach of Jefferson
is the best, after all!

April 30, 1953
Wellfleet

Dear Dos: I think that only the last of
those titles — <u>The White Porch of the Republic</u> —
is any good, & that even that doesn't have quite
the right rhythm to be spoken in bookstore
or conversation. If you made the accented
+ unaccented syllable. You see, it would be
be better from this point of view if it were
<u>The Porch of the Great Republic</u> or <u>The Pergola of</u>
<u>The Republic</u> — not that I mean to suggest
these: they are dummies.

See letter to John Dos Passos, 1953

. . . The ideal title is short, easy to remember and pronounce, and imaginatively stimulating.   (To Helen Muchnic, 1970)

To John Dos Passos   1953

Dear Dos: I think that only the last of those titles—*The White Porch of the Republic*—is any good, and that even that doesn't have quite the right rhythm to be spoken in bookstores or conversation. If you mark the accented and unaccented syllables, you see what is the matter: there would be a tendency to say *The White Porch*, but this is impossible. It would be better from this point of view if it were *The Porch of the Great Republic* or *The Pergola of the Republic*—not that I mean to suggest these: they are dummies.

Maybe *Portrait of Jefferson* is the best, after all.

How about *Dos Passos on Jefferson*? I can't really advise, because I haven't read the book* . . .

---

* *The Head and Heart of Thomas Jefferson*, 1954.

LAST YEARS

But isn't literature simply a part of life, as much as conversation?

CHRONOLOGY

1969	THE DEAD SEA SCROLLS and an account of the work that has been done in connection with the scrolls since 1955 THE DUKE OF PALERMO AND OTHER PLAYS, *with an Open Letter to Mike Nichols*
APRIL	We have just come back from five weeks in Jamaica.
SUMMER	Wellfleet, Talcottville, Wellfleet.
SEPTEMBER	I expect to go up to Talcottville for 2–3 weeks.
1970	
MARCH	New York.
APRIL	Cape Cod Hospital, Hyannis: Coronary.
MAY	Talcottville.
JUNE– JULY	Wellfleet.
AUGUST– SEPTEMBER	Talcottville.
DECEMBER	I had a slight stroke around Christmas.
1971	UPSTATE
JANUARY	The Russian book is all but finished* . . . The Introduction to *Finland Station* I'll do when I finish this.†
FEBRUARY	c/o Lillian Hellman, 630 Park Avenue, New York: I'm just out of a week in the Doctors Hospital.
MARCH	Wellfleet: I'm getting together a volume of my Russian articles.‡
MAY	Talcottville.

---

* *A Window on Russia*, 1972.
† *To the Finland Station*, new edition, 1972.
‡ *A Window on Russia*.

JUNE	Wellfleet: The book of miscellaneous essays is mostly all pasted up.*
AUGUST	Boston: Hospital.
SEPTEMBER 22– OCTOBER 2	Talcottville.

1972

JANUARY– MARCH	Naples, Florida: How boring this place is . . . We are going to stop off in March to see my cousin [Susan Wilson] in [Charlottesville] Virginia.
APRIL	New York and Wellfleet.
MAY	Hyannis hospital
MAY 27	I am going over to my Boonville address on Wednesday [May 31] and expect to stay till the middle of June.
JUNE	Talcottville: Edmund died on June 12 and was buried in Wellfleet on June 15.

---

* *The Devils and Canon Barham.*

1969

January 1, 1969
                                                         Wellfleet

Dear Alfred: Have just read your *Harper's* article with much interest.
You are mistaken about Dos Passos's being a Middle Westerner. He
happened to be born in Chicago simply because his parents were traveling
at the time. His family connections were all with New York and Washington. Washington seemed to be his city more than any other. He has
seen very little of the Middle West. You don't speak of Dawn Powell,
who is the perfect example of the Westerner coming to New York and
becoming a New Yorker, but observing it with the eye of someone who
has come to it from outside. חגים לשמחה.*

Get Ann to translate this—and best wishes to you both.   Edmund W

To Alfred Kazin   April 18, 1969
                                                         Wellfleet

Dear Alfred: That was an excellent article on Dos Passos—I wish you
had gone on to his later books. Corrections: The writers of his generation
you mention were not all, as you say, "close friends." Cummings knew
Dos Passos because they had been at Harvard together, but he did not
know Scott Fitzgerald; he could only barely have met Hemingway, if at
all. I have just got the Baker biography of Hemingway, however, and find
that Hemingway greatly admired *The Enormous Room* and "introduced"
Cummings to Sylvia Beach—whether personally is not clear. In general,
Cummings refused to meet other writers—the few he saw were mostly
either admirers like Hart Crane or people he could condescend to like Joe
Gould. The section called "Vag" was not added as an epilogue when the
three volumes of *U.S.A.* were published in one volume. It was in the first
edition of *The Big Money.* Dos Passos's father wrote other books besides

---

* Happy holidays.

those on corporation law, etc. There were *The Anglo-Saxon Century* and the rather grandiloquent *The American Lawyer*, of which I have a copy because it was in my own father's library.   Best regards, Edmund

To MORLEY CALLAGHAN   February 1969
[Postcard]   Runaway Bay, Jamaica

Dear Morley: This is not at all what Jamaica is like. It is rather a miserable little country, full of terrible problems since the English pulled out. Also full of Canadians, who are doing a lot of business here. The climate and general atmosphere are debilitating, and one feels that if one stayed here long enough, one might begin to write like Ian Fleming or Noel Coward, who are, or were, habitués of the island. Love to all the family.   Edmund

To WILLIAM SHAWN   February 5, 1969
The New Yorker   Jamaica

Dear Shawn: I should like to do an article on [Richard Harris] Barham, have been intending to do so for years. He is a great favorite of mine, and I have been collecting material on him . . .   As ever, Edmund W

To CELIA GOODMAN   Spring, 1969
                                                               Wellfleet
Dear Celia: I have sent you a little book of plays of mine.* They wouldn't be understood by many people in England, so I am not even trying to get them published there. You will see that one of my heroes is translating Pindar.

We have just come back from five weeks in Jamaica, which is a poor and sad little country, rather at a loss since the British left . . . But we lived mostly in a vacuum in a little cottage on the water and escaped from the horrible weather here and got over our ailments and worries—which, however, were only lying in wait to descend on us when we got back. Aside from our personal troubles, there has just been a series of murders up here, in the next town to ours, of a gruesomeness that rivals the Moors murder. My daughter [Rosalind] says she thinks that there is a cult of murder among the hippies, and I am not sure it isn't true.

I'd be very glad to have [Arthur] Waley's "Chinese Poems" . . . Bertrand Russell was never a hero of mine. You are right: his accounts of his love affairs are most unpleasant. I did not know any of his wives, but I knew an American who had had two children by him with whom he ran that school. I was told she had a fatal predilection for "international cads." I have heard that he was seriously worried for fear one of these

---

* *Five Plays.*

700

children, who were given his name, might someday inherit his title. He simply skips this in his autobiography.

I'm correcting final proofs on my scrolls book—shall send you a copy later. The inclusion in the *New Yorker* articles from it of a few Greek and Hebrew words threw the printers and the office into such a confusion that I had to come back from Jamaica in order to straighten it out. I have never had this kind of trouble with *The New Yorker* before, and I felt from this and other signs that the magazine is rather demoralized, as I believe the whole of the East is since Nixon was elected. There has been a general letdown, and we don't know whether or not he is capable of any kind of leadership. I've always thought him an empty valise. I'm afraid that his much advertized whirl through Europe was nothing but a "public relations" job. This is rather a somber letter.   Love from us both, Edmund

To Jason Epstein   April 23, 1969
                                                    Talcottville
Dear Jason: This article by Gross is really a fake. There is a fragmentary line (385) in the *Ichneutae* which has been filled in various ways. The satyrs are trying to find out who has stolen Apollo's oxen and where they are. They trace them to a cave where Hermes is hidden. He has presumably used an oxskin for making his lyre. Richard Walker makes their chorus say, "Now can I judge of these oxen by the evidence of their dung"—which may very well be correct. But it is silly to call this *bullshit* and make a sensation of it. There is nothing in the ragged text that justifies the German reconstruction Gross gives; and in any case *bullshit* in the correct sense is not the same thing as *ox dung*. Besides, there is nothing surprising in the use by the Greeks of plain words. It is true that the nineteenth-century English liked to play down what they thought was improper and coarse, but it is no shock to anyone who knows anything of the classics to hear that they are sometimes what we call indecent—if you think that ox dung is indecent. Aristophanes is extremely indecent. Gross hasn't really read much or any Greek. It sounds as if he hadn't.

I'm going to Talcottville the second week in May. Please let Barbara know—and ask her to send me (to Wellfleet) half a dozen more M.L.A. pamphlets. I forget whether I told her on the phone that the last issue of the *Review* was particularly good.   As ever, Edmund

To Mary Meigs   June 19, 1969
                                                    Talcottville
. . . I never met Wallace Stevens. I think you must have heard at second or third hand the story of his eruptive visit to Dos Passos. He was, I'm told, in the habit of getting away once a year from his insurance-law business in Hartford and going for a big drunken spree in Florida. You can see it in the poems he wrote about clouds, etc. In that state, he sud-

denly descended on Dos and kept saying, "I thought you were a serious radical, and here you are surrounded with women, drinking cocktails, with the phonograph playing!" Dos said that he was the only visitor that he ever wanted to throw out of the house. I think he was an extremely dull fellow. Have you looked at his letters, which seem to me deadly? The idea of the Hartford insurance man who has never been abroad but fancies himself as a wistful Pierrot inhabiting the *fin de siècle* I have always found somewhat repellent. His early book *Harmonium* has some nice—purely verbal—writing, but his more pretentious stuff bores me . . .

To HELEN MUCHNIC   July 1, 1969
                                                     Talcottville
Dear Helen: I was glad to get your letter—had been wondering about you. We more or less enjoyed Jamaica, but I seem to have brought back some sort of tropical malaria and have been having most unpleasant attacks. Could we stay over with you the night of the 22nd? on our way back to Boston.

I have read Svetlana's new book, which is terrific—quite different from the first—and I am afraid it may get her into trouble. I have written about it for *The New Yorker*, and the *Review* says that it is going to send it to you. I have told Harper's to send you also the Russian edition, which is supposed to be out in August. I have been reading Tolstoy's plays, but the peasant language in some of them gets me down.

Плоды Просвещения [*Fruits of Enlightenment*] anticipates Chekhov. И Светь во Тьме Светит [*And Light Shines in Darkness*] is no good as a play, but immensely interesting as a picture of his struggles with his family at the time of his conversion. He couldn't resist entering imaginatively into a family situation, and he makes the protesting friends and relatives of the convert so much more sympathetic than the convert is. This is a good way to get at Lev Nikolaevich's religious ideas reduced to their simplest form. Живой Труп [*The Living Corpse*] is not interesting. I should like to discuss these plays with you.

Please tell Dorothy that my Jesuit dropout friend has been able to throw a good deal of light for me on the problem of succubae and incubi. He has all the doctrine at his finger ends. Vampires, it seems, also present a special problem.   Love to you both as ever, Edmund

To DOROTHY WALSH   September 10, 1969
                                                     Talcottville
Dear Dorothy: I have finally cleaned up my study and found your book, which I have just read with much interest.* You approach the problem

---

* *Literature and Knowledge.*

in such a different way from the way I do that it is hard for me to see it as you do. For me, all the constructions of intellect and imagination, from poetry, drama, and fiction through Whitehead (metaphysics is the poetry and fiction of people who do not produce concrete images) to Einstein, are inventions directed to enabling us to get through life and explain the world. I have always made "validity" rather than "authenticity" the criterion—although I do not think that this term is much more susceptible of definition. In regard to detail:

Chapter VII. Doesn't the word *experience* here stand for two distinct things?—the short, more or less self-contained experience of something out of the ordinary that happens, as when we speak of "a strange experience," and the experience of long duration such as the experience of grief.

p. 105. We *can* speak of having been a Marxist or a Christian Scientist as an "experience."

p. 104. "Life is one thing and literature is another." But isn't literature simply a part of life, as much as conversation?

p. 118. I don't think that one could suppose that the music of Mozart had been composed by an angel or was the music of the spheres. Hearing it, one does learn something about his personality—for example, from the strain of sadness.

p. 127. I don't think that the poetic conceptions of the moon will ever be the same again. They will always have against them, to impede the ancient images, the new picture of an arid waste.

p. 139. You mention written history only twice, near the end, and you class it with anthropology and social and political theory. But history is literature as much as poetry and fiction. (I'm just finishing Macaulay's history.) One enjoys it in the same way as any other kind of literary art.

I think you write with great lucidity and elegance. I always know exactly when I disagree with you and greatly enjoyed reading the book. I hope that, now you're retired, you will go on to write a lot more.

Love to Helen. As ever, Edmund

MAX BEERBOHM
1912–1971

To Alfred Bellinger   December 22, 1912
                                                    Red Bank
. . . I have lately been reading more of Max Beerbohm, who is certainly
an artist of the first rank . . .

You are one of the few critics now functioning who have any real
love of writing as an art.   (1948)

To Louis Kronenberger   June 24, 1947
                                          The New Yorker
Dear Kronenberger: I was very much interested in your piece about Max
Beerbohm, because I have just been rereading him with the idea of writing
something about him. I am so glad you had the courage to insist on the
defects of *Zuleika Dobson*. You say just the right thing about it. The
trouble is that, though it's full of amusing moments and patches of brilliant
writing, it's not clear precisely what he's trying to do and the whole thing
seems rather pointless. I think in general that these fairy-tale fantasies are
the weakest part of his work. It seems to me that *The Dreadful Dragon
of Hay Hill* is the only really bad thing he has written.

My only complaint about your essay is that you don't bring out quite
enough his sound and sensible side, with its strong independence and
audacity—which, for some reason, appears in his caricatures and in his
dramatic criticism more plainly than in his other writing. His caricatures,
too, constitute a social criticism in a way that most of his writings do not
(the John Bull series, for example, done at the time of the Boer War)—
so much so that it was possible for Shaw to say that he was "the most
savage radical cartoonist since Gillray," or something of the kind. (The
real reason that we call him Max is that he has always signed his carica-

tures so.) It would be interesting to consider his work from the point of view of the "social slant." In spite of his exploitation in the writings of his youth of the glamour of the Regency and all that, he has always loved to kid the royal family, and not always altogether good-naturedly; and in his caricatures up through the end of the First World War there was a pretty consistent bias in the direction of middle-class liberalism. After that, he seems to have been scared by the Russian Revolution and the rise of labor. The fact that he is half English, half foreign, has complicated his talent and his point of view; and his work is full of what the Marxists call contradictions which would require a delicate analysis. It is significant that in his essay on servants he should call himself a "Tory anarchist."

I agree that his coyness is sometimes trying—a queer weakness in his admirable taste—as well as with most that you say on the positive side. I'm sure he'll outlive Chesterton and a lot of others.

I hadn't meant to write at such length, but it is so rare to find anything nowadays—especially in *The Saturday Review!*—that shows any real interest in writing as writing that your essay seemed extravagantly stimulating. Yours sincerely, Edmund Wilson

To MAMAINE KOESTLER March 18, 1954
Hotel Danieli, Venice
. . . I went off on what has proved to be a most delightful holiday of three days in Italy. I went to Rapallo (which I thought was wonderful), where a friend of mine [S. N. Behrman] who knows Max Beerbohm arranged for me to come and meet him. He is a most distinguished person —over eighty, but still amusing. It is impressive to see how he has lived in retirement there for, I think, fifty-four years. He has the peculiar sense of dedication to his work that all the rest of his generation had . . .

To ELENA WILSON March 15, 1954
Rapallo
. . . We went to Max's villa this afternoon. It is pretty, looks right down on the sea, has a pleasant sunny terrace. He has just recovered from flu and received us in a bathrobe, sitting up in a chair. He makes an extraordinarily distinguished impression, and his head and face have more weight and strength than I had gathered from photographs of him and from his caricatures of himself. He talked extremely well and is not in the least gaga, remembered with perfect accuracy every detail of his own and other people's work. He gave us a long physical description of Bernard Shaw as he had looked when Max had first known him in London that showed how minute his observation of people is. He hadn't cared for Virginia Woolf's diary, had been struck, as I was, by her preoccupation with her own worries and her lack of consideration for other people—but

then he doesn't in the least appreciate the things that are good about her, can't see anything in her books. He said a lot of amusing things; but there is a mischievous-small-boy side of him that finally becomes a little tiresome—not in his conversation, but in the innumerable books (of other people) that he has doctored in various comic ways, and too many of which we were shown, not at his instance, but by the faithful Mme Jungmann (a very able, amiable, and well-read German, who came to his rescue after his wife's death—she had before that taken care of [Gerhardt] Hauptmann). He has lived here for forty-four years, lately on a diminishing scale—Sam [Behrman] says that he is now very poor, and that it is hard to do anything for him: he has refused a large fee to appear on television, etc. I felt that it had been worthwhile to come here to see him (may go back tomorrow if she phones that he is up to it). He is certainly a remarkable person, more continental than English (he has charming portraits of his grandparents that make them look like idealized characters in eighteenth-century operas, the eye in both cases *espiègle* and the mouth as if it were just about to smile). Seeing him out here makes you feel that he is independent and self-sufficing, quietly and scrupulously devoted to his own ideals. He said that most caricaturing nowadays was ugly, whereas "though I am not the person to say it—and I had half a mind to leave it unsaid—my drawings are pretty and agreeable to have around." He showed us a little watercolor in pink and blue that he had lately made of Edward VII and said, "Now, you see that's a pretty little drawing." He told us that he had stopped doing caricatures when he came to the time of life at which he realized that what he was producing were simply painstaking likenesses that showed pity for their subjects instead of making them amusing. "Pathos," he said, "is no quality for a caricaturist." He was interesting about Walter Sickert, whose painting he does not think successful: he had too much theory, would have made perhaps a good critic: "A painter ought not to be too clever in that way. He should be a passionate gaze, putting down what he sees or what he thinks he sees" . . .

To Elena Wilson   March 17, 1954
                                                        Venice

. . . We went up at half past four to see Beerbohm again. This time he sat up at the table and presided at tea. His head is quite sunk between his shoulders, and he has great red circles around his round blue eyes. Where he still has hair at the back of his head, it hangs down uncut below his collar. I have never seen hands like his: his fingers are not fine and tapering—they are very long and of uniform thickness till the ends, where they look as if they had been sharpened into thin pencils. They resemble large engraver's tools rather than fingers.

I asked him about Sem,* and he said that Sem's method of work was entirely different from his. Sem made sketches on the spot, as Max never did; would come to England and go to the races, then ask who the people were that he'd drawn. Max always had to have seen quite a lot of the people, heard their voices, and known what they thought, before he could caricature them. He said that he had never been able to caricature Somerset Maugham, had tried it several times, then given it up; but that [Graham] Sutherland, in his recent portrait, had made up for any failure on Max's part by "carrying caricature as far as it could go." After he had done Maugham, Sutherland had written to Max asking him to sit for a portrait, and Max had replied that, having seen the Maugham portrait, he was sorry to have to decline. He had sometimes made monsters of people himself, "but the bully is always a coward." He told us that it was impossible to caricature women, whereas Sem was brilliant at this. The truth is, I think, that Max is too much of an old-fashioned gentleman to be willing to make real women ridiculous. He has sometimes invented imaginary ones . . .

For his *Portrait of Max*, S. N. Behrman sent this account to Edmund: In March of 1954, the American critic, Edmund Wilson, paid several visits to Max at the Villino. Afterward, he told me that Max and André Malraux—a startling juxtaposition—were the two strongest literary personalities he had ever met. "He's secure," Mr. Wilson said. "He knows the worth of what he has done. He doesn't give a damn about where his caricatures or his book rights are, because he knows someone else will have to worry about all these things someday. He has been writing and illustrating a Divine Comedy for fifty years.

To S. N. Behrman   December 1959
                                                              Cambridge
Dear Sam: If I didn't say exactly this, it was what was in my mind. We are hoping you will make Boston—let us know in advance, if possible. In the meantime, greetings of the season.   Edmund

Edmund's version: In March of 1954, I paid two visits to Max at the Villino in company with the American critic, Edmund Wilson. He told me afterward that he had just seen André Malraux in Paris, and that in the cases of both men he had been much impressed—a startling juxtaposition, it seemed to me—by their self-confidence and strength of char-

---

* "Sem, the great French caricaturist . . . he caricatured year after year the whole social, artistic, and literary world."   —*The Bit Between My Teeth*

acter. "He's quite sure of himself," Wilson said of Max. "He knows the value of what he has done. He doesn't give a damn about having all his caricatures collected and published, as I suggested they ought to be. He doesn't even know where many of them are. He knows very well that somebody else will have to worry about all that someday." He said that Max had a strong head, but that he had never brought this out in his drawings of himself, had always represented himself as a wide-eyed and wispy little dandy. In connection with a mural that Max had painted in the hallway, Wilson was struck by the fact that he had brought to Rapallo with him all of his favorite characters: Chesterton, Balfour, etc. "It is a kind of Divine Comedy," he said, "that he has been working at all his life. The celebrities he has been caricaturing have come to play significant roles. There is a whole hierarchy of values: people like Conrad and Henry James that he both admires and likes; people like Bernard Shaw, that he admires but doesn't like; people like some of the politicians —Lloyd George, for example—that he loathes." He said that he thought Max was the greatest caricaturist of the kind—that is, portrayer of personalities—in the history of art.

(Maybe this is more than you want—if it is, cut it.)

To Sir Rupert Hart-Davis   January 20, 1967
Rupert Hart-Davis Limited, London   Wellfleet
. . . I agree with you about Max as a watercolorist, but I never knew how very good he was till I saw the Guedalla collection in the Ashmolean. I think that he is much underrated as an artist. I am sure you know the series in an office in London about Bernard Shaw's infatuation with Mrs. Patrick Campbell. I wanted to see it when I was last there, but didn't have time. You don't happen to have reproductions of which you could send me photostats? . . .

To Sir Rupert Hart-Davis   February 10, 1967
                                                         Wellfleet
. . . I am very glad to hear that the Shaw–Campbell caricatures are coming out with the Shaw letters. Have you ever seen the drawing of Frank Harris attempting to seduce Shakespeare? . . .

To Sir Rupert Hart-Davis   September 13, 1968
                                                         Wellfleet
Dear Sir Rupert: I suppose you know Max's *One Fine Morning*, in which all his favorite victims parade past him, either dressed differently or wearing their hair or whiskers differently from formerly, so that his caricatures no longer resemble them? It was published, with a note by him, in Part

Ten of an American publication called *The Colophon: A Book Collectors'*
Quarterly, in 1932.   Sincerely, Edmund Wilson

To Sir Rupert Hart-Davis   August 16, 1969
                                                          Wellfleet
Dear Sir Rupert: Thank you very much for the Beerbohm book.* It
arrived at a particularly propitious moment: I have been rereading *Around*
Theatres in order to lift my morale by an application of some clear and
easy English prose—of which there is now a great scarcity—and had been
wishing I could read the rest of it. I look forward to the second volume.

I have this morning only looked through *More Theatres*, but I note
that on the third page of your introduction one of the p's has been
dropped out of *appeared*, and that on page 311, in the Greek phrase, *un*
has been printed for an upsilon.   Yours sincerely, Edmund Wilson

To Sir Rupert Hart-Davis   October 28, 1970
                                                    The New Yorker
Dear Sir Rupert: Thank you for having the new Max Beerbohm sent me.†
It seems to me much more interesting than the other volume. He has got
hold of his subject better and has better plays to deal with. It is probably
a pity that all the articles could not have been published in chronological
order. The book is also better proofread. I noticed, however, the follow-
ing‡ . . .

The Greek is a little bit off. According to my Oxford text, p. 135
should read: τ᾽ ἄπη τῇ βακτηρίᾳ and κ᾽ ἀγὼ μὲν τοιοῦτος ἀνὴρ ὢν
ποιητὴς οὐ κομῶ; and p. 136: δέξασθέ μου θοἰμάτιον.§
                                                 Sincerely, Edmund Wilson

To Sir Rupert Hart-Davis   November 10, 1970
                                                          Wellfleet
Dear Sir Rupert: I can't find any of these supposed quotations anywhere
and am almost forced to conclude that Max made them all up. The
Amyclaean brothers, Castor and Pollux, and the Dodonian oak were more
or less familiar properties of Latin poetry. That Max could invent Greek
is shown in *Zuleika Dobson*, where the Greek version of "For people who
like that sort of thing," etc., is obviously Max's invention. Liddell and
Scott and Lewis and Short do not throw any light on the Latin and

---

* *More Theatres.*
† *Last Theatres.*
‡ Eight corrections omitted.
§ I (he) was away from the staff. And such a man as I, being a poet, do not
cut my hair. Receive (take) my cloak.

Greek. My set of the Delphin Classics has word concordances for all the Latin authors, and I cannot find these lines in any of the writers that Max would be likely to have read. They are not beyond the competence of a clever young classical student. (Shouldn't οἶδα, as you have it, be οἶδα?*) The English lines might easily be improvised. I have sometimes invented quotations myself, not naming the authors, as if they ought to be familiar, and nobody has ever questioned them. You might send these to Maurice Bowra.

I am glad to know about Erardian. I had already made an incorrect emendation—in one of the texts of the now sanctified Scott Fitzgerald.

I wish you would get together a volume of Max's uncollected pieces other than the dramatic reviews—Andrew Lang, the old lady who is writing her memoirs, etc.　　　　　　　　Yours sincerely, Edmund Wilson

To Sir Rupert Hart-Davis　　　　　　　　　　November 20, 1970
　　　　　　　　　　　　　　　　　　　　　　　　　Wellfleet
Dear Sir Rupert: I am further puzzled by the Latin elegiacs that are apparently supposed to be quoted in "The Pervasion of Rouge." They are followed by a reference to Ovid. I have tried to run down these lines in the indices to two editions of Ovid, one of them an index of names, by looking up Maro, who is mentioned, but I cannot find any such reference.

I suppose you know the expanded version of "The Mote in the Middle Distance" that Max sent to Edmund Gosse. It was sent me by a Mr. John Felstiner. It is evident from one of his letters that he has seen you.

Another error in *More Theatres*: Graigie on p. 471 should be Craigie. I have been trying to find out something about Mrs. Craigie, who seems at one time to have been quite well known for her many novels and plays, published under the name of John Oliver Hobbes. Max reviewed her plays and she is included in the D.N.B., but I cannot find anything about her in the memoirs of that period. A memoir published by her father does not throw any light on her personal life. I have read only one book of hers, and did not think very much of it; but am going to look up some of the rest.　　　　　　　　　Sincerely, Edmund Wilson

To Sir Rupert Hart-Davis　　　　　　　　　　December 7, 1970
　　　　　　　　　　　　　　　　　　　　　　　　　Wellfleet
Dear Sir Rupert: I think *Unto This Last* is excellent. People who are old enough to know about Ruskin will understand that it is being used humorously; and other younger people won't know or care about Ruskin at all. Had you thought of enclosing it in quotation marks?

———————————
* I know.

710

Quotations: The English quotation in the Maurice Baring parody—
"of the stuff that can affront despair"—*must* surely be an invention. My
reason for thinking that the other English quotations must be inventions,
too, is that they are not good enough lines for Milton or any other poet
that one would be likely to remember . . .

Yours sincerely, Edmund Wilson

To Sir Rupert Hart-Davis   December 14, 1970
                                                             Wellfleet
Dear Sir Rupert: I'm sorry that I can't throw any light on the Beerbohm
caricature. As you know, he did a drawing of Birrell and Whitley in
A Book of Caricatures of 1907, apropos of the Education Act. Thank you
for the corrections of the errors in "Men's Clothes."* I'll correct them if
the book is ever reprinted.†   Yours sincerely, Edmund Wilson
    In connection with the dubious quotations: there are faked pieces of
scholarship in his theater articles. I taxed him, when I met him, with
having invented his statement that Shakespeare had originally played
Lady Macbeth, and he laughed and confessed that he had.

To Sir Rupert Hart-Davis   June 10, 1971
                                                             Wellfleet
Dear Sir Rupert: Do you know Max's very funny caricature inspired by
Mrs. Conrad's book on her husband? It is in the Benjamin Sonnenberg
collection and is reproduced in a catalogue called *Artists and Writers*, just
published in New York by the Pierpont Morgan Library. I have just seen
it for the first time.   Sincerely, Edmund Wilson

To Sir Rupert Hart-Davis   June 17, 1971
                                                             Wellfleet
Dear Sir Rupert: I have been sent two copies of the album of the
Sonnenberg collection and am forwarding one to you in case it might
be of use.   Yours sincerely, Edmund Wilson

To Barbara Epstein   November 19, 1971
The New York Review of Books   Wellfleet

. . . I forgot to ask you the other day about doing a very short piece on
two books that Hart-Davis is getting out for a Max Beerbohm anni-

---

* Beerbohm's notes for an essay.
† *The Bit Between My Teeth.*

versary: a catalogue of his caricatures, which will contain reproductions, and a collection of his hitherto uncollected writings. I simply want to bring these to the attention of people over here. The books will be sent directly to me . . .*

---

* ". . . I had long admired his writing, and I was astonished to find how interested he was in my catalogue of Max's caricatures, and what an amazing amount he knew about the minor figures of the period. It was a great sorrow to me that he didn't live to see (and perhaps even to write about) the catalogue, which appeared in August 1972."
—Rupert Hart-Davis to Elena Wilson

1970

To Hugh MacLennan   January 18, 1970
                                                                Wellfleet
Dear Hugh: Yes, "squalid" is the word for the last decade—though it has
evidently been worse for us than for you. Trudeau makes a very good
impression in comparison with the oafs who are supposed to be the
heads of the other countries. I have just been reading the book that he
and Jacques Hébert wrote about their visit to China. Do you ever come
to the States? We wish you would come to see us. By plane it is only
about an hour from New York to Boston, and about half an hour from
Boston here. What are you writing? I am too depressed by a feeling of
old age and helplessness to have any effect on anything that is going on.
I've fallen back on a kind of autobiography.
                                            Best regards as ever, Edmund W

To Glyn Morris   January 14, 1970
                                                                Wellfleet
Dear Glyn: Do you know why the Mennonites did not believe in buttons?
I have looked it up in a huge four-volume Mennonite encyclopedia, but
it doesn't give any explanation. I am well into my upstate New York book
and want to include this detail. I hope that you will persist in your intention of coming back [to Lewis County]. You have left a gap which is
hard to fill. I expect to go over in the middle of May.   As ever, Edmund

> Margaret Edmunds [Rullman], about my own age, was at that time
> [1908] my closest friend in Red Bank.   (A Prelude)

To Margaret Rullman   January 17, 1970
                                                                Wellfleet
Dear Margaret: We had been wondering what had become of you, and
were very glad to hear from you. We are leading our same monotonous

life up here, and, due to lack of funds, don't expect to get away this winter.

If Red Bank names a school after me, it would amount to naming it after my father, who, with Eisner, did more for public schools than anybody else in Red Bank. This would mean more to the Board of Education than my reputation as a writer . . .

Love from both of us, Edmund

To Helen Muchnic   January 18, 1970
                                                    Wellfleet

Dear Helen: Here is Sinyavsky's Медвежонок.* I can't detect any political implications except perhaps in the pitiless shipping him off to Poland. I imagine that it is a true story, picked up by Sinyavsky in Siberia.

I had already written you about your first suggested title. The Shakespeare phrase is almost as bad. The ideal title is short, easy to remember and pronounce, and imaginatively stimulating. Something about "survivors" would be all right if you made a point of saying somewhere that it was even more difficult for a serious writer to survive in Russia now than it had been before the Revolution.   Love to you both, Edmund

To Paul Horgan   April 1, 1970
[Postcard]   Wellfleet

Dear Paul: . . . What do you think of Father D'Arcy running away with Rebecca West? I didn't expect the breakdown of celibacy to go so far.

As ever, Edmund W.

To Glyn Morris   April 6, 1970
                                                    Wellfleet

Dear Glyn: I am delighted about your getting your house back. I had really become attached to it, was depressed when you left, and couldn't imagine you as living anywhere else. I had hoped to get up there the second week in May; but I had a heart attack when I last went to New York, have spent some time in the Hyannis hospital, and my plans must depend partly on the readings of cardiograms. There is a new wing to the hospital which, as a gadget laboratory, rivals yours. They do what they call "monitor" your heartbeats. They wire you to a box, the action of your heart is projected, in jewel-like green or amber lights, against a black background, as little elf-like signs that hop downward. These are read on another TV box by the doctors and nurses in a separate room. Some-

---

* The Bear Cub.

714

body has suggested that the next step will be interpolated commercials. Since I have been back here, at home, however, I have been thoroughly enjoying myself. My bed has been moved downstairs just across from the table where I write, and since I don't have to do anything about anything else, I have been making great progress with my Talcottville book. I am pleased with it, but don't know how far it will be possible to interest other people in my own and the local affairs. Lots of points I want to ask you about. Love to Gladys. As ever, Edmund

To John Dos Passos April 19, 1970
Wellfleet

Dear Dos: I am writing you on behalf of the Cape Cod Cardiac Writers Association, recently organized by Paul Chavchavadze, Charley Walker, and myself, in order to defend the rights of cardiac sufferers. As a veteran of long residence on the Cape, we believe that you should be recruited. Our main objectives are as follows:

1. The abolition of the unnecessary blood tests to which the patient is constantly subjected and which reduce him, on leaving the hospital, to a condition much weaker than that in which he entered.

2. Prevention of the proposed leasing to TV networks of the parade of the heartbeats of the patient as made visible on the so-called monitor boxes, whose exhibits may be projected in the same way as television shows. These little green and amber elf-like lights give a pretty and lively performance and many people, of course, would be interested in watching these distinguished hearts. But we believe that the indiscriminate showing is an invasion of personal privacy.

3. Opposition to the interpolated commercials which it is proposed to introduce into such leased or unleased shows.

4. The use of pornographic matter to be synchronized into the rhythm of the heartbeats.

I regretted to know that you were a sufferer from a cardiac ailment— as to which I have been hearing conflicting rumors—that it was caused by your expedition to Easter Island—to your report on which I am eagerly looking forward; and that it resulted from the strain of your public statement that Agnew is the "greatest Greek since Pericles." But I believe that a determined solidarity may be made to alleviate our situation.

Actually, since I have left the hospital, I have been having a most enjoyable life: bed moved downstairs to my study, so that I only have to crawl from the bed to the writing table.

Do come to see us if you ever get up here. We would love to see you all. They tell me that Lucy is marvelous. Elena sends much love.

Bunny

To WILLIAM SHAWN   May 4, 1970
The New Yorker   Wellfleet

. . . I write my articles as a journalist in the expectation of getting printed
fairly promptly . . .

To V. S. PRITCHETT   March 17, 1970
                                                         Wellfleet
Dear Victor: I wanted to see you again, but had been so prostrated that
I tottered back here. Thanks so much for the books. By the time I got
them, however, I had started Graham Greene's *Aunt*—which is mildly
amusing, but not serious. I think, though, that he is better when he is
not serious. I have never very much believed in him.

   Have since read most of your stories, which I much enjoyed, especially,
as in the last one, when you are being funny. I have always been curious
about Queiroz, but my prejudice against translations has hitherto prevented
me from reading him. Your sending me these books, however, now makes it
obligatory. I may still get a chance to see you again. If it is a choice
between New York and Smith, I strongly recommend the latter. I think
that New York now is hell.   Best regards to you both, Edmund W

   The Secret Agent bored me. There is too much psychologizing of an
old-fashioned kind that piles up without being convincing. Leavis is certainly remarkable in illustrating his lack of taste by picking out second-
rate books for special praise.

                                 Part II
Since the above was written,* I have read all the stories in your book—
I find it hard to read a whole volume of short stories through like other
kinds of books. I have always been rather baffled by your short stories—
though not by *Key to My Heart*. They don't have the kind of ending one
expects. I suppose that Maupassant and O. Henry have between them
established a tradition. But I seem now to have got the hang of your
method and have been coming under your spell. The point is that in your
masterly use of detail you so exactly hit the nail on the head that the
reader expects a more usual kind of point at the end, and I haven't
always grasped that the final details, though they may seem as much at
random as the things that actually happen, are equally significant in their
accuracy. "Skeleton" and "Birds" are particularly good. In any case, your
stories are quite unlike anybody else's.

   We hope you can come up here sometime this month, and I'll write
you after I've had my next cardiograph . . .   EW

---
* Part II was written after E. had spent six days in the Hyannis hospital.

To V. S. Pritchett   May 4, 1970
                                                      Wellfleet
Dear Victor: Just got your letter. We have tried several times to call you
and decided you were away. Tried again this morning, with no luck. I
am going over to New York State next Monday . . . We wanted to have
you come up here, but it hasn't been possible. My cardiograms are supposed to show improvement, but I am hardly allowed to move and am
finding it rather enjoyable. Have broken down on three novels, *Mlle de
Maupin* [Théophile Gautier], *Peregrine Pickle* [Tobias Smollett], and
Nostromo; but am reading a Russian nineteenth-century dramatist,
Sukhovo-Kobylin—of such unmitigated cynicism that his plays were suppressed under the Tsar—who perfectly suits my present mood. I fall back
on rereading Saintsbury and soothe myself at night by hearing that he
thinks Trollope somewhat overrated and noting that he thinks *The Vicar
of Bullhampton* a little better than Trollope's worst. I've never taken
Graham Greene very seriously. We're sorry not to see you again before
you leave, but may see you in the fall at Northampton.
                    Best from both of us to both of you. Edmund W.

To V. S. Pritchett   June 1, 1970
                                                      Talcottville
Dear Victor: Thank you for the Meredith. It strikes me as the best thing
I have read about him. He seems always to have been a writer that is hard
for English critics to handle. I think that you perhaps overdo *brilliant*
and *brilliantly* a little. But this seems hard to avoid nowadays. I have to
struggle against it myself. And Angus Wilson, in his book on Dickens,
has been having the same trouble.   Best to Dorothy. Edmund

To Helen Muchnic   July 16, 1970
                                                      Wellfleet
Dear Helen: Приживалка's* privilege of complaining was meant to be
partly humorous. It was Nina Chavchavadze who spoke of it. The equivalent for бабник is the horrible British word *womanizer*, American skirt-
chaser. I am much interested in the Сухово-Кобылин† case and am
reading the literature on the subject. It is one of those Russian affairs that
is argued about for years and never gets cleared up—like the fate of the
Grand Duchess Anastasia, the death or non-death of Alexander I, and
the identity of the writer of the anonymous letters to Pushkin. (Not that
we don't have our uncleared-up mysteries—the death of President Kennedy
—but they seem to me somewhat different.)   Love, Edmund

---

* A hanger-on.
† Sukhovo-Kobylin.

To Glyn Morris   November 8, 1970
                                                              Wellfleet

Dear Glyn: I am back from six days in New York, which nearly finished me—I don't think I'll ever feel able to go there again. But my book has gone over well both with my publisher and with the *New Yorker* editor, who is running two installments of it. I regard this as the high point of my journalistic career—to induce *The New Yorker* to print an account of twenty years of Talcottville.

I saw *Conduct Unbecoming* [Rupert C. Cooke], which I understand you also saw. It preserves the suspense through a fairly long performance, but it seems to me the end is rather confusing and implausible. And everybody shouted too much. New York is worse hell than ever. I really can't struggle with it any longer.

I hope you have recovered by this time . . . I know that it must be hard for you to adjust yourself to so relatively inactive a life, but I have great hopes in your book. Would you like to have me read it in MS?

My difficulty is the opposite one nowadays of adjusting myself, as in New York, to seeing and doing business with people. It fatigues me, and my memory breaks down. When alone with one person and my work, I don't have to worry about other people—can always simply write them letters. I've decided not to sell Talcottville. That provides almost the only real story to my book. In the Prologue I'm deciding to give it up; in the Epilogue, not to.

. . . Don't forget the Hebrew motto חזק חזק, etc.,* which is still tacked up behind the oxygen tank in my bedroom-study.   As ever, Edmund

---

* Be strong, be strong.

"UPSTATE"

1933–1971

To Louise Bogan

July 19, 1933
Talcottville

Dear Louise: . . . I have come up here for a few days to the old family place. My mother spends a couple of months here every summer, but I haven't been here for years. It gave me an awful turn at first, made me horribly gloomy the first night—everybody I ever knew here is dead, gone, or taken to drink and debt. The little town, which used to be populated by my relatives, is practically deserted. But the place here is still attractive and very interesting. My family came over here from New England in the latter part of the eighteenth century—this house was built 1800–4; I suppose it was a first Westward migration. You can get a very good idea of how people lived in America a century and a half ago. The house includes all the things usually found in antique stores, and my constant thought has been—how like an antique store! There are comb-back chairs, curly-maple chairs; bedsteads with faces like figureheads sticking out of the top of them; bed quilts in bright and faintly phallic patterns; engravings of Washington and his family and other standard historical subjects; spinning wheels, bootjacks, berry baskets; a footstool which opens into a cuspidor when you press a little wooden flap (there used to be a chair that played tunes when you sat on it, but I don't know what has become of it); a hideous bust of one of my cousins, done in Germany, and with the hair ribbon and ruffles all carefully reproduced in marble; a stuffed heron; many religious works, annals of the state legislature, and a book called *The Young Wife, or Duties of Woman in the Marriage Relation*, published in 1838 in Boston and warning against the effects of tea and coffee, which "loosen the tongue, fire the eye, produce mirth and wit, excite the animal passions, and lead to remarks about ourselves and others that we should not have made in other circumstances, and which it were better far, for us and the world, never to have made"; perforated tin boxes to be filled with hot coals for warming the feet on sleigh rides and in church; a wooden pestle and mortar; iron cranes and other instruments

Helen Muchnic

Edmund at Talcottville

for cooking things in the fireplaces; jars of dried rose leaves and colored pebbles; a decanter which says "J. Rum"; an old wooden flute, brought over, my great-uncle told me, in an ox-team load from New England. Big rooms, well proportioned; chastely elegant fireplaces, all different; an amplitude and completeness of the large old-fashioned family (my great-grandfather had three wives and his children must have run to a dozen) whose house is a whole city in itself. Currants, gooseberries, red and white raspberry bushes, stone hitching posts; stifling attics with hoopskirts and beaver hats in old hide-covered trunks (there used to be a sealed-up place, where somebody was supposed to have been hidden). There is a gray dappled effect about the side of the house where the plaster has been dropping off the stone which resembles the light and shade in shallow rivers and recalls certain effects in your poetry. The country—hills, pastures, and forests of the first uplands of the Adirondacks—is magnificent—almost too much so: it has never been civilized, humanized, as a good deal of New England has been.

When I was a kid, I used to love coming up here with my little cousins; but when I got older, I used to be depressed and irked when my parents came back every summer. It seemed like moping around in a tomb when life was going on elsewhere. And the old gloom came down on me, as I saw, when I first arrived. Yet I find I take a certain pride in it—and satisfaction in something that stays the same through all the upheavals. Yet, though it stay the same, there is nothing alive in it any longer. The state road now runs directly in front of it, the little town is dwindling to nothing, and there will presently be nothing left but the old house confronting a hot-dog stand and gas station. Maybe I will turn the whole place into an antique shop!

What is really needed here, however, rather than a refined *Atlantic Monthly* essay like the above, is a thorough-going drinking party—such as those at which you are so much missed nowadays in New York in the role of the gracious and stimulating hostess . . . Well, love and good luck! I have greatly enjoyed hearing from you and miss you constantly.

Edmund

To Philippe Thoby-Marcelin August 19, 1950
Talcottville

. . . We are spending a few days up here at a house belonging to my mother, in which her family lived—built at the end of the eighteenth century. Nobody has been here for eight years, and I wanted to see what sort of shape it was in. I have only one relative left in this part of the world: the cousin who came to get us at Yaddo. The people here are much solider (as you can see from him) and more good-natured than on Cape Cod, where the natives are rather dried up and decadent. It is all dairy country here—everybody raises cows. We went to the County Fair yesterday and inspected the prize cattle. Elena says I have a stock-farmer side that she did not know before . . .

To JOHN DOS PASSOS   August 2, 1952
                                                           Talcottville
. . . It is wonderful up here. I prefer it to any other country in the world, and it is the only place where I feel that I can see at something like first-hand how Americans used to live in the days—this community here mostly dates from the end of the eighteenth century—when the country had just been settled. I have been fascinated going through the things here and talking to my local relatives and clearing up the various mysteries connected with the rather curious history of this house. It is too long to write about, but I hope you will come to see me here sometime . . .

To DAWN POWELL   June 18, 1954
                                                             Wellfleet
Dear Dawn: I am getting away to Talcottville immediately after the Fourth. The family are not joining me till the first of August. Why don't you come up and visit me in the meantime? . . . Say, the weekend of the 17th or 24th, though it doesn't matter a bit whether you come on a weekend or not. It is very simple to get there from New York: you just take a train to Utica, where I'll meet you. Hoping to hear from you favorably.   Wig
    . . . This visit would enable you to contrast Dos's large-scale farming with my failure to do anything whatever. My great-grandfather sold the farm, so I don't have to worry about it. I think this was very sound of him.

To LOUISE BOGAN   August 9, 1954
                                                           Talcottville
. . . I wanted to have you come up here, but maybe it would be better another summer. The whole family will be here, and we have invited one or two other people. In having the furniture reupholstered before Elena came, I have filled the place with red plush—much to her horror—not knowing that "mohair" was plush. The Persian kittens on the red plush Victorian furniture are something absolutely Tate Gallery. The landscape outside the windows is like paintings on the walls . . .

To LOUISE BOGAN   June 22, 1956
                                                             Wellfleet
Dear Louise: Thank you for your note. It's a wonder that you haven't been honored by somebody nearer home than Ohio. These degrees and things are beginning to make me feel that I'm a certified old stuffed shirt.

I'm arranging a unique anthology at my Talcottville house. I get the better poets to write poems on the panes with a diamond pencil. I've got Auden, Nabokov, and Edwin Muir, and eventually want to get you. The poems on the windows of the bedrooms all have to do with sleep, and I want to have you put "Song for a Lyre" on one of them.

Love, Edmund

To Van Wyck Brooks
June 8, 1958
Talcottville

. . . I should have told you that the postal address is Boonville, R.F.D. 1, Oneida County, New York . . . This village of eighty inhabitants has no post office. When I first arrive up here, it is likely to seem rather empty, then everything fills in around me, and it becomes far more real than Wellfleet . . .

To Robert Lowell
July 13, 1960
Talcottville

Dear Robert: Why don't you come over here for a visit? also, Elizabeth, if possible. The weather is divine, with a touch of tornado, the countryside is magnificent and full of natural wonders, and you know my richly stocked mind . . .
Edmund

To Mary Meigs
July 14, 1960
Talcottville

Dear Mary: I was so glad to get your letter. Since you people left, I have had a solid spell of work, but I sometimes miss you acutely. I wish you were here to see certain things with me. My non-formal garden is now quite beautiful. It reminds me of the work of some painter—nineteenth-century or early nineteen-hundreds—but I can't think who it is. You would probably know. It is all grown up with a high little white flower—probably Barbara's daisy fleabane. Behind and above this and scattered among it are bright hollyhocks, pink, dark red, rose madder, and lemon. In the front right-hand corner are a mixture of garden and wild flowers, black-eyed susans and some little yellow daisylike flower that must be one of the things I planted, sweet william, red and gingham pink and white, and sprigs of wild blue-purple bells. Malcolm Sharp took me to see one sight that I hadn't ever known existed. Do you remember a sign that said Whitestone Gulf—or State Park? I told you that it was boring, but I found that I had never seen the interesting part—which is a huge and deep canyon of curious gray stone that is almost white, with a little stream at the bottom. You walk along it in a path through the woods above. When you come again, you must see it.

A local Indian came to see me today: a Mohawk who is the school superintendent of the little town of West Leyden. He is the son of a hereditary chief who graduated from Cornell. I had never met him before, but he had written me about my book. I can't get over the superior brains and character of some of these Iroquois and how the families with hereditary titles still retain their dignity and sense of importance. This man tells me that, nevertheless, growing up on the Iroquois reservation, Catholic-dominated and without much community solidarity of the kind the Senecas have, he had to brace himself against the contempt that was felt for them by the surrounding world. Now he says he finds difficulty in making his young sons—his wife is also a Mohawk—understand that they are Indians and what Indians are. All they know is the nonsense they see on TV . . . Do write me again sometime. When I am living alone, I count a good deal on the mail . . . Good night, my dear.   Love, Edmund

To Philippe and Eva Thoby-Marcelin   August 22, 1960
                                                        Talcottville

. . . I had an unsatisfactory feeling about your visit. I had been preoccupied up here with my book, living the life of a hermit, and then everybody arrived at once. I see you nowadays only once a year, and I like to have a little more leisure. I didn't even show Phito his verses, which had been set in the third-floor window in such a way as to balance Léger's [Saint-John Perse]. Stephen Spender, who was up here after you, admired them . . .

To Lewis M. Dabney   November 24, 1962
Smith College, Northampton   Cambridge

Dear Mr. Dabney: I was very much pleased, of course, by your article on *Patriotic Gore*. But you mustn't say that my roots are in New England. My father's family all came from central New York—were among the first settlers. My Wilson grandmother's family were Dutch, and it was from her that I got in my childhood my first intimations of Calvinism. My mother's family all came from New England, but were established in upstate New York by the beginning of the last century. I have always felt myself something of a foreigner in New England, and find myself quite at home when I get back to New York. It is only in the last few years since we have been spending the winters in Cambridge that I have been paying any attention to the original New England stock of the Mathers and Kimballs. (I have been delighted to discover that the Boston Judge [Otis Phillips] Lord, whom Holmes succeeded in the Massachusetts Supreme Court and with whom Emily Dickinson, when they were both rather elderly, carried on an amusing flirtation, was a remote relative of mine.) This is important because the New York point of view is quite distinct from the New England one. Henry James, you know, was always rather irritated when he was taken for a New Englander, and in *Notes of a Son and Brother*, he says that no one with any knowledge of regional differences in America could have taken the Jameses for New Englanders. I purposely left out of *Patriotic Gore* the disaffection of New York toward the Civil War—which I suppose is behind my own attitude—Horatio Seymour, Harold Frederic, the Copperheads, and all that; but I am now going to write about it.

It was not, as you say, during the thirties that I invited my cousins to Talcottville. My mother was still living, and I would simply spend a few days with her there in the summer (see *American Earthquake*). It was in my childhood that the family reunions took place; and it has only been recently, since the house has been mine, that I have been getting my cousins to come back in the summer—the few that still feel any ties with the place. I hope that we may meet again in Northampton.

Yours sincerely, Edmund Wilson

To Tony Garrett   June 1, 1966
Bury St. Edmunds, Suffolk, England   Wellfleet

. . . The Kimball family had a crest which delights me: two lions rampant —one gilded, one bright red—with the device: *Fortis non Ferox* . . .

To Arthur Schlesinger, Jr.   June 10, 1964
                                                                     Wellfleet
. . . I suppose that there is no chance whatever of your being in the neighborhood of Talcottville, New York. I used to think it a refuge, where one could have long conversations and engage in long, undisquieted work; but it is now only a little way from Rome, New York, one of the most important nuclear-warfare centers (they have stacks of bombs right there), where squads of pilots are on duty night and day and ritualistically, at intervals, fly out in the direction of Russia. Last winter I learned with dismay that there were local John Birchers in the neighborhood . . . who had been putting up posters of the "Lynch Warren" type, which would be taken down and then put up again . . .

To Thomas F. O'Donnell   July 24, 1964
Utica College, Utica, N.Y.   Talcottville

Dear Mr. O'Donnell: What I expect to write next summer is a long general article on Harold Frederic—which would not confine itself to his war stories. It would have to appear first in *The New Yorker*, but after that I'd be glad to have it included in your book.

I much enjoyed seeing you and Mrs. O'Donnell and hope we can arrange something soon again.   Sincerely, Edmund Wilson

To Thomas F. O'Donnell   July 20, 1965
                                                     Wellfleet
Dear O'Donnell: I have almost finished all the Harold Frederic books
that I brought with me over here. Could you send me *Mrs. Albert
Grundy* and *A Day in the Wilderness?* I think that the later novels that
take place in England are more interesting than they are usually said to
be. They are full of the social issues—socialism, crooked finance, the new
woman—that were then appearing in fiction. It is interesting to see that
they are almost contemporary with Bernard Shaw's first plays, the first
volume of which came out in 1898.   Best regards, Edmund Wilson

To Thomas F. O'Donnell   October 5, 1965

Dear Tom: This is not brilliant but will, I hope, provide some useful
information. Please be sure to have them send me proof.*
                                              Best regards, Edmund W

To Clelia Carroll   September 22, 1967
                                                     Wellfleet
. . . I have arranged with a man at Utica College, who has written a
book on the subject, for a celebration on the 19th in honor of the
novelist Harold Frederic, the only really first-rate writer who ever came
out of that part of the world. (He died in the late nineties.) Have you
read *The Damnation of Theron Ware?* Our evening performance will
be followed by a colossal party at my local club, which will be paid for
by the college as a public-relations promotion but enable me to pay off
social debts without having, as we used to do, an end-of-the summer party
in our house. The occasion has amusing aspects, because it follows a celebration for another illustrious Utican for whom we feel that extravagant
claims are being made by a man who has just discovered him and has
become fanatical on the subject. A competitive spirit has got into the
thing, and we feel that we are running Frederic against this hitherto
unknown other man. Not that he may not have merit: he was a pioneer
in the field of semantics, about which I know nothing. In his lifetime he
was only known as a successful businessman and banker, who had married
John Adams's granddaughter. My co-organizer tells me with glee that
the other celebration drew only about fifty people. We are hoping to do
much better . . .

---

* Introduction to *Harold Frederic's Stories of York State*, edited by Thomas F.
O'Donnell.

To Thomas F. O'Donnell   November 11, 1967
                                                   Wellfleet
Dear Tom: I have been wondering whether it would be possible to make
our cultural demonstration an annual affair. (1) Minor regional writers:
You and John Gaus; (2) Lewis Morgan: Fenton and me; (3) architecture:
Palmer and ? (I was told that the museum had a lot of pictures of buildings
that no longer exist); (4) early travelers: a number of people, I should
think, could contribute to this; (5) the Oneida Community: Constance
Robertson, who has just written me, as well as other people . . .
                    Best regards to you and Gertrude. Edmund Wilson

To Thomas F. O'Donnell   December 1, 1967

. . . I expect to come up in May, and we can discuss our [cultural]
explosion then. I neglected to mention the possible inclusion of a session
on the local flora and fauna . . .

> Our session on the Iroquois on October 16 . . . Bill Fenton read an
> admirable paper on Lewis Morgan, Tom O'Donnell one on Robert
> W. Chambers and I read the chapter from my Iroquois book on the
> Little Water Ceremony.   (*Upstate*, 1968)

To Thomas F. O'Donnell   September 17, 1968
                                                   Wellfleet
Dear Tom: The 16th is O.K. for me. I think it would be a good idea to
have Fenton perform first, before dinner, and explain who the Iroquois
are and who Lewis Morgan was. Then you do Robert W. Chambers and
the Indians, and I'll end up with a description of the Little Water Ceremony and, if that is too short, some other ceremony. You, of course,
will preside and explain what it is all about.
    I hope to come up sometime next week. I am suffering from shingles,
a horrid ailment that is most uncomfortable and goes on and on.
                                          As ever, Edmund

To Isaac Bashevis Singer   January 31, 1967
                                                   Wellfleet
Dear Mr. Singer: Thank you for your letter, but you overrate the importance of any recommendation of mine.
    About the ghost seen by my wife: we were staying in an old house that
belonged to my family—built at the end of the eighteenth century. I have
never seen a ghost there, but my wife, who does not like ghost stories and
has no interest in the supernatural, got up, as is her habit, very early

one morning and, coming down the stairs, saw a woman in an old-fashioned pleated dress going from the front hall into the living room. Later, we looked at old family pictures in which the women wore such dresses. I have been reading an English book which describes a number of such occurrences and am almost convinced that it is possible for moments of the past to seem to repeat themselves.

Yours sincerely, Edmund Wilson

To Mary Meigs   August 14, 1967
                                                              Talcottville
. . . I doubt whether I shall ever again come up for all summer as I used to do. It gets to be too lonely, and I have by this time pretty well explored the place . . .

To Glyn Morris   December 21, 1969
                                                               Wellfleet
. . . I have really got rolling now with my book on that part of the world. Hope to finish it up there next summer. My cousin Dorothy Mendenhall has written an autobiography which I hadn't known about—which I am now reading with fascination. It tells a lot about the earlier life there which I otherwise shouldn't have known. I now know where my Indian blood comes from—the Wampanoags in this part of the New England world . . .

To Joseph Alsop   February 6, 1970
                                                          The New Yorker
Dear Mr. Alsop: I am writing about upstate New York, and I want to locate an article that you and your brother wrote about your grandmother, Mrs. Robinson, in, I think, *The Saturday Evening Post* a few years ago. I should be grateful if you would let me know in what issue it appeared . . .

Yours sincerely, Edmund Wilson

To Joseph Alsop   February 15, 1970
                                                               Wellfleet
Dear Mr. Alsop: Thank you very much for your letter and the article. I am writing a book about that part of the world which is partly regional history and partly a personal memoir. My family house in Talcottville, Lewis County, built 170 years ago, is not very far from Herkimer, and your grandmother's place as you describe it seemed typical of that semi-feudal and semi-detached society. The information in your letter is very much to the point for me. I don't know the Hyde Park place, and shall make a point of going there next summer. Does somebody live in it or can you go to see it? I have noticed signs near Herkimer directing you

to "the Castle." Is that your grandmother's house? The arrogance of which you speak was a characteristic of that part of the world on the part of people who owned big estates. But it all turned out to be something that, in the long run, had no development.

Yours sincerely, Edmund Wilson

To Joseph Alsop

May 25, 1970
Talcottville

Dear Mr. Alsop: I went over to Henderson House the other day. It is still very impressive, and the view is tremendous. It has been turned, as you know, into a "home for the handicapped"—that is, I gathered, from seeing some of the rather dimwitted old ladies who are encouraged to do ceramics. Mrs. Blair, the wife of the owner, is a very straight, clear-eyed Scotch woman (by way of New Jersey), who seems to have been rather hurt to learn that you regretted the use to which the place has been put. She says that she wrote your brother rather a bitter letter of protest. She declares that if it had not been for her and her husband, the place would soon have collapsed—and this may very well be true. But they have apparently been dealers in antiques and have the most awful taste—they have filled the big downstairs room with a miscellany of unsightly objects. The only things left from the original furnishings are the barrel organ, which they don't know how to work, and the carved marble fireplace. We had some difficulty in finding the place, but happened, at lunch in a restaurant, to sit at a table next to a couple who lived near Henderson House and were able to direct us. They said they had bought from the house a set of Chippendale chairs—I am going to try Hyde Hall presently.

Yours sincerely, Edmund Wilson

To Joseph Alsop

June 4, 1970
Talcottville

Dear Mr. Alsop: I went over to Hyde Hall yesterday. It is a dark desolation now—peeling wallpaper, fallen plaster, and signs saying "Unsafe," where they are afraid the floors may go through. It seems very much less attractive and in less good taste than Henderson House. They must have gone in for grandeur rather than elegance. The Historical Association wants to have it restored, but seems to be short of money. It would be a terrific job to put it into any kind of shape. But I am glad you told me about it. It fits perfectly into my book, a copy of which I'll send you. I'd be grateful if you could arrange to have me visit the Whitehead house and let me know where they live. What you say about their house being eighteenth-century and still inhabited by the original family is also true of ours here. I am conveying to Mrs. Blair your instructions for starting the organ.

Sincerely, Edmund Wilson

To Clelia Carroll   September 2, 1970
                                                           Talcottville
Dear Clelia: My researches have led me to explore the Spiritualist community at Lily Dale, New York, which is a very queer place in every
sense of the word: 80 percent of the mediums are women, and the rest
homosexuals. The village is shut off from the rest of the world, and you
feel that you are surrounded by a conspiracy of a different kind of creatures.
Did you ever read Algernon Blackwood's stories of the supernatural? Have
also been visiting old mansions, which, like mine, have become white
elephants for the owners. They are all being sold as museums or institutions
for feeble-minded old ladies or something of the kind. I'm going back to
Wellfleet when I get near the end of my book. Chautauqua County,
where Lily Dale is, is very flat and unattractive. Even the thunderstorms
are flat. The people seem on such a low level that you wonder that they
are able to get to the point of mating and producing more of the same
kind. Here we at least have mountains, and the inroads of the wild
animals, which, as the farms are being abandoned, seem now to be
moving in on the countryside.

I expect to be in New York sometime about the second week in
October. If you should be there, couldn't we have an evening together?
                                                  Love as ever, Edmund

To William Shawn   July 19, 1971
The New Yorker   Wellfleet

. . . I have been surprised to get more letters about my *Upstate* pieces
than for anything I have written for *The New Yorker* since my detective-
story articles. That is evidently a part of the world that doesn't get written
about, and the people are overjoyed that anybody should know they
exist . . .

To Roger W. Straus, Jr.   January 26, 1971
Wellfleet

Dear Roger: This seems a good moment to give you an account of the present state of my various books:

1. The *Upstate* manuscript you already have, but I think I'll have to make quite a few revisions in proof.

2. The Russian book* is all but finished. I want to add something about Solzhenitsyn and about Nabokov's fiction. (The Introduction to *Finland Station* I'll do when I finish this.)

3. The part of the diary that covers the twenties has been edited in such a way that it is publishable; but I plan to write in a good deal more: character sketches of the Algonquin group, *Vanity Fair*, the Paramore family, etc. The last of these will be found in an article written for *The New Republic*, and there is also a *New Republic* article written when I came back from Europe that I want to include.

4. The book of miscellaneous essays is mostly all pasted up.† I think there are now eight of them, and I expect to be writing others from time to time.

5. I don't believe that my lectures on the representational powers of literature are in any shape now to make a book, but I am hoping eventually to get one out of them. In the meantime, you have my permission to get what you can out of the rest of the diaries.   As ever, Edmund

To Helen Muchnic   February 11, 1971
c/o Hellman, 630 Park Avenue, N.Y.

Dear Helen: I have been going through Solzhenitsyn and last night read your essay on the subject, which seems to me one of your very best. If anybody wanted a summary of these books explaining what they are really

---

* *A Window on Russia.*
† *The Devils and Canon Barham.*

about and what Solzhenitsyn's point of view is, he couldn't do better than read it.

I don't know whether I told you that I had a slight stroke around Christmas, which has somewhat affected my right hand, and gives me some trouble in writing. We have come down to New York and shall be at the above address all through February.   Love, Edmund

To Helen Muchnic   March 4, 1971
                                                              The New Yorker
Dear Helen: I am just out from a week in the hospital, feeling much depleted, though I hope it did me some good. All the time I have been reading Solzhenitsyn and Mrs. Mandelstam's memoirs, which have not made me feel any more cheerful. Have also been reading you on Mandelstam, Akhmatova, and the rest, about whom I think you are excellent. You managed to put into these little reviews a good deal of very telling criticism. Since you are writing in such detail about the steeplechase in *Anna Karenina*, I think you ought to tell exactly how it might have been due to a kind of triumphant thoughtlessness. After the leap, he sat back too hard, didn't he?

I don't quite understand your dedication. I don't have it here in the office with me; but what I don't understand is the relation of the plural second line to the first line.   Love, Edmund

To Helen Muchnic   March 18, 1971
                                                                   Wellfleet
Dear Helen: I am still reading your book. Elena believes that Vronsky did wreck Anna very much as he did the mare; he plunged back into his relation with her impulsively very much as he sat back on the horse.

I have thought about the obvious derivation of the O'Neill play from Gorky. I am not sure that you make it plain to the reader exactly what happens in these plays, and that both Luka and Hickey are complete fakes. I did see Pritchett's review and was very much pleased by it.

You tell me to "do what the doctors order," without realizing, I think, that the doctors all order different things—sometimes two drugs that contradict one another. We are slowly recovering up here after six more or less terrible weeks in New York. You and I are both lucky to have comfortable country places to live in.

By the way, "it has been brought to my attention" that, as usual, there are errors in my article about Tolstoy in *The New York Review*. Воскресенье* and Воскресение† are not the same word and are

---

* Sunday.
† Resurrection.

spelled slightly differently; and Father Sergius did not apparently go to bed with his woman visitor but cut off his finger instead. Nabokov has suddenly written me a letter telling me that he values my friendship and that all has been forgiven. He has been told that I have been ill, and it always makes him cheerful to think that his friends are in bad shape. He was mourning for Roman Grynberg at least ten years before he died.

Much love to you both, Edmund

To HELEN MUCHNIC   April 23, 1971
                                                                    Wellfleet

Dear Helen: I have only just finished reading all the pieces in your book. It has been very useful to me in getting together my own book on Russian writers. You fill in for me many gaps. You write much better now and have learned to make terse formulations. You are particularly good on the NEP and on Solzhenitsyn. I should like to refer to your chapter on the latter, but again you have somewhat embarrassed me by dedicating the book to me. My only suggestion would be that when you are not writing for *The New York Review* you sometimes take for granted a knowledge of matters which the reader is not likely to know about. I think, too, that you ought to make your acknowledgments to periodicals at the beginning of the book instead of scattering them, as you have done, at the beginning of each piece. And please don't use the vulgar expression "That is something else again" (page 218), which was taken over from Yiddish . . . Why don't you say "that is another matter"?   Love as ever, Edmund

To VLADIMIR NABOKOV   March 8, 1971
                                                              The New Yorker

Dear Volodya: I was very glad to get your letter. I am just now getting together a volume of my Russian articles. I am correcting my errors in Russian in my piece on Nabokov–Pushkin; but citing a few more of your ineptitudes. I don't agree that Solzhenitsyn is third-rate. I think he is remarkable, though somewhat monotonous—not in a class with Pasternak, but, after all, he has nothing to tell but the story of illness and imprisonment. I am trying to write something about him for a final chapter. I find I have some difficulty in reading Soviet Russian.

I have included an account of my visit to you in Ithaca in a book that will be out this spring (don't read the stripped version in *The New Yorker*), based on twenty years of Talcottville diary. I hope it will not again impair our personal relations (it shouldn't).

. . . Best regards and love to Vera. EW

According to the Soviet edition of Chekhov, you have the date slightly wrong about the letter in which he tells of your relatives' encounter with him.

To ELENA LEVIN   February 1, 1968
                                                                Wellfleet
Dear Elena: Do you know of any place in Cambridge—or New York—
that would have a grammar of Old Slavonic? It is the Dead Sea scrolls
that are getting me into this. Certain apocrypha only exist in Old Slavonic.
There are translations, but having the Old Slavonic text has made me
curious about it. Regards to Harry . . .   Преданы Вам* Edmund

To EUGENIE LEHOVICH   April 14, 1971
                                                                Wellfleet
Dear Evgenia: Thanks so much for the Old Church Slavonic testament. I
have been struggling with it, with the aid of a Slavonic grammar. One
thing for which I can find no explanation is the meaning of the little
signs over the vowels—as Ŭ. Do you know what these are? Some of them
probably show the accentuation.   As ever, Edmund

To JEANNE BALLOT (MRS. ALBERT E. WINHAM)   April 23, 1971
                                                                Wellfleet
Dear Jeanne: I was so sorry about your having been attacked and injured.
Our friend at *The New Yorker* told me about it. Something of this kind
has happened to a number of my friends. It is disgusting. I hope you
have recovered now. I am sorry not to have seen you for such a long
time.   As ever, Edmund Wilson

To JEANNE BALLOT   May 5, 1972
                                                                Wellfleet
Dear Jeanne: I hope you have recovered from that mugging. I have often
thought about you with sympathy.
   Have you any way of finding out how much I was getting at the end
of my period at *Vanity Fair*? I am writing a sort of book of memoirs, and
I should like to know.† I should be grateful if you could look this up or
happen to remember about it.   As ever, Edmund Wilson

To STANLEY DELL   August 24, 1971
                                                                Wellfleet
Dear Stanley: On top of my other misfortunes, I managed to fall in the
Princeton Club and fracture one of my vertebrae. I have been more or
less incapacitated ever since. I have not yet gone up to Talcottville and

---

* Yours devotedly.
† *The Twenties.*

734

they tell me the new road is making it so awful that I had better not come. I am getting a brace made and hope this may help with my back.

Love to Jean. Edmund

To HARRIET WALDEN   September 7, 1971
The New Yorker   Wellfleet

Dear Mrs. Walden: Scribner's years ago published a complete Ibsen, which may now be out of print. I should like to get the volumes with the following plays: *The League of Youth, The Pillars of Society, Emperor and Galilean, Love's Comedy, Lady Inger of Østeraad, The Feast at Solhaug, The Pretenders, The Vikings at Helgeland.*

Could you find out whether they still have these and whether they will sell the volumes separately? The easiest thing would be just to call them up and ask them. If the books are available, please buy them and send the bill to me. Thank you and best regards. I am still laid up but I think getting somewhat better.   Sincerely, Edmund Wilson

To DOROTHEA STRAUS   September 19, 1971
                                                         Wellfleet

Dear Dorothea: Your book* helped me through some depressed moments. I found it consoling to read in the hospital about well-to-do people living with comfort and dignity. Elena says that your German family were even more old-fashioned than hers. The curious thing is that it has been possible to exert a spell in a book in which nothing very startling ever happens. Prohibition apparently did not upset your family as it did my poor old friend Paul Rosenfeld, whose money also came from Rheingold. In his case, it was tragic and changed all his habits of life. I read the book straight through without ever being bored one moment. I think you write extremely well. Your choice of words is perfect, and you never use a word too many. I wonder what you will write next.   As ever, Edmund

To ERICH SEGAL   September 19, 1971
                                                         Wellfleet

Dear Mr. Segal: Thank you very much for the Plautus, with its inscription, which I have been reading with approval. You have been extremely successful in catching the sense and following the meter. And you have managed to avoid Gilbert and Sullivan, to which the translators of Aristophanes have found it difficult not to succumb. I don't quite like "Greeking it up," "Boozing it up," etc. (Wouldn't "going Greek" be

---

* *Thresholds.*

better?) But I know that Plautus is not fastidious. Again, I wish you had avoided the unnecessary near-rhymes such as *depth* and *death* on page 318. The drawing by Hirschfeld on the cover made me a little nervous while I was reading the book. Those Menaechmi rather annoy me, anyway.

If you ever get up this way again, do be sure to look us up. We promise not to bore you about *Love Story*.   Sincerely, Edmund Wilson

I find that you were right about [Gilbert] Highet on Juvenal's sexual habits. Please don't forget to send me your article on the Fellini *Satyricon*.

To Angus Wilson   October 29, 1971
                                                            Wellfleet
Dear Angus: Penelope Gilliatt tells me that you are now in this country. If you should ever come to Boston, do let us know, as we'd be delighted to have you visit us. An hour and a half by plane from New York.

I enjoyed your book on Dickens. I suppose that you have discovered that an illustration by Catermole is attributed to Cruikshank.

                                         Best regards, Edmund Wilson

I am having Roger Straus send you the novel about Hollywood [*Play It As It Lays*] by Joan Didion. It represents a further phase of the horrors that you have already depicted.
                                              (To Anita Loos, 1970)

To Joan Didion   October 25, 1971
                                                            Wellfleet
Dear Joan: I was really particularly pleased by your letter. I have never read Henry Adams's *Mont-Saint-Michel;* I esteem him without being very crazy about him. I lately tried to go back to what he calls his "dreary history," which I dropped something like fifty years ago, and found it just as unreadable as it was then. Nonetheless, I have found him interesting on the American politics of his period.

I have been wondering what you were able to do about that delinquent girl.   Best regards to your husband. Edmund W

To Alison Lurie   November 19, 1971
                                                            Wellfleet
Dear Alison: . . . I have been reading your article in the *Review* with interest. I don't know why you should have been at a loss for a modern example of the Cinderella story. Shaw's *Pygmalion*, which has been such a success as *My Fair Lady*, is an outstanding example of this. So was Pushkin's *Evgeni Onegin*, also a permanent success.

736

I have it on my mind that I wrote about your upstate novel in my Dead Sea scrolls book rather than in my book about upstate New York, where it would have been much more appropriate.

Barbara Epstein has been telling me about your new novel, which I am eager to read. I am glad to hear that Jonathan's book is going to be published.　　　　　　　　　　Best regards to both of you. Edmund W

To Leonard Kriegel　　　　　　　　　　　November 14, 1971
　　　　　　　　　　　　　　　　　　　　　　　　Wellfleet

Dear Mr. Kriegel: I have just read your book on me* with much interest, and I am grateful for the time and thought you have devoted to it. Aside from questions of opinion, which can only be argued about, the only actual inaccuracy I have found was your saying that I had learned Russian in order to read Lenin in the original. This made me laugh, because Lenin is a very dull writer who would never inspire anybody to learn Russian in order to read him. I learned Russian primarily, I think, in order to read Pushkin, inspired by D. S. Mirsky's book on the subject, as I had learned Italian in order to read Dante.

When you write about *Patriotic Gore*, I think you are still under the influence of the old myths about American history; and I think you are too much obsessed with the idea of Black Power. I certainly didn't leave any doubt that I disapproved of slavery, though I don't think it had much to do with the reasons of the North for subduing the South. Beginning at the bottom of page 76, you begin using "us" and "our" in a way that always makes me wince, because I want to ask who are "we," who is the author speaking for. You are surely mistaken in thinking that the readers of my book† already knew about biological warfare. I had some difficulty myself in getting accurate information about it.

Harry Moore is mistaken in thinking that *Patriotic Gore* is a "shapeless hodgepodge." It was actually very much organized. I regret now that I didn't put the two long extracts from De Forest in appendices. It would have made that chapter less lumpy. I don't think that Moore understands that with such books I am always working with a plan and structure in mind. As a journalist, I sell the various sections to magazines as I can. You seem to understand this process better than he does. He is also incorrect in implying, as several other people have, that I studied Hebrew for the purpose of writing on the Dead Sea scrolls. It was the other way around: it was from studying Hebrew that I became curious to find out what was going on in connection with the scrolls. You once fall into an error which Sherman Paul is very much prone to: suggesting originals for

---

* *Edmund Wilson*, preface by Harry T. Moore.
† *The Cold War and the Income Tax.*

invented characters. The character in *Daisy* was derived from a combination of people, among whom my father played very little part. It was closer to J. J. Chapman, though really an imaginary person.

Though I doubt whether your book will ever get into a second printing, I may note that there are misprints on pages 18, 47, 49. The word "bourgeois" has no *e* at the end. The grammar breaks down toward the beginning of page 62. In dealing with *The Boys in the Back Room*, you evidently base your criticisms on the little book published in California rather than on the version, which is somewhat different, included in *Classics and Commercials*. The poem called "Night in May" has nothing to do with the war: it was written very much earlier, when I was doing my labor reporting. But thank you again for your trouble and intelligence.

Yours sincerely, Edmund Wilson

To Barbara Epstein   November 19, 1971

. . . I was delighted with the ragtime record*—hadn't heard anything like that since my youth . . .

To Jonathan and Susanna Wylie   December 4, 1971
                                                                  Wellfleet

Dear Wylies: I am sending you George Borrow† for a Christmas present. It may help to get you through the long winter. The two volumes are really all one story. He was dissatisfied with the reception of the first volume, and characteristically—for he was very peculiar—did not publish the second for six years, and then began it with the characters simply waking up, with no explanation of who or where they are. They used to be among my favorite books.

We were much interested in your account of the Faroes. Have you heard anything about a character from the Faroes named Magnus Heinesson, about whom Ibsen once thought of writing a play?

Holiday greetings, EW

To Harriet Walden   February 15, 1972
The New Yorker   Naples, Florida

Dear Mrs. Walden: In a day or two I'll be sending you a first installment of my memoirs of the twenties. There's no hurry about it, and don't send it back. I'll pick it up when I get to New York in the spring. The pages are not numbered correctly and the numbering ought to be done, in

---

* *Piano Rags* by Scott Joplin.
† See letter to Alfred Bellinger, p. 4.

738

copying it, by the typist. I hope she understands about printer's signs: how capitals and lower case are indicated, etc.

Yours sincerely, Edmund Wilson

To GLYN MORRIS   February 19, 1972
Naples, Florida

Dear Glyn: I had already written you when I just got your letter. I had forgotten you had lots down here. They will probably go up in value. The developments are going forward at breakneck speed. When I read that story about the White House dinner for the *Reader's Digest*, I at first thought of doing an article about it, but gave up the idea because I realized that it could only be abusive and that it wouldn't look well because the "Freedom Medal" that Nixon gave Wallace was the same thing that Kennedy gave me. A man I know—not a writer, but a banker whose judgment I think is pretty good—predicts that we are in for another mediocre president—McGovern is "too pure." The Americans won't do anything until they feel a severe economic pinch. I don't feel any enthusiasm for either Muskie or Lindsay. About the *Reader's Digest*: Harold Ross forbade his contributors to allow any article to be reprinted in it.

I think I wrote you before how boring this place is. It is largely populated by elderly parties who are delighted to get away from the blizzards and winds of the Great Lakes and who are shocked and uncomprehending when you say you find it dull. I hope to be back in April rather than in May, but we are going to stop off in March to see my cousin in Virginia. Then the Cape, thank God.   As ever, Edmund

To MARY MEIGS   May 18, 1972
Wellfleet

Dear Mary: I am getting off another copy of my book to you.* Please let me know if it arrives.

The shadbushes are all in bloom here now and the arbutus is threading its way under the old leaves. Otherwise, there are not many signs of spring.

I had a slight stroke the other day and now can't talk distinctly—spent a week in the Hyannis hospital, but they weren't able to do much for me.

I read Mrs. Mandelstam last winter. It is impressive and very depressing.

I don't know about Mandelstam and Akhmatova in French. I have only read the latter's "Requiem" in Russian, and it is almost too painful to read. I thought that *The Sense of the Past* was quite successful.

. . . I still look rather longingly at your house when I pass it and wish you were still here.   Love to both of you, Edmund

---

* *Upstate.*

739

To WILLIAM SHAWN   May 27, 1972
The New Yorker
Dear Shawn: I'm going over to my Boonville address on Wednesday and
expect to stay till the middle of June. Roger Straus will send you a
complete proof of my book on the twenties. Please send me your selections
from it so that I can see what has been done.

                                        Sincerely, Edmund Wilson

This writing of books is an endless matter.—Ecclesiastes 12:12*

---

* Edmund requested that the ninetieth Psalm and the last chapter of Ecclesiastes be
read at his funeral.

INDEX

Mendenhall, Dorothy, 728
Menjou, Adolphe, 277
Menotti, Gian-Carlo: *The Consul*, 482; *The Medium*, 482
Meredith, George, 5, 11, 13, 19, 27–8, 511, 717; *The Amazing Marriage*, 27n; *The Egoist*, 5; *The Letters*, 11; *One of Our Conquerors*, 11
Mérimée, Prosper: *Une Amitié littéraire*, 579
Merrill, Stuart, 163
Merz, Charles, 56
Metropolitan, The, 73, 85
Meyer, Sheldon, 615–16, 671, 683
Meyerbeer, Giacomo, 27
Michelet, Jules, 229, 246–51, 358
Milano, Paolo, 512, 520–1, 672
Milhaud, Darius, 117
Milholland, Inez, 71
Mill, John Stuart, 22, 64; *Autobiography*, 22
"Mill Stream, The" (Wilson), 90
Millay, Edna St. Vincent, 53, 67–8, 70–72, 89, 106, 115, 118, 134, 136, 153–154, 166, 174, 222, 227, 232, 293, 305, 329, 392, 452, 473, 491–2, 508, 518; *The Buck in the Snow*, 153–4; *Conversation at Midnight*, 293n; *Epitaph for the Race of Man*, 166–7; *Fatal Interview*, 71; "Figs from Thistles," 70; "Justice Denied in Massachusetts," 154n; "Shroud," 71–2
Miller, Arthur, 540, 570
Miller, Henry, 537, 663
Milton, John, 98, 124, 213, 303, 376, 711; *Paradise Lost and Regained*, 98, 124
Mindszenty, Joseph, 650
Minor, Robert, 257
Miracle, The, 497
Mirbeau, Octave, 39–40, 665, 670; *Sébastien Roch*, 40, 665, 670
Mirsky, D. S., 271, 276, 282, 375–6, 576–7, 737
"Mr. More and the Mithraic Bull" (Wilson), 190n, 208n, 229
Mitchell, Weir, 494
Mizener, Arthur, 14n, 233–4, 475–80, 487, 494, 562–4, 689; "Edmund Wilson: A Checklist," 233n; *The Far Side of Paradise*, 234n, 475–81
Modern Language Association, xxi, 370, 685–6, 688, 701; *Professional Standards and American Editions: A Response to Edmund Wilson*, 686
Modern Library, 231, 309, 337

Modern Quarterly, The, 225
Modern Music, 412, 443
Modigliani, Amedeo, 641
Moe, Henry Allen, 304–6, 382, 517
Moeller, Philip, 87
Molière, 64, 81, 450
Montaigne, Michel de, 685
Montesquieu, 227
Moore, David, 413
Moore, George: *Memoirs of My Dead Life*, 438
Moore, Harry T., 737
Moore, Marianne, 114–15, 126, 382, 399, 518, 524; *La Fontaine*, 518
Moore, T. Sturge, 298
Moravia, Alberto, 413, 418, 487; *Agostino*, 413; "L'Ufficiale Inglese," 413
More, Paul Elmer, xviii–ix, 193, 195, 208, 229–30, 240, 288, 291, 293, 459; *The Demon of the Absolute*, 459; *Pages from an Oxford Diary*, 291
"More Notes on Current Clichés" (Wilson), 569n
Morgan, Lewis, 727
Morgenthau, Robert, 634
Morley, Christopher, 108
Morrell, Ottoline, 682
Morris, Glyn, 656, 671, 713–15, 718, 728, 739
Morris, William, 100, 118
Moscow Art Theatre, 101, 112, 677
Moses, Robert, 552, 557
Mourontzov, Barbara Wolkov, 576–7
Mozart, Wolfgang Amadeus, 395, 703; *The Marriage of Figaro*, 395
Muchnic, Helen, 376–80, 394, 401, 411–412, 415, 451, 497–8, 524, 577–82, 584, 595, 603–5, 617–19, 637, 638, 668, 670, 694, 702, 714, 717, 731–3; *An Introduction to Russian Literature from Gorky to Pasternak*, 380n; *Russian Writers*, 603n
Muir, Edwin, 440, 723
Mumford, Lewis, 215, 222, 685
Munson, Gorham, 225
Murdoch, Iris: *A Severed Head*, 634, 641
Murphy, Esther, 96n, 106, 111, 119–20, 191, 263; *see also* Strachey, Esther
Murphy, Gerald, 96n, 254, 347, 638–9, 665
Murray, Gilbert, 291
Murray, Natalia, 676
Murset, Polly, 506
Muskie, Edmund S., 739
Musorgsky, Modest P., 395, 640; "Bal-

Nouvelle Revue Française, 103–4
Novy Zhurnal, 576
Nowell-Smith, Simon: The Legend of the Master, 479
Noyes, Alfred, 80–1
Noyes, Laurence, 5, 9, 11, 17–18, 25, 39, 44, 536

Ober, Harold, 348
Observer, The, 550, 607, 678
O Canada (Wilson), 594, 632–6
O'Connor, Edwin, 628, 680
O'Connor, Frank, 365
O'Donnell, Thomas F., 680, 725–7; Harold Frederic's Stories of York State (ed.), 726
Oelrichs, Hermann, 435
Ognyov: Communist Schoolboy, 374
Oh, You Beautiful Doll, 464–5
O'Hara, John, 328–9, 338, 570, 652
Old Testament, 521n, 522–3, 529, 532, 612–13
Olmsted, Frederick, 610
"Omelet of A. MacLeish, The" (Wilson), 307–8
"On First Reading Genesis" (Wilson), 521n, 527n
O'Neill, Eugene, 52, 86–7, 117, 134–5, 199–200, 202, 212, 497–8, 603, 732; All God's Chillun Got Wings, 117n, Anna Christie, 87; Desire under the Elms, 52, 125; The Hairy Ape, 85, 87; The Iceman Cometh, 450, 497–8, 603
Orage, Alfred Richard, 195, 596
Origo, Iris, 518
Ornstein, Leo, 51, 117, 121
Országh, László, 647
Orwell, George, xxvii, 450–1, 486–7; Animal Farm, 409, 450; Burmese Days, 450; Dickens, Dali & Others, 450; The English People, 450; Inside the Whale, 450; Keep the Aspidistra Flying, 450
Osbert's Career or the Poet's Progress (Wilson), 160–1
Osborn, William, 5, 8, 11, 40, 43
Osborne, John, 678
Ostrovsky, Alexander, 271, 377; Talents and Admirers, 377
Oswald, Lee Harvey, 646
Ottley, Roi: Black Odyssey, 490
Our Exagmination (Wilson), 183
Ovid, 435, 710; Metamorphoses, 435
Oxford Dictionary, 170

Paderewski, Ignace, 22
Paget, Celia, see Goodman
Paget, Mamaine, 417–23, 427–8, 430–1, 438–41, 454, 485–6, 491–2, 509, 511, 515, 610–11, 705
Paine, Thomas, 453, 639
Panama-Pacific International Exposition, 22
Paramore, E. E. Jr., 5, 51, 59, 79, 80, 85, 105, 119, 202, 340, 731
Pareto, Vilfredo, 283
Paris Express, 645
Parker, Dorothy, 85, 136, 155, 234, 485
Parkman, Francis, 552
Partisan Review, 116, 301, 307, 309–310, 320–1, 360, 369, 371, 382, 393, 402, 437, 443, 567
Pascal, Blaise, 64
Pasternak, Boris, 568, 573, 580, 582–6, 588–9, 670, 733; Dr. Zhivago, 573, 582n, 584–6, 588, 670; "An Essay in Autobiography," 586; I Remember, 586; Safe Conduct, 586
Pater, Walter, xxxi, 19–20, 37, 321, 399; Marius, 19
Patriotic Gore (Wilson), xxiii, 474n, 520n, 521n, 566n, 593, 601n, 605, 608n, 608–23, 627, 630, 633, 724–5, 737
Paul, Sherman, 737
"Paul Rosenfeld: Three Phases" (Wilson), 445
"Paul Valéry" (Wilson), 115n
Pcolar, Mary, 602
Pearce, Charles (Cap), 333, 362, 406–7
Pearlman, Moshe, 673–4
Pemberton, Brock, 87
Pennell, Joseph, 22
Pepys' (Samuel) Diary, 9
Péguy, Charles Pierre, 475
Percy, Thomas: Reliques, 687
Perelman, S. J., 411
Perelman, Mrs. S. J., 245
Perkins, George, 6, 42–4
Perkins, Maxwell, 52, 147–53, 159–61, 166, 168, 173–4, 191, 200–2, 209–10, 214–15, 244, 254, 272–3, 312–13, 323, 328, 337–43, 347–8, 350, 382, 387–8, 433–4, 447, 516
Perse, Saint-John, see Léger, Aléxis
Petöfi, Sandor: "Az Alföld," 648
Petrarch, 524
Petronius, 534
Phillips, David Graham, 385
Philo Judaeus, 517

Ransom, John Crowe, 214, 399–400, 443, 452
Rascoe, Burton, 79, 88, 92–4, 97, 105, 112, 119, 127, 133, 168–70, 173, 175, 178, 195, 215, 240, 364–5, 542; *Diary*, 97
Rascoe, Hazel, 87, 93, 168
Ray, Gordon N., 686–7
Read, Herbert, 170, 517
Reader's Digest, The, xxii, 439, 739
Red Army Star, 287
Red, Black, Blond and Olive (Wilson), 474, 521n, 533–4, 683
Reed, John, 71, 122, 283
Reinhardt, Max, 515–16
Renan, Ernest, 22, 39, 59, 64, 114, 122, 212, 246–50, 458, 509, 523, 525, 654; *Les Apôtres*, 39, 122; *Histoire générale des langues sémitiques*, 654; *Histoire du peuple d'Israël*, 509, 523; *Saint Paul*, 458; *Vie de Jésus*, 22, 525
Repin, Ilya, 675
Reporter, The, 356, 462–3, 570, 619
"Reversals, or *Plus ça change*" (Wilson), 432n, 496
Revue des Deux Mondes, La, 579
Rexroth, Kenneth: "Assays," 626
Rhodes, James Ford, 565–6
Rice, Elmer: *The Adding Machine*, 105
Rickword, Edgell: *Rimbaud: The Boy and the Poet*, 298
Riley, James Whitcomb, 253
Rilke, Rainer Maria, 289, 321
Rimbaud, Arthur, 80, 203, 210, 296–9, 448, 457, 464; "*L'Automne déjà*," 297; "*Bateau ivre*," 297, 299; *Les Illuminations*, 298; "*Ô saisons, ô chateaux!*", 297; *Reliques*, 298; *Une Saison en enfer*, 297–300, 476; "*Tête de Faune*," 297
Rimbaud, Isabelle, 298
Rivera, Diego, 230
Robertson, Constance, 727
Robeson, Paul, 117n
Robinson, Edwin Arlington, 114, 136, 458
Robinson, Noel, 6, 11–12, 14, 16–17
Robles, José, 357–8, 665
Rochefort, Christiane: *Les Stances à Sophie*, 647–8
"Rockets" (Wilson), 407
Rodbertus, Johann Karl, 316,
Roditi, Edouard, 428–9
Roland, Colonel, 468
Rolland, Romain: *Au-dessus de la mêlée*, 34

Roosevelt, Eleanor, 558
Roosevelt, Franklin D., 245, 266, 419, 565, 567, 600, 618
Roosevelt, Theodore, 197, 538, 613
Root, Esther, 106
Rootham, Helen, 298
Rose, William K., 371–2
Rosenberg, Julius and Ethel, 512, 643
Rosenfeld, Paul, 64, 88, 92, 109, 115, 121–2, 127, 169, 173, 191, 258, 288, 292, 348, 412–13, 445, 447, 544, 735
Ross, Harold, 401–6, 451, 482, 739
Roth, Cecil, 519
Roth, Philip, 652
Roth, Samuel, 341, 344, 347
Roumain, Jacques, 462, 469; *Bois-d'ébène*, 469; *Gouverneurs de la rosée*, 469
Roumer, Émile, 469, 476
Rousseau, Jean-Jacques, 42, 83, 108–9, 126, 225, 227; *Confessions*, 83, 108–9; *Contrat social*, 109
Rowlandson, Thomas, 599
Rukeyser, Muriel, 307
Rullman, Margaret Edmunds, 713–14
Ruskin, John, 710
Russell, Bertrand, 37, 566, 682, 700–1
Russia, 190, 214–15, 251–3, 255–7, 259, 263–4, 267, 269, 271–3, 275, 279, 282, 286–8, 296, 311, 389, 394, 441, 477, 486, 490–1, 506, 530, 533–4, 591, 596, 619–22, 642–3, 645, 651, 656, 714

S4N, 119
Sacco and Vanzetti, xxiv, 135n, 137, 145, 154, 197, 278, 504, 512
Sade, Marquis de, 362, 498–9, 516; *120 Journées de Sodome*, 499
Sailors of Cattaro, 258
Saint Jerome, 673
St. Nicholas, 506
Saint-Simon, 260, 685
Sainte-Beuve, Charles A., 108, 458
Saintsbury, George, 661, 717
Salinger, J. D., 545, 605
Salzburg Seminar of American Studies, 474, 512, 514–16, 526, 609, 611
Samuel, Mar Athanasius Yeshue, 530n
Sand, George, 605
Sand, Maurice, 623
Sandburg, Carl, 610
Santayana, George, 390, 420, 426, 532–533, 608; *The Last Puritan*, 533

Surkov, Alexei, 588
Sutherland, Graham, 707
Sutton, Barbara, 653
Svengali, 208
Swedish Ballet, 113, 117, 120–1
Sweet, Henry, 375
Swift, Jonathan, 37, 81, 100, 207, 265, 289, 291, 551; *Gulliver's Travels*, 265
Swinburne, Algernon, 172, 458, 460, 617, 623–4, 661–2; *La Fille du policeman*, 625; "Hesperia," 458; *Heptalogia*, 624; "Pasa Thalassa Thalassa," 458; *La Soeur de la Reine*, 625; *The Whippingham Papers*, 625
Sylvain, Yvonne, 467
Symonds, John Addington, xxxi, 37
Symons, Arthur, 93, 171

Taine, Hippolyte Adolphe, 64, 246–50, 317; *L'Ancien Regime*, 248; *The History of English Literature*, 250
Tandy, Jessica, 473, 488
Tate, Allen, xxiii, xxvi, 101, 104, 127–130, 142, 145, 154, 158–9, 162–8, 174–175, 191, 193, 196–200, 211–14, 220–221, 225–6, 228, 279–80, 292, 301, 308, 318, 321, 323–4, 330–1, 358, 370–1, 393–4, 399–401, 412–14, 436, 443, 453, 471, 476, 483n, 483–5, 492, 495–7, 508, 615, 625–6; "Alice," 225; "American Poetry Since 1920," 158n; "Bored to Choresis," 128; "The Death of Little Boys," 128; "The Duchess of Malfi," 128; "Emblems," 225; "The Ivory Tower," 279; *The Mediterranean and Other Poems*, 279n; "Mr. Pope," 128; *Pervigilium Veneris*, 393, 399; "The Robber Bridegroom," 279
Taub, Allen, 222
Taylor, Myron C., 419
Taylor, William: *Cavalier and Yankee*, 607, 623
Tchaikovsky, Peter Ilich, 271, 380; *Pique Dame*, 362, 380
Tchelichev, Pavel, 380
Tead, Ordway, 56
Temps Modernes, 487
"Tennessee Agrarians" (Wilson), 214n
Tennyson, Alfred Lord, 245
Ternan, Ellen, 507
Thackeray, William Makepeace, 13, 344, 687
Thayer, Scofield, 115, 126
Theatre Guild, 84, 86, 87, 204, 489

Theatre Union, 258
Theodoric, 491
This Quarter, 123
This Room and This Gin and These Sandwiches: Three Plays (Wilson), 190, 474n, 598n
Thoby-Marcelin, Eva, 470, 724
Thoby-Marcelin, Milo, 466–7, 470
Thoby-Marcelin, Philippe (Phito), 461–462, 466–70, 476, 494, 512, 631–2, 721–2, 724; *La Bête de Musseau*, 461–462; *Canapé Vert*, 461–2; *Le Crayon de Dieu*, 462, 469
Thoby-Marcelin, Pierre, 466–7, 470, 476, 513; *La Bête de Musseau*, 461–2; *Canapé Vert*, 461–2; *Le Crayon de Dieu*, 462, 469.
Thomas, Dylan, 627
Thompson, Dorothy, 420
Thomson, Virgil, 412
Thoreau, Henry David, xxiv, 110–11, 165, 390, 538, 684; *Walden*, 110, 212
Thorne, Mrs. Oakleigh, 214
Thucydides, 565
Thurber, James, 239, 275, 344, 405–6, 570; *The Years with Ross*, 405n, 570
Tibbett, Lawrence, 362
Tiger, The (Princeton), 5, 9, 12
Tillich, Paul, 520n, 521
Tillyard, E. M. W., 303
Time, 426, 585, 595, 618
Times Literary Supplement (London), *The*, 548, 551, 610, 678, 681
Tindall, William Y., 182–3
To the Finland Station (Wilson), xxiii, 190, 247–9, 276, 283, 290, 292–3, 312, 317, 322, 327, 355, 357n, 359, 381, 479, 524, 533, 610, 697, 731
Toklas, Alice B., 257
Tolkien, J. R. R., 543, 660n; *The Hobbit*, 660
Tolstoy, Leo, 19, 304, 319, 367, 376n, 377–8, 459, 490, 526, 551, 570, 578–579, 588, 604, 682, 702, 732; *And Light Shines in Darkness*, 702; *Anna Karenina*, 377, 732; *A Confession*, 377; *The Death of Ivan Ilyich*, 377, 578; *The Devil*, 376n; *The Fruits of Enlightenment*, 702; *The Kreutzer Sonata*, 19; *The Living Corpse*, 702; *War and Peace*, 284, 377, 389, 524, 570, 618
Torrence, Ridgely, 226
Tosca, 660
Toussaint L'Ouverture, 464